GATES ON UNDERSTANDING COMPANY LAW:
A Conceptual and Functional Approach

GATES ON UNDERSTANDING COMPANY LAW:
A Conceptual and Functional Approach

By

R. Blankfein Gates, LLB (UNZA), AHCZ

Advocate
MAINZA & CO

Lecturer of Contract and Company Law
Cavendish University Zambia

Formerly Assistant Senior Research Advocate
Judiciary of Zambia

Published in 2018 by Reagan Blankfein Gates
MAINZA & CO
Lusaka, Zambia

Typeset by Mwanida Banda: bmwanida@gmail.com

For further information on this and other works by this author and updates generally, visit our facebook page: *Gates on Corporate and Commercial Law.*

Reagan Blankfein Gates has asserted his right to be known as the author of this work in accordance with the Copyright and Performance Rights Act, Chapter 407 of the Laws of Zambia.

Contents

7 SHAREHOLDERS' RIGHTS AND OBLIGATIONS 159

PREFACE TO THE FIRST EDITION

This first edition of *Gates on Company Law: A Conceptual and Practical Approach* follows hot on the heels of this author's first foray into company law with the publication of *Gates Company Law and Practice in Zambia* in May of 2017. The writing and publication of that text had caused the author considerable anxiety having been done at a time when work on an Act to replace the 1994 Companies Act had reached an advanced stage a fact clearly spelt out by Professor Mwenda in his foreword to that text. At the urging and encouragement of Mr. Justice Mumba Malila SC, PhD that work was completed and published.

At the end of 2017 two bills which would have considerable consequences on company law and procedure in this jurisdiction were tabled before parliament. Passed as Act No 9 and receiving presidential assent on 20 November 2017 was the Corporate Insolvency Act. Its preamble states that it is,

[a]n Act to provide for corporate receiverships, appointment of receivers and the duties and responsibilities of receivers; business rescue, appointment, duties and responsibilities of business rescue administrators, rights of affected persons during business rescue proceedings and business rescue plans; schemes of arrangements or compromise with creditors; winding up of companies, appointment of liquidators and the duties and responsibilities of liquidators, committees of inspection, special managers and the Official Receiver; insolvency practitioners and the duties and responsibilities of insolvency practitioners; cross-border insolvency; and matters connected with, or incidental to, the foregoing.

For the first time, corporate insolvency will now have separate legislation instead of being bound together with corporate law proper in the Companies Act. It is a change that many corporate law and corporate insolvency law practitioners had called for and which is now a reality. The Companies Bill No 10 of 2017 soon followed and, like the Corporate Insolvency Bill, received presidential assent on 20 November 2017. Quite clearly, as Paul L. Davies has noted in his preface to *Gower and Davies' Principles of Modern Company Law* 7th edn, '[l]legislation is necessarily an uncertain activity, so that it is difficult to predict precisely when a new Act will be on the statute book or still less, when its various parts might be brought into force'.

The writing of this text is borne of necessity. Many readers of my first text have asked me whether I was going to review *Gates Company Law and Practice in Zambia* in view of the legislative changes referred to above. This publication answers their questions somewhat. Though it is not meant to succeed or as a replacement to, or revision of *Gates Company Law and Practice in Zambia,* which will have its own successor, replacement and/or revision in due course, it is an easy to use text for purposes of understanding company law in Zambia within the context of the Companies Act, 2017. The structure that is followed is therefore uncommon in that it veers away from the traditional and familiar topical approach which usually does not follow provisions as they are laid out in company legislation and may be in the eyes of some, liable to criticism. Be that as it may, it has much to commend it. In a text of this kind which is meant to be used both as a main text and a complement to other text books on the subject, by undergraduates and post graduate candidates for the Legal Practitioners' Qualifying Examinations administered by the Zambia Institute of Advanced Legal Education (ZIALE), it was thought necessary to follow closely the law as it is set out in the Companies Act, 2017. At the same time, nothing is lost as a pithy easy to use approach is used for first time readers which will enable them to compare and contrast the Companies Act, 1994 and the Companies Act, 2017, and in many places and where necessary, the UK Companies Act, 2006. The text also continues the practice of highlighting Zambian cases where these are available. Where the law as set out in the CA 2017 is clear, no additions or subtractions are made. Additionally, the text encourages readers to do further research not only on the many cases that are cited but not quoted but from other works that have been published on the topics covered in this text.

It is my sincere hope that the text will be a welcome resource to many Judges, Legal Practitioners, Research Advocates, lecturers of company law, post-graduate and undergraduate students alike.

While every effort has been made to acknowledge sources in keeping with good academic practice, I apologise if for some reason, I inadvertently left unacknowledged any sources used in this publication and will gladly take any required measures at the first opportunity.

It is hoped that the Law is as stated at the end of March, 2018. This means that I have not been able to refer to draft clauses in the Regulations to the Companies Act, 2017. Any errors and omissions are down to me.

Reagan Blankfein Gates
Lusaka, February, 2018

LAW REPORT ABBREVIATIONS

ACSR	Australian Corporations and Securities Report
All ER Rep	All England Reports Reprint
All ER (D)	All England Reports
All ER	All England Reports
ALR	Administrative Law Reports
App Cas	Appeal Cases
B & Ad	Barnwell & Adolphus' King's Bench Reports
B & CR	Reports of Bankruptcy and Companies Winding up Cases
BCC	British Company Law and Practice
BCLC	Butterworths Company Law Cases
Ch app	Law Reports Chancery appeals
Ch/D	Law Reports Chancery Division
CLR	Commonwealth Law Reports
Com Cas	Commercial Cases
Comp Cas Mad	Company Cases Madras (India)
Con LR	Construction Law Reports (UK)
CP Law	Reports Common Pleas
CPD	Law Reports Common Pleas Division
DLR	Directors Law Reports
DLR(2d)	Dominion Law Reports Second Series
Dr & Sm	Drewly and Smale's Vice-Chancellor's Reports
EB & E	Ellis, Blackburn & Ellis' Queen's Bench Reports
ER	English Reports
Eq	Equity Cases
Eq Cas Abr	Equity Cases Abridged
EWCA	England and Wales Court of Appeal
EWHC	High Court of England and Wales Reports
Ex Law	Reports Exchequer Division
F	Federal Reporter (USA); Fraser's Court of Session Cases
Fam	Family Law Reports
HCA	Hong Kong Court of Appeal
H Ct of Australia	High Court of Australia
H & M	Henning and Munford's Reports
HK	Ndola High Court Registry (Zambia)
HP	Lusaka High Court, Principal Registry (Zambia)
HPC	High Court for Zambia, Commercial Division

Hare	Hare Law Reports
IRLB	Industrial Relations Law Bulletin
IRLR	Irish Law Reports
JBL	Journal of Business Law
Jur	Juridical Review
KB/D	Kings Bench Division
LSG	Law Society Gazette
LJPC	Law Journal Privy Council
LJQB	Law Journal Queens Bench
LR	Law Reports
LR app Cas	Law Reports appeal Cases
LR Eq	Law Reports Equity
Lloyd's	Lloyd's Law Reports
LS Gaz	Law Society Gazette
Macq	Macqueen's Scotch Appeal Cases
Meg	Megone's Companies Act Cases
NE	North Eastern Reporter
NI/NILR	Northern Ireland Law Reports
NIJB	Northern Ireland Judgments Bulletin
NLJ	New Law Journal
NZCA	New Zealand Court of Appeal
NZLR	New Zealand Law Report
PCC	Palmer's Company Cases
P. Wms	Peere Williams' Reports
QB/D	Queens Bench
QdR/QR	Queensland Reports
Qd Sup Ct	Queensland Supreme Court
R	The Reports in all the Courts
SCLR	Scottish Civil Law Reports
SE	South Eastern Reporter (United States)
SJ	Solicitor's Journal
SLR	Scottish Law Reports
SLT	Scottish Law Reports
SN	Session Notes
Sol Jo	Solicitor's Journal and Reporter
TC	Tax Cases (United Kingdom)
The Times	The Times Reports
TLR	Times Law Reports
UKSC	United Kingdom Supreme Court
VLR	Victorian Law Report
WLR	Weekly Law Reports

WN	Weekly Notes
WR	Weekly Reporter
CAZ	Zambian Court of Appeal (Neutral Citation)
ZMHC	Zambian High Court (Neutral Citation)
ZMSC	Zambian Supreme Court (Neutral Citation)
ZR	Zambia Law Report

TABLE OF CASES

TABLE OF STATUTES

INTRODUCTION

The Companies Act[1] (the Act) received presidential assent on 20 November 2017.[2] The preamble to the Act provides that it is an '[a]n Act to promote the development of the economy by encouraging entrepreneurship, enterprise efficiency, flexibility and simplicity in the formation and maintenance of companies; provide for the incorporation, categorisation, management and administration of different types of companies; provide the procedure for the approval of company names, change of name and conversion of companies; provide for shareholders' rights and obligations, the conduct of meetings and the passing of resolutions by shareholders; to encourage transparency and high standards of corporate governance by providing for the functions and obligations of company secretaries and directors; provide for issue of shares, share capital requirements, procedures for alteration and reduction of share capital and disclosure requirements of companies; provide for the public issue of shares, the issue and registration of charges and debentures; incorporate financial reporting provisions, maintenance of accounting records, and access to financial information of companies; provide for amalgamations; provide for the registration of foreign companies doing business in Zambia; provide for the deregistration of companies; repeal and replace the Companies Act, 1994;[3] and provide for matters connected with or incidental to the foregoing.[4]

In terms of section 2, '[s]ubject to [the] Act, the Act shall also apply to—
  (a)   a body corporate; and

---

[1] No 10 of 2017.

[2] Replacing Companies Act 1994.

[3] The Act provides for repeal under section 376. It further provides for transitional provisions in section 377 in the following terms:
   (1) A company incorporated under the repealed Act shall continue to operate as if incorporated under this Act.
   (2) A charge relating to movable assets under the repealed Act shall continue in force as if registered in accordance with this Act and shall be registered within a period of twelve months in accordance with this Act and the Movable Property (Securities) Act, 2016.
   (3) A church of faith based organisation that was incorporated as a company before the commencement of this Act shall continue as if incorporated under this Act.

[4] As of this writing the Act had not yet become law owing to the fact that shall come into operation on a date that the Minister had not, as provided for under section 1 of the Act appointed a date by Statutory Instrument for said coming into operation.

(b) an existing company incorporated in accordance with the repealed Act as if it was incorporated in accordance with this Act'.[5]The use of the term *"also"* in the section is rather curious considering that there is no suggestion that the Act was crafted to or is meant to apply to any other entities or unincorporated bodies such as clubs, co-operative societies (unless incorporated) or indeed, partnerships.[6]

In an effort to maintain consistency and perchance, to avoid duplication and a drafting debacle 'unless the context otherwise provides, words and expressions used in [the] Act and which are not defined, but are defined in the Corporate Insolvency Act[7] the Movable Property (Security Interest) Act[8], the Securities Act[9], the Banking and Financial Services Act[10] or any other relevant Act, shall have the meaning assigned to them in those Acts'.[11]In terms of section 5 of the Act, inconsistencies between the Act and the Constitution[12]are resolved in favour of the Constitution. This is an obvious fact as the Constitution is the supreme law of the land. An entire Act or provisions thereof may be struck out as being unconstitutional. It follows that this part of the provision adds no value to the Act. It is superfluous. It is not a silver bullet preventing the striking out of the Act or provisions in the event that same were deemed unconstitutional.[13] Subjecting the provisions of the Act to those of the Banking and Financial Services Act[14], and the Securities Act[15] on the other hand is in line with public and economic policy given that the banking industry has as its regulator, not the Patents and Companies Registration Agency (PACRA) but the Bank of Zambia[16]. Further, the Securities Act[17] creates the Securities and Exchange Commission as regulator of the securities industry, given the specialised and

---

[5] Section 3, the definition section provides for definitions of terms in the Act from "Agency" to "wholly owned subsidiary".

[6] In Zambia clubs are registered under the Societies Act, partnerships under the Business Regulatory Act and regulated under the Partnership Act 1891, and cooperatives (unless they are incorporated), under the Co-operatives Act.

[7] No 9 of 2017.

[8] No 3 of 2017.

[9] No 41 of 2016.

[10] No 7 of 2017.

[11] Section 4.

[12] 1991 as amended by Act No 2 of 2017.

[13] This power is reposed in the Constitutional Court of Zambia by way of the Constitutional Court Act No 8 of the Laws of Zambia.

[14] No 7 of 2017 which provides for the legal framework for the regulation of banks and other financial institutions.

[15] No 41 of 2016 which provides for the legal framework for the regulation of securities which include shares, bonds, collective investment schemes and other debt instruments which go beyond the scope of the companies Act and as such beyond the competence of PACRA.

[16] Created under the Bank of Zambia Act.

[17] No 41 of 2016.

highly complex nature of securities. However, where there is any inconsistency between the provisions of the Act and the provisions of any other written law, the provisions of the Act shall prevail to the extent of the inconsistency.

I

INCORPORATION AND REGISTRATION OF COMPANIES[1]

AIMS AND OBJECTIVES

 After reading this chapter you should appreciate the following:

- ➤ The types of companies that can be incorporated under the Act
- ➤ How the incorporation of Companies is done
- ➤ The significance of the Certificate of incorporation and share capital Certificate to the incorporation process
- ➤ The legal status of registered company specifically, the implications of a separate legal personality
- ➤ The contractual effect of incorporation
- ➤ The legal status of pre-incorporation contracts
- ➤ The importance of the register of Companies and register of Beneficial Owners
- ➤ Circumstances under which companies may be deregistered
- ➤ Why the Registrar can act as representative of a deregistered company in certain events

1.1   Introduction

The incorporation and registration of companies is encompassed in Part II of the Act. Our exploration under this chapter therefore relates to types of companies; declaration of compliance; Certificate of incorporation; and share capital Certificate which according to the Act will be evidence of incorporation We further and briefly, discuss the legal status of a registered company; the contractual effect of incorporation; the requirement to display the Certificate

---

[1] According to section 364(1), it is an offence to fail to comply with requirements of registration as stipulated under Part II: sections 6 – 21 making one 'liable, on conviction, to a fine not exceeding one hundred thousand penalty units'.

of Incorporation; instances in which the application for incorporation may be rejected by the registrar; pre-incorporation contracts; Finally, we turn to a brief discussion of the Registrar of Companies and Register of the Beneficial Owners.

1.2   Types of companies

In terms of section 12 which we discuss later, only the types of companies listed under section 6 of the Act may be incorporated, that is to say-

(a)   public company; or

(b)   private company, being—

  (i)   a private company limited by shares;

  (ii)   a private company limited by guarantee; or

  (iii)   an unlimited private company. There is no room for creativity in what type of company may be incorporated as section 6 is couched in mandatory terms. We now turn to a more detailed discussion of the types of companies capable of being incorporated under the Act in terms of sections 6 and 12.

1.2.1   Public company

The regulatory provisions relating to public companies are to be found in section 7 which must be read together with section 12, the enabling provision. In terms of section 7(1), '[a] public company shall have share capital. Further and in terms of section 7(2), '[t]he articles of a public company shall state the—

(a)   rights, privileges, restrictions and conditions attaching to each class of shares; and

(b)   authority given to the directors to determine the number of shares in, the designation of, and the rights, privileges, restrictions and conditions attaching to, each series in a class of shares. The long held rule that all shares, unless a contrary intention can be noted, will rank *pari passu* applies to a public company. What is envisaged and provided for in this respect and in terms of section 7(3) is the exception 'for differences relating to the classes or series of shares'. It is patent here that recognition for classes of shares and therefore creativity in this aspect of company law and practice is given. Further, this allows for, it may be argued, room for manoeuvre for boards of directors and shareholders.

The concept of limited liability first pronounced in *Salomon v A Salomon & Co Ltd*[2] is retained in section 7(4) wherein it is provided that in the event of a winding up in accordance with the Corporate Insolvency Act[3] a member is liable to contribute, an amount not exceeding the amount, if any, unpaid on the shares held by that member. The specificity in what limited liability as concept means even for a Public Limited Company (Plc) as provided for hereunder is worthy of note. The Act in no way limits the liability of the company which in fact must be pursued to the last fathom of its indebtedness. However, shares will only be liable to pay that which they owe in the shares they own in the Plc at the point of the winding up order being made by the High Court of Judicature for Zambia.

It is submitted that the articles of a Plc cannot be crafted so as to impose '[…] any restriction on the right to transfer shares of the company other than a—

(a) restriction on the right to transfer a share which has not been fully paid for; or

(b) provision for the compulsory acquisition, or rights of first refusal, of shares referred to in paragraph *(a)*, in favour of other members of the company or assignees'.

It is worth mentioning that this provision is taken from section 57(1) of the previous Act.[4] More importantly, the prohibition by the Act for a Plc to craft articles that restrict the transferability of shares is grounded in the simple fact that shares are property and as such, must be freely transferrable by the owners who have paid for them and whose rights to so own and deal as they please with their property is protected by Part III of the Zambian Constitution referenced in section 5 of the Act. The right for a company to restrict the transfer of shares for which full payment has not been made must be understood within the context of the fact that strictly speaking, shares not fully paid are not legally owned by the owner as to enjoy free transferability under the Zambian Constitution. Nor

---

2 [1897] AC 22 HL; an interesting American case that further illustrates how important the concept of separate personality is to Anglo-American legal jurisprudence and just how far courts will go to protect it, is *People's Pleasure Park Co v Rohleder* 1 61 SE 794 (Va 1908). In this case a former slave and later major commanding the Virginia Sixth Negro Regiment, Joseph B Johnson, bought land which was subject to a number of covenants restricting transfer to 'colored persons'. Fifty years later such covenants would be declared unconstitutional but at the beginning of the twentieth century they were commonplace. In order to side-step the covenants, Johnson incorporated a company to hold the title. The company, 'People's Pleasure Park Company', was owned entirely by 'colored persons' and the company's stated object was to create an amusement park for the enjoyment of 'colored persons'. The question before the court was whether the company itself could be said to have a colour and thus be restricted from owning the property. The court held that a corporation was incapable of having a colour, the company was a legal being distinct and separate from its owners and incorporators. As the company was not coloured, it was not restricted from holding the property because in law the company and not Johnson was the owner of the property.- Excerpted from Talbot LE *Critical Company Law* (Taylor & Francis Group New York 2008) 23.

3 No 9 of 2017.

4 CA 1994.

can the law restrict a company to compulsorily acquire shares in favour of other members if its constitution allows it to, much like the Zambian Constitution allows for compulsory acquisition of property under certain circumstances.

1.2.2   Private companies

The first port of call so far as regulation of this type of company is concerned is section 8 which mandates the articles of the company to limit the membership to no more than fifty.[5]

1.2.2.1 Private Companies Limited by shares

Additionally and in terms of section 8(3) read together with section 8(1)—
- *(a)*   joint holders of a share shall be counted as one shareholder; and
- *(b)*   a member shall not be counted as a member, if the member is—
    - (i)   in the employ of the company or of a related corporate; or
    - (ii)   became a member while previously in the employ of the company or a related corporate and has been a member since.

In terms of section 9(1), the articles of a private company limited by shares shall state the—
- *(a)*   rights, privileges, restrictions and conditions attaching to each class of shares; and
- *(b)*   authority given to the directors to determine the number of shares in, the designation of, and the rights, privileges, restrictions and conditions attaching to each series, in a class of shares. Further, and as in the case of Plcs, [a]ll shares in a private company limited by shares rank equally except for differences relating to the classes or series. By section 9(3), [w]here a private company limited by shares is wound-up in accordance with the Corporate Insolvency Act,[6] a member shall be liable to contribute an amount not exceeding the amount, if any, unpaid on the shares held by that member.

1.2.3   Company limited by guarantee

A company limited by guarantee is one in which the members agree to contribute a certain amount in the event of the company being wound-up. To that end and in terms of section 10(1), '[a] subscriber to an application for incorporation for a company limited by guarantee shall make a declaration of guarantee specifying the amount that the subscriber undertakes to contribute to the assets of the company in the event of the company being wound-up'. In terms of

---

[5]   Section 8(1). We must note though that in terms of section 8(2) and by comparison, (2) '[t]he articles of an unlimited company may, subject to any specified conditions, have more than fifty members.
[6]   No 9 of 2017.

section 10(2), '[a] subscriber to an application for incorporation for a company limited by guarantee shall, on incorporation of the company, be a member of the company. By section 10(3), '[a] declaration of a guarantee made under subsection (1) shall state that a member undertakes to contribute an amount not exceeding the amount specified in the declaration of guarantee made by the member, if the company is wound-up in accordance with the Corporate Insolvency Act[7], or within one year after the member ceases to be a member'.

1.2.3.1 Membership, ceasure of membership and type of business

While section 10(2) of the Act provides for a subscriber to the application becoming a member upon such incorporation, it is provided under section 10(4) that it is, as is the case with other types of companies under the Act, possible for others who so will, to join a company limited by guarantee as members in line with requirements if any 'imposed by the articles and this Act' under the following circumstances:

(a)   on approval of the members by special resolution, and by signing a declaration of guarantee delivered to the company; or

(b)   cease to be a member, by delivering to the company a signed notice to that effect in the prescribed form. Within seven days after a person becomes or ceases to be a member of the company, a company limited by guarantee is mandated to, within seven days, lodge with the Registrar the declaration of guarantee and a notice in the prescribed form'.

A company limited by guarantee is proscribed from carrying on business for the purpose of making profit for its members or anyone concerned in its promotion or management.[8] If it so desires, it would have to convert to a private company limited by shares as an initial step.

Failure to comply with the provisions of section 10 is a serious matter with the result that, the directors and each officer in default commit an offence and are liable, on conviction, to a fine not exceeding three hundred penalty units for each day that the failure continues.

1.2.4 Private unlimited companies

As the name suggests, a private company unlimited company is one where the concept of limited liability is none-existent. In essence, it is a partnership with corporate clothing and no different from a sole trader operation. *A fortiori* and in terms of section 11(3), in the event of a winding up order being granted, in accordance with the Corporate Insolvency Act[9], a member will be liable to

---

[7]   No 9 of 2017.
[8]   Section 10(6).
[9]   No 9 of 2017.

contribute without limitation of liability to the last fathom of company's liability. Be that as it may, '[a] private unlimited company shall have share capital and its articles shall state the—

(a) rights, privileges, restrictions and conditions attaching to each class of shares; and

(b) authority given to the directors to determine the number of shares in, the designation of, and the rights, privileges, restrictions and conditions attaching to each series, in a class of shares.

According to section 10(2), '[a]ll shares in a private unlimited company shall rank equally, except for differences relating to classes or series'.

1.3   Incorporation of Companies

The Act provides the legal framework for the incorporation[10] and regulation[11] of companies. Section 12 which replaces section 6 of the previous Act[12] represents a return to the original section 6 when the Companies Act 1994 was first enacted.

In terms of section 12(1) and '[s]ubject to the other requirements of [the] Act, two or more persons may apply to incorporate a company specified in section 6[13] for a lawful purpose[14], by subscribing their names to an application for incorporation in accordance with this section.[15] To the extent that the inclusion of the phrase *for a lawful purpose* was meant to bring clarity as to what kind of incorporation is permissible under the law, the phrase serves no useful purpose given that the provision states already that the two or more people mentioned in section 12(1) must subject such incorporation to, in addition to those under section 12 which we discuss shortly, 'other requirements' of the Act. It is highly unlikely that a company would go through the incorporation process having proposed a business activity the nature of which quite clearly is, under section

---

[10] The enabling function.

[11] The regulatory function. It must be remembered that even though all companies will start their life with incorporation under the Act, regulation of certain types of companies such as banks is the preserve of the Bank of Zambia under the Banking and Financial Services Act No. 7 of the Laws of Zambia. Further, securities, insurance and pension firms, mining companies for example, have individual statutes with agencies for their regulation quite apart from the Act.

[12] CA 1994.

[13] That is to say, *(a)* public company; or*(b)* private company, being—(i) a private company limited by shares;(ii) a private company limited by guarantee; or (iii) an unlimited private company.

[14] By comparison section 7 of the UK CA 2006 provides that '[a] company is formed under [that] Act by one or more persons—(a) subscribing their names to a memorandum of association.., and (b) complying with the requirements of [that] Act as to registration....' We must also note that the inclusion of the phrase for a "lawful purpose" is not only a return to section 4 of the CA 1921 which provided that "any two or more people associated for a lawful purpose" may incorporate a company but also in keeping with section 7(2) of the UK CA which provides: '[a] company may not be so formed for an unlawful purpose'.

[15] (2) An application for incorporation of a company, specified in subsection (1), shall be made in the prescribed manner and form and shall be lodged with the Registrar.

12(4) (viii), illegal e.g. to 'to grow, possess, and traffic drugs and psychotropic substances'. If the argument is that the incorporation can be invalidated because the company was, having passed through the cracks, incorporated for an illegal purpose, then the addition of the phrase is justified. The problem, it may be contended, is that once incorporated, a company becomes a legal person and any defect in its incorporation is irrelevant to its being and the rights it must now enjoy and the protection it must receive from the Constitution of the land. While this argument could hold under CA 1994, it would appear that in terms of section 14(2) incorporation *for an illegal purpose* would be grounds for invalidating the incorporation of a company if same could be added to the ground that an individual or individuals subscribed to the application for incorporation in contravention of section 12(8) for instance.

In terms of section 12(3), the following shall accompany an application for incorporation of a company:

   (a)   a copy of the proposed articles of the company, or a statement that it has adopted the Standard Articles;
   (b)   declaration of compliance made in accordance with section 13;
   (c)   signed consent from each person named in the application as a director or secretary of the company;
   (d)   declaration of guarantee by each subscriber, if the company is limited by guarantee;
   (e)   a statement of beneficial ownership which shall state, in respect of each beneficial owner—
       (i)   the full names;
       (ii)   the date of birth;
       (iii) the nationality or nationalities;
       (iv)   the country of residence;
       (v)   the residential address; and
       (vi)   any other particulars as maybe prescribed; and
   (f)   a declaration by the applicants that the particulars stated in accordance with paragraph *(e)* have been submitted to the Registrar with the knowledge of the individuals to whom the particulars relate.

Further and in terms of section 12(4), [a]n application for incorporation specified in subsection (1), shall state—

   (i)   the name and address of the individual lodging the application;
   (ii)   the proposed name of the company;
   (iii) the physical address of the office to be the registered office of the company;
   (iv)   the registered postal address, electronic mail address and phone number of the company where available;

(v)   the type of company to be formed;

(vi) the particulars of persons who shall be the first directors of the company;

(vii) the particulars of persons who shall be the first secretary or joint secretaries of the company; and

(viii) the nature of the company's proposed business or proposed activity.

Additionally and by section 12(5), '[w]here a company being incorporated is required to have share capital, the applicant shall state on the application for incorporation the—

(a)   amount of share capital of the company;

(b)   the division of the share capital into shares of a fixed amount; and

(c)   number of shares each subscriber has agreed to take. Moreover, section 12(6) provides that '[a]n applicant shall specify, on the application for incorporation, the date on which the first financial year of the company shall end, which shall not be more than twelve months from the date of incorporation'.

There is an interesting provision in section 12(7) which now requires, unlike before, '[a]n application for incorporation to be signed by each subscriber *in the presence of at least one witness who attests to the signature*'.[16] This addition adds a solemnity equivalent to that of a Will under section 6 of the Wills and Testamentary Succession Act.[17]

Though section 12(8) which replaces section 6(2) (under CA 1994), provides that an individual shall not subscribe to an application for incorporation if that individual is—

(a)   under eighteen years of age;

(b)   an undischarged bankrupt; or

(c)   of unsound mind and has been declared to be so by a court of competent jurisdiction, section 14(2) to which section 12(8) is subject provides that the incorporation of a company shall not be invalid by reason only that an individual or individuals subscribed to the application for incorporation in contravention of section 12(8).

In essence, while section 12(8) of the Act is meant, as the previous section 6(2) of CA 1994 attempted, to qualify the "two or more persons" who may incorporate a company, and to preclude persons or entities under a disability from incorporating a company is in fact of no consequence when this is put forward for purposes of invalidating a company's incorporation. The rationale as before, and the preamble to the Act would seem to suggest that the foregoing is meant to encourage commerce and enterprise. There also is a more fundamental and solemn reason for this crafting which is to protect third parties not in the know and for whom the company in question may seek to avoid liability from being prejudiced were the company's incorporation to be deemed invalid.

---

[16] Emphasis added.

[17] Chapter 60 of the Laws of Zambia.

Excluded from incorporation as companies, are entities created for purposes of carrying out religious or faith based activities.[18] Religious organisations have always been considered societies and not-for-profit organisations whose proper place for registration and regulation should be the Societies Act.[19] The fact that they have been allowed in the past to be incorporated as companies is a misnomer which this provision seeks to put right.

1.4   Declaration of compliance

The seriousness of complying with the requirements for incorporation in section 12 are brought to the fore under section 13(1) which stipulates that an application for incorporation, specified in section 12, shall be accompanied by a declaration made in the prescribed form stating that the requirements of the Act relating to incorporation, have been complied with. There is no room for crafting a tailor made declaration as the same shall, in terms of section 13(2), be made in the prescribed manner and form by not just any person but either a legal practitioner (i) holding a valid practicing certificate and (ii) who was engaged in the formation of the company; or a person named, as a first director or secretary of the company, in the application for incorporation.[20]

That the foregoing provision with reference to a legal practitioner involved in the formation of the company or first directors so named in the 'application for incorporation' making the 'declaration' must be read with Part VII[21] headed "Corporate Governance" which replaces Part X headed "Directors and Secretary" in CA 1994, is patent. Section 82(5) in particular provides that '[a] person shall not be eligible for appointment, as company secretary if the person, in the case of—

(a)   an individual, is not—

    (i)   a legal practitioner, a chartered accountant or a member of the chartered institute of secretaries; and

    (ii)   resident in Zambia; or

(b)   a body corporate—

    (i)   is not incorporated in Zambia; and

    (ii)   does not have an officer who qualifies to be appointed as company secretary'.

It must be remembered though that the preamble of the Act states in part that it aims to simplify the incorporation of small companies and to that end section 82(6) qualifies the foregoing by providing that '[t]he qualifications for

---

[18] Section 12(9).

[19] Chapter 119 of the Laws of Zambia.

[20] Section 13 is what used to be the old section 9 in CA 1994.

[21] Sections 82–122.

a company secretary set out in subsection (5) shall not apply to a small private company'.[22]

In terms of section 13(3), the Registrar is under no obligation nor is he mandated to accept the declaration as *prima facie* evidence of compliance with the requirements of the Act. In practice though, and barring some serious irregularity or glaring errors or omission, the Registrar will accept said 'declaration as such'. This is because '[a] person who makes a declaration in accordance with this section, without having reasonable grounds for believing that the requirements of [the] Act have been complied with, commits an offence and shall be liable, on conviction, to a fine not exceeding fifty thousand penalty units[23] or to imprisonment for a period not exceeding six months, or to both'.[24]

1.5   Certificate of incorporation and share capital Certificate to be evidence of incorporation

Where, in terms of section 14(1), '[…] an applicant meets the requirements of [the] Act, the Registrar shall within five days—
  (a)   register the proposed company;
  (b)   issue a certificate of incorporation in the prescribed form;
  (c)   issue a certificate of share capital in the prescribed form, where a company has share capital; and
  (d)   assign a designating number to the company as its registration number.[25]
Further and as we have already noted above, '[t]he incorporation of a company shall not be invalid by reason only that an individual or individuals subscribed to the application for incorporation in contravention of section 12(8)'.[26] However, in terms of section 19(1) and the foregoing notwithstanding, '[t]he Registrar shall reject an application for incorporation of an entity where an applicant—
  (a) does not meet the requirements of this Act; or
  (b) submits false information in the application for incorporation.
By section 19(2), '[w]here the Registrar rejects an application for incorporation, the Registrar shall inform the applicant of its decision, in writing, within fourteen days of making the decision and shall give reasons for the rejection'.

It must be noted that the role of Registrar in the foregoing process, namely, deciding whether in terms of sections 14 and 19 to register a company are

---

[22] In terms of section 2, a "small private company" means any business enterprise whose total investment, excluding land and buildings, annual turnover and the number of persons employed by the enterprise, does not exceed the prescribed numerical value'.

[23] A *penalty unit* is as of this writing valued at ZMW 0.30 in terms of the Fees and Fines (Fees and Penalty Unit Value) Amendment Regulations 2014 (made pursuant to the Fees and Fines Act Chapter 45 of the Laws of Zambia) which came into force on 14 June 2015.

[24] Section 13(4).

[25] A refusal to so register is subject to judicial review.

[26] Section 14(2); Similar provisions are to be found in section 14 of the UK CA 2006.

merely administrative. In terms of section 322, '[t]he Registrar shall exercise the powers and perform the functions assigned to the Registrar by the Act and the Patents and Companies Registration Agency Act.[27] He must satisfy himself that the incorporation documents as prescribed by section 12 are in order and that all the formalities mandated by the Act have been followed.

For this reason, a refusal by the Registrar to register a company pursuant to section 19 is in terms of section 341[28] appealable to the High Court. The section provides that 'a person aggrieved by a decision of the Registrar may within thirty days after the date on which the person is notified of the decision, *appeal* to the Court against the decision, and the Court may confirm, reverse or vary the decision or make such order or give such directions in the matter as it considers just and equitable'. The necessary predicate is section 340 which provides that 'where any discretionary or other power is given to the Registrar, the Registrar shall not exercise that power adversely or arbitrarily and a person challenging a decision of the Registrar shall have the right to apply to the Court'. The chances of success are however slim.[29] The case of *R v Register of Joint Stock Companies*[30] demonstrates this. In that case an application for *mandamus* for an order for the Registrar to register a company whose objects included ticket sales in England relating to the Irish Hospital Lottery was thrown out on the ground that the Registrar had correctly drawn the conclusion that the said sales were illegal in England.

In the Zambian context however, the proper procedure to follow from the decision of the Registrar is by way of appeal and not judicial review as shown in *R v Register of Joint Stock Companies*.[31] Having said that, there is nothing to stop a person with standing, where there are good and compelling reasons, to challenge the Registrar's decision. In that case, the Registrar must act in accordance with any confirmation, reversal or variation of the Registrar's decision or any order or directions in the matter as the court 'considers just and equitable'.[32] The Registrar is also expected to act in accordance with any decision of the Court to an appeal made in any matter brought before him and in which he is required to sit with assessors to make a decision as provided for under sections 342 to 346.

The significance of the certificate of incorporation issued in accordance with section 14 is asserted in section 15(1) to '[…] be conclusive evidence that—

---

[27] No 15 of 2010. It is further provided under the same section that the power reserved to the Registrar by the Act 'may be exercised or performed by the Registrar personally or by an officer acting under the delegation or control or direction of the Registrar'.

[28] Which replaces section 379 of CA 1994 with nothing more or less.

[29] Davies PL *Gower and Davies's Principles of Modern Company Law* 7th edn.

[30] [1931] 2 KB 197.

[31] [1931] 2 KB 197; In *Newplast Industries v Commissioner of Lands and Attorney General* [2001] ZR 51 it was held that a litigant had no choice on the mode of commencement of an action where legislation or statutes have provided for a specific mode of commencement.

[32] Section 341.

(a)   the requirements of [the] Act regarding the incorporation of the company have been complied with;

(b)   from the date of registration stated in the certificate, the company is incorporated in accordance with [the] Act'.

The foregoing was illustrated in the case of *Jubilee Cotton Mills Ltd v Lewis*[33] where the company had allotted shares to one Lewis on May 6 1924 which was the day on which the Registrar had issued the certificate of incorporation. It was however not signed until two days later. Lewis, in breach of his duties as promoter sold the shares allotted to him making a profit for himself. Sued by the liquidator to account, he asserted that there was nothing to account for as the company was not in existence on the date the shares were allotted. It was held *inter alia* that a company comes into existence from the first moment on the date mentioned in its certificate of incorporation. Lewis was therefore required and expected to account for the profit made. Section 15(1)(b) must be read together with section 22 of the Act which provides for capacity, power and rights of an incorporated company.[34]

The conclusive nature of the certificate of incorporation as provided for under section 15(1) means that ordinarily, the registration of the company cannot be contested or invalidated.[35] Davies[36] suggests that '[t]his, happily, has rendered [Zambian] company law virtually immune from the problems arising from defectively incorporated companies which have plagued the United States and many continental countries'. Be that as it may, and on the strength of the decision in *R v Registrar of Companies Ex p. Central Bank of India*[37] the apparent imperviousness of section 15(1) is not complete. Further and as suggested by the decision in *R v Registrar of Companies Ex p. HM's Attorney General*[38] since section 15(1) is not crafted to bind the Republic, it is conceivable that the Attorney-General for Zambia may apply to the High Court to have the decision of the Registrar to register a company quashed by way of *certiorari*.[39]

There is a precedent for the foregoing position. In *R v Registrar of Companies Ex p. HM's Attorney General*[40] a prostitute succeeded in incorporating a company under the name "Lindi St Claire (Peronal Services) Ltd" the Registrar having rejected her preferred names of "Prostitutes Limited" or "Hookers Ltd" or "Lind St Claire (French Lesson) Ltd" with the objective 'to carry on the

---

[33] [1924] AC 958.

[34] Similar provisions are to be found in section 15 of the UK CA 2006.

[35] See further, Gates RB *Gates Company Law and Practice in Zambia....*

[36] Davies PL *Gower and Davies's Principles of Modern Company Law* 7th edn 84 referencing the research by Drury, on "Nullity of Companies in English Law" [1985] 48 MLR 644.

[37] [1986] QB 1114 CA.

[38] [1991] BCLC 476.

[39] See how this procedure was put to use albeit unsuccessfully in *Bowman v Secular Society* [1917] AC 406 HL.

[40] [1991] BCLC 476.

business of prostitution'. On an application for judicial review by the Attorney General, the registration was quashed on grounds of it being illegal and contrary to public policy.

It must be further submitted that in view of the clear and mandatory provision in section 12(9) that '[a] person *shall* not apply to incorporate an entity as a company, *for purposes of carrying out religious or faith based activities* ',[41] it is arguable that were a company to be registered in contravention of this provision the certificate of incorporation would not be conclusive of valid incorporation as envisaged in section 15(1). It is inconceivable that were a situation to arise such as in *R v Registrar of Companies Ex p. HM's Attorney General*[42] or in contravention of section 12(9) and an application was brought before the High Court, section 15(1) would come to the rescue of the promoters or indeed the company in question. It would be an affront to public policy and a stain on the Court were it to hold that under those circumstances, the certificate of incorporation was still conclusive as to the validity of the incorporation now impugned.[43]

In view of the foregoing, there is a point to be made here about the appeal procedure envisaged in section 341 discussed in chapter 14 in this work. It is that the said procedure is meant for persons, promoters or entities whose desire to incorporate in terms of sections 6-16 has been rejected by the Registrar in terms of section 19; or in terms of section 41-43, the Registrar rejects a proposed name by a company that has passed a resolution to change its name under Part IV of the Act; or the Registrar refuses to issue a new certificate of incorporation following a company's expression of its desire to convert and after following the procedure for conversion provided for under Part V of the Act to another type other than its present form or where the Registrar refuses to accept the lodgment of a notification for a share transfer which transfer the company has accepted among other scenarios which call for a judicious use of the Registrar's discretionary power in terms of section 340 of the Act.

The appeal procedure as we show elsewhere in this work is also applicable in all proceedings brought before the Registrar and against which a party can appeal to the High Court in terms of section 342 to 346 of the Act. However, where public policy is involved as was the case in *R v Registrar of Companies*

---

[41] There is a similar is a similar provision in the UK proscribing Trade Unions from registering under the Companies Act in section 10(3) of the Trade Union and Labour Relations (Consolidation) Act 1992.

[42] [1991] BCLC 476.

[43] See further for historical significance only (as it is doubtful if they are still good law) *Edinburgh & District Water Manufacturers Association v Jenkinson* [1903] 5 Sessions Cases 1159; and *British Association of Glass Bottle Manufacturers v Nettlefold* [1911] 27 TLR 527 which were based on what is now section 15(1) of the Act but which provision was less comprehensive and related to ministerial rather than substantive issues leading to registration such as those envisaged in sections 6-12 of the Act.

Ex p. HM's Attorney General[44] the right procedure, it is submitted, would not be by appeal but judicial review to the High Court so as to obtain *certiorari* to quash the registration.

In addition to the foregoing, we must add that the post-incorporation injunctive procedure envisaged in section 330(1) and discussed further in chapter 14, where '[the High] Court may, on the application of a person referred to in [section 330](2), make an order restraining a company or a director from engaging in conduct that contravenes or would contravene the articles or [the] Act is restricted, so far as standing as to who can make the said application is concerned, to-

(a) the company;

(b) a director or member;

(c) an entitled person; or

(d) the Registrar.

That notwithstanding, the Attorney-General[45] would still apply under section 330(1) where the company involved is a *parastatal*[46] as an *entitled person* defined in section 3 as 'a member or other person recognised under the articles as enjoying a shareholder's rights and having a shareholder's obligations'.

1.6   Legal status of registered company

'A company registered in accordance with [the] Act, acquires a separate legal status, with the name by which it is registered, and shall continue to exist as a corporate until it is removed from the Register of Companies'.[47] The basis of this provision is the common law principle founded on the case of *Salomon v Salomon & Co Ltd*.[48] The consequences of incorporation include the fact that, as provided for in section 22 which we discuss in chapter 3 below, '[a] company shall have—

(a) perpetual succession[49] and a common seal,[50] capable of suing and being sued in its corporate name and shall, subject to [the] Act, have power to do all such acts and things as a corporate may by law, do or perform; and

---

[44] [1991] BCLC 476.

[45] See section 12(1) of the State Proceedings Act Chapter 71 of the Laws of Zambia which provides that 'subject to the provisions of any other written law, civil proceedings by or against the State shall be instituted by or against the Attorney-General as the case may be'.

[46] By which is meant a company owned by the government.

[47] Section 16.

[48] [1897] AC 442. The principle in *Salomon* has been affirmed in the following cases: *Macaura v Northern Assurance*[1925] AC 619 HL; *Lee v Lee's Air Farming* [1961] AC 12 PC; *Secretary of State for Trade and Industry v Bottrill*[1999] EWCA Civ 781; *R v Philippou* [1989] 5 BCC 665 and *Foss v Harbottle* [1843] 2 Hare 461 CH.

[49] See *Noel Tedman Holdings Pty Ltd, Re* [1967] QdR 56.

[50] Compare this to section 45 of the UK CA 2006.

(b) subject to [the] Act and to such limitations as are inherent in its corporate nature, the capacity, rights, powers and privileges of an individual; and

(c) the capacity to carry on business and exercise its powers in any jurisdiction outside Zambia, to the extent that the laws of Zambia and of that jurisdiction permit'.

The *Salomon* principle now codified in section 16 has proved to be an extremely potent artifice which has allowed companies the room to incur risk without interference from their members. Be that as it may, it has also been abused by many an incorporator for fraudulent enterprises. The concept also extends to groups of companies. In terms of *Salomon,* each subsidiary has a separate legal personality and as such cannot be deemed to be subsumed into the holding company. It was shown in *Lonrho Ltd v Shell Petroleum Co Ltd*[51] by Shaw LJ that allowing Lonrho the disclosure of documents which they sought and which were held by a wholly-owned subsidiary of shell '…would [have involved] not merely raising the corporate veil, but committing an affront to the *persona* of the company itself'.[52]

1.7 Contractual effect of incorporation

In terms of section 17,[53] '[s]ubject to [the] Act, the incorporation of a company has the same effect as a contract under seal[54] between the company and its members and between the members themselves, in which they agree to form a company whose business shall be conducted in accordance with the articles and [the] Act'.[55] This section replaces section 21 in CA 1994. It is important to state that it is the act of incorporation, not the company concluding any contract in any way shape or form, separate and distinct from the process of

---

[51] [1980] QB 358.

[52] But see the decision in *Lake Kariba Boating Services Ltd v Kariba North Bank Company Limited* [1982] ZR 35 SC where the appellants were the registered proprietors of leasehold properties in Siavonga. The respondent lodged caveats on the said properties maintaining that it had a beneficial interest in the properties having acquired complete control of the assets of the appellant company through purchasing all the shares in the latter. An application by the appellants for the removal of the caveats was refused. They appealed against the refusal. It was held that: (i) One company can acquire complete control over the assets of another company by the acquisition from the shareholders of the whole of the issued share capital of the company whose assets it is sought to control and (ii) that a company having such control has legitimate beneficial interest the assets arising out of the trust created and is in a proper position to lodge a caveat over the said assets.

[53] Compare this with section 33(1) of the UK CA 2006 which provides that 'the provisions of a company's constitution bind the company and its members to the same extent as if there were covenants on the part of the company and of each member to observe those provisions'.

[54] 'A contract under seal is a formal contract which does not require any consideration and has the seal of the signer attached. A contract under seal must be in writing or printed on paper. It is conclusive between the parties when signed, sealed, and delivered.' from *https://definitions.uslegal.com/c/contract-under-seal/* (retrieved on 10 December 2017).

[55] In terms of section 18, a company registered in accordance with [the] Act shall display its certificate of incorporation in a prominent place at its business premises.

incorporation, beginning with the requirements in terms of section 12 within the context of section 6 as the case may be, being complied with, culminating in the issuance of the certificate of incorporation in accordance with section 14 and having the significance exemplified in section 15(1) of the Act, that constitutes a contract having the same effect as one made under seal.   More to the point, '[t]he ownership of shares in a company gives rise to certain rights and obligations'.[56] From the date of incorporation, a company does not only become a *persona* at law in its own right but also an association of those who constitute its membership, 'and is therefore able to contract with its members'.[57]

We must briefly discuss the significance, if any, of the phraseology that 'the incorporation of a company has the same effect as *a contract under seal*....' The term 'seal' has as its origin, the wax seal which throughout history has been used for purposes of authentication. While originally only wax seals were accepted by the courts as authenticating documents including contracts, the advent of the 19th century saw a relaxation of the rules in this respect. This resulted in the definition of a seal encompassing an impression; a scroll made using a ball pen; and/or printed words "seal" or "L.S."[58]

At common law, contracts made under seal have always been treated differently from those made under hand (simple contracts). It has always been the case that the existence of a seal will eliminate the need for consideration. Given the common law indispensability of the element of consideration to a valid contract, the seal was (or has always been) seen as an alternative to the requirement for consideration. It followed therefore that a seal was considered not as a species of consideration but a presumption thereof.[59] The justification for this singular treatment of contracts under seal can best be appreciated, *inter alia*, within the context of legal formalities associated with the sealing of a document with a wax seal:

(i)   Affixing a seal or following the formalities associated with such affixing to a deed evidenced the contract's existence;

(ii)   Using a seal impressed upon the parties (as should the incorporation of a company within the context of our discussion) the implication of the contract being made; and

(iii)   Following formalities in affixing the seal demonstrated beyond doubt the fact that the parties involved intended to create legal relations.

It follows from the foregoing discussion that following the incorporation requirements as set out in section 12 *inter alia*, impresses upon promoters or those that subscribe to the incorporation documents that their actions are an expression of intent, a crafting of terms and conditions by way of articles by

---

[56] Ridley A and Shepherd C *Company Law: Key Facts Key Cases* (Routledge New York 2015) 52.

[57] Ridley A and Shepherd C *Company Law: Key Facts Key Cases* (Routledge New York 2015) 52.

[58] Latin term for *locus sigilli* (place of the seal).

[59] As was shown in *Marine Contractors Co Inc. v Hurley,* 365 Mass. 280, 285-86 (1974) though, courts have arrived at different conclusions as to whether this presumption was a rebuttable one.

which their relationship with the company, once it is created, will be governed and that by the same token, they accept that the same terms and conditions as contained in the articles will govern the members' rights and obligations *interse*. Further, that by following formalities relating to incorporation as set out in the Act, the eventual members, demonstrate beyond doubt that they intended to create legal relations between themselves and the company. Additionally, the certificate of incorporation, like the object used to imprint the wax such as an engraved signet ring, identifies the company to which it relates and thereby provides evidence that the owner of the certificate of incorporation is party to the contract provided for under section 17 of the Act.

Having said that, it is quite clear that the language and extent of this particular section is briefer and narrower than the section it replaces namely section 21 under CA 1994. While the contract referred to under section 17 is still '[s]ubject to [the] Act', and as we have already seen, such incorporation shall have the same effect as a contract under seal, the basis of which we have discussed above, there are a few changes to be noted and capable of extensive analysis but not in a work such as this one. While the old section 21 provided, like the new section 17, that the contract will be between the company and its members, section 17 has dropped the part *'from time to time'* because it is not possible to entrench a provision in the articles of association.[60] Further, while the contract is still said to be, in addition, 'between those members themselves, in which they agree to form a company', the manner in which this company's business will be conducted has been altered. Section 17 excludes 'the application for incorporation', and 'the certificate of share capital' and only limits same to 'the articles of the company' (where from the phrase 'from time to time' is dropped) and the Act.

As a starting point in discussing the foregoing, we must state that the contract mentioned in section 17 limits the rights and obligations thereunder to the members and the company and the members *interse*. In fact, section 26 of the Act provides:

(1) that '[t]he articles shall have the effect of a contract between—
    (a) the company and each member; and
    (b) amongst the members; and
(2) that [t]he articles shall bind the company and its members.

This imports the concept of privity of contract into statutory company law. The concept of privity[61] 'consists of two general rules.'[62] The first rule states that a third party cannot be subject to the obligations of a contract to which he is not a party. The second, which has proved more controversial, is the rule that a third party could not enforce a contract or benefit from a contract to which he was not

[60] See section 27 discussed in chapter 2 below.
[61] For a historic and critical analysis of the concept of privity see generally Mckendrick E *Contract Law* 7th edn. (Palgrave Macmillan Hampshire 2007) Chapter 7 137-175.
[62] Mckendrick E *Contract Law* 7th edn 137.

a party the fact that it was concluded for his benefit notwithstanding. In England, this second limb has seen changes made to it via the Contracts (Rights of Third Parties) Act. However, section 6(2) of the Act does not apply to the Company's constitution. We must then draw the conclusion that in terms of section 17, 'since only the members who are party to the contract with the company, it would follow that non-members cannot enforce the contract, even if they are intimately involved with the company, for example, as directors'.[63] It has been held in *Hickman v Kent or Romney Marsh Sheepbreeders' Association*[64] that:

> An outsider to whom rights purport to be given by the articles in his capacity as such outsider, whether he is or subsequently becomes a member, cannot sue on those articles, treating them as contracts between himself and the company, to enforce those rights.

It would follow that the same principle will apply to members *interse* in that it would be inconceivable to imagine that the provisions of section 17 have the expressed intention of placing an obligation on third parties or indeed to benefit such third parties not privy to the contract between the company and its members, and members *interse*. The holding in *Hickman* has meant that an advocate who later becomes a member of the company cannot enforce a provision stating that he shall be the company's solicitor[65] nor can a promoter who becomes a member enforce a provision to the effect that he ought to be reimbursed for his expenses.[66]

Finally, the restriction of the contract to the members and the company and members *interse* and the exclusion of the 'application for incorporation' and 'the certificate of share capital' is deserving of anecdotal postulations as is the dropping of the phrase 'from time to time' as it relates to articles of association. If it be argued that the application for incorporation which among other things is still required under section 12(4) to state 'the nature of the company's proposed business or proposed activity' is equivalent, albeit in a diminished sense, to the memorandum of association restricted to company's proposed objects, it must also be remembered that it represents nothing more and nothing less than the promoters' intent to transact their business affairs through the vehicle of the company. Its immutability means that 'key information regarding the internal allocation of powers between the directors and members of a company will be set out in one place: the articles of association'.[67]

---

[63] Davies PL *Gower and Davies' Principles of Modern Company Law* 7th edn (Sweet & Maxwell London 2007) 62.

[64] [1915] 1 Ch 881 at 897.

[65] *Eley v Positive Life Association* [1876] 1 Ex D 88 CA.

[66] *Re English & Colonial Produce Co* [1906] 2 Ch 235.

[67] Companies Act 2006 – Explanatory Notes www.legislation.gov.uk. See also section 8 of the UK CA 2006: Memorandum of Association sections 31-5.

It can therefore not be argued that the business of the company will be transacted through the application of incorporation which will usually for the most part, be overtaken by events, through alterations to the articles of the association brought about by changing needs and the company's operational environment. As regards the issue of the certificate of share capital not being part of the contract envisaged in section 17, it was rather anomalous to include it in a global provision such as section 21 of CA 1994 as share capital has, for instance, no relevance to a company limited by guarantee. Further, a company's business is strictly speaking run through its articles and pursuant to the regulatory provisions of the Act. Share capital is an issue provided for in the constitution and therefore played no useful purpose as it stood in section 21 of CA 1994.

The dropping of the term 'from time to time' should be seen within the context of section 22(1) which provides in part that '[a] company shall have— *(a)* perpetual succession....'[68] As it relates to articles of association, it should be seen within the context of section 27(1) discussed in chapter 2 below which provides that '[s]ubject to [the] Act, and its articles, a company may amend its articles by passing a special resolution'.

1.8   Pre-incorporation contracts[69]

At common law, unless and until a company is incorporated, it cannot contract[70] nor can it, after incorporation envisaged in section 14, be made liable for contracts purportedly made on its behalf before its birth. The statutory position in this regard which in CA 1994 was found in section 28 is now to be found in section 20 of the Act which apart from slight changes in syntax has been retained in its previous form hook line and sinker. As before,[71] section 20(1) provides that '[w]here a person purports to enter into a contract not evidenced in writing in the name or on behalf of an entity before it is incorporated, that person is bound by the contract and shall incur any liability and be entitled to the benefits arising therefrom. Further and by section 20(2), '[…] where a person purports to enter into a contract evidenced in writing in the name or on behalf of an entity before it is incorporated, the person shall be bound by the contract and entitled to the benefits thereof, except as provided in this section'.

---

[68] The company is not subject to treachery of mortality nor is it subject to incapacity resulting from physical or mental ailments. Members can come and go but the company, barring dissolution, can go on forever. See *Re Noel Tedman Holding Pty Ltd [1967] QdR 561, Qd.Sup.Ct* where the only members in a company were killed in a road accident.

[69] For a more detailed discussion based on the old section 28 see generally, Gates RB *Gates Company Law and Practice in Zambia* 1ˢᵗed (Reagan Blankfein Gates Lusaka 2017) pp 55-61; *Western Driveways Ltd v Mistry House Hardware Ltd and Masauso Banda* 2009/HP/1532 (ZMHC); *Phonogram Ltd v Lane* [1981] 3 All ER 182.

[70] See *Kelner v Baxter* [1866] LR 2 CP 174; *Natal Land Co v Pauline Syndicate* [1904] AC 120 PC; Per Herman J in *Rover International Ltd v Canon Film Sales Ltd* [1987] 1 WLR 1597 at 1599:'If someone does not exist they cannot contract'

[71] Under section 28(1), CA 1994.

In terms of section 20(3), '[a] company may, not later than fifteen months after its incorporation, adopt the contract specified in subsection (1) and (2) by an ordinary resolution, and on the adoption, subject to subsection (4) the—

(a)   company shall be bound by the contract and entitled to the benefits thereof, as if the company had been incorporated at the date of the contract and had been a party thereto; and

(b)   person who purported to act in the name or on behalf of the company shall cease to be bound by the contract or entitled to the benefits thereof'.

The use of the term 'adopt' in section 20(3) is significant in that a principal that was not in existence at the time the contract in question was concluded is incapable of ratifying it as would an existent principal at the material time.

According to section 20(4), '[s]ubject to subsection (5), whether or not a contract specified in subsection (3) is adopted by the company, a party to the contract, may apply to the Court for an order fixing obligations under the contract as a joint party or joint and several parties, or apportioning liability between or among the company and, the person who purported to act in the name or on behalf of the company, and on such application, the Court may make any order it considers appropriate in the circumstances'.

Finally and in terms of section 20(5), '[s]ubsection (4) shall not apply if the relevant contract expressly provides that the person who purported to act in the name or on behalf of the company before it was incorporated shall not be bound by the contract nor entitled to the benefits thereof'. The provisions in section 28 must be analysed within the context of sections 15(1)(b) which provides that 'from the date of registration stated in the certificate, the company is incorporated in accordance with [the] Act' and section 22 which provides for capacity, power and rights of an incorporated company.

1.9   Register of Companies and Register of Beneficial Owners[72]

Section 21(1) enjoins the Registrar to establish and maintain a Register of Companies in manual or electronic form in which shall be entered, in respect of each company a—

(a)   chronological record of the prescribed particulars, and of any other particulars as prescribed in relation to the company; and

(b)   record of the documents lodged in compliance with this Act in respect of the company, other than documents whose only effect is to amend particulars recorded in accordance with paragraph *(a)*.

By section 21(2), '[t]he Registrar shall establish and maintain a Register of beneficial owners in manual or electronic form in which shall be entered

---

[72] In terms of section 3, '"beneficial owner" means a natural person who—*(a)* directly or indirectly, through any contract, arrangement, understanding, relationship or any other means ultimately owns, controls, exercises substantial interest in, or receives substantial economic benefit from a body corporate; or *(b)* exercises ultimate and effective control over a legal person or legal arrangement....'

(a)   the information provided in accordance with section 12(3)*(e)*;

(b)   the following information relating to a legal person—

    (i)   the body corporate name;

    (ii) head office address;

    (iii) identities of directors, shareholders and beneficial owners;

    (iv) proof of incorporation or evidence of legal status and legal form;

    (v) provisions governing the authority to bind the legal person; and

    (vi) such information as is necessary to understand the ownership and control of the legal person;

(c)   with respect to other legal entities or arrangements the name of trustees, settler and beneficiary of a trust, and any other parties with authority to manage, vary or otherwise control the entity or arrangement; and

(d)   any other information as maybe prescribed'.

Finally in terms of section 21(3), '[a] company shall, where a change occurs with respect to the particulars of shareholding or beneficial ownership stated in a register maintained in accordance with this Act, notify the Registrar in the prescribed form, within fourteen days of such change'.

1.10   Deregistration of companies

We have noted that the Act gives the Registrar the power to register the company if satisfied that the requirements for incorporation have been met in terms of sections 6 and 12 of the Act. That power would however be incomplete if the Registrar did not have the power to deregister a company for cause or the company could not by its own volition apply to be deregistered. For that reason, the Act in part XV specifically sections 317 to 319, provides for situations in which the Registrar can on the one hand deregister a company either at his own instance or by order and on the other, the company itself can apply to be deregistered.

We must hasten to explain that the situations envisaged under Part XV are independent[73] of those envisaged under and for which the Corporate Insolvency Act[74] makes provision such as receivership;[75] business rescue proceedings;[76]

---

[73] Except those situations under section 317(1)(a)(b) of the Act. Section 317(9) provides that '[t]he Corporate Insolvency Act, 2017, shall apply to a company which has been deregistered due to the reasons specified in subsection 1*(a)* or *(b)*'.

[74] No 9 of 2017.

[75] Part II: Sections 3 – 20.

[76] Part II: Sections 21 – 45.

winding up by court;[77] voluntary winding up;[78] miscellaneous provisions on winding up.[79]

1.10.1   Power of Registrar to deregister company

The power for the Registrar to deregister a company is found under section 317. Under section 317(1) despite the relevant provisions of the Corporate Insolvency Act, 2017, the Registrar may deregister a company under any of the following scenarios:

(a)   company has not filed annual returns for two consecutive years;

(b)   Court, on an application by the Registrar, issues an order that the company be deregistered;

(c)   Registrar has reasonable cause to believe that a company is a dormant company; or

(d)   company applies for de-registration for reason that it is a dormant company.

However, the power under subsection (1) cannot be exercised with automatism because under subsection (2) the Registrar is mandated to, 'before de-registering a company in accordance with subsection (1), give notice in writing, in the prescribed manner and form to the company or shareholders or promoters of the company, of the intention to de-register the company and shall—

(a)   give reasons for the intended de-registration; and

(b)   require the company to show cause, within a period of thirty days, why the company should not be deregistered'.

In the event that 'a company takes remedial measures to the satisfaction of the Registrar, within the period referred to in subsection (2), the Registrar shall not de-register the company'.[80]   However, despite the mandatory nature of subsection (2), the decision by the Registrar to not de-register the company in question must be seen within the context of subsections (4) and (5). In terms of subsection(4) '[t]he Registrar shall, in making the Registrar's final determination on the de-registration of the company consider the submissions made by the company, in accordance with subsection (2), and shall consider any remedial measures taken in accordance with subsection (3). However, by subsection (5), '[t]he Registrar may de-register a company if after being notified, in accordance with sub-section (2), that the company failed to show cause why it should not be de-registered or did not take any remedial measures to the satisfaction of the Registrar, within the specified period'.

---

[77] Part VI: Sections 55 – 87.

[78] Part VII: Sections 88 – 98.

[79] Part VIII: Sections 99 – 139.

[80] Section 317(3).

The consequences of de-registration as envisaged in section 317 are far reaching. According to subsection (6), '[a] company on being de-registered shall—

(a) cease to be entitled to the rights and benefits, conferred in [the] Act, with effect from the date of the deregistration;

(b) take down any certificate or licence on display in every place of business of the company; and

(c) if the de-registration is due to subsection 1(a) or (b), being a company which is not a dormant company, comply with the Corporate Insolvency Act, 2017'.

Further and in terms of section 317(7), '[t]he Registrar shall, on de-registration of a company, in accordance with…section [317]—

(a) publish a notice of the de-registration, in the prescribed manner and form, in the *Gazette* and may be published in a daily newspaper or other media of general circulation in Zambia; and

(b) take any additional steps necessary to inform the public of the de-registration of the company'.

It is to be further noted that '[a]company that has been de-registered in accordance with this section, shall not, from the date it receives a notice of deregistration from the Registrar—

(a) enter into any new contract or business relating to the affairs of the company;

(b) renew or vary a contract relating to the affairs of the company'.[81]

1.10.2 Deregistration on application by company

According to section 318(1), '[a] company may, in the prescribed manner and form, request the Registrar to deregister the company in accordance with section 317(1)(d)'. In terms of section 318(2), '[a] request made, in accordance with subsection (1), shall be accompanied by the prescribed fee and a—

(a) copy of the special resolution signed by the members of the company to have the company de-registered;

(b) summary of accounts, if any; and

(c) statutory declaration by two or more directors of the company on the assets of the company stating that the company has no debts or liabilities'.

The Registrar is under obligation to 'cause to be published in the *Gazette* and in a daily newspaper of general circulation in Zambia or other media a notice of intention to deregister the company as requested'.[82]

---

[81] Section 317(8).
[82] Section 318(3).

Following 'the expiration of ninety days from the publication of the notice, referred to in subsection (1), the Registrar shall, unless cause to the contrary is shown, deregister the company and shall cause notice thereof to be published in the *Gazette* and in a daily newspaper of general circulation in Zambia'. Subsection (5) provides that '[o]n the publication of the notice that a company has been deregistered the liability, if any, of every officer and member in respect of any act or omission that arose before the company was de-registered, shall continue, and may be enforced in accordance with this Act as if the company had not been de registered'.

1.10.3   *Registrar to act as representative of deregistered company in certain events*

For purposes of continuing obligations which the company was, prior to its de-registration and rights that may have accrued to the now de-registered company that need to be acted upon, among other things, section 319 allows the Registrar to act as representative of the de-registered company under certain circumstances. Specifically, section 319(1) provides that '[t]he Registrar may, after a company has been deregistered in accordance with this Part, represent the company if satisfied that—

(a) if the company was still existing, it would be bound to carry out, complete or give effect to a transaction or matter; or

(b) an administrative act or decision requires to be done by or on behalf of the company.

However, '[d]espite the generality of subsection (1), the Registrar shall have power to execute or sign any relevant instrument or document and when so executing or signing an instrument or document, endorse thereon a note or memorandum to the effect that the Registrar has done so in accordance with this section, and such an execution or signature shall have the same force, validity and effect as if the company had been in existence and had executed the instrument or document'. Further, by subsection (3), '[t]he Registrar shall not incur any liability to any person by reason of any act done or caused to be done by the Registrar in accordance with this section. Finally, according to subsection (4) '[a] person aggrieved by a decision of the Register may appeal in accordance with this Act'.

1.11   Conclusion

In this chapter we have discussed that the Act mainly provides for two types of companies namely Public companies and Private companies. The Private companies are further divided into Private Companies Limited by shares; Company limited by guarantee; and Private unlimited companies. We have further seen that Members can cease to be such by informing the company or by selling off their shareholding and procuring the removal of their names from the register of members. The chapter has also considered the specifics of company incorporation including the necessity of a declaration of compliance; the significance of a Certificate of incorporation and share capital Certificate as evidence of incorporation. Once incorporated, a company becomes a persona at law with an existence separate and distinct from its members and with perpetual succession. Further, incorporation in and of itself brings into being a contract between the company and its members and members *inter se*. Pre-incorporation contracts will only bind parties involved unless they are reduced in writing and adopted by the company after its formation. Additional issues considered include the de-registration of companies; the power of Registrar to deregister companies of his own volition or on application by the company and finally the fact that the Registrar is empowered act as representative of the deregistered company in certain events.

FURTHER READING

Articles

Bourne, N, 'Pre-incorporation contracts' (2002) 28 Bus LR 110.

Cain, B, 'Company Names Adjudicator Rules' (2008) 32 CSR 25.

Conaglen, M, 'Equitable compensation for breach of fiduciary dealing rules' (2003) 119 LQR 246.

Ireland, P, 'Capitalism Without the Capitalist: the Joint Stock Company Share and the Emergence of the Modern Doctrine of Separate Corporate Personality' (1996) 17 *Journal of Legal History* 63.

Mayer, T, 'Personal liability for trading in prohibited name: sections 216–217 Insolvency Act 1986' (2006) 27 Comp Law 14.

Pekmezovic, A, 'Determinants of corporate ownership: the question of legal origin: Part 1' (2007) 18 ICCLR 97.

Pekmezovic, A, 'Determinants of corporate ownership: the question of legal origin: Part 2' (2007) 18 ICCLR 147.

Pennington, R, 'The Validation of Pre-Incorporation Contracts' (2002) 23(9) Comp Law 284.

Books

Davies PL *Gower and Davies' Principles of Modern Company Law* 7th edn. (London Thomson Sweet & Maxwell 2003).

Dine J and Koutsias M *Company Law* 6th edn (Palgrave Macmillan Hampshire 2007).

Farrah JH and Hannigan BM *Farrar's Company Law* 4th edn (Butterworths London 1998).

Gates RB *Gates Company Law and Practice in Zambia* (Reagan Blankfein Gates Lusaka 2017).

Harris R *Industrializing English Law Entrepreneurship and Business Organization, 1720–1844* (Cambridge University Press Cambridge 2000).

Keenan D *Smith and Keenan's Company Law* 13th edn (Pearson Longman Essex 2005).

McCahery J and Vermeulen E *Corporate Governance of Non-listed Companies* (Oxford University Press Oxford 2008).

Mclaughlin S *Unlocking Company Law* 3rd edn (Routledge New York 2015).

Ridley A and Shepherd C *Company Law: Key Facts Key Cases* (Routledge New York 2015).

Sealy L and Worthington S *Sealy & Worthington's Cases and Materials in Company Law* 10th edn (Oxford University Press Oxford 2013).

Talbot LE *Critical Company Law* (Taylor & Francis Group New York 2008).

Wild C and Weinstein S *Smith and Keenan's Company Law* 15th edn (Pearson Education Ltd London 2011).

Reports

Company Law Review 1998 Steering Group and Government documents (available at BIS Companies Act 2006).

European Commission Communication, Implementing the framework for financial markets:action plan (COM(1999) 232 final).

European Commission Green Paper, The EU corporate governance framework (COM (2011) 164).

European Commission Internal Market and Services, Report of the Reflection Group on the Future of EU Company Law, Brussels 5 April 2011.

Memorandum to the Business, Innovation and Skills Select Committee, Post-Legislative Assessment of the Companies Act 2006 (Cm 8255) (January 2012).

2

CORPORATE CAPACITY AND ADMINISTRATION

AIMS AND OBJECTIVES

After reading this chapter you should appreciate the following:
- ➤ The capacity, powers and rights of company
- ➤ The validity of acts by a company
- ➤ presumption of knowledge
- ➤ The provisions relating to articles of association
- ➤ The effect of articles of association
- ➤ The process of amending articles of association
- ➤ The nature and significance of the registered office and how change of the registered office should be effected
- ➤ The obligation and manner in which the name of a company may be published
- ➤ records kept at company's registered office
- ➤ register of directors and secretaries
- ➤ seal of company and execution of documents
- ➤ common seal for use abroad
- ➤ How service of documents on company may be effected
- ➤ How service of documents by company may be made.

2.1   Introduction

According to section 14 of the Act, '[w]here an applicant meets the requirements of [the] Act, the Registrar shall within five days—
- *(a)*   register the proposed company;
- *(b)*   issue a certificate of incorporation in the prescribed form;
- *(c)*   issue a certificate of share capital in the prescribed form, where a company has share capital; and
- *(d)*   assign a designating number to the company as its registration number.

In terms of section 14(2), '[t]he incorporation of a company shall not be invalid by reason only that an individual or individuals subscribed to the application for incorporation in contravention of section 12(8). By section 15(1), '[a] certificate of incorporation issued in accordance with section 14 shall be conclusive evidence that—

(a)   the requirements of this Act regarding the incorporation of the company have been complied with; and

(b)   from the date of registration stated in the certificate, the company is incorporated in accordance with this Act'.

Our discussion hereunder must therefore turn to the consequences of incorporation as outlined in Part III of the Act[1] specifically capacity, powers and rights of company; validity of acts; presumption of knowledge; Articles of association; Effect of articles of association; Amendment of articles of association; registered office and change of registered office; Publication of name of company; records kept at company's registered office; register of directors and secretaries; seal of company and execution of documents; common seal for use abroad; and service of documents on company service of documents by company.

2.2   Capacity powers and rights of company

Once incorporation requirements are met and the certificate of incorporation is issued in terms of section 14, the company shall stand incorporated as an independent juristic/artificial person in the eyes of the law.[2] A company so incorporated, 'shall [in terms of section 22] have—

(a)   perpetual succession and a common seal,[3] capable of suing and being sued in its corporate name and shall, subject to this Act, have power to do all such acts and things as a corporate may by law, do or perform;

(b)   subject to [the] Act and to such limitations as are inherent in its corporate nature, the capacity, rights, powers and privileges of an individual;[4] and

(c)   the capacity to carry on business and exercise its powers in any jurisdiction outside Zambia, to the extent that the laws of Zambia and of that jurisdiction permit.

Perpetual succession such as the one provided for under section 22(a) is one of two core consequences of incorporation the other being limited liability also codified under sections 7(4), 9(3), 10(3) and 11(3) of the Act relating to public

---

[1] SS 22-35.

[2] It falls under what section 3 defines as a 'company' or 'corporate' respectively with the former being an entity incorporated in accordance with [the] Act and section 6 of CA 1994 and the latter meaning 'an entity, including a company or body corporate, that is separate and distinct from its owners and which is recognised as such by law and acts as a single entity.

[3] In terms of section 45(1) of the UK CA 2006 'a company may have a common seal, but need not have one'. It appears that the Act does not give an incorporated company the option of opting out of having a seal like its UK counterpart.

[4] There is a striking resemblance between this section and section 39(1) of the UK CA 2006 which provides under '[a] company's capacity': that '[t]he validity of an act done by a company shall not be called into question on the ground of lack of capacity by reason of anything in the company's constitution. The section must however be read within the context of section 42 (companies that are charities)'.

companies; Private companies limited by shares; private companies limited by guarantee; and private companies unlimited by shares respectively. By perpetual succession is meant the continued existence of the company in spite of changes in the nature, character or complexion of its members. While as exemplified in *Daimler Co v Continental Tyre and Rubber Co*[5] where the majority of the directors became enemy aliens, certain events including the number of directors falling below the statutory minimum[6] or are imprisoned or cannot form a coram will necessary be disconcerting to the company, the company is immune to frailties of natural persons. As Grcer LJ has said in *Stepney Corporation v Osofsky*[7] a company incorporated pursuant to, *inter alia*, sections 6, 12, 14 and 15 of the Act has 'no soul to be saved or body to be kicked'.[8] The concept of perpetual succession may also be helpful in avoiding problems that may arise in the event that an individual sells a business as regards the performance of subsisting contracts by the new owner,[9] 'the assignment of rights of a personal nature,[10] and the validity of agreements made with customers ignorant of the change of'[11] ownership.[12] Where the company has been incorporated will have, in terms of section 14(b), 'subject to [the] Act and to such limitations as are inherent in its corporate nature, the capacity, rights, powers and privileges of an individual.' As such, the company will remain the owner of any and all contracts which it will perform within the context of its being, rights and obligations in the said contract. It will also be at liberty to enter into new contracts. Indeed, it will have 'the capacity to carry on business and exercise its powers in any jurisdiction outside Zambia, to the extent that the laws of Zambia and of that jurisdiction permit'.[13]

We must now turn to the issue of a company having a 'common seal' whose history we discussed at length in chapter 1. A common seal is an official seal routinely used by an incorporated company. Seals are generally used for only two

---

[5] [1916] 2 AC 307 HL.

[6] See interplay between section 85(2)(a)(b) on requisite number of directors and section 90 relating to the consequences of a company carrying on business for a period of more than ninety days with less than the minimum number of directors specified in section 85(2)(a)(b).

[7] [1937] 3 All ER 289 at 291, CA.

[8] See the interesting decision in *Rolloswin Investments Ltd v Chromolit Portugal SARL* [1970] 1 WLR 912 where the court unaware that before the case was heard, the Sunday Observance Act 1677 with which the case was concerned and on whose interpretation the decision lay, had been repealed by the Statute Law (Repeals) Act 1969, held that since a company was incapable of public worship it could not be said to be a 'person' within the meaning of the Sunday Observance Act 1677. As a consequence said the court, a contract made by it on a Sunday was not void.

[9] See *Robson v Drummond* [1831] 2 B. & Ad. 303 for instance.

[10] *Griffiths v Tower Publishing Co* [1897] 1 Ch 21; *Kemp v Baerselman* [1906] 2 KB 604 CA; and *Tolhurst v Associated Portland Cement* [1902] 2 KB 660 CA.

[11] Davies PL *Gower and Davies' Principles of Modern Company Law* 7th edn 35-36.

[12] *Boulton v Jones* [1857] 2 H & N 564.

[13] Section 14(c).

purposes today by companies namely: (i) documents that need to be executed as deeds such as assignments, debentures, mortgages and the like may be executed under a company's common seal; and (ii) certain company documents including share certificates will ordinarily be issued under a company's common seal. Despite the loss of its significance in most common law jurisdictions such as the United Kingdom and Canada, the Act has provided specifically for the common seal in great legislative detail. As such, section 22(a) with reference to the common seal must be read together with sections 32 and 33.[14]

Section 33(1) for instance provides that '[a] company shall have a common seal bearing its name and the words "common seal" in legible letters'. In terms of section 33(2), '[t]he chairperson, vice-chairperson and the secretary or any other person authorised by a resolution of the Board, shall authenticate the affixing of the seal. By section 33(3), '[a] common seal referred to in subsection (1), shall not be used for any purpose, except in accordance with the articles and [the] Act. According to section 33(4), '[a] document or deed shall be validly executed by or on behalf of a company—

(a)   by the affixing of the common seal; or

(b)   if the document or deed bears the signatures or signature of—

      (i)   two authorised signatories; or

      (ii)   a director whose signature is attested by a witness'.

Hence by section 33(5), '[a] document signed, in accordance with subsection (4)(b), shall have the same effect as if executed under the common seal of the company. Finally, in terms of section 33(6), '[a] seal may be kept in electronic form in accordance with the Electronic Communications and Transactions Act'.[15]

In terms of section 34(1), '[a] company may, subject to its articles, have for use outside Zambia, a common seal stating, on its face, the name of the country where the seal is to be used'. By section 34(2), '[a] company may, in writing, under its common seal specified in subsection (1), authorise an agent or appoint an attorney to affix the common seal to a document or execute a deed to which the company is a party to outside Zambia'. According to section 34(3), '[a] person dealing with a person authorised or appointed as specified in subsection (2), shall be entitled to assume that the authority of the person is valid, unless that person has actual notice of the revocation of the appointment or determination of the authority'. Section 34(4), additionally provides that '[a] person affixing the common seal specified in sub-section (1), shall certify on the document or deed to which the seal is affixed the date and the place at which the seal is affixed'.

The former section 22 has, as we have already noted, now been expanded with the addition of section 22(a) codifying inter alia, the concept of perpetual succession. Interestingly, the new section 22(a) provides for a company to 'have

---

[14] A provision similar to section 33 in the UK CA is section 49 headlined: 'Official seal for use abroad'

[15] Act No 21 of 2009.

power to do all such acts and things as a corporate may by law, do or perform'; Section 22*(b)* appears to qualify section 22*(a)* in one breath by implying that the power 'to do all such acts and things as a corporate may by law do or perform', must be exercised within the context of 'such limitations as are inherent in its corporate nature'. In another, as was the case in the old section 22, the company will still have the capacity, rights, powers and privileges of an individual. This provision as do sections 23 and 24 discussed below, ensures the continuation of the debate of whether the *ultra-vires* doctrine[16] has been abolished or is retained in some form by the Act. We must note though that the crafting of section 22 suggests that save for instances where its articles restrict the type of business a company can engage in,[17] a company is free to engage in any business even against or beyond its objects as stated in its application for incorporation pursuant to section 12(4)(viii). The rationale has always been and will, under the Act, continue to be the protection of third parties dealing with the company in good faith and not for those who seek to invoke the provisions if only to perpetuate fraudulent or nefarious activities despite being in the know.

2.3   Validity of acts and presumption of knowledge

The new section 23 is a merger of the former sections 23 and 25 of CA 1994 and except for a few grammatical realignments makes no changes to the old sections 23 and 25. Perchance, a noticeable change from the old section 23 is the specificity of the reasons by which a third party dealing with a company in good faith may not be prejudiced. It cannot be invoked by those in the know or dealing with the company in bad faith.[18]

In terms of section 23(1), '[a] person dealing with the company or any person who has acquired rights from the company, in good faith, shall not be prejudiced by the company or a guarantor of an obligation of the company by reason only that—

(a)   the articles have not been complied with;

(b)   a person named as director of the company in the most recent notice received by the Registrar is not—

　　(i)   a director or an employee of the company;

　　(ii)   duly appointed; or

　　(iii)   authorised to exercise powers performed by a director or executive officer; or

---

[16] For a detailed discussion complete with case analysis see generally, Gates RB *Gates Company Law and Practice in Zambia* 1st edn 72-77 para 4.16; Mwenda KK *Legal Aspects of Banking Regulation: Common Law Perspectives from Zambia* (PULP Pretoria 2010) 44-53.

[17] Section 25(2) provides that [t]he articles may contain restrictions on the type of business that a company may carry on or the powers exercisable by the company while section 25(3) provides that '[a] company shall not carry on any business or exercise a power which the company is restricted by its articles from carrying on or exercising, or exercise any of its powers in a manner that is contrary to its articles.

[18] *Royal British Bank v Turquand* [1843-60] All ER Rep 435; 119 ER 886.

(c)   a director, nominee or chief executive officer of the company acted fraudulently or forged a document, that was signed on behalf of a company'.[19]

By section 23(2), '[s]ubject to subsection(3), a document executed on behalf of a company by a director, nominee or chief executive officer of the company with actual authority to execute the document, shall be valid'. Finally, by section 23(3), '[a] document specified in subsection (2), shall be void if, at the time the document was executed, a person dealing with the company or acquired rights from the company, knew or ought to have known, by virtue of that person's relationship with the company, of the facts specified in subsection (1).

In terms of section 24, '[a] person shall not be affected by, or presumed to have notice of the contents of the articles or any other document of a company, by reason only that the articles or document is—

(a)   registered or has been lodged with the Registrar; or

(b)   available for inspection at the office of the company'.

Sections 23 and 24[20] must be read and appreciated within the context of the law of agency[21] to determine whether the agent through whom the company has acted, specifically a director or board of directors, is clothed with the required authority. As was said in *BP Zambia Plc v Interland Motors Ltd*[22] '[a]s a metaphysical entity or fiction of law which only has legal, but no physical existence, a company (though being a separate and distinct legal person members or shareholders), can only act through the humans charged with its management and conduct of its affairs'.

These persons referred to as directors and provided for under part VII of the Act will act on behalf of the company by way of actual authority[23] described in *Freeman & Lockyer v Buckhurst Properties (Mangal) Ltd*[24] as 'a legal relationship between the principal [the company] and the agent [the director] created by a consensual agreement [in terms of the articles and the Act pursuant to section 17] to which they alone are the parties'. It may also be by way of ostensible (apparent) authority. A key case in this respect is *Armagas Ltd v Mundogas SA*[25] wherein Lord Keith of Kinkel opined that: 'Ostensible authority comes about where the principal, by words or conduct, has represented that the agent has the requisite actual authority, and the party dealing with the agent has entered into a contract with him in reliance on that representation.'

---

[19] *Mahoney v East Holyford Mining Company* [1875] LR 7 HL 869, HL.

[20] Formally sections 23-5 under CA 1994.

[21] For a detailed and systematic discussion of the law of agency in the Zambian context complete with case law, see generally, Malila M *Commercial Law in Zambia: Cases and Materials* (UNZA Press 2007 Lusaka) 115-119.

[22] [2001] ZR 37 (Coram: Ngulube CJ, Chirwa and Muzyamba, JJS).

[23] See sections 85-87 of the Act.

[24] [1964] 2 QB 480 CA.

[25] [1986] AC 717 HL.

So far as company-director relations are concerned, ostensible authority must be seen and determined within the context of section 85(5) which provides that '[a] person who, not being a duly appointed director, holds oneself out, or knowingly allows another to hold that person out, as a director—

(a)   shall be considered to be a director for the purposes of all duties and liabilities, including liabilities for criminal penalties imposed on directors by this Act; and

(b)   commits an offence and is liable, on conviction, to a fine not exceeding one hundred thousand penalty units'.

(c)   The point to be made in this regard is that ostensible authority is predicated, not on the intention of the principal [the company], but perceptions of the third party. For this reason and as section 85(5) shows, one who holds himself out as a director when in fact not, must take responsibility for his actions and shall not bind the company, unless, the company also held him out to be such director in contravention of section 85(6).[26]

Quite apart from the foregoing, sections 23 and 24[27] must be seen within the context of problems that have arisen regarding want of authority by directors and a company acting *ultra vires*,[28] and which, it may seem, the Act has gone some way to try and resolve. They must also be seen within the context of what has been referred to as the indoor management rule or the rule in *Turquand's* case which we discuss below.

2.3.1   *The indoor management rule: the rule in Turquand's case*

As sections 23 and 24 make plain, the mischief they seek to cure are the challenges that result from the application of the rules of agency referred to above 'particularly in the context of limitations on the authority of directors imposed by the company's'[29] articles of association. This is because as section 23(1) shows, '[a] person dealing with the company or any person who has acquired rights from the company, in good faith', may not know that

(a)   the articles have not been complied with;

(b)   a person named as director of the company in the most recent notice received by the Registrar is not—

---

[26] For purposes of protecting third parties acting in good faith section 85(7) provides that '[a] limitation on the authority of a director, whether imposed by the articles or otherwise, shall not be effective against a person who has no knowledge of the limitation, unless, taking into account that person's relationship with the company the person ought to have had knowledge of the limitation'.

[27] Equivalent to sections 40 and 41 of the UK CA 2006.

[28] For a more detailed discussion of the *ultra vires* doctrine see generally, Gates RB *Gates Company Law and Practice in Zambia*….65-73; Griffin S 'The Rise and Fall of the *Ultra-Vires* Rule in Corporate Law', *Mountbatten Journal of Legal Studies*, 1998, ssudl.solent.ac.uk/954/1/1998_2_1.pdf; and Mwenda KK *Legal Aspect of Banking Regulation: Common Law Perspective from Zambia* (PULP Pretoria 2010) 21-64.

[29] Ridley A and Shepherd C *Company Law: Key facts key cases* (Routledge New York 2015) 80.

> > (i)   a director or an employee of the company;
> > (ii) duly appointed; or
> > (iii) authorised to exercise powers performed by a director or executive officer; or
>
> *(c)*   a director, nominee or chief executive officer of the company acted fraudulently or forged a document, that was signed on behalf of a company.[30]

In addition to the foregoing and compounding the problem further was the fact that a third party dealing with a company was taken 'or presumed to have notice of the contents of the articles or any other document of a company, by reason only that the articles or document in question had been registered or had been lodged with the Registrar'; 'or' was 'available for inspection at the office of the company'[31] This problem referred to as constructive notice gave way to the development of the *Turquand* (or indoor management) rule which mitigated the unfair consequences of constructive notice. In *Royal British Bank v Turquand*[32] a company's articles of association obliged its directors to, before the company could borrow money, obtain authorisation for such borrowing by way of an ordinary resolution. The directors, in contravention of this requirement borrowed £2,000.00 from the plaintiff, which claimed in the company's winding up. It was held that the plaintiff bank was entitled to assume, as it did, that 'matters of indoor management' as they related to the money borrowed had been complied with. As such, the court determined, the company was liable whether or not the requisite ordinary resolution had been passed. Similarly, in *Mahony v East Holyford Mining Co*[33] where a bank was instructed to honour the company's cheques as long as same signatures of two named directors appended and countersigned by the secretary and in which the liquidator sought repayment by the bank owing to an unbeknown fact that the directors who signed on cheques relating to the money being claimed had not been properly appointed, it was held, relying on *Turquand* that the bank was permitted to assume that the directors in question had been properly appointed and as such was not liable. The liquidator's claim would fail.

Similar conclusions have been reached in several Zambian cases: In *Zambia Bata Shoe Company v Vin-Mas Ltd*[34] the managing director of the appellant company instructed one of his subordinates, one Mr. Mbewe to advertise some of the company's houses for sale. Mr. Mbewe issued the advertisements. The managing director then left the country but while he was away Mr. Mbewe went ahead and sold one of the company houses to a prospective buyer. Upon

---

[30] *Mahoney v East Holyford Mining Company* [1875] LR 7 HL 869 HL.

[31] Section 24.

[32] [1856] 6 E & B 327; [1843-60] All ER Rep 435; 119 ER 886.

[33] [1875] LR 7 HL 869.

[34] [1993-94] 136; approving *Royal British Bank v Turquand* [1843-60] All ER Rep 435; 119 ER 886.*Mahoney v East Holyford Mining Company* [1875] LR 7 HL 869, HL.

his return, the managing director was surprised to find that the house had been sold and told Mr. Mbewe that he was not authorised to sell the house as that power rested in the Board of Directors. Mr. Mbewe consequently resigned. The appellant company attempted to overturn the contract of sale but the trial court dismissed the action and on appeal it was held that (i) In practice most people dealing with companies rely on the rule of *Turquand*'s case and do not bother to inspect the Articles. They assume that they are not concerned with domestic or "indoor" formalities. (ii) Applying the fiction of constructive notice, both the vendor and the purchaser were aware of the need for a special resolution and the binding contract for sale was entered into on that basis. As in cases where there is failure to apply for state consent, the courts will not allow a vendor to avoid liability under a contract of sale by pleading his own default. In this case the company's authorised agents bound the company to comply with the contract and such liability cannot be avoided.

In *National Airport Corporation v Reggie Ephraim Zimba and Savior Konie*[35] the appellant company was desirous of employing a Managing Director. The short listed candidates were interviewed and it appears that during such exercise the sort of remuneration package expected and that to be offered were discussed.

The position was offered to the first respondent in a letter dated 6th August 1996, written on behalf of the appellant by the second respondent who was at the time the Chairman of the Board of Directors of the appellant company. Consequently, the first appellant was offered a two year contract to run from 1st September 1996, to 30th August 1998. The first respondent worked for four months and a few days until 14th January 1997, when his contract was terminated quite summarily. The learned trial Judge found for the first respondent in respect of the claim for breach of contract and awarded him damages. The appellant appealed. It was held in*ter alia*, that an outsider dealing with a company cannot be concerned with any alleged want of authority when dealing with a representative of appropriate authority or standing for the class or type of transaction.

In *Bank of Zambia v Chibote Meat*[36] the Zambian Supreme Court interpreted the present section 23 and 24 (formerly 24 and 25 in CA 1994) as being intended for the protection of third parties who dealt with the company and that matters of internal procedure should not be imputed on people.

Given the foregoing, it is conceivably not surprising that the former section 24 has been retained in the Act in the same form as before and still provides that '[a] person shall not be affected by, or presumed to have notice of the contents of the articles or any other document of a company, by reason only that the articles or document is—

[35] SCZ Judgment No 34 of 2000.
[36] SCZ Judgment No 14 of 1999.

(a)   registered or has been lodged with the Registrar; or

(b)   available for inspection at the office of the company'.

Be that as it may, and considering that section 23(2) provides, for purposes of protecting third parties dealing with the company in good faith, that 'a document executed on behalf of a company by a director, nominee or chief executive officer of the company with actual authority to execute the document, shall be valid', the same is subject to section 23(3) which provides that '[a] document specified in subsection (2), shall be void if, at the time the document was executed, a person dealing with the company or acquired rights from the company, knew or ought to have known, by virtue of that person's relationship with the company, of the facts specified in subsection (1).[37] 'The spirit of the law in this respect is not, as may be mistakenly believed, to protect without qualification, all third parties irrespective'.[38]   If there was any doubt in this respect, the same has been removed by section 23(3). Sections 23 and 24 are thus wider than the rule in *Turquand* since knowledge of a defect prevents the third party from relying on *Turquand*.

The foregoing notwithstanding, the rule in *Turquand* has limitations which as demonstrated in *B liggit (Liverpool) v Barclays Bank Ltd,*[39] *Morris v Kanssen*[40] and *Fresh Mint Ltd, Heman Jallan, Thompson Lloyd and Ewart Ltd v Kawambwa Tea Company Ltd*[41] include, but are not limited to the fact that where the articles explicitly prohibit certain actions by a director, such director cannot rely on the internal management rule, nor can (an issue that is now clearly provided for under section 23(2)), a third party who has been put on enquiry or notice as to the want of authority due to his dealings with the company.

2.4   Articles of association

Articles of association are the rules selected by a company to regulate the company's affairs which include rights and obligations of members and how the business of the company will be run. To that end and in terms of section 25 which replaces and expands section 7 of CA 1994 '[a] company *shall* have articles of association that regulate the conduct of the company'.[42] It is immediately

---

37   Which provides that '[a] person dealing with the company or any person who has acquired rights from the company, in good faith, shall not be prejudiced by the company or a guarantor of an obligation of the company by reason only that—*(a)* the articles have not been complied with; *(b)* a person named as director of the company in the most recent notice received by the Registrar is not—(i) a director or an employee of the company; (ii) duly appointed; or (iii) authorised to exercise powers performed by a director or executive officer; or *(c)* a director, nominee or chief executive officer of the company acted fraudulently or forged a document, that was signed on behalf of a company'.

38   Gates RB *Gates Company Law and Practice in Zambia....*

39   [1928] 1 KB 48.

40   [1946] AC 459 HL.

41   [2008] 2 ZR 32 (SC).

42   Section 25(1).

evident from this provision that the confusion and uncertainty brought about by the previous section 7(1) of CA 1994 which provided in permissive terms that '[a] company *may* have articles regulating the conduct of the company' and thereby implied that a company could exist without articles of association has been removed.[43] Having articles of association is now mandatory under the Act without more.

In terms of section 25(2), '[t]he articles may contain restrictions on the type of business that a company may carry on or the powers exercisable by the company. The permissive crafting in this subsection must be understood within the context of section 12(4)(viii) which provides as already noted that an application for incorporation specified in section 12(1), shall, among other things, state 'the nature of the company's proposed business or proposed activity'. This is important because in terms of section 25(3), '[a] company shall not carry on any business or exercise a power which the company is restricted by its articles from carrying on or exercising, or exercise any of its powers in a manner that is contrary to its articles'. Whether or not contravening this part of the section will negatively affect a third part dealing with the company will depend on the circumstances and facts of the transaction concerned and the application of sections 23 and 24 to the particular transaction and whether the third party was acting in good faith or by his dealings, he ought to have known that the company or any of its directors were acting contrary to restrictions placed on them by the articles within the context of section 25(3).[44]

Articles, including standard articles provided for in the first schedule pursuant to section 12(3) cannot be put on the same operational plain with statutory law in terms of significance. Even though a company will be run in terms of the articles and the Act, articles of association are subject to statutory law including but not limited to the Act. *A fortiori,* section 25(4) provides that '[a] provision in the articles which is inconsistent with this Act or any other law is invalid to the extent of the inconsistency'. 'The articles shall be divided into paragraphs numbered consecutively'.[45] We must add that articles ought not, for ease of reference, be scattered in different documents but must be contained in one document. In terms of section 25(6), '[t]he articles shall be signed by persons who are the first members of the company.

---

[43] Having said that, the continued use of the word '*shall*' must, in light of the fact that it appears to lack a single meaning, and may be a cause for litigation apart from the fact that it is nearly absent from ordinary every day parlance, be reconsidered. By way of comparison, section 18 of the UK CA 2006 provides that '[a] company *must* have articles of association prescribing regulations for the company'.

[44] See *Zambia Bata Shoe Company v Vin-Mas Ltd*[1993-94] 136; approving *Royal British Bank v Turquand* [1843-60] All ER Rep 435; 119 ER 886; *Mahoney v East Holyford Mining Company* [1875] LR 7 HL 869 HL; see further, *B liggit (Liverpool) v Barclays Bank Ltd*[1928] 1 KB 48; *Morris v Kanssen*; [1946] AC 459 HL; and *Fresh Mint Ltd, Heman Jallan, Thompson Lloyd Ewart Ltd v Kawambwa Tea Company Ltd* [2008] 2 ZR 32 (SC).

[45] Section 25(5).

There is the option that also existed in section 7(5) of the CA 1994 and has been retained in section 25(7) which is that '[a] company may adopt the Standard Articles set out in the Schedules or any specified regulation therein. However, interestingly and unlike in the past section 25(8) provides that '[w] here a company adopts the Standard Articles set out in the Schedules, the company shall not be required to file the Standard Articles with the Registrar'. This provision which dispenses with the filing of Standard Articles where such are adopted in the incorporation process must be read and understood within the context of section 12(3)(a) which provides that among documents that 'shall accompany an application for incorporation of a company is 'a copy of the proposed articles of the company, or *a statement that it has adopted the Standard Articles*'.[46]

As is discernible from the Standard Articles in the schedules of the Act, articles of association will ordinarily include the following:

1. Interpretation
2. Share Capital and Variation of Rights
3. Calls on Shares
4. Lien
5. Forfeiture of Shares
6. Transfer of Shares
7. Transmission of Shares
8. Conversion of Shares into Stock
9. Alteration of Capital
10. General Meetings
11. Proceedings at General Meetings
12. Directors
13. Borrowing Powers
14. Proceedings of Directors
15. Managing Director
16. Associate Directors
17. Secretary
18. Seal
19. Inspection of Records
20. Dividends and Reserves
21. Capitalisation of Profits
22. Winding up
23. Indemnity

---

[46] Emphasis added.

2.5   Effect of articles of association[47]

The satisfaction of the procedures in sections 12 through 15 leads to the incorporation of a company. This incorporation, according to section 17, 'has the same effect as a contract under seal between the company and its members and between the members themselves, in which they agree to form a company whose business shall be conducted in accordance with the articles and [the] Act'. Given that the articles will be the constitution through which the company is run, subject to the Act, '[t]he articles [themselves] shall have the effect of a contract between—

(a)   the company and each member; and

(b)   amongst the members[48].

Further and in terms of section 26(2), '[t]he articles shall bind the company and its members'. It is worth noting that while the incorporation of a company 'has the same effect as a contract under seal' the binding nature of articles has the 'effect of a [simple] contract'. The distinction is important. The general rule is that a contract need not be concluded in a particular form. The fact is though that most contracts will be reduced in writing so that parties have a record to refer to should they be victims of the 'treachery of memory'. Be that as it may, some contracts, such as incorporation of the company, are required by law to follow a certain form or be under seal or by deed.

A deed must make it clear that it is such and intended to be so. The incorporation of a company and the form in which it is to be done, is prescribed. It must state that it is intended to be an incorporation of a company in terms of section 6 and 12. Further, there must be a declaration in terms of section 13 'that the requirements of the Act relating to incorporation, have been complied with'.[49] This is in keeping with the position that a deed will require additional procedures regarding signatures or execution for purposes of enforceability.

A [simple] contract, (which is statutorily provided for under section 25(5)), the effect of which articles of association once registered, are said to have can be concluded orally except that in the case of articles, as is the case with most simple contracts, they must be in writing in according with section 25(5) which mandates that the articles 'shall be divided into paragraphs numbered consecutively'. Additionally, and unlike incorporation, which requires no consideration, the contract which the articles bring about is one which will

---

[47] Provided for under section 26.

[48] Section 26(1).

[49] In terms of section 13(2), '[t]he declaration, referred to in subsection (1), shall be made in the prescribed manner and form by a—*(a)* legal practitioner holding a valid practicing certificate who was engaged in the formation of the company; or *(b)* person named, as a first director or secretary of the company, in the application for incorporation. The importance of this is shown in section 13(3) in that '[t]he Registrar may accept the declaration as *prima facie* evidence of compliance with the requirements of this Act'.

require each member and the company to provide consideration of some sort, a price paid by each party, which in the case of the company, may be the allotment of shares and for the members, payment for the shares allotted to them.[50] Below, we dissect section 26 of the Act.[51]

2.5.1   '[t]he articles shall have the effect of a contract between'—

2.5.1.1 (a) 'the company and each member'

By this is meant that by virtue of his capacity as a member of the company, the member is bound by the provisions of the articles of association. In *Hickman v Kent or Romney Marsh Sheepbreeders' Association*[52] the defendant, an association registered as a company under the UK CA 1895 refused to register the plaintiff's certain of his sheep in the flock book for which he sought damages in his action against the company. By summons the defendant sought to stay the proceedings on the strength of the fact that the articles of association provided that any disputes between the company and the members were to be referred to arbitration. It was held that being a statutory contract [under what is now section 33 UK CA equivalent to section 26 of the Act] between the members and the company and amongst the members themselves, the plaintiff was bound to submit his dispute to arbitration.[53]

2.5.1.2 (b) 'amongst the members'

Section 26(1)(b) codifies a common law position which is that the articles are a contract between the members themselves. It means that a member can invoke section 26(1)(b) in bringing an action against another member who has breached any of the provisions of the articles to the exclusion of the company. The scenario was played out in the case of *Rayfield v Hands*[54] where the company's articles provided in Art II that 'Every member who intends to transfer shares shall inform the directors who will take the said shares equally between them

---

[50] Under section 33(2) of the UK CA 2006, 'Money payable by a member to the company under its constitution is a debt due from him to the company. In England and Wales and Northern Ireland it is of the nature of an ordinary contract debt'.

[51] Compare this to the UK CA section 33(1) which provides as follows: '(1) The provisions of a company's constitution bind the company and its members to the same extent as if there were covenants on the part of the company and of each member to observe those provisions'.

[52] [1915] 1 Ch 881.

[53] See further, *Pender v Lushington* [1877] 6 Ch D 70 where the plaintiff whose resolution was lost thanks to the chairman of the meeting refusing to accept the plaintiff's votes succeeded in stopping the directors from acting contrary to the resolution because according to the court, the articles were a contract binding the company to the members; and *Beattie v E&F Beattie Ltd* [1938] Ch 708 where a similar provision in the articles was held not to apply to a person who dispute with the company fell in the realm of his being a director, the fact that he was a member notwithstanding.

[54] [1958] 2 All ER 194; [1960] 1 Ch 1.

at a fair value'. The plaintiff who held 725 fully-paid up shares valued at £1 each accordingly notified the directors of his intention to transfer his shares to them. They refused have the transfer effected. The plaintiff sought an order of specific performance. It was held by Vaisey J that the directors were bound to take the shares. As the court saw it, having regard [to what is now section 26(1)(b) in the Act], Art II constituted a binding contract between the directors (who were required to hold qualification shares thus making them members) and the plaintiff as a member in respect of his rights as such member.[55]

2.5.2 'The articles shall bind the company and its members'

This provision excludes the application of the rights inherent in the articles and resulting obligations from those not privy to the contract. The articles can generally not be construed to be a contract with third parties but strictly between the company and its members.[56] The case of *Eley v Positive Government Security Life Assurance Co*[57] demonstrates the foregoing. In that case, the plaintiff who was appointed pursuant to the articles of the company which stipulated that he could not be dismissed but for misconduct, sued the company for breach when, after he had become a member following his service to the firm for a time, the company appointed other lawyers to handle their legal matters. The action failed because according to the court, there was no contract between the plaintiff and the company under the articles. He was an outsider who could not rely on the contractual effect of the articles, the fact that he was now a member of the company notwithstanding.[58] This latter fact was in fact irrelevant as the dispute related not to his rights as a member as against the company's obligations towards him but his rights as a solicitor, an outsider.

---

[55] The fact that the obligation even though relating to directors was construed as falling upon the said directors within the context of them being members is an important distinction between the *ratio decidendi* in *Rayfield* and that in *Beattie* failing which the contractual aspect of the provision in article II would not have applied.

56 However see *Re New British Iron, Ex parte Beckwith* [1898] 1 Ch 324; *Read v Astoria Garage (Streatham) Ltd* [1952] Ch 637; and *Salmon v Quin & Axtens Ltd* [1909] 1 Ch 311 for instances where a provision in the articles can translate into a contract between the company and a member or third party.

[57] [1876] 1 Ex D 88.

[58] Be that as it may, given the circumstances and facts of the case and the fact that the decision was predicated on section 4 of the Statute of Frauds 1677 (applicable to Zambia by virtue of the English Law (Extension of Application) Act Chapter 11 of the Laws of Zambia) now repealed and re-enacted by section 1 of the Law Reform (Enforcement of Contracts) Act, 1954 (itself applicable to Zambia by virtue of section 2 of the British Acts Extension Act Chapter 10 of the Laws of Zambia) the case must be read within the context of the decisions in *Re New British Iron, Ex parte Beckwith* [1898] 1 Ch 324; *Read v Astoria Garage (Streatham) Ltd* [1952] Ch 637; and *Salmon v Quin & Axtens Ltd* [1909] 1 Ch 311.

2.6   Amendment of articles of association

2.6.1   *General*

Articles of association are not unassailable. They are, as section 27(1) provides, amenable to amendment by the passage of a special resolution.[59] It follows, given the foregoing, that the 'from time to time' phrase, as it appeared in section 21 of CA 1994 was superfluous. All articles are subject to amendment and as such any attempt to craft an article to the effect that the articles will not be subject to amendment would be contrary to section 27(1) and as such illegal.[60] In any case, such an amendment would not be accepted for lodgment under section 27(2) and even if for some administrative error, it was, it would not be valid under section 27(3) for contravening section 27(1).

In terms of section 27(2), '[a] company shall, where it amends its articles, in accordance with subsection(1), within twenty-one days after the date of passing the resolution, lodge a copy of the resolution with the Registrar, together with a copy of each paragraph of the articles affected by the amendment, in its amended form'. The provision in section 27(3) that '[t]he articles shall take effect, in their amended form, on and from the day of their lodgement with the Registrar, or such later date as may be specified in the resolution shows several things. Firstly, that the provisions by which the articles are amended are as valid as the original provisions now replaced; secondly, that the amended articles can they themselves only be amended following the same procedure stipulated in section 27(1)-(3); and thirdly, that the amendment of articles are subject to the regulatory power of the Act as (i) they should be amended subject to the Act and (ii) that they will only take effect on lodgement and the registrar being informed or such later date thereof. This last point is significant in that the company cannot act in tandem with the amended articles until this critical stage provided for in section 27(3) is fulfilled. It follows therefore that any purported actions based on provisions in articles for which amendment is sort will still be valid and any action based on amended articles before lodgment pursuant to section 27(2) will, in terms of section 27(3) be invalid. So serious is the lodgment requirement that '[i]f a company fails to comply with' it, 'the company, and each officer in default, commits an offence and is liable, on conviction, to a fine not exceeding three hundred thousand penalty units for each day that the contravention continues'.

Having said that, we must make the point that as shown in *Allen v Gold Reefs of West Africa Ltd*[61] section 27(1) does not stop a company from amending its

---

[59] In terms of section 3 "special resolution" means a resolution passed by not less than seventy-five per cent of the votes of members of a company, entitled to vote in person or by proxy at a meeting duly convened and held at which the resolution is moved as a special resolution, or such higher majority percentage as the articles of association may require.

[60] See *Punt v Symons & Co* [1903] 2 Ch 506.

[61] [1900] 1 Ch 656.

articles the effect of which is to have retro-effective consequences on present rights enjoyed by members if the said amendment is for the benefit of the company unless the articles themselves provide against such amendment.

2.6.2 Restrictions on amendment of articles

Be that as it may, one must note the following restrictions, among others, regarding amendment of articles:[62]

(i) No amendment to the articles the effect of which is to permit a company to engage in illegal activities is permissible.[63]

(ii) No amendment that contravenes the Act is permissible.

(iii) 'Despite anything in the articles, a shareholder is not bound by an amendment of the articles that—

(a) requires the shareholder to acquire or hold more shares in the company than the number held on the date the amendment takes effect; or

(b) increases the liability of the shareholder to the company, unless the shareholder agrees, in writing, to be bound by the amendment, before or after it is made'.[64]

(iv) No amendment requiring the company to alter the articles below the statutory threshold is permissible.

(v) No amendment in contravention of a court order is permissible.

(vi) The High Court[65] has, as shown in *Allen v Gold Reefs of West Africa Ltd*[66] jurisdiction to deem an amendment of articles as unenforceable unless it can be shown that said amendment was done for the benefit of the entire body of membership. To do this the Court uses an objective test. Essentially the Court sees the company in equipoise. By that is meant that the Court imagines a hypothetical company in which shareholding and by implication voting power are evenly distributed and shareholders vote independent of each other and not combine to foist their voting pattern on others.[67] 'The difficulty is that the court sometimes assumes, probably rightly, that those who are managing the company's affairs and, on occasion, a majority of the shareholders,

---

[62] See generally, Keenan D *Smith and Keenan's Company Law* 13th edn (Pearson Longman London 2005) 105-6.

[63] See section 12(1).

[64] Section 128.

[65] In terms of section 3 "Court" means the High Court for Zambia.

[66] [1900] 1 Ch 656; *Shuttleworth v Cox Brothers & Co (Maidenhead) Ltd* [1927] 2KB 9; *Citco Banking Corp NV v Pusser's Ltd* [2007] UKPC 13; [2007] Bus LR 960.

[67] See generally, Keenan, D *Smith and Keenan's Company Law* 13th edn.

know better than the court what is for its benefit'.[68] The problem that arises with this approach as one can imagine is the variance between the conclusions the court is likely to draw in the event that the impugned amendment meets the *Allen* test as against minority shareholders feeling had done by said amendment.[69]

In any event, the result of the objective test employed by the court is that most amendments will be deemed valid including those relating to expulsion of members where there are good and compelling reasons for doing so among them that the expelled member's activities which may have include fraud or direct competition with the company were inimical to the company and or the membership as a whole. The cases of *Dafen Tinplate Co Ltd v Llanelly Steel Co [1907] Ltd[70], Sidebottom v Kershaw, Leese & Co[71] Shuttleworth v Cox Brothers & Co (Maidenhead) Ltd[72]* illustrate this point.

2.6.3 *Amendment of articles and consequential breaches of contract with third parties*

The consequences of amendment may well result in breaches to subsisting contracts with third parties. This is because a company cannot knowingly or unknowingly escape its liability by using the device of amendment of articles allowed under section 27 of the Act. Considerable judicial difficulties have been witnessed with regard to what remedies are open to an innocent third party[73] with it being said in *Punt v Symons & Co Ltd[74]* that while the third party could claim for damages, he could not obtain an injunction to stop the amended articles from taking effect (which would have to be before they are lodged in accordance with section 27(2) or such later date as provided in the articles as provided for in section 27(3) of the Act). In *Baily v British Equitable Assurance Co Ltd[75]* the EWCA seemed to indicate that both remedies were available to the third party. The law appears to have been settled in *Southern Foundries (1926)*

---

[68] Keenan, D *Smith and Keenan's Company Law* 13th edn 106.

[69] See *Greenhalgh v Arderne Cinemas Ltd* [1951] Ch 286.

[70] [1920] 2 Ch 124.

[71] [1920] 1 Ch 154.

[72] [1927] 2 KB 9.

[73] Where an article is included in a contract putting a third party on notice that the company may alter its articles thus affecting the contract, the third party is taken to know that the risk that the contract may fail and prevent him from claiming damages: See *Shuttleworth v Cox Brothers & Co (Maidenhead) Ltd* [1927] 2KB 9. However, see limitations to this rule regarding rights that have already accrued in a contract in *Swabey v Port Darwin Gold Mining Co* [1889] 1 Meg 385 and amendment of articles being inconsequential to express terms of the contract in *Southern Foundries (1926) Ltd v Shirlaw* [1940] AC 701.

[74] [1903] 2 Ch 506.

[75] [1904] 1 Ch 374.

Ltd v Shirlaw[76] where Porter J opined orbiter[77] that only the remedy of damages was open to the third party. It follows therefore that while a company is free to alter or amend its articles, and cannot be estopped from doing so by an outsider whose contract may be affected by such amendment, should the amendment breach a subsisting contract, the company may be liable to pay damages in an action for breach of contract resulting from the amendment.

2.6.4 *Amendment of articles by the court*

The fact that articles of association are said to, as we have already noted under section 25, form a contract (albeit a statutory one) means that they are amenable to consideration and adjudication by the High Court. It is however doubtful that the High Court would go so far as to amend articles if called upon to do so. The first reason for the disinclination to do so would be the concept of 'freedom of contract' and the other more significant and fundamental reason is that section 27(1) provides that articles can only be amended by special resolution. This was the conclusion reached in *Scott v Frank F Scott (London) Ltd.*[78] Be that as it may, where, as in *Folkes Group Plc v Alexander,*[79] an absurdity may result from following the general rule set in *Scott,* the High Court ought to depart from the principle in *Scott.* In the *Folkes* case, the court was compelled to order the addition of five words to a badly drafted amended article in order to give it the intended effect, as to leave the article as it was, would defy business sense.[80] This was a case, as the court admitted, where judicial decisions might on occasion profit from collective commercial logic.

2.7   Shareholders' agreements

Shareholders' agreements have increasingly come to supplement statutory documents specifically the articles of association. Like articles and other constitutive documents mentioned in Section 17, those shareholders' agreements are binding contracts as between the parties to the exclusion of everyone else. In addition to the foregoing, articles deal with rights and duties of members of a particular company to which they apply. A great advantage of having shareholders' agreements is that unlike articles of association, they remain secret since they are not registered and are thus not open to public scrutiny.

As seen in *Mwamba v Nthenge, Kaing'a, Chekwe* (below*)*, courts can adjudicate upon shareholder agreements due to their contractual force. This principle had been discussed ten years earlier in *Euro Brokers Holdings Ltd v*

---

[76] [1940] AC 701.

[77] Approving *Punt v Symons & Co Ltd* [1903] 2 Ch 506.

[78] [1940] Ch 794.

[79] [2002] 2 BCLC 254.

[80] *Investors Compensation Scheme Ltd v West Bromwich Building Society* [1998] 1 BCLC 493 followed.

Monecor (London) Ltd[81] which was to the effect 'that the informal and unanimous assent of all the company's shareholders can override formal requirements as where a particular course of action requires a meeting and resolution of the shareholders, either under statutory provisions or because of the requirements of the company's articles, and no such meeting and/ or resolution has been held or passed or written resolution made.'[82]

2.7.1   Why shareholders should have agreements[83]

While it is trite that articles of association bind shareholders from the date of the formation of the company, there are good and compelling reasons why members should craft shareholder agreements. Articles of association are public documents registrable with the Registrar of companies and are available to all and sundry. So shareholders who are desirous of agreeing on certain matters to keep away from public domain ought to conclude, as between them, a shareholders agreement.

An inherent disadvantage of articles of association is that they are alterable, as discussed above, at any time with a special resolution. This is preventable if there exists a shareholders' agreement that fixes a higher threshold or imposes other conditions relating to articles. Minority shareholders can thus expect to be protected from what may be called the inherent oppression of the minority by the majority. A rule of thumb is that where it is important to have a 3rd party put on notice, or even crucially a prospective state as regards any restrictions which many be contained in a shareholder agreement, it is important that such a restriction be replicated in the articles of association. Typical examples of the above include: Issue/issuance of shares; transfer of shares/pre-emptive rights; and conducting business.

2.7.2   The nature and effect of shareholders Agreements

A 'shareholder[s'] agreement is a contract between persons who are parties to it and is enforceable in accordance with normal contractual principles'.[84] Shareholders' agreements are described as useful in conferring rights on shareholders, which rights would not be enforceable if contained in the articles of association. Some Jurists[85] have note that,

> Since 1856, the Companies Acts have provided for a constitution
> in the form of memorandum and articles of association. The

---

[81] [2003] 1 BCLC 506; approving *Re Duomatic* [1969] 2Ch 365.

[82] Paraphrased in *Smith and Keenan's Company Law* 15th edn...110.

[83] Taken from Gates RB *Company Law and Practice in Zambia*...

[84] Steadman G and Jones J *Shareholders' Agreements* 3rd edn (...1998) 58.

[85] Farrah JH and Hannigan BM Farrar's Company Law 4th edn...135.

proprietors of a company sometimes wish to supplement these for a variety of reasons. Although they value the limitation of personal liability as regards the outside world, they wish to agree among themselves how risk, profit and control shall ultimately be distributed.

Further, it has been observed[86] that quite apart from those terms in the articles of the company designed to police the affiliation of members among themselves, it is lawfully permissible for the shareholders to bind themselves through an independent and supplemental shareholders' agreement with contractual force predicated on common law principles to enable them act and/or vote 'in a specific way on issues governed by the terms of the agreement....' The agreement seeks to regulate matters of internal management with the effect that members who are a party to the agreement must act and vote on specific issues in a predetermined way'.

What is apparent is that shareholders are not precluded from concluding a contract amongst themselves through a shareholder agreement specific rights or obligations. 'Such shareholders' agreements will be personally binding on each shareholder who has executed the same, courts will honour such agreements'.[87] We must further note that shareholders' agreements are classified as follows:[88]

(a)   An agreement between the company and the members collateral and supplementary to the articles;[89]

(b)   An agreement between all the shareholders inter se;[90]

(c)   An agreement between some of the shareholders.[91]

2.7.3   *Construction of shareholders' agreements*

Normal rules of construing contracts apply to shareholders' agreements. The starting point is that words ought to be given their natural meaning[92] unless this

---

[86]   Griffin S *Company Law Handbook* 2nd edn (...2010) quoted in *Mwamba Nthenge* at J 13.

[87]   *Mwamba Nthenge* at J14 – 15.

[88]   For a detailed discussion see generally, Farrah JH and Hannigan BM *Farrar's Company Law* 4th edn...136 – 9.

[89]   See Salmond J's lucid description of this at law in *Shalfoon v Cheddar Valley Co-operative Dairy Co Ltd* [1924] NZLR 561.

[90]   See *Greenhalgh v Mallard* [1943] 2 All ER 234, CA; *Elliot v Richardson* [1870] LR 5 CP 744; *Coronation Syndicate Ltd v Lilienfeld and New Fortuna Co Ltd* 1903 TS 489 at 497; *Puddenphatt v Leith* [1916] 1 Ch 200; *Ringuet v Bergeron* [1906] 24 DLR (2d) 449; *Pennell Securities Ltd v Venida Investments Ltd*, 25 July 1974, noted (1981) 44 MLR 40 245 (See article by Susan Bridge [1984] 44 MLR 40); *Russell v Northern Bank Development Corp Ltd* [1992] BCLC 1016 (See analysis in *Sealy & Worthington's Cases and Materials in Company Law* 10th edn (Oxford University Press Oxford 2013) 265/ Sealy [1992] CLJ 437).

[91]   'The principles are the same as in (b) above but the exercise of the contractual provisions can work oppressively on members who are not parties to the contract' giving rise to minority shareholders remedies under section 330.- *Farrar's Company Law*...139.

[92]   *Chitty on Contracts General Principles*, Vol. 1 20th edn.

would lead to absurdity. It follows that,[93] as with any written agreement, the court is permitted to gaze at any and all substantiation 'of the objective factual background known to the parties at or before the date of the contract, including evidence of the "genesis" and objectively the "aim" of the transaction'. Be that as it may, the court is precluded to and should not attempt or be misled into looking at evidence relating to the parties' subjective intentions no matter how seemingly telling. It has further been observed by some[94] that,

> The cardinal presumption is that the parties have intended what they in fact said, so that their words must be construed as they stand. That is to say, the meaning of the document or a part of it is to be sought in the document itself: one must consider the meaning of the words used, not what one may guess to be the intention of the parties. However, no contract is made in a vacuum. In construing a document, the court may resolve the ambiguity by looking at its commercial purpose and the factual background against which it was made.[95]

It is therefore clear that the factual background leading to the execution of these agreements is an important part when considering the meaning of the agreements. As it has been repeatedly stated, that an agreement is not made in a vacuum. shareholders' agreements are accepted as being capable of departing from articles of association in the manner directors are appointed and, or, in the management of a company.[96]

2.7.4   Relationship between shareholders' agreements and articles of association

Articles of association deal with membership rights while shareholders' agreements are not restricted to dealing with membership rights only. A point to note is that what is contained in a shareholder agreement is largely a matter of test. In *Wilkinson v West Coast Capital,*[97] a shareholders' agreement provided (a) in Clause 5 that specific actions could only be pursued by the company if 65 per cent of the shareholders provided their consent; and (b) in Clause 7 that the shareholders should use all reasonable and proper means to promote the interests of the company. The combination of these two clauses meant that shareholder-directors are to use their vote so as to prevent the company from pursuing certain opportunities and thereby preventing them from being classified as 'corporate opportunities' and subsequently enabling them to pursue them themselves. A

---

[93] Lewison K *The Interpretation of Contracts* 2nd edn (...1997).
[94] Lewison K *The Interpretation of Contracts* 2nd edn (...1997).
[95] Quoted in *Mwamba Nthenge* at J16 - 17.
[96] *Palmer's Company Law Manual* 2000 edn.
[97] [2005] EWHC 3009 (Ch); summarised in *Smith and Keenan's Company Law* 15th edn 109.

minority shareholder unsuccessfully brought an action under s 994, CA 2006 on the grounds that this was unfairly prejudicial conduct.

Unlike articles which are subject to an alteration threshold of 75 percent or more under section 27, the alteration of shareholders' agreements or clauses thereof can only be done upon 100 percent of the members who executed the agreement agreeing to such alteration. Furthermore, as shown in *Mwamba Nthenge* (below) and *Russell v Northern Bank* (below), the courts seem to agree to take the existence of shareholders' agreements as normal contractual activity, 'providing them with a degree of legitimacy, power and scope'.[98] Additionally, the foregoing authorities also show that courts will resort to shareholders' agreements in the event of a dispute between the shareholders. As shown in *Russell v Northern Bank* (below) however, problems may arise where there is an inconsistency between the terms of the articles and those of the shareholders' agreement.

In *Russell v Northern Bank Development Corporation Limited,*[99] the House of Lords upheld the validity of a membership agreement by which all five (current) members of the company were bound. In that case, the company's five shareholders agreed to refrain from voting to increase the company's share capital, save in a situation where all parties consented in writing to the increase. Subsequently, as the company's circumstances changed, four of the members proposed that the company should increase its issued share capital. However, the fifth member challenged the proposal in so far as it contradicted the terms of the membership agreement. The House of Lords held the agreement to be binding as it was separate and distinct from the company's articles and was of a personal nature.

2.7.5 *Enforceability of shareholders' agreements*

The starting point is that since shareholders' agreements are considered as falling squarely under the law of contract, their enforceability failing performance by either party will be guided by the said principles. Concerning the law of contract, it has been said that:

> The Law of contract is perceived as a set of power conferring rules which enable individuals to enter into agreement of their own choice on their own terms. Freedom of contract and sanctity of contract are the dominant ideologies. Parties should be as free as possible to make agreements on their own terms without the interference of the courts or parliament and their agreements should be respected, upheld and enforced by the courts.[100]

---

[98] *Smith and Keenan's Company Law* 15th edn.
[99] [1992] 1 WLR 588; summarised in Griffin S *Company Law Handbook* 2nd edn (...2010) quoted in *Mwamba Nthenge* at J 13.
[100] Mckendrick E *Contract Law* 3rd edn [(....)] 3.

In *Mwamba v Nthenge, Kaing'a, Chekwe* (below), it was observed that shareholders' agreements were voluntary and unanimous. That '[a]ll shareholders agreed to sign the Agreements which are now binding on them personally, *inter se* and which must be interpreted according to the principles on interpretation of contracts'. In *Printing and Numerical Registered Company v Simpson*[101] it was decided that:

> ...if there is one thing more than another which Public Policy require, it is that men of full age and competent understanding shall have the utmost liberty in contracting and that their contract when entered into freely and voluntarily shall be held sacred and shall be enforced by courts of justice.

Further, in *National Drug Company Limited and Zambia Privatization Agency v Mary Katongo,*[102] the Supreme Court held that it was,

> ...trite law that once the parties have voluntarily and freely entered into a legal contract, they become bound to abide by the terms of the contract and that the role of the Court is to give efficacy to the contract when one party has breached it by respecting, upholding and enforcing the contract.

The case of Mwamba v Nthenge, Kaing'a, Chekwe[103] which we alluded to earlier is the leading Zambian authority on the matter of shareholders' agreements. This was an appeal against the judgment of the High Court. At issue was the interpretation of a shareholders' agreements executed by the appellant and the respondents regarding the management of two Zambian registered companies namely, NECOR (Z) Limited and Application Solutions (Z) Limited. The trial court summarized that the dispute was about the interpretation of two similar shareholders' agreements with common clauses executed by and between the shareholders concerning the two companies.

The shareholding between the parties was that the 1st, 2nd and 3rd respondents held 48.5%, 1.5 % and 1.5% shares respectively, whereas the appellant held 48.5% in NECOR (Z) Ltd, whereas NECOR (Z) Limited held a 51% share interest in Application Solutions (Z) Ltd. The appellant held 17.82%, 2nd respondent held 0.18%, the 3rd respondent also held 0.18% whereas the 1st respondent held 17.82% in Application Solutions (Z) Ltd. There were other minority shareholders in the two companies concerned which however were not parties to the appeal.

---

[101] [1875] LR19 462.
[102] Appeal No. 79/2001.
[103] Coram: Mumba, Ag/DCJ, Chibomba and Wanki JJS.

The dispute arose when the annual general meeting for the two companies concerned was convened after a High Court order and after the parties agreed to adjourn in order to resolve the question of appointment of directors to the boards of the two companies. The two shareholders' agreements which were due for interpretation in the trial court were signed by all the shareholders and their witnesses. The relevant common clauses of the shareholders' agreements hinged on the status of director for the two companies.

As is common practice in many companies, said the Court, directors for the board need not be shareholders. Qualifications for the board, in the relevant sections of the CA 1994, did allow non-shareholders to be appointed to the board of a company provided that such appointees or nominees met qualifications spelt out in those relevant sections. In the case at hand, the parties decided to place qualifications for those who could sit on the board of the two companies by executing the two shareholders' agreements. The parties understood, said the Court, the purpose of the agreements because they already knew the existing provisions of company law as well as the provisions in the articles of association of the two companies concerned. As the Court saw it, the shareholders agreements in this appeal were meant to regulate the way the two companies were going to be managed. Articles of association were thus varied by these unanimous and voluntary agreements.

In the class of shareholders, the agreements created two classes, those with 10% or more and those with less than 10% shares. It followed that those who could sit on the board could also nominate others who could sit on the same board. Similarly, those who could not sit on the board could also not nominate anyone to sit on the said board. On account of this distinction, those not eligible were not expected, as such, in terms of status and entitlement, to sit on the board. In the view that the Court took, it would be absurd to allow those who were not entitled to sit on the board, *ab initio*, to nominate directors to sit on the board. The Court thus reversed the decision of the High Court which had held that that those with less than 10% shareholding could be nominated to the board.

All the shareholders in the companies concerned understood that those holding less than 10% shareholding could not sit on the board and could not nominate anyone to sit on the board. Other persons who were not shareholders with less than 10% shareholding in the two companies concerned, could be nominated to sit on the board if they qualified according to the provisions of the law and if they were nominated by the shareholders holding 10% or more shareholding. It follows that persons who are not shareholders have no shareholding impediment unlike the shareholders with less than 10% shareholding. These agreements provided for one process only for purposes of constituting the boards of the companies concerned.

Section 206(13), CA 1994 provided for replacement of directors out of office. For the two companies concerned, this was open only to those shareholders with 10% or more shareholding. The restriction to entitlement and nomination to the board to those with 10% or more shareholding was the chosen mode of control of the two companies concerned by the shareholders themselves.

It was held as follows:

(1) That the common clauses, that is, 8.1.2 in both shareholders' agreements created two classes of shareholders; those shareholders with 10% or more and those with less.

(2) The Court held that the two agreements were designed to specifically deal with the circumstances of the two companies which required a particular type of management to run them.

(3) That the shareholders bound themselves to those shareholders agreements which determine the level of shareholding for purposes of directorship on the board.

(4) That where eligible persons voluntarily and unanimously enter into a contract, the contract will be personally binding and will be honoured by the courts except where there is a legal impediment. In this appeal, parties to the said shareholders agreements were unanimous. In the face of no evidence to the contrary, the Court assumed that the parties understood the implications of the agreements to which they appended their signatures.

(5) That as parties sign contracts consciously they cannot say that what was agreed upon had become untenable or unconscionable. The courts can only offer equitable intervention. In this appeal, facts did not permit such intervention.

(6) That the shareholders themselves decided through their agreements to vary the manner in which directors of the board would be appointed, that was perfectly legal. Clause 8.1.2 meant exactly what it said, that only members with 10 or more per centum shareholding may sit on the board of directors. Clause 8.2.0 simply protected those shareholders with 10 or more per centum shareholding from losing their entitlement. This clause completed a factual expectation of those entitled to sit on the board of directors as prescribed in Clause 8.1.2, notwithstanding the changes that might occur in terms of shareholding.

2.7.4 *Typical contents of shareholders' agreements*

A typical shareholders agreement may include the following:

(i)   undertakings and agreements from perspective shareholders before the company was formed;

(ii)   matters that it would be inappropriate to put on the public record such as confidentiality undertakings and non-competition restrictions;

(iii) the rights of shareholders to appoint directors;

(iv) dispute resolution;

(v) protection of the minority (Note: Section 27 requires ¾ majority for alteration; shareholders agreement can require written consent from all shareholders thus protecting those with minority holding); and

(vi) internal management issues which the members wish to keep off the public record, for example, choice of banker, loan policies and cheque signatories.

In conclusion and as shown in *Mwamba v Nthenge, Kaing'a, Chekwe*[104], the prominence of shareholders' agreements cannot be overemphasised. Their contractual nature and being means that they will convey substantial authority in swaying the court's decision especially in instances where there are endeavours to fissure the terms of the shareholders' agreement if only to treat unwilling minority shareholders from tolling the majority line under the guise of following articles of association.

2.8   Registered office and change of registered office

2.8.1   General

In terms of section 3 of the Act " registered office " means, in relation to a—

(a)   company, the registered office of the company as provided in section 28 (discussed below); and

(b)   foreign company, the established place of business of the company as provided in section 300.[105]

The fact that there is a definition for a registered office is a departure from CA 1994 which provided no definition at all except to say in section 190(i) that it was 'the physical place notified in the place for incorporation'.

Section 28(1) mandates a company to 'have a registered office in Zambia to which all communications and notices may be addressed'. It further provides in subsection (2) that '[t]he registered office shall be the address for service of legal proceedings on the company'. A company is not precluded from changing its registered office[106] as long as it notifies 'the Registrar in the prescribed manner and form, within fourteen days of that change.[107] In terms of section 28(5), '[a] change of the registered office shall take effect on the date the notice referred to in subsection (4), is lodged with the Registrar. Failure to comply with the requirement to notify the registrar is a serious matter. In terms of section 28(6), '[w]here a company fails to comply with subsection (4), every

---

[104] (Appeal No 174 2010) [2013] ZMSC 5 (17 May 2013).

[105] Which sets out what, for a foreign company amounts to an "established place of business".

[106] Section 28(3).

[107] Section 28(4).

officer of the company commits an offence and is liable, on conviction, to a fine not exceeding one hundred thousand penalty units.

There does not appear to be any mention of a registered records office which in CA 1994 was provided for under section 191. This should be of no consequence because even under section 191, where a company had registered records office, the registered office served as the records office. This change is in line with the reality of most companies which in the Zambian context tend to be small, have bad record keeping practices and are rarely called to account.

2.8.2   *Records kept at company's registered office*

This is provided for under section 30 which in subsection (1) provides that '[a] company shall, at its registered office, keep the following records':

- *(a)*   the articles of association;
- *(b)*   a register of—
  - (i)   members indicating separately for each class of equity and preference shares held by each member residing in or outside Zambia;
  - (ii)   beneficial owners, specifying the particulars in section 12(3) *(e)*;
  - (iii) debenture holders; and
  - (iv) any other security holders;
- *(c)*   the full names and addresses of the current directors;
- *(d)*   minutes of all meetings and resolutions of shareholders for the preceding ten years;
- *(e)*   an interests register;
- *(f)*   minutes of all meetings and resolutions of directors and directors' committees within the last ten years;
- *(g)*   copies of all financial statements for the preceding ten years;
- *(h)*   the accounting records for the preceding ten years;
- *(i)*   copies of instruments creating or evidencing charges required to be registered in accordance with this Act or any other written law; and
- *(j)*   any other document or record as may be prescribed by the Minister.

There is a further requirement regarding a register of members under section 30(2) which provides that '[a] register of members maintained in accordance with subsection (1) *(b)* shall have an index of the names contained in it'. In keeping with the times, section 30(3) allows documents required to be maintained under it to 'be kept in electronic form'. Also, in keeping with a globalised dispensation, in terms of section 30(4), '[a] company may, if authorised by its articles, keep in a country outside Zambia, in such a manner as may be prescribed, a part of the register, referred to in subsection (1) *(b)*, except that such part of the register shall be publicly available in Zambia in accordance with this Act'.

According to section 30(5), '[i]f a company fails to maintain a document in accordance with this section, the company and every officer of the company in default commit an offence and are liable, on conviction, to fine not exceeding one hundred thousand penalty units'.

2.9   Publication of name of company

This is provided for under section 29.[108] Section 29(1) mandates '[a] company to—

(a) paint or affix, and keep painted or affixed, the name of the company, in easily legible Roman letters or a combination of Roman letters with Arabic numerals, above or adjacent to the principal entrance to the company's registered office, its registered records office and to every other office or place in which the company's business is carried on; and

(b) have its name accurately stated in Roman letters or a combination of Roman letters with Arabic numerals on all business letters, invoices, receipts, notices and other publications of the company, and in all negotiable instruments or orders for money, goods or services issued or signed by or on behalf of the company. In the event of failure to comply with subsection section 29(1) the 'company and each officer in default commit an offence and are liable, on conviction, to a fine not exceeding one hundred thousand penalty units'. The said fines to which the company and each officer in default may be subject may arise in the following circumstances:

  (i)   Where, as in *Penrose v Martyr*[109] and *Stacey & Co Ltd v Wallis,*[110] the words 'Limited' or 'Plc' are omitted[111]

  (ii) Where, as in *Hendon v Adelman*[112] and *Durham Fancy Goods Ltd v Michael Jackson (Fancy Goods) Ltd,*[113] the name of the company is styled erroneously.[114]

---

[108] This section must be read together with sections 36 (under paragraph 3.2) and 42 to 47 (under paragraph 3.6) on name change and the authorities discussed thereunder.

[109] [1858] EB & E 499.

[110] [1912] 28 TLR 209.

[111] See requirement under section 36.

[112] [1973] 117 SJ 63; but see section 45 of the Act and also decision in *Jenice Ltd v Dan* where the view seems to now be that where a third party is in the know small errors will not automatically trigger liability.

[113] [1968] 2 All ER 987; *S.J. Patel (Zambia) Ltd v D.V. Cinamon (Male)* [1970] ZR 68 (HC); *Maxform SPA v B Mariani & Goodville Ltd* [1979] 2 Lloyd's Rep 385 affirmed in [1981] 2 Lloyd's Rep 54; *Lindholst & Co A/S V Fowler* [1988] BCLC 166; and *Blum v OCP Repartition SIA* [1988] BCLC 170.

[114] There is nothing in sections 36 and 45 to suggest that if the error is committed by a third party or with his knowledge, he would still enforce his claim against individual officers of the company nor can such a third party expect to succeed under the rule of equitable estoppel.

2.10   Register of directors and secretaries

Part III provides for a register of directors and secretaries in section 31. In terms of section 31(1), '[a] company shall keep a register of its directors and secretaries. By section 31(2), '[t]he register shall contain the following particulars of each director and secretary:*(a)* forenames and surname; *(b)* residential and postal address; *(c)* business or occupation, if any; *(d)* nationality and national identity card number or passport number; *(e)* any directorship held in another corporate, whether or not formed in Zambia, during the preceding five years; and *(f)* any local directorship held in a foreign company during the preceding five years.

In terms of section 31(3), '[w]here the secretary is a body corporate, the register, specified in section 31(1), shall contain the—

(a)   name of the body corporate;

(b)   registered office and registered postal address and, if different, the address of its principal office; and

(c)   name of a body corporate in which the body corporate holds the position of secretary.

So that it is possible for the company to comply with the requirements of section 31(2), in terms of section 31(4), '[a] director or secretary shall, at the time of being appointed or employed, furnish to the company all the documents, information and particulars, as may be necessary for purposes of this section.

According to section 31(5), '[i]f a company or individual fails to comply with this section, the company, individual and each executive officer in default commits an offence and is liable, on conviction, to a fine not exceeding one hundred thousand penalty units'.

2.11   Service of documents on company and service of documents by company

2.11.1 Service of documents on company

The procedure is provided for in section 34. By section 34(1), [despite the] Act or any other law, a document may be served on a company by—

(a)   delivery of the document to the registered office of the company; or

(b)   personally serving a director or secretary of the company.

In terms of (2), '[w]here service in the manner specified in subsection (1) is not possible, a document may be served on a company by registered mail or electronic mail'.

2.11.2 Service of documents by company

The procedure is in this respect provided for under section 35. Section 35(1) provides that, [...] a document may be served by a company on any member, debenture holder, director or secretary of the company—

(a) personally;

(b) by sending it by registered post in a prepaid letter addressed to that member, debenture holder, director or secretary of that company at the registered postal address or at any other address supplied by that member, debenture holder, director or secretary to that company for the giving of notices to that member, debenture holder, director or secretary to that company; or

(c) by leaving it for that member, debenture holder, director or secretary of that company at the registered address of that member, debenture holder, director or secretary of that company with a person apparently over the age of eighteen years.

Further and in terms of section 35(2), '[a] document may be served by a company on the joint holders of a share or debenture of the company by serving it on the joint holder named first in the register of members or debenture holders in respect of that share or debenture. By section 35(3), '[a] document may be served by a company on the person upon whom the ownership of a share or debenture has devolved by reason of the person being a legal personal representative, receiver, or trustee in bankruptcy of a member or debenture holder—

(a) personally;

(b) by sending it by registered post in a prepaid letter addressed to the person at a postal address notified by the person to the company;

(c) by leaving it in any manner in which it might have been served if the death, receivership or bankruptcy had not occurred, if the company has not received notice of a postal address for the person;

(d) by leaving it for the person at a place the address of which has been notified by the person to the company, with a person apparently over the age of eighteen years; or

(e) by electronic means'.

According to section 35(4), '[w]here a document is sent by registered post, service shall be deemed to be effected by properly addressing, prepaying and posting the letter accompanying the document and to have been effected at the expiration of seven days or, if it is sent to an address outside Zambia, twenty-one days, after the letter containing the same is posted. By section 35(5), [w]here a document is sent by electronic means, service shall be deemed to be effected when the complete data message enters an information system designated or used for that purpose in accordance with the Electronic Communications and Transactions Act, 2009.

'For purposes of subsections (4) and (5), where a document is sent to an address outside Zambia, the letter accompanying the document shall be dispatched by registered or electronic mail, as applicable'.[115]

2.12   Conclusion

In this chapter we have discussed the fact the company has the capacity powers and rights similar to those of a natural person and as are inherent in its corporate nature. We have also noted that the validity of acts cannot be invalidated by reason only that the company acted in contravention of the Act or its articles unless the third party involved knew through his dealings with the company that the act now impugned was one that the director had no power to authorise or the company was restricted by its articles from doing. We have further considered the fact that knowledge on the side of third parties can generally not be presumed reference the indoor management rule: the rule in *Turquand's* case. We have considered articles of association, their effect and the fact that '[t]he articles shall have the effect of a contract between'—

(a)   'the company and each member'; and

(b)   'amongst the members'.

Further, that '[t]he articles shall bind the company and its members'. That articles can be amended but that there are restrictions and consequences that may follow such amendment including breach of contract for which the company may be liable to pay damages. Allied to the foregoing we examined the concept of shareholders' agreements, why shareholders should have agreements, the nature and effect of shareholders Agreements, construction of shareholder agreements, the relationship between shareholders' agreements and articles of association, enforceability of shareholders' agreements, and typical contents of shareholders' agreements. We have also discussed the company's registered office and change of registered office, records kept at company's registered office, publication of name of company, the register of directors and secretaries and various modes of service of documents.

FURTHER READING

Articles

Cheng, T K, 'The Corporate Veil Doctrine Revisited: A Comparative Study of the English and the U.S. Corporate Veil Doctrines' (2011) 34 BC Int'l & Comp. L. Rev. 329.

---

[115] Section 35(6).

Conaglen, M, 'Sham Trusts' (2008) 67 CLJ 176.

Ferran, E, 'Corporate Attribution and the Directing Will' (2011) 127 LQR 239.

Hargovan, A, and Harris, J, 'Piercing the Corporate Veil in Canada: A Comparative Analysis' (2007) 28 Comp Law 58.

Griffin, S, 'The Rise and Fall of the *Ultra-Vires* Rule in Corporate Law', *Mountbatten Journal of Legal Studies*, 1998, ssudl.solent.ac.uk/954/1/1998_2_1.pdf.

Kahn-Freund, O, 'Some Reflections on Company Law Reform' (1944) 7 MLR 54.

Linklater, L, 'Piercing The Corporate Veil – The Never Ending Story' (2006) 27 Comp Law 65.

Moore, M, 'A Temple Built on Faulty Foundations: Piercing the Corporate Veil and the Legacy of *Salomon v Salomon*' [2006] JBL 180.

Rixon, J, 'Lifting the Veil between Holding and Subsidiary Companies' [1986] 102 LQR 415 (on *Woolfson*).

Sullivan, G R, 'The Attribution of Culpability to Limited Companies' [1996] CLJ 515.

Books

Davies PL *Gower and Davies' Principles of Modern Company Law* 7th edn (London Thomson Sweet & Maxwell 2003).

Dine J and Koutsias M *Company Law* 6th edn (Palgrave Macmillan Hampshire 2007).

Farrah JH and Hannigan BM Farrar's *Company Law* 4th edn (London Butterworths 1998).

Gates RB *Gates Company Law and Practice in Zambia* (Reagan Blankfein Gates Lusaka 2017).

Keenan D *Smith and Keenan's Company Law* 13th edn (Pearson Longman Essex 2005).

Mclaughlin S *Unlocking Company Law* 3rd edn (Routledge New York 2015).

Mwenda KK *Legal Aspect of Banking Regulation: Common Law Perspective from Zambia* (PULP Pretoria 2010).

Ridley A and Shepherd C *Company Law: Key Facts Key Cases* (Routledge New York 2015).

Sealy L and Worthington S *Sealy & Worthington's Cases and Materials in Company Law* 10th edn (Oxford University Press Oxford 2013).

Wild C and Weinstein S *Smith and Keenan's Company Law* 15th edn (Pearson Education Ltd London 2011).

Websites

The Human Rights of Companies website: http://www.thehumanrights of companies.com

Understanding the Corporate Manslaughter and Corporate Homicide Act 2007 (Ministry of Justice, 2007), accessible at: www.justice.gov.uk/docs/manslaughterhomicideact07.pdf.

3

COMPANY NAME AND
NAME CHANGE

AIMS AND OBJECTIVES

 After reading this chapter you should appreciate the following:
- ➢ The requirements for name endings such as "Ltd" and "Plc"
- ➢ Provisions on application to omit or dispense with "Limited" in name of company limited by guarantee
- ➢ Instances under which the Registrar may revoke the approval to dispense with the word "Limited" at the end of the company name
- ➢ The requirement for company names to end with Plc or Ltd
- ➢ Reservation of company name
- ➢ Clearance and approval of proposed names
- ➢ Rejection of application for approval of name
- ➢ How the change of name may be effected
- ➢ Circumstances that may necessitate the registrar to direct change of name
- ➢ Why a document with incorrect name may not be void
- ➢ Liability where the company name is incorrectly stated.

3.1   Introduction

This chapter explores the provisions in Part II of the Act specifically sections 36 to 47. Our discussion is therefore centered on provisions relating to company names and the procedure for change. Quite apart from analysing the requirements for name endings, we explore provisions on application to omit or dispense with "Limited" in name of company limited by guarantee; revocation of approval to dispense with "Limited"; the requirement for company names to end with Plc or Ltd; reservation of company name ;clearance and approval of proposed names; rejection of application for approval of name; change of name; Circumstances that may necessitate the registrar to direct change of name; why a document with incorrect name may not be void; and finally, liability where company name is incorrectly stated.

3.2   Names to end with "Plc" or "Ltd" as the case may be[1]

In terms of section 36(1), '[t]he name of a public limited company shall end with the words "Public Limited Company" or the abbreviation "Plc".[2] By section 36(2), '[…] the name of a private limited company shall end with the word "Limited" or the abbreviation "Ltd".[3] The statutory provision for the alternative of "Ltd" to the full term "Limited" in section 36(2) is rooted, it may be argued, in the decision in *Stacey & Co Ltd v Wallis*[4] where a bill was drawn on a company in terms of 'J & TH Wallis Ltd' and accepted by three persons in the usage: 'James Wallis, Thomas Wallis, Henry Bowles, Secty'. It was held firstly, that the name of the company was correctly stated and thus complied with the requirements of the Companies Act; and secondly, that the abbreviation 'Ltd' could be used for the word 'Limited'. It followed therefore that the persons who had appended their signatures to the bill were not liable on the said bill.

The importance of the foregoing was exemplified in the case of *S.J. Patel (Zambia) Ltd v D.V. Cinamon (Male)*.[5] This was an appeal by the plaintiff against the decision of the Registrar in which he granted unconditional leave to defend the plaintiff's claim brought in respect of three dishonoured cheques. The plaintiffs supplied goods to Longacres Stores Limited and three cheques were drawn in their favour signed by the defendant in his capacity as managing director of the company over a rubber-stamp bearing the inscription "Longacres Store", without the word "Limited" appearing on the cheques. Subsequent to the issue of these cheques the company went into voluntary liquidation and on presentation of the cheques they were dishonoured. The issue as to whether the defendant had a statutory liability for the amount claimed by the plaintiff was considered. It was held:

(i)   that the Companies Ordinance [equivalent to section 36(2) of the Act] required that the company's name in full be engraved on its seal and

---

[1] According to section 364(2)(a), '[a] person who, not being a body corporate trades or carries on business in Zambia under a name or title which includes the word "Limited", "Plc", "Corporation" or any contraction or imitation thereof, or any equivalent in a language other than English'.

[2] See, for purposes of comparison, section 58 of the UK CA 2006.

[3] See, for purposes of comparison section 59(1) of the UK CA 2006 where a private company is normally required to have "Ltd" at the end of its name unless it is a 'community interest companies (but see section 33(1) and (2) of the [UK] Companies (Audit, Investigations and Community Enterprise) Act 2004) or otherwise exempt from such use by sections 60-62 of that Act. The Welsh equivalent is "Cyfyngedig" or "cyf". (See section 59(2) of the UK CA 2006).

[4] [1912] 28 TLR 209; Lord Goff would use Stacey in *Bancque de l'Indochine et de Suez SA v Euroseas Group Finance Co* [1981] 3 All ER 198 to hold that the abbreviation of 'company' to 'Co' on a cheque was an apposite reference to the company's name in terms of the UK CA.

[5] [1970] ZR 68 (HC); See also *Penrose v Martyr* [1858] EB & E 499 where, Crompton J in justifying the need to include "Limited" in a private company (or for that matter Public company) limited by shares, opined that '[t]he intention of the enactment plainly was to prevent persons from being deceived into the belief that they had security with the unlimited liability of common law when they had but the security of a company Limited'.

mentioned in documents to be signed by or on behalf of the company and that the last word of the name should end with the word "Limited". Failure to comply with the provisions made the person who signed the documents personally liable if the company failed to pay.[6]

(ii)   By failing to comply with the statutory provisions the defendant rendered himself liable to the plaintiffs for the amount payable in respect of the three cheques.

In coming to its decision, the court relied on two earlier English cases: In *Atkins and Co. v Wardle*[7] the court considered the personal liability of directors under section 42 of the UK CA 1862. The facts of that case were that a company was registered by the title of "The South Shields Salt Water Baths Company (Limited)". The plaintiffs drew the following bill of exchange, "Six months after date pay to our order the sum of £125 for value received. - Salt Water Baths Company (Limited), South Shields", which was accepted as follows: "Accepted payable Messrs. Hodgkin, Barnett & Co.'s Bank, So. Shields. - John P. Wardle Chairman, Thomas S. Blues and Joseph Pollard Directors, South Shields Salt Water Baths Co." The company later fell into difficulties and the bill was dishonoured, an action having been brought upon the bill by the plaintiffs against the chairman and directors. It was held that the two variations from the proper designation of the company were sufficient to bring the defendants within the provisions of section 42 of the UK CA 1862, the intention of which was to insure extreme strictness in regard to the use of the registered name of the company, not only enforcing the use of the word "Limited", but in all other respects. The plaintiffs were entitled to judgment.

In *Durham Fancy Goods Ltd v Michael Jackson (Fancy (goods) Ltd*[8], the court considered the provisions of section 108 (4) of the UK CA 1948. In that case the plaintiffs drew a bill of exchange on a company called M. Jackson (Fancy Goods) Ltd. but addressed it to "M. Jackson (Fancy Goods) Ltd." and inscribed the words of acceptance: "Accepted payable [....] for and on behalf of M. Jackson (Fancy Goods) Ltd., Manchester." On receiving the bill the second defendant, who was a director and secretary of the company, merely signed his name and returned the bill. The bill was dishonoured upon maturity and the company went into liquidation. On a claim by the plaintiffs against the second defendant on the grounds that he had become personally liable on the bill by

---

[6] Companies Ordinance, Cap 216, sections 8 (1) (a), 80 and 81.

[7] [1889] LJQB 377.

[8] [1968] 2 All ER 987; See further, *Hendon v Adelman* [1973] 117 SJ 63 where a cheque apparently signed on behalf of 'L&R Agencies' but printed on its cheques erroneously as 'LR Agencies Ltd' omitting the ampersand. The directors who signed on the cheques were held to have contravened (the equivalent of section 36(2)) and as such, personally liable. However, see distinction drawn by Mocatta J in *Maxform SPA v B Mariani & Goodville Ltd* [1979] 2 Lloyd's Rep 385 and affirmed by the UK CA [1981] 2 Lloyd's Rep 54.

signing it on behalf of the company contrary to s. 108 of the 1948 Act, as the bill did not mention the proper name of the company. It was held: "(i) that 'M' was not an acceptable abbreviation for 'Michael' and that accordingly, the second defendant had committed an offence under section 108, which had not been sufficiently complied with, and was liable to the plaintiffs who were holders of the bill of exchange. (ii) but that the plaintiffs' action would be dismissed because that could not enforce that liability, for they had inscribed the words of acceptance and had chosen the wrong words, thereby implying that acceptance of the hill in that form would be, or would be accepted by them as, a regular acceptance off the bill: in seeking to rely on their own error, coupled with the second defendant's failure to detect and remedy it, as entitling them to relief, they were bound by the equitable principle of promissory estoppel.

Personal liability as exemplified in the foregoing authorities is predicated on the legislative basis for the concept of limited liability which is that the inclusion of the term "Limited" or "Ltd" will put persons dealing with the company on notice, not that the company itself has limited liability (for it will be followed to the last fathom of its assets in the event of a winding-up) but that the liability of its members is, in the event of a winding up, limited to what they owe on the shares they own in the company in question or indeed nothing, if their shares are fully paid up. The metaphysical or artificial nature of the company entails that it can only act through its officials, namely directors. That means that 'since the officials of the company are the only persons who can ensure that the company's documents convey this impression, it seems right to subject them to fines and personal liability where this is not so'. This position applies to name change as exemplified in section 45. Be that as it may, and as exemplified in *Jenice Ltd v Dan*[9] discussed below, it appears that where a third party knows that he is dealing with a company with limited liability, minor mistakes in the name of the said company ought not to trigger liability.[10]

3.3   Application to omit or dispense with "Limited" in name of company limited by guarantee and Revocation

The Act enables those who would be minded under certain specified circumstances to apply to omit or dispense with the use of the word "Limited" at the end of the company name. The procedure is provided for under sections 37 and 38. In terms of section 37(1), '[t]he Registrar may, on application in the prescribed manner by a—

(a)   person applying to form a company limited by guarantee; or
(b)   company, that is, or has use of the word "limited" from the name of the company, on such terms and conditions as the Registrar considers necessary.

[9]   [1993] BCLC 1349.
[10]   See section 45(2).

'The Registrar shall, on granting the approval specified in [section 37](1), enter the company name on the register without the word " Limited " and issue a certificate of incorporation or replacement certificate of incorporation worded to meet the circumstances of the case.[11]   Further, '[a] replacement certificate referred to' above 'shall be conclusive evidence of the alteration to which it relates'.[12] Despite the foregoing, '[w]here the Registrar considers that the reasons given by an applicant for omitting or dispensing with the word "Limited" from the name of a company limited by guarantee have ceased to be valid, the Registrar may revoke the approval granted in accordance with section 37 and the revocation shall take effect on a date that the Registrar determines'.[13]

3.4   Clearance and approval of proposed name and/or rejection of application thereof

'A person intending to incorporate a company may apply to the Registrar, for clearance and approval of a proposed name, in the prescribed manner and form'.[14] 'If the Registrar considers that a proposed name of a company does not contravene section 40 (discussed below), the Registrar may approve the name and shall notify the applicant in writing of the approval'.[15]

As the foregoing suggests, having a desired name does not guarantee the company being incorporated using it. The basis for this is section 40, a regulatory provision. In terms of section 40(1), '[t]he Registrar may reject an application for approval of a proposed name made in accordance with section 39, where

(a)   the name, if registered, is likely to cause confusion with a name or trademark of a registered company or a well-known name or trademark[16];

(b)   registration of the name is sought to prevent another person who is legitimately entitled to use that name from using it;

(c)   registration of the name is otherwise undesirable or inimical to the public interest;

(d)   the name denotes the patronage of the State or of the President, Government or administration of any foreign state, or of any department or institution of any foreign state;

---

[11] Section 37(2).

[12] Section 37(3).

[13] Section 37(4).

[14] Section 39(1).

[15] Section 39(2).

[16] This is a foray into intellectual property law. By section 40(3) a "well-known name or trademark" means a name or trademark associated generally by the Zambian public with a registered company, products whether within or outside the Republic, and in respect of which confusion is likely to arise if the proposed name or trademark is registered by a company other than the company generally associated with that name. According to section 40(4), '[t]he Registrar shall, in determining whether a name is well known in Zambia take into account the degree of association of the name with a registered company by the Zambian public'.

(e)   the name is calculated to deceive or mislead the public, cause annoyance or offence to any person or is suggestive of blasphemy or indecency; or

(f)   registration would suggest or imply a connection with a political party or a leader of a political party. The registrar is mandated, where he rejects an application made in accordance with section 39, to, within seven days of the decision, notify the applicant of the refusal and give reasons for the refusal.[17]

3.5   Reservation of company name

'[A] person or persons who propose to incorporate a company may reserve a proposed name for the company, by making an application in the prescribed manner and form to the Registrar'.[18] In terms of section 41(2), '[t]he Registrar may approve a reservation of a name if satisfied that the—

(a)   name proposed for reservation is—

(i)   a registered business name of the person or persons registered in accordance with any other law; or

(ii)   the name of an unincorporated association consisting of, or represented by the person or persons; or

(b)   applicant is a body corporate, other than a company, and the name is of the body corporate or that name with minor modifications.

According to section to section 41(3), '[t]he Registrar shall, on approving a reservation of a name in accordance with subsection (2), notify the applicant, in writing, and shall register the name as reserved for a period of ninety days from the date of the notice'. By section 41(4), '[...] where a name is registered as specified in subsection (3)—

(a)   the applicant shall be entitled to incorporate a company under the reserved name; and

(b)   the Registrar shall treat the proposed name as the name of a company incorporated by the person for the purposes of determining the acceptability of any other name'.

3.6   Change of name

The law regarding name change which was contained in sections 40 and 41 of CA 1994 is now to be found in sections 42 through 47 with expanded regulations for the company and an expanded regulatory reach for the Registrar. Our interest must first turn to sections 42 and 43 which have been transplanted from CA 1994 hook line and sinker into the Act and with that, the same legal nightmare that has been present under the CA 1994.[19] Section 42(1) therefore still provides that 'a company may pass a special resolution to change its name. The use of

---

[17] Section 40(2).

[18] Section 41(1).

[19] See generally Gates RB *Gates Company Law and Practice in Zambia* para 1.12.

the permissive term 'may' suggests the obvious fact that while this option is available to a company, it is one the company is not mandated to take unless it be minded to do so owing to changed circumstances among them a merger, a de-merger, reorganisation, conversion[20] or takeover by another. 'Within twenty-one days after the date of the resolution, the company shall notify the Registrar in the prescribed form that the company intends to change its name to the name specified in the resolution'.[21] Further and by section 42(3), '[t]he Registrar, after considering the new name, shall notify the company that—

(a) the new name is acceptable; or

(b) in the opinion of the Registrar, the new name of the company would be likely to cause confusion with the name of another company or is otherwise undesirable, and that the Registrar will not register the new name. According to section 42(4), '[i]f the new name is acceptable, the company shall, within twenty-one days after receiving the notice of the fact, lodge with the Registrar—

    (a) the company's certificate of incorporation; and

    (b) a copy of the resolution'.

Further to the foregoing, '[o]n receiving the documents referred to in subsection (4), the Registrar shall enter the new name on the Register in place of the former name, and shall issue a replacement certificate of incorporation worded to meet the circumstances of the case'.[22] Significantly, '[a] change of name by a company shall not affect any rights or obligations of the company nor render defective any legal proceedings that could have been continued or commenced against it by its former name, and any such legal proceedings may be continued or commenced against it by its new name'.[23]

Even if the foregoing has been adhered to, there is still a chance that the Registrar may, where he deems it necessary, invoke section 43. Section 43(1), provides that '[…] where [the Registrar] considers that the name of a registered company subsequently contravenes section 40, [he may] direct that the company changes its name in accordance with this Part'. If so directed and a company fails to change its name, within fifty days or such longer period as the Registrar may allow, the Registrar may register the designation number of the company, together with the word "Limited" or "Plc" if required by section 38, as the name of the company, and shall issue a new certificate of incorporation for the company worded to reflect the change in name of the company. Under section 43(3), '[w]here the Registrar directs a company to change its name, the Agency shall not compensate any person in respect of such matter.

'A contract or legal obligation of a company evidenced on a document on which the name of the company is incorrectly stated shall not be void, at the

---

[20] Under part V: sections 48-55.
[21] Section 42(2); in this section called the "new name".
[22] Section 42(6) provides that '[a] certificate under this section shall be conclusive evidence of the alteration to which it relates'.
[23] Section 42(7).

instance of the company, by reason only of the company's name being incorrectly stated'.[24] Additionally, '[w]here the name of a company is incorrectly stated in a document which evidences a legal obligation of the company, and the document is issued or signed by or on behalf of the company, every person who issues or signs the document is liable to the same extent as the company unless the—

(a)   person who issues or signs the document proves that the person in whose favour the obligation was incurred was aware at the time the document was issued or signed, that the name was incorrectly stated and the obligation was incurred by the company; or

(b)   Court before which the document is produced, is satisfied that it would not be just and equitable for the person who issued or signed the document to be held liable'.[25]

The case of *Jenice Ltd v Dan*[26] demonstrates this. The defendant, Mr Dan who at the material time was a director of Primekeen Ltd, signed a cheque which was incorrectly printed by the bank in the misspelled name 'Primkeen Ltd'. Owing to its winding up and dissolution, the company was unable to honour the cheque. It was nonetheless held that the defendant was not liable on the said cheque as it was clear that outsiders would have known they were dealing with a limited company and from the evidence, no harm had been occasioned by the defendant's actions.

Section 44 is meant to prevent fraud or a denial of liability being perpetuated by a company or individual directors given the somewhat complex and unsatisfactory procedure outlined under sections 42 and 43. It is quite possible in practice that a company may pass a resolution to change its name and in anticipation of it being accepted by the Registrar prepare documentation with the proposed name on it which may mistakenly or fraudulently be used in contracts with third parties. Amidst this, the Registrar, may, as he is empowered to do, under section 42(3)(b) inform the company that in his opinion, 'the new name of the company would be likely to cause confusion with the name of another company or is otherwise undesirable, and that the Registrar will not register the new name'.

At this point as one can imagine, the company will be required to pass a new resolution scrapping the first resolution proposing a new name and scrap plans for name change or pass another resolution proposing a new name. It is in theory, a process that can go on forever with no end in sight with presumably different documents using different names emerging and purportedly binding the company. This has potential to create a legal mess fraught with denial of liability predicated on the company's name being incorrectly stated.

---

[24] Section 44.
[25] Section 45.
[26] [1993] BCLC 1349.

The Registrar's decision making power in this whole process, it must be remembered, is subjective-it is *'in his opinion'*. The crafting of sections 42 and 43 has the potential to undo the premise on which the Act is built which is to encourage commerce and protect third parties acting in good faith. Add to this the fact that the Registrar may accept the name change as valid and thereafter, in terms of section 43 order a name change 'where [the Registrar] considers that the name of a registered company subsequently contravenes section 40', and the relevance of adding section 45 becomes even the more clearer.

A company is required, in the event of its name changing to, 'within a period of twelve months prior to the company's release of any public notice, cause to be published in the *Gazette* a notice stating the—

(a)   new name of the company;

(b)   specific date on which the name of the company changed; and

(c)   former name or names of the company'.[27]

Further, '[i]f a company fails to comply with subsection (1), the company and each officer in default commits an offence is liable, on conviction, to a fine not exceeding three thousand penalty units for each day that the failure continues'.[28]

Finally, [t]he change of name of a company in accordance with this Part shall—

(a)   not affect the rights or obligations of the company nor render defective legal proceedings by or against it;

(b)   not affect any legal proceedings that could have been continued or commenced against the company by or under its former name; and

(c)   take effect from the date specified in the replacement certificate of incorporation.

3.7   Conclusion

In this chapter we have considered the statutory requirement that registered companies ought to have their names end with "Plc" or "Ltd" as the case may be. Be that as it may, the Act does allow applications to omit or dispense with "Limited" in names of companies limited by guarantee and but that where granted such omission may be revoked by the Registrar for cause. We have further considered the Act's provisions relating to clearance and approval of proposed name and/or rejection of application thereof. We have also examined the specific mechanics relating to the reservation of company name and the change of the company's name

---

[27] Section 46(1).

[28] Section 46(2).

FURTHER READING

Books

Adams MA *Essential Corporate Law* (Newport Cavendish Publishing (Australia) Pty Ltd 2002)

Davies PL *Gower and Davies' Principles of Modern Company Law* 7th edn (London Thomson Sweet & Maxwell 2003).

Dine J and Koutsias M *Company Law* 6th edn (Hampshire Palgrave Macmillan 2007).

Farrah JH and Hannigan BM *Farrar's Company Law* 4th edn (London Butterworths 1998).

Gates RB *Gates Company Law and Practice in Zambia* (Reagan Blankfein Gates Lusaka 2017).

Keenan D *Smith and Keenan's Company Law* 13th edn (Essex Pearson Longman 2005).

Mclaughlin S *Unlocking Company Law* 3rd edn (New York Routledge 2015).

Ridley A and Shepherd C *Company Law: Key Facts Key Cases* (New York Routledge 2015).

Sealy L and Worthington S *Sealy & Worthington's Cases and Materials in Company Law* 10th edn (Oxford University Press 2013).

Wild C and Weinstein S *Smith and Keenan's Company Law* 15th edn (London Pearson Education Ltd 2011).

4

CONVERSION 0F COMPANIES

AIMS AND OBJECTIVES

 After reading this chapter you should appreciate the following:
> The conversion of private company limited by shares into company limited by guarantee;
> The conversion of private company limited by shares into unlimited company;
> The conversion of company limited by guarantee into company limited by shares or unlimited company;
> The conversion of unlimited company into private limited company;
> The conversion of public company into private company limited by shares;
> The conversion of private company limited by shares into public company;
> The process of conversion; and
> The imposition of penalty by Registrar for non-compliance.

4.1   Introduction

The incorporation of the company in any of the types provided for under section 6 and in terms of section 12 of the Act is not cast in stone. Changes in a company's internal and external environment such as change of objects; an amalgamation provided for under section 282; merger; de-merger; legislation; regulation; competition; change of business foisted upon it by competitors or consumer tastes; and/ or new growth areas the company desires to take advantage of may necessitate the need to change its type at some point in its corporate life. It may decide to convert itself into a type other than the one it was incorporated as or the form it presently exists in without the necessity of effecting the procedure under Part III: sections 21 – 45 relating to Business Rescue Proceedings; Part IV: sections 46 – 48 relating to Schemes of Arrangements, Compromise,

Reconstruction and amalgamation; Part V-VIII: sections 49 – 139 relating to winding up under the Corporate Insolvency, 2017; and the amalgamation procedure in Part XIII: sections 282 – 296 of the Act.

Our discussion will therefore focus on the following modes of conversion:

(i)   Conversion of private company limited by shares into company limited by guarantee;

(ii)   Conversion of private company limited by shares into unlimited company;

(iii) Conversion of company limited by guarantee into company limited by shares or unlimited company;

(iv)   Conversion of unlimited company into private limited company;

(v)   Conversion of public company into private company limited by shares;

(vi)   Conversion of private company limited by shares into public company;

(vii) Process of conversion; and

(viii) Imposition of penalty by Registrar for non-compliance.

4.2   Conversion of private company limited by shares into company limited by guarantee

For a private company limited by shares to be converted into a company limited by guarantee 'all its members agree in writing to such a conversion; there is no unpaid liability on any of its shares; *(c)* the members surrender their shares for cancellation, despite section 150 (1) (c) on reduction of share capital by way of accepting the surrender of shares by shareholders; the members pass a special resolution to amend the articles to convert the company to a company limited by guarantee complying with section 10;[1] and [finally], each member makes a declaration of guarantee'.[2]

4.3   Conversion of private company limited by shares into unlimited company

When one considers the central role of limited liability to incorporation, this type of conversion is the riskiest for members of the company. Be that as it may, members may have come to the conclusion that the ability to run the company as a partnership in the form of an incorporated body with all its advantages but for liability being unlimited may be a better approach for their company going forward. They can attain a level of privacy that they may otherwise not have under limited liability. To that end, section 49 provides that '[a] private company limited by shares may be converted into an unlimited company if—

---

[1] Provides for manner of incorporation and registration of a company limited by guarantee. It is to be read together with sections 12-16.

[2] Section 48 of the Act.

(a) all its members agree in writing to such a conversion;

(b) there is no unpaid liability on any of the company's shares;

(c) the members pass a special resolution to amend the articles to convert the company to an unlimited company complying with section 11;[3] and

(d) each member agrees, in writing, to take up a specified number of shares'.

4.4 Conversion of company limited by guarantee into company limited by shares or unlimited company

This is provided for under section 50 which states that '[a] company limited by guarantee may be converted into a company limited by shares or an unlimited company if—

(a) all its members agree in writing to—

    (i) convert it into a company limited by shares or an unlimited company; and

    (ii) a share capital for the company; and

(b) each member agrees, in writing, to take up a specified number of shares; and

(c) the members pass a special resolution to amend the articles to convert the company to a company limited by shares or an unlimited company complying with section 9 or 11'.

4.5 Conversion of unlimited company into private limited company

According to section 51(1), '[a]n unlimited company may be converted into a company limited by shares or a company limited by guarantee if—

(a) all its members agree in writing to its conversion;

(b) in the case of conversion to a company limited by guarantee, each member makes a declaration of guarantee as provided in section 10; and

(c) the members pass a special resolution to amend the articles to convert the company to a private limited company complying with section 8.[4] In terms of section 51(2), '[t]he company may, by special resolution, in the case of a conversion to a company limited by shares—

    (a) increase the nominal amount of the company's share capital by increasing the nominal amount of each of its shares, subject to the condition that no part of the increased capital shall be capable of being called up except in the event of the company being wound-up; or

---

[3] Which provides for manner of incorporating and registration of private unlimited companies. Section 11(3) provides that at winding up, all members will be liable to the last fathom of the company's liability.

[4] Relating to the incorporation and registration of private companies in general.

(b)   provide that a specified portion of the company's uncalled share capital shall not be capable of being called up except in the event, and for the purpose of, the company being wound-up.

It is clear that in this case, unlike that under para 4.4 above, it is the present company's creditors who will need protection. That is afforded by section 51(3), which provides that '[w]here an unlimited company is converted into a private limited company and is wound-up within three years after the conversion, a member of the company who was a member immediately before the conversion, shall not be entitled to a limitation of liability'. In any other case, the suffix 'Ltd' to the company's name will alert creditors and any other person of the conversion of the company from one with members with unlimited liability to one where shareholders' liability will be limited to the unpaid amounts on the shares they own and no more.

4.6   Conversion of public company into private company limited by shares

This type of conversion may, because of the nomenclature be confused with the process of privatisation (de-nationalisation)[5] The procedure for this type of conversion is provided for under section 52. Thereunder, '[a] public company may be converted into a private company limited by shares by—

(a)   its members passing a special resolution to convert the company into a company limited by shares;

(b)   amending the articles to satisfy sections 8 and 9;[6]

(c)   its members agreeing in writing to a share capital for the company; and

(d)   each member agreeing, in writing, to take up a specified number of share'.

4.7 Conversion of private company limited by shares into public company

Converting a company from a private one limited by shares to a public one still limited by shares is, barring any discord among the members a fairly straight forward matter. In terms of section 53, [a] private company limited by shares may be converted into a public company by—

(a)   passing a special resolution to convert the company into a public company;

(b)   amending the articles to satisfy section 7;[7] and

(d)   its members agreeing in writing to a share capital for the company.

---

[5] Davies PL Gower and Davies' Principles of Modern Company Law 7th ed.

[6] Relating the incorporation and registration of private companies limited by shares.

[7] Relating to the incorporation and registration of public companies.

4.8   The process of conversion

'A company shall, within twenty-one days of satisfying the requirements of sections 47, 48, 49, 50, 51 or 52, as the case may be, lodge with the Registrar a notice, in the prescribed form',[8] together with the following documents:

(a)   the company's certificate of incorporation;

(b)   a copy of each amended paragraph in the articles;

(c)   a copy of the special resolution or written agreement by the members as specified in the relevant conversion section;

(d)[9]   a statutory declaration by a director and the secretary of the company stating that—

   (i)   the conditions for converting the company as specified in the relevant section have been complied with; and

   (ii)   in their opinion, the company is solvent as evidenced in a report by the auditors of the company, made not more than ninety days before the date of the notice referred to in section 54(1);

(e)   if the company is being converted from a public company to a private company and has been incorporated as a public company for not less than fifteen months, certified copies, signed by not less than two directors of the company or, where the company has one director, by that director, of every financial statement, statement of comprehensive income, group accounts, directors' report and auditor's report sent to the members of the company in the preceding twelve months.[10]

In terms of section 54(3), '[t]he Registrar shall, on receipt of the notice referred to in [section 54](1), together with the documents specified in section 54(2)—

(a)   issue a replacement certificate of incorporation in the prescribed form, worded to meet the converted status of the company and stating the date of conversion of the company; and

(b)   make such entries in such registers as the Registrar considers appropriate'.

Further and in terms of section 54(4), '[f]rom the date of conversion stated in the certificate of incorporation the—

(a)   company shall stand converted into a company of the status specified on the replacement certificate of incorporation;

(b)   articles shall stand amended in accordance with the documents lodged with the notice of conversion; and

---

[8] Section 54(1). So important is this requirement that in terms of section 54(6) '[i]f a company fails to comply with [it] the company and each officer in default commit an offence and are liable, on conviction, to a fine not exceeding three thousand penalty units for each day that the failure continues'.

[9] This is a serious requirement with grave consequences if flouted. In terms of section 54(7), '(7) If a director or secretary of a company makes a declaration, for purposes of subsection (2)*(d)* that in the director's or secretary's opinion, the company is solvent, without having reasonable grounds for the opinion, the director or secretary commits an offence and shall be liable, on conviction, to a fine not exceeding one hundred thousand penalty units.'

[10] Section 54(2).

    (c)   name shall be as stated in the replacement certificate of incorporation.

It is significant to note that according to section 54(5), '[t]he conversion of a company [hereinbefore described] shall not—

    (a)   alter the identity of the company;

    (b)   affect any rights or obligations of the company, except as specified in this section; or

    (c)   render defective any legal proceedings by or against the company'. In essence, conversion cannot be used as a device for a company to avoid or escape from any subsisting liability, legal, contractual or otherwise.

4.9   Imposition of penalty by Registrar for non-compliance

Where a private company—

    (a)   has more members than permitted by its articles; or

    (b)   invites the public to acquire shares or debentures in the company in contravention of section 210',[11] the Registrar will 'give notice in the prescribed form to the company, of the Registrar's intention to impose a penalty for failure to comply with the Act'. 'The Registrar shall, in said notice:

        (a)   give reason for the intended penalty;

        (b)   require the company to show cause within a period of thirty days, why the penalty should not be imposed'.[12]

In the event that 'a company takes remedial measures to the satisfaction of the Registrar, within the period specified in [section 55(2)], the Registrar shall not impose the intended penalty'.[13] In terms of section 55(4), '[w]here a company fails to take remedial measures within thirty days, the Registrar shall impose a penalty not exceeding three hundred penalty units for each day that the failure to comply continues'.

4.10 Conclusion

In this chapter we have noted that the Act does permit companies to convert from one form to another. That, as the process involves the change of the

---

[11] Section 210 reserves the right to invite the public to acquire shares and debentures public companies. It makes the money paid to acquire shares and debentures in contravention of the section payable to the members of the public who responded to the invitation. Further and in terms of section 210(7), '[i]f an invitation to the public is made, in contravention of this section, each person making the invitation and, where such a person is a body corporate, each officer in default commits an offence and is liable, on conviction, to a fine not exceeding two hundred thousand penalty units or to imprisonment for a period not exceeding two years, or to both'.

[12] Section 55(2).

[13] Section 55(3).

character of the company, it may also be referred to as re-registration as is the case under the UK CA 2006. We have noted that the Act allows for conversion of private company limited by shares into company limited by guarantee; conversion of private company limited by shares into unlimited company; conversion of company limited by guarantee into company limited by shares or unlimited company; conversion of unlimited company into private limited company; conversion of public company into private company limited by shares; conversion of private company limited by shares into public company; and the process of conversion. We finally observed that in its regulatory role, the Act allows the Registrar to impose a penalty on companies that fail to comply with the requirements of conversion irrespective.

FURTHER READING

Articles

Francies, M, McLaughlin, C & Hardy, A, 'From public to private: changing direction' (2003) 14 Plc 21.

Ireland, P, 'Capitalism Without the Capitalist: the Joint Stock Company Share and the Emergence of the Modern Doctrine of Separate Corporate Personality' (1996) 17 *Journal of Legal History* 63.

Books

Davies PL *Gower and Davies' Principles of Modern Company Law* 7th edn (Thomson Sweet & Maxwell London 2003).

Dine J and Koutsias M *Company Law* 6th edn (Palgrave Macmillan Hampshire 2007).

Farrah JH and Hannigan BM *Farrar's Company Law* 4th edn (Butterworths London 1998).

Gates RB *Gates Company Law and Practice in Zambia* (Reagan Blankfein Gates Lusaka 2017).

Sealy L and Worthington S *Sealy & Worthington's Cases and Materials in Company Law* 10th edn (Oxford University Press Oxford 2013).

Wild C and Weinstein S *Smith and Keenan's Company Law* 15th edn (Pearson Education Ltd London 2011).

5

MEETINGS AND RESOLUTIONS

AIMS AND OBJECTIVES

 After reading this chapter you should appreciate:
- ➢ What an Annual General Meeting is
- ➢ The business to be transacted at an Annual General Meeting
- ➢ What an Extraordinary General Meeting
- ➢ Instances in which the High Court may order a company to convene a meeting
- ➢ How a requisition of General Meeting is supposed to be made
- ➢ What a Class Meetings is
- ➢ The concept of entitlement to receive notice of meetings *vs.* attendance at meetings
- ➢ The length of notice for convening meeting
- ➢ The place of meeting
- ➢ How meetings of the company are to be conducted and procedure for voting
- ➢ The significance of a Quorum
- ➢ The role of the Chairman at a meeting of the company
- ➢ The concept of proxies
- ➢ Provisions relating to representation of body corporates and unincorporated associations at meetings
- ➢ Articulate the concept of Resolutions by comparing and contrasting:
  - ▪ Special resolution
  - ▪ Extraordinary resolution
  - ▪ Ordinary resolution
- ➢ Matters relating to the circulation of members' resolutions and supporting documents
- ➢ Matters relating to the circulation of members' statements vs. refusal to circulate member's statements
- ➢ Matters relating to the concept of written resolutions for private companies
- ➢ The need and manner of resolution lodgement
- ➢ The importance of writing and retaining Minutes

5.1   Introduction

A company's important decisions are, so far as they are not reserved for directors, made by the membership through resolutions in general meetings. The general meetings are usually held once every year hence the term *Annual General Meeting* (AGM) for purposes of electing directors and auditors, declaring dividends, considering accounts and reports of directors and auditors. When exigencies arise, an *Extraordinary General Meeting* (EGM) may be called. Where there is more than one class of shares, there will invariably be more than one class of shareholders. To them is given the right to call what is termed a class meeting (CM) to which only members of that class are entitled to attend.[1]

This chapter therefore discusses Part VI of the Act specifically sections 56-81 which provides for meetings and resolutions. To that end we will explore and critically analyse provisions relating to types of meetings; annual general meeting; imposition of penalty by Registrar for noncompliance; business to be transacted at annual general meeting; extraordinary general meeting; class meetings; requisition of general meeting; entitlement to receive notice of meetings; length of notice for convening meeting; place of meetings; attendance at meetings; conduct of meetings and voting; meeting by order of Court; chairperson's declaration as to result of vote; right to demand poll; voting on poll; proxies; representation of body corporates and unincorporated associations at meetings; circulation of members' resolutions and supporting documents; circulation of members' statements; refusal to circulate member's statements; reference to ordinary, extraordinary, and special resolutions in other documents; written resolutions for private companies; lodgement of resolutions; and date of certain resolutions.

5.2   Types of meetings under the Act

5.2.1   General

In terms of section 56(1), '"meeting" means any of the following meetings of a company:
- *(a)*   an annual general meeting;
- *(b)*   an extraordinary general meeting; or
- *(c)*   a class meeting.

'A meeting called in accordance with this Part, at which voting will be conducted or documents tabled, may be held by teleconferencing or other electronic means'.[2] We discuss these three types in turn.

---

[1]   See the comments of Lord Russell of Killowen in *Carruth v Imperial Chemical Industries Ltd* [1937] AC 707.

[2]   Section 56(2). In fact the UK HC has held in *PNC Telecom Plc v Thomas* [2003] BCC 202 that so far as a members' requisition to convene an extraordinary general meeting goes, under section 61 a fax will do

5.2.2 Annual General Meeting[3]

A company is mandated to, 'within ninety days after the end of each financial year[4] of the company, [hold] an annual general meeting'.[5] In the event that an annual general meeting is not held, the '...Registrar may, ...on the application of a member, direct the convening of an annual general meeting and give such directions as the Registrar considers expedient, including directions to modify or supplement the convening, holding and conducting of the meeting; or operation of the company's articles'.

In terms of section 57(3), '[a] private company may dispense with the holding of an annual general meeting required in accordance with this Part, other than the first financial year, if all the members entitled to attend and vote at the annual general meeting agree in writing, before the end of the financial year, and notify the Registrar in the prescribed form. By section 57(4), '[i]f a company fails to comply with this section, the company and each officer in default commit an offence and shall be liable, on conviction, to a fine not exceeding three thousand penalty units for each day that the failure continues'.

5.2.2.1 Business to be transacted at an Annual General Meeting

The business to be transacted at an annual general meeting is in terms of section 58, to include the following:
- *(a)* consideration and approval of the financial statements and annual report;
- *(b)* the declaration of a dividend;
- *(c)* the consideration of the directors' and auditors' reports;
- *(d)* the election of directors in place of those retiring;
- *(e)* the fixing of the remuneration of the directors; and
- *(f)* the appointment of the auditors and the fixing of their remuneration.

5.2.3 Extraordinary General Meeting

Though section 3 unhelpfully defines an "extraordinary general meeting" '[as] a special meeting of a company as specified in section 59', it is submitted that an extraordinary general meeting is a general meeting other than an annual general meeting but which is also not a class meeting. It is ordinarily called to deal with exigencies that cannot wait until the next annual general meeting. 'An extraordinary general meeting may be convened in accordance with [the] Act or by—

---

[3] Previously provided for under section 138 in CA 1994.
[4] According to section 3 " financial year " means, in relation to—*(a)* a company, the period, that begins on the first or subsequent accounting date, whether or not it constitutes a period of twelve months; *(b)* a foreign company, the financial year of the foreign company as specified in section 301; and *(c)* any other body corporate, the period specified in the law establishing or incorporating the body corporate;
[5] Section 57(1).

(a)   the board of directors whenever it considers necessary; or

(b)   any other person in accordance with the articles'.[6]

5.2.3.1 Court order to convene a meeting[7]

The Court may, in instances where it is unworkable to convoke a meeting of a company in accordance with the provisions of the Act or/and its articles and following the application of a director or a member entitled to vote at the meeting—

(a)   order a meeting of the company to be convened, held and conducted in such a manner as the Court considers appropriate; and

(b)   give such ancillary or consequential directions which the Court considers expedient, including a direction that one member shall make resolutions relating to the matters for that meeting which resolutions shall be deemed to be resolutions of the company. A meeting convened, held and conducted under the foregoing circumstances, will 'for all purposes be considered to be a meeting of the company duly convened, held and conducted'.

This was exemplified in *Re British Union for the Abolition of Vivisection*[8] where it appeared that in 1994 an extraordinary general meeting had been so disrupted that a near riot had broken out as a result of animosity between opposing factions within the Union and no business had been done. The Union's articles stated that no votes by proxy were allowed at annual general meetings or extraordinary general meetings, but the committee members of the union wished to change that provision, allowing proxies so that it would be possible for members to vote without actually attending the meeting. The committee members asked the court to direct them to hold an extraordinary meeting at which only 13 committee members would be present, i.e. 13 out of 9,000 members. The change to proxy voting could then be resolved upon at the meeting. The court made the necessary direction under section 371.[9]

Another case worth considering is *Re Sombrero Ltd.*[10] The applicant held ninety per cent of the shares of a private company, which was incorporated in March, 1956, and each of the two directors of the company held five per cent of the shares. By the company's articles of association, the quorum for general meetings of the company was two members present in person or by proxy, and, if within half an hour from the time appointed for a meeting a quorum was not present, the meeting, if convened on the requisition of members, was dissolved.

---

[6] Section 59.

[7] Section 64 which replaces section 144 of CA 1994.

[8] [1995] The Times, 3 March.

[9] Of the UKCA 2006.

[10] [1958] 3 All ER 1.

No general meeting of the company had ever been held. On 11 March 1958, the applicant requisitioned an extraordinary general meeting, under s 132 of the Companies Act, 1948, for the purpose of passing resolutions removing the two directors and appointing two other persons as directors. The directors having failed to comply with the requisition, the applicant himself convened an extraordinary general meeting for 21 April 1958. The directors deliberately did not attend the meeting either in person or by proxy, and, as a quorum was not present, the meeting was dissolved. On 29 April 1958, the applicant served a special notice, under s 142 of the Act of 1948, of his intention to move the same resolutions, under s. 142 and s 184, at the next extraordinary general meeting of the company. On the same day he took out an originating summons asking for a meeting to be called by the court, under s. 135(1)a, for the purpose of passing the resolutions, and for a direction that one member of the company should be deemed to constitute a quorum at such meeting. The application was opposed by the directors.

It was held as follows:

(1) As a practical matter the desired meeting of the company could not be conducted in accordance with the articles of association and the court had jurisdiction under s 135(1) of the Companies Act, 1948, to order a meeting to be held notwithstanding opposition by the shareholders other than the applicant.

(2) an order for the meeting to be held and that one member present should constitute a quorum would be made because (a) to refuse the application would be to deprive the applicant of his statutory right under s 184 to remove the directors by means of an ordinary resolution, and (b) the respondent directors had failed to perform their statutory duty to call an annual general meeting for the reason that, if they had convened a general meeting, they would have ceased to be directors.

Other than the circumstances envisaged in section 59 and 64, the extraordinary general meeting may, as was shown in *Re State of Wyoming Syndicate*,[11] be convened by the directors whenever they think fit.; or if the articles so provide, by any other person in accordance with those provisions.

5.2.3.2 *Requisition of General Meeting*[12]

Any member of a company may make a requisition for a general meeting to be held.[13] A requisition made in accordance with section 61(1), may be made

[11] [1901] 2 Ch 431.
[12] Section 61 which replaces section 141 CA 1994.
[13] Section 61(1). However note the difference in the UK as exemplified in the decision in *Morgan v Morgan Insurance Brokers Ltd* [1993] BCC 145; See generally Keenan D Smith and Keenan's Company Law 13th edn 406-7.

by any member who at the time when the requisition is made, holds not less than five percent of the total voting rights of all the members having a right to vote at a general meeting of the company. Further, '[t]he requisition, made in accordance with section 61(1), shall—

(a)   state the nature of the business to be transacted at the meeting;

(b)   be signed by the member making the requisition; and

(c)   be deposited at the registered office of the company or posted to the company's registered postal address; and may consist of several documents in like form, each signed by the member making the requisition'.[14]

The board is obliged, 'where a requisition is made in accordance with section 61(1), to proceed to convene a general meeting of the company'. If for any reason be it negligence or indifference, 'the board does not proceed to convene a meeting to be held within the period requested for the convening of the meeting, the members requesting the meeting may, convene the meeting, which shall be held not more than ninety days after receipt of the requisition by the company'.[15]

In terms of section 61(6), '[d]espite anything in the articles, the notice period for a meeting convened in accordance with [section 61] shall be—

(a)   twenty-eight days, if the meeting is an annual general meeting or a meeting at which a special resolution shall be passed; or

(b)   twenty-one days, in any other case; beginning on the date of receipt by the company, of the requisition to convene a general meeting'. Finally, and in terms of section 61(7), '[t]he company shall refund, any reasonable expenses incurred by a member requesting a meeting specified in this section'.[16]

5.2.4   Class Meetings

'Unless the articles provide otherwise, a meeting of members of a particular class may be convened by—

(a)   the board of directors whenever it considers necessary; or

(b)   two or more members of that class, holding, at the time the notice of the meeting is sent out, not less than five percent of the total voting rights of all the members having a right to vote at meetings of that class'.[17] Under those circumstances, only the members of a particular class for which the meeting has been called may attend'.

---

[14]   Section 61(3).

[15]   Section 61(5).

[16]   By section 61(8), '[t]he company shall, for purposes of making a refund in accordance with subsection (6), draw the necessary funds from the sums payable as remuneration or fees to the board'.

[17]   Section 60.

Lord Russell has opined in *Carruth v Imperial Chemical Industries Ltd* [18] as follows: *Prima facie* a separate meeting of a class should be a meeting attended only by members of the class, in order that the discussion of the matters which the meeting has to consider may be carried on unhampered by the presence of others who are not interested to view those matters from the same angle as that of the class; and if the presence of outsiders was retained in spite of the ascertained wish of the constituents of the meeting for their exclusion, it would not, I think, be possible to say that a separate meeting of the class had been duly held.

5.3   Entitlement to receive notice of meetings *vs* attendance at meetings

In terms of section 62(1), '[t]he following are entitled to receive notice of a meeting of the company':
(a)   a member having the right to vote at such meeting;
(b)   a person on whom the ownership of a share devolves by reason of that person being a legal personal representative, receiver or assignee in bankruptcy of a member, and of whom the company has received notice;
(c)   a director;
(d)   an auditor of the company; or
(e)   a person entitled under the articles to receive such notice.
The issue of notice arose in *International Trades Crystals Societe Anonyme v Northern Minerals (Zambia) Limited*.[19] The plaintiff sued the defendant for certain sums of money. The defendant applied to have the writ set aside on the ground that the resolution passed by three out of five directors of the plaintiff company authorising the institution of the proceedings was not valid because one of the directors had not been notified of the meeting at which the resolution was passed. The director to whom notice should have been given became aware of the decision taken in his absence and took no steps to require a second meeting to be held so that he could vote on the resolution. It was held that as the director affected had not called for another meeting within a reasonable time or at all, he could be regarded as having waived the irregularity which would otherwise have attached to the meeting at which the resolution was passed.

However, in terms of section 66, the following persons are entitled to attend and to speak at a meeting of a company—
(a)   a member with the right to vote at the meeting;
(b)   a person on whom the ownership of a share devolves, by reason of that person being a personal representative, successor in title, receiver or assignee in bankruptcy of a member;
(c)   director of the company;

---

[18] [1937] AC 707.
[19] [1985] ZR 27 (SC).

(d)   the secretary of the company;

(e)   auditor of the company;[20]

(f)   a person entitled under the articles to do so; and

(g)   any other person permitted to do so by the chairperson.

What is patently clear is that the secretary is not included among those entitled to receive notice. This is because as the chapter relating to Part VII: Corporate Governance will shows, the company secretary will ordinarily be present 'at all meetings of the company, and of the directors, and will make proper minutes of the proceedings'.[21] Further, '[h]e will issue, under the direction of the board, all notices to members and others. If that be the case, it is unnecessary even absurd for him to issue a notice to himself when he will have to attend irrespective'.[22]

'It would appear that contravening [section 62(1)] including deliberately omitting to give notice of a meeting to person entitled to receive such notice or for any reason conceivable, meddling with the receipt of such notice will invariably invalidate any resolution passed at the meeting in question'.[23] The case of *Young v Ladies Imperial Club*[24] demonstrates this. In that case, one of the rules of a ladies' proprietary club provided that if the conduct of any member should, in the opinion of the executive committee, be injurious to the character and interests of the club, the committee should have power to suspend the member from the use of the club and to recommend her to resign, and if she did not do so within a certain time, the committee should erase her name from the list of members, provided that no member could be so suspended or recommended to resign unless a resolution to that effect should have been passed by a certain majority of the members of the committee actually present at a meeting especially convened for the purpose.

Acting under the rule the committee of the defendant club recommended the plaintiff, who was a member, to resign, and, as she did not do so, the committee erased her name from the list of members. The notice convening the meeting of the committee stated that the object of the meeting was "to report on and discuss the matter concerning [the plaintiff] and Mrs. L.," and it was sent to each member of the committee except one, who had previously intimated to the chairman that she would be unable to attend meetings of the committee. In an action for a declaration that the plaintiff was still a member of the club, it was held as follows:

(1)   that the omission to summon the absent member of the committee invalidated the proceedings of that body; and

(2)   that the notice did not state the object of the meeting with sufficient particularity. On both these grounds the plaintiff was entitled to succeed.

---

[20] Must be read together with section 261.

[21] Gates RB *Gates Company Law and Practice in Zambia* 288.

[22] Gates RB *Gates Company Law and Practice in Zambia* 288.

[23] Gates RB *Gates Company Law and Practice in Zambia* 288-9.

[24] [1920] 2 KB 523.

However, section 62(2)[25] provides that the proceedings of a meeting shall not be invalid by reason only of the—

(a)   accidental omission to give notice of the meeting to a person entitled to receive notice; or

(b)   non-receipt of a notice of the meeting duly sent to a person entitled to receive notice.[26]

Two cases demonstrate how the courts have decided such a question: The first is *Re West Canadian Collieries Ltd.*[27] By section 141 (5) of the Companies Act 1948: "For the purposes of this section, notice of a meeting shall be deemed to be deemed to be duly given and the meeting to be duly held when the notice is given and the meeting held in manner provided by this Act or the articles." The Registrar of a company, in sending out to members of the company notices of a special resolution for the reduction of capital to be proposed at the annual general meeting, inadvertently omitted to send notices to nine of the members. Article 75 of the company's articles of association, which was identical in terms with article 51 of Table A, provided that the accidental omission to give notice of a meeting to, or the non-receipt of notice of a meeting by, any person entitled to receive notice should not invalidate the proceedings at that meeting. The special resolution was passed at the meeting. On a petition for confirmation of the reduction of capital, it was *held* that the omission to give notice of the meeting to the nine members was "accidental" within the meaning of article 75 and that, therefore, it did not invalidate the proceedings at that meeting. It must be implicit in article 75 that a meeting, the proceedings of which were to be taken to be valid notwithstanding the omission to give notice to the members, was to be deemed to have been duly convened for the purposes of the articles, including in those purposes the of convening the meeting, since in the absence of such an implication there could be no meeting the proceedings of which could be validated by article 75. Accordingly, the notice of the meeting had been duly given and the resolution duly passed for the purposes of section 141 of the Companies Act, 1948, and the reduction would therefore be confirmed.

The second case is *Musselwhite v C H Musselwhite & Son Ltd and Others*[28] where the share capital of a company incorporated in 1933 was divided into 8,000 £1 shares. 7,200 of these shares were issued fully paid up. The plaintiffs, A. and his wife, were the registered holders of 3,599 and one of the shares respectively, and the individual defendants, B. and his wife, were also the registered holders of 3,599 and one of the shares respectively. A. was the managing director and secretary of the company, and A.'s wife, B. and B.'s wife were directors. The company's articles of association incorporated Table

---

[25] Section 143(2) under CA 1994.

[26] Further and by section 62(3) subject to subsection 62(1), 'a notice of a meeting of a company shall be in writing and served on each person entitled to receive the notice'.

[27] [1962] Ch 370.

[28] [1962] Ch 964.

A set out in the First Schedule to the Companies Act, 1929, article 43 of which provided: "The accidental omission to give notice of a meeting to...any member shall not invalidate the proceedings at any meeting." By an agreement dated May 21, 1958, A. agreed, on behalf of himself and his wife, to sell their shares in the company and another company to B. for £10,000, of which sum £7,500 was to be paid by three-monthly installments of £375 over five years. The agreement also provided that transfers and the relevant share certificate should be deposited with the company's solicitors until payment had been made in full. In accordance with the agreement, the relevant transfers and certificates were deposited with the solicitors and the plaintiffs resigned as directors and A. also resigned as secretary. The plaintiffs remained on the company's register of members as the holders of the shares. The installments of the purchase price were being duly paid; at the date of the hearing about £2,600 was still outstanding.

On December 30, 1958, the annual general meeting of the company for the year ending May 31, 1958, was purported to be held. No notice of such meeting was given to either of the plaintiffs. The omission to give such notice resulted from the then directors of the company being under the erroneous impression that the plaintiffs, having executed transfers of their shares to B., were no longer members of the company and were not, therefore, entitled to receive such notice. In October, 1959, a further 50 shares of the original share capital were issued to B.'s wife. It was held as follows:

That the omission to give notice of the meeting of December 30, 1958, to the plaintiffs prima facie invalidated the meeting, and that an omission arising from an error was accidental, so that article 43 of Table A did not operate to prevent the omission from invalidating the meeting which was, therefore, a nullity.

That, when a meeting would take place after the end of the period required by law for its holding, there was no justification for determining the voting rights at that meeting by reference to the state of the share register on the last date allowed by law for the holding of it.

But that an unpaid or partly-paid vendor of shares remaining on the register of members after the execution of the contract for sale retained, vis-à-vis the purchaser, the right to decide how to, exercise the voting rights in respect of those shares; and that, therefore, the plaintiffs were not bound to vote in accordance with the directions of B., and were entitled to complain of the defect in the meeting. Accordingly, the plaintiffs were entitled to a declaration that the meeting was a nullity.

5.4   Length of notice for convening meeting[29]

The law and procedure in this regard is to be found in section 63 of the Act. By section 63(1), '[a] notice of a company meeting shall be given not less than—

---

[29] Formerly under section 143 CA 1994.

(a)   twenty-one days, in the case of an annual general meeting;

(b)   twenty-one days, in the case of a meeting at which a special resolution will be proposed; or

(c)   fourteen days, in any other case; and not more than fifty days before the meeting is to be held'.

In terms of section 63(2), '[t]he articles may substitute for the minimum periods of notice provided in subsection (1) longer periods, being periods of not more than thirty days. However, '[w]here a meeting of the company is convened with a shorter period of notice than that required under this section, full notice shall be deemed to have been given if it is so agreed—

(a)   by all the members entitled to attend and vote at the meeting, in the case of a meeting convened as the annual general meeting;

(b)   by a majority in number of the members having a right to attend the meeting and vote on the resolution concerned, being a majority holding not less than ninety-five percent of the total of such voting rights, in the case of a meeting convened as a meeting at which a special resolution will be moved, and in relation to that resolution; and

(c)   by a majority in number of the members having a right to attend and vote at the meeting, being a majority holding not less than ninety-five percent of the total of such voting rights, in the case of any other meeting'.[30]

Section 63(2) and 63(3) are derived from sections 369(3)(4) and 378(3) of the UK CA 1985 which themselves grew from the decisions in several cases including *Re Express Engineering Works Ltd*[31] where five persons incorporated a private company in which they were sole shareholders. They sold to the company for £15,000.00 a property which they had bought for £7,000.00. The price was to be paid by the issue of debentures for £15,000.00 by the company. The transaction was carried out at a "board" meeting of the five individuals who appointed themselves directors. The articles forbade a director to vote in respect of a contract in which he was interested. It was held that there was no fraud and the company was bound in the matter by the unanimous agreement of the members. Consequently the debentures were valid. In *Re Oxted Motor Co Ltd*'[32] both members of a company waived the normal length of notice of a meeting at which an extraordinary resolution for voluntary winding up was validly passed. Another interesting case is *Parker & Cooper Ltd v Reading*[33] where there was no actual meeting but the members individually and at different times informally ratified a debenture granted by the directors which, although

---

[30] Section 62(3) of the Act.
[31] [1920] 1 Ch 466 (CA) applied in *Re Bailey, Hay & Co Ltd* [1971] 1 WLR 1357.
[32] [1921] 3 KB 32.
[33] [1926] Ch 975.

intra vires the company, was beyond the powers of the directors because two directors had been invalidly appointed.[34]

5.5 Place of meeting

Unless the articles provide otherwise or all the members entitled to vote at that meeting agree in writing,[35] to hold the meeting at a place outside Zambia, a meeting of the company will ordinarily be held in Zambia.

5.6   Conduct of meetings and voting

5.6.1   General

In terms of section 67(1), '[u]nless the articles provide otherwise, a member
 (a)   shall have one vote for each share and whole unit of stock that the member is registered as holding; and
 (b)   of a private company limited by guarantee, shall have one vote.[36] 'A person who is not a member shall not be entitled to vote at a meeting of the company'.[37]

5.6.2   Quorum

The notion of a quorum is used with respect to the minimum number of persons appropriately qualified who must be in attendance at a properly called meeting in order that the business of the company may be validly conducted. According to 67(4), '[t]he quorum for a meeting of a company shall be [*two members present*][38] of the company, holding not less than one third of the total voting rights in relation to the meeting, unless the articles or an order of Court provide otherwise'. However, in terms of section 67(6), '[t]he articles may provide that a member shall not be entitled to attend a meeting of the company, unless all outstanding sums payable by the member, in respect of shares in the company, have been paid'.[39] If the articles so provide, any member who attends a meeting will, for purposes of determining whether a quorum has been formed, not, in

---

[34]   Applied *in Re Duomatic Ltd* [1969] 2 Ch 365.

[35]   For an illuminating discussion of the concept of 'Decision-Making without meetings' see Davies PL *Gower and Davies' Modern Principles of Company Law* 7th edn 328-336.

[36]   In terms of section 67(2), '[t]he articles may provide that a member shall have rights in respect of shares not registered to that member.

[37]   Section 67(3).

[38]   See however section 7 of the UK CA 2006 which provides for the formation of one member companies; see further Gates RB *Gates Company Law and Practice in Zambia* 16-19 para 1.8: "The case for a Single-member Private Limited Company".

[39]   In terms of section 67(7), ' For the purposes of this section, a " unit of stock " of a company is the amount of stock with a nominal value arrived at by adding together the nominal value of all the shares of the company other than stock, and dividing the sum by the number of those shares'.

terms of section 67(4) be counted as constituting a quorum. Contravention of section 67(4) and 67(6), were applicable has serious consequences in that unless there is a quorum present, the meeting is null and void. However, sections 67(4) and 67(6) must be understood within the context of the articles of the company if a claim of validity or lack thereof for want of quorum arises at the beginning of the meeting or at any time during the meeting.

5.6.3   Chairman

In terms of section 67(5), '[a] meeting of the company may, unless the articles or this Act provide otherwise, elect a chairperson and determine the conduct of business in that meeting'. The importance of the chairman cannot be underestimated. By section 68, '[a] statement by the chairperson and secretary at a meeting of the company that a motion or resolution at a meeting was passed by a specified majority, shall be conclusive evidence that it was so passed, unless a poll was demanded on the motion or resolution and unless the articles provide otherwise'. While it may seem from the permissive crafting of section 67(5) that the company has the option of choosing whether or not to have a chairman for 'a meeting of the company' in practice, any meeting of the company will have a chairman. His main duties include, but are not limited to preservation of order; call on members to speak; to decide points of order; acceptability of amendments; and to take the vote after a proper discussion in order to ascertain the sense of the meeting, though not bound to hear everyone.

Additionally, the chairman must be fair to the minority. This point was, among others, illustrated in *Wall v London Northern & Assets Corporation*.[40] The objects of the A. company as stated by art. 3 of its memorandum were (inter alia) (a) to raise capital and invest it in such bonds, stocks, and securities as therein mentioned; (i) to sell any part of the assets and to accept the consideration in cash, shares, or other securities, and to divide any assets of the company in specific among its shareholders; (o) to amalgamate with any persons, companies, or firms carrying on business of a like nature. The D. Company carried on a similar business. The A. Company agreed with the D. Company to sell to the D. Company all its assets (except £33252 shares in the D. Company which the A. Company held) for £60,991, to be satisfied as to £59,736. by allotment of 29,868 fully paid-up shares of £2. each in the D. Company, and the balance of £1,255. in cash or fully paid-up shares at the option of the A. Company. It was provided by the agreement that the shares so allotted and the shares in the D. Company already held by the A. Company were to be divided among the shareholders of the A. Company in manner therein mentioned. It was doubtful

---

[40] [1898] 2 Ch 469.

whether the mode of division was not illegal as interfering with the rights of the shareholders under the memorandum and articles. It was held as follows:

(1) that the proposed sale being a sale of the assets of the A. Company with a substantial exception was within (i), and that the transaction was also warranted by (o) as being an amalgamation;

(2) that the proposed division of shares, being a matter with which the D. Company had nothing to do, did not, even if illegal, affect the validity of the agreement for sale. And that an interlocutory injunction to prevent the A. Company from carrying the agreement into effect had been properly refused on an undertaking by the A. Company not to divide the shares till after the trial otherwise than in accordance with the rights of the shareholders under the memorandum and articles.

(3) At a meeting of shareholders it is not competent to the majority to come determined to vote in a particular way on any question, and to refuse to hear any arguments to the contrary; but when the views of the minority have been heard, it is competent to the chairman with the sanction of a vote of the meeting to declare the discussion closed and to put the question to the vote.

(4) At a meeting held to confirm a resolution passed by the requisite majority at a former meeting so as to make it a special resolution, it is irregular to propose an amendment to that resolution.

5.6.4 Right to demand poll and voting on poll

A poll is a process of voting whereby each member is permitted to vote for or against a resolution based on the voting power of the number of shares such a member holds. Any shareholder has a right to demand a poll. Section 69[41] provides that '[a] poll may be demanded, at a meeting of a company on any question other than the election of the chairperson of the meeting or the adjournment of the meeting, by not less than—

(a) three members with the right to vote on the question, representing not less than five percent of the total voting rights of all members having the right to vote on the question, where there are more than eight members present; or

(b) one-third of the members present with the right to vote on the question, where the members present are eight or less'. These rather stringent requirements are meant to stop unfounded demands for polls being made every time the default method of voting, by show of hands, is used.

The issue of demanding for a poll came up in two cases the salient facts of which follow below:

---

[41] Which replaces section 149 CA 1994.

The case of *Sharp v Dawes*[42] was an appeal from an order of the Queen's Bench Division making absolute an order to increase the amount of a verdict for the plaintiff. At the trial it appeared that the Great Caradon Mine was a mining company in Cornwall carrying on business on the cost-book system. The company had offices in London, and on 22 December 1874, a notice was duly given that a general quarterly meeting of the shareholders would be held on 30 December at the London offices for the purpose of passing the accounts, making a call, receiving a report from the agent, and transacting any ordinary business of the company. The only persons who attended at the time appointed for the meeting were the secretary G. Sharp and one shareholder, R.H. Silversides, who held twenty-five shares. A circular was then sent to the shareholders with the accounts and the following notice:-

R.H. Silversides, Esq., in the chair,

The notice convening the meeting having been read,

The minutes of the last meeting were confirmed.

The financial statement, ending the 28th of November, shewing a balance of 83l.11s. 5d. against the shareholders, having been read, it was

Resolved-"That the same be received and passed."

Captain William Taylor's report having been read, it was

Resolved-"That the same be received and passed, and, together with the financial statement, be printed and circulated among the shareholders."

Resolved-"That a call of 4s. 6d. per share be now and is hereby made payable to the secretary, and that a discount of 5 per cent. be allowed if paid by the 20th of January, 1875."

Resolved-"In consequence of the death of Lieut.-Col. W.T. Nicolls, and until the appointment of a shareholder to act in his stead, that all cheques be signed by Mr. R.H. Silversides and Mr.. Granville Sharp jointly."

(Signed)   R.H. Silversides,   Chairman.

Resolved-"That a vote of thanks be given to the chairman."

(Signed)   Granville Sharp, Secretary.

There was no rule of the company varying the requirements of the Stannaries Act (32 & 33 Vict. c.19). By rule 4,-

The secretary shall call a general meeting of the shareholders one in every three calendar months, to be held at such time and place as shall be appointed by the committee of management.

The defendant, one of the shareholders, refused to pay this call, and the action was brought against him, in the name of the secretary, for the amounts due on a previous call and on this call. Judgment was given for the plaintiff for

---

[42] [1876] 2QBD 26.

the amount due on the previous call, with leave to move to increase it by the amount due on the second call.

The plaintiff accordingly moved Blackburn and Quain, JJ., who made the rule absolute.

It was held for the defendant that the call was invalid; one shareholder could not constitute a meeting and make a call under the powers of the Stannaries Act, 1869 (32 & 33 Vict.c. 19) (1) and the rules of this company. It was clearly the intention of the legislature that there should be a discussion. In no sense of the word could one person constitute a meeting; the use of the word shareholders, in the plural, showed this. In fact the meeting was abortive, as it would have been if no shareholder had attended. Another meeting ought to have been called. Neither the words nor the spirit of the Act had been complied with.

In *Re London Flats Ltd*[43] a private company which had been incorporated in February 1936 had an authorised issued share capital of 45,000 shares of £1 each. The respondent's mother, Mrs. O., held 39,900 of the shares, 15,000 of them being held by her as nominee for her husband, 5,000 of the remainder were held by the respondent, and the balance of 100 by the applicant. In February 1963 the company went into a members' voluntary liquidation, Mrs. O. being appointed liquidator, but she died in March 1963. Under her will her husband, O., who survived her but who himself died in October 1963, became entitled to all her shares in the company. As a result of an action begun by O as his wife's executor to establish her will and codicil, to which the respondent was defendant, the 39,900 shares in the company became sterilised and could not be voted on. In this situation, there being no liquidator following Mrs. O.'s death, the applicant called an extraordinary general meeting of the company for 26 July 1963, the notice convening the meeting stating that it would be proposed as an ordinary resolution that L be appointed liquidator of the company to fill the vacancy caused by the death of Mrs. O. The applicant and respondent were in the circumstances, the only persons entitled to attend and vote as members.

At the meeting the respondent, having declared himself to be chairman although the applicant objected, invited the applicant to propose the resolution set out in the notice which the applicant then read out in full. The respondent then stated that he proposed an amendment that he would propose himself as liquidator, but the applicant left the room before he, in fact, did so. The amendment was put to the vote and there being one vote in favour and none against the respondent declared the amendment carried. The applicant now took out a summons under s 304a of the Companies Act 1948 asking for an order appointing W as liquidator of the company or, alternatively, an order removing the respondent from the office and an order appointing W in his place.

---

[43] [1969] 2 All ER 744 applying *Sharp v Dawes* supra note 302 above.

On the question whether the respondent was validly appointed liquidator by the company in general meeting under s. 286(1) of the Companies Act 1948.

It was held that the respondent's purported appointment of himself as liquidator was a nullity because at the moment when he was proposing himself as liquidator the applicant left the meeting, and from that moment, there was only one member present and, therefore, no meeting, a single shareholder being unable, as a general rule, to constitute a meeting.

The foregoing notwithstanding, in terms of section 70, '[t]he articles shall not require a member entitled to more than one vote on a poll taken at a meeting of the company, if the member votes to use or cast all the member's votes in the same way'.

5.6.5 *Proxies*

Section 71 which replaces section 151 CA 1994 provides for the law and procedure on proxies. In terms of section 71(1), '[a] member entitled to attend and vote at a meeting of the company is entitled to appoint another person as a proxy. By section 71(2), '[a] member shall appoint a proxy in writing, in the prescribed form, in the case of—

(a) an individual member, under the hand of the appointing member or the appointing member's authorised agent; or

(b) a member that is a body corporate, under seal or under the hand of an officer or authorised agent'.

According to section 71(3), '[a] proxy, appointed in accordance with this section, shall have, in relation to the meeting and subject to any instructions in the instrument of appointment, all the rights and powers of the appointing member. By section 72(4), '[w]here voting rights attach to shares held in a company with share capital, a shareholder may, appoint separate proxies to represent the member on each of the shares held, in a manner specified in the instrument of appointment'.

There are however restrictions placed on directors who may be appointed as proxies in section 71(5). They cannot vote on the following business transacted at an annual general meeting:

(a) declaration of a dividend;

(b) consideration of the accounts and the directors' and auditors' reports;

(c) election and fixing of remuneration of directors; and

(d) appointment and fixing of remuneration of auditors.

It is apparent that the reason for the restrictions is predicated on the fact the potential for a conflict of interest were a director to vote behind the cloak of a proxy are high.

'In a notice convening a meeting of a company, there shall appear, with reasonable prominence, a statement to the effect that a member entitled to attend and vote is entitled to appoint one or more proxies and, unless the articles provide otherwise, such a proxy need not be a member'.[44] According to section 71(7) which is subjected to section 71(5), 'a company shall not provide a member with a form for the appointment of a proxy unless the form permits the member to direct the proxy as to how to use that member's vote on different matters'. Further, 'the articles shall not provide that an appointment of a proxy shall only be valid if received by the company or any other person more than forty-eight hours before a meeting is to be held'.[45] The reason is simple, the provision for a proxy is a statutory acknowledgement of the agency relationship between a member of the company and the proxy to which the company is not privy and with which it ought not to interfere.

So serious are the requirements in section 71(6)(9) that (9) failure to comply with them means 'the company and each officer in default commit an offence and are liable, on conviction, to a fine not exceeding two thousand five hundred penalty units. Further, and in terms of section 71(10), '[w]here a company fails to issue a form for the appointment of a proxy to every member entitled to receive a notice and vote at a meeting, the company and every officer in default commit an offence and are liable on conviction to a fine not exceeding two thousand five hundred penalty units in respect if each member not issued with a notice'.

As in any contract, the appointment of a proxy can be revoked at any time expressly, that is, by letting the proxy know that his appointment has been revoked and that his services relating to the voting process at a general meeting are no longer required. The member may also imply the revocation by exercising his right to vote in which case his vote will supersede that of the proxy.[46] Revocation may also occur because the principal has died. Be that as it may, the foregoing issues must be looked at within the context of the articles of the company which may provide for specifics in any of the foregoing circumstances.[47]

5.6.6 Representation of body corporates and unincorporated associations at meetings

The metaphysical nature of a company or an unincorporate body means that that they will invariably act through their agents. It therefore follows that where a body corporate or an unincorporated association is a member of a company a certain procedure has to be followed to enable it attend a meeting of the company in which it is a member. Section 72(1) therefore provides that '[a] body corporate or an unincorporated association that is a member may,

---

[44] Section 71(6).
[45] Section 71(8).
[46] See *Cousins v International Brick Co Ltd* [1931] 2 Ch 90.
[47] *Spiller v Mayo (Rhodesia) Development Co (1908) Ltd* [1926] WN 78.

by resolution of its board of directors or other governing body, authorise any person it considers appropriate to act as its representative at a meeting of the company. In terms of section 72(2), '[a] person authorised, in accordance with [section 72](1), may exercise the same powers on behalf of the body corporate or unincorporated association in the same manner that an individual member of the company would exercise those powers'.[48]

5.7   Resolutions

5.7.1   General

A company primarily makes its decision through the device of resolutions. There are basically three types of resolutions namely:

(1)   special;
(2)   extraordinary; and
(3)   ordinary.

We must note that there is no relationship between the type of meeting called and the type of resolution passed. The validity of the resolution by whatever name called is therefore dependent on the procedure as provided for in the articles of the company and the Act being followed. It therefore follows that anyone of the foregoing types of resolutions may be passed at any meeting of the company provided for in section 56(1). We now turn to the discussion of types of resolutions hereinbefore mentioned.

5.7.2   Special resolution

A special resolution is the kind 'passed by not less than [75] per cent of the votes of members of a company, entitled to vote in person or by proxy at a meeting duly convened and held at which the resolution is moved as a special resolution, or such higher majority percentage as the articles of association may require'. The following matters can only be decided upon by way of special resolution and no provision of the articles may provide otherwise as they are statutorily provided for:

Under the Act

Action	*Section*
(i) Alteration of articles	27
(ii) Change of company's name	42
(iii) Conversion of company from one form to another	48, 49, 50, 51, 52 and 53

---

[48] This is because once incorporated a company becomes a persona at law with, according to section 22(b) 'the capacity, rights, powers and privileges of an individual'.

Under the Corporate Insolvency Act[50]

5.7.3 *Extraordinary resolution*

In terms of section 3 an '"extraordinary resolution" means a resolution passed by a majority of not less than seventy-five percent of the votes of the members entitled to vote in person or by proxy at a meeting duly convened and held'.

5.7.4 *Ordinary resolution*

An '"ordinary resolution" means a resolution passed by more than half of the votes cast by the members entitled to vote in person or by proxy at a meeting duly convened and held'.[51] The articles of association will ordinarily provide for instances when an extraordinary resolution. We must however add that in the event that notice is given for such a resolution, and it must be, those who vote for the passage of the resolution must outnumber those against it. A further point in this regard is that the majority to which the foregoing refers is not the majority of the entire membership but a majority of those who are present and vote on the resolution. As a rule of thumb, whenever the articles of association or the Act

---

[49] According to section 3, '"amalgamation" means the combination of two or more companies to form a new body corporate as provided for in section 282 and the word amalgamating shall be construed accordingly'.

[50] No 9 of 2017.

[51] Section 3.

provide that the approval of members is required, an ordinary resolution will be sufficient unless there are statutory provisions or provisions in the articles specifying some other resolution for the matter at hand.

A case in point is section 85(1) for the appointment of a director or section 87(1)(a) where, in limiting the powers of directors it is provided that the board of directors shall not, without the approval of the members, '*by ordinary resolution*'(emphasis added)—

(a)   sell, lease or otherwise dispose of the whole, or substantially the whole, of the undertaking or assets of the company;

(b)   issue any new or unissued shares in the company;

(c)   create or grant any rights or options entitling the holders to acquire shares of any class in the company; or

(d)   enter into a transaction that has or is likely to have the effect of the company acquiring rights or interests or incurring obligations or liabilities, including contingent liabilities, the value of which is the value of the company's assets before the transaction'. Another, is section 118 which provides that '[t]he remuneration of directors shall be proposed by the board of directors and approved by the members by ordinary resolution'.[52]

5.7.5   Reference to ordinary, extraordinary, and special resolutions in other documents

We must add that '[a] reference in the articles, any debenture or debenture trust deed to—

(a)   an ordinary resolution;

(b)   extraordinary resolution; or

(c)   special resolution; of a meeting of creditors or debenture holders or of any class of creditors or debenture holders shall have the same meaning as defined in this Act, with necessary modifications'.[53]

5.8   Circulation of members' resolutions and supporting documents

According to section 73(1), '[a] member entitled to attend and vote at a meeting of the company may, in accordance with this section, request the company to

---

[52] But see section 119(1) which provides that '[d]espite [s]ection 118, the members may, *by special resolution*, approve any payment, provision, benefit, assistance or other distribution proposed by and payable to the directors. Further and importantly section 119(2) provides that '[a]n approval, referred to in subsection (1), shall only be made where there are reasonable grounds to believe that, after the distribution, the company will be able to satisfy the solvency test. (emphasis added)

[53] Section 76.

circulate, at the company's expense, a notice of any resolution, which is intended to be moved at the meeting accompanied by a statement with respect to the matter referred to in the proposed resolution. 'A request made, in accordance with subsection (1), shall be in writing and posted to the company's registered postal address or deposited at the company's registered office'.[54] Further and in terms of section 73(3), '[t]he company shall, if a meeting is proposed and the company receives a request—

(a)   not less than seven days before the end of the period during which notice of the meeting is required to be given; or

(b)   at a time when it is practicable to include the notice and statement required with the notice of the meeting; send the notice and statement to each person entitled to receive notice of the meeting before the end of the period within which notice of the meeting is required to be given.

There is a requirement under section 73(4) that '[w]here a company receives a request and subsection (3) does not apply, the company shall include the notice and statement required in a notice for the next meeting'. Additionally, under section 73(5), '[w]here a request is made in accordance with this section and the resolution is not passed, a request for the same resolution to be moved shall not be made at a meeting held within ninety days after the meeting at which the resolution was first moved unless the—

(a)   board agrees otherwise; or

(b)   request is supported, in writing, by members representing not less than five percent of the total voting rights of all the members having at the date of the request a right to vote on the resolution to which the request relates'.

5.9   Circulation of members' statements *vs.* refusal to circulate member's statements

5.9.1   *Circulation of members' statements*

By section 74(1), '[a] company shall, at the written request of a member entitled to attend and vote at a meeting, circulate to members, a statement of not more than one thousand words with respect to any business to be dealt with at that meeting'. '[t]he circulation of the statement, referred to in subsection (1), shall be at the expense of that member, unless the company otherwise resolves'.[55] It is a requirement under section 74(3) that '[t]he statement referred to in subsection (1),.. be circulated to the members in any manner permitted for service of a notice of the meeting at the same time as the notice of the meeting'. However,

---

[54] Section 73(2).
[55] Section 74(2).

'[a] company shall not be required to circulate a statement in accordance with this section, unless the request is—

(a)   received by the company not less than ten days before the meeting; and

(b)   accompanied by a sum reasonably sufficient to meet the company's expenses in circulating the statement'.[56]

5.9.2   *Refusal to circulate member's statements*

Section 75 provides for an instance when the company may refuse[57] to circulate a member's statement, the provisions of section 73 and 74 notwithstanding. It may do so if it 'is satisfied that the rights conferred by those sections are being abused so as to secure publicity of defamatory matter'.[58] This is however tempered by the fact that '[a] person aggrieved by the company's decision to refuse to circulate a resolution or a statement,..may appeal to the [High] Court against the decision'.[59] No liability can be incurred by the company 'by reason only that it has circulated a resolution or statement in compliance with section 73 or section 74'.[60] So serious is the requirement for the company to follow the provisions of section 75 that failure by the company to comply means that 'the company and each officer in default commit an offence and are liable, on conviction, to a fine not exceeding two thousand five hundred penalty units'.[61]

5.10   Written resolutions for private companies

As part of the its goal to encourage entrepreneurship, enterprise efficiency, flexibility and simplicity in the formation and maintenance of companies and the conduct of meetings and the passing of resolutions by shareholders, the Act provides for a varied procedure to that public companies are generally required and expected to follow. To that end section 77 provides for written resolutions for private companies instead of meetings being called for resolutions to pass in the conventional way.

By section 77(1), '[t]he members of a private company may, in accordance with this section, pass a resolution in writing, without holding a meeting, and such a resolution shall be valid and have the same effect as if it had been passed at a meeting of the appropriate kind, duly convened, held and conducted. Further and in terms of section 77(2), '[t]he resolution, referred to in subsection (1), shall be—

---

[56] Section 74(4).
[57] See *Ball v Metal Industries Ltd* [1957] SC 315.
[58] Section 75(1).
[59] Section 75(2).
[60] Section 75(3).
[61] Section 75(4).

(a)   signed by each member who is entitled to vote on the resolution, if it was moved at a meeting of the company or by the member's authorised representative; and

(b)   passed when signed by the last member, or member's representative, referred to in paragraph *(a)*, whether or not the member was a member when the other members signed.

Additionally and in terms of section 77(3), '[i]f the resolution proposed is described as a special resolution, it shall be treated as a special resolution for the purposes of [the] Act. Further and according to section 77(4), '[i]f the resolution states a date as being the date of the signature by a member, the statement shall be *prima facie* evidence that it was signed by the member on that date.

Before moving on, we must briefly discuss the above statutory provisions from a common law perspective. Lord Davey has suggested in *Salomon v Salomon & Co Ltd*[62] that a company will be bound by the unanimous consent of shareholders even when such unanimity is concerned with a matter or matters reserved to the board.[63] The unanimous consent rule at common law is therefore meant to allow shareholders in small private companies to act informally in matters that are within their competence and thereby bind the company. In fact a wholly informal when given by all the members entitled to vote may, as much as any resolution at a meeting or the written resolution referred to in section 77(2), bind the company. In *Wright v Atlas Wright (Europe) Ltd*[64] the negotiation by the managing director of the parent company with the managing director of its wholly owned subsidiary regarding the terms of a consultancy agreement which the second had proposed to enter into with said subsidiary was held to be an informal unanimous consent on the part of the parent company. 'Thus, as its name suggests, the written resolution procedure allows shareholders to adopt resolutions outside meetings; the unanimous consent rule permits wholly informal methods of giving shareholder consent'[65]

That this principle is well established in law is beyond doubt. 'In a series of case, the courts have come to recognise that "individual assents given separately" by all members entitled to vote are "equivalent to the assent of a meeting" and that the assent may be no more than passive acquiescence in the

---

[62] [1897] AC 22 at 57.

[63] See *Re Empress Engineering Works Ltd* [1920] 1 Ch 466 CA where shareholders were held to have default power to purchase property which ordinarily was within the realm of the board, given that all the directors had been disqualified from acting.

[64] [1999] 2 BCLC 301 CA.

[65] Gower and Davies' *Principles of Modern Company Law* 334.

result'[66] In view of the provisions of section 77, the case of *John Joseph Baker v The Raine Engineering Co. Ltd*[67] wherein it was held that (i) in the absence of a specific provision in the articles of association of a private company authorising the passing of a resolution by the signing of it by the shareholders without any meeting having been convened, any such resolution was null and void and (ii) that as a consequence the proceedings of directors' meeting of which notice was not given to any of the directors were null and void, is no longer good law.

The foregoing notwithstanding, the provisions of section 77 are not applicable to 'a resolution proposed for the removal of an auditor or a director'.[68] There are several reasons for this, the most obvious being that the auditor or director in question must be given an opportunity to be heard: *audi alteram partem,*[69] in writing together with the notice of the meeting at which the resolution will be tabled or orally before the resolution is voted on.

5.11   Lodgement of resolutions

A company is required to, 'within twenty-one days after the passing of a special resolution, lodge with the Registrar a certified copy of the resolution'.[70] Additionally, '[e]very copy of the articles shall have embodied in, or attached to it, a copy of every special resolution passed by the company'.[71] In terms of section 78(3), 'where the sole effect of a special resolution is to amend the articles, a copy of the articles that embodies the amendment, embodies the resolution'.[72]) '[I]f a company fails to comply with the requirements of section 78, 'the company and each officer in default commit an offence and are liable, on conviction, to a fine not exceeding one thousand penalty units in respect of each copy that is not in compliance with this section'.[73]

---

[66] Gower and Davies' *Principles of Modern Company Law* 334-5; For an appreciation of developments in this area see: *Re Express Engineering Works Ltd* [1920] 1 Ch 466 CA; *Wright v Atlas Wright (Europe) Ltd* [1999] 2 BCLC 301 CA; *Parker & Cooper Ltd v Reading* [1926] Ch 975; *Re Pearce Duff & Co Ltd* [1960] 1 WLR 1014; *Re Duomatic Ltd* [1969] 2 Ch 365; *Re Bailey Hay & Co Ltd* [1971] 1 WLR 1357; *Re Gee & Co (Woolwich) Ltd* [1975] Ch 52; *Cane v Jones* [1980] 1 WLR 1451; *Re Moorgate Mercantile Holdings Ltd* [1980] 1 WLR 227 at 242G; *Multinational Gas Co v Multinational Gas Services* [1983] 1 Ch 258 at 289 CA; and *Re Torvale Group Ltd* [1999] 2 BCLC 605.

[67] [1971] ZR 23 (ZMHC).

[68] Section 77(5).

[69] Also *audiatur et altera pars* is a latin maxim loosely translated as "listen to the other side", or "let the other side be heard as well". The principle is that no person may be judged without a fair hearing in which each side is given the opportunity to give a response to any evidence against them.

[70] Section 78(1).

[71] Section 78(2).

[72] Section 78(3).

[73] Section 78(4).

5.12   Date of certain resolutions

In terms of section 79(1), '[w]here a resolution is passed on a poll, it shall for all purposes be considered to have been passed on the day on which the result of the poll is declared. By section 79(2) Subject to subsection (1), where a resolution is passed at an adjourned meeting of a company or the board, it shall be considered to have been passed on the date of the adjourned meeting'.

5.13   Minutes

Matters relating to minutes are provided for under section 80.[74] In terms of section 80(1), '[a] company shall cause minutes to be entered in books kept for that purpose, the proceedings of meeting of—

(a)   the company;
(b)   the board of directors and any committee of the directors; and
(c)   meetings of its debenture holders or other creditors.

According to section 80(2), '[a] minute, referred to in subsection (1), if purporting to be signed by the chairman of the meeting at which the proceedings took place or of a subsequent meeting, shall be *prima facie* evidence of the facts stated in the minute in relation to the proceedings. Further and in terms of section 80(3), '[w]here minutes have been made, in accordance with [section 80] , a meeting shall be presumed to have been duly convened, held and conducted and all appointments of directors, officers, auditors and liquidators shall be presumed to be valid. Failure to comply with section 80(1) means that 'the company and each officer in default commit an offence and shall be liable, on conviction, to a fine not exceeding two thousand five hundred penalty units'.[75] Finally, the books, referred to in section 80(1), shall be kept at what is mistakenly referred to as 'the registered records office'[76] of the company and shall be open for inspection by any member, officer, auditor, receiver or liquidator of the company and the Registrar or a delegate of the Registrar.

5.14   Conclusion

In this chapter we have looked at the types of meetings under the Act which include the Annual General Meeting; Extraordinary General Meeting; and Class Meetings and business transacted at each. We have further discussed the

---

[74] Which replaces section 160 CA 1994.

[75] Section 80(4).

[76] The inclusion of a *'Registered Records office'* which is no longer provided for in the Act is a bit curious and must be considered to be a drafting or typographical error. Section 28 only provides for a 'Registered office and change of registered office'. Section 30 further provides that 'records will be kept at company's registered office'. It is clear that the Act has now dispensed with the useless distinction between 'Registered Office' and 'Registered Records Office' provided for in sections 190 and 191 of the CA 1994.

concept of entitlement to receive notice of meetings *vs* attendance at meetings; the length of notice for convening meeting; place of meeting; conduct of meetings and voting; the importance of the quorum; the role of the chairman. We have additionally discussed proxies and resolutions in the form of special, extraordinary and ordinary resolutions. We have also examined the concept of written resolutions for private companies; the lodgement of resolutions; date of certain resolutions and the requirement to take Minutes.

FURTHER READING

Articles

De Lacey, J, 'The Concept of a Company Director: Time for a New Expanded and Unified Statutory Concept' [2006] JBL 267.

Books

Davies PL *Gower and Davies' Principles of Modern Company Law* 7th edn (Thomson Sweet & Maxwell London 2003).

Gates RB *Gates Company Law and Practice in Zambia* (Reagan Blankfein Gates Lusaka 2017).

Sealy L and Worthington S *Sealy & Worthington's Cases and Materials in Company Law* 10th edn (Oxford University Press Oxford 2013).

Wild C and Weinstein S *Smith and Keenan's Company Law* 15th edn (London Pearson Education Ltd 2011).

6

CORPORATE GOVERNANCE

AIMS AND OBJECTIVES

 After reading this chapter you should appreciate:
- ➤ The company secretary with respect to the following:
  - ▪ Qualifications for a company secretary
  - ▪ Responsibilities of a company secretary; and
  - ▪ the Appointment of a body corporate as company secretary.
- ➤ The appointment of directors
- ➤ Powers and duties of directors
- ➤ Limitations on powers of directors
- ➤ Delegating powers of board and constitution of board committees
- ➤ Number of directors; qualifications of director
- ➤ Disqualification by court from holding office of director
- ➤ Consent before appointment as director or secretary
- ➤ First and subsequent directors
- ➤ Appointment of directors by court
- ➤ Alternate directors
- ➤ Removal of director from office
- ➤ Vacancy in office of director and filling up of casual vacancy
- ➤ Notice of change of directorship and particulars
- ➤ Executive director; acts done in dual capacity as director and secretary
- ➤ Loans to directors by company
- ➤ general responsibilities of directors
- ➤ Fiduciary responsibilities of directors
- ➤ Duty to avoid conflict of interest and meaning of interest
- ➤ Duty not to accept third party benefits
- ➤ Disclosure of interest of director
- ➤ Avoidance of transaction in which director has interest
- ➤ Effect of avoiding transaction on bona fide purchase
- ➤ None disclosure of information
- ➤ Disclosure of interest in shares issued, acquired or disposed of by director

➢ Restrictions on director regarding disposal of shares
➢ Director's liability on share dealing
➢ Exception for companies dealing in securities
➢ Remuneration for directors
➢ Approval of other distributions by special resolution
➢ Liability of director for breach of duty
➢ Validity of decisions by executive officer
➢ Liability and indemnity with regard to decisions made bona fide.

6.1 Introduction

This chapter focuses on 'Part VII: Corporate Governance'. The part has been rechristened and replaces what was 'Part X: Directors and Secretary' under CA 1994. We therefore explore matters relating to the Company secretary; Qualifications for a company secretary; Responsibilities of a company secretary; and the Appointment of a body corporate as company secretary. Thereafter we explore and discuss in some detail provisions relating to the appointment of directors; powers and duties of directors; limitations on powers of directors; delegating powers of board and constitution of board committees; number of directors; qualifications of director; disqualification by court from holding office of director; consent before appointment as director or secretary; first and subsequent directors; appointment of directors by court; alternate directors; removal of director from office; vacancy in office of director and filling up of casual vacancy; notice of change of directorship and particulars; executive director; acts done in dual capacity as director and secretary; loans to directors by company; general responsibilities of directors; fiduciary responsibilities of directors; duty to avoid conflict of interest and meaning of interest; duty not to accept third party benefits; disclosure of interest of director; avoidance of transaction in which director has interest; effect of avoiding transaction on *bona fide* purchase; none disclosure of information; disclosure of interest in shares issued, acquired or disposed of by director; restrictions on director regarding disposal of shares; director's liability on share dealing; exception for companies dealing in securities; remuneration for directors; approval of other distributions by special resolution; liability of director for breach of duty; validity of decisions by executive officer; and finally, liability and indemnity with regard to decisions made *bona fide.*

6.2   Company secretary

6.2.1   *General*

A company incorporated under the Act is mandated to have a company secretary. Section 82(1) provides that a company 'shall' appoint a company secretary. The requirement for a company secretary applies to both small and big companies as well as to public and private companies and is subject to the qualifications discussed below and provided for in section 82(5)(6). In terms of section 82(2), '[a] person who is named as the first company secretary or joint company secretary in the application for incorporation shall, on the incorporation of the company, be deemed to have been appointed as such for a term of one year. Where, in terms of section 82(3) the company secretary is not the first company secretary referred to in section 82(2), he shall be appointed by the board of directors for such a term as the board considers appropriate, unless the articles provide otherwise. This section brings to the fore the fact that5 the company secretary's appointment will be pursuant to the a contract of employment and not in accordance with the provisions of the Act which do not provide for the terms and conditions which will be the preserve of the company's agents to determine as provided for in the company's articles of association. In fact section 82(4) does provide that '[a] company secretary shall be appointed on such remuneration and other conditions as the board of directors considers appropriate and may be removed by the board, subject to the company secretary's right to claim damages from the company if removed in breach of contract'.

6.2.2   *The common law history of the company secretary*

The Act has, as we will further see below, expanded and codified the role of the company secretary. But we can ill afford to recognise the fact that as the following brief discussion demonstrates, the office of company secretary has come a long way.

As early as 1887, Lord Esher M.R. said in *Barnett, Hoares & Co v South London Tramways Co*[1] that 'a secretary is a mere servant; his position is that he is to do what he is told, and no person can assume that he has authority to represent anything at all; nor can anyone assume that statements made by him are necessarily to be accepted as trustworthy without further inquiry, any more than in the case of a merchant it can be assumed that one who is only a clerk has authority to make representations to induce persons to enter into

---

[1] [1887] 18 QBD 815 (CA) at 817.

contracts.[2] In *Barnett,* Lopes LJ considered it most irrational 'to infer from the mere fact that a person was the secretary of a tramway company that he had authority to make representations with regard to the financial situation and relations of the company, although there was no evidence that the making of such representations was within the scope of his duty.'[3]

A rather striking case in how inconsequential the company secretary was considered was the case of *Ruben v Great Fingall Consolidated.*[4] In that case, the appellants advanced in good faith a sum of money to the secretary of the respondent company for his own purposes on the security of a share certificate of the company issued to them by the secretary certifying that the appellants were registered in the company's register of shareholders as transferees of shares. This certificate was, in point of form, in accordance with the company's articles of association, in as much as it bore the seal of the company, and appeared to be signed by two of the directors and counter-signed by the secretary. The seal of the company was however, affixed to it by the secretary fraudulently and without authority, and the signatures of the two directors were forged by him. In an action against the company for damages for refusing to register the appellants as owners of the shares. It was held that, in the absence of any evidence that the company ever held out the secretary as having authority in this behalf to do anything more than the mere ministerial act of delivering share certificates, when duly made, to the owners of shares, the company were not estopped by the forged certificate from disputing the claim of the appellants, or responsible to them for the wrongful action of their secretary.

The foregoing notwithstanding, it was shown in an earlier case[5] that 'the secretary is, [...]the proper official to issue share certificates, and so the company is estopped or barred from denying the truth of genuine share certificates issued by him without the authority of the company.'[6]

Later authorities did nothing to raise the profile of the company secretary. As a consequence, he was understood to have no autonomous power to, through his office bind the company for which he was secretary by way of contract.[7] Additionally, that he could not borrow money for and on behalf of the company. In *Re Cleadon Trust, Ltd,*[8] one of the two directors of a company paid money at the request of the secretary in discharge of debts owed by two subsidiary

---

[2] Approving his earlier judgment in *Newlands v National Employer's Accident Association* 54 LJ (QBD) 428; Lord Macnaghten would, in 1902 approving *Barnett,* describe a secretary's duties in *George Whitechurch Ltd v Cavanagh* [1902] AC 117, at page 124 as being well known, specifically that, 'they are of a limited and of a somewhat humble nature'.

[3] Supra note 255 at p.818;

[4] [1906] A.C. 439.

[5] *Clavering, Son & Co v Goodwins, Jardine& Co Ltd* [1891] 18 R.

[6] Charlesworth's Company Law 13th edn 418.

[7] *Williams v The Chester and Holyhead Rly Co* [1851] 15 Jur 828; *Houghton & Co v Nothard, Lowe & Wills Ltd* [1928] AC 1.

[8] [1939] Ch 286.

companies and guaranteed by the company, in expectation that the company which benefited thereby would repay him. The secretary and the directors were also the secretary and directors of the subsidiary companies. At a meeting of the directors a resolution was passed purporting to confirm some of the advances, and they were treated in the books of the company as advances to the company. The quorum for such meetings was two, but by the company's articles of association no director could vote in respect of any contract or agreement in which he was interested. The company and the subsidiary companies subsequently went into voluntary liquidation. The assets of the subsidiary companies were insufficient to discharge the amounts owing on their debentures. It was held that the resolution had not been validly passed by an independent board and that on the facts there was neither knowledge nor acquiescence on the part of the company rendering it liable at common law under an implied contract to repay the director. The Court in this case came to the conclusion that the secretary had no power to borrow, as he had done, on behalf of the company.

It was held in *Daimler Co Ltd v Continental Tyre Co Ltd*[9] that a company secretary has no authority to institute an action on behalf of the company. Lord Parker of Waddington in finding that the articles of association did not contemplate or provide for the continuance of the company's trading without directors and the secretary not having convened a general meeting where he could have appointed himself director as he was not the King's enemy, also mentioned that the secretary of a company was not 'an official who *virtute officii*[10] can manage all its affairs, with or without the help of servants, in the absence of a regular directorate.'[11]

Further limitations were attached to the position of company secretary including the assertion that he could not, without the authority of directors, register a transfer[12] nor strike a name off the members' register[13] nor summon an annual general meeting.[14]

While as we have mentioned and we will soon see from an exploration of additional provisions in the Act relating to the company secretary, his stature has improved to a considerable if not indispensable statutory degree, the tide turned some 46 years earlier in the watershed judgment in *Panorama Development (Guildford) Ltd v Fidelis Furnishing Fabrics Ltd.*[15] The brief facts were that the company secretary of the defendant company rented a number of cars from the plaintiff by deceitfully claiming that same were needed for purposes of picking up customers from the airport. He signed the forms relating to the transaction:

[9] [1916] 2 AC 307.
[10] Latin phrase meaning "by virtue of his office."
[11] *Mohoney v East Holyford Mining Co* [1875] LR 7 HL 869.
[12] *Chida Mines Ltd v Anderson* [1905] 22 TLR 27.
[13] *Re Indo-China Steam Navigation Co* [1917] 2 Ch. 100.
[14] *Re State Wyoming Syndicate* [1901] 2 Ch 431.
[15] [1971] 2 QB 711 (CA); [1971] 3All ER 16; See further, *B. Liggett (Liverpool) Ltd v Barclays Bank* [1982] 1 KB 48.

'company secretary'. He used the rented cars for his own purposes. When called upon to pay, the defendant denied liability on grounds that the company secretary lacked authority. Lord Denning rejecting the 1887 position in *Barnett, Hoares & Co v South London Tramway Co*[16] of the secretary being 'a secretary is a mere servant; his position is that he is to do what he is told, and no person can assume that he has authority to represent anything at all[...]' judged that times had changed. As such, the great judge opined,

> A company secretary is a much more important person nowadays than he was in 1887. He is an officer of the company with extensive duties and responsibilities. This appears not only in the modern Companies Acts, but also by the role which he plays in the day-to-day business of companies. He is no longer a mere clerk. He regularly makes representations on behalf of the company and enters into contracts on its behalf which come within the day-to-day running of the company's business. So much so that he may be regarded as held out as having authority to do such things on behalf of the company. He is certainly entitled to sign contracts connected with the administrative side of a company's affairs, such as employing staff, and ordering cars, and so forth. All such matters now come within the ostensible authority of a company's secretary.

6.2.3 Responsibilities of a company secretary

Section 83 is a huge departure from section 205 CA 1994 which left the responsibilities to common law. It therefore codifies what was recognised in *Panorama* and what over the years has become the reality surrounding this important interlocutor in the company. The company secretary is responsible for the following:

(a) providing the directors, collectively and individually, with guidance as to their duties, responsibilities and powers;

(b) informing the board of directors on—
(i) legislation relevant to or affecting the meetings of members and the board;
(ii) the reports relating to the operations of the company; and
(iii) submission of documents to relevant authorities, as required by statute, as well as the implications of failure to comply with such requirement;

(c) ensuring that minutes of the members' meetings and of the meetings of the board of directors are properly recorded and registers are properly maintained;

---

[16] [1887] 18 QBD 815.

(d)   ensuring that the company maintains and updates information on the beneficial ownership of all the shares of the company and their associated voting rights;

(e)   ensuring that the company is in compliance with this Act in relation to lodging of documents with the Registrar; and

(f)   bringing to the attention of the board of directors any failure on the part of the company or a director to comply with the articles or this Act.

As exemplified in *Re Morvah Controls Tin Mining Company McKay's case*[17] and section 83, the company secretary owes fiduciary duties similar to those of a director. As such, he ought to ensure that the company acts in accordance with the Act, articles and relevant legislation.

6.2.4 *Qualifications for a company secretary*

The provisions in the Act relating to qualifications for a company secretary are a patent departure from CA 1994 which did not explicitly provide for qualifications. In terms of section 82(5), a person will only be eligible for appointment, as company secretary if the person, in the case of—

(a)   an individual, is—

(i)   a legal practitioner, a chartered accountant or a member of the chartered institute of secretaries; and

(ii)   resident in Zambia; or

(b)   a body corporate[18]

(i)   is incorporated in Zambia; and

(ii)   has an officer who qualifies to be appointed as company secretary.

However, by section 82(6), '[t]he qualifications for a company secretary set out in section 82(5) shall not apply to a small private company'. The reasons for this exception as regards small companies are obvious and rational in view of the reality of the state of small companies in Zambia. In addition to a non-existent corporate culture, there are no rules of procedure. Their lack of access to capital and the fact that most will fail within a few years makes it impossible to meet the stringent requirements for the appointment of a company secretary set out in section 82(5).

The foregoing notwithstanding, a person who occupies this important position will need to possess strong leadership, negotiation and motivational skills. He will no doubt need to have strong analytical, modelling, oral and written communication skills and all the experience upon which the foregoing skills will be predicated.

According to section 82(7), '[t]he [c]ourt may, on application by a company, a creditor of the company or the Registrar, disqualify a person from being

[17] [1875] 2 Ch D 1.
[18] Section 84 provides that '[a] body corporate may be appointed to hold the office of company secretary'.

appointed as secretary of a company, for a period not exceeding five years on conviction for an offence or breach of any of the duties of a secretary as specified in the Act.[19] Where the application for disqualification is granted, the board of directors is obliged to, 'within sixty days after a vacancy arises in the office of company secretary, fill the vacancy by appointing a person qualified to be so appointed in accordance with this Act'. In the event that 'a company carries on business for more than sixty days without a company secretary or in contravention of [section 82(8)], each officer of the company commits an offence and is liable, on conviction, to a fine not exceeding three thousand penalty units.

6.3   Directors

6.3.1   General

The very juristic, metaphysical and artificial nature of a company even though it is said to have only subject to the 'Act and to such limitations as are inherent in its corporate nature, the capacity, rights, powers and privileges of an individual' and 'the capacity to carry on business and exercise its powers in any jurisdiction outside Zambia, to the extent that the laws of Zambia and of that jurisdiction permit' entails that the full remit of the capacity and power granted to it by law cannot turn it into a self-operating organism to have such capacity or enjoy such power or indeed carry out business within and without Zambia devoid of human agents charged with its management and control of its affairs pursuant to the Act and articles of association.

In terms of section 3, "director" means a person appointed as a member of the board of directors and includes an *alternate director*, by whatever name designated. In *Brown-Wilkinson v Cin Re Lo-Line Electric Motors Ltd*[20] it was observed that the words "whatever name [designated]" (whether or not he is called a director in the Act) show that the subsection is dealing with nomenclature; for example where the company's articles provide that the conduct of the company is committed to "governors" or "managers".

It is perchance important to point out that though our exploration of Part VII of the Act adopts the term 'director', for that is the term the Act uses, other terms have been and continue to be used in literature, case law and statutes to denote a person occupying the office of director. They include 'managers', 'governors', 'counsellors' and 'management committee/board' among others.[21] It therefore follows that 'a director is anyone occupying the role of director

---

[19] Mainly those set out Section 83.

[20] [1988] 2 All ER 692 at 699.

[21] See *Brown-Wilkinson v Cin Re Lo-Line Electric Motors Ltd* [1988] 2 All ER 692 at 699 where it was said that the title/nomenclature is not the determining factor as to who is and who is not a director.

by whatever name called'[22] and regardless of his title. Two cases illustrate the foregoing with different conclusions but based on the same principle.

In *Re Sykes (Butchers) Ltd*[23] a person who denied being a director and whose appointment the company knew nothing of as it had not been formerly notified, was held to be liable to disqualification as a *de facto* director on account of various defaults which included among others, preference in which he paid a bank overdraft off using the company's money and to the disadvantage of other creditors where he had guaranteed said overdraft; and led the company, thanks to his trading practices down the road of virtual insolvency.[24]

Conversely, in *Secretary of State for Trade and Industry v Tjolle*[25] *where* a woman called herself a director, it was held that for purposes of ineligibility as she had no participation with anything financial and did not form part of the company's real governance.

6.3.2 Appointment of directors[26]

6.3.2.1 General

A company is under obligation to, unless the articles provide otherwise, appoint a person as a director by ordinary resolution[27] passed at a general meeting of the company.[28] Therefore, two pre-requisites must be met in order for the appointment of the director to be valid:

(i)   it must be by ordinary resolution; and

(ii)   the said ordinary resolution must be passed at a general meeting of the company.

Only provisions in the company's articles to the contrary can override the foregoing. That in and of itself is not enough. Attention must be paid to section 94 which proscribes the appointment of a person as director or secretary without that person's consent to be appointed being given in prescribed form. A further requirement is a declaration predicated on section 92 relating to the qualifications pertaining to directors, that such a person is not disqualified from holding the office of director in terms of sections 92 and/or 93.

We must also allude to two other ways in which people are appointed as directors provided for under sections 95 and 96.

---

[22] Keenan D *Smith and Keenan's Company Law* 13th ed 307.

[23] [1998] 1 BCLC 110.

[24] We must add that in coming to its decision, the court did not lay down a test to determine whether the person in question was a de facto director saying instead that all material factors relating to a person's involvement in management needed to be considered.

[25] [1998] 1 BCLC 333.

[26] Section 85 under which this now falls replaces section 203 of CA 2017; For a more detailed discussion see generally, Gates RB *Gates Company Law and Practice in Zambia* under chapter 11 200-247.

[27] See section 3 for definition.

[28] Section 85(1).

6.3.2.1.1 First and subsequent directors

In terms of section 95(1), '[a] person named in an application for incorporation or in an amalgamation proposal as a director shall, on the date of incorporation or of the amalgamation, as the case may be, be a director from that date until that person ceases to hold office as a director in accordance with this Act'. Section 95(2) makes reference to '[a]ll subsequent directors' being 'appointed at a general meeting of the company in accordance with section 85' discussed above.

6.3.2.1.2 Appointment of directors by Court

'A shareholder or creditor of a company may apply to the Court to appoint a director and the Court may, on such terms and conditions as the Court considers just in the circumstances, make the appointment where—
- (a) there are no directors of a company, or the number of directors is less than the—
    - (i) statutory minimum number; or
    - (ii) quorum required for a meeting of the board of directors; and
- (b) it is not possible or practicable to appoint directors in accordance with the articles'.[29]

6.3.2.2 Composition and power of board to fill casual vacancies

There is a stipulation as to the composition of the board of directors[30] in terms of section 85(2) which is that '[t]he board of directors shall comprise, in the case of a—
- (a) private company, not less than two directors; or
- (b) public company, not less than three directors'.[31] The board of directors is empowered to, 'where there are less directors than the minimum number prescribed in this section, subject to ratification at the next general meeting of the company, appoint a person to be a director'.[32]

6.3.2.3 De facto director

A *de facto* director is one who is 'such in effect though not formally recognised'.[33] That the concept of *de facto* director has received statutory recognition is evidenced by section 85(5) which provides that '[a] person who, not being a

---

[29] Section 96.
[30] Other names include but are not limited to board of advisors; board of governors; board of trustees; board of visitors; executive board (in relation to the supervisory board in a two tier system common in mainland Europe and Asia); board of regents.
[31] Section 85(4) permits a company to appoint a higher number of directors than the minimum specified in section 85(2) if its articles allows this.
[32] Section 85(3).
[33] Latin term when translated.

duly appointed director, holds oneself out, or knowingly allows another to hold that person out, as a director—

    (a)   shall be considered to be a director for the purposes of all duties and liabilities, including liabilities for criminal penalties imposed on directors by this Act; and

    (b)   commits an offence and is liable, on conviction, to a fine not exceeding one hundred thousand penalty units'.

As section 85(5)(b) demonstrates, the recognition that there will be instances where a *de facto* director exists does not mean its condonation. This is why from a plain reading of section 85(5), the title of *de facto* director will only be ascribed to a person for purposes of duties and liabilities which include criminal liability and secondly, as has been observed the question whether someone is a *de facto* director is likely to arise where a penalty or liability is imposed on a director, such as disqualification[34] or liability for wrongful trading,[35] or misfeasance[36] and the individual attempts to evade the penalty or liability by relying on the fact that he is not a *de jure* director.[37]

Historically under the common law, the term '*de facto* director' was used to refer to a director who was appointed but whose appointment was in some way defective or a director who had been properly appointed but who carried on acting as a director after the appointment was terminated.[38] Lord Collins seems to have given a settled definition of the term *de facto* director in the case of *Commissioners of HM Revenue and Customs v. Holland*[39] which definition was for the purpose of deciding whether a person is subject to the fiduciary duties of a director and for that purpose it must be shown that the person was part of the corporate governing structure and assumed a role in the company sufficient to impose fiduciary duties.

Further, section 85(5)(a) provides that it relates not only to a person who 'holds oneself out', but also one who 'knowingly allows another to hold that person out' as director. As Lord Collins citing *Secretary of State for Trade and Industry v. Tjolle*[40] in *Re Paycheck Services 3 Ltd, Revenue and Customs Commissioners v. Holland*,[41] opines, in determining whether someone is a *de facto* director or not, the court will consider *inter alia* whether there is a holding out by the company of the individual as a director and whether he used the title and whether taking all the circumstances into account the individual is part of the corporate governing structure of the company.

---

[34] *Re Lo – Line Electric Motors Ltd* [1988] Ch 477.

[35] *Re Hydrodam (Corby) Ltd* [1944] 2 BCLC 666.

[36] *Re Paycheck Services 3 Ltd, Revenue and Customs Commissioners v Holland* [2011] 1 BCLC 141.

[37] See also: *Secretary of State for Trade and Industry v Laing* [1996] 2 BCLC 324.

[38] *Secretary of State for Trade and Industry v Laing* [1996] 2 BCLC 324.

[39] [2010] WLR 2793 at 58 – 93.

[40] [1998] 1 BCLC 333.

[41] [2010] UKSC 51.

6.3.2.4   *Types of directors*

As exemplified in *Buchan v Secretary of State for Employment*,[42] the board of directors may be composed of different types or classes of directors. Unlike CA 1994, which provided or recognised three types namely *de jure, de facto* and shadow, the Act only provides for the first two. We will however discuss all three.

6.3.2.4.1   *De jure[43] director*

What is clearly missing from the new section 85 is any explicit reference to a *de jure* director but this is not necessary as this is the kind that section 85(1) provides for. It follows that a person is deemed as a *de jure* director of a company if the following have happened:[44]

 (1)   The person has been appointed to the office of director in accordance with the rules governing such appointment;
 (2)   The person has agreed to hold office;
 (3)   The person is not disqualified from being director of the company; and
 (4)   The person has not vacated office.

Therefore, a *de jure* director is a person who has lawfully and validly been appointed as such.

6.3.2.4.2   *Shadow director*

The Act has, in breaking with CA 1994 which provided for a shadow director under section 203(4)(7), neither defined nor provided for a shadow director. That notwithstanding, it is worth mentioning that a shadow director is one who though not duly appointed as director of a company, on whose directions or instructions the duly appointed directors are accustomed to act shall be deemed to be a director for the purposes of all duties and liabilities (including criminal penalties) imposed on directors by the Act. It would appear from the foregoing that professional advisors including advocates and accounts do not come within the purview of the Act. However, it has been suggested in the case of *Secretary of State for Trade and Industry v Deverell*[45] that those who give advice other than that which is purely professional may be held liable.[46]

It has been observed that determining whether a person is a shadow director is a matter not of law but fact to be determined on the circumstances and facts

---

[42] [1997] 565 IRLB 2.

[43] Latin maxim meaning 'based on or according to law'.

[44] Mayson S French D Ryan C Mayson *French and Ryan on Company Law* 31st edn (Oxford University Press Oxford 2014-15).

[45] [2000] 2 BCLC 133; under common law, the definition of a shadow director is similar to that in section 203(4) and (7) of CA 1994.

[46] See Morrit LJ's 4 propositions in *Deverell*.

of each case. There has been uncertainty expressed over what duties a shadow director owes. For example, while in *Ultraframe (UK) Ltd v Fielding*[47] the court expressed the view that shadow directors do not ordinarily owe duties to the company, in *Vivendi SA v Richards*[48] the court came to the conclusion that they did. Facts in the latter case were that nine payments to the tune of £10 Million were made to the plaintiff. The plaintiff was subsequently wound-up. It was alleged that B, a *de jure* director had made the said payments in breach of duty while acting under instructions of the defendant. It was held *inter alia* that there was a breach not only by B as *de jure* director but also by Richard in his capacity as shadow director. As the court saw it, Richard had dishonestly assisted B in his breach of duty thus making him liable. Be that as it may, the following may be indicative of one being a shadow director:

    (a)   being a signatory to the company's bank account and/or attendance at interviews with bank officials;

    (b)   the ordering by the person concerned of goods and/or services for the company;

    (c)   the signing of contracts and/ or letters in the capacity of director;

    (d)   attendance at meetings of the board;

    (e)   possession of detailed information about the company[49]

It must be pointed out that as shown in *Secretary of State for Trade and Industry v Laing*[50] persuading the High Court (should one be minded to bring a matter of this sort before it) that one has acted as shadow director is a lofty endeavour that few have managed to pull off. 'It is necessary to present to the court specific evidence of the alleged 'directions' given by the person concerned, plus evidence that they were acted upon by the company to satisfy the test for a shadow director.'[51]

In terms of section 85(6), '[a] company shall not, knowing that a person is not a duly appointed director—

    (a)   hold that person out; or

    (b)   allow that person to hold out as a director'.

By section 85(7), '[a] limitation on the authority of a director, whether imposed by the articles or otherwise, shall not be effective against a person who has no knowledge of the limitation, unless, taking into account that person's relationship with the company the person ought to have had knowledge of the limitation'. Finally, and in terms of section 85(8), '[…] the directors shall act collectively as a board'.

---

[47] [2005] EWHC 1638 (Ch).

[48] [2013] EWHC 3006; [2013] BCC 771.

[49] Keenan D *Smith and Keenan's company* 13th edn 354.

[50] [1996] 2 BCLC 324.

[51] [1986] AC 207 (HL).

6.3.3 *Powers and duties of directors*

6.3.3.1 *General*

The powers and duties of directors are wide ranging. By 'powers' is meant the extent and breadth of authority to act that directors in a company enjoy and are expected to exercise primarily in the best interest of the company. By duties is meant the obligations that accrue to a director by virtue of his office in relation to the company, to employees, to shareholders in their individual capacity and third parties which may but usually include those with whom the company may contract for goods and services, creditors and debenture holders as provided for in the Act or/and articles of association. One convenient way to classify powers and duties of directors is to pigeonhole them into statutory duties which arise by way of statutory provisions;[52] '...fiduciary (or equitable) duties which arise because [the directors] are quasi-trustees of the assets of the company (and may, as is the case with the Act, also be statutorily provided for), and duties of skill and care which arise at common law'[53]

6.3.3.2 *Statutory duties*

The relevant provision regarding powers and duties of directors in the Act is section 86.[54] In terms of section 86(1) '...the business of a company shall be managed by, or under the direction or supervision of, a board of directors...' This includes—

(a) pay all expenses incurred in promoting and forming the company; and
(b) exercise all such powers of the company as are not, by this Act or the articles, required to be exercised by the members'.[55]

The powers and duties that follow may be exercised by the board of directors[56] where the articles have no provisions to the contrary:

(a) borrow money;
(b) charge any property or business of the company, including any of its uncalled capital; and
(c) issue debentures or give any other security for a debt, liability or obligation of the company or of any other person'.

Additionally and in terms of section 86(3), '[t]he board of directors may, by power of attorney, appoint a person to be the attorney of the company for

---

[52] See section 86.
[53] Keenan D *Smith and Keenan's Company Law* 13th edn 354; The duty of skill and care is an aspect of the tort of negligence.
[54] Formerly section 215 under CA 1994.
[55] See *Automatic Self-Cleansing Filter Syndicate Co Ltd v Cuninghame* [1906] 2 Ch 304 where it was held that the general meeting has no power to interfere with the management of the company by the directors by simply passing an ordinary resolution.
[56] Without limiting the generality of [section 86](1).

such purposes, with the powers, authorities and discretions that are vested in or exercisable by the board of directors, for such periods and subject to such conditions as the board of directors considers appropriate'. According to section 86(4), '[a] power of attorney, made in accordance with [section 86(3)], may contain provisions for the protection and convenience of persons dealing with the attorney, as the board considers necessary, including an authorisation to the attorney to delegate all or any of the powers, authorities and discretions vested in that attorney'.

By section 86(5), '[a]ll cheques, promissory notes, bankers drafts, bills of exchange and other negotiable instruments, including receipts for money paid to the company, shall be signed, drawn, accepted, endorsed or otherwise executed by two directors or as the board may determine'.

It is clear from the foregoing that the powers and duties of directors are quite extensive. However, there are statutory limitations provided for in section 87 relating to how the said powers may be exercised. We turn to this discussion next.

6.3.3.2.1   Limitations on powers of directors

In terms of section 87(1), '[t]he board of directors shall not, without the approval of the members, by ordinary resolution—

   (a)   sell, lease or otherwise dispose of the whole, or substantially the whole, of the undertaking or assets of the company;
   (b)   issue any new or unissued shares in the company;
   (c)   create or grant any rights or options entitling the holders to acquire shares of any class in the company; or
   (d)   enter into a transaction that has or is likely to have the effect of the company acquiring rights or interests or incurring obligations or liabilities, including contingent liabilities, the value of which is the value of the company's assets before the transaction.

Section 87(2) qualifies section 87(1) by providing that '[t]he approval of a transaction relating to the 'sell, lease or otherwise dispose of the whole, or substantially the whole, of the undertaking or assets of the company'…shall be an approval of the specific transaction proposed by the board to the members. The directors are, at least as far as the specified transactions are concerned, to seek shareholders' approval on a transaction by transaction basis. Whether this improves corporate governance or stands in its way is subject to anecdotal postulations. What is clear though is an attempt by the draftsperson to balance the powers and duties of directors and how they are exercised or carried out respectively with the ultimate authority that shareholders have in all matters reserved to them by the Act or the articles of association.

In terms of section 87(3), '[n]othing in [the] section prohibits the issue—

(a)   of shares under a good faith underwriting agreement; or

(b)   to a director of such shares, if any, as the articles require the director to hold by way of share qualification.

By section 87(4), '[t]he validity of any transfer or disposition of property to a person dealing with the company, in good faith, shall not be affected by a failure to comply with this section. Finally, according to section 87(5), the provisions of section 87 'shall not limit the powers exercisable by an insolvency practitioner appointed in accordance with the Corporate Insolvency Act.'[57]

6.3.3   Fiduciary duties

6.3.3.1   General

In *Re City Equitable Fire Insurance Co*,[58] Romer J expressed the view that the use of the term 'trustees' with respect to directors and their duties should only be limited to 'no more than directors in the performance of their duties' standing in a fiduciary relationship with the company. It logically follows that when we speak of directorial duties we, in the strictest sense, are referring to the duties directors owe to the company for which they act as quasi trustees.

We cannot emphasise enough the holding in *Interland* of the indispensability of directors and the negative consequences that may follow if they fail to carry out their duties properly as exemplified in *Nkongolo Farm Ltd v Zambia National Commercial Bank Limited, Kent Choice Ltd (In Receiver Ship), Charles Haruperi.*[59] In that case, the plaintiff's director signed a director's guarantee, believing the said document to be related to maize transactions in which the parties were dealing. The plaintiff's director released the certificate of title for Farm No. 3342 Chisamba to the 3rd defendant, believing that the 3rd defendant wanted to obtain a bank loan to pay for the purchase of the same farm and not as security for the 3rd defendant's bank loan in form of a third party mortgage. It was held *inter alia* that the plaintiff was negligent and the admission that the directors did not read the documents that tied the plaintiff's company property to a debt for K750 million was an oversight or mistake which can only react against the plaintiff.

We further cannot emphasise enough that because he holds a position of trust, the common law duties of care, good faith and loyalty are inextricably linked to the position of director. It has been held in *Multinational Gas and Petroleum Co v Multinational Gas and Petrochemical Services ltd*[60] that directors are

---

[57] Act No 9 of 2017.

[58] [1925] Ch 407.

[59] [2005] ZR 78 (SC).

[60] [1983] 2 All ER 563.

agents of the company and as such they owe their general duties to the company and not the shareholders individually or collectively. 'As such, directors are required to act in the best interest of the company as opposed to the members who appointed them'.[61]

For the foregoing reasons, section 105[62] provides regarding the general responsibilities of directors that a director shall—

(a)   take necessary measures to prevent, reduce and manage any attendant risks to the business of the company;

(b)   not cause, allow or agree for the business of the company to be conducted in a manner that is likely to create a substantial risk of serious loss to a member or creditor of the company; and

(c)   when exercising powers or performing duties of a director—

    (i)   act in good faith and in the best interests of the company; and

    (ii)   exercise the degree of care, diligence and skill that may reasonably be expected of a person carrying out the functions of a director.

From the foregoing, we must proceed on the basis of the new reality which is that the Act, unlike CA 1994, has in ways not done before, codified fiduciary duties of directors. Specifically, section 106 which builds on section 105 provides that '[a] director shall—

(a)   exercise that director's power—

    (i)   in accordance with this Act and act within the articles; and

    (ii)   for the purpose for which the power is conferred;

(b)   promote the success of the company;

(c)   exercise independent judgment; and

(d)   disclose information about that director's remuneration in the financial statements of the company.

We explain the foregoing in turn bearing in mind that unlike section 170(4) of the UK CA which provides that the general duties enumerated therein, similar to the duties in the Act, shall be interpreted and applied in the same way as common law rules or equitable principles', and that 'regard shall be had to the corresponding common law rules and equitable principles in interpreting and applying the general duties', no equivalent provision can be found in either section 105 or 106 of the Act. It is quite possible to reason that any duties excluded and not specifically mentioned cannot be said to accrue to directors. This would however be untenable not only in view of Article 118(2)(e) of the Zambian Constitution[63] which enjoins the courts to administer justice without undue regard to procedural technicalities but also the provisions of section 10

---

[61] Gates RB *Gates Company Law*...212.

[62] Compare this with section 170 in the UK CA which provides for general responsibilities of directors.

[63] As amended by Act No 5 of 2016.

of the High Court Act but also the fact that courts in Zambia have jurisdiction to administer common law and equity concurrently. It would appear that section 106 notwithstanding, the cases decided before the Act will continue to be relevant.

6.3.3.2 Duty to exercise director's power in accordance with the Act and articles

Directors are mandated to exercise their power in accordance with the Act and the company's articles. For example, if the Act or articles have, as already discussed, restricted their powers or the proposed nature of business to be done by the company is restricted this must be respected. It also includes using the said powers for the purpose for which the power is conferred and nothing else.[64] It has been shown in *Extrasure Travel Insurances Ltd v Scattergood*[65] that a director owes a fiduciary duty to the company to exercise his powers firstly, in what he honestly believes to be the company's best interests, and secondly, for the purpose for which, as provided in section 105(a)(ii), those powers have been conferred on him. The case further established that in a claim that the director in question did not exercise his powers for the proper purpose, it became unnecessary to show that the director was dishonest or that he was pursuing a secondary purpose. In circumstances where the foregoing was the case, the job of the court must apply a four stage objective test:

  (a) Identify the power whose exercise is in question;
  (b) Identify the proper purpose for which that power was delegated to the directors;
  (c) Identify the special purpose for which the power was in fact exercised; and
  (d) Decide whether that purpose was proper.

There has been a recent clarification on establishing a breach of duty against a director in the case of *Grand Field Group Holdings Ltd v Chu King Fai and Others*[66] which cited *Extrasure* with approval. In *Grand Fields* a shareholder commenced a statutory derivative claim of the plaintiff claim in its name against eight erstwhile directors for breaches of fiduciary duties under section 168BC of the Hong Kong Companies Ordinance.[67] It was claimed by the plaintiff that the said directors had caused the plaintiff's subsidiary to be conceived and incorporated in Shenzhen, Mainland China and then caused HK$50 million to be transferred to it, which, said the shareholder, was used by the first and second defendants as a vehicle for providing rolling facilities to companies related to or

---

[64] Section 105(a) (ii).
[65] [2003] 1 BCLC 598; Followed in the Hong Kong case of *Grand Field Group Holdings Ltd v Chu King Fai and Others* HCA771/2009.
[66] HCA771/2009.
[67] Chapter 32 of the Laws of Hong Kong.

controlled by them. Further, it was claimed that the first defendant had sought to improperly gain influence over other members of the board by bribing them to vote in accordance with his wishes and that of his family. It was held, in rejecting the plaintiff's claim that when determining a claim of bribery, the burden of proof was on the plaintiff to prove allegations of corruption and that where very serious allegations were levelled against the defendant, very cogent evidence must logically be provided.[68]

In relation to the claim for breach of duty the court citing *Extrasure* clarified that mere incompetence is not sufficient to establish a breach of fiduciary duty, but it could nonetheless, give rise to a claim for breach of the duty of care. Further, that, '[f]iduciary duties are concerned with concepts of honesty and loyalty, not with competence. Accordingly, a director is not in breach of his fiduciary duty if he honestly, but unreasonably and mistakenly, believes he is pursuing the company's best interests'.

It follows, the foregoing notwithstanding, that any improper use of directorial powers to for example, issue shares to avoid a takeover as demonstrated in *Hogg v Cramphorn, Ltd and Others*[69] or as in *Howard Smith Ltd v Ampol Petroleum Ltd,*[70] to alter the weight of votes by shareholders in order to influence the outcome of a takeover bid will be deemed invalid and of no consequence. Having said that, it has been held in *Hogg* that acts in breach of the proper purpose tenet can nonetheless be ratified by a majority of members in a general meeting.

Finally, according to section 104(1), '[a] director shall not act, or agree to the company acting, in a manner that contravenes this Act or the articles'. In fact, '[a] director who contravenes [section 104](1) commits an offence and is liable, on conviction, to a fine not exceeding one hundred thousand penalty units or imprisonment for a period not exceeding twelve months, or' more seriously, 'to disqualification from being eligible for appointment as a director, as specified in section 85'.[71]

6.3.3.3   Duty to promote the success of the company

The duty to promote the success of the company has as its basis the equitable doctrine for directors to act *bona fide*. This must be with respect to what they, holistically consider to be in the best interests of the company. In *Re Smith &*

---

[68] Following *Re H & Others (Minors) (Sexual Abuse: Standard of Proof)* [1996] AC 563; and *Mohammad Jafara-Fini v Skillglass Ltd & Others* [2007] EWCA Civ 261.

[69] [1966] 3 All ER 420; *Criterion Properties Plc v Stratford UK Properties LLC* [2002] 2 BCLC 151; *Howard Smith Ltd v Ampol Petroleum Ltd* [1974] AC 821.

[70] [1974] AC 821.

[71] Section 104

Fawcett, Ltd[72] the articles of association of a private company provided that 'the directors may at any time in their absolute and uncontrolled discretion refuse to register any transfer of shares'. The appellant, as executor of his father, claimed to be registered in respect of 4,001 shares. The directors refused to register a transfer unless he was willing to sell 2,000 of the shares to a named director at a certain price, in which case they would register a transfer of the remainder. It was held, having regard to the terms of the articles, the only limitation on the directors' discretion was that it should be exercised *bona fide* in the interests of the company. There was no ground for saying that the directors' refusal to register the transfer was not due to a *bona fide* consideration of the interests of the company as seen by them.

That the test is subjective[73] has received judicial recognition. Parker J has observed in *Regentcrest Plc v Cohen*[74] for example, that 'the question is not whether, viewed objectively by the court, the particular act or omission which is challenged was in fact in the interest of the company; still less is the question whether the court, had it been in the position of the director at the relevant time, might have acted differently. Rather, the question is whether the director honestly believed that his act or omission was in the interest of the company. The issue is as to the director's state of mind'. In *Re Smith and Fawcett Ltd*[75] Lord Green MR noted that directors must act '*bona fide* in what they consider - not what a court may consider - is in the interests of the company, and not for any collateral purpose'. Further, in *Percival v Wright*[76] it was held that the directors are not trustees for the individual shareholders and may purchase their shares without disclosing pending negotiations for the sale of the company. However, from the facts and circumstances of the case, the evidence leads the court to conclude that the directors have failed to promote the success of the company as they are statutorily expected and required to do *Allen v Hyatt*[77] where the Privy Council held that the directors had made themselves agents for the shareholders and must consequently account for the profit which they had obtained.

It has been held in *Mills v Mills*[78] that a director cannot arbitrarily choose the views of one group of shareholders over another. Further, a director who is nominated by a holding company to sit on the board of a subsidiary as in *Hawkes v Cuddy*[79] cannot choose to bind himself to follow the wishes of the

---

[72] *Re Smith & Fawcett Ltd* [1942] 1 All ER 542.

[73] See however, *HLC Environment Projects Ltd* [2013] EWHC where it was shown that though the test is generally subjective, objective may sometimes be necessary in order for the Court to come to a just conclusion.

[74] [2001] 1 BCLC 80 at 105.

[75] See note 462 above.

[76] [1902] 2 Ch 421.

[77] [1914] 30 TLR 444.

[78] [1938] 60 CLR 150 H. Ct. Aust.

[79] [2009] 2 BCLC 427; EWCA Civ 291; *Re Neath Rugby Club Ltd* [2008] All ER (D) 42 (Apr).

nominating company. His primary consideration should be to work in the best interest of the company. It would appear as a result, that the concept of best interests of the company is seen in terms of what is not acceptable conduct rather than what is acceptable conduct by a director as regards his position relative to the company.[80]

A recent decision[81] in *Ball (liquidator of PV Solar Solutions Ltd) and another v Hughes and Another*[82] has applied the duty to act in the best interests of the company to directorial duties when a company is insolvent or of dubious solvency. Prior to its liquidation the company had two successful years trading in the supply and installation of solar panels, having benefitted from a government incentive in place at the time. The liquidator claimed that the directors caused the company to make three unjustified credit entries against their directors' loan accounts in breach of their duties in breach, it was claimed, of section 172(3) of the UK CA 2006 to act in the interest of the creditors of the company.

According to the court, the duty to act in the best interest of the company is to be regarded as a duty to act in the best interest of the creditors at the point when a company is "insolvent or of dubious solvency". The key take away it would appear is that 'directors are not free to take action which puts the creditors' prospects of being paid at real, as opposed to remote, risk, without first having considered their interests'.

6.3.3.4   Duty to exercise independent judgment[83]

Broadly speaking, this may well be said to fall within the ambit of the duty to act *bona fide* and in the best interests of the company. This duty encompasses not just third parties or shareholders but other directors on the board. A director is appointed in his personal capacity and as a fiduciary should be able to act with independence of thought to justify his continued stay on the board. The reason this is provided as a separate and distinct duty under section 106 is that once appointed, directors cannot enter into agreements that fetter their discretion to act independently and in the best interests of the company. The collapse of WorldCom in 2002, Enron in 2004, Lehman Brothers and Bear Stearns in 2008 among others, showed how in most instances, powerful directors on a board can influence less influential and more malleable directors to the company's detriment and ultimately, that of shareholders. This is however not new. The matter had arisen as early as 1925 in the case of *Re City Equitable Fire*

---

[80] *Item Software (UK) Ltd Fassihi* [2004] EWCA Civ 1244; [2005] ICR 450, CA.

[81] See summary in 'Directors must repay sums withdrawn from company in liquidation, rules High Court' retrieved from http://www.out-law.com on 17/01/2017.

[82] [2017] EWHC 3228 (Ch); approving *Guinness v Saunders* [1990] 2 AC 663(HL).

[83] Formerly under section 212(1) CA 1994 which provided as follows: '[a] person shall not give directions or instructions to the duly appointed directors of a company if the person is not eligible to be a director of the company'.

Insurance Co Ltd.[84] In the winding up by the Court of the above mentioned company, an investigation of its affairs disclosed a shortage in the funds, of which the company should have been possessed, of over £1,200,000, due in part to depreciation of investments, but mainly to the instrumentality of the managing director and largely to his deliberate fraud, for which he had been convicted and sentenced.

However, as has been shown in *Fulham Football Club v Cabra Estates Plc,*[85] it may not ordinarily be deemed to be a failure to act independently if a director were to enter into an agreement that later fetters his discretion if in his judgment, entry into such an agreement is in the best interest of the company. In this case then, and given that acting independently appears subject to the duty to act in the best interest of the company, the exception is warranted.

6.3.3.5   Duty to disclose information about director's remuneration in the financial statements of the company

6.3.3.5.1   General

Responsibility to determine policy regarding remuneration along with setting the structure and level of compensation for the CEO and other senior members of management falls to the board of directors. That this duty is specifically provided for in the Act speaks to the great interest that has arisen over the last few decades in the level of pay or in American corporate parlance, 'compensation' for directors which has been deemed excessive and unrelated or divorced from company performance and creation of shareholder value. It also speaks to the disconect that has developed between directors as agents of the company and shareholder perception of the appropriateness of compensation. In the face of the 2008 financial crisis the public and the media in major economies but much less so in this jurisdiction where corporate governance remains enigmatic and expertise lacks, have compelled companies, especially Plcs to be more transparent on the remuneration front in order to encourage market confidence and to allow current shareholders, would-be investors or/ and creditors such as banks to easily and informatively compare one company to another.

The duty to disclose information about directors' remuneration is a serious one. In so far as preparing remuneration reports is concerned the following advice is appropriate:

---

[84] [1925] Ch 407.
[85] [1994] 1 BCLC 363 (CA); [2012] Ch 333; *Dawsons International Plc v Coats Patons Plc* (No 1) [1989] SLT 655; 1989 SCLR 452 1 Div.

Directors must approach the issue of remuneration reporting with the dispassionate intent of 'arming investors with comprehensive information'.[86] Rather than be superficial and obfuscatory, '[t]he remuneration report should explain the relationship between the company performance and the remuneration of [directors]. This approach will inform shareholders and help limit surprises and controversy in the event of particular payments being made, especially termination payments'.[87]

6.3.3.5.2   What disclosure involves

The disclosure envisaged in section 106(b) is not intended to lead to economy of the truth on the part of directors. Rather, it is intended to compel the board of directors to disclose, without reserve, what the company is spending on them for their services and to justify the subsistence of the current level of remuneration in comparative terms. It therefore follows that '[c]omprehensive disclosure involves discussing the board's policy for determining the nature of remuneration, not simply the board's policy for determining the amount. Companies should also explain how the policies and arrangements aim to influence executives to achieve the company's objectives. Companies often pay executives "at risk" remuneration subject to one or more performance conditions under an incentive plan. These performance conditions may be a mix of financial and non-financial performance conditions'.[88]

Additionally, [b]oards should disclose a detailed summary of the performance conditions and what an executive needs to do to meet those conditions. The remuneration report should also explain why the performance conditions have been chosen and provide details about any discretions given to the board under the company's incentive plan. This information helps shareholders assess whether the performance measures are appropriate to the company's circumstances and whether an executive will have earned the remuneration offered.[89]

In any case, section 118 provides that the remuneration of directors shall be proposed by the board of directors and approved by the members by ordinary resolution.[90]

---

[86] Gibson B *Company Director*, 'Fine-tuning your AGM reporting', September 2011 retrieved from aicd.companydirectors.com.au retrieved on 25 January 2017.
[87] Gibson B *Company Director*....
[88] Gibson B *Company Director*....
[89] Gibson B *Company Director*....
[90] *Guinness Plc v Sanders* [1990] 2 AC 663, HL; Note further that section 119(1) provides that '[d]espite [s] ection 118, the members may, by special resolution, approve any payment, provision, benefit, assistance or other distribution proposed by and payable to the directors. (2) An approval, referred to in subsection (1), shall only be made where there are reasonable grounds to believe that, after the distribution, the company will be able to satisfy the solvency test.

6.3.3.6   Duty to avoid conflict of interest[91] and meaning of interest

6.3.3.6.1   Duty to avoid conflict of interest[92]

A director is obliged to avoid a situation or situations 'in which that director has, or is likely to have, a direct or indirect interest that conflicts, or is likely to conflict, with the interests of the company'.[93] He, as has been shown in *Item Software (UK) Ltd v Fssihi,*[94] ought to, more than anything else, be loyal to his principal, the company. In *Aberdeen Railway Company v Blaikie Bros*[95] the plaintiff made an order of several iron chairs from the defendant. JB, was on the one hand a partner in the defendant and on the other hand, the chairman of the plaintiff's board. On this account the plaintiff refused to complete the contract. It was held that the contract was voidable on account of a breach of the duty to avoid conflict of interest which JB had breached. Lord Cranworth went so far as to opine that 'so strictly [was] this principle adhered to that no question [was] allowed to be raised as to the fairness or unfairness of a contract so entered into'.

The foregoing will apply especially where the situation or situations referred to relate 'to the exploitation of any property, information or opportunity,[96] whether or not the company takes advantage of the property, information or opportunity'.[97] The case of *Regal (Hastings) Ltd v Gulliver*[98] exemplifies this. In that case, the plaintiff possessed and at the same time managed a cinema. The directors of the company expressed the desire to acquire two other leases relating to two other cinemas, and sought, to sell these together with the first as a going concern. To execute this plan, they incorporated a subsidiary to purchase the said two leases. However, the landlord conditioned the transactions on the directors guaranteeing the rent except where the paid-up capital of the subsidiary was £5,000. As Regal could only raise £2,000, the rest of the £3,000 was purchased by the directors with the help of their sponsors. As it turned out, the initial plan to sell the three cinemas as a going concern did not materialise.

---

[91] Also provided for under section 218 CA 1994.

[92] See also: *Imperial Mercantile Credit Assoc. v Coleman* [1873] LR 6 HL 189; *Peso Silver Mines Ltd (NLP) v Cropper* [1966] 58 DLR (2d) 1; and *Foster Bryant Surveying Ltd v Bryant, Savernake Property Consultants Ltd* [2007] BCC 804.

[93] Section 107(1).

[94] [2004] EWCA Civ 1244; [2005] ICR 450.

[95] [1843-60] All ER Rep 249.

[96] See *Industrial Development Consultants Ltd* [1972] 1 WLR 443 where it has been held that an opportunity is a company asset and the fact that the company itself would not have exploited the opportunity is irrelevant; *Bhullar v Bhullar* [2003] EWCA Civ 424; [2003] 2 BCLC 241 for an extreme application of the no-conflict rule. However, see *Island Export Finance Ltd v Umunna* [1986] BCLC 460 where the court found in favour of the director showing that much will depend on the nature of the opportunity and the impeccability of the timing by the director in question.

[97] Section 107(2).

[98] [1942] 1 All ER 378; see also *Boulting and Another v Association of Cinematograph, Television and Allied Technicians* [1963] 2 QB 606.

In its stead, the directors sold the shares in both Regal and the subsidiary. In an action brought by the company's new owners to recover the profit the directors made as a consequence of selling the said shares. It was held inter alia, that the directors had profited from their fiduciary relationship with the subsidiary concern and as such were liable to account. According to Lord Russell, '[t]he liability arises from the mere fact of a profit having, in the stated circumstances, been made. The profiteer, however honest and well intentioned, cannot escape the risk of being called upon to account'.

It must be noted from the comments of Lord Porter that had the directors obtained prior approval from the members in a general meeting, they would have been allowed to retain the profit and the action against them would either not have been commenced, or had it been, would have not succeeded.

We can add that other situation captured by the no-conflict duty in section 106(b) include a director competing with the company on whose board he serves.[99] However, difficult situations may arise with regard to whether any and all competition by directors will be deemed to breach the no-conflict duty in view of the decision in *Bhullar v Bhullar*[100] where Parker LJ that the no-profit and no-conflict rules were universal and inflexible and more importantly, in view of section 107(1)(2)'s mandatory provision for a director not to directly or indirectly act in a manner that conflicts with the interests of the company. This issue arose in the case of *Plus Group Ltd v Pyke*.[101] Pyke and Plank were the only directors and shareholders of the company. Their business relationship broke down. Pyke was excluded from the management of the company; denied access to the company's financial statements; denied a monthly salary; and barred from entering the company's premises to access his office. Pyke set up a new company which incidentally began doing business with C, a significant customer of the company. On a claim for an accounting, for competing with the company it was held *inter alia* that competing in and of itself was not a breach with the court opting to take a wait and see approach.

The foregoing holdings must however be understood within the context of contractual liability so far as the company is concerned but only in so far as it can be proved that the conflict of interest arising was unknown to the third party at the time the director in question caused the company to enter the contract now impugned. They must be understood within the context of sections 23 and 24 which provide for validity of acts of a company and presumption of knowledge respectively.

---

[99] See *Hivac Ltd v Park Royal Scientific Instruments Ltd* [1946] 1 All ER 350.
[100] [2003] EWCA Civ 424; [2003] 2 BCLC 241.
[101] [2003] BCC 332.

However, in terms of section 107(3), '[t]he duty to avoid a conflict of interest shall not be considered to be infringed if the—

(a)   situation cannot reasonably be regarded as likely to give rise to a conflict of interest; or

(b)   matter has been authorised by the board of directors'.

As regards section 107(3)(a) the case of *O'Donnell v Shanahan*[102] is instructive. The plaintiff, defendant and a third director TD were directors in a company that had as its business, the provision of financial advice and assistance. A property owner inquired if the company could find a purchaser for the property in question which purchase would have resulted in the company earning £30,000. Shanahan and TD and another one of the company's clients decided to purchase the property themselves for £1.35 million and thereby deprived the company of the commission it could have earned. O'Donnell sued Shanahan and TD claiming that the purchase was a breach of the no-conflict rule. It was held that as the opportunity to purchase the property in question came to the directors in question in their capacity as directors of the company the purchase was a breach of duty. According to the court, it made no difference that the company itself would not have been in a position to purchase the property or that this had not been in the company's line of business, it being restricted to estate agency.

The strictness of the approach taken in this case harkens back to the *Bhullar* decision and conflicts with the *Plus Group* decision. It is submitted that section 107(3)(a) gives the court the power to use an objective approach in coming to a decision of whether the no-conflict rule has been breached or not. To that end, the *Plus Group* is more in line with section 107(3)(a) and given that it is a later case must be taken to have precedence over *Bhullar.*

Before leaving this part we must briefly comment on section 107(3)(b) and the meaning of authorisation by the board of directors. The said authorisation will only be deemed to be valid if it is made to the exclusion of the director(s) in question. Additionally, this provision must be seen as being independent of and not subject to section 88.[103] In any case, the use of the permissive 'may' in section 89 which permits the board to form committees must also be understood to mean that their ability to do so may be restricted by articles, the Act or a court decision brought under an action allowed under section 330.[104] As such, disclosures such as are envisaged under section 107(3)(b) may not, as was shown in *Guinness Plc v Sanders*[105] be delegated to a committee.

---

[102] [2009] EWCA Civ 751; [2009] BCC 822.

[103] Which provides for the delegation of the 'powers of board'.

[104] Under section 330(1), '[t]he [High] Court may, on the application of a person referred to in subsection (2), make an order restraining a company or a director from engaging in conduct that contravenes or would contravene the articles or this Act'.

[105] [1990] 2 AC 663 HL.

6.3.3.6.2   *Meaning of interest*

What amounts to interest within the context of section 107 is to be found in section 108. In terms of section 108(1), '[…] a director has interest in a transaction in which the company is a party if the director—

    (a)   is a party to, or is likely to derive a material financial benefit from, the transaction;

    (b)   has a material financial interest in, or with another party to, the transaction;

    (c)   is the parent, child or spouse of another party to, or person who is likely to derive a material financial benefit from, the transaction; or

    (d)   is otherwise directly or indirectly materially interested in the transaction'.

The scenarios covered under section 108(1) are however subject to section 108(2). They should therefore be read within the context of the latter subsection. Section 108(2) provides that '[a] director, shall not be considered to be interested in a transaction to which the company is a party, if the transaction relates to the company—

    (a)   giving security to a third party on the request of that third party who or which is not connected to the director; and

    (b)   with respect to a debt or obligation of the company for which the director or another person has personally assumed responsibility in full or in part under a guarantee, indemnity or deposit of a security'.

6.3.3.7   *Duty not to accept third party[106] benefits*

Section 109(1) provides that '[a] director shall not accept a benefit from a third party, conferred by reason of—

    (a)   being a director of the company; or

    (b)   doing or not doing anything as a director of the company'.

A helpful case in this regard and of which section 109(1) appears to be a restatement of the principle thereof is the classic authority for the position that an agent ought not to take a bribe: *Boston Sea Fishing & Ice Co Ltd v Ansell.*[107] In that case, a director acting on the company's behalf, as he ordinarily should have, made an order for the construction boats and the supply of ice. He received a secret commission/bonus on the shares being a shareholder in the ice company from which the order was made. It was held that he had breached his duty and as such had to account for the commission and the bonus. It is therefore safe to conclude that section 109(1) appears to be a restatement of the *Boston Sea Fishing* principle.

There are, however, qualifications to the foregoing in that by section 109(2), '[b]enefits received by a director from a person by whom that director's services

---

[106] In terms of section 109(4), … '"third party" means a person other than a body corporate or a person acting on behalf of the body corporate'.

[107] [1888] 39 Ch D 339.

as a director or otherwise are provided to the company shall not be regarded as conferred by a third party'. Additionally, 'the duty not to accept third party benefits, in [accordance with section 109], shall not be considered to have been infringed if the acceptance of the benefit does not give rise to a conflict of interest'.

6.3.3.8   Duty to disclose interest

Section 110[108] mandates a director to disclose interest in a transaction or proposed transaction. Specifically, section 110(1) provides that '[a] director shall, if interested in a transaction or proposed transaction with the company—

(a) cause to be entered in the interests register and disclose to the board—
(i) the nature and monetary value of the director's interest where the monetary value of that interest is quantifiable; or
(ii) where the monetary value of the director's interest cannot be quantified, the nature and extent of that interest; and
(b) not vote on a matter relating to the transaction'.

By section 110(2), '[a] failure by a director to comply with [section 110(1)(a), may not affect the validity of a transaction entered into by the company or the director, if the other party was not aware of the director's interest'. Further, and for obvious reasons, in terms of section 110(3), '[w]here a director with an interest in a matter votes on it the vote shall be null and void. It is an offence for any director to fail to comply with section 110(1)(a)'.

The seriousness of this duty is illustrated in the case of *Neptune (Vehicle Washing Equipment) Ltd v Fitzgerald.*[109] In that case, the defendant who was the sole director of the company called a meeting in which the only other person in attendance was the secretary. He passed a resolution terminating his contract of employment and as compensation, authorised the payment of £100,000.00. He consequently retired as director. In an action by the company for breach of duty to disclose interest, it was held that Fitzgerald ought to have declared the interest to himself and recorded same in the minutes. We must note that even though the case concerned a single member company which in terms of sections 6 and 12 is incapable of incorporation under the Act, the principle still holds and should, to all intents and purposes be deemed to be persuasive so far as interpreting section 110 is concerned. As may be remembered, the decision in Neptune was predicated on section 375 of UK CA 1985, now section 177 of the UK CA 2006 on which section 110 of the Act appears to be premised.

The foregoing notwithstanding, in terms of section 111(1), '[a] transaction entered into by a company, in which a director has an interest known to the

---

[108] Section 220 under CA 1994. Section 110 is similar to section 177 in the UK CA 2006.
[109] [1996] Ch 274.

other party, may be avoided by the company within six months after the transaction is disclosed to all the shareholders'. This is however not possible where the company receives fair value for the transaction in question.[110] In terms of section 111(3), '[t]he question, as to whether a company receives fair value under a transaction, shall be determined on the basis of the information known to the company and to the interested director at the time the transaction is entered into'. It would appear that the circumstances envisaged in section 111(2)(3) are ones in which no breach is intended or effected. The provisions, it appears, are intended to separate acts in which a director acts for the benefit of the company from those in which he acts in his own interest and to the detriment of the company. At the same time, they are meant to estop the company from denying liability for a transaction just because it can or in circumstances where complying with the obligations under said contract become difficult. Section 111(2)(3) can thus be best understood when read together with section 23 on validity of acts by the company and 24 on constructive notice.

It is also worth noting what the effect of avoiding a transaction under section 111 on *bona fide* purchase is. Section 112 provides that '[t]he avoidance of a transaction shall not affect a person's title to, or interest in, property which that person has acquired—

(a)   from a person other than the company;

(b)   for an appropriate price or fair value; or

(c)   without actual knowledge of the circumstances of the transaction under which the person, referred to in paragraph *(a)*, acquired the property from the company'.

6.3.3.9   *None disclosure of information*

Given the fiduciary nature of his duties upon appointment to the board, it is not surprising that section 113(1) provides that '[a] director shall not, except as required by [section 113(2)] or in circumstances authorised by the articles, disclose to any person or use or act on information which is in the director's possession, by virtue of the director's position as a director or employee of the company and to which the director would not otherwise have had access'.

In terms of section 113(2) referenced in section 113(1), '[a] director may, on written approval of the board, use or act on, or disclose information… to a person authorised to be informed in accordance with guidelines, instructions, powers and responsibilities of the company. Further and by section 113(3), '[t] he board of directors may authorise a director to disclose, use information or act on the information, if the board is satisfied that the interests of the company shall not be prejudiced. According to section 113(4), '[a] director shall inform

---

[110] Section 111(2).

the company of any benefit that the director obtains from using or acting on information acquired as a director or employee of the company'.

6.3.3.10   *Disclosure of interest in shares issued, acquired or disposed of by director*

The duties to be loyal, to act *bona fide* and in the best interest nay avoiding conflict of interest seem to converge in a director's obligation to disclose interest in shares issued, acquired or disposed of by the director. How a director deals with shares, when he deals with them be in in acquiring them or disposing them off may be an indicator of the company's health or the lack thereof.[111]It may be a sign for investors to buy into the company or flee. For this reason section 114(1) provides that '[a] director who has an interest in any shares issued by the company, shall—

(a)   disclose the interest to the board of directors as specified in [section114 (2) discussed below]; and

(b)   ensure that the particulars disclosed to the board are entered in the interests register'.

In terms of section 114(2), [a] director who acquires or disposes of an interest in shares issued by the company, shall within seven days after the acquisition or disposal, disclose to the board of directors the—

(a)   number and class of shares in which the interest has been acquired or disposed of, as the case may be;

(b)   nature of the interest;

(c)   consideration paid or received; and

(d)   date of the acquisition or disposal.

By section 114(3) … a director has an interest in a share issued by a company, if the director—

(a)   is a beneficiary of the share or has power to—

   (i)   exercise a right to vote attached to the share;

   (ii)   control the exercise of the right to vote attached to the share;

   (iii) acquire or dispose of the share; and

   (iv)   control the acquisition or disposition of the share by another person; or

(b)   has any of the powers referred to in subsection (3) *(a)* (i) and (ii) following an agreement or consensus   between that director and the board of directors.

---

[111] See section 115 below.

6.3.3.11   Restrictions on director regarding disposal of shares

Section 115 places restrictions on directors regarding the disposal of shares. In terms of section 115(1),[112] '[w]here a director has information which is material to an assessment of the value of shares or debentures issued by the company or subsidiary that would not be available to that director, the director may acquire or dispose of those shares or debentures in the case of—

(a)   an acquisition, where the consideration given for the acquisition is not less than the fair value of the shares or debentures; or

(b)   a disposition, where the consideration received for the disposition is not more than the fair value of the shares or securities'.

'The fair value of shares or debentures shall be determined on the basis of all information known to the director or publicly available at the time of the acquisition or the disposition, as the case may be'.[113] It is worth noting that '[w]here a director acquires or disposes of shares or debentures, in contravention of section 115, the director shall be liable to the person who, or from whom, the shares or debentures were acquired or disposed to, for the amount by which the consideration received by the director exceeds the fair value of the shares or debentures'.[114] However, in terms of section 117 and for perfectly obvious reasons, '[t]he restrictions specified in sections 115 and 116 with regard to disposal of shares by directors shall not apply in relation to a company dealing in shares on the capital market'.

6.3.4   Duty to exercise reasonable care, skill and diligence[115]

Directors ought to exercise reasonable care, skill and diligence in the execution of their duties. This is important for if it were determined that a director had fallen below the basic standard of skill and care, he may personally be liable to compensate the company for any loss resulting from such negligence. A director would therefore be expected to have the necessary level of expertise in order to serve as such and effectively manage the business of the company on whose board they serve. And because directors will ordinarily be selected on the basis of their competence, a higher standard is expected and required.

It has been shown in *Re City Equitable Fire Insurance Co Ltd*[116] that the manner in which the work of a company is to be distributed between the board of directors and the staff is a business matter to be decided on business lines.

---

[112] In terms of section 115(3), '[s]ubsection (1), shall not apply to a share or security that is acquired or disposed of by a director only as a nominee for the company or a related company'.

[113] Section 115(2).

[114] Section 116.

[115] See also *Dorchester Finance Co Ltd v Stebbing* [1989] BCLC 498; and *Thomas Saunders Partnership v Harvey* [1989] 30 Con LR 103.

[116] [1925] Ch 407.

The larger the business carried on by the company the more numerous and the more important the matters that must be necessity be left to the managers, the accountants and the rest of the staff. Further, that in ascertaining the duties of a director of a company, it is necessary to consider the nature of the company's business and the manner in which the work of the company is, reasonably in the circumstances and consistently with the articles of association, distributed between the directors and the other officials of the company.

In discharging those duties, a director (a) must act honestly, and (b) must exercise such degree of skill and diligence as would amount to the reasonable care which an ordinary man might be expected to take, in the circumstances, on his own behalf. But, (c) he need not exhibit in the performance of his duties a greater degree of skill than may reasonably be expected from a person of his knowledge and experience; in other words, he is not liable for mere errors of judgment; (d) he is not bound to give continuous attention to the affairs of his company; his duties are of an intermittent nature to be performed at periodical board meetings, and at meetings of any committee to which he is appointed, and though not bound to attend all such meetings he ought to attend them when reasonably able to do so; and (e) in respect of all duties which, having regard to the exigencies of business and the articles of association, may properly be left to some other official, he is, in the absence of grounds for suspicion, justified in trusting that official to perform such duties honestly.[117]

In view of the foregoing, it is perchance appropriate to end this section with some thoughts on the important role of directors from the late Enron Chairman, Kenneth Lay in his speech entitled 'What a CEO Expects from a Board'[118] delivered in 1999:

> [A] strong, independent, and knowledgeable board can make a significant difference in the performance of any company.... [O]ur corporate governance guidelines emphasize "the quality of strength of character, an inquiring and independent mind, practical wisdom and mature judgment...." It is no accident that we put "strength of character" first. Like any successful company, we must have directors who start with what is right, who do not have hidden agendas, and who strive to make judgments about what is best for themselves or some other constituency....
>
> [W]e look first and foremost for the principle-centered leaders. That includes principle-centered directors. The second thing we look for are independent and inquiring minds. We are always thinking about the company's business and what we are trying

[117] Overend & Gurney Co v Gibb [1872] LR 5 HL 480; Lagunas Nitrate Co v Lagunas Syndicate [1899] 2 Ch 392; In re National Bank of Wales [1899] 2 Ch 629; [1901] AC 477 (sub nom. Dovey v Cory); and In re Brazilian Rubber Plantations and Estates, Ltd [1911] 1 Ch 425, applied.
[118] Quoted in preface to Monks RAG and Minow N Corporate Governance 5th edn.

to do.... We want board members whose active participation improves the quality of our decisions.

Finally, we look for individuals who have mature judgment – individuals who are thoughtful and rigorous in what they say and decide. They should be people whom other directors and management will respect and listen to very carefully, and who can mentor CEOs and other senior managers.... The responsibility of our board – a responsibility which I expect them to fulfill – is to ensure legal and ethical conduct by the company and by everyone in the company. That requirement does not exist by happenstance. It is the most important thing we expect from board members....

What a CEO really expects from a board is good advice and counsel, both of which will make the company stronger and more successful; support for those investments and decisions that serve the interests of the company and its stakeholders; and warnings in those cases in which investments and decisions are not beneficial to the company and its stakeholders.

6.4   Balance of power between directors and shareholders

Good corporate governance involves limiting the powers and duties of directors and shareholders using their bundle of rights including voting at general meetings or in any other way provided for in the Act or by the company's articles of association to watch director actions in relation to the company. That said, the notion, as expressed in section 86, of a separate and distinct board charged with the management, governance and oversight of a company has been augmented over a long period of legal history. It would appear that until the beginning of the 19th century, the assumption had been that the general meeting (of shareholders) was the supreme decision making organ of the body in the corporate management space with the board being no more than mere agents acting as agents of the company subject to control of the shareholders in a general meeting.

This archaic notion appears to have persisted in the minds of Zambian courts[119]despite the changes we explore below. As early as 1906 the EWCA had in *Automatic Self – Cleansing Filter Syndicate v Cunningham,*[120] held that the articles of association which specifically provided that 'the directors were responsible for the management of the business and the control of the company' empowered [the directors] to sell property on such terms and conditions as they would deem fit. At the general meeting of the company, a resolution was passed

[119] See generally, Gates RB *Gates Company Law and Practice in Zambia* 239-245; See also decisions in *Boxtel v Kearney* [1987] ZR 63; *Bank of Zambia v Chibote Meat Corporation* [1999] ZR 103; *ZCCM v Kangwa & others* [2000] ZR 109; and *John Kasengele & Others v Zanaco* [2000] ZR 72.
[120] [1906] 2 Ch 34.

directing the board to sell the company's undertaking to a new company formed for that purpose. It was held that shareholders had no say in the matter, which was for the board alone to decide.[121] Though not securing immediate approval this new approach would receive approval by the House of Lords[122] in *Quin & Axtens v Salmon*.[123] Perchance, the best expression of this modern doctrine is to be found in Greer LJ's decision in *Shaw and Sons (Salford) Ltd v Shaw*,[124]

> ...a company is an entity distinct alike from its shareholders and its directors. Directors may, according to its articles, exercise some of its powers; certain other powers may be reserved for the shareholders in a general meeting. If power of management is vested in the directors, they and they alone can exercise these. The only way which the general body of shareholders can control the exercise of the powers vested by the Articles in the directors is by altering their articles, or, if an opportunity arises under the articles, by refusing to re – elect the directors of whose actions they disapprove they cannot themselves usurp the powers which by the articles are vested in the directors any more than the directors can usurp the powers vested by the articles in the general body of shareholders.[125]

That the instances in which shareholders can act are specified and limited pursuant to the Act and articles of association is settled. Indeed, unless the board is acting in contravention of the Act or provisions of the articles, their power to conduct the management of the company cannot be impugned by a general meeting of members. To that end, at least, the members cannot be said to have 'overriding authority'[126] over directors nor can directors be liable to 'dance the shareholders' tune' no matter how legally out of tune the song is. Shareholder control over the board of directors is not without limits.   It cannot, as seems to have been suggested by the Supreme Court in the case of *Boxtel v Kearney*[127] and affirmed in three subsequent cases, namely *Bank of Zambia v Chibote Meat Corporation*,[128] *ZCCM v Kangwa & others*[129] and *John Kasengele & Others v Zanaco,*[130] be exercised irrespective. It certainly does not extend to instances where directors have acted within the confines of their authority as provided for

---

[121] Affirmed in *Gramophone and Typewriter Ltd v Stanley* [1908] 2KB 89.
[122] The precursor to the UK SC.
[123] [1909] AC 442.
[124] [1935] 2 KB 113.
[125] This position was affirmed in *Howard Smith Ltd v Ampol Petroleum Ltd* [1974] AC 821.
[126] See generally Gates RB *Gates Company Law and Practice in Zambia* 239-45 for a detailed analysis.
[127] [1987] ZR 63.
[128] [1999] ZR 103.
[129] [2000] ZR 109.
[130] [2000] ZR 72.

in section 86. It will be remembered that section 86(1)(b) specifically provides that directors will 'exercise all such powers of the company as are not, by this Act or the articles, required to be exercised by the members.' It has been held in *Breckland Group Holdings v London & Suffolk Properties Ltd*[131] that the commencement of litigation on behalf of the company is a duty reserved to directors in their managerial capacity.[132] The general meeting is therefore not competent to interfere with matters that have been reserved for the board of directors by the Act or the company's articles.

6.5   Default powers reserved to the general meeting

Section 131(1) provides that '[t]he shareholders of a company shall, exercise the powers reserved to shareholders as specified in [the] Act or the articles—
(a) at a meeting of the shareholders; or
(b) *in lieu* of a meeting, by a resolution made in accordance with section 77'.[133]
In terms of section 131(2), '[a] power reserved to shareholders shall be exercised by ordinary resolution, unless the articles or [the] Act specify otherwise'. The Supreme Court has observed in *Edgar Hamuwele (appealing in his capacity as joint liquidator of Lima Bank Ltd (in Liquidation)) and Christopher Mulenga (appealing in his capacity as joint liquidator of Lima Bank (in Liquidation)) v Ngenda Sipalo and Brendah Sipalo*[134] that a board of directors and shareholders are two distinct entities. 'While shareholders are members who own shares in a company, the court said, 'a board of directors is the governing body of the company'. Further, that '[a]company can continue to exist even without a board of directors'. Finally, that '[i]f a board of directors is dissolved, members can appoint or elect another one'. Additionally and has been held in another case,[135] where the board of directors is deadlocked or incapable of meeting, the powers of management provided for in section 86 revert to the general meeting. As such the company may take appropriate action in a general meeting.[136]

6.6   Delegating powers of board and constitution of board committees

6.6.1   *Delegating powers of board*

The delegation of powers of the board is provided for in section 88. In what is a direct deviation from the *delegatus non protest delegare*[137] principle, section

---

[131] [1989] BCLC 100.
[132] However see section 330 and 331.
[133] Which provides for written resolutions for private companies.
[134] SCZ Judgment No 4 of 2010.
[135] *Barron v Potter* [1914] 1 Ch 895
[136] See *Barron v Potter* [1914] 1 Ch 895.
[137] 'One to whom power is delegated cannot himself further delegate that power'.

88(1), allows the board of directors, subject to the company's articles, to delegate to a director or committee of directors any one or more of its powers. 'Rather than all directors discussing and debating every issue [a company] faces, committees allow a small group of directors to investigate issues in detail and report back to the board with recommendations for actions'.[138] However, in terms of section 88(2), '[a] board of directors that delegates any power, in accordance with subsection (1), cannot absolve itself of responsibility in matters that they have delegated to a committee or a single director.[139] This is a basic principle of agency law where the principal is generally responsible unless he can prove otherwise. To that end and following the Latin principle: *qui facit per alium facit per se*[140] the board of directors 'shall be responsible for the exercise of that power, as if the power had been exercised by the board itself'.[141]

That this delegation should be allowed at all is borne of necessity and the reality of corporate management more than anything else. The board of directors' duties including establishing broad strategic policies and objectives for a company; the selection, appointment, supporting and appraising the performance of and termination of the Chief Executive Officer; resource mobilization and availability financial and otherwise; budget approval; explanation of the company's performance to the shareholders; and setting remunerations, compensation and related benefits of senior management, are generally taken once every three months (or quarterly). It is impractical and would be suicidal for a company to subject its day to day running of affairs to decisions made every three months.

Additionally, the creation of any board committees is a means of ensuring that the board of directors is able to manage its workload efficiently and effectively. It has therefore been the tradition that the board of directors has in practice delegated the day to day running of the company to a management team which until now has not been recognised in the Act. There are further provisions regarding the extent of the board of directors' power to delegate their authority in section 89 discussed below.

6.7   Constitution of board committees

In terms of section 89(1), '[t]he board of directors may constitute committees of the board and appoint any number of directors as members of the committee, unless the articles otherwise provide'. The use of the permissive term 'may' means that the board may choose not to constitute any such committees. In practice though the board will almost always constitute said committees the most important of which appear to be, for obvious reasons the compensation

---

[138] 'Director Remuneration': http://www.aicd.companydirectors.com.au.
[139] See *Re Queens Moat Houses Plc* (No 2) [2005] 1 BCLC 136.
[140] 'He who does (something) through another does it through himself'.
[141] Section 88(2).

committee and the audit committee. Others include but are not limited to the nominating and governance committees. However, in terms of section 89(2), '[a] committee constituted, in accordance with [section 89(1)], may to the extent provided by the articles or a resolution constituting the committee—

(a)   include a person who is not a director but such person shall not—
      (i) be eligible or qualified to be appointed as director; and
      (ii) vote on any matter to be decided by the committee;
(b)   consult with or receive advice from any person; and
(c)   have the full authority of the board of directors in respect of a matter referred to it'.

The foregoing seeks not only to signify a delineation between the board of directors and those who are not part of the board but to whom for purposes of convenience and efficiency, the board of directors may delegate its powers and duties. These persons who are not directors but who may serve on board constituted committees regardless will ordinarily be members of the senior management team to whom the day to day running of the company is delegated. This marks a departure from section 217 CA 1994 which section 89 replaces in that, for the first time in Zambian company law jurisprudence, a cadre other than the board of directors has received mention and recognition. Be that as it may, they serve at the pleasure of the board and their engagement will be pursuant to the terms and conditions of a contract of employment pursuant to the articles of association.[142]

6.8   Minimum number of directors

Section 85(2)(a) or (b), requires that '[t]he board of directors shall comprise, in the case of a—

(a)   private company, not less than two directors; or
(b)   public company, not less than three directors'.[143]

This section replaces the rather obtuse section 204 in the CA 1994 which in subsection (1) of that Act provided that a company shall have at least two directors. Unlike section 85, the section made no distinction between private and public companies. While section 204(2) made it an offence for a company to carry on business for a period more than two months with fewer than two directors, whatever that meant, section 90 makes it an offence for a company to carry 'on business for a period of more than ninety days[144] with less than the minimum number of directors specified in section 85(2) providing that in such a case, 'the company and each officer of the company commit an offence and are liable, on conviction, to a fine not exceeding two hundred thousand penalty units'.

---

[142] See *Re Equitable Fire Insurance Co* [1925] Ch 407.
[143] By comparison section 154(1) of the UK CA 2006, requires every company to have at least one director whereas section 154(2) requires a public company to have at least two directors.
[144] Thereby increasing the default period by 30 days.

In terms of section 91(1), '[t]he number of directors, including an executive director, resident in Zambia, shall not be less than half the number of directors appointed'. Additionally and by section 91(2), '[t]he Minister may, by statutory instrument, permit a company which after 1st February, 2000, entered into a Development Agreement in accordance with the Mines and Minerals Act, 1995, to have not less than thirty percent of its directors resident in Zambia'. The subsection is permissive and not mandatory. A rather and novel and grave provision is that '[a] contravention of subsection (1) which continues for more than sixty days shall constitute grounds for winding-up of the company, in accordance with the Corporate Insolvency Act, 2017 by the Court on the application of the Registrar'.[145]

The point to note here is that like a floating charge that will not become fixed, unless some step is taken,[146] the contravention of section 91(1) will not in and of itself lead to automatic winding-up as there is no such thing as automatic winding-up. The contravention may well go on for 59 days without the risk of winding-up. Even after the 60 day period, no winding-up order may be made by the court unless and until the Registrar takes the necessary step of making an application. Even then, the mere fact of an application by the Registrar will not guarantee a company being wound-up. The Court must be convinced that it will be just and equitable to wind-up the company under the circumstances.

6.9   Qualifications of director

The qualifications of a director are set out in section 92. Section 92(1) provides that '[a] company shall appoint a natural person as director'.[147] While the language is slightly different from that used under section 207(1) CA 1994 which this subsection replaces, it has the clarity that the previous section lacked. Further, while under English company law as established in *Re Bulawayo Market and Officers Company Ltd*[148] a company may have another company as a *de jure* director called a corporate director, this, by implication, is not possible in Zambia by virtue of section 92(1)(2). In addition to the foregoing, '[a] director may not be a member or hold shares in the company, unless the articles provide otherwise'.[149]

---

[145] Section 91(3).
[146] *The Government Stock and Other Securities Investment Co. Ltd v The Manila Railway Co Ltd and Others* [1897] AC 81 HL.
[147] Section 155(1) of the UK CA 2006 only imposes a requirement that every company must have at least one director who is a natural person. It does not prevent a company from being a director in another. Known as a corporate director, any action done in the exercise of the power such corporate director will ordinarily be done by a human agent acting on its behalf: *Secretary of State for Trade and Commerce v. Hall* [2006] EWHC 1995 (Ch).
[148] [1907] 2 Ch 58.
[149] Section 92(2).

Further, and in terms of section 92(3), '[a] person shall not be appointed as a director if that person—

(a)   is under eighteen years of age;

(b)   is an undischarged bankrupt;

(c)   is disqualified by section 93[150] from being a director;

(d)   has been declared by a court of competent jurisdiction to be of unsound mind; or

(e)   fails to satisfy any additional qualifications for directors provided in the articles'.

In terms of section 92(4), '[t]he articles may provide further restrictions or qualifications on the appointment or continuation in office of a director'. These may include:

(i)   General misconduct;

(ii) Unfitness; and

(iii) Wrongful trading.

6.10   Disqualification by court from holding office of director

Apart from the disqualification that may arise under section 93, in terms of section 93(1), '[t]he Court may, on the application of a company, a creditor of the company or the Registrar, prevent a person from being appointed as director in any company, for a period not exceeding five years, for committing an offence or breaching any of the duties of a director specified in [the] Act'. By section 93(2), '[a] person who is disqualified from appointment as a director but continues to act as a director, is liable for any purported actions as a director, for the purposes of the duties and liabilities of a director as specified in [the] Act'. Further, and in terms of section 93(3), '[a] person who is disqualified from appointment as a director shall during the period of disqualification remain disqualified to act as director in any other company'.

It has been shown by *Brown – Wilkinson v Cin Re Lo – Line Electric Motors Ltd*[151] the inspiration for the statutory provisions under section 93, that directorial disqualification is designed for the protection of the public from directors who are unfit or otherwise incompetent from running companies in which the public may invest endangering their investments. He may for example have been a director in insolvent companies. In *Sevenoaks Stationers (Retail) Ltd*[152] for example, C's CV was an impressive one: he had an MBA from Harvard and was an erstwhile merchant banker and a member of the Institute of Chartered Accountants. He was a director in five companies all of which had gone into liquidation between the years 1983 and 1986. The debts totalled £559,000 with

---

[150] Which provides for the disqualification by court from holding office of a director.

[151] [1988] 2 All ER 692 at 699.

[152] [1990] 3 WLR 1165.

£116,000 representing Crown debt. He was disqualified for 7 years. On appeal, the disqualification was reduced to 5 years on the facts and circumstances of the case which were deemed by Dillon LJ to be relatively not very serious even though C was deemed to be incompetent to a marked degree.

6.11   Alternate directors

Section 97[153] provides for the manner of appointment of alternate directors. In terms of section 97(1), '[a] director may, subject to any restriction provided in the articles, with the approval of the board of directors, appoint a person who is not a director as an alternate director'. It is mandatory for such an appointment to be in writing, signed by the director making the appointment and the person being appointed with the same being lodged with the company.[154] In terms of section 97(3), '[a] person shall not be appointed as an alternate director by more than one director'. By section 97(4), '… the provisions on registration of directors' particulars and interests shall apply to an alternate director as if the alternate director were a director'.

However, '[a]n appointment of a person as an alternate director shall confer on that alternate director the right to—

(a)   attend any meeting of the board of directors or any committee of directors at which the director who appointed the alternate director is not present; and

(b)   vote at a meeting of the board of directors or committee of directors'.[155] *A fortiori* '[a]n alternate director may not hold shares in a company'[156] or have 'power to appoint an alternate director'.[157]

Subject only to the articles providing otherwise as we see shortly, 'a company may not pay any remuneration to an alternate director or be liable to pay additional remuneration by reason of the appointment of an alternate director, except that an alternate director may be remunerated by the director who appointed the alternate director'.[158]

The provisions of section 97(8) notwithstanding, '[t]he articles may provide that—

(a)   an alternate director shall be entitled to receive from the company, during the period of the alternate director's appointment, the remuneration to which the director who appointed the alternate director is entitled; and

(b)   the director who appointed the alternate director shall not be entitled to that remuneration.

---

[153] Replaces section 213 under CA 1994.
[154] Section 97(2).
[155] Section 97(5).
[156] Section 97(6).
[157] Section 97(7).
[158] Section 97(8).

In terms of section 97(9), '[t]he appointment of an alternate director shall cease—

(a) at the expiry of the period for which the alternate director was appointed;

(b) if the director who appointed the alternate director—

  (i) gives written notice to that effect to the board of directors; or

  (ii) ceases for any reason to be a director; or

(c) if the alternate director resigns by notice in writing to the board of directors'.

6.12 Removal of director from office

The removal of a director from office is provided for under section 98.[159] In terms of section 98(1), '[a] company may remove a director from office by an ordinary resolution passed at a general meeting of the company'. This provision must be seen in the context of the philosophy that he who hires must also have the right to fire and as such be seen as the antithesis of section 85 that provides the shareholders at a general meeting with the power to appoint shareholders. There is a set procedure to removing a director set in section 98(2). It provides that '[a] member shall, not less than twenty eight days before the meeting referred to in [section 98](1), give the company secretary notice of intention to move a resolution to remove a director, in the prescribed manner and form'. On receipt of such notice the secretary is obligated to send a copy of the notice to the director concerned and that director shall be entitled to—

(a) be heard at the meeting;

(b) submit a written statement to the company regarding the notice..; and

(c) require that the director's written statement, made in accordance with paragraph *(b)*, be read at the meeting'.[160]

Further to the foregoing and in terms of section 98(4), '[a] notice of the general meeting, at which a notice referred to in [section 98](2) is to be considered, shall be sent to every person entitled to receive the notice, which shall be accompanied by a copy of the written statement referred to in [section 98](3)*(b)*'. Further, and according to section 98(5), '[t]he company shall not be obliged to send or circulate the director's statement if it is received by the company less than seven days before the meeting'. Finally, by section 98(6), '[a] vacancy created by the removal of a director in accordance with this section, if not filled at the meeting at which the director is removed, may be filled as a casual vacancy'.

---

[159] Replacing section 211 under CA 1994.
[160] Section 98(3).

6.13   Vacancy in office of director and filling up of casual vacancy

Section 99 provides instances under which the office of director may fall vacant. They include the following:

(a)   resignation;

(b)   removal from or vacating of office in accordance with the articles or the Act;

(c)   becoming 'disqualified to hold the office of director as specified in [the] Act; or

(d)   death.[161]

As regards resignation, section 99(2) provides that such resignation may be by written notice in the prescribed form and delivering the notice to the company secretary. Though it may appear that resignation by written notice is optional, the context appears to show that this is mandatory in any orderly resignation. This is because by section 99(3), '[t]he notice, specified in [section 99(2), shall be effective when received by the company secretary or at a later time as specified in the notice'. In terms of section 99(4), '[a] director who vacates office in accordance with this section shall within the five years following that vacation of office continue to be liable, for acts, omissions and decisions made during the period that person was a director'.

The curious thing about the foregoing is it does not seem to envisage a situation where the resignation is effected contrary to section 99 for example, orally and outside any of the instances listed under section 99(1). One possibility is for any of the persons with standing under section 330 to commence an action to compel the departing director to follow the procedure as laid down in the Act or the company's articles. The company may itself bring an action against him and to continue to consider him a director until he follows the procedure. Finally, and in order to protect the company, the director may be formally removed from office by any of the methods provided for in company's articles which provisions may go beyond envisaged under section 99(1).

Finally, in terms of section 99(5), '[w]here the office of a director becomes vacant before the expiry of the term of office, the company may in accordance with section 85, appoint another director in place of the director who vacates office but such director shall hold office only for the unexpired part of the term'.

6.14   Notice of change of directorship and particulars Executive director

It is a requirement in terms of section 100(1) that a company lodges with the Registrar, in the prescribed form, notice of a change in the—

(a)   directorship of the company, whether as a result of a director ceasing to hold office under any of the circumstances enumerated under section 99

---

[161] Section 99(1).

or appointment of a new director in terms of section 85 irrespective of the reasons for the vacancy or

(b) particulars of a director, such as the name, residential address or other particulars as may be prescribed.

A notice required to be lodged aforesaid will, in addition to the requirements specified in section 100(1), include the—

'*(a)* date of the change;

(b) full name, residential address and other particulars, as may be prescribed, of every person who is a director from the date of the notice; and

(c) consent to be appointed director as specified in section 94'.[162]

Further, and in terms of section 100(3), '[a] notice required to be lodged in accordance with section 100(1) shall be lodged with the Registrar within twenty-one days of the following—

(a) change occurring, in the case of an appointment or resignation of a director; or

(b) company first becoming aware of the change, in the case of the death of a director or a change in the name or residential address or other particulars of a director.

Should a company fail to comply with the foregoing requirements, 'each officer of the company commits an offence and is liable, on conviction, to a fine not exceeding one hundred thousand penalty units'.[163]

6.15 Executive director

In terms of section 101(1), '[a] company may appoint an executive director for such period and on such terms as the company considers appropriate, unless the articles provide otherwise'. Following his appointment, the executive director's remuneration will be determined by the members, pursuant 'to the terms of a contract of employment executed by the company on the one hand and the executive director'[164] on the other. It is open to the company to, 'subject to the articles and the terms of any agreement entered into'[165] with an executive director, revoke his appointment. Revocation of an agreement is a province of contract law and whatever the articles provide and the agreement contains, common law principles and those of equity must be adhered to. Otherwise the revocation may be of no consequence, and may indeed be deemed to be a breach of contract were an action to be brought by the director affected by the revocation.

Unlike non-executive directors, '[a]n executive director shall not, while holding that office, be subject to retirement by rotation or be taken into

---

[162] Section 100(2).
[163] Section 100(4).
[164] Section 101(2).
[165] Section 101(3).

account in determining the retirement of directors by rotation'.[166] However, the subsistence of the position of executive director is inextricably linked to his continued occupation of the office of director. As such, 'an executive director's appointment shall terminate automatically if the executive director ceases for any reason to be a director'.[167]

Having discussed the separate and distinct roles of the secretary on the one hand, and the directors on the other, it is important to note that according to section 102, where there is (or are) provision(s) 'that require(s) or authorises an act to be done by a director and the company secretary shall not be satisfied if it is done by the same person in that person's capacity both as a director and company secretary'. The importance of this provision in delineating the functions of the director and secretary in company operations and corporate governance in particular is patent.

Further to the foregoing, we must consider statutory provisions as they relate to the validity of decisions by executive officer in terms of section 121 which provides that, [a] decision made by an officer of a company shall, subject to the requirements as to disclosure, be considered valid if the—

(a) decision is made in good faith for a proper purpose;

(b) officer does not have a personal interest in the decision;

(c) company is appropriately informed of the subject matter of the decision; and

(d) officer reasonably believes that the decision is in the best interests of the company.

Finally, as regards liability and indemnity with regard to decisions made *bona fide,* section 122 provides that '[w]here a company establishes that a decision made by an officer is—

(a) not valid, the officer shall be held personally liable for any obligation or liability that arises as a result of that decision; or

(b) valid, the officer shall be indemnified for that decision'.

6.15   Loans to directors by company

The provisions relating to loans to directors by the company are to be found in section 103. Section 103(1) makes the point that the said provisions will only apply to—

(a) public company;

(b) a related company to a public company; and

(c) company in a prescribed class of companies.

---

[166] Section 101(4).
[167] Section 102(5).

Further, a company to which section 103 applies is mandated not to do the following:

(a)   make a loan to a director or related company;

(b)   give a guarantee or provide security in connection with a loan made by any person to a director or related company; or

(c)   subject to this section—

(i)   make a loan; or

(ii)   give a guarantee or provide security in connection with a loan made by any person; to a company in which a director or nominee of a director holds twenty percent or more of the company's issued shares'.[168]

However, in terms of section 103(3), a company is not prohibited—

(a)   from making a loan to a related company, or entering into a guarantee or providing security in connection with a loan made by any person to the related company;

(b)   whose ordinary business includes the lending of money or the giving of guarantees in connection with loans made by other persons from making a loan to, or giving a guarantee or providing security in connection with, a director or a company referred to in [section 103(2).

(c)   if prior written approval of the company has—

(i)   been obtained at a general meeting; or

(ii)   not been obtained within 12 months of a general meeting being held, on condition that the loan shall be repaid or the liability under the guarantee or security shall be discharged within 18 months.

The provisions of section 103(2) notwithstanding,

> [a] company may advance to a director or related company, funds to meet expenditure incurred or to be incurred by the director for the purposes of the company or for the purposes of enabling that director to properly perform that director's duties, except that the total amount advanced to that director does not exceed one per centum of the assets of the company, less the liabilities of the company as shown in the last audited statement of financial position of the company.[169]

In terms of section 103(3), in the event of failure by the company to comply with section 103, the—

---

[168] Section 103(2).

[169] Section 103(4).

(a) company and each officer in default commit an offence are liable, on conviction, to a fine not exceeding one hundred thousand penalty units; and

(b) directors, who authorised the making of the loan or the giving of the guarantee or provision of the security, shall be jointly and severally liable to indemnify the company against any loss arising therefrom.

However, section 103 'shall not', in terms of section 103(6), 'apply to a loan, guarantee or security made or provided before the commencement of this Act'.

6.16   Liability of director for breach of duty

'Where a director of a company wilfully commits a breach of any duty or responsibility specified in this Act, the director—

(a) is liable to compensate the company for any loss the company suffers as a result of the breach;

(b) may be removed from the board of directors in accordance with this Act; and

(c) is liable to account to the company for any profit made as a result of the breach'. [170]

Additionally, '[a] contract or other transaction entered into between a director and the company in breach of any duty of the director as specified in this Act, may be rescinded by the company'. [171]

6.17   Conclusion

In this chapter we have explored two different matters. The first is the Company secretary. We have looked at the common law history of the company secretary; the responsibilities of a company secretary; and qualifications for a company secretary. The second matter we have covered is that of directors including their appointment; types of directors under which we have examined the *de facto* director; Types of directors; *de jure* director; and the shadow director. We have also explored the powers and duties of directors as provided for in the Act. We additionally have examined fiduciary duties now statutorily provided for among them: duty to exercise director's power in accordance with the Act and articles; duty to promote the success of the company; duty to exercise independent judgment; duty to disclose information about director's remuneration in the financial statements of the company. We have also explored the important issue of the balance of power between directors and shareholders noting that any power not explicitly given to directors is reserved to shareholders. We have also noted that the Act specifies qualifications of a director; and that a director

---

[170] Section 120(1).
[171] Section 120(2).

may be disqualified by the court from holding office of director for cause. We have noted that in addition to there being power by the board to fill a vacancy should one arise, a director may also be removed by the shareholders for cause. Finally, it must be remembered that with duties and powers come liability for breach of duty by directors.

FURTHER READING

Articles

Ahern, D, 'Directors' duties, dry ink and the accessibility agenda' (2012) 128 LQR 114.

Boros, E, 'The duties of nominee and multiple directors', Part 1 (1989) 10 Comp Law 211; Part 2 (1990) 11 Comp Law 6.

Conaglen, M, 'The nature and function of fiduciary loyalty' [2005] LQR 469.

Crutchfeld, P, 'Nominee directors: the law and commercial reality' (1991) 12 Comp Law 136.

Davies, P, 'Directors' Creditor-Regarding Duties in Respect of Trading Decisions Taken in the Vicinity of Insolvency' [2006] EBOR 30.

Griffths, B, 'Dealing with directors' conflicts of interest under the Companies Act 2006' (2008) 23 BJIB & FL 292.

Keay, A, 'Formulating a Framework for Directors' Duties to Creditors: An Entity Maximisation Approach' [2005] CLJ 614.

Keay, A, 'The duty of directors to exercise independent judgment' (2008) 29 Comp Law 290.

Keay, A, 'Ascertaining the Corporate Objective: An Entity Maximisation and Sustainability Model' (2008) 71 Modern Law Review 663.

Lowry, J, & Sloszar, L, 'Judicial pragmatism: directors' duties and post-resignation conflicts of duty' [2008] Journal of Business Law 83.

Books

Davies PL *Gower and Davies' Principles of Modern Company Law* 7th edn (Thomson Sweet & Maxwell London 2003).

Dine J and Koutsias M *Company Law* 6th edn (Palgrave Macmillan Hampshire 2007).

Farrah JH and Hannigan BM *Farrar's Company Law* 4th edn (Butterworths London 1998).

Gates RB *Gates Company Law and Practice in Zambia* (Reagan Blankfein Gates Lusaka 2017).

Mayson S French D Ryan C Mayson *French and Ryan on Company Law* 31st edn (Oxford University Press Oxford 2014-15).

Sealy L and Worthington S *Sealy & Worthington's Cases and Materials in Company Law* 10ᵗʰ edn (Oxford University Press Oxford 2013).

Wild C and Weinstein S *Smith and Keenan's Company Law* 15ᵗʰ edn (Pearson Education Ltd London 2011).

Reports

European Commission Communication, Modernising Company Law and Enhancing

Corporate Governance in the EU – A Plan to Move Forward (COM (2003) 284).

7

SHAREHOLDERS' RIGHTS AND OBLIGATIONS

AIMS AND OBJECTIVES

 After reading this chapter you should appreciate:
- ➤ the concept of beneficial owner
- ➤ The declaration in respect of beneficial interest in share
- ➤ The beneficial ownership of shares
- ➤ The liability of shareholders
- ➤ The liability of former shareholders
- ➤ The liability of person ceasing to be shareholder before shareholders' liability becomes unlimited
- ➤ The fact that shareholders are not required to acquire shares by alteration to articles
- ➤ The liability of personal representative
- ➤ The liability of assignee
- ➤ The exercise of powers reserved for shareholders
- ➤ The power to acquire shares of minority on takeover
- ➤ The rights of minority on takeover
- ➤ The remedy against oppression of minority on takeover
- ➤ The classes and interest groups
- ➤ The alteration of shareholder rights
- ➤ The shareholder requiring the company to purchase shares
- ➤ The right of a shareholder to commence action under certain specified circumstances

7.1 Introduction

Shareholders' rights and obligations are concepts not borne so much of statutory law as in common law specifically, the law of contract and the doctrine of equity. The Act however seeks to, and has codified to a large degree within the Zambian context, the said shareholders' rights to curb, it appears, the apparent weaknesses in the CA 1994 regarding this matter. As has been observed,[1] [s]hareholders are both ['partners'] with voting rights, who can take part in collective decisions concerning the company, and owners of equity securities, who are entitled to profit from selling them on. In view of this dual aspect, it seemed that legal efficiency in terms of their rights and obligations could be improved by (i) recognising the primacy of corporate benefit and (ii) making concerted action possible.

The new provisions in the Act are an attempt by its framers 'to identify legal avenues for achieving a fair balance between these rights and obligations so as to create value overall, both for the holder of these rights and for the issuing company towards which the shareholder has obligations'.[2] Whether or not the statutory provisions in the Act will be effective in strengthening corporate governance in companies incorporated under CA 1994 and those under the Act remains to be seen.

In the present discussion though, we focus on the substance of the provisions and their possible motivation, and implications. To that end, we explore the concept of beneficial owner; declaration in respect of beneficial interest in share; beneficial ownership of shares; liability of shareholders; liability of former shareholders; liability of person ceasing to be shareholder before shareholders' liability becomes unlimited; the fact that shareholders are not required to acquire shares by alteration to articles; liability of personal representative; liability of assignee; exercise of powers reserved for shareholders; power to acquire shares of minority on takeover; rights of minority on takeover; remedy against oppression of minority on takeover; classes and interest groups; alteration of shareholder rights; shareholder requiring company to purchase shares; and the right of a shareholder to commence action under certain specified circumstances.

7.2   Declaration in respect of beneficial interest in share

In terms of section 3 '"beneficial owner" means a natural person who—
- *(a)* directly or indirectly, through any contract, arrangement, understanding, relationship or any other means ultimately owns, controls, exercises substantial interest in, or receives substantial economic benefit from a body corporate; or
- *(b)* exercises ultimate and effective control over a legal person or legal arrangement'.[3]

It has also been defined as '...the right to receive benefits on shares held by another party. That it 'is often referred to in matters concerning trusts, whereby

---

[1] Laprade, F M 'Rights and obligations of shareholders National regimes and proposed instruments at EU level for improving legal efficiency' retrieved from http://www.europarl.europa.eu/activities/committees/studies.do?language=FR on 14/01/2017.

[2] Laprade, F M 'Rights and obligations of shareholders....'

[3] Further, 'the terms "beneficially own" and "beneficial ownership" shall be construed accordingly'.

one has a vested interest in the trust's assets' or as "that right which a person has in a contract made with another (third party)."[4] Black's Law Dictionary[5] defines 'beneficial interest' as '[a] right or expectancy in something (such as a trust or an estate), as opposed to legal title to that thing'.

In view of the foregoing, section 123(1) provides that '[w]here the name of a person who is not the beneficial owner, is entered in the register of members as the holder of a share, the person shall make a declaration to the company within such time and in such form as may be prescribed, specifying the name and other particulars of the beneficial owner of the share'. While this part of the section puts the obligation on the person entered on the register of members, who incidentally is not the same as a beneficial owner, section 123(2), places the same obligation on the beneficial owner defined in section 3 as shown above, or/ and his 'agent' providing that '[a] beneficial owner or a person acting or holding a share on behalf of a beneficial owner, shall make a declaration to the company, specifying—

(a) the nature of the interest and voting rights held;
(b) particulars of the person in whose name the share is registered in the books of the company; and
(c) such other particulars as may be prescribed'.

We must note that unlike the rights of someone like a trustee or official who has responsibility to perform and/or [has] title to the assets [in question] but does not share in the benefits',[6] the beneficial owner like the name suggests, benefits from his connection in any of the terms or situations included under section 3(a) and (b). A common method in the use of the device of beneficial ownership has been by way of incorporating a wholly-owned subsidiary company and thereby subscribing to the shares in the said company 'through a person or persons who act as the nominee of the company to fulfill the criteria of minimum number of members. Upon incorporation, the company becomes a beneficial owner and nominee becomes a registered member of the subsidiary company'.[7]

In *Lake Kariba Boating Services Ltd v Kariba North Bank Co Ltd*[8] the appellants were the registered proprietors of leasehold properties in Siavonga. The respondent lodged caveats on the said properties maintaining that it had a beneficial interest in the properties having acquired complete control of the assets of the appellant company through purchasing all the shares in the latter. An application by the appellants for the removal of the caveats was refused. They appealed against the refusal. It was held as follows:

---

[4] Saar G 'Beneficial Interest in any share (Sec 89)' retrieved from http://www.icsi.edu on 14/01/2012.
[5] 9th edn 913.
[6] Saar G 'Beneficial Interest in any share....'
[7] Saar G 'Beneficial Interest in any share....'
[8] [1982] ZR 35, Ngulube DCJ, Muwo JS and Bweupe, AG JS.

(i)   One company can acquire complete control over the assets of another company by the acquisition from the shareholders of the whole of the issued share capital of the company whose assets it is sought to control

(ii)   A company having such control has a legitimate beneficial interest in the assets arising out of the trust created and is in a proper position to lodge a caveat over the said assets.

Comment: We must note that though this case involved a corporate having beneficial interest which section 3 excludes by limiting the beneficial interest to a natural person, the principle still holds and the provisions of section 123 must be adhered to.

In the event that an adjustment arises as respects beneficial ownership, the person whose name is entered on the register but who is not a beneficial owner in terms of section 3 must, together with the beneficial owner, 'within fourteen days from the date of the change, make a declaration to the company, in the prescribed form, giving such particulars as may be prescribed'.[9] The foregoing provisions are open to change or enhancement as needs be for in terms of section 123(4) the Minister responsible for commerce 'may make rules on beneficial ownership, beneficial owners and the identification, verification and disclosure of beneficial ownership'. Additionally, '[i]t is an offence for any person whose name is entered on the register in terms of section 123(1) to fail to 'make a declaration in accordance with provisions of section 123 as a whole or regulations made pursuant to the said section'.[10]

Failure to comply with the declaration provisions under section 123 has consequences. Section 123(8) specifically provides that '[w]here a beneficial owner or a person acting or holding a share on behalf of a beneficial owner fails to make a declaration in accordance with [section 123], a right in relation to that share shall not be enforceable'. We must consider this provision within the context of the definition offered by Farewell J in *Borland's Trustee v Steel*[11], perhaps the most comprehensive legal definition of the term 'share' in company law jurisprudence:

> A share is the interest of a shareholder in the company measured by a sum of money, for the purpose of liability in the first place, and interest in the second, but also consisting of a series of mutual covenants entered into by all the shareholders interse in

---

[9]   Section 123(3). In terms of section 123(6), '[a] company shall, where a declaration referred to in subsection (3) is made— *(a)* record the declaration in the Register of beneficial ownership established in accordance with section 21(2); and *(b)* within thirty days from the date of receipt of the declaration, and on payment of such fees or additional fees as may be prescribed, file with the Registrar a return in the prescribed form in respect of the declaration'. In terms of section 123(7), '[f]ailure to comply with subsection (6) the company and every officer of the company in default commit an offence'.

[10] Section 123(5).

[11] [1901] 1 Ch 279 at 288.

accordance with [section 21 of the Act]. The contract contained in the articles of association is one of the original incidents of the share. A share is not a sum of money...but is an interest measured by a sum of money and made up of various rights contained in the contract, including the right to a sum of money of a more or less amount.[12]

The interest spoken of here is what empowers a shareholder or shareholders to derive benefits from what may be termed a bundle of rights founded on share ownership. They include the right to vote, to earn dividends as and when they are declared, to attend meetings as and when they are called, and to 'share in the surplus assets at winding up or when there is capital reduction as already discussed. The shareholder thus gains proprietary interest in the company but not in its property. In essence, as a result of owning a share or shares in a company, the shareholder enjoys rights in the company and against it. The definition also imports into it the binding contractual nature of owning shares in a company as codified in section [17] of the Act'.[13]

The implication of section 123(8) therefore is that none of the rights which ordinarily should be available to a shareholder whose name has been entered on the members' register will be enforceable against the company. The consequences also extend to the rights the shareholder has under section 330 to seek injunctive relief against a company; the right to bring an action against a director of the company under section 335; the right to bring an action against the company under section 336; the right to bring a representative action or to be part of such an action under section 338; the right to appeal a decision of the Registrar under section 341; or to bring proceedings before the Registrar under sections 342 and 343.

In the Indian case of *PR Ramakrishnan and Others v A. Mounaguruswami*[14] the issue that fell to be considered by the court was whether the registered (but not beneficial) owners could depose against the purported beneficial owners without making a declaration under section 187C (similar to section 123 of the Act) of the Indian Companies Act, 1956. It was held as follows:

> It would, therefore, not only be inadvisable, but also dangerous, for any court to accept the evidence of someone regarding the purchase of shares by third parties *benami*[15] for another and render any finding, because the holder of the shares will be greatly

[12] Approved by the House of Lords (present: Viscount Hailsham LC, Lord Blanesburgh, Lord Russell of Killowen, Lord Macmillan, and Lord Roche) in *IRC v Crossman* [1937] AC 26.
[13] Gates RB *Gates Company Law and Practice*...
[14] [1985 57 Comp Cas 477 Mad].
[15] In India, a *benami* is a transaction made in another person's name in order to avoid taxation or other legal sanctions.

prejudiced by any adverse finding rendered against him by the court. In fact, if a person holds a share *benami* for another and fails to disclose it, he becomes punishable under section 187C(5) for contravention of section 187C(1). The punishment is as high a fine which may extend to one thousand rupees for every day during which the failure continues. Having regard to the serious nature of the offence and the penalty provided for it, it would be highly improper for any court to render a finding against anyone that he is holding shares in a company *benami* for another, on the evidence of some other shareholder or shareholders ... Sub-ss. (1) and (2) of section 187C are of such a nature that a court cannot act on the unilateral statement of either party along in court against the other without making a declaration under section 187C(1) or (2), for it will lead to unhealthy practices by the shareholders and directors of a company.

The foregoing notwithstanding, section 123(9) provides that '[n]othing in [section 123] shall prejudice the obligation of a company to pay dividends to its members in accordance with this Act and the obligation shall, on such payment, stand discharged'.

7.3   Beneficial ownership of shares

7.3.1   General

The Registrar is obliged under section 124(1) to 'ensure that the beneficial ownership of shares is known, ascertained and verified before the shares can be registered and transacted in'. In terms of section 124(2), '[w]here the Registrar, considers it necessary to ascertain and verify the beneficial ownership of a share or class of shares of a company, the Registrar may serve on the company a notice to furnish the Registrar, within a period specified in the notice, specified information with regard to the beneficial ownership of the share'.

The foregoing procedure would appear to guard against the sought of issues that came before court in *Pan Electronics Limited and Savvas Panayiotides and Others v Andereas Miltiadous and Others*.[16] The 1st appellant was owner of a company which he ran with the respondents as his employees. In the course of time, the 1st appellant had to leave the country for Cyprus because he ran into trouble with the government of Zambia. Before he left, he was advised by a lawyer that he should form another company with the respondents as shareholders to which he agreed. Later the respondents filed a petition for winding up of the company. High Court Judge who determined that the

---

[16] [1988] SJ 1 (ZMSC).

Respondents were beneficial owners of the shares they hold in Pan Electronics Limited and that their petition for the winding-up of the company should be upheld on the ground that it was just and equitable so to do. A major issue at the trial was whether or not the Respondents were the beneficial owners of the shares registered in their names or if in fact, as was contended by the appellants, they were simply nominees and held the shares in trust for the first appellant.

The Court observed that that an examination of the return of allotments filed with the Registrar was not a relevant method in deciding a question of fact which could only be received on the basis of the evidence tendered by the parties. Additionally, that it is inappropriate to raise questions of beneficial ownership in shares in a winding-up petition and the better approach may be to stand over the petition while the ownership question is determined in proceedings constituted in the ordinary way. It further held:

(i)   Where there is a relationship of trust and confidence, and inexplicably large gifts are made, the presumption of undue influence will be rebuttable only on proof of full, free and informed thought on the part of the donor.

(ii) The Respondents were and continue to be nominees.

(iii) It was not just and equitable to wind up the company at the instance of the nominees over the wishes of their beneficiary, the principal and true owner.

Section 124(3) makes reference to the provisions of section 329 'as far as possible', 'applying as if the enquiry provided for in [section124](1), were an investigation conducted in accordance with that section'.'A person who fails to comply with a notice provided for in [section 124](2) commits an offence'.[17]

7.3.2   *Maintenance of share and beneficial ownership register*

7.3.2.1   *Company to maintain a share and beneficial ownership*

In terms of section 195(1), '[a] company shall maintain a share and beneficial ownership register, in any form and manner, that records the shares issued by the company and states—

(a) whether, under the articles or terms of issue of the shares, there are any restrictions or limitations on the transfer; and

(b) where the inspection of any document that contains the restrictions or limitations may be done'.

According to section 195(2), [t]he share and beneficial ownership register shall state, with respect to each class of shares, the—

(a) names and the latest known address of each person who is, or has within the last ten years been, a shareholder or a beneficial owner;

---

[17] Section 124(4).

(b)   number of shares of that class held by each shareholder or a beneficial
        owner within the last ten years;

(c)   the nature of the associated voting rights of the shares in respect of
        beneficial owners; and

(d)   date of any—
   (i)   issue of shares to;
   (ii)   repurchase or redemption of shares from; or
   (iii) transfer of shares by or to; each shareholder within the last ten
          years, and in relation to the transfer, the name of the transferor
          or transferee'. The Act allows '[a]n agent of the company' to
          'maintain the share and beneficial ownership register of the
          company'.[18] Failure by a company to comply with subsections
          (1) and (2), means 'the company commits an offence.

7.3.2.2 *Directors' duty to supervise share and beneficial ownership register*

The board of directors is obliged under section 198(1) to take reasonable steps
to ensure that the share and beneficial ownership register is properly kept and
that matters to be recorded therein are promptly entered on it in accordance with
section 195'. It is an offence for a director to fail to comply with subsection
(1).[19]

7.3.3   *Those to be entered on beneficial register*

In terms of section 200, '...a notice of a trust, express, implied or constructive,
shall be entered in the share and beneficial ownership register and lodged with
the Registrar'. By section 201(1), a personal representative—

(a)   whose name is registered in the share and beneficial ownership register
        of a company as the holder of a share in that company; or

(b)   beneficially entitled to a share in a company, with the consent of the
        company; is entitled to be registered as the holder of that share as
        personal representative'.

However, in terms of section 200(2), '[t]he registration of an assignee, executor,
or administrator in terms of this section, shall not constitute notice of a trust
despite anything contrary'.

Section 202 provides for the entry of the assignee of a bankrupt on the
registered. Specifically, section 202(1) provides that despite any provisions to
the contrary, 'an assignee of the property of a bankrupt is entitled to be registered
as the holder of a share held by the bankrupt'. By section 202(2), '[t]he assignee
of the property of a bankrupt beneficially entitled to a share in a company shall,
with the consent of the company and the registered holder of that share, be

---

[18] Section 195(3).
[19] Section 191(2).

entitled to be registered as the holder of the share as the assignee of the property of the bankrupt'.

7.3.4   Power of court to rectify share register

Section 199 gives the High Court power to rectify the share register. Specifically, section 199(1) provides that '[w]here the share and beneficial ownership register of a company has an error and the company fails to correct the error within reasonable time, after it is brought to the attention of the company, or the error causes loss to a person'. However, the court will not act unless and until the person aggrieved or a shareholder of the company makes an application to the Court for—

(a)   rectification of the share and beneficial ownership register;

(b)   compensation for loss sustained as a result of the error; or

(c)   both rectification and compensation.

In terms of section 199(2), upon such application, '[t]he Court may decide on a question—

(a)   relating to the entitlement of a party to the application to have the applicant's name entered in, or omitted from, the share register; and

(b)   for rectification of the register'.

7.3.5   Place of share and beneficial ownership register

According to section 196(1), '[a] company may, if expressly permitted by its articles, divide its share and beneficial ownership register into two or more registers which may be kept in different places'. By section 196(2), '[t]he principal register[20] shall be kept at the company's registered office'.

Section 196(3)[21] provides that, [w]here a share and beneficial ownership register is divided into two or more registers kept in different places—

(a)   otice of the place where each register is kept shall be lodged with the Registrar within fourteen days after the share register is divided or the place where a register is kept is altered;

(b)   a copy of every register shall be kept at the same place as the principal register; and

(c)   if an entry is made in a register other than the principal register, a corresponding entry shall be made, within fourteen days, in the copy of the register kept with the principal register.

---

[20] In terms of section 196(4), "principal register" means, if the share and beneficial ownership register is—
(a) not divided into two or more registers, the share and beneficial ownership register; and (b) divided into two or more registers, the register described as the principal register in the last notice sent to the Registrar.

[21] In terms of section 196(5), '[i]f a company fails to comply with subsection (2) or subsection (3), the company and every director of the company commit an offence'.

7.4   Statement of shareholder's rights

The premise for this discussion is section 187. In terms of section 187(1), [t]he board of directors shall issue to a shareholder, on request, a statement that sets out the—

(a)   class of shares held by the shareholder, the total number of shares of that class issued by the company, and the number of shares of that class held by the shareholder;

(b)   rights, privileges, conditions and limitations, including restrictions on transfer and attaching to shares held by the shareholder; and

(c)   relationship of the shares held by the shareholder to other classes of shares.

By section 187(5), '[i]f the board of directors fails to comply with subsection (1), every director of the company commits an offence and shall be liable, on conviction, to a fine not exceeding one hundred thousand penalty units'.

According to section 187(2), [t]he board of directors is not obliged to provide a shareholder with a statement if—

(a)   a statement has been provided within the previous six months;

(b)   the shareholder has not acquired or disposed of shares since the previous statement was provided;

(c)   the rights attached to shares of the company have not been altered since the previous statement was provided; and

(d)   there are special circumstances that make it reasonable for the board to refuse the request.

In terms of section 187(3), '[a] statement issued in accordance with this section, is not evidence of title to the shares or matters set out in it'. By section 187(4), '[a] statement issued in accordance with this section, shall state in a prominent place that it is not evidence of title to the shares or of the matters set out in it'.

7.5   Liability of shareholders

In terms of section 125(1), 'a shareholder is not liable for an obligation of the company by reason only of being a shareholder; and 'the liability of a shareholder, to the company, is limited to any amount unpaid on a share held by the shareholder[22] as demonstrated in the case of *Re European Society Arbitration Acts*[23] where under a deed of settlement which provided that every instrument whereby the company became liable to pay money should contain a clause limiting the liability of shareholders to the amount payable on their shares. The other common law position can be derived from the definition of a share by Farewell J. in *Borland's Trustee v Steel*[24] wherein he said that 'a share

---

[22] See *Borland's Trustees v Steel* [1901] 1 Ch 279 at 288.

[23] [1878] 8 Ch D 679.

[24] [1901] 1 Ch 279 at 288.

is not a sum of money...but is an interest measured by a sum of money and made up of various rights contained in the contract, including the right to a sum of money of a more or less amount'.[25] The fact that this imports limited liability as described in section 125(1)(i) cannot be doubted and is settled at common law.

Section 125 provides further, that liability of shareholder will arise where such liability is expressly provided for in the articles; the liability arises by reason of the shareholder exercising powers, or carrying out the duties of a director, as provided in the Act; or 'other incidental liability'.[26] Be that as it may, in terms of section 125(2), '[n]othing in this section shall affect the liability of a shareholder to a company under a contract, including a contract for the issue of shares, or for any tort or other actionable wrong committed by the shareholder'.

7.6   Liability of former shareholders

A former shareholder who, while a member, was liable 'to the company in respect of any amount unpaid on the shares' held by that former shareholder or any liability provided for in the articles, cannot, by virtue of ceasing to be a shareholder be absolved of his responsibility or liability 'until the amount or liability has been fully paid or discharged'.[27] It would appear that the same principle applies to liability of a person ceasing to be shareholder before shareholders' liability becomes unlimited provided for under section 127. He will, according to that section, be liable 'to the same extent as if the liability of the shareholders had remained limited'. A recent American case demonstrates this point in rather detailed and clear fashion:

In *William Scott Stuart, Jr., Transferee, et al., v Commissioner of International Revenue*[28] William Stuart, Arnold Walters Jr., James Stuart Jr., and Robert Joyce (the taxpayers) were the shareholders of Little Salt Development Co. (Little Salt), a Nebraska C corporation. Little Salt owned 160 acres of saline wetlands on the outskirts of Lincoln, Neb., that it sold to the City of Lincoln on June 11, 2003, for $472,000. After it sold the land, Little Salt's only asset was cash. Little Salt realized a gain of $432,148 on the land sale, and, after the sale, the company did not engage in any business activity.

The taxpayers then entered into an agreement to sell their stock in Little Salt to MidCoast Investments Inc. for a price equal to the cash held by Little Salt on the date of sale closing reduced by 64.92% of the company's combined state and federal corporate income tax liability for its current tax year (i.e., its tax liability related to the sale of the land). As part of the transaction, Little Salt was

---

[25] Approved by the House of Lords (present: Viscount Hailsham LC, Lord Blanesburgh, Lord Russell of Killowen Lord Macmillan and Lord Roche) in *IRC v Crossman* [1937] AC 26.

[26] Section 125(ii)(iii)(iv).

[27] Section 126(1).

[28] 144 TC NO 12. The facts are as summarised in Beavers J A 'Former Shareholders Held Liable for Corporate Tax Debt' retrieved from http;//www.thetaxadviser.com on 14/01/2018.

required to transfer on or before the closing date its cash on hand (which was not to be less than $467,721) to MidCoast's attorneys' trust account.

MidCoast agreed to "cause" Little Salt to file its returns for 2003 and to pay its federal and state tax liabilities arising from the land sale. According to their later testimony in Tax Court, before they signed off on the sale agreement, none of the taxpayers made any real effort to understand the terms of the agreement, and none of them knew why MidCoast was purchasing Little Salt or what it planned to do with the corporation after the purchase.

Pursuant to the sale agreement, on Aug. 7, 2003, the attorney for the taxpayers wired the cash held by Little Salt at that time ($467,721) to MidCoast's attorney, and minutes later MidCoast's attorney wired back to the taxpayers the agreed-upon purchase price for the stock ($358,826, or the total cash reduced by 64.92% of Little Salt's tax liability). The following day, the taxpayers' attorney distributed the cash from the purchase to them pro rata. MidCoast's attorney distributed the cash transferred to him from Little Salt to an account in the name of Little Salt and on the next day to an account held by MidCoast. Little Salt treated the transfer of funds on its books at the end of its fiscal year on Sept. 30, 2003, as a shareholder loan of $327,000, with the remainder of the money transferred apparently representing payment of operational expenses and fees to MidCoast.

On Dec. 15, 2003, Little Salt filed its 2003 Form 1120, *U.S. Corporation Income Tax Return*. It reported taxable income of $432,148, total tax of $146,930, and tax due of $148,456. No payment was made with the return. The company reported on Schedule L, "Balance Sheets per Books," that, as of the end of the year, it had cash of $278, a loan of $467,000 due from MidCoast, and no other assets; it reported no liabilities.

On Feb. 18, 2005, Little Salt filed its 2004 Form 1120. It reported interest income of $1,739, a bad debt deduction of $450,370 resulting from the worthlessness of the shareholder loan, and, taking into account certain other deductions, negative taxable income of $483,970. It reported no gross receipts or cost of goods sold. The bad debt deduction produced a net operating loss that Little Salt carried back to, and deducted for, 2003. It reported on Schedule L that, as of the end of the year, it had trade notes and accounts receivable of $903 and no liabilities.

The IRS examined Little Salt's 2003 and 2004 returns and disallowed both the 2004 bad debt deduction and the loss carried back to, and deducted for, 2003. On Oct. 5, 2007, the IRS determined a deficiency in Little Salt's 2003 federal income tax of $145,923 and an accuracy-related penalty of $58,369. The IRS later issued Little Salt a notice of deficiency for these amounts. Little Salt did not challenge the notice, and the IRS assessed the deficiency; however, it was unable to collect the amounts assessed from Little Salt.

The IRS, after it failed to collect the tax due from Little Salt, sent the taxpayers notices of transferee liability in November 2010. In the notices, the IRS recast the transaction by which the shareholders disposed of their shares in Little Salt as a liquidating distribution of all of Little Salt's cash to its shareholders in redemption of its outstanding shares, followed by the shareholders' payment of a portion of that cash to MidCoast as an accommodation fee for its participation in the assumed sale. The taxpayers in turn petitioned the Tax Court, disputing the deficiency the IRS claimed Little Salt owed and their liability for any amount owed as transferees of Little Salt's assets.

Sec. 6901 Transferee Liability: Sec. 6901 provides that the liability, at law or in equity, of a transferee of property "shall . . . be assessed, paid, and collected in the same manner and subject to the same provisions and limitations as in the case of the taxes with respect to which the liabilities were incurred." Sec. 6901(h) provides that the term "transferee" includes "donee, heir, legatee, devisee, and distributee." However, Sec. 6901 only provides the mechanism through which the IRS may collect unpaid taxes owed by a transferor; whether a basis exists for holding a transferee liable for a transferor's debts is determined under the applicable state or federal law.

The IRS argued that, in determining whether under Sec. 6901 it could use administrative procedures to collect Little Salt's unpaid 2003 tax liability from the taxpayers, the Tax Court should engage in a two-step analysis. First, it said, the court should determine under federal law whether the transaction that gave rise to the liability was properly characterized and whether the recipients were transferees under Sec. 6901(h). If the court recasts the transaction or otherwise disregards it under federal tax law and finds that the recipients were transferees in the first step, it should then determine under state law whether the transferees received fraudulent transfers.

The IRS contended that under federal tax law the transaction by the taxpayers, Little Salt, and MidCoast was a sham transaction that should be recharacterised as a liquidation of Little Salt and that under Nebraska corporate law and Nebraska's version of the Uniform Fraudulent Transfer Act (UFTA), the IRS could collect Little Salt's liability from the taxpayers as its shareholders.

The taxpayers argued that under the applicable state law, they were not liable for Little Salt's debts because none of the proceeds of the land sale were ever transferred directly to them. Further, they claimed it would be improper to recharacterise the overall transaction as a redemption of their shares because they did not know that MidCoast would never pay Little Salt's taxes on the land sale.

The Tax Court held that the taxpayers were liable as transferees for the taxes owed by Little Salt. However, in making its decision, it rejected, based on its own precedent, that the IRS's two-step analysis should be applied to the case. Rather, it looked first at whether a state law basis existed for transferee liability for the taxpayers and then at whether the taxpayers were transferees for purposes of Sec. 6901.

With respect to whether it should use the IRS's two-step analysis, the Tax Court found that this method of analysis was foreclosed by its decision in *Swords Trust*, 142 T.C. 317 (2014). In addition to the reasons set out in that case, the court offered an additional reason for rejecting the analysis because the IRS had, since that case, persisted in pushing its arguments for using the two-step analysis.

The Tax Court explained that the purpose of the change in the law in Sec. 6901 was to provide for the enforcement of third-party liability to the IRS by the procedures already in existence for the enforcement of tax deficiencies. The procedures were to be effective against a transferee of property of the taxpayer without in any way changing the extent of the transferee's liability under existing law. Also, nothing in the statute was to afford the IRS any rights it would not have if it sought to enforce a tax liability through judicial mechanisms outside of Sec. 6901. The court noted that if the IRS cannot fix the liability on the transferee without invoking Sec. 6901, it cannot use Sec. 6901 to obtain a different result. Thus, transferee liability must exist under applicable state or federal law before Sec. 6901 is considered.

Having concluded that it must first determine whether there was a basis under state or federal law for the IRS's claim that the taxpayers were liable for Little Salt's taxes, the Tax Court analyzed Little Salt's transfer of its cash to MidCoast's lawyer under the Nebraska version of the UFTA (Neb. Rev. Stat. §§36-701 through 36-712). In particular, the court evaluated whether Little Salt, a debtor of the IRS for the taxes on its land sale, made the transfer "without receiving a reasonably equivalent value in exchange for the transfer," which, pursuant to Nebraska Revised Statutes Sections 36-705(a)(2) and 36-706(a), was constructively fraudulent with respect to the IRS as a creditor of Little Salt. After identifying the requirements of these two statutes and reviewing the transactions, the court found that under the Nebraska UFTA, the transfer of funds to MidCoast's lawyer was constructively fraudulent with respect to the IRS.

Because the transfer was fraudulent, the court further found that under the Nebraska UFTA, the transfer was voidable and that the IRS could have the transfer voided and could recover the amount necessary to satisfy its claim (i.e., the tax and penalties owed due to the land sale, which were $145,923 and $58,369, respectively). However, with respect to the taxpayers, the court determined that they were only liable for the benefit they received from the transfer, which the court concluded was the difference between the after-tax amount they would have received if they had simply liquidated Little Salt and the amount that they received in the sale of their shares to MidCoast. This was a very favourable finding for the taxpayers, as the court calculated that this amount was only $58,842.

Finally, the Tax Court considered whether the taxpayers were transferees for purposes of Sec. 6901. After reviewing the applicable precedent, the court said that "[t]he determinative factor is liability to a creditor (the Commissioner) for the debt of another under a State fraudulent conveyance, transfer, or similar law." Since it had found that the shareholders were collectively liable for $58,842 as persons for whose benefit Little Salt transferred its cash holdings to MidCoast, it accordingly concluded that the taxpayers were transferees within the meaning of Sec. 6901.

We must note however, that in terms of section 126(2), '[a] former shareholder is not liable, as specified in [section 126](1), for any debt or liability of the company contracted after ceasing to be a shareholder'. *Starnes v CIR*[29] in which the taxpayers were held not to be liable for corporate taxes as transferees after selling their stock to MidCoast demonstrates this point. In that case, the Tax Court held, and the Fourth Circuit affirmed, that the IRS had failed to prove an independent substantive basis for liability for the taxpayers under the applicable North Carolina fraudulent transfer law. As the Tax Court pointed out, a crucial distinction between the this case and *William Scott Stuart*[30] in determining whether the taxpayers were liable as transferees was that the agreement between the taxpayers and MidCoast in *Starnes* obligated MidCoast, after the stock sale closed, to return the cash its attorney received before closing from the corporation being sold, whereas the Little Salt agreement was silent on this point.

7.7   Shareholders not required to acquire shares by alteration to articles

Evershed MR has observed in *Greenhalgh v Arderne Cinemas*[31] that '… when a man comes into a company, he is not entitled to assume that the articles will always remain in a particular form'.[32]A company may subject to the provisions of the Act or to the provisions in the articles of association, amend its articles of

---

[29] 680 F.3d 417 (4th Cir. 2012), EWCAs for the Fourth Circuit. Except for a few marginal additions, the facts are as summarised in Beavers J A 'Former Shareholders Held Liable for Corporate Tax Debt' retrieved from http://www.thetaxadviser.com on 14/01/2018.

[30] 144 TC NO 12.

[31] [1951] Ch 286.

[32] In the case of *Russell v Northern Bank Development Corporation Ltd* [1992] 1WLR 588; [1992] 2 All ER 161, the House of Lords held *inter alia* that 'the company's agreement that it would not increase its capital without the consent of each of the shareholders was unenforceable as being contrary to art 131 of the Companies (Northern Ireland) Order 1986 because it amounted to an undertaking not to exercise its statutory powers for a period which could last for as long as anyone of the parties to the agreement remained a shareholder and after the control of the company had passed to other shareholders and, as such, was as obnoxious as if it had been contained in the articles of association. It followed that company's undertaking was unenforceable….'

association by passing a special resolution (3/4 majority).[33] As shown in *Allen v Gold Reefs of West Africa Ltd*[34] the power to pass resolutions is reposed in its members. Once a company has passed a special resolution approving the amendment of its articles, it must within 21 days lodge a copy of the resolution together with a copy of the amended articles. As already discussed elsewhere in this text, there are restrictions relating to the alteration of articles. For example, the provisions of the articles notwithstanding, a shareholder is, in terms of section 128, not under any obligation to act in accordance with an amendment of the articles that *(a)* requires the shareholder to acquire or hold more shares in the company than the number held on the date the amendment takes effect; or *(b)* increases the liability of the shareholder to the company, unless the shareholder agrees, in writing, to be bound by the amendment, before or after it is made'.

Lindley MR has opined in *Allen v Gold Reefs*[35] that the court has jurisdiction to regard an alteration of the articles as invalid unless it is made for the company as a whole, that is, the whole body of members. Using an objective approach assuming, rightly it may appear, that those managing the company know better than the court. The significance of this approach is that it hints to most alterations being declared valid. This however is not always the case. It would appear from case law[36] that the focal point of court decisions has been on the rules relating to the interpretation of the articles of association under consideration and which have birthed the dispute before court.

Primarily, the rules of interpretation are those relating to the law of contract. The main principle of construction known as the *contra proferentem* rule provides that clauses will be construed strictly against those who crafted them and who now seek to rely on them. Additionally, rather than looking at individual clauses, the Court will seek to look at the whole document in order to draw the full and relevant meaning of the articles in question. As noted already however, articles, among other things, constitute a special contract said to be such as it is codified under section 17[37] and subject to the statutory limitations contained in the Act and individual provisions in the articles of association as they stand.[38]

A useful case in this regard is *Scott v Frank F Scott (London)*.[39] In that case three brothers were the registered holders of all the shares in a private company. They were also the directors of the company and the signatories of the articles

---

[33] Section 27 of the Act, formerly under section 8 of CA 1994.

[34] [1900] I Ch 656.

[35] See section 203.

[36] See: *Punt v Symons & Co Ltd* [1903] 2 Ch 506; *Greenhalgh v Arderne Cinemas Ltd and Others* [1951] Ch 286; *Allen v Gold Reefs of West Africa Ltd* [1900] 1 Ch 656; *Clemens v Clemens Bros Ltd*[1976] 2 All ER 268; *Dafen Tinplate Co Ltd vs. Llanelly Steel Co(1907) Ltd* [1920] 2 Ch 124; *Sidebottom v Kershaw, Leese & Co* [1920] 1 Ch 154; *Shuttleworth v Cox Bros & Co Ltd* [1927] 2 KB 9; *Northern Counties Securities Ltd v Jackson & Steeple Ltd* [1974] 1WLR 1133; and *Puddephatt v Leith* [1916] 1 Ch 200.

[37] Previously section 21 under CA 1994.

[38] A similar provision in the UK CA 2006 is section 33.

[39] [1940] 3 All ER 508; [1940] Ch 794 CA.

of association. One of the brothers died, and his widow was his sole executrix. She claimed that they were entitled to acquire the shares at par, or, alternatively, rectification of the articles so as to give them that right. Article 11 provided that no share should be transferred to a person who was not a member, and article 18 provided that all ordinary shares of deceased member should be offered to the principal shareholders. It was held (i) upon the proper construction of the articles of association, the widow was entitled to be registered as the holder of the ordinary shares standing in the name of the deceased brother and (ii) the court has no jurisdiction to rectify articles of association, signatories at the time when they were entered into.[40]

7.8   Liability of personal representative and assignee

7.8.1   Liability of personal representative

This is provided for under section 129, the liability of a personal representative of the estate of a deceased person, who is registered as the holder of a share comprised in the estate, shall not, in respect of that share, exceed the proportional amount available from the assets of the estate, after satisfaction of prior claims, for distribution among creditors of the estate.

7.8.2   Liability of assignee

The term '"assignee" is in terms of section 130(2), [said to mean one] in whom the property of a bankrupt is vested pursuant to the Bankruptcy, Act'.[41] 'The liability of an assignee of the property of a bankrupt, who is registered as the holder of a share which is comprised in the property of the bankrupt, shall not, in respect of that share, exceed the proportional amount available from the property of the estate of the bankrupt, after satisfaction of prior claims, for distribution among creditors of the estate, being property of the bankrupt which, at the time when demand is made for the satisfaction of the liability, is vested in the assignee'.[42]

7.9   Power to acquire shares of minority on takeover[43]

7.9.1   General

It has been said in in *Lake Kariba Boating Services Ltd v Kariba North Bank Company Limited*[44] that 'one company can acquire complete control over the

---

[40] Approving *Evans v Chapman* [1902] 86 LT 381.
[41] Chapter 82 of the laws of Zambia.
[42] Section 130(1).
[43] This subject should be considered within the context of Part XI: Sections 131-136 of the Securities Act No 41 of 2016 and Part IV: sections 24-37 of the Competition and Consumer Protection Act No 24 of 2010.
[44] [1982] ZR 35 (SC).

assets of another company by the acquisition from the shareholders of the whole of the issued share capital of the company whose assets it is sought to control.'[45] In this section we therefore set out and explore the provisions relating to take-overs and how minorities are protected during this process.

The provisions relating to the procedure as respects the power to acquire shares of a minority as described in *Lake Kariba Boating*[46] are set out in section 132.[47] It is safe to proceed on the basis that this section is inapplicable to companies whose securities are either traded or listed on any securities exchange also known as Plcs.[48] This is because such are registered with the Securities and Exchange Commission. Therefore, in terms of section 131(1) of the Securities Act,[49] '[n]otwithstanding any other written law, every merger or take-over of listed companies or companies whose securities are registered with the Commission shall be subject to this Part'.[50]

However, by section 131(2), '[a]n approval of a merger or take-over by the Commission in accordance with this Part shall not relieve a listed company from complying with any other applicable law'. This part of the section references the need to comply with the requirements of sections 24 to 37 under the Competition and Consumer Protection Act[51] and not the Act not only because this is clear from the margin but also because the Act subjects itself[52] to the Securities Act on this and other matters where there is conflict as it does to the Constitution and the Banking and Financial Services Act.[53]

The rationale for this process otherwise and widely known as a mandatory offer is that a certain threshold say 35 percent[54] once reached even though not giving a transferee company formal control will be sufficient to give the transferee company effective control.[55] A change of control is directly linked to the share price based on perception. This unavoidable result may lead minority shareholders to worry that the company will be run in line with the majority

---

[45] Coram: Ngulube DCJ, Muwo, JS and Bweupe Ag JS.

[46] [1982] ZR 35 (SC).

[47] This is a renumbering of section 237 under CA 1994 while retaining the same content.

[48] See *Chanda Mutoni & 7 Others v Bharti Airtel Zambia Holdings BV, Celtel Zambia Plc* 2011/HPC/013 4.

[49] No 41 of 2016.

[50] Which is why in terms of section 132 of the Securities Act No 41 of 2016, 132(1) '[a] person shall not make or pursue an offer in respect of a take-over or substantial acquisition of the securities of any listed company or company whose securities are registered with the Commission except in accordance with this Act and the conditions and procedures prescribed by regulations made in accordance with this Act.

[51] No 24 of 2010.

[52] See section 5 of the Act discussed elsewhere within the text in this respect.

[53] No 7 of 2017.

[54] See Securities (Takeover and Mergers) Rules of the Securities Act Cap 354 (Statutory Instrument number 170 of 1993); see application *per* Chishimba J in *Chanda Mutoni & 7 Others v Bharti Airtel Zambia Holdings BV, Celtel Zambia Plc* 2011/HPC/0134.

[55] See *Philip Morris Products Inc. v Rothmans International Enterprises (No 2)* [2000] The Times, 10 August where the EW HC applied the 30 percent mandatory offer bid rule.

shareholder's wishes. For this reason, the provisions in section 132 are designed, in theory at least, to afford the minority shareholders an opportunity to sale out at the price the majority shareholder paid out before assuming control.[56]

Section 132(1) specifically stipulates in what instances the provisions under section 132 as a whole will apply, that is to say 'where a transferee company[57] makes an offer to shareholders in a transferor company[58] and the following conditions are satisfied:

(a) the offer by the transferee company is made to all the shareholders in the transferor company, other than those shares already held by the transferee company, its related companies or its nominees, for the transferee company or any of its related companies;

(b) the consideration for the acquisition or a substantial part of the consideration, is an allotment of shares in the transferee company or, at the option of the holders, a payment of cash;

(c) the same terms are offered to all the shareholders to whom the offer is made or, where there are different classes of shares, to all shareholders of the same class;

(d) the notice of the offer sent to the shareholders includes a—

    (i) description of the effect of this section;

    (ii) statement that, if paragraph *(e)* is satisfied, the transferee company intends to take advantage of this section; and

    (iii) statement that a shareholder may apply to the Court, in accordance with subsection (4); and

(e) within four months after making the offer, the offer has been accepted in respect of sufficient shares in each class to make up, together with any shares held by the transferee company, ninety percent of the shares of that class'.

7.9.2   *Compulsory acquisition*

We must now turn to the issue of compulsory acquisition. '[W]here section 132(1) applies, the transferee company may, 'within sixty days from when [section132](1) is satisfied, give to each shareholder who has not accepted the offer, in respect of all of that member's shares, a notice in the prescribed form stating that—

(a) the company intends to acquire that member's shares;

(b) if no action is taken by the shareholder, the shares shall be compulsorily acquired in accordance with this section; and

---

[56] 'Mandatory Offer' http://moneyterms.co.uk retrieved on 15/01/2018.

[57] In terms of section 132(b), '"Transferee Company" means a company to which an interest in shares is conveyed'.

[58] In terms of section 132(b), '"Transferor Company" means a company that conveys an interest in shares'.

(c)   if the offer consists of alternatives, the alternatives shall apply, unless the shareholder directs otherwise'.[59]

'A copy of the notice, referred to in section 132(2), shall be sent to the shareholder and the transferor company'.[60] Following this, '[t]he shareholder may, within the period beginning when the offer is made and ending ninety days after [section 132](1) is satisfied, apply to the Court for an order—

(a)   prohibiting the compulsory acquisition of shares pursuant to this section; or

(b)   that the terms of the offer applying to the shareholder, in respect of the shares or of the shares of a particular class, be varied as the Court directs'.[61]

Where an application is made in terms of section 132(4), [t]he transferee company shall—

(a)   where the Court makes an order that the terms of the offer shall be varied, give notice of the varied terms to all other shareholders of the same class and, within sixty days after receiving the notice, a shareholder of that class shall be entitled to accept the original offer or the offer as varied by the Court; or

(b)   where a shareholder does not accept an offer on the acquisition day, within seven days after the acquisition day, send to the transferor company a share transfer instrument executed—

 (i)   on behalf of the shareholder by a person appointed by the transferee company; and

 (ii)   by the transferee company on its own behalf; and shall transfer to the transferor company, the consideration payable by the transferee company for the shares, and the transferor company shall register the transferee company as the holder of those shares.[62]

The procedure set out in section 132(2)-(5) is meant to protect minority shareholders so as to allow for minorities to opt out of a company whose effective control by a majority shareholder will leave them with no say in the operations and direction of the company in question. At the same time it is meant to allow compulsory acquisition as long as all the rules have been followed by the offeree company. The tenor of section 132(4) appears to suggest that '[t]he court will seldom interfere if the offer is fair but will not allow [section 132] to be used for

---

[59] Section 132(2).

[60] Section 132(3).

[61] Section 132(4)

[62] Section 132(5); In terms of section 132(6), '...acquisition day" shall be the day—*(a)* ninety days after subsection (1) is satisfied; or *(b)* on which the last of any applications made in accordance with subsection (4), is disposed of; whichever occurs later'.

improper purposes such as the expulsion of a minority'.[63] The following cases demonstrate this. We start with a case that was decided on the interpretation of section 237 CA 1994, the precursor to section 132.

In *Chanda Mutoni & 7 Others v Bharti Airtel Zambia Holdings BV, Celtel Zambia Plc*[64] the facts of the case as disposed by the applicants were that on the 8 June 2011 Bharti Airtel International (Netherlands) BV, a company incorporated in the Netherlands, using its wholly owned subsidiary the 1st respondent herein acquired 78.9 percent shares in the 2nd respondent, a company listed on the Lusaka Securities Exchange. The 1st respondent thereafter made a mandatory offer on the 22nd November, 2010, to acquire the shares of all the other shareholders in the 2nd respondent company pursuant to and in accordance with clause 56 of the third schedule of the Securities (Takeover and Mergers) Rules, Statutory Instrument No. 170 of 1993 under the Securities Act Chapter 354 of the Laws of Zambia.[65]

The applicants were minority fully paid up registered holders of about 139,000,000 ordinary shares of nominal value of K1 each in the capital of the 2nd respondent.

On the 18 February 2011, the respondent issued a notice for compulsory acquisition of ordinary shares in the 2nd respondent held by the minority shareholders. The Applicants refused to accept the Mandatory offer made pursuant to Section 237(2) of the CA 1994. The terms of the mandatory offer and the acquisition notice was at a consideration of K710.00 cash per share. According to the applicants clause 58(1) of the 3rd schedule to the Securities (Takeover and Mergers) Rules of the Securities Act Cap 354 (Statutory Instrument number 170 of 1993) (Takeover and Mergers Rules), the offers should have been at a value of not less than the highest price paid by the 1st Respondent or Bharti Airtel International (Netherlands) BV for the shares or voting rights in the 2nd Respondent Company within six (6) months.

It was stated that the respondents had provided inadequate information and not availed the applicants the price at which Bharti Airtel International purchased the shares in the 2nd respondent company making it difficult for them to make an informed decision.

The applicants state inter alia that the acquisition notice stated that having acquired more than ninety percent shares in the 2nd respondent, the 1st respondent was desirous of acquiring their shares under section 237(2) unless an application was made to this Court, the 1st respondent would be entitled and bound to acquire the applicants' shares on the stipulated terms.

The affidavit further disclosed that the mandatory offer made by the respondent under the Securities (Takeover and Mergers) Rules is mandatory

---

[63] Keenan D *Smith and Keenan Company Law*...502.

[64] 2011/HPC/0134.

[65] Repealed by Act No 41 of 2016.

to anyone acquiring more than thirty five percent shares in a Public Company. Further, the said mandatory offer does not require the 1st respondent or any person acting in concert with it such as Bharti Airtel International (Netherlands) to give the holders of shares in the 2nd respondent an option to acquire shares in the 1st respondent whereas under section 237 (1) of the CA 1994 there was such a requirement.

It was further stated that the 1st respondent did not offer to the applicants a statutory option to acquire shares in the 2nd respondent company as required by Section 237(1)(b) of the CA 1994. The said failure to comply with Section 237(1) by the 1st respondent rendered the subsequent acquisition notice impotent and invalid due to non-compliance.

The terms of the offer by the respondent were not fair and the applicants were opposed to the compulsory acquisition of their shares on grounds of non-compliance and in the alternative that the terms of the offer by the respondent ought to be varied by adjusting the value for each share upwards.

The main gist of the applicants' submission was that the option to acquire shares in the 1st respondent's company which was a pre-condition for compulsory acquisition under section 237 was not one of the terms of the offer. Therefore the 1st respondent could not take advantage of section 237 to compulsorily acquire shares of the minority and as such the compulsory notice for acquisition under section 237 was made in violation of the section and was invalid.

Chishimba J, rejecting arguments to the contrary by the respondents held as follows by:

(i)   As regards the issue of the option of allotment of shares, that the 1st respondent did not as a transferee company offer the applicants (the minority shareholders) the statutory option required under section 237(1)(b)(i)(ii) of CA 1994. The said requirements are mandatory requirements under compulsory acquisition. The purported choice given under the offer relates to the takeovers and mergers rules and did not apply under the compulsory acquisition made pursuant to the Companies Act.[66]

(ii)   As regards whether the value proposed under the offer conformed to statutory provisions, that in determining the above recourse is had to section 58(1) and section 56 of the 3rd schedule to the Securities (Takeovers and Mergers) Rules (Statutory Instrument No 170 of 1993) Chapter 354 of the Laws of Zambia. Clause 58 (1) sets the guidelines on how offers should be treated in terms of value that is; "Offers made under Clause fifty six must in respect of each class or equity share

---

[66] Agreeing with the holding in the *Re-Carlton Holdings Limited* [1971] ALL ER where it was stated that as much as a transferee company has the right to acquire other shares, the terms must be defined with some strictness.

capital involved, be in cash or be accompanied by a cash alternative at not less than the highest price paid by the offeror or any person acting in concert with it for voting rights of the offeree within the preceding six months". The Applicants were offered the value price of K710 per share. The 1st respondent had not complied with section 58(1). The price offered should not be less than the highest price paid by the 1st respondent for the shares acquired within the preceding six months. It was irrelevant and immaterial that other shareholders had consented to the terms of the offer or in this case the offer price of K710 per share.

(iii) As much as the Court agreed with the 1st respondent's argument that a transferee company ought not to be prevented from compulsorily acquiring the shares in question by a dissenting minority of 3 per cent Holders in Celtel Zambia Plc, the acquisition should have been in accordance with the Law by offering a fair price. In order for the applicants to consider whether the price offered was fair, adequate information relating to the price at which the 1st respondent acquired the shares in the 2nd respondent ought to be made available. The court rejected the argument that Zain (Z) Limited was purchased in a group of 14 companies across Africa and therefore it is not possible to particularize the price for Zain (Z) Limited or any other group calling it misconceived. Adding that it was possible to particularise the value of Zain (Z) Limited or to assess its value separate from the other companies across Africa.

Having taken into account all the evidence and authorities, Chishimba J came to the inescapable conclusion that the applicants had proved their case on a balance of probability. The Court applied its power under Section 237(4)[67] and gave the following Orders:

i)   That the terms of the compulsory acquisition notice in respect of the shares are hereby varied to the extent that a provision be included giving the applicants' herein the option of allotment of shares in the transferee company and or at the option of the holders, a payment of cash;

ii)   That the consideration price at which the 1st respondent acquired the shares in the 2nd respondent company be furnished to the applicants to enable them to determine whether to exercise the option for a cash consideration; and

iii) That the transferee company was to give the notice of the varied terms to the applicants within twenty one (21) days from date of the judgment.

In *Re Bugle Press Ltd*[68] the holders of 90 percent of the shares in a company formed a new company which made an offer for the shares of the old company.

---

[67] See section 132(5) of the Act.
[68] [1960] 3 All ER 791.

As was to be expected, 90 percent of the shareholders accepted the offer and the new company then served notice on the holder of the other 10 percent of the shares stating that it wished to purchase his holding. It was held by the EWCA that in substance the new company was the same as the majority shareholders, and the scheme was in effect an expropriation of the minority interest. According to Evershed, referring to section 429 (similar to section 132 of the Act), '[w] hat the section is directed to is a case where there is a scheme or contract for the acquisition of a company, its amalgamation, re-organisation or the like, and where the offeror is independent of the shareholders in the transferor company, or at least independent of that part or fraction of them from which the 90 percent is to be derived'.

In *Re Joseph Holt Plc Winpar Holdings Ltd v Joseph Holt Group Plc*[69] the EWHC ruled that section 429 (similar to section 132 of the Act), allows a bidder (offeree company) which holds 90 percent in shares in the offeror company (or victim) to compulsorily acquire the shares of the remaining member even though the said minority shareholders did not receive the offer documents.

Finally and in terms of section 132(7), '[a]ny sums received by the transferor company in accordance with subsection (5)*(b)*, shall be paid into a separate bank account, and any such sums and all shares or other consideration so received, shall be held by the transferor company in trust for the several persons entitled to them.

7.10   Rights of minority on takeover

Section 133 looks at the rights of minority on takeover from the perspective of the minority shareholder in that in terms of section 133(1), [a] transferee company is obliged to, where—

(a)   an offer is made to the shareholders of a company or to any of them for the purchase of their shares;

(b)   in pursuance of an offer, shares in the transferor company are transferred to another body corporate; and

(c)   after the transfer of shares, the transferee company holds more than seventy-five percent of the shares in the transferor company or in a class of those shares; within thirty days after the date of the transfer, give notice of that fact to the remaining shareholders of the company or the remaining shareholders of a particular class, as the case may be; and a shareholder may, within ninety days after receiving notice, require the transferee company to acquire all or any of that holder's shares.

The circumstances envisaged under section 133(1) are not different so far as the protection of shareholders is concerned. However, unlike section 132 where it is the offeree who is obliged to make a mandatory offer upon reaching the 35

---

[69] [2000] 97 (44), LSG 44. Appeal case available at www.lawtel.com, under case Law-CO100109.

percent shareholding threshold, in this particular case, the offeree company is obliged to accept the offer of shares by a minority shareholder within 90 days without the option of passing the offer should the offeree company bring itself within the purview of the instances mentioned under section 133(1). Here again as in section 132 the minority, shareholders can opt out of having shares in a company which will but in name only, be controlled by just one shareholder with them having no say.

Further and according to section 133(2), ...where a share is transferred to or held by a—

(a) company related to the transferee company; or

(b) nominee of the transferee company or of a related company to the transferee company; the share shall be considered to be transferred to, or held by, the transferee company.

By section 133(3), [t]he transferee company shall, where a shareholder requires the transferee company to acquire any shares as specified in [section 133](1), be bound to acquire those shares—

(a) on the terms of the offer or on such other terms as may be agreed; or

(b) in the manner as may be directed by the Court, where the transferee company or the shareholder applies to the Court for such an order.

7.11   Remedy against oppression of minority on takeover

The Court has the option, on the application of a member, to make an order, in accordance with section 134(3),[70] if it is satisfied that—

(a) the affairs of the company are being conducted, or the powers of the directors are being exercised, in a manner that is oppressive;

(b) an act or omission, or proposed act or omission, by or on behalf of the company has been done or is threatened, which was or is likely to be oppressive; or

(c) a resolution of the members, or any class of them, has been passed or is proposed which was or is likely to be oppressive.

A common theme in the foregoing is the term 'oppressive'. The term 'oppressive' is in terms of section 134(9) taken to mean one of two things:

(a) unfairly prejudicial to, or unfairly discriminatory against, a member or members of a company; or

(b) contrary to the interests of the members as a whole'.

An order made in accordance with section 134(1), 'may include the following:

(a) directing or prohibiting an act, or cancelling or varying a transaction or resolution;

(b) regulating the conduct of the affairs of a company;

---

[70] Section 134(3) provides that '[d]espite [the] Act, where the Court makes an order in accordance with subsection (1), which alters the share capital or articles, the company shall not, without leave of the Court, make any further alteration to the share capital or articles that is inconsistent with the order'.

(c)   purchasing of the shares of any members by any other member or by the company and, in the case of a purchase by the company, for the reduction of the company's capital accordingly;

(d)   winding up of the company; or

(e)   appointing a receiver of the property of the company'.[71]

It is an offence for any person to contravene an order, made in accordance with section 134. It makes such a person 'liable, on conviction, to a fine not exceeding one hundred thousand penalty units or to imprisonment for a period not exceeding twelve months, or to both'.[72]

7.12   Alteration of shareholder rights

A company is not allowed[73] to 'take any action that will affect the rights ascribed to shares, except where such action has received the approval by a special resolution of each interest group.[74] Section 136(2) stipulates that the rights devoted to a share include but are, by the tenor of the section, not limited to the…

(a)   rights, privileges, limitations, and conditions attached to the share by [the] Act or the articles, including voting rights and rights to distributions;

(b)   pre-emptive rights as provided in [the] Act;

(c)   right to have the procedure set out in…section [136] and any further procedure required by the articles for the amendment or alteration of rights observed by the company; and

(d)   right that a procedure required by the articles for the amendment or alteration of rights be not amended or altered.

Included in actions the company is proscribed from taking which may, according to section 136(1) affect the rights ascribed to shares, is 'the issue by a company of further shares ranking equally with, or in priority to, existing shares, whether

---

[71] Section 134(3). In terms of section 134(4), '[w]here the Court makes an order in accordance with subsection (2)*(d)*, the Corporate Insolvency Act, 2017 shall apply to the winding up, with the necessary modifications, as if the order had been made on an application by the company for winding up by the Court'. Further, in terms of section 134(5), '[a] company shall lodge, with the Registrar, a copy of an order altering a company's share capital or articles, within fifteen days of the order being made by the Court'. Additionally, according to section 134(6), '[t]he Registrar shall, where an order is lodged in accordance with subsection (5), issue a replacement certificate of share capital to the company, which shall be worded to meet the circumstances of the case'. Finally, in terms of section 134(8), '[i]f a company fails to comply with [section 134](5), the company and each officer in default commit an offence and is liable, on conviction, to a fine not exceeding six thousand penalty units for each day that the failure continues'.

[72] Section 134(7).

[73] Section 136(1).

[74] In terms of section 135(1), '[f]or purposes of [the] Act—*(a)* one or more interest groups may exist in relation to an action or proposal; and *(b)* shareholders in the same class may fall into two or more interest groups if—(i) action is taken in relation to some holders of shares in a class and not others; or (ii) a proposal expressly distinguishes between shareholders in a class'.

as to voting rights or distributions, shall be considered to be action affecting the rights attached to the existing shares....'[75]   The rationale behind this requires some further explanation.

The usual motivation for companies making what is referred to as a secondary offer (as opposed to an initial public offer (IPO)) is to raise more capital on the financial markets. Thus for Plcs, secondary issuance of shares is a more straight forward way of raising additional funds which they may use to deal with some difficulties or to finance further expansion of acquisitions. Be that as it may, secondary offerings have the tendency to dilute existing stock sending the share price lower and affecting the current shareholders' investments. This phenomenon may be explained as follows: Following an IPO, a company's shares trade on the open market with the perception and the company's performance affecting how buyers and sellers through the laws of demand and supply value a company's shares.

A company's current stock market share price sets what may be termed an upper limit so far as the amount the company can expect to get should it want to make a secondary offer. It follows that if the company's current share price is K10, it cannot ordinarily expect to sell the shares under a secondary offering for more than K10 for the simple reason that potential purchasers will simply purchase the shares on the open market instead of participating in the secondary offering.

To cajole buyers into taking part in the secondary offering, a company archetypally offers to sell its shares at a discount to the current market value. The consequence of this is that the price that buyers and sellers on the open market will be willing to pay for the shares will usually follow the discounted price of the new shares resulting into, as we indicated earlier, what is termed a dilution.[76] By way of example, if the company was initially valued at K15, 000.00 with 1, 000.00 shares valued at K15, in the event that the company does a secondary offering of another 1, 000 shares at K14 per share, what it will raise is K14, 000.00 in the secondary offering. The K14, 000 in cash would increase the value of the company to K29, 000, but there will now be 1, 000.00 shares outstanding. That works out to K14.50 per share, or a K0.50 reduction from the original price. It also means that the company's market capitalisation falls to K14, 500.00 down from the original K15, 000.00 before the secondary issue.

While dilution may not always result from a secondary offering, 'even the fear of potential dilution is often enough to send the share price downwards, at least temporarily. Shareholders need to be wary of secondary offerings to make sure they do not see their existing holdings lose too much value'.[77]

---

[75] Section 136(3).

[76] See discussion below on pre-emptive rights provided for under section 144 of the Act.

[77] The Motley Fool 'What Happens to the Share Price When New Shares Are Issued?' retrieved from http://www.fool.com on 15/01/2018.

For the foregoing reasons and the potential loss of value by shareholders from any secondary offerings, a secondary offering will only escape the purview of section 136(1) if 'the—

(a) articles expressly permit the issue of further shares ranking equally with, or in priority to, those shares; or

(b) issue is made in accordance with the pre-emptive rights of shareholders in accordance with this Act or the articles'.[78]

7.13   Shareholder requiring company to purchase shares

In terms of section 137, [a] shareholder is entitled to require a company to purchase shares where—

(a) an interest group has, in accordance with section 136(1),[79] approved, by special resolution, an action that affects the rights attached to the shares;

(b) the company becomes entitled to take the action, referred to in paragraph *(a)*, and a shareholder, who was a member of the interest group, casts all the votes attached to the shares registered in that shareholder's name; or

(c) a resolution approving an action was passed in accordance with section 77,[80] and a shareholder who was a member of the interest group did not sign the resolution.

7.14   Right of a shareholder to commence action

The principle in *Foss v Harbottle*[81] is that since the company is a separate legal entity and with an existence independent of its members, the rightful plaintiff in redressing a wrong against the company is the company and not any of its members.[82] However, section 138(1) provides that '[a] shareholder may commence an action against the company or a director for—

(a) breach of a duty owed by the company or director to the shareholder; or

(b) an illegal act done by the company or a director'.

Section 138(2) however provides limitations to matters amenable to member action by providing that '[a]n action may not be commenced as specified in subsection (1) (a), to recover any loss arising from a reduction in the value of shares of a company or failure of the shares to increase in value, by reason only of a loss suffered, or gain forgone, by the company'.

---

[78] Section 136(3).

[79] Which provides for the procedure for the alteration of shareholder rights'.

[80] Which provides for '[w]ritten resolutions for private companies'.

[81] [1843] 2 Hare 461, 67 ER 189.

[82] See *Edward v Halliwell* [1950] 2 All ER 1064, CA in which Jenkins LJ identified two limbs of the rule in *Foss*.

Suffice to say at this point that section 138 to the extent that it allows the shareholder to sue a director, like Part 11, Chapter 1 UK Companies Act 2006 (UK CA 2006),[83] provides the derivative claim with a statutory foothold and introduces a flexible legal framework which once only lay at common law.[84] Inexorably, it enables a shareholder to pursue an action in specific instances arising out of those mentioned and provided for under section 138. However, the ability of the shareholder to sue the company (which must be distinguished from his right to sue a director because a wrong against the company has been committed by a director due to his negligence, and in the process contravening the shareholder's) cannot, strictly speaking, be said to be within the *Foss* principle. The reason appears to be that what section 138 envisages is the right to sue arising not because a wrong has been committed against a company itself in which case the company would, generally speaking, be the rightful plaintiff, but because the company itself has breached a duty owed to the shareholder or has committed an illegal act for which section 138 gives the shareholder recourse against the company before a court of the law. The rationale seems to be that as in the case of a director who has or directors who have committed a wrong, it is difficult for a company to bring its wrong doing to the attention of the court of its own volition or to correct course once the wrong has been brought to its attention.

It is submitted that 138 ought to be read, where applicable, together with section 330 which provides for injunctive relief procedure. It may also be read with section 335 relating to actions by a member or former member for breach of duty against such a member or former member. It may further be read with section 336 which provides that '[a] member may bring an action against the company for breach of a duty owed by the company to the member'. In terms of section 330(1), '[t]he Court may, on the application of a person referred to in subsection (2), make an order restraining a company or a director from engaging in conduct that contravenes or would contravene the articles or the Act'. By section 330(2), '[f]or the purposes of [section 330(1), an application may be made by—

(a)   the company;
(b)   a director or member;

---

[83] Specifically sections 260-264 and by comparison, section 331(1). It must be noted though that in terms of section 331(1) of the Act, common law derivative actions can no longer be commenced as they have survived the relevant provisions in the Act. It will be good to note that as shown in *Universal Project Management Services Ltd v Fort Gilkicker Ltd* [2013] All ER (D) 313, only double derivative actions are permissible under the UK CA 2006.

[84] See as discussed under chapter 14, the cases of *Cook v Deeks* [1916] 1 AC 554, PC; *Wallersteiner v Moir* (No 2) [1975]; *Smith v Croft* [1986]; *Prudential Assurance Ltd v Newman Industries* (No 2) [1981] Ch 257; [1982] Ch 204 (Ch and CA); *Smith v Croft* (No 2) [1988]; *Cooke v Cooke* [1997] 2 BCLC 28; *Mumbray v Lapper* [2005] All ER (D) 294; *Barrett v Duckett* [1995]; *Daniels v Daniels* [1978] Ch 406, CH.

(c)   an entitled person; or

(d)   the Registrar'.

As is standard procedure in interlocutory proceedings including applications for injunctive relief, in accordance with section 330(3), '[t]he Court may not make an order in terms of this section, in relation to conduct or a course of conduct that has been completed'. This is because there will be nothing to stop.

7.15   Conclusion

In this chapter we have discussed the new requirement by the Act for there to be a declaration in respect of beneficial interest in shares. Beneficial ownership has to do with natural persons who are the actual beneficiaries of the shares but whose names are not entered on the register of members. The Act now requires that each company maintains a register of such beneficial ownership. Directors have a duty to supervise share and beneficial ownership register. The court is empowered to rectify the share register. We have also looked at the extent liability for shareholders, former shareholders, personal representatives and assignees. The Act proscribes a company from compelling shareholders to acquire shares by alteration to articles. We have further examined the following: that a company can, under certain specified circumstances, compulsorily acquire shares. Further, that in the event of a takeover, there are remedies open to minorities against oppression. It is also permissible for a company to, subject to the relevant provisions of the Act and articles of association, alter shareholder rights. It will be remembered that the Act provides for instances and in what fashion a shareholder may require the company to purchase shares. Where the shareholder thinks that his rights have been contravened, he has the right to commence action against the company or director as the case may be.

FURTHER READING

Articles

Fisher, D, 'The Enlightened Shareholder – Leaving Stakeholders in the Dark: will section 172(1) of the Companies Act 2006 make directors consider the impact of their decisions on third parties?' (2009) 20 International Company and Commercial Law Review 10.

Keay, A, 'Enlightened Shareholder Value, the Reform of the Duties of Company Directors and the Corporate Objective' [2006] Lloyd's Maritime and Commercial Law Quarterly 335.

Kiarie, S, 'At Crossroads: Shareholder Value, Stakeholder Value and Enlightened Shareholder Nakajima, C, 'Whither "enlightened shareholder value"' (2007) 28 Company Lawyer 353.

Sealy, L, '"Bona fides" and "proper purposes" in corporate decisions' (1989) 15 Mon UL Rev 265.

Books

Dine J and Koutsias M *Company Law* 6th edn (Palgrave Macmillan Hampshire 2007).

Farrah JH and Hannigan BM *Farrar's Company Law* 4th edn (London Butterworths 1998).

Gates RB *Gates Company Law and Practice in Zambia* (Reagan Blankfein Gates Lusaka 2017).

Sealy L and Worthington S *Sealy & Worthington's Cases and Materials in Company Law* 10th edn (Oxford University Press Oxford 2013).

Wild C and Weinstein S *Smith and Keenan's Company Law* 15th edn (Pearson Education Ltd London 2011).

Websites

'Mandatory Offer' http://moneyterms.co.uk

The Motley Fool 'What Happens to the Share Price When New Shares Are Issued?' http://www.fool.com

8

SHARES AND SHARE CAPITAL

AIMS AND OBJECTIVES

 After reading this chapter you should appreciate:

- ➤ the concept of share capital
- ➤ The different types of capital
- ➤ The alteration of share capital
- ➤ The rights and powers attaching to shares
- ➤ The types of shares and rights conferred
- ➤ The paripassu principle
- ➤ Classes of shares
- ➤ Class rights and their variation and/or abrogation
- ➤ Pre-emptive rights
- ➤ Issue of shares on incorporation and amalgamation
- ➤ Issue of other shares
- ➤ Rights and options to subscribe for share issue to directors, officers and employees
- ➤ Consideration for shares
- ➤ Consideration to issue of options and convertible securities
- ➤ Allotment and return on allotment of shares
- ➤ Forfeiture and surrender of shares
- ➤ Reduction of share capital
- ➤ Dividends
- ➤ Acquisition of fully paid-up shares by company and related matters
- ➤ Holding companies and subsidiary companies
- ➤ Restrictions on transferability
- ➤ Transmission of shares by operation of law
- ➤ Evidence of legal title to shares
- ➤ Procedure for Issuance of share certificate

8.1   Introduction

This chapter explores provisions under Part IX specifically sections 139 through 207. It examines the concept of share capital, the different types of capital; alteration of share capital; rights and powers attaching to shares; types of shares and rights conferred; the paripassu principle; Classes of shares; class rights and their variation and/or abrogation; pre-emptive rights; issue of shares on incorporation and amalgamation; issue of other shares; rights and options to subscribe for share issue to directors, officers and employees; consideration for shares; consideration to issue of options and convertible securities; allotment and return on allotment of shares; forfeiture and surrender of shares; reduction of share capital; dividends; acquisition of fully paid-up shares by company and related matters; holding companies and subsidiary companies; restrictions on transferability; transmission of shares by operation of law; Evidence of legal title to shares; and procedure for Issuance of share certificate.

8.2   Share capital

Like CA 1994 which it replaces, the Act does not define the term 'share capital'. The rationale for this is open to anecdotal postulations which may include but cannot be limited to the philosophy that the notion of share capital is kaleidoscopic and to constrain its definition to a few statutory terms would be to constrain creativity in the commercial space. Conceivably, it is one of those instances in which the law has taken a backseat and let commerce lead the way. Be that as it may [t]he word 'capital' sometimes means the 'nominal' capital of the company, namely that which is stated in the [articles] of association of any company limited by shares or by guarantee with a share capital, or in the articles of an unlimited company which has a capital divided into shares, and any increase of that nominal capital which has been made in the manner required by statute.[1]

Share capital has further been defined as consisting '...of all funds raised by a company in exchange for shares of either common or preferred shares of stock. The amount of share capital or equity financing a company has can change over time. A company that wishes to raise more equity can obtain authorization to issue and sell additional shares, thereby increasing its share capital'.[2] It is different from loan capital. The importance of share capital cannot be overstated. According to section 139(1), '[a] company other than a company limited by guarantee shall have share capital as prescribed'. However, and for obvious reasons inherent in a company limited by guarantee's corporate nature, in terms of section 139(2), '[a] company limited by guarantee shall have a guaranteed amount'.

---

[1] Halsbury's Laws of England 4th edn. page 141 para 173.

[2] 'Share Capital' retrieved from https://www.investopedia.com/terms/s/sharecapital.asp on 18/01/2017.

The notion of capital is no mean matter. The issue arose and was dealt with in the case of *Ooregnum Gold Mining Company v Roper*[3]. In that case, the memorandum of association of a company registered under the Act of 1862 stated that the capital of the company registered under the Act of 1862 stated that the capital of the company was £125,000.00 divided into £125,000.00 shares of £1.00 each, and that the shares of which the original or increased capital might consist might be divided into different classes and issues with such preference, privilege, or guarantee as the company might direct. The company being in want of money and the original shares being at a great discount, the directors in accordance with resolutions duly passed issued preference shares of £1.00 each with 15s. credited as paid, leaving a liability of only 5s. per share. A contract to this effect was registered under the Companies Act 1867 s. 25. The transaction was bona fide and for the benefit of the company. In an action by an ordinary shareholder to test the validity of the issue it was *held,* affirming the decision of the EWCA, that reading the Companies Acts 1862 and 1867 together the issue was beyond the powers of the company, and that the preference shares so far as the same were held by original allottees were held subject to the liability of the holder to pay to the company in cash the full amount unpaid on the shares.

8.3   Different types of capital

The term 'share capital' may be used in relation to the following:

8.3.1   Nominal value of shares

Also known as the par value or book value, nominal capital is the price of a share at the time of issue. This is a rather uncertain concept for several reasons: it does not indicate in anyway the price at which the share is likely to be issued to investors. Ordinarily, the issue value will be higher than the nominal/par/book value. Additionally, the market value of the share, which the nominal value oddly seems not to take into account, is a more treasured conception as far as creditors and investors are concerned.[4] The difference between the nominal value and the issue price is referred to as the share premium. Therefore, if the nominal value of a share is K1 and that same share is issued at K1.50, the share premium is K0.50.

The significance of nominal capital lies in the fact that it can be used 'to work out the proportion, or rateable share, of the residual wealth of the company to which each shareholder is entitled. If a company has share capital of [K15, 000.00] made up of [15, 000.00 X K1] ordinary shares, each share entitles its owner to one-hundredth of the residual wealth of the company'.[5]

---

[3] [1892] AC 125.

[4] Section 4 of the Companies (Amendment) Act No 12 of 2010 repealed section 18 of CA 1994 which provided for minimum capital for private companies limited by shares. There is no provision relating to this concept in the Act.

[5] McLaughlin S *Unlocking Company Law* 3rd edn (Routledge London 2015) 199.

8.3.2   Authorised Capital

This is the capital stated in the company's incorporation document as the capital with which it intends to be registered. How much authorised capital the company decides on will be determined by the nature of business it intends to engage in. A company is not allowed to issue shares in excess of its authorised capital unless the capital is altered to the extent required by way of a special resolution.

8.3.3   Issued capital

This is that part of the company's authorised capital which is issued and allotted to the public for subscription. A company is under no obligation to issue or alter all its authorised capital and frequently there is a variation between authorised and issued share capital. The capital which a company retains after it has issued its authorised capital is what is called 'un-issued share' capital. In Lake Kariba Boating Services Ltd v Kariba North Bank Co Ltd[6] the appellants were the registered proprietors of leasehold properties in Siavonga. The respondent lodged caveats on the said properties maintaining that it had a beneficial interest in the properties having acquired complete control of the assets of the appellant company through purchasing all the shares in the latter. An application by the appellants for the removal of the caveats was refused. They appealed against the refusal. It was held as follows:

(i)   One company can acquire complete control over the assets of another company by the acquisition from the shareholders of the whole of the issued share capital of the company whose assets it is sought to control.

(ii)   A company having such control has a legitimate beneficial interest in the assets arising out of the trust created and is in a proper position to lodge a caveat over the said assets.

8.3.4   Subscribed capital

It is that part of the issued capital for which applications have been received from the public and for which shares have been allotted.

8.3.5   Uncalled Capital

This is that part of the subscribed capital which is yet to be called. It represents capital which has been issued but not paid for. The reason is that the company may not be in need of all of its authorised capital and may only call on this capital as and when circumstances demand it through what is termed a call by the directors of the company.

---

[6] [1982] ZR 35, Coram: Ngulube DCJ Muwo JS and Bweupe AG JS.

8.3.6   Called-up capital

This is that part of subscribed capital for which a call has been made by directors, that is, a demand that the money owed in the shares owned by shareholders be paid.

8.3.7   Paid-up capital

This is the amount actually contributed for the shares issued but excludes premium capital and any calls made but not yet paid.

8.3.8   Reserved capital

This is that part of uncalled capital which cannot be called up except in the event that there are winding up proceedings. 'This capital is not under the control of the directors and cannot be reconverted into ordinary uncalled capital, or charged by the company, e.g. as security for debentures.'[7]

8.3.9   Premium capital

This is the amount paid over and above the nominal value when the shares are allotted by the company. Section 145(1) provides that '[w]here a company issues shares at a premium, whether for cash or otherwise, a sum equal to the total amount of value of the premiums on these shares shall be transferred to an account, to be called "the share premium account" and the provisions of this Act relating to the reduction of share capital of a company shall, except as provided in this section, apply as if the share premium account were paid up share capital of the company'.

The premium must be put in a special share premium account the usage of which is restricted to very few matters. In terms of section 145(2), '[t]he share premium account may [only] be applied by the company—

    (a)   in paying up unissued shares of the company to be issued to members of the company as fully paid bonus shares;

    (b)   in writing off—

        (i)   the preliminary expenses of the company; or

        (ii) the expenses of, the commission paid or the discount allowed on any issue of shares or debentures of the company; or

    (c)   in providing for the premium payable on redemption of any redeemable preference shares or of any debenture of the company'.

---

[7] Morse G *Charlesworth's Company Law* 13th edn 184; See: *Re Midland Rlwy. Carriage Co* [1907] 23 TLR 661.

8.4   Alteration of share capital

The law and procedure relating to the alteration of share capital is found in section 140.[8] Section 140(1) allows a company, 'unless its articles provide otherwise, by special resolution', to 'alter its share capital as stated in the certificate of share capital by' any of the following means:

(a)   increasing its share capital by issuing new shares of such an amount as it considers expedient;[9]

(b)   consolidating and dividing all or any of its share capital into shares of a larger amount than its existing shares;

(c)   converting all or any of its paid-up shares into stock and re-converting that stock into paid-up shares of any denomination;

(d)   subdividing its shares, or any of them, into shares of smaller amounts than is stated in the certificate of share capital; or

(e)   cancelling shares which, at the date of the passing of the resolution, have not been allotted to any person, and diminishing the amount of its share capital by the amount of the shares so cancelled'.

What is manifest from the foregoing is that the alteration of capital even though authorised by the Act does not subtract from the importance of provisions in the articles of association to permit such alteration or prohibit it. It is also clear from section 140(1) that the articles may provide 'otherwise' or disallow any alteration relating to share capital. Under such circumstances, any alteration by any of the methods available under section 140(1) will be null and void. Invariably, to go around this difficulty, the company will have to pass a special resolution altering the articles and insert a provision allowing for the alteration of capital. Only after that has been done as provided for under section 27 can the process under section 140 be engaged in.

However, where the articles allow for such alteration, its validity will not be complete unless the alteration is by special resolution. In the case of *Re Patent Invert Sugar Co*[10] a company, the regulations of which did not authorise a reduction of capital, passed on the 30 October (1) a resolution inserting in the articles a power to reduce its capital, and (2) a resolution for reducing the capital. Both these resolutions were confirmed at a meeting on the 16 November. It was held, by Kay, J., and by the EWCA, that the Court could not confirm the resolution for the reduction of capital, for that a special resolution for that

---

[8] Replaces section 74 of CA 1994.

[9] There are several reasons why a company may desire to have its share capital altered by way of increasing its share capital which may include the need to raise money as *Punt v Symons & Co Ltd* [1903] 2 Ch 506; or/ and as exemplified in *Salomon v A Salomon & Co* [1897] AC 22 (HL), to issue shares in return for assets transferred to the company. However, increasing share capital to, as in *Hogg v Cramphorn Ltd* [1967] Ch 254, prevent a takeover bid or as in *Howard Smith v Ampol Petroleum Ltd* [1974] AC 821 (PC)), to change the company's headquarters have been held to be undesirable.

[10] [1886] 31 Ch D 166.

purpose could not be passed until after the regulations of the company had been altered so as to make them authorise a reduction of capital.

In terms of section 140(2), '[w]here shares are subdivided, in accordance with [section 140](1)*(d)*, the proportion between the amount paid and the amount, if any, unpaid on each reduced share shall be the same as it was in the case of the share from which the reduced share is derived. By section 140(3), '[a] cancellation of un-allotted shares, in accordance with subsection (1) *(e)*, shall be considered not to be a reduction of share capital for the purposes of this Act'.

There are additional requirements to be adhered to under section 140(4)[11] for a company that 'has made any alteration, referred to in [section 140](1). The company, '…shall within thirty days after making the alteration lodge with the Registrar a—

(a)   notice in the prescribed form specifying, as the case may be, the shares increased, consolidated, divided, subdivided, converted, redeemed or cancelled, or the stock reconverted; and

(b)   copy of the resolution authorising the alteration.

Further, and in terms of section 140(5), '[t]he Registrar, where an alteration is made in accordance with subsection(1), shall alter a particular stated in the company's certificate of share capital and issue a replacement certificate of share capital which is worded to meet the circumstances of the case'.

8.5   Rights and powers attaching to shares

Replacing section 57[12] under CA 1994, section 141 not only provides for the legal nature of a share but in its more expansive form, compared to the section it replaces, provides for rights conferred on the holder of a share. Specifically, section 141(1)[13] confirms that '[a] share in a company is personal property'.[14] The House of Lords held in *Colonial Bank v Whinney*[15] that a share was a chose in action. This classification is relevant in so far as determining the rules of transfer are concerned. In England and Wales for example, the assignment of choses in action is the province of the Law of Property Act 1925.

---

[11] In terms of section 140(6), '[i]f the company fails to comply with subsection (4), each officer of the company commits an offence and is liable, on conviction, to a fine not exceeding one hundred thousand penalty units'.

[12] Which incidentally provided in subsection (1) that 'the shares or other interest of a member in a company shall be personal estate and movable property, transferable by a written transfer in a manner provided by the articles of the company or by this Act.'

[13] Compare section 541 of the UK CA which in similar terms but with a bit more finesse provides in part: '[t]he shares or other interest of a member in a company are personal property…and are not in the nature of real estate'.

[14] There is nothing illuminating in the Act's definition of "share" which is said simply to include 'stock'. A more helpful definition is to be found in section 2 of the Securities Act No 41 of 2016 which provides that "shares" means an ownership interest or stocks issued or proposed to be issued by a company in the capital of the company'.

[15] [1886] 11 App Cas 426.

The crafting of the old section 57 in CA 1994 appears to have followed this philosophy stating in section 57(1) that 'the shares or other interest of a member in a company shall be personal estate and movable property, transferable by a written transfer in a manner provided by the articles of the company or by this Act.' Section 141(1) seems to have gotten rid of this detailed definition partly, it seems, because the status of a share being a chose in action is limited by the fact that the Act and the articles provide specific rules to govern the transfer of shares.

Section 140(2) which should be read within the context of section 140(3) provides that a share in a company confers on the holder the right to—

(a)   one vote on a poll at a meeting of the company on any resolution, including a resolution to—

   (i)   appoint or remove a director or auditor;
   (ii)   adopt and alter the articles;
   (iii) approve an amalgamation of the company; and
   (iv)   put the company into liquidation in accordance with the Corporate Insolvency Act; and

(b)   an equal share in dividends authorised by the board of directors and in the distribution of the surplus assets of the company.

However, in terms of section 140(3) '...the rights specified in [section 140](2) may be negated, altered or added to by the articles or in accordance with the terms on which the share is issued'.

Section 140 harkens back to Farewell J's archetypal statement in *Borland's Trustee v Steel*[16] considered the most comprehensive legal definition of a share in company law jurisprudence:

> A share is the interest of a shareholder in the company measured by a sum of money, for the purpose of liability in the first place, and interest in the second, but also consisting of a series of mutual covenants entered into by all the shareholders interse in accordance with [section 17 of the Act]. The contract contained in the articles of association is one of the original incidents of the share. A share is not a sum of money...but is an interest measured by a sum of money and made up of various rights contained in the contract, including the right to a sum of money of a more or less amount.[17]

Present in the foregoing illuminating observation as regards the ownership of a share are not only the interest exemplified by the bundle of rights provided for

---

16 [1901] 1 Ch 279 at 288.
17 Approved by the House of Lords (present: Viscount Hailsham LC Lord Blanesburgh Lord Russell of Killowen Lord Macmillan and Lord Roche) in *IRC v Crossman* [1937] AC 26.

under section 140(2) but the liability arising therefrom and contractual nature of the relationship between the company and the shareholders and shareholders *inter se* within the context of section 17[18] of the Act.[19]

The foregoing principles are exemplified in the case *Short and Others v Treasury Commissioners*[20] where the court was compelled to deal with the legal nature of shares. It was shown that in as much as the expression "as between a willing buyer and a "willing seller" in reg. 78 (5) of the Defence (General) Regulations, natural meaning, the conception of a separate bargain of sale by an individual seller to an individual buyer, a shareholder of an undertaking taken over under reg. 55 of the Regulations of 1939 only on the basis of the value of a single, and no account is to be taken, in assessing the compensation payable to him, of the fact that the competent authority in acquiring all the shares is acquiring, in addition, the exclusive control of the undertaking; for to add to each parcel of shares, as sold separately, a rateable proportion of the added or "control" value of the totality of the shares would be to add to each holding an item of value which the shareholder, as an individual, did not, in fact, possess

Moreover, shareholders are not, in the eye of the law, part-owners of the undertaking. They are also not entitled to have their shares valued by the method of apportioning among all the shares in the undertaking as a whole. The value of an individual share is not necessarily the price quoted for it on the Stock Exchange. It is open to a shareholder to displace that evidence of value by any other evidence which is directed solely to the value as between a willing buyer and a willing seller of the holding *per se*.

8.6   Types of shares and rights conferred

The Act allows a company, subject only to stipulations in its articles, the right to create and issue different classes of shares.[21] Both section 7(2)[22] relating to public companies and section 9(1)[23] relating to private companies limited by shares provide that [t]he articles of a public company shall state the—

(a)   rights, privileges, restrictions and conditions attaching to each class of shares; and

(b)   authority given to the directors to determine the number of shares in, the designation of, and the rights, privileges, restrictions and conditions attaching to, each series in a class of shares.

This rather open ended crafting has meant that legal practitioners, specifically corporate lawyers, have been very creative in terms of the types of shares they

---

[18] Which provides for the '[c]ontractual effect of incorporation'.
[19] See further Gates RB *Gates Company Law*....131-4.
[20] [1948] AC 534.
[21] Section 142(1).
[22] Replacing section 14(2), CA 1994.
[23] Replacing section 17(2), CA 1994.

have created and the rights attaching to the created shares. This is done mainly to attract different types of shareholders to the company with each class of shares created having different rights.

8.6.1   The paripassu[24] presumption

In terms of section 7(3), '[a]ll shares in a public company rank equally except for differences relating to the classes or series of shares'. The meaning of this can be explained thus; unless there is something to the contrary, that is, an agreement in the articles of association providing for the creation of different classes of shares, the shares and those who hold them will rank equally or be on the same footing. Ordinarily, this means that the shareholders will enjoy equal rights and also be liable to the same extent as regards liability. In the first case this means the right to receive dividends when they are declared (or in the case of preference shares a percentage of the nominal value); voting; and return of capital and participation in surplus assets (or where there is a reduction of capital); attendance at meetings and voting at the said meetings. We must make the point however of the indispensability of unequivocal provisions relating to the right or power of directors to create new classes of shares, it cannot be implied. If no such power is provided for but the need to create new classes of shares arises, the company will have to pass an extraordinary resolution in terms of section 27.

The foregoing has been exemplified in the case of *Andrews v Gas Meter Company.*[25] Overruling the earlier case of *Hutton v Scarborough Cliff Hotel Co*[26] it was held that a limited company, having no authority under its articles of association to create any preference between different classes of shares, may by special resolution alter its articles so as to authorise the directors to issue preference shares by way of increase of capital. In the second case, it means the obligation to pay what a shareholder owes on the shares he owns in a company when a call is made.

8.6.2   Classes of shares

The crafting of section 142(1) means that there is no statutory requirement for a company to issue all its shares with the same rights. As a consequence, a company may grant variable rights on disparate classes of shares. It follows that a company can create any number of class of shares. There are however limits to this. The difficulty of dealing with numerous types has limited the types of class of shares to two, generally preference and ordinary shares. The

---

[24] The Latin term literally means side by side; at the same rate or on an equal footing.
[25] [1897] 1 Ch 361.
[26] [1865] 2 Dr. & Sm. 521.

classification is significant. For starters, in gauging what rights relate to the share in question in a particular company, one has to look to the label attached to the share in question. The articles of association, as is clear from section 142(1), regulate what type of shares are created and the peculiar rights associated with them as is the power given to directors to create different classes of shares or withhold it.

8.6.2.1 Preference shares

The issuance of preference shares is regulated by articles of association. Preference shares enjoy the rights accorded to them in a preferred manner relative to ordinary shares. There will be clarity with respect to the said rights. Priority with respect to preference shares will relate to payment of dividends, if one is declared, at a fixed rate; and payment of capital in a winding up unless the company prescribes otherwise in its articles. Whether or not a specific right attaches to preference shares is a question of interpretation of the articles or related agreements.

Whether the rights stated above will be enjoyed by holders of preference shares is largely dependent on whether the company is (i) a going concern (ii) being wound-up. The two scenarios are discussed below.

(i)   *Where a company is a going concern the following will be the case:*

A right to a preferential dividend, unless a contrary intention can be found, means a right to a cumulative dividend. It follows that if a dividend is not declared and thus not paid in a particular year, it will be carried over to the next financial year and will be paid in arrears and must be paid before a dividend is paid to other shares such as ordinary shares.[27] It must be noted that the shares will not be cumulative if declared to be non-cumulative. Non-cumulative preference shares enjoy no right to a cumulative dividend. The effect is the same if, as shown in *Adair v Old Bushmills Distillery,*[28] it is decided that the preferential dividend will be paid out of yearly profits or that net profits of each financial year as the case may be, will form the basis of the dividend payment.

The foregoing was exemplified in the case of *Staples v Eastman Photographic Materials Co*[29] in which the memorandum of association of a company contained this clause: "The capital of the company is £150,000," divided into 10,000 ordinary shares of £10 each, and 5000 preference shares of £10 each. The holders of preference shares shall be entitled out of the net profits of each year to a preference dividend at the rate of £10 percent per annum on the amount

[27] See *Webb v Earle* [1875] LR 20 Eq 556.
[28] [1908] WN 24.
[29] [1896] 2 Ch D 303 (CA).

for the time being paid or deemed to be paid up thereon. After payment of such preferential dividend the holders of ordinary shares shall be entitled to a like dividend at the rate of £10 per cent per annum on the amount paid on such ordinary shares. Subject as aforesaid, the preference and ordinary shares shall rank equally for dividend." It was held (reversing the decision of Chitty J. in the EWCA), that the preference shareholders were not entitled to a cumulative dividend of £10 per cent so as to have the deficiency in one year paid out of the profits of a subsequent year before paying anything to the ordinary shareholders.

Additionally, where preference shares are designated as non-participating, the articles of association must specifically provide that the preference shares are conferred with the right to a participation in the surplus profits of the company subsequent to the payment of a precise rate of dividend amount to ordinary shares, failing which they will have no right to a participation in the surplus profits of the company. In *Will v United Lankat Plantations Co Ltd and Another*[30] a company which had power under its articles to issue new shares upon such terms, including preference, as the company in a general meeting might direct passed a resolution that the capital of the company be increased by the issue of certain new shares to be called preference shares and that the holders thereof be entitled to a cumulative preferential dividend at the rate of 10 percent per annum on the amount for the time being paid up on such shares, and that such preference shares rank, both as regards capital and dividend, in priority to the other shares. Preference shares were issued in accordance with this resolution. The articles further provided that, subject to any priorities that might be given upon the issue of any new shares, the profits of the company available for distribution should be distributed as dividend among the members in accordance with the amounts paid on the shares held by them respectively.

It was held, that in the distribution of profits holders of the preference shares were not entitled to anything more than a 10 percent dividend.[31] The foregoing holding notwithstanding however, it is not inconceivable to imagine that preference shares may be formed with the right to take part in surplus profits up to a certain percentage.

(ii)   Where a company is being wound-up

Where a company is being wound-up and in the absence of a provision relating to the issue of arrears in terms of a cumulative dividend as they relates to preference shares are not payable out of the assets in a dissolution of the company. The only way dividend arrears are payable is if the dividend has

---

[30] [1914] AC 11.
[31] Affirming the decision of the EWCA.

been declared. In *Re Crichton's Oil Co*[32] the capital of a trading company consisted of £10 shares, preference and ordinary, all paid up in full, the former being entitled to a cumulative preferential dividend. The articles of association empowered the directors to set aside out of the profits sums as they thought proper as a reserve fund. For some years the preferential dividend was paid, and then for three years the business was carried on at a loss, the result being a loss of capital to the amount of £4,346. In the next year there was a profit of £1,675 on the year's trading, but the directors did not declare a dividend or make any appropriation of that sum. The company went into voluntary liquidation, the debts were all paid, and the capital, to the extent of £7 per share, was returned to the shareholders. The sum of £1,675 remained in the hands of the liquidator. It was held, upon the construction of the articles, that the preference shareholders were not entitled to have this sum applied in paying them dividends for the four years in which they had received none, but that it must be divided as capital rateably among all the shareholders.[33]

There is authority for the proposition that in the event that the articles of the company do provide for the payment of arrears, the same are payable out of the surplus of the assets of the company, after the payment of debts and following the pecking order in section 127 of the Corporate Insolvency Act[34] irrespective of the provision relating to undistributed profits. The case of *In re Springbok Agricultural Estates, Ltd*[35] illustrates to what extent arrears are payable in a winding up where there are no profits earned and no dividend declared. In that case a company incorporated in 1903 passed a special resolution in 1905 sanctioning the issue of preference shares and providing that the dividends on them should be paid out of profits only and that "In the event of the winding up of the company the holders of the preference shares shall be entitled to have the surplus assets applied first in paying off the capital paid up on the preference shares...., secondly, in paying off the arrears, if any, of the preferential dividend.... to the commencement of the winding up and thereafter to participate rateably with the holders of other shares in the residue, if any, of such surplus assets which shall remain after paying off the capital paid up on such other shares." In 1919 the company went into voluntary liquidation and there were surplus assets in the hands of the liquidators. No preference dividends had ever been declared

---

[32] [1902] 2 Ch D 86.

[33] A similar decision was reached in *Re Catalinas Warehouses & Mole Co Ltd* [1947] 1 All ER 51 where on similar facts the Court held that on the true construction of the company's articles, the right to payment of a dividend arose only after a dividend had been declared, and therefore, as no dividend for 1945 had been declared or recommended and the company had gone into liquidation, the shareholders had no right to dividend out of the profits for that year. However, see *In re Bridgewater Navigation Co* [1891] 1 Ch 155 for a different take.

[34] No 9 of 2017.

[35] [1920] 1 Ch D 563.

nor profits earned.   It was held[36], that all unpaid preferential dividends were "arrears" of preferential dividends although no profits had been earned by the company, so that subject to the payment off of the preference shares the surplus assets were applicable in the first place in paying off the whole of the unpaid preferential dividends down to the commencement of the winding up.

By the same token, in *Re Wharfedale Brewery Co Ltd*[37] a company incorporated in 1896, passed a resolutions in 1896 and 1897 sanctioning the issue of preference shares with the right to a fixed cumulative dividend and providing that those shares should rank "both as regards dividend and capital in priority to the other shares but shall not confer any further right to participate in profits or surplus assets." In 1952 the company went into voluntary liquidation and there were, at the date of the commencement of the winding up, profits amounting to approximately £1, 700.00. The dividends on the preference shares were in arrears to the extent of over £112,000.   There were, in due course, surplus assets in the hands of the liquidator amounting to £62, 887.00.   It was held, that, on the true construction of the resolutions, the whole of the fund which constituted the surplus assets was distributable among the holders of the preference shares.

Further to the foregoing, where the articles of association provide that payment of arrears in terms of dividends will be made for those arrears due at the date of winding up, no arrears will be paid unless dividends have been declared.   The point is well illustrated in the case of In *re Roberts and Cooper, Ltd.*[38] The memorandum of association of a company provided that in the event of a winding up the preference shareholders should be entitled to receive in full out of the assets the amount of capital paid up on their shares, and also all arrears of dividend due thereon at the date of winding up. A resolution was passed for the winding up of the company in April, 1925, at which date no dividends on the preference shares had been declared or paid for over four years past. After the winding up there was a surplus sufficient to pay arrears of dividend due.   It was held that no dividends having been declared between 1921 and 1925, none were due, and the preference shareholders were not entitled to be paid anything in respect of arrears.[39]

We must now deal with the question of what should happen in the event that there are surplus assets available subsequent to discharge of all of the company's liabilities in accordance with the pecking order in section 127 of the Corporate

---

[36] Following Dicta of Neville J in *In re New Chinese Antimony Co* [1916] 2 Ch D 118;

[37] [1952] Ch D 913.

[38] [1929] 2 Ch D 383.

[39] *In re Springbok Agricultural Estates, Ltd* [1920] 1 Ch D 563 and *In re New Chinese Antimony Co* [1916] 2 Ch 115 *distinguished*. See further, *Re Walter Symons Ltd* [1934] Ch D 308; *Re Wood Skinner & Co Ltd* [1944] Ch D 323;and *Re Wood, Skinner& Co Ltd* [1944] Ch D 323

Insolvency Act.[40] In the early case of *Monkland Iron Co Ltd v Henderson*[41] it was shown that such surplus, if there be any, ought to be proportionately divided among all shareholders. The articles will ordinarily provide for explicit exhaustive rights attaching to preference shareholders. More to the point, articles of association have for example attached to them a preferential right 'in the repayment of capital in a liquidation but containing no reference to any further rights in the capital do not entitle the preference shareholders to participate in such surplus assets.'[42]

Finally, the case of *Dimbula Valley (Ceylon) Tea Co Ltd v Laurie*[43] is authority for the position that 'if articles give preference shareholders an express right to participate equally with the ordinary shareholders in surplus assets, they are entitled to share in such assets'[44] the fact being that the said assets may include profits from past years which instead of being distributed to ordinary shareholders were placed in reserve.

8.6.2.2 Ordinary/equity shares

Ordinary or equity shares represent the most common class of shares. In this class is vested all the rights that remain after rights relating to preference shares have been taken care of. They are said, as the name suggests, to hold the equity of the company. Not only do they bear the most risk of any class in th e lean years, but by the same token, take immense benefits in terms of dividends in the good years. Ordinarily, ordinary shareholders will enjoy all the rights expected of shareholders unless otherwise a contrary intention can be proved or there is an explicit limitation in this regard. The privileges include but may not be limited to receiving notices for meetings; attendance and participation at the meetings; but also voting and earning a dividend if one is declared after the directors and other company officers have been remunerated and extra capital after the company has been wound-up.

Ordinary shareholders are the closest thing there is to the definition of ownership of the company if the term be broadly interpreted.

It follows that a company cannot issue shares completely devoid of ordinary shares. If there is only one class of shares, they will be ordinary shares. There must be at least one ordinary share if different classes are created. The reason is simple: unlike preference shares which, in the rights they enjoy including cumulative dividends and priority in the pecking order[45] at winding-up, where

---

[40] No 9 of 2017.

[41] [1883] 10 R 494.

[42] Morse G *Charlesworth's Company Law* 13th edn 269; See *Scottish Insurance Corp Ltd v Wilsons and Clyde Coal Co Ltd* [1949] AC 462.

[43] [1961] Ch D 353; See also, *Saltdean Estate Co Ltd, Re* [1968] 1 WLR 1844. It would appear that on the basis of these decisions *In re Bridgewater Navigation Co* [1891] 2 Ch.D.317 ought to be disregarded.

[44] *Smith and Keenan's Company Law*....161.

[45] Section 127 of the Corporate Insolvency Act No 9 of 2017.

there is a provision to that effect, may be akin to debentures, ordinary shares fit the conventional definition of shares without anything more. Be that as it may, '...ordinary shares may shade off imperceptibly into preference [shares], for, when the latter confer a substantial right of participation in income or capital, or a *fortiori* both, it is largely a matter of taste whether they are designated "preference" or "preferred ordinary" shares.'[46] It also not inconceivable nor is it impermissible to divide ordinary shares into classes "A""B" or "C" each enjoying varying rights if not in voting power then in financial participation at winding up stage. Finally, there has been a recent creation called non-voting ordinary shares which it appears are for people that would not want to participate in the management of a company – a bank, for example.

Section 142(2) further provides that '[d]espite the generality of section 142] (1), shares in a company may—

(a)   be redeemable;

(b)   confer preferential rights to distributions of capital or income;

(c)   confer special, limited, or conditional voting rights; or

(d)   not confer voting rights.

8.7   Variation of class rights

8.7.1   *General*

Should a company wish to vary the rights of a class of shareholders, it must observe statutory provisions found under section 143.[47] Section 143(1) stipulates what in terms of the Act is considered a variation of the rights of that class, that is to say:

(a)   the abrogation of any rights attached to a class of shares; and

(b)   any resolution of a company, other than a resolution for the creation or issue of further shares, the implementation of which would have the effect of—

(i)   diminishing the proportion of the total votes exercisable at a general meeting of the company by the existing shareholders of a class; or

(ii)   reducing the proportion of the dividends or other distributions payable to the existing shareholders of a class.

8.7.2   *Class rights*

It would appear that the protections envisaged in section 143 are meant, at least in terms of section 143(2), to extend to instances '[w]here the shares of a company are divided into different classes'. In such an instance, 'the *rights attached to any class* may not be varied, except to the extent and in the manner provided

---

[46]   *Gower and Davies' Principles of Modern Company Law* 9th edn 870.

[47]   Which is replaces section 62 of CA 1994 but retains its contents.

for under section 143. A useful case in this respect is *Cumbrian Newspapers Group Ltd v Cumberland & Westmoreland Herald Newspaper & Printing Co Ltd.*[48] The plaintiff and defendant who were both publishers of newspapers, negotiated a transaction whereby the defendant would acquire inter alia one of the plaintiff's newspapers and the benefit of certain advertising arrangements and the plaintiff would acquire *inter alia* 10 per cent of the defendant's share capital. The defendant duly issued 10 per cent shareholding to the plaintiff and as part of the agreement under which the shares were issued amended its articles to grant to the plaintiff rights of pre-emption over other ordinary shares, rights in respect of unissued shares and the right to appoint a director. The purpose of such rights was to enable the plaintiff, in its capacity as shareholder, to be in a position to be able to prevent a take-over of the defendant. After the arrangements so embarked on had continued for several years, the directors of the defendant proposed to convene an extraordinary general meeting and to pass a special resolution to cancel the articles which gave such special rights to the plaintiff.

In an action by the plaintiff for (1) a declaration that the rights were class rights which could not be abrogated without its consent and (2) an injunction restraining the defendant from convening or holding the extraordinary general meeting:

It was held, granting the declaration,

(1) that the special rights granted by the defendant's articles were rights that although not attached to any particular shares were conferred on the plaintiff in its capacity as shareholder in the defendant and were attached to the shares for the time being held by the plaintiff without which it was not entitled to the rights; that accordingly the plaintiff had "rights attached to a class of shares" and since section 125 of the Companies Act 1985 provided that class rights could not be valid or abrogated without the consent of the class members the special rights enjoyed by the plaintiff could not be varied or abrogated without the consent of the plaintiff.

(2) That on the facts, the adoption of articles by the defendant conferring the special rights on the plaintiff was a condition precedent to the agreement between the parties and was not a contractual obligation of the defendant that, accordingly, it was not a term of the agreement between the plaintiff and the defendant that the plaintiff would have the benefit of the special rights conferred on it by the articles, nor could such a term be implied.[49]

---

[48] [1986] 3 WLR 26.
[49] Applying *Bushnell v Faith* [1970] AC 1099 HL (E).

Per Scott J:

> In my judgment, if specific rights are given to certain members in
> their capacity as members or shareholders, then those members
> become a class. The shares those members hold for the time
> being, and without which they would not be members of the
> class, would represent, in my view, a "class of shares".

What is manifest from the foregoing is the court adopting a wide definition of
the phrase *'rights attached to any class'* in section 143(2). We must add that
the implications of the decision in *Cumbrian* would appear to be that 'where
particular rights are granted to an individual shareholder they would not be
alterable without the consent of that shareholder'.[50] The individual shareholder
would thereby constitute a class whose rights are protected from variation or
abrogation under section 143. One way around this would be to claim that the
rights which a class of shareholders claim should not be varied or abrogated
were granted to them, not in their capacity as shareholders, but some other
capacity.[51]

8.7.3   *Variation or abrogation?*

The meaning of the terms 'variation' and 'abrogation' under section 143 is
deserving of further interrogation. It seems that in 'general there will be a
variation if the alteration directly affects the way the rights are described, but
not if the alteration directly affects the way the rights are described, but not if
the value of the shareholding has been altered in some way, for example, by
varying the rights of another class of shares'.[52] It appears to be the case under
section 143 that the variation of class rights encompasses among other things,
their abrogation. Put another way, while all abrogation of class rights in terms
of section 143 amount to variation of class, not all variations of class rights are
by way of abrogation as variation can be by 'any resolution of a company, other
than a resolution for the creation or issue of further shares, the implementation
of which would have the effect of—
  (i)   diminishing the proportion of the total votes exercisable at a general
         meeting of the company by the existing shareholders of a class; or
  (ii)   reducing the proportion of the dividends or other distributions payable
         to the existing shareholders of a class'.[53]
We must invariably turn the discussion to court decisions and see how the term
variation of class rights which under section 143(1) includes, but is not limited
to their abrogation, has been interpreted.

---

[50] Dine J and Koutsias M *Company Law* 6th edn (Hampshire Palgrave Macmillan 2007) 284.

[51] Dine J and Koutsias M *Company Law*....

[52] Dine J and Koutsias M *Company Law*....284

[53] Section 143(1)(b).

In *Greenhalgh v Arderne Cinemas*[54] the company passed 2 resolutions, the first to subdivide some 50p ordinary shares into 10p ordinary shares. The second, which was as a consequence of the votes created by the first was to increase the capital of the company. Greene MR observed thus, '[a]s a result of those two resolutions, if they are valid, the voting power of the appellant, which previously gave him a satisfactory measure of voting control, is liable to be completely swamped by the votes of the other ordinary shareholders'. That notwithstanding, the resolution was still held to be valid. Although, as Lord Greene himself admitted, the resolution by way of abrogation, varied the right of the minority relating to pre-emption, under the articles, the plaintiff was unable to prove that such variation was not *bona fide* for the benefit of the company. Nor was it shown that variation engendered discrimination between the majority and the minority as all members were at liberty to sell their shares to outsiders.

Another general point to note in this respect is that the court will have to consider whether the scheme envisaged under section 143 is fair, just and equitable not only between the shareholders of the classes but also the shareholders of the same class.[55] In *Re Old Silkstone Collieries*[56] the company having decided that that its share capital was in excess of its needs following the nationalisation of the coal industry, decided to reduce its share capital in stages by repaying preference shareholders. The consequence was the preference shareholders losing their right to any compensation that was due to them from a government compensation scheme. It was held that the reduction constituted a variation of the preference shareholders' rights. As such, the court would decline to confirm the reduction for being unfair and inequitable as between the preference and ordinary shareholders.

Variation of class rights is restricted under section 143(3). According to that section, '[i]f the articles expressly forbid the variation of the rights of a class or specify the manner in which such a variation may be carried out and expressly forbid any alteration of the articles in that respect, the rights or the variation may not be made except in accordance with the written consent of all the members of that class or with the sanction of the Court under a scheme of arrangement made in accordance with the Corporate Insolvency Act'.[57]

Further, and in terms of section 143(4), '[w]here [section 143](3) is not applicable, the rights attached to a class of shares may be varied with the written consent of the holders of seventy-five per cent of the issued shares of that class, or by a special resolution passed at a meeting of the holders of shares of that

---

[54] [1951] Ch 286.
[55] See *Re Holders Investment Trust Ltd* [1971] 1 WLR 583 Ch D; and *Re Northern Engineering Industries Plc* [1994] BCC 618 CA.
[56] [1954] Ch 169.
[57] No 9 of 2017.

class'. There is no role for any resolution by any member or members of the company who are not members of the class in question to make decisions at any general meeting. Any resolutions outside section 143(3)(4) would be *void ab initio* and of no effect and cannot be enforced in any way shape or form. Lord Russell has opined in *Carruth v Imperial Chemical Industries Ltd*[58] that:

> *Prima facie* a separate meeting of a class should be a meeting attended only by members of the class, in order that the discussion of the matters which the meeting has to consider may be carried on unhampered by the presence of others who are not interested to view those matters from the same angle as that of the class; and if the presence of outsiders was retained in spite of the ascertained wish of the constituents of the meeting for their exclusion, it would not, I think, be possible to say that a separate meeting of the class had been duly held.

Section 143(4) must be read together with section 143(5)(6)(7) on the one hand and section 143(8) on the other. In terms of section 143(5) and despite the provisions of section 143(4), '[t]he holders of not less than fifteen per cent of the issued shares of a class may, within twenty-one days after the date of the resolution referred to in [section 143](4), apply to the Court for the resolution to be cancelled and the Court may confirm or cancel the resolution'. The said application 'may be made on behalf of the persons referred to in [section 143(5)] or by such of their number as they may appoint in writing for that purpose'. Indeed, it has been shown in *Carruth v Imperial Chemical Industries Ltd*[59] that there exists a common law right to challenge a variation on, among others, the foundation that the resolution to achieve the variation was not passed in good faith or for the good of the company or the shareholders in question or as a whole. As section seems to suggest, the said application under section 143(4) need not have the concurrence of all members having no less than 15 percent of the shareholding, it may be made 'by such of their number as they may appoint in writing for that purpose'

Where on the one hand the application envisaged in section 143(4)(5) is not made, the company is obliged to, 'within fourteen days after the end of the period prescribed in that subsection for making such an application, lodge with the Registrar a copy of each paragraph of the articles affected by the variation, in its amended form'.[60] On the other hand, '[i]f an application is made, in

---

[58] [1937] AC 707.
[59] [1937] AC 707 at 756-7.
[60] Section 143(7).

accordance with section 143(5), and the Court makes an order, the company'
will be obliged to, 'within fourteen days after the date of the order, lodge with
the Registrar—

(a) the Court order; and

(b) a copy of each paragraph of the articles affected by the variation, in its
amended form, if the order confirms the resolution'.[61]

Failure to comply with section 143(7) or 143(8), means 'the company and each
officer in default commit an offence and are liable, on conviction, to a fine not
exceeding three thousand penalty units for each day that the failure continues'.[62]

Though the expressed intention of the framers of the Act so far as section
143 is concerned appears to mainly minority shareholders in a class from
the oppression of the majority in another, and from the oppression within a
particular class from those having majority shareholding by regulating how
and restricting the manner in which a variation of class rights may be done, a
line of English cases on similar provisions[63] in various UK CA over the years
seem to indicate that the protection offered under section 143 is not fool proof.
We briefly discuss a few of those cases bearing in mind that they are only of
persuasive value in the Zambian context.

In *Re Schweppes Ltd*[64] the court declined to hold that an issue regarding shares
ranking *paripassu* with existing ones was a variation. In *Re Mackenzie & Co
Ltd*[65] a reduction of capital carried out by cancellation of paid-up capital in two
instances to an equal extent was made. The consequences were a reduction of the
amount payable under the fixed dividend payable to preferential shareholders.
At the same time, the ordinary shareholders could share a bigger chunk of the
residual dividend declared. It was held however that this was not a variation
because, as the court saw it, the percentage of the dividend was not affected.
Put another way, no alteration had, *prima facie*, been effected on the actual
description of the rights in question and as such, there was no variation of class
rights as envisaged under section 143.

In *Greenhalgh v Arderne Cinemas*[66] considered elsewhere in this text, the
subdivision of shares and consequential attenuation of voting rights was held
not to amount to a variation of class rights.

---

[61] Section 143(8).

[62] Section 143(9). It is also worth noting that in terms of section 143(10), '[n]othing in...section [143]
shall affect or derogate from the powers of the Court in relation to schemes of arrangement, takeovers
and protection of minorities as provided in the Corporate Insolvency Act'.

[63] See section 125 UK CA, 1985 on which *Cumbrian Newspapers Group Ltd v Cumberland &
Westmoreland Herald Newspaper & Printing Co Ltd* [1986] 3 WLR 26 was decided; and sections 629
– 634 of the UK CA 2006.

[64] [1914] 1 Ch 322.

[65] [1916] 2 Ch 450.

[66] [1951] Ch 286.

Similarly, in *White v Bristol Aeroplane Co Ltd,*[67] the issuance of bonus shares to one class significantly snowballing its voting power in contradistinction to another class was held not to be a variation of the latter class's rights.

In *House of Fraser Plc v ACGE*[68] preference shareholders protested the compulsory payment-off of their shares at par with the consequence of reducing of the company's capital by way of paying off and cancelling of the company's preference shares. No meeting of preference shareholders had been called or held to discuss or approve the said reduction despite the existence of an article which compelled the company to call and hold such a meeting if the rights relating to preference shares were 'modified, affected or dealt with'. It was held that the proposed cancellation of preference shares did not attract the protection of that article, because the cancellation of the shares was in accordance with the rights originally attached to those shares, specifically, the right to return of capital in priority to other shareholders where any capital was in excess of the company's needs. The cancellation of the shares did not constitute a modification, commutation, affecting or dealing with rights attached to them.[69]

Per Lord Keith of Kinkel:

> The reduction of capital now proposed to be made gives effect to that right [that the second preference shareholders were entitled to priority of repayment after certain preferences shares and before any other shareholders on a reduction of capital]. This necessarily involves, of course, that all other rights attached to the shares will come to an end, but that is something to which the holders of the shares must be taken to have agreed as a necessary consequence of their right to prior repayment receiving effect. Upon no view of the matter can it be said that as a result any of the special rights attached to the shares has been 'modified, commuted, affected or dealt with' within the meaning of article 12. These words all contemplate that after the relevant transaction the shareholders in question will continue to possess some rights, albeit of a different nature from those which they possessed before the transaction. The proposal for reduction of capital involves complete cancellation of the shares.

---

[67] [1953] Ch 65.

[68] [1987] 1 AC 387.

[69] See further, *Dimbula Valley (Ceylon) Tea Co v Laurie* [1961] Ch 353 where an issue of bonus shares to one class which would have as a consequence, a substantial reduction of the amount receivable when participating in surplus assets on a winding-up was similarly not held to be a variation.

In view of the foregoing, the case of *Re Old Silkstone Collieries Ltd*[70] appears to be a rare oddity in which the court deemed the paying of preference shareholders, as a class, on a reduction of share capital following the nationalisation of the coal industry, as amounting to a variation of class rights envisaged under section 143. It would appear that 'only in the most obvious cases, usually when the rights attaching to shares have been [modified] by alteration of the actual wording describing those rights, where the special protection afforded by'[71] [section 143] will be enforced. Legalistic and technical as this may otherwise seem from a lay person's perspective, discernible from the foregoing cases is the fear the courts entertain which is that 'by using a wide definition of 'variation' the courts would be allowing one class a veto over a scheme which might benefit the company as a whole'.[72] It remains to be seen how Zambian courts will approach with the issue of variation as envisaged under section 143 of the Act.

In view of the approach taken by the courts, it is suggested that bringing a claim and seeking injunctive relief under section 330[73] of the Act may be a better course of action.

8.8   Pre-emptive rights[74]

Also known as 'first option to buy', a pre-emptive right or the right to pre-emption is a contractual right to acquire certain shares newly coming into existence before they can be offered to someone else or entity.[75] It may also be said to be 'a potential buyer's contractual right to have the first opportunity to buy, at a specified price, if the seller chooses to sell within the contractual period [....]'[76] While the articles of a private company will typically contain a pre-emptive clause to the effect that no shares will be sold to an outsider as long as a subsisting shareholder can be found to buy any shares that become available for purchase, the Act has codified the issue in section 144. Section 144(1) provides that '[a] company shall, offer for acquisition to the existing shareholders shares, which are issued or proposed to be issued by a company, that rank or would rank as to voting or distribution rights, or both, equally with shares already issued, in a manner and on terms that would, if accepted, maintain the existing voting or distribution rights, or both, of those shareholders'.[77]

---

[70] [1954] Ch 169.

[71] Dine J and Koutsias M *Company Law* 6th edn 286.

[72] Dine J and Koutsias M *Company Law* 6th edn 286.

[73] Compare with section 994 UK CA 2006 headed 'Petition by company member'.

[74] Derived from the latin verb *emo, emere, emi, emptum* meaning to buy plus the inseparable preposition *pre,* before.

[75] For a detailed discussion the right of pre-emption see generally, Keenan D *Smith and Keenan's Company Law* 13th edn 241-246.

[76] Garner BA (Ed) *Black's Law Dictionary* (St. Paul, Minnesota Thomson Reuters 2009).

[77] In terms of section 143(2), '[a]n offer, made in accordance with subsection (1), shall remain open for acceptance for a reasonable time or for the period as may be specified in the Articles'.

It has been held in *Lyle & Scott Ltd v Scott's Trustees*,[78] that shareholders who, on a take-over bid accepted an outside offer to buy their shares, received the price, gave the purchaser general proxies, and agreed to execute transfers and deliver up the share certificates when called upon to do so, were "desirous of transferring" their shares and had to comply with the pre-emption clause, unless they gave notice that they had changed their minds before the other shareholders exercised their pre-emption rights. Implicit in the foregoing ruling is the important point that the offer for sale and acceptance of such an offer are guided by the basic principles of the law of contract. To that end, any offer made with respect to a pre-emptive rights clause can be withdrawn at any time before acceptance is made either explicitly or steps are taken to accept the offer in line with the clause on pre-emption in the articles. It has been suggested that the decision in *Lyle & Scott Ltd* has the potential to prevent a takeover bid for a private company because where a pre-emptive clause exists, the board of directors may seek an injunction within the context of section 330 to compel the shareholder to offer his shares to another shareholder in the bidder's stead.[79]

The EWCA has indicated that where a pre-emptive clause provides that shares may not be transferred to an outsider if there is an indication of the willingness on the part of an existing shareholder, then sensible steps ought to be taken by the transferor to give the other members a realistic opportunity to make offers to purchase the shares in question at what it termed a fair value.[80] A curious scenario arose in *Theakston v London Trust Plc*[81] where the purchase of shares was financed by an outsider even though the agreement was to the effect that the member was the person to whom the shares were to be transferred. The shares were charged to the name of the outsider who retained an equitable interest in them. The court held that this amounted, despite the facts, to a transfer between members and as such was not captured by the pre-emptive clause. The *raison d'être* for the foregoing holding is that a company cannot be expected to police the sources of or/and should not require its members to disclose the financing for the purchase of shares for that is a contract to which it would not be privy.[82]

While it is possible for a transfer of shares to occur outside the terms of the pre-emptive procedure, it must be shown that there has been to a substantial degree, compliance with the procedure relating to pre-emption including the fact that shareholders may, in compliance with a provision in the articles of association be unavoidably compelled to buy shares which a member wishes to

[78] [1959] AC 763.
[79] Keenan D *Smith and Keenan's Company Law*....
[80] *Tett v Phoenix Property and Investment Co* [1986] BCLC 149.
[81] [1984] BCLC 390.
[82] This may well fall within the province of the Drug Enforcement Commission in their role as enforcers of the Narcotic Drugs and Psychotropic Substances Act Chapter 96 of the Laws of Zambia and The Prohibition and Prevention of Money Laundering Act No 14 of 2001.

dispose of. Otherwise, the transfer will be ineffective. This situation arose in the case of *Rayfield v Hands*.[83] the plaintiff was a shareholder in a company, article 11 of the articles of association of which required him to inform the directors of his intention to transfer shares in the company, and which provided that the directors "will take the said shares equally between them at a fair value". In accordance with article 11 the plaintiff so notified the directors, who contended that they need not take and pay for the plaintiff's shares, on the ground that the articles imposed no such liability upon them. On the plaintiff's claim for the determination of the fair value of his shares, and for an order that the directors should purchase such shares at a fair value it was held,

(1)   That upon their true construction the articles required the directors to purchase the plaintiff's shares at a fair price.

(2)   That article 11 was concerned with the relationship between the plaintiff as a member and the defendants, not as directors, but as members of the company.

(3)   That it was not necessary, for the plaintiff to succeed in his action, that he should join the company as a party in addition to the directors.

The foregoing notwithstanding, it is, as exemplified in *Scotto v Petch*,[84] possible to transfer control over shares without triggering the pre-emption clause. It is also possible to for the members, in writing, waive of their right to pre-emption. Directors have no discretion to register a transfer that breaches the pre-emption clause. Be that as it may, and as has been shown in *Re Accidental Death Insurance Co Allin's case*[85] where the articles give the directors the discretion to approve or refuse a transfer the same must be exercised in good faith as their decision can be challenged in court for bias. At the same time, where the articles explicitly provide grounds under which a transfer may not be accepted/approved, the transferee has no right to demand specificity as to why the transfer has not been approved.[86]

The position is the same where the articles specifically provide that the directors may reject a transfer without assigning cause. In this light we must consider the reality of articles that prohibit the transfer of shares by an executor or personal representative to himself and as such stop him from voting on the shares of the deceased. These provisions must be contrasted with the usual position taken in articles as regards a trustee in bankruptcy.[87] He is able to direct how the debtor votes. Additionally, and as exemplified in *Safeguard Industrial Investments Ltd v National Westminster Bank*[88] any restriction in a company's

[83] [1960] Ch D 1.
[84] [2001] *The Times*, 8 February.
[85] [1873] LR 16 Eq 449.
[86] See *Berry and Stewart v Tottenham Hotspur FC Ltd* [1935] Ch 718.
[87] See section 2 of the Bankruptcy Act Chapter 82 of the Laws of Zambia.
[88] [1982] 1 All ER 449.

articles relating to share transfer while covering the transfer of legal title, that is, the transfer of a registered member's title, does not extend to the transfer of beneficial interest.

Re Hackney Pavilion Ltd[89] is authority for the position that a transfer must be accepted where there is an equality of votes between those for and those against a particular transfer. Further and as shown in *Re Copal Varnish Co*[90] 'a transferee can ask the court to rectify the register so that his name is included on it where one director, by refusing to attend board meetings, is preventing a directors' meeting from being held to consider the registration because of lack of quorum'.[91] It is worth remembering the foregoing notwithstanding that as shown in *Re Swaledale Cleaners*,[92] the powers to refuse or approve a transfer of shares cannot be delayed in perpetuity. It must be exercised within a reasonable time.

As shown in *Re Pool Shipping Ltd*[93] generally and unless a contrary intention can be distilled from the articles, pre-emptive rights and rights of refusal only encompass a transfer of shares by a member under sections 188 and 189 and can in no way be construed to extend to the transmission of shares under section 190 nor in a scenario where the shares in question are represented by an allotment subject to renunciation.

Finally, if there is no such compliance with section 144, the court can grant an injunction upon application, to prevent such transfers under section 330 as exemplified in *Curtis v J.J. Curtis & Co Ltd*.[94]

8.9   Issue of shares on incorporation and amalgamation

A company limited by shares is in terms of section 146 required to,

   (a)   issue to each qualified person named in the application for incorporation as a shareholder, within a reasonable time after its incorporation, the number of shares specified in the application as being the number of shares to be issued to that person; and

   (b)   in the case of an amalgamated company,[95] issue to each person entitled to a share or shares, in accordance with the amalgamation proposal, the share or shares to which that person is entitled, within reasonable time after the amalgamation comes into effect'.

---

[89] [1924] 1 Ch 276.
[90] [1917] 2 Ch 349.
[91] Keenan D *Smith and Keenan's Company Law*....244.
[92] [1968] 3 All ER 619.
[93] [1920] 1 Ch 251.
[94] [1986] BCLC 86 (NZ).
[95] "[A]malgamation" means the combination of two or more companies to form a new body corporate as provided for in section 282....'

8.10   Issue of other shares

The board of directors is empowered to issue shares to any person or entity and is not limited, as long as it considers it appropriate, to issue as many shares as it deems necessary under the circumstances.[96] Be that as it may, the board, is mandated, in issuing shares in accordance with section 147 to do the following:

(a)   determine the consideration for, and the terms on which, the shares shall be issued;

(b)   if the shares are to be issued for consideration other than cash, determine the reasonable present cash value of the consideration; and

(c)   resolve that the—

(i)   consideration for, and terms of, the issue are fair and reasonable to the company and to all existing shareholders; and

(ii)   present cash value of the consideration to be paid for the issue of the shares is not less than the amount to be credited for the issue of the shares'.[97]

We must add that in terms of section 156(1) is precluded from, without the consent of a shareholder, 'issuing new shares that increase the liability of that shareholder to the company'. By section 156(2), '[a]ny issue of shares that is done contrary to subsection (1) is void'.

In addition the directors who vote in favour of a resolution, required by section 147(1), must sign a declaration—

(a)   stating the consideration for, and the terms of, the issue;

(b)   describing the consideration in sufficient detail to identify it;

(c)   where a present cash value has been determined in accordance with subsection (1) (b), stating the value and basis for assessing it;

(d)   stating that, in their opinion, the consideration for and terms of issue are fair and reasonable to the company and to all existing shareholders; and

(e)   if the shares are to be issued other than for cash, stating that, in their opinion, the present cash value of the consideration to be provided for the issue of the shares is not less than the amount to be credited for the issue of the shares.[98]

Further, and in terms of section 153(3), '[t]he board of directors shall, before the issued shares are credited as fully or partly paid up, other than for cash—

(a)   determine the reasonable present cash value of the consideration; and

(b)   resolve that, in its opinion, the present cash value of the consideration is—

(i)   fair and reasonable to the company and to all existing shareholders; and

(ii)   not less than the amount to be credited in respect of the shares.

---

[96] Section 147.
[97] Section 153(1).
[98] Section 153(2).

In addition to the declaration they are required and expected to sign under section 153(2), section 153(4) mandates the directors who vote in favour of a resolution to issue shares as envisaged in section 147, and which is share issuance is captured under section 153(3), to sign 'a declaration—

(a) describing the consideration in sufficient detail to identify it;

(b) specifying the present cash value of the consideration and the basis for assessing it; and

(c) tating that the present cash value of the consideration is—

(i) fair and reasonable to the company and to all existing shareholders; and

(ii) not less than the amount to be credited in respect of the shares'.

The board of directors should then 'deliver copies of the declarations, made in accordance with sections 153(2) and (4), to the Registrar for registration, within ten days of the declarations being signed'.[99] In terms of section 153(7) '[a] director who fails to comply with this section commits an offence'. We must end by observing that none of the provisions of section 153 apply to the issue of shares in a company on the—

(a) conversion of convertible securities; or

(b) exercise of an option to acquire shares in the company'.[100]

Section 207 provides for shareholding in regulated companies. Specifically, section 207(1) provides that '[t]he Registrar shall, on being notified by a regulator that the shareholding in a regulated company requires to be altered and on payment of prescribed fees by the company, alter the shareholding accordingly'. By section 207(2) '[d]espite section 193,[101] the Registrar shall not register a transfer of shares in a regulated company if the transfer would contravene any other written law'.

8.11 Rights and options to subscribe for share issue to directors, officers and employees

The rights and options to subscribe for share issue to directors, officers and employees is provided for under section 193.[102] In terms of section 193(1), '...

[99] Section 153(5); by section 153(9), '[i]f the board of a company fails to comply with subsection (5), every director commits an offence. It is also worth noting that in terms of section 153(6), 'shares that are, or are to be, credited as paid up, whether wholly or partly, as part of an arrangement that involves the transfer of property or the provision of services and an exchange of cash or cheques or other negotiable instruments, whether simultaneously or not, shall be treated as paid up other than in cash to the value of the property or services'.

[100] Section 153(8).

[101] Which provides for '[r]ights and options to subscribe for share issue to directors, officers and employees'.

[102] Section 193 will not, according to subsection (8), 'apply to the right of holders of convertible debentures to acquire shares on the exercise of a conversion option.

and subject to the articles, the board of directors may create and issue, whether in connection with the issue of any of the company's shares or otherwise, rights or options in favour of a director, officer or employee of the company or of any subsidiary of the company which entitle the holder to acquire shares of any class from the company, on such consideration, terms and conditions as may be fixed by the board of directors'. By section 193(2), '[t]he terms and conditions of rights or options, referred to in subsection (1), including the time within which and the value at which they may be exercised and any limitations on transferability, shall be incorporated in the instrument evidencing the rights or options'.

Where, according to section 193(2), 'the board of directors proposes to issue rights or options to—

    (a)   one or more of the persons, referred to in subsection (1), as an incentive to continued service with the company or a subsidiary company; or

    (b)   an assignee on behalf of the persons, referred to in subsection (1); the issue shall be authorised at a general meeting, by the passing of a special resolution, or shall be authorised by and be consistent with, a scheme adopted at a general meeting, by special resolution.

In terms of section 193(4), '[i]f there are pre-emptive rights in any of the shares proposed to be issued, in accordance with subsection (3), the issue or scheme, as the case may be, shall be approved by the vote or written consent of the holders of more than fifty percent of the shares, who are entitled to exercise pre-emptive rights with respect to the shares, and the vote or written consent shall release the pre-emptive rights'.

In terms of section 193(5), '...a special resolution authorising the issue of rights or options, or a scheme adopted by special resolution, shall include the—

    (a)   material terms and conditions upon which the rights or options are to be issued, including any restrictions on the number of shares that eligible individuals may have the right or option to acquire;

    (b)   method of administering the scheme, in the case of a scheme;

    (c)   terms and conditions of payment for shares in full or by instalments;

    (d)   limitations on the transferability of the shares; and

    (e)   voting and dividend rights to which the holders of the shares may be entitled'.

'The terms and conditions referred to in subsection (5)*(a)*, prior to the full payment for shares, shall not provide for a share certificate to be delivered to a shareholder or confer a right to vote in respect of such shares'.[103] By section 193(7) ,'[i]n the absence of fraud in a transaction, the decision of the—

    (a)   board of directors; or

---

[103] Section 193(6).

(b) general meeting, where the directors or a quorum are not disinterested in the issue or scheme; shall be conclusive as to the adequacy of the consideration received or to be received by the company for the issue of rights or options and for the acquisition of shares in the company'.

8.12   Consideration for shares

The consideration referenced in section 153(1)*(a)*, '…may be in the form of cash, promissory notes, contracts for future services, real or personal property, or other securities of the company'.[104] The foregoing notwithstanding, in terms of section 153(2), [a] shareholder is not liable to pay or provide any consideration in respect of an issue of shares unless the—

(a) articles of the company specify the consideration to be paid or provided for those shares; or

(b) shareholder is liable to pay or provide consideration for those shares pursuant to a pre-incorporation contract or a contract entered into after the incorporation of the company.

However the provisions of section 152 are, in terms of section 154, inapplicable to the—

(a) issue of shares that are fully paid up from the reserves of a company to all shareholders of the same class in proportion to the number of shares held by each shareholder;

(b) consolidation and division of the shares or any class of shares in a company in proportion to those shares or the shares in that class; and

(c) sub-division of the shares or any class of shares in a company in proportion to those shares or the shares in that class.

8.13   Consideration to issue of options and convertible securities

In terms of section 155(1), [t]he board of directors shall, before issuing any securities that are convertible into shares in the company or any options to acquire shares in the company—

(a) determine the consideration payable with respect to the convertible securities or options and, in either case, the shares and the terms on which the shares shall be issued;

(b) if the shares are to be issued for consideration, other than cash, determine the reasonable present cash value of the consideration;

(c) resolve that the consideration payable and the terms of the issue of the convertible securities or options and, in either case, the shares are fair and reasonable to the company and to all existing shareholders; and

(d) if the shares are to be issued, other than for cash, resolve that the

---

[104] Section 152(1).

present cash value of the consideration to be provided is not less than the amount to be credited for the issue of the shares.

According to section 155(2), [t]he directors who vote in favour of a resolution, required by subsections (1)*(c)* and *(d)*, shall make a declaration—

(a)   stating the consideration for, and the terms of the issue of, the convertible securities or options and, in either case, the shares;

(b)   describing the consideration in sufficient detail to identify it;

(c)   where a present cash value has been determined, in accordance with subsection (1) *(b)*, stating that value and the basis for assessing it;

(d)   stating that the consideration for and terms of issue of the convertible securities or options and, in either case, the shares are fair and reasonable to the company and to all existing shareholders; and

(e)   if the shares are to be issued, other than for cash, stating that the present cash value of the consideration to be provided is not less than the amount to be credited for the issue of the shares'. By section 155(5), '[a] director, who fails to comply with subsection (2), commits an offence.

In terms of section 155(3), '[t]he board of directors shall within ten days of the declarations being signed, deliver copies of the declarations, made in accordance with subsections (2) *(d)* and *(e)*, to the Registrar, in the prescribed form, for registration. According to section 155(6), '[i]f the board of directors fails to comply with subsection (3), every director of the company commits an offence'.

For purposes of section 155 as a whole, 'shares that are to be credited as paid up, whether wholly or partly, as part of an arrangement that involves the transfer of property or provision of services and an exchange of cash or cheques or other negotiable instruments, whether simultaneously or not, shall be treated as paid up, other than in cash, to the value of the property or services'.[105]

8.14   Allotment and return on allotment of shares

Allotment of shares simply means the appropriation to a person of a specified number of shares. It is a direct divestiture of shares by the company itself at any time after incorporation as envisaged in section 149. While the terms 'allotment' and 'issue' are used interchangeably, they should, strictly speaking, and as regards the process of one becoming a shareholder, be understood as distinct. Agreements to take shares in a company are governed by principles of contract law. Allotment entails that there has been acceptance of the offer by the allottee to acquire the right to have his name entered on the register of members. This allotment is distinguishable from share transfer because in this case, the

---

[105] Section 155(4).

company itself has allotted to a member and is involved in the "transfer" of shares. Allotment is then followed by the actual issuance of the shares already allotted as envisaged in sections 146 and 147 when the name of the owner of the shares is formally entered on the register of members of the company.[106] It was held in the case of *National Westminster Bank v IRC*[107] that 'shares are allotted when a person acquires the unconditional right to be included in the company's register of members in respect of those shares....' The allottee thus acquires a legal right to the shares and the bundle of rights that come with share ownership and membership of the company. Sometimes we talk of shares in the context of a prospectus. Where there is a prospectus - it is an invitation to treat which asks the public to make offers on the shares on "offer." This matter is discussed under chapter 9.

The trigger and authority for an allotment of shares by the board of directors is a special resolution of the shareholders.[108] Within ten days of such allotment the company must 'lodge, with the Registrar, a notice in the prescribed form, accompanied by the special resolution for the allotment of the shares by the company'.[109] Failure by the company to fulfil the requirements of section 149 means, 'each officer of the company commits an offence'.[110] As shown in *Pan Electronics Ltd and Savvas Panayiotides and Others v Andreas Miltiados & Others*[111] however, an examination of the return of allotment filed with the Registrar is not a relevant method in deciding a question of fact which could only be received on the basis of the evidence tendered by the parties.

8.15   Forfeiture and surrender of shares

The circumstances under which forfeiture or surrender of shares may occur are stipulated in section 148. They include any instances stipulated in the articles as grounds for forfeiting or surrender of shares;[112]and failure to pay a call on shares[113] though it may be noted that failure to pay a call may not result in

---

[106]Section 157; It is also worth mentioning that in terms of section 156(1), '[t]he board of directors shall not, without the consent of a shareholder, issue new shares that increase the liability of that shareholder to the company. By section 156(2), '[a]ny issue of shares that is done contrary to subsection (1) is void'.

[107] [1995] 1 AC 111 (HL).

[108] Section 149(1).

[109] Section 149(2).

[110] Section 149(3).

[111] [1988-9] ZR 19.

[112] Section 148(1).

[113] Section 148(2).

automatic forfeiture.[114] The articles may stipulate otherwise and it is to them that one should look for guidance. We must acknowledge though that a company will have a *lien* over any share for which no full payment has been received.[115] Once the board resolves that the unpaid for shares ought to be forfeited, the person who has held such shares will cease to be a member. In terms of section 148(3), '[t]he Registrar shall register a forfeiture or surrender of shares lodged in the prescribed manner and form'. Given its drastic and castigatory nature, the directors must guarantee that the method for the forfeiture process is stringently followed failing which, it will be rendered irrelevant.

The case of *Johnson v Lyttle's Iron Agency*[116] demonstrates the foregoing. The directors of a company, which was governed by the regulations of Table A. in the UKCA, 1862, resolved on 16 September that a call of £2 per share be made, and that the shareholders be requested to pay the same as soon as possible. They afterwards, on the same day, gave verbal instructions to the secretary to make the call payable on the 16 December, and he sent a circular notice to the shareholders accordingly. J., one of the shareholders, did not pay the call, and on 21 December the secretary wrote to him, telling him that if he did not pay the amount of the call together with interest at 5 per cent from the date of the call, on or before 31 December his shares would be liable to forfeiture. J. did not pay, and on 4January the directors passed a resolution forfeiting his shares. It was held that, as the notice of the 21 December claimed interest from the date of the call, instead of from the day fixed for its payment, as provided by clause 6 of Table A., it was a bad notice, and the forfeiture was invalid, and an injunction was granted restraining the company from proceeding further under the resolution of forfeiture.

Re Esparto Trading Co[117]is authority for the position that the power reposed in the directors to forfeit shares ought to be exercised *bona fide*. It is not, as was attempted in that case, to relieve shareholders who owe money on the shares they own but who are in good books with the directors from fulfilling their obligation to pay in the event that a call is made.

The following cases further illustrate the law of forfeiture as it relates to different scenarios. While not a comprehensive exposition of the law on the matter, they paint a picture of dos and don'ts for directors, members and others when it comes to the matter of forfeiture:

---

[114] The recognition of the concept of surrender of shares is a fundamental departure from CA 1994 as the surrender of shares was not referred to anywhere in CA 1994 and in fact the standard articles of association did not even mention it. Therefore, while under CA 1994 company's articles would make provision for surrendering of shares in *lieu* of forfeiture, nothing of the sort is required though the articles may regulate the surrender of shares beyond what is provided for under section 148. Finally, surrender of shares may also entail surrendering of shares by the owner.

[115] The basis for this is section 192 which provides that '[a] company shall not have or claim a lien on shares on which there is no unpaid liability nor shall any lien extend to sums due from a shareholder, except in respect of the unpaid liability on the shares'.

[116][1877] 5 Ch D 687.

[117][1879] 12 Ch D 191.

Hopkinson v Mortimer, Harley & Co[118]

Article 22 of the articles of association of a limited company, as altered by a special resolution, provided that the company should have a first and paramount lien upon all the shares registered in the name of each member for the debts, liabilities, and engagements of such member. Articles 23 provided that the board might sell the shares for the purpose of enforcing the lien, and might also by a resolution to that effect, forfeit the shares subject to such lien.

The holder of fully-paid shares brought an action against the company and its directors asking for a declaration, in effect, that his fully-paid shares were not subject to the power of forfeiture for debts on the ground that it was ultra vires and illegal. There had been no threat to forfeit the plaintiff's shares. It was held,

(1) That the plaintiff was not premature in coming to Court, as his rights had already been invalid and his property damaged.

(2) That under this power the forfeiture for debts due from a member generally, as distinct from those due from him as a contributory, would amount to an illegal reduction of capital.

(3) That the lien being an equitable charge in the nature of a mortgage, the power to forfeit the plaintiff's shares, on his failure to redeem on a seven days' notice, was a clog on the equity of redemption and as such invalid and ultra vires and the plaintiff was therefore entitled to the declaration claimed.

Hope v International Financial Society[119]

A company, having 150,000 shares issued and half paid up, passed a special resolution that the directors should have to apply the company's assets in purchasing from any shareholders willing to sell, ay number of shares not exceeding 100,000; and that such shares should not be re-issued by the directors without the authority of a general meeting. The company had no power under its memorandum of association or articles to purchase or deal in its own shares or accept surrenders. It was held, (affirming the decision of Bacon, V.C.), that the scheme was *ultra vires* and invalid, being either an attempt to reduce the capital of the company without complying with the provisions of the Companies Act, 1867, ss. 9-13, or else a trafficking in the shares of the company which was not authorised by the memorandum of association.

---

[118] [1917] 1 Ch 646.
[119] [1876] 4 Ch D 327.

Re Exchange Trust, Limited, Larkworthy's Case[120]

The articles of association of a company provided that on on-payment of a call on shares the directors might forfeit the shares; that the forfeited shares should be the property of the company; that before the shares were disposed of the directors might "annual forfeiture" upon such conditions as they thought fit; and that notwithstanding the forfeiture the shareholder should be liable to pay all calls, interest, and expenses owing in respect of the shares at the time of forfeiture.

The directors passed a resolution forfeiting the shares of L. for non-payment of a call, and gave him notice of the forfeiture. On demand L. paid the call, interest, and expenses, and at the same time wrote that he repudiated any further liability on the shares.

Nine months afterwards the directors passed a resolution purporting to rescind the forfeiture and giving notice to L. that he was registered in respect of the shares. L. replied declining to have his name registered as owner of the shares. It was held, that the company had no power adversely to L. to reinstate him with the liability of a shareholder.

New Balkis Eersteling Ltd and Randt Gold Mining Co[121]

When shares which have been forfeited for non-payment of a call are sold, and a certificate of proprietorship is delivered to the purchaser under art. 22 of Table A of the Companies Act, 1862, stating that he is to be deemed to be the holder of the shares "discharged from all calls due prior to the date" of the certificate, he is liable for the payment of future calls duly made. The decision of the EWCA, [1903] 1 KB 461, affirmed.

Shares in the respondent company were issued by the respondents at the nominal value of 5s. a share. Upon these shares 3*s*. 4*d*. was paid, and in 1898 a call of 1*s*. 8*d*. was made upon the then holders, who failed to pay it. The shares were then duly declared forfeited to the respondent company, and in 1900 they the shares to the appellants and gave them a certificate under art. 22 of Table A of the Companies Act, 1862. The terms of the certificate are stated in Lord Macnaghten's judgment.

Afterwards a call of 1s. 3d. was duly made by the respondents, and an action against the appellants brought by the respondents to recover it. Bucknill J. gave judgment for the respondents, and this decision was affirmed by the EWCA (Earl of Halsbury L.C., Lord Alverstone C.J., and Sir F. H. Jeune.

---

[120] [1903] 1 Ch D 711.
[121] [1904] AC 165.

Re Randt Gold Mining Company[122]

Where a company in pursuance of its articles of association has forfeited shares for non-payment of calls, and the articles provide that notwithstanding forfeiture the ex-shareholder shall be liable to pay the amount of the calls, and the shares are subsequently reallotted to another person, that person is entitled on the winding-up of the company to be credited with all sums paid by the previous holder, whether in respect of moneys paid by him as a shareholder in respect of the shares, or as a debtor in respect of liability under the articles to pay calls notwithstanding forfeiture.

Re Bolton, Ex parte North British Artificial Silk Ltd[123]

Where a company in pursuance of its articles of association has forfeited shares for non-payment of moneys due on allotment and calls, and the articles provide that notwithstanding forfeiture the ex-shareholder shall be liable to pay all calls or other money owing upon the shares at the time of the forfeiture, and the shares are subsequently sold and re-alloted to other persons with the result of a loss to the company, the company on the subsequent bankruptcy of the ex-shareholder is only entitled to prove for the actual loss suffered, that is the difference between the amount received on the re-allotment of the forfeited shares and the amount due at the date of the forfeiture. Any payment of the uncalled capital by the now allottees must ensure for the benefit of the original allottee who has forfeited the shares and release him *pro tanto* in respect of the damages for which his breach of contract in failing to pay the calls rendered him liable.[124]

Ladies' Dress Association, Limited v Pulbrook[125]

The articles of association of a company provided an that any member whose shares had been forfeited should, nevertheless, be liable to pay all calls owing upon the shares at the time of the forfeiture. The defendant had been the owner of shares in the company, but his shares had been forfeited for non-payment of calls. More than a year after the forfeiture the company went into liquidation, and the defendant was then sued for the unpaid calls. It was held,

(1)   That, notwithstanding the provisions of s. 38 of the Companies Act, 1862, sub-ss. 1, 3, the action was maintainable, inasmuch as the defendant was liable, not as a contributory, but as a debtor to the company. Where the resolution confirming a resolution by a company to reduce its capital did not comply with the terms of s. 51 of the Companies Act, 1862, because

---

[122] [1904] 2 Ch D 468.
[123] [1930] Ch D 48.
[124] The principle laid down in *Re Randt Gold Mining Company* [1904] 2 Ch D 468 considered and applied.
[125] [1900] QBD 376.

there was not an interval of fourteen days between the passing of the two resolutions, but an order of the Court had been made in accordance with the resolutions under s. 11 of the Companies Act, 1867, and the Registrar of Joint Stock Companies had certified the registration of the order, together with a minute approved by the Court, in conformity with s. 15 of that Act.

(2)   That the certificate of the registrar was conclusive evidence that a special resolution to reduce the capital of the company had been duly passed in accordance with s. 51 of the Companies Act, 1862, and s. 9 of the Companies Act, 1867.

Re Darwen and Pearce[126]

On December 29, 1920, D. and P. - who afterwards became bankrupt - joined with others in entering into an agreement with a company whereby they guaranteed to them the payment of all the installments then owing upon the shares in the company specified in the schedule to the agreement, the amount of D. and P.'s liability being limited to the sum therein mentioned. The shareholders having been served with notice calling upon them to pay the installments due on their respective shares on pain of forfeiture, and D. and P. also having been required to pay the same on or before February 17, 1925, in case of non-compliances by the shareholders with the notice, and default in payment having been made both the shareholders and by D. and P., the company forfeited the bulk of the shares in pursuance of the power conferred upon them by their articles of association. Article 31 was as follows: "Any member whose shares have been forfeited shall notwithstanding such forfeiture, be liable to pay to the company all calls or other moneys, interest and expenses, whether presently payable or not, owing in respect of such shares at the time of forfeiture, together with interest thereon from the time of forfeiture until payment at the rate of 10 per cent, per annum or such less rate as may be fixed by the Board." On September 9, 1925, a receiving order in bankruptcy was made against D. and P., and on April 10 the company lodged their proof for the amount claimed to be due on the guarantee. Upon a motion by the company for the reversal of the decision of the trustee in rejecting their proof, it was held,

(1)   That the right created by art.31 was a new right which arose upon the forfeiture of the shares and one which placed a more onerous obligation upon the shareholders than if the shares had not been forfeited. The forfeiture, therefore, was an interference with the rights of the sureties as against the principal debtors.[127]

---

[126] [1927] Ch D 176.
[127] Applying the principles in *Stocken's Case* [1868] LR 3 Ch 412 and *Ladies Dress Association v Pulbrook* [1900] 2 QB 376.

(2)   That the company had by exercising their option to forfeit the shares deprived the sureties of their lien on the shares which they would have been entitled to, had the company, in lieu of forfeiture, compelled them to pay the calls; with the result that, upon the principles stated in *Polack v Everett*[128] D. and P. were discharged from their liability as sureties under the guarantee, and the decision of the trustee in their bankruptcy in rejecting the proof of the company was right.

Trevor and Another v Whitworth and Another[129]

A limited company was incorporated under the Joint Stock Companies Acts with the objects (as stated in its memorandum) of acquiring and carrying on a manufacturing business, and any other businesses and transactions which the company might consider to be any way conducive or auxiliary thereto or in any way connected therewith. The articles authorized the company to purchase its own shares. The company having gone into liquidation a former shareholder made a claim against the company for the balance of the price of his shares sold by him to the company before the liquidation and not wholly paid for. It was held, reversing the decision of the EWCA that such a company has no power under the Companies Acts to purchase its own shares, that the purchase was therefore ultra vires, and that the claim must fail.[130]

8.16   Reduction of share capital

There is no definition of what the term reduction of capital is. Be that as it may, Lord Macnaghten seemed to imply in the case of *Poole and others v Bank of China*[131] that a reduction of share capital is a diminution or extinguishment of a share capital of a company affecting two things namely: (1) the funds available to creditors or (2) the rights of different classes of shareholders as between themselves and the interest of the members of the public who may be induced to buy shares in the company. Section 150[132] provides the procedure as regards ways and means through which a company may reduce its share capital. Section 150(1) provides for three necessary predicates a company must comply with in order to be permitted to reduce its share capital, i.e. such a proposed reduction must be authorised by the company's articles; the company must pass a special

---

[128] [1876] 1 QBD 675.

[129] [1887] 12 App Cas 409.

[130] The reasoning of the EWCA in *Re Dronfield Silkstone Coal Company* (17 Ch D 76) disapproved.

[131] [1907] AC 229.

[132] We must note that by section 150(7), section 150 in its entirety 'shall, unless the Court directs otherwise, apply to any reduction of share capital if the—*(a)* proposed reduction of share capital involves either diminution of liability in respect of unpaid share capital; or *(b)* payment to any shareholder of any paid-up share capital'. Further and by section

resolution relating to the reduction;[133] and thirdly confirmation by the Court in accordance with section 150(3) which mandates a company to, 'within twenty-one days after passing the resolution to reduce its share capital, apply to the Court for an order confirming the reduction'. The court is unlikely to condone a reduction in capital which has not been met with its approval.[134]

The following are methods through which, in terms of section 150(1), a reduction of share capital may be accomplished by a company, that is:

(a) by extinguishing or reducing 'the liability on any of its shares';

(b) with or without extinguishing or reducing 'liability on any of its shares—

    (i) cancel any paid-up share capital which is lost or is unrepresented by available assets; or

    (ii) pay off any paid-up share capital which is in excess of the wants of the company';

(c) accepting the surrender of shares by any of its shareholders; and where necessary, reducing the amount of its shares accordingly, except that the share capital shall not be reduced below the prescribed minimum.

Section 150(4) envisages the application to court in accordance with section 150(3) discussed above receiving the Court's confirmation. Where such is the case, the company is instructed to 'give notice of the reduction to the Registrar, in the prescribed manner and form, specifying the amount of the reduction and the reduced amount of its share capital'. Upon receipt of the notice hereinbefore mentioned which must be accompanied by a, prescribed fee, the Registrar must 'issue the company with a replacement certificate of share capital'. It is only after lodgment and issuance of new certificate, the resolution will take effect. The issuance of a replacement certificate is conclusive evidence that all the requirements as regards reduction of share capital have been complied with and that the share capital is as reflected.

In terms of section 150(6), '[a] company shall not take an action to—

(a) extinguish or reduce liability in respect of an amount unpaid on a share; or

(b) reduce its share capital for any purpose, other than for declaring that its share capital is reduced by an amount that is not represented by the value of its assets; unless there are reasonable grounds on which the directors may determine that, immediately after the taking of such action, the company will be able to satisfy the solvency test'.

---

[133] In terms of section 150(2), '[t]he company shall, not less than thirty days before passing the resolution to reduce the share capital in accordance with [section 150(1), issue a notice, of the proposed reduction, in a daily newspaper of general circulation in Zambia'.

[134] *Alexander Henderson Ltd., Petitioners,* 1967 S.L.T. (Notes) 17. However, see the rather unique judgment in *Re Barry Artist Ltd* [1985] BCLC 283 where the court allowed a written resolution signed by all members to authorise a reduction instead of a special resolution. It must be noted though that the Court indicated that it would not be prepared to decide as it did in this case going forward.

Section 150(10) permits a company to reach an agreement 'in writing, with a creditor that the company shall not reduce its share capital—

(a)   below a specified amount without the prior consent of the creditor; or

(b)   unless specified conditions are satisfied at the time of the reduction'. For that reason, '[a] resolution to reduce the share capital passed in breach of an agreement, referred to in [section 150(10), is invalid'.[135]

The foregoing requirements are stringent. The requirement that there be a provision in the articles allowing for a reduction failing which a company cannot even take further steps including the passage of a special resolution unless it first passes a special resolution to amend its articles in terms of section 27 to insert the provision to allow for a reduction and thereafter pass another special resolution in terms of section 150(1) after which the High Court's confirmation can be sought illustrates the seriousness of the process of reduction of share capital and for good reason as we show below.

An elementary principal of English company law is that capital cannot generally be reduced without the approval of the Court. The case of *Trevor v Whitsworth*[136] demonstrates this. In that case, a limited company was incorporated under the Joint Stock Companies Acts with the objects (as stated in its memorandum) of acquiring and carrying on a manufacturing business, and any other businesses and transactions which the company might consider to be in any way conducive or auxiliary thereto or in any way connected therewith. The articles authorised the company to purchase its own shares. The company having gone into liquidation a former shareholder made a claim against the company for the balance of the price of his shares sold by him to the company before the liquidation and not wholly paid for. It was held, reversing the decision of the EWCA that such a company had no power under the Companies Acts to purchase its own shares, that the purchase was therefore ultra vires, and that the claim must fail.[137]

8.16.1   *Reasons for capital reduction*

There are several reasons that may necessitate the reduction of capital:

Firstly, some of the capital of the company may have been lost and it has now become doubtful whether the share capital on the certificate is an accurate representation of the real world situation as it relates to the company. It would appear from the comments of Lord Parker in *Caldwell & Co Ltd v Caldwell*[138] logical for the court to probe into the reasons as to why the company is of

---

[135] Section 150(11).

[136] [1887] 12 App Cas 409.

[137] Disapproving *Re Dronfield Silkstone Coal Company* (17 Ch D 76).

[138] 1916 SC (HL) 120 *per* Lord Parker at 121.

the view that its share capital has been lost or that the assets available do not accurately represent the company's share capital. It has been shown in *Re Hoare & Co Ltd and Reduced*[139] that the court has jurisdiction to sanction a scheme for the reduction of the capital of a company, part of which has been lost or is unrepresented by available assets, whereby it is proposed to treat the loss as apportioned rateably between a sum placed to reserve and the capital account properly so called, i.e., the share capital. The fact that too large a proportion of the loss has been attributed to the reserve and too small a proportion to the share capital does not deprive the company of its right to such sanction.

Secondly, the company's share capital may be in excess of its needs. This includes directors acting to refinance the company specifically, replacing expensive share capital with debt financing. Ordinarily, the return of capital to shareholders under these circumstances will have to follow the order of priority outlined in section 127 of the Corporate Insolvency Act.[140] This situation was illustrated in the case of *Prudential Assurance Co Ltd and Others v Chatterley-Whitfield Collieries Co Ltd.*[141] In that case, a colliery company, whose capital of £400,000 was divided into 20,000 six per cent preference shares of £10 each and the same number of ordinary shares of a like nominal value, passed a special resolution, as empowered by its articles of association, to reduce its capital to £200,000 but returning to the preference shareholders the whole capital paid up on their shares. The articles conferred on the preference shareholders a right to a cumulative preference dividend of 6 per cent., and on winding up, in priority to ordinary shareholders, to repayment of capital together with any arrears of dividend down to the date of such repayment in priority to the claims of the holders of ordinary shares, but to no other participation in the assets. On Jan. 1, 1947, under the Coal Industry Nationalisation Act, 1946, the company's colliery undertaking became vested in the National Coal Board, and, pending the payment of compensation, the company was entitled under s.22(3) of the Act to interim income, and under s.22(2) to interest on the amount of the compensation. The Act provided in s.25: "(1) Provision shall be made by regulations for due regard being had, as between classes...of members...of a company being an owner of transferred interests, to what their relative expectations of income yield from their respective interest in the company would have been if this Act for the transferred interests of the company so as to give effect, so far as may be, on the one hand to the said expectations and on the other hand to the rights of priority conferred on such classes respectively by the...memorandum and articles of association of the company." Certain preference shareholders dissented from the resolution to reduce capital in the proposed manner and opposed the petition

---

[139] 1904-1907] All ER 635.
[140] Act No 9 of 2017 which replaces section 346 of CA 1994.
[141] [1949] All ER 1094; [1949] AC 512 (HL) *sub nom Re Chatterley-Whitfield Collieries Ltd* [1948] 2 All ER 593 CA.

to confirm it. It appeared that the company was not contemplating liquidation, but was prospecting for coal in Ireland and had other activities in view.

It was held that the jurisdiction of the court to adjudicate on the proposed reduction of capital was unaffected by the provisions of s.25, and it was the duty of the court not to postpone consideration of the proposed reduction, but, giving such weight as it thought proper to s.25, to dispose of the matter; in accordance with the principles on which the jurisdiction was exercised the proposal in the present case was fair and equitable; and, therefore, it was proper to be confirmed.[142]

Per Lord Greene MR:

> A company which has issued preference shares carrying a high rate of dividend and finds its business so curtailed that it has capital surplus to its requirements and sees the likelihood, or at any rate the possibility, that its preference capital will not, if I may use the expression, "earn its keep", would be guilty of financial ineptitude if it did not take steps to reduce its capital by paying off preference capital so far as the law allowed it to do so. That is mere common-place in company finance.

Thirdly, shareholders may have taken out shares but not paid for them. When reduced, the shareholder will no longer have the obligation to pay for what they hitherto owed on the shares they will now own. By the same token and as in *Westburn Sugar Refineries Ltd., Petitioners*[143]
shown in the company has no obligation to pay dividends on the shares affected.

Where, as discussed elsewhere in this text, a reduction of capital results in the variation of class rights as envisaged in section 143 and the relevant clause in the articles is contravened, the court is unlikely to grant an order for leave for the company to reduce its capital. In *Re Old Silkstone Collieries Ltd*[144] the court refused to confirm a reduction of share capital by a company drawing the conclusion that it was neither fair nor equitable between the classes of preference and ordinary shareholders.[145]

8.16.2   *Reduction of capital vs interest of creditors*

We have already seen that in terms of section 150(3) a company must, 'within twenty-one days after passing the resolution to reduce its share capital, apply

[142] *Scottish Insurance Corp Ltd v Wilsons and Clyde Coal Co Ltd* [1949] 1 All ER 1068 applied.
[143] [1951] AC 625.
[144] [1954] Ch 169 (CA).
[145] Observations of Bowen LJ in *Birmingham & District Land Co v London and North Western Railway Co* [1888] 40 Ch D 268, 286 and those of Maugham J. in *In re Dorman, Long & Co Ltd* [1934] Ch 635 applied.

to the Court for an order confirming the reduction'.[146] Such an application is by way of a petition ordinarily supported by an affidavit verifying the facts in the petition. It has been observed in *Poole v National Bank of China Ltd*[147] that to give the Court jurisdiction to entertain a petition for the reduction of capital it is not essential to prove that the capital which the company proposes to cancel is lost or unrepresented by available assets and that creditors not being concerned the questions to be considered are:

(1)   ought the Court to refuse its sanction to the reduction out of regard to the interests of those members of the public who may be induced to take shares in the company?; and

(2)   is the reduction fair and equitable as between the different classes of shareholders?

Where the proper reduction to share capital involves either a diminution/ reduction of liability in respect of share capital among other things, the creditors who are entitled to object should be duly advised so that on the date on which the petition is presented, they can have an opportunity to object to the reduction as they are entitled to do.[148] By the same token, in any reduction of capital, where there is no diminution of liability relating to any unpaid up capital or payment to any paid up capital shareholder, it follows that creditors will have no basis for objecting to a company's proposal to reduce its capital.[149] The reason is that 'no asset out of which their claims could be satisfied is being given up or returned to shareholders'.[150]

In *re Meux's Brewery Company Ltd*[151] the company was incorporated with a fully paid share capital of £1,000,000, in addition to which it had issued £1,000,000 perpetual debenture stock secured by certain trust deeds constituting a floating security. In 1904 the company had incurred losses amounting to upwards of £800,000, since which year no dividend had been declared, the profits in each year being applied in reduction the of the deficiency, which now amounted to £649,000 or upwards. In 1917, by special resolution, the company resolved to reduce its capital to £360,000 by writing off the lost capital. The reduction did not involve the diminution of any liability in respect of any unpaid capital or the payment to any shareholder of any paid-up capital. This petition by the company to confirm the special resolution was opposed by certain holders of debenture stock on the ground that the proposed reduction would be prejudicial to their security by enabling the company to pay dividends out of profits instead of such profits being applied in making good the lost capital. The assets according to the

---

[146] Replacing Section 77 CA 1994.
[147] [1907] AC 229.
[148] Section 150(12).
[149] *Re Meux's Brewery Co Ltd* [1919] 1 Ch D 28.
[150] Supra note 275 at 210.
[151] [1919] 1 Ch 28.

latest balance sheet exceeded the amount of the debenture debt by £500,000 and upwards. No evidence was adduced to show what part of the lost capital was attributable to circulating capital. It was held that the holders of the debenture stock were not entitled to object to the reduction.

We also noted that section 150(13) empowers the Court to '…settle a list of creditors entitled to object, and for that purpose' mandates it to 'ascertain, as far as possible without requiring an application from any creditor, the names of the creditors and the nature and amount of their debts or claims'. The Court may, if it deems it necessary, 'publish notices fixing a day within which creditors, not yet entered on the list, shall lose their right to object, if they have not presented a claim to be entered on the list'.[152] Where a creditor on the list referred to in section 150(13), is unable or refuses to consent to the reduction, the court will dispense with that creditor's consent but only if the company secures payment of that creditor's debt or claim by appropriating—

(a) the full amount of the debt or claim, if the company admits the full amount of the debt or claim, or undertakes to provide for the debt or claim; or

(b) an amount fixed by the Court, if the company fails to admit, and is not willing to provide for, the full amount of the debt or claim, or if the amount is contingent or not ascertained'.[153]

8.16.3   *Confirmation of reduction by Court*

Confirmation of the reduction of share capital by the court is provided for under section 151.[154] In terms of section 151(1), '[t]he Court may make an order confirming the reduction of share capital, if satisfied that every creditor of the company who is entitled to object to the reduction—

(a) consented to the reduction; or

(b) the creditor's debt or claim has been discharged, determined or secured. In terms of section 151(2), '[t]he Court may, on making an order in accordance with [section 151](1)—

    (a) direct that the company shall, during a period specified in the order, add to its name, as the last words thereof, the words "and reduced";[155] or

---

[152] In terms of section 150(8), '[t]he Court may direct that subsections (12) and (13) do not apply to a specified class or classes of creditors'. By section 150(9), '[i]f section 150(7) which provides for exceptions under section 150, 'is not applicable, section 150 (12) and (13)' will not 'apply unless the Court directs that they apply'.

[153] Section 150(14).

[154] Which replaces section 78 of CA 1994.

[155] For an example of this, see: *Re Hoare & Co., Ltd and Reduced* [1904-1907] All ER 635.

    (b)   require the company to publish—

        (i)   a notice of the reduction, in the prescribed form, on receipt of the replacement certificate of share capital; or

        (ii)   the reasons for the reduction or such other information, with regard to the reduction, as the Court may consider expedient for purposes of giving proper information to the public. Further, '[w]here a company is ordered to add to its name the words "and reduced" as specified in subsection (2)*(a)*, those words shall, until the expiry of the period specified in the order, be treated as part of the name of the company'.

The confirmation procedure and the circumstances under which it is made is meant to ensure fairness regarding three stakeholders: (1) the creditors; (2) the shareholders;[156] and (3) the public who may have dealings with the company or may invest in its shares as illustrated in the case of *Westburn Sugar Refineries Ltd., Petitioners.*[157] In the case of *Re Lucania Temperance Billiard Halls (London) Ltd,*[158] a company's proposed reduction of capital involved payment of paid-up share capital to certain shareholders. The company had sufficient cash resources to cover those payments and its liabilities, apart from those under certain leases. The majority of those leases were beneficial to the company, the remainder were neither beneficial nor onerous. On a summons by the company under section 671 of the companies Act, 1948, for an order that settlement of a list of creditors entitled to object be dispensed with. It was held *inter alia* that before giving a direction dispensing with a list of creditors under section 67(3) the court must be satisfies, having regards to the company's liquid assets, or for some other reason, that no creditor who might be entitled to object to the reduction of capital would be prejudiced by it.

If the company does not admit the debt and is unwilling to settle it in full, the court can go into adjudication to determine the veracity/legitimacy of the claim. Upon establishment of the true position it will make determination.

The court will also, in considering what is just proceed on the basis, so far as shareholders and creditors are concerned, of the pecking order in section 127 of the Corporate Insolvency Act 2017.[159] It stands to reason that in any other case

---

[156] As regards shareholders we must make the point that consideration of whether the reduction is fair and equitable must relate to shareholders *interse* whether they are of the same or different classes (see *Scottish Insurance Corporation Ltd v Wilson & Clyde Coal Co Ltd* [1949] AC 462 HL). A reduction which varies the rights of shareholders must by necessary implication be amenable to the variation procedure under section 143.

[157] [1951] AC 625; [1951]1 All ER 881.

[158] [1966] Ch D 98.

[159] For case law consider on the point see: Bannatyne*v Direct Spanish Telegraph Co* [1886] 34 Ch D 287 CA*; Re Floating Dock Co of St. Thomas Ltd* [1895] 1 Ch D 691*;* and *Re Mackenzie & Co Ltd* [1916] 2 Ch 450.

outside the foregoing tests, the court is empowered to allow a creditor to object to a reduction and where this is the case, the creditor ought to prove his case before the court makes any determination in this respect.

8.17   Dividends

8.17.1 General

The term 'dividend' comes from the late 15c., middle French *dividende* meaning 'a number divided by another', or /and from the latin word *'dividendum'* meaning 'a thing to be divided'.[160] It is a payment made by a company to its shareholders as a distribution of profits. When a company earns a profit several options are open to it. One is to reinvest the profit in the business; another is to distribute a portion of the profit to its shareholders as a dividend. This may be by way of cash or where there is a dividend reinvestment plan, by way of issuance of additional shares; or indeed share repurchase.[161] A dividend will ordinarily be allocated as a fixed amount per share owned. This entails a shareholder receiving a dividend in direct proportion to his shareholding. Our discussion in this section therefore focuses on provisions relating to the board's authority to authorise the distribution of dividends; the concept of shares being issued in *lieu* of dividends; and the recovery of distributions of dividends; and the matter of reduction of shareholder's liability and distribution.

8.17.2   Board to authorise distribution of dividends

The authorisation for the distribution of dividends is to be found under sections158, 159 and is also provided for under clause part 20 clauses 71-9. In terms of section 158(1) '…the board of directors may, if satisfied that the company shall immediately after a distribution of dividends satisfy the solvency test, authorise a distribution of dividends by the company, in an amount stated, and to a shareholder that may be entitled'.[162] This marks the first time that authority to declare dividends and their distribution has been provided for in the substantive part of the Act. In the past it has only been mentioned in the standard articles, a practice which has continued with the standard articles in schedule 1 of the Act. By section 158(2), '[t]he directors who vote in favour of a distribution of dividends shall sign a declaration stating that, in their opinion the company shall immediately after the distribution satisfy the solvency test and specifying the grounds for that opinion'. Further and according to section

---

[160] http://www.etymonline.com retrieved on 22/01/2018.
[161] Simkovic M "The Effect of Enhanced Disclosure on Open Market Stock Repurchases", 6 Berkeley Bus. L.J. 96 (2006).
[162] In terms of section 159, '[a] company shall not distribute dividends to shareholders, except out of the profits arising or accumulated from the business of the company.

158(3), '[i]f, after a distribution of dividends is authorised but before it is made, the board of directors ceases to be satisfied that the company shall, immediately after the distribution is made, satisfy the solvency test, a distribution made by the company shall be considered not to have been authorised'. Section 158(3) must be read together with section 161 discussed below.

Section 158(4) provides that '[i]n applying the solvency test for the purposes of this Act—

(a)   debts include fixed preferential returns on shares ranking ahead of those in respect of which a distribution is made, except where that fixed preferential return is expressed in the articles, as being subject to the power of the directors to make distributions, but does not include debts arising by reason of the authorisation; and

(b)   liabilities include the amount that would be required, if the company were to be removed from the Register after the distribution, to repay all fixed preferential amounts payable by the company to shareholders at that time, or on earlier redemption, except where such fixed preferential amounts are expressed in the articles as being subject to the power of directors to make distributions, subject to paragraph (a), excluding dividends payable in the future'. Finally, '[a] director who fails to comply with subsection (2) commits an offence'.[163]

8.14.3   Shares in lieu of dividends

The board of directors may, according to section 160 and subject to the company's articles, 'issue shares to shareholders who have agreed to accept the issue of shares, wholly or partly, in lieu of a proposed dividend or proposed future dividends if any of the following conditions have been complied with—

(a)   the right to receive shares, wholly or partly, in lieu of the proposed dividend or proposed future dividends has been offered to all shareholders of the same class on the same terms;

(b)   all shareholders elected to receive the shares in lieu of the proposed dividend and relative voting or distribution rights, or both, would be maintained;

(c)   the shareholders to whom the right is offered are afforded a reasonable opportunity of accepting it;

(d)   the shares issued to each shareholder are issued on the same terms and subject to the same rights as the shares issued to all shareholders in that class who agree to receive the shares; and

(e)   the provisions governing issue of shares are complied with by the board of directors'.

---

[163] Section 158(5).

8.17.4   *Recovery of distributions of dividends*

In terms of section 161(1), '[a] company may recover a distribution of dividends made to a shareholder at a time when the company did not, immediately after the distribution, satisfy the solvency test unless the—

    (a)   shareholder—

        (i)   received the distribution in good faith and without knowledge of the company's failure to satisfy the solvency test; or

        (ii)   has altered the shareholder's position in reliance on the validity of the distribution; and

    (b)   Court is satisfied that it would not be just or equitable to require repayment in full or in part, from the shareholder.

According to section 161(2), '[i]f, in a distribution of dividends made to shareholders—

    (a)   the procedure set out in this Act has not been followed; or *(b)* reasonable grounds for believing that the company would satisfy the solvency test, in accordance with this Act, did not exist at the time the declaration was signed; a director who failed to take reasonable steps to ensure compliance with the procedure or signed the declaration, as the case may be, shall be personally liable to the company, to repay to the company the portion of the dividends distributed that cannot be recovered from the shareholders'.

If it is determined that a distribution of dividends was not authorised in accordance with this Act, a director who—

    (a)   ceased, after authorisation but before the making of the distribution, to be satisfied on reasonable grounds that the company would satisfy the solvency test immediately after the distribution is made; and

    (b)   failed to take reasonable steps to prevent the distribution being made; shall be personally liable to repay to the company so much of the dividends distributed as cannot be recovered from shareholders.[164]

According to section 161(4), '[t]he Court may, in an action against a director or shareholder, in accordance with this section, if satisfied that the company could, by making a distribution of dividends of a lesser amount, have satisfied the solvency test—

    (a)   permit the shareholder to retain; or

    (b)   relieve the director from liability in respect of; an amount equal to the value of any dividends distributed that could properly have been made'.

8.17.5   *Reduction of shareholder's liability and distribution*

Section 162(1) expressly provides that '[i]f a company proposes to alter its articles, acquire shares issued by itself or redeem shares, in a manner which

---

[164] Section 161(3).

would cancel or reduce the liability of a shareholder to the company in relation to a share held prior to that alteration, acquisition, or redemption, the proposed cancellation or reduction of liability shall be treated for purposes of—

(a)　sections 159 and 160, as if it were a dividend; and

(b)　section 161, as if it were a distribution of dividends'.

Further, '[w]here a company alters its articles, acquires shares or redeems shares in a manner which cancels or reduces the liability of a shareholder to the company, in relation to a share held prior to that alteration, acquisition or redemption, that cancellation or reduction of liability shall be treated for purposes of this section as a distribution of the amount by which that liability was reduced'.[165]

By section 162(3), [i]f the liability of a shareholder of an amalgamating company in relation to a share held before the amalgamation is—

(a)　greater than the liability of that shareholder to the amalgamated company, in relation to a share or shares into which that share is converted; or

(b)　cancelled by the cancellation of that liability; the reduction of liability effected by the amalgamation shall be treated for the purposes of this Act, as a distribution by the amalgamated company of the amount by which that liability was reduced to that shareholder, whether or not that shareholder becomes a shareholder of the amalgamated company.

8.17.6　*Power to return accumulated profits in reduction of paid-up share capital*

According to section 194(1), '[a] company may, where it has accumulated a sum of undivided profits which, with the approval of the shareholders may be distributed among the shareholders in the form of a dividend or bonus, by special resolution, return the same, or any part thereof, to the shareholders in reduction of the paid-up capital of the company, the unpaid capital being thereby increased by a similar amount'. Further, and in terms of section 194(2) '[t]he company shall, in the case of a special resolution reducing share capital, within twenty-one days after making the special resolution, in accordance with subsection (1), lodge with the Registrar a return in the prescribed form giving the details required'. Additionally, section 194(3) clearly provides that '[t]he resolution, lodged in accordance with subsection (2), shall take effect from the date of lodgement'.

There are two more matters to consider the first being that in terms of section 194(4), '[a] reduction of share capital, as provided in [the] Act, shall not apply to a reduction of paid-up share capital, in accordance with this section,

---

[165] Section 162(2).

except as provided in subsection (2)'. Secondly, in terms of section 194(5), '[t]he Registrar shall not register a reduction of paid-up share capital made, in accordance with this section, unless the Registrar is satisfied that the relevant tax laws have been complied with'.

8.18   Acquisition of fully paid-up shares by company

The procedure for the acquisition of fully paid-up shares by the company is provided for under section 163. In terms of section 163(1) the right to acquire fully-paid up shares is subject to sections 170,[166] 171[167] and 172[168] which we discuss below and open to 'a company which is not a public limited company'. According to the section, this right can only be exercised by way of special resolution for a consideration as specified in section 163. It is a requirement for the board of directors to, 'within fourteen days of acquisition of the shares, lodge with the Registrar a notice in the prescribed form of such acquisition accompanied by a declaration by the directors that the company shall remain solvent after the acquisition'.[169] It is also open to '[a] member or creditor of the company or the Registrar to, if they be minded to so do, 'to apply to the Court, prior to the acquisition, for an annulment of the special resolution, made in accordance with subsection (1)'.

In terms of section 163(4), '[a] director who makes a declaration of solvency as referred to in [section 163](2), without reasonable grounds for believing that the company will remain solvent after the acquisition commits an offence and is liable, on conviction, to a fine not exceeding two hundred thousand penalty units or to imprisonment for a period not exceeding two years, or to both'.

8.19   Acquisition of company's own shares

8.19.1 General

The acquisition of a company's own shares is expressly provided for in 164. Section 164(1) subjects such acquisition to section 162[170] a company may purchase or acquire shares issued by the company if it is expressly permitted to do so by its articles. However, section 162(2) additionally provides that '[n]othing in the Act limits or affects—

---

[166] Which provides that securities exchange acquisitions are not subject to prior notice to shareholders.
[167] Which provides for cancellation of shares repurchased.
[168] Which provides for enforceability of contract to repurchase shares.
[169] Section 163(2); In terms of section 163(5), '[i]f the board of directors fails to comply with subsection (2), every director of the company commits an offence and is liable, on conviction, to a fine not exceeding two hundred thousand penalty units or to imprisonment for a period not exceeding two years, or to both'.
[170] Which provides for '[r]eduction of shareholder's liability and distribution.

(a)   an order of the Court that requires a company to purchase or acquire its own shares; or

(b)   any provision of this Act which relates to the right of a shareholder to require a company to purchase shares'.

8.19.2   *Board may make offer to acquire shares*

The starting point in this regard is section 165(1) which provides that, [t]he board of directors may make an offer to acquire shares issued by the company, if the offer is to—

(a)   all shareholders to acquire a proportion of their shares that—
  (i)   if accepted, would not affect relative voting and distribution rights; and
  (ii)   give an opportunity to accept the offer; or

(b)   one or more shareholders to acquire shares and—
  (i)   to which all shareholders have consented in writing; or
  (ii)   which is expressly permitted by the articles and is made in accordance with the procedure set out in this Act.

Where, according to section 165(2), 'an offer is made, in accordance with section 165(1) *(a)*—

(a)   the offer may permit the company to acquire additional shares from a shareholder to the extent that another shareholder does not accept the offer or accepts the offer only in part; and

(b)   in which the number of additional shares exceeds the number of shares that the company is entitled to acquire, the number of additional shares shall be reduced proportionately'.

Further and in terms of section 165(3), [t]he board of directors may make an offer, in terms of [section 165](1), if it has resolved that the—

(a)   acquisition is in the best interests of the company and its shareholders;

(b)   terms of the offer and the consideration offered for the shares are fair and reasonable to the company its shareholders; and

(c)   board is not aware of any information that has not been disclosed to the shareholders—
  (i)   which is material to an assessment of the value of the shares; and
  (ii)   as a result of which the terms of the offer and consideration offered for the shares are unfair to shareholders accepting the offer. 'The resolution, required by [section 165](3), shall set out in full the reasons for the board of director's resolutions'.[171]

---

[171] Section 165(4).

Also, '[t]he directors who vote in favour of a resolution, required by subsection (3), shall sign a declaration as to the matters set out in that subsection'.[172]

The foregoing notwithstanding, in terms of section 165(6), '[t]he board of directors shall not make an offer in terms of subsection (1) if, after the passing of a resolution required by [section 165](3) but before the making of the offer to acquire the shares, the board—

(a)   ceases to be satisfied that the—
    (i)   acquisition is in the best interest of the company; and
    (ii) terms of the offer and the consideration offered for the shares are fair and reasonable to the company; or
(b)   becomes aware of information that has not been disclosed to the shareholders—
    (i)   which is material to an assessment of the value of the shares; or
(ii) as a result of which the terms of the offer and consideration offered for the shares would be unfair to the shareholders accepting the offer'.

8.20   Special offers to acquire shares

The Act makes categorical provision that '[t]he board of directors may make an offer to acquire shares in terms of this Act, if the board resolves that the

(a)   acquisition shall benefit the remaining shareholders; and
(b)   terms of the offer and the consideration offered for the shares are fair and reasonable to the remaining shareholders'.[173]

The resolution to be made by the board of directors as specified above, it is provided, 'shall set out, in full, the reasons for the board's resolutions'.[174] 'The directors who vote in favour of a resolution, made in accordance with [section 166](1)', are required to 'sign a declaration as to the matters set out in that [section 166](1)'.[175]

However, if, after the passing of a resolution required by section 166(1), but before the making of the offer to acquire the shares, the board has a changed view and as such is no longer 'satisfied as to the matters resolved in terms of that [section 166](1)', '[t]he board of directors shall not make an offer, as specified in [section 166](1)'.[176] We must explain that 'before an offer is made in accordance with section 166(1), the board of directors is mandated to 'send

---

[172] Section 165(5). By section 165(7), '[a] director who fails to comply with [section 165](5) commits an offence'.
[173] Section 166(1).
[174] Section 166(2).
[175] Section 166(3). In terms of section 166(9), '[a] director who fails to comply with [section 166](3) commits an offence'.
[176] Section 166(4).

to each shareholder a disclosure document[177] that complies with [section 166] (3)'.[178] Further, '[a]n offer, in accordance with [section166](1), shall be made not less than fourteen days and not more than twelve months after the disclosure document, specified in [section 166(5), has been sent to each shareholder'.[179] In terms of section 166(7), '[section 166(5) and (6)] shall not apply to an offer to a shareholder by a company, if the offer is in relation to shares quoted on a registered securities exchange market and the number of those shares is less than the minimum holding of shares prescribed by that exchange'.

According to section 166(8), '[a] shareholder or the company may apply to the Court for an order restraining the proposed acquisition of shares on the grounds that—

(a)   it is not in the best interest of the company or for the benefit of the remaining shareholders; or

(b)   the terms of the offer and the consideration offered for the shares are not fair or reasonable to the company or the remaining shareholders'.

8.21   Securities exchange acquisitions subject to prior notice to shareholders

Section 168(1) overtly provides that, [t]he board of directors may make offers on one or more securities exchanges to all shareholders to acquire shares, if the board resolves—

(a)   to acquire not more than a specified number of shares, by means of offers on one or more securities exchanges;

(b)   that the acquisition is in the best interest of the company and its shareholders;

(c)   that the terms of the offer and the consideration offered for the shares are fair and reasonable to the company and its shareholders; and

(d)   that the board is not aware of any information that has not been disclosed to shareholders—

(i)   which is material to an assessment of the value of the shares; and

(ii)   as a result of which the terms of the offer and consideration offered for the shares are unfair to shareholders accepting the offer.

---

[177] According to section 167, '[f]or the purposes of section 166, a disclosure document is a document that sets out the—*(a)* nature and terms of an offer, and if made to specified shareholders, the names of those shareholders; *(b)* nature and extent of any interest of a director in any share which is the subject of the offer; and *(c)* text of the resolution required by section 166 (2), together with such further information and explanation as may be necessary to enable a shareholder to understand the nature and implications, for the company and its shareholders, of the proposed acquisition of shares'.

[178] Section 166(5). In terms of section 166(10), '[i]f the board of directors fails to comply with [section 166](5), every director of the company commits an offence'

[179] Section 166(6).

In terms of section 168(6), '[t]he board of directors shall, before an offer is made, in accordance with [section 168](1), send to each shareholder a disclosure document that complies with sections 166 and 167'. By section 168(7),'[t] he offer, made in accordance with subsection (1), shall be made not less than fourteen days and not more than twelve months after the disclosure document, specified in subsection(6), has been sent to each shareholder'.

According to section 169(1), [f]or purposes of section 168, a disclosure document is a document that sets out the—

(a)   maximum number of shares that the board of directors resolves to acquire;

(b)   nature and terms of the offer made;

(c)   nature and extent of any relevant interest of a director in the shares to be acquired; and

(d)   text of the resolution required by section 168, together with such further information and explanation as may be necessary to enable a shareholder to understand the nature and implications, for the company and its shareholders, of the proposed acquisition of shares.[180]

'The resolution to be made, as specified in [section 168](1), shall set out in full the reasons for the board's resolution'.[181] Additionally, '[t]he directors who vote in favour of a resolution, made in accordance with [section 168](1), shall make a declaration as to the matters set out in that subsection'.[182] In terms of section 168(4), '[a] director, who is authorised by a resolution of the board of directors, may make any of the offers specified in [section 168](1)'.

By section 168(5)[183] '[a]n offer, referred to in [section 168](1), shall not be made if—

(a)   the number of the shares to be acquired, when aggregated with any shares already acquired, would exceed the maximum number of shares the board of directors resolved to acquire in accordance with that subsection;

(b)   after the passing of a resolution, required by that subsection, but before the making of the offer to acquire the shares, the board of directors ceases to be satisfied that the—

(i)   acquisition is in the best interest of the company and its shareholders; and

(ii)   terms of the offer and the consideration offered for the shares are fair and reasonable to the company and its shareholders; or

---

[180] By section 168(2), '[n]othing in subsection (1) shall require the board of directors to disclose the consideration the board of directors proposes to offer for the acquisition of the shares'.

[181] Section 168(2).

[182] Section 168(3). According to section 168(9), '[a] director who fails to comply with [section 168(3), commits an offence'.

[183] By section 168(10), '[i]f the board of directors fails to comply with [section 168](5) every director commits an offence'.

(c)   the board of directors becomes aware of any information specified in section168(1)*(d)'*.

A shareholder or the company is permitted, if he/it be minded to, to make an application before the High Court 'for an order restraining a proposed acquisition of shares on the grounds that—

(a)   it is not in the best interest of the company or the shareholders; or

(b)   the terms of the offer and, if it is disclosed, the consideration offered for the shares are not fair or reasonable to the company or its shareholders'.

8.22   Securities exchange acquisitions not subject to prior notice to shareholders

Despite the provisions of section 163, section 170(1)[184] unambiguously provides that 'the board of directors may acquire shares on a securities exchange from its shareholders if—

(a)   prior to the acquisition, the board resolves that the—

(i)   acquisition is in the best interest of the company and the shareholders;

(ii)   terms of, and consideration for, the acquisition are fair and reasonable to the company; and

(iii)   board is not aware of any information that is not available to shareholders, which is material to an assessment of the value of the shares and as a result of which, the terms of, and consideration for, the acquisition are unfair to shareholders from whom any share is acquired; and

(b)   the number of the shares to be acquired, when aggregated with any other shares acquired pursuant to this section in the preceding twelve months, does not exceed five percent of the shares in the same class as at the date twelve months prior to the acquisition of the shares'.

In terms of section 170(2), '[t]he board of directors shall, within fourteen days after shares are acquired, send to each securities exchange on which the shares of the company are listed, a notice in the prescribed form containing the—

(a)   class and number of shares acquired;

(b)   consideration paid or payable for the shares acquired; and

(c)   identity of the seller, if known to the company and if the seller was not the beneficial owner, the identity of the beneficial owner'. Within three months after the acquisition of shares, the board of directors shall 'send to each shareholder a notice in the prescribed form containing the particulars referred to in [section 170](2)'.[185] According to section

---

[184] According to section 170(4), '[a] director who is authorised by a resolution of the board, may make an acquisition specified in subsection (1)'.

[185] Section 170(3).

170(5) '[i]f the board of directors fails to comply with [section 170](2) or [section 170](3), every director commits an offence'.

8.23   Cancellation of shares repurchased

According to section 171(1), '[s]hares that are acquired by a company other than in accordance with this Act, shall be considered to be cancelled immediately on acquisition'. Further and in terms of section 171(2) and for purposes of section 171(1), 'shares shall be acquired on the date on which the company would, if it were not for this section, become entitled to exercise the rights attached to the shares'. Finally and in terms of section 171(3), '[o]n the cancellation of a share, in accordance with this section, the—

(a)   rights and privileges attached to that share shall expire; or

(b)   share may be reissued in accordance with this Part'.[186]

8.24   Enforceability of contract to repurchase shares

'A contract with a company, providing for the acquisition by the company of its shares, shall be specifically enforceable against the company, unless the performance of the contract by the company would result in the company being unable to satisfy the solvency test'.[187] The 'burden of proving that performance of the contract would result in the company being unable to satisfy the solvency test' is borne by the company.[188]   In terms of section 170(3), '[a] party to a contract with a company, for purposes of this section, shall retain the status of a claimant entitled to be paid as soon as the company is lawfully able to pay or, prior to the removal of the company from the Register, to be ranked subordinate to the rights of creditors but in priority to the other shareholders, until a company has fully performed a contract referred to in [section 170(1)'.

8.25   Company may hold its own shares

The provisions of section 171 notwithstanding, in terms of section 173(1), '[a] share acquired by a company, shall not be considered to be cancelled…, if the—

(a)   articles expressly permit the company to hold its own shares;

(b)   board of directors resolves that the share shall not be cancelled on acquisition; and

(c)   number of the shares acquired, when aggregated with shares of the same class held by the company in terms of this section at the time of the acquisition, does not exceed five percent of the shares of that

---

[186] But See Section 173 which provides for a company holding its own shares.
[187] Section 172(1).
[188] Section 172(2).

class previously issued by the company, excluding shares previously considered to be cancelled in accordance with section 171'.

Further, and in terms of section 173(2), '[a] share acquired by a company, in accordance with section 171, which, as provided in this section, is not considered to be cancelled, shall be held by the company in itself'. By section 173(3), '[t]he board of directors may, by resolution, cancel a share that the company holds in itself'.

In terms of section 174(1), '[t]he rights and obligations attaching to a share held by a company in itself, in accordance with this Act, shall not be exercised by or against the company while it holds the share'. However, '[d]espite the generality of subsection (1), a company shall not, while holding a share in itself, in accordance with this Act—

    (a) exercise any voting rights attaching to the share; or

    (b) make or receive any distribution authorised or payable in respect of the share'.

Section 175 provides for reissue of shares held by company in itself. Section 175(1) makes reference to section 189[189] as applying 'to the transfer of a share held by a company in itself, as if the transfer was an issue of the share in accordance with section 147.[190] Section 175(2) subjects 'the transfer of a share by a company in itself to section 175(1) but at the same time makes the point that such transfer as is envisaged under section 175(2) itself 'is not subject to [the] Act or the articles in relation to the issue of shares, except to the extent that the articles expressly apply to the transfer of shares'.

8.26   Redeemable shares

8.26.1 General

The redemption of redeemable shares at the option of the company or shareholders was provided for under section 59 of CA 1994 and is a standard feature of Zambian company law. Unless it has in existence shares which are not redeemable, a company is proscribed from issuing redeemable shares. It follows that the action to issue redeemable shares is only exercisable when a company has other classes of shares that are non-redeemable. The following provisions demonstrate the law according to the Act.

For purposes of the Act, 'a share shall be redeemable if the articles—

    (a) provide for the company to issue redeemable shares; or

    (b) the terms of issue of the share provide for the redemption of that share by the company—

        (i)   at the option of the company or the holder of the share; or

---

[189] Which provides for restrictions on transferability of shares.

[190] Which provides for issue of shares.

      (ii)   on a date specified in the articles or the terms of issue of the share'.[191]

According to section 176(2), '[t]he consideration for the redemption of a share, in accordance with subsection (1), shall be—

    (a)   specified;

    (b)   calculated by reference to a formula; or

    (c)   required to be fixed by a suitably qualified person who is not associated with or interested in the company'.

8.26.2   Redemption at option of company

In terms of section 177(1), '[a] company shall not exercise an option to redeem shares, unless the option is exercised in relation to—

    (a)   all shareholders of the same class and in a manner that shall not affect relative voting and distribution rights;

    (b)   one or more shareholders and—

        (i)   all shareholders have consented in writing; or

        (ii) the option is expressly permitted by the articles and is exercised in accordance with the relevant procedure set out in this Act'.

Further, and in terms of section 177(2), '[a] company shall not exercise an option to redeem shares unless, before the exercise of the option, the board of directors has resolved that the—

    (a)   redemption of the shares is in the best interest of the company;

    (b)   consideration for the redemption of the shares is fair and reasonable to the company; and

    (c)   board is satisfied, on reasonable grounds, that the company shall, immediately after the share is redeemed, satisfy the solvency test'. By section 177(3), '[t]he resolution, required to be made as specified in subsection (2), shall set out, in full, the grounds for the board of director's resolution'. It is a requirement under section 177(4) that '[t]he directors who vote in favour of a resolution, made in accordance with subsection (2), shall sign a declaration as to the matters set out in that subsection'. It is an offence for any director to fail to act in accordance with section 177(4).[192]

We must note that under section 177(5) a company is proscribed from exercising 'an option to redeem shares, in terms of [section 177](1) if, after the passing of a resolution made in accordance with this section but before the exercise of the option to redeem the shares, the board of directors ceases to be satisfied that the—

    (a)   redemption of the shares is in the best interest of the company; or

---

[191] Section 176(1).

[192] Section 177(7).

(b)   consideration for the exercise of the option is fair and reasonable to the company'.

Additionally, section 177(6) makes section 160[193] applicable 'in relation to the redemption of a share at the option of the company, with such modifications as may be necessary'.

8.26.3   *Special redemption of shares*

A company may, in terms of section 178(1), exercise an option to redeem shares, in accordance with section 176,[194] if the board of directors resolves that the—

(a)   redemption of the shares is of benefit to the remaining shareholders; and

(b)   consideration for the redemption of the shares is fair and reasonable to the remaining shareholders. It is a requirement that '[t]he resolution to be made as specified in subsection (1), be set out, in full, the grounds for the directors' resolution.[195]It is also a requirement that '[t]he directors who vote in favour of a resolution, made in accordance with subsection (1), shall sign a declaration as to the matters set out in that subsection'. Section 178(8) makes failure to comply with section 178(3) by any director an offence.

If, following the passage of a resolution in accordance with section 178(1), but before the option is exercised, the board of directors is no longer of the view that the—

(a)   redemption of the shares is of benefit to the remaining shareholders; or

(b)   consideration for the redemption of the shares is fair and reasonable to the remaining shareholders, the company is obliged, under section 178(4), not to exercise the option to redeem shares.

The board of directors is directed to, 'before exercising the option referred to in section 178(1), send to each shareholder, a disclosure document that complies with [section 179],[196] after the resolution is passed'. Section 179 defines a disclosure document in terms of section 178 as being 'a document that sets out the—

(a)   nature and terms of the redemption of the shares, and if the option to redeem the shares is to be exercised in relation to specified shareholders, the names of those shareholders; and

(b)   text of the resolution specified in that section, together with such further information and explanation as may be necessary to enable a reasonable shareholder to understand the nature and implications, for the company and its shareholders, of the proposed redemption'.

---

[193] Which provides for distributions by way of Shares in *lieu* of dividends.
[194] Relating to redeemable shares.
[195] Section 178(2).
[196] Disclosure document.

It is worth remembering that section 178(6) puts a time limit on the exercise the option referred to in section 178(1) to 'not less than fourteen and not more than thirty days after the disclosure document [defined under section 179] has been sent to each shareholder'. It is worth explaining that there always remains recourse to the High Court for any shareholder who so wishes, or the company, if it so desires, by way of application 'for an order restraining the proposed exercise of an option on the grounds that—

(a) it is not in the best interest of the company or to the benefit of the remaining shareholders; or

(b) the consideration for the redemption is not fair or reasonable to the company or the remaining shareholders'.[197]

Section 180 does authorise a company to cancel redeemed shares. In terms of section 180(1), '[w]here a company redeems shares, in accordance with section 177, the redeemed shares shall be considered to be cancelled immediately on redemption'. In addition, section 180(2) clearly states that '[o]n the cancellation of a share in terms of this section the—

(a) rights and privileges attached to that share shall expire; and

(b) share may be reissued in accordance with this Part'.

8.26.4   *Redemption at option of shareholder*

In instances where, as envisaged under section 181, the redemption is at the option, not of the company but a shareholder upon the holder giving proper notice, in the prescribed form, to the company requiring the company to redeem the share the following may, according to section 181(1), ensue—

(a) the company may redeem the share on the date specified in the notice, or if no date is specified, on the date of receipt of the notice;

(b) the share shall be considered to be cancelled on the date of redemption; and

(c) from the date of redemption, the former shareholder ranks as an unsecured creditor of the company for the consideration payable on redemption. Section 181(2) makes the point that '[a] redemption in terms of this section is not a distribution for the purposes of section 158'.[198]

8.26.5   *Redemption on fixed date*

Section 182 provides for what should occur in the event that a share is redeemable on a specified date, specifically, that—

---

[197] Section 179(7).

[198] Which empowers the board of directors to authorise a distribution of dividends.

(a) company shall redeem the share on that date;

(b) share shall be deemed to be cancelled on that date; and

(c) former shareholder ranks as an unsecured creditor of the company for the consideration payable on redemption from that date. As in the case of a redemption at the option of a shareholder, '[a] redemption in accordance with section 182 'is not a distribution for the purposes of sections 157[199] and 158.[200]

8.26.6 *Restriction on financial assistance in acquisition of shares*

There are strict requirements that need to be met by a company under the provisions of section 183 regarding financial assistance in acquisition of shares. Section 183(1) for example proscribes a company from giving 'financial assistance to a person for purposes of acquiring shares in the company'. In terms of section 183(2) '...where a person has acquired shares in a company and liability has been incurred by that person or any other person, for the purpose of the acquisition, the company shall not give any financial assistance, directly or indirectly, for the purpose of reducing or discharging the liability incurred'.[201]

Under section 183(3) the following are not prohibited—

(a) a distribution of a company's assets by way of dividend lawfully made or a distribution made in the course of winding up of the company;

(b) the allotment of bonus shares;

(c) anything done in terms of an order of the Court, as specified in this Act;

(d) anything concerning a scheme of arrangement as provided in the Corporate Insolvency Act, 2017;

(e) anything done in accordance with an arrangement made between a company and its creditors which is binding on the creditors as provided in the Corporate Insolvency Act, 2017;

(f) a reduction of a company's share capital confirmed by order of the Court, as specified in this Part; or

(g) redemption of a share as specified in this Part.

Section 183(4) which is the antithesis of section 183(3) provides that the following will not be prohibited—

(a) lending of money by a company in the ordinary course of its business, if the lending of money is part of the ordinary business of the company;

---

[199] Which provides that '[a] share shall be considered issued when the name of the holder is entered on the share register of the company'.

[200] Which empowers directors to authorise the distribution of dividends.

[201] In terms of section 183(7), '[i]f a company fails to comply with subsection (1) or (2), the company and each officer in default commit an offence and are liable, on conviction, to a fine not exceeding two hundred thousand penalty units or, in the case of each officer in default, to imprisonment for a period not exceeding two years, or to both'.

(b) provision by a company, in accordance with an employee's share scheme, of money for acquisition of fully paid-up shares in the company to be held by, or for the benefit of, employees of the company, including any director holding a salaried position in the company; or

(c) making, by a company, of loans to persons, other than directors, employed in good faith by the company, with a view to enabling those persons acquire fully paid-up shares, other than as nominees of the company. However, by section 183(5), '[a] public company shall not, in giving financial assistance to a person, in accordance with [section 183](4), reduce its net assets, other than distributable profits'.

"[A] person incurring any liability" under section 183, includes, so far as section 183(6) is concerned, 'a reference to a person changing that person's financial position by making any agreement or arrangement, whether enforceable or unenforceable and whether made on the person's own account or with any other person, or by any other means'.

8.26.7 Relaxation of restrictions for private companies

The stringent requirements relating to financial assistance under section 183 are somewhat relaxed under 184 with respect to private companies. For this reason section 184(1) provides that '[a] private company may give financial assistance for the acquisition of shares in—

(a) itself as specified in with this section;

(b) another private company that is its holding company as specified in this section, unless it is the subsidiary of a—

    (i) body corporate not incorporated in Zambia; or

    (ii) public company; that is also a subsidiary of the holding company concerned'.

Be that as it may, in terms of section 184(2), '[f]inancial assistance shall not be given, in accordance with [section 184], unless the—

(a) company proposing to give the financial assistance is a wholly owned subsidiary; or

(b) giving of the assistance is approved by a special resolution of the company'.

Additionally, '[a] company shall not give financial assistance for the acquisition of shares in its holding company, unless approved by special resolution of —

(a) the holding company; and

(b) any other company which is both the company's holding company and a subsidiary of the holding company, referred to in paragraph (a), other than a wholly owned subsidiary'.

According to section 184(4), '[w]here the board of directors is proposing to give financial assistance and, where the shares to be acquired are shares in its holding company, the boards of directors of the companies referred to in subsections (3) *(a)* and *(b)* shall, not more than seven days before the special resolution is put to a meeting, make a statutory declaration in the prescribed form complying with subsection (5), and shall make the declaration available, together with the auditors' report, for inspection by members at a meeting at which the resolution is to be voted on'.

In terms of section 184(5), '[a] statutory declaration, for the purposes of [section 184](4), shall—

(a) contain particulars of the assistance to be given and of the business of the company of which they are directors, as may be prescribed;

(b) identify the person to whom the assistance is to be given;

(c) state that, to the best of the board's knowledge and belief, the company shall be able to pay its debts—

    (i) in full, within twelve months of the commencement of the winding up of the company, if it is intended to commence the winding up of the company within twelve months of the date of the declaration; or

    (ii) as they fall due during the year immediately following that date, in any other case'.[202]

We must add that '[t]he board of directors shall, in forming its views for the purposes of the statutory declaration, take into account any liabilities of the company which the Court would be required by the Corporate Insolvency Act, 2017, in relation to winding up, to take into account in determining whether the company is insolvent'.[203]

It is also important to realise that '[w]here a special resolution is required by this section to be passed approving the giving of financial assistance, financial assistance shall not be given less than thirty days after the date on which the—

(a) special resolution is passed; or

(b) last of the resolutions is passed, where more than one such resolution is passed; unless every member which passed the resolution who was entitled to vote on the resolution, or any of the resolutions, voted in favour of the resolution'.[204]

Further, '[w]here a special resolution is passed by a company, in accordance with this section, an application may be made to the Court for the cancellation of that resolution, by not less than twenty percent of the members, being persons who did not consent to, or vote in favour of, the resolution, within twenty-one

[202] Intrinsic to the requirements under section 184(5) is the auditor's report which in terms of section 184(7) ought to be—'*(a)* be addressed to the directors who made the declaration; and *(b)* state that the auditors have enquired into the state of affairs of the company and are not aware of any thing to indicate that the opinion expressed by the directors in the declaration is unreasonable in all the circumstances'.
[203] Section 184(6).
[204] Section 184(8).

days after the making of the resolution'.[205] The consequence of an application being made in terms of section 184(9) is that 'financial assistance shall not be given before the final determination of the application, unless the Court orders otherwise'.[206]

One must be mindful of the fact that despite the foregoing, section 184(11) provides that '[f]inancial assistance shall not be given...,more than sixty days after the date on which the—

(a)   directors of the company proposing to give the financial assistance made the statutory declaration required by subsection (4); or

(b)   earliest of the declarations required by the subsection is made, where the company is a subsidiary and both its directors and the directors of any of its holding companies made such a declaration; unless the court, on an application for the cancellation of any of the resolutions, orders otherwise'.

In terms of section 184(12), '[a] company shall lodge with the Registrar, a statutory declaration referred to in subsection (4), together with the auditors' report and a copy of the special resolution, within twenty-one days after the—

(a)   passing of the special resolution, if there was no application in terms of subsection (9); or

(b)   Court's decision, if such an application was made but rejected by the Court'.

By section 184(13), '[i]f a company fails to comply with subsection (12), the company and each officer of the company in default commit an offence and shall be liable on conviction to the general penalty specified in this Act'. According to section 184(14), '[a] director who makes a statutory declaration, for the purposes of this section, without having reasonable grounds for the opinion expressed in that declaration, commits an offence and shall be liable, on conviction, to a fine not exceeding one hundred thousand penalty units or to imprisonment for a period not exceeding twelve months, or to both'.

8.27   Holding companies and subsidiary companies

8.27.1   General

Our discussion must invariably turn to holding companies and subsidiaries within the context of section 185. According to section 185(1), '...the composition of a company's board of directors is controlled by another company, if more than half of the directors—

(a)   of the other company is able, without the consent or concurrence of any other person, to appoint or remove a director; or

(b)   a person's appointment as a director follows from the person's appointment as a director of the other company'.

---

[205] Section 184(9).
[206] Section 184(10).

In 'determining whether the composition of a company's board of directors is controlled by another company, shares held or power exercisable—

(a) by a person—

    (i)   who is an effective nominee of the other company shall be deemed to be held or exercisable by the other company;

    (ii) by virtue of a debenture of the company or trust deed for securing any issue of debentures shall be disregarded; and

    (iii) only by way of security for the purposes of a transaction entered into in the ordinary course of business, shall be disregarded, if the ordinary business of the person includes the lending of money; or *(b)* in a fiduciary capacity, shall be disregarded'.[207]

In terms of section 185(3), '…a member is the effective nominee of another company if the member is—

(a) a nominee of the other company;

(b) a subsidiary of the other company; or

(c) nominated by a person who is an effective nominee of the other company, in accordance with paragraph *(a)* or *(b)*'.

8.27.2 *Subsidiary may not hold shares in holding company*

There are mandatory provisions in section 186 in this regard. Section 186(1) provides that a subsidiary shall not hold shares in its holding company. *A fortiori* neither '[a]n issue of shares by a holding company to its subsidiary'[208] nor a 'transfer of shares in a holding company to its subsidiary'[209] are valid. However, '… where a company which holds shares in another company, becomes a subsidiary of the other company, the company may continue to hold the shares, but shall not exercise any voting rights attaching to the shares'. Further, '[n]othing in [section 186] 'shall prevent a subsidiary from holding shares in its holding company, in the subsidiary's capacity as a personal representative or an assignee, unless the holding company or another subsidiary has a beneficial interest under a trust, other than an interest that arises by way of security, for the purposes of a transaction made in the ordinary course of business relating to the lending of money'. Section 186, it must be realised, is applicable to a nominee of a subsidiary in the same way it applies to the subsidiary'.[210]

8.28 Transfer of shares

The transfer of shares is a voluntary *inter-vivos* (between living people) disposition characterised by three elements namely (1) that it is voluntary; (2)

---

[207] Section 185(2).
[208] Sections 186(2).
[209] Sections 186(3).
[210] Section 186(6).

it is *inter-vivos;* and (3) there is divestiture of interest. We have already made the point that '[a] share in a company is personal property'. Being such, and in terms of section 188(1) subject only to the articles, 'fully paid-up shares in a company may be transferred by entry of the name of the transferee on the share and beneficial ownership register and evidenced by registration with the Registrar'.

Section 188(2) adds to the foregoing providing that '[f]or the purpose of transferring shares, a share transfer form signed by the present holder of the shares or by the personal representative of the present holder shall be delivered to—

(a) the company; or

(b) an agent of the company who maintains the share register in accordance with section 195'.[211]

There is a requirement under section 188(3) for '[a] share transfer form' to, 'where registration as holder of the shares imposes a liability to the company on the transferee, be signed by the transferee'. By section 188(4), '[t]he personal representative of a shareholder may transfer a share without being a shareholder at the time of transfer'. According to section 188(5),'[w]ithin twenty-one days of receipt of a share transfer form, in accordance with subsection (2) and, if applicable, subsection (3)', a company shall 'enter or cause to be entered the name of the transferee on the share register as holder of the shares, unless—

(a) the board of directors resolves, within that period, to refuse or delay the registration of the transfer, and the resolution sets out in full the reasons for doing so;

(b) notice of the resolution, made in accordance with paragraph *(a)*, is sent within seven days of the resolution being passed, to the transferor and the transferee, and lodged with the Registrar; and

(c) this Act or the articles expressly permit the board of directors to refuse or delay registration for the reasons stated in the resolution'. By section 188(9), '[i]f a company fails to comply with subsection (5), the company and each officer in default, commits an offence and is liable, on conviction, to a fine not exceeding twenty thousand penalty units'.

Further and according to section 188(6), '[a] transferee of shares, in a company, shall, within fourteen days of the transferee's name being entered on the share register, as specified in subsection (1), notify the Registrar in the prescribed form and pay a fee as may be prescribed'. 'The prescribed form, referred to in subsection (6), shall be signed by both the transferor and the transferee'.[212] In terms of section 188(10), '[a] person who fails to comply with subsection (6) commits an offence'.

---

[211] Which provides for the '[p]ower to return accumulated profits in reduction of paid-up share capital'.

[212] Section 188(7).

While the general rule is that shares must be freely transferable, section 188(8) takes cognisance of the fact that this may not always be possible. It in fact indicates that the articles may provide the directors with the power of refusal under certain circumstances specifically, 'that the board of directors may refuse or delay the registration of a transfer of shares, if the shareholder fails to pay to the company, an amount due in respect of those shares, either by way of consideration for the issue of the shares or in respect of sums payable by the shareholder in accordance with the articles'.

It has been shown in the case of *In re Discoverers Finance Corporation, Ltd, Lindlar's case*[213] that where the articles contain no clause authorising directors to reject a transferee, a shareholder may up to the last moment before liquidation, and for the express purpose of escaping liability, transfer his partly paid shares to a transferee, even though he be a pauper, and may compel the directors to register that transfer, provided it be an out and out transfer reserving to the transferor no beneficial right to the shares direct or indirect. Whether the transfer is of that character is a question of fact. Where the articles contain a clause empowering the directors to reject a transferee whom they do not approve, the transferor cannot escape liability if he has actively or passively induced the directors to pass and register a transfer (even though it be an out and out transfer) which, but for his conduct, they would have refused to register. Here again the question is one of fact. Whether directors refuse registration, the transferor cannot escape liability where he has obtained the advantage of executing and registering his transfer upon an opportunity obtained by him fraudulently or in breach of some duty which he owed the company.

8.29   Restrictions on transferability

Restrictions on the transferability of shares are subject only to limitations or restrictions on such transfer in the articles and the Act. Outside that, shares in a company shall be transferable without restriction—

(a)   provided they are fully paid up; and

(b)   by a transfer in accordance with section 187.[214]

An important provision to take note of is section 189(2) which provides that 'the articles of a private company shall not impose any restriction on the transferability of shares after they have been issued, unless all the shareholders have agreed in writing'. It has been shown in the case *Borland's Trustees v Steel Bros & Co Ltd*[215] that provisions in a company's articles of association compelling a shareholder at any time during the continuance of the company to

---

[213] [1910] 1 Ch D 312.

[214] Section 189(1) which replaces section 65(1) but retains its contents as do other subsections under it.

[215] [1901] 1 Ch 279.

transfer his shares to particular persons at a particular price are not void as being repugnant to absolute ownership, or as tending to perpetuity. [In essence t]here is nothing obnoxious to bankruptcy law in articles which bona fide provide that a shareholder shall, in the event of his bankruptcy, sell his shares to particular persons at a particular price, which is fixed for all persons alike, and is not shown to be less than the fair price which might otherwise be obtained.[216]

In *Jarvis Motors (Harrow) Ltd and Another v Carabott and Another*[217] the articles of association of a private company formed in 1959 restricted the transfer of shares and by article 15 required that "on the death of a member his...shares must be offered to the other "member at par." K. and N. the sole shareholders and subscribers to the company's articles, held 250 1*l*. shares each, and on the death of K. in 1962, N. tendered 250*l*. to K's executors and required them to implement the provision in the articles, but they refused. N. brought an action claiming specific performance of the obligation imposed on them. It was held that no contrary intention appeared in article 15 to offset, the usual rule that the plural included the singular and, therefore, on its true construction, the articles required that shares should be offered to a sole surviving member; that requirement was not invalidated by any statutory provision as to the minimum number of members of a limited company; and that, accordingly, the shares should be transferred to the plaintiff in return for the amount tendered less the taxed cost of the action.

The foregoing notwithstanding, section 189(3) provides quite obviously that the board of directors shall refuse to register a transfer of shares to any person who—

(a) is under eighteen years of age;

(b) has been declared by the Court or a court of competent jurisdiction of another country to be of unsound mind; or

(c) is an undischarged bankrupt. This provision must be seen within the context of section 12(8) which precludes these same classes of people from subscribing to an application for incorporation. Further, if one appreciates that in terms of section 146 a company is mandated at incorporation to 'issue to each qualified person named in the application for incorporation as a shareholder' it becomes apparent why no board would confirm any transfer to any of the persons disqualified by sections 12, 146 and 189(3). In fact, were a board to accept such transfer, it would trigger the kind of injunctive relief envisaged in section 330 by any of the persons entitled to commence such action thereunder.

A few other points may be made regarding the directors' power to refuse the transfer of shares. As exemplified in *Tett v Phoenix Property and Investment*

[216] See further, *The Ocean Coal Co Ltd v The Powell Duffryn Steam Coal Co* [1932] 1 Ch 654.
[217] [1964] 1 WLR 1101.

Co,[218] the directors have no power to refuse to effect a transfer already made but in breach of the pre-emption rights. Additionally, it is unlikely that a court would interfere with the company exercising its power pursuant to section 189(3). Be that as it may, as was the case in *Stewart v James Keiller & Sons Ltd*[219] the improper exercise of discretion by directors can be a valid basis for a court interfering in their refusal to allow a transfer of shares by a member.

Further to the foregoing, the directors' right to refuse a transfer is well within their fiduciary powers. To that end, they are destined to act in the best interests of the company, fairly table the issue at a properly constituted board meeting recognising a shareholder's right to transfer his shares in accordance with sections 146 and 189(1) of the Act. In *Re Smith and Fawcett Ltd*[220] where the articles of association of a private company gave the directors absolute and uncontrolled discretion of refusal as regards the registration of any transfer of shares. It was shown that the only limitation on the directors' discretion was that it should be exercised bona fide in the interests of the company.

The directors' motives for declining to agree to a transfer may range from them not approving of the transferee to the transferor being indebted to the company. Where such reasons are explicitly provided for in the articles of association, the directors' motives cannot be questioned. Nor can they be compelled to disclose any reasons unless a contrary intention can be found in the company's articles.[221] The preponderant reason for the foregoing is that there is a presupposition that the directors have, under the circumstances, acted *bonafide* and unless this deduction can be rebutted as exemplified in *Barry v Artist Ltd,*[222] they should be taken to have acted sensibly.

However, a disclosure pertaining to the reasons for refusal to transfer inexorably opens the directors up to an inquiry by the court to resolve the question of whether there were reasonable grounds to justify the refusal. This was demonstrated in the case of *Re Bede Steam S. Co Ltd*[223] where the majority[224] held that a power for directors to refuse to register transfers of shares if "in their opinion it is contrary to the interests of the company that the proposed transferee should be a member thereof" only justifies a refusal to register upon grounds personal to the proposed transferee. It does not justify refusal to register

---

[218] Supra note 340.

[219] [1902] 4 F 657; [1902] SLR 39_353.

[220] [1942] Ch D 304 (CA).

[221] *Berry and Stewart v Tottenham Hotspur Football Co Ltd* [1935] Ch D 718.

[222] [1985] BCLC 283.

[223] [1917] 1 Ch D 123 (CA); See further, *Re Hackney Pavilion Ltd* [1924] 1 Ch 276; *Re Copal Varnish Co. Ltd* [1917] 2 Ch 349; *Re Swandale Cleaners Ltd* [1968] 1 WLR 1710 (CA); *Re Zinotty Properties Ltd* [1984] 1 WLR 1249; and *Charles Forte Investments Ltd v Amanda* [1964] Ch D 240 (CA) for an insight into other issues that have arisen with respect to the exercise of the power to refuse the transfer of shares.

[224] Lord Cozen-Hardy M.R. and Warrington LJ affirming the decision of Eve J and approving the judgment of Chitty J in *In re Bell Brothers* [1891] 65 LT 245 while Scrutton LJ dissented.

transfers of single shares or shares in small numbers because the directors do not think it desirable to increase the number of shareholders, or because they think that the transfer is not bona fide, but that the transferee is the mere nominee of the transferor, and the transfer is made to increase the number of shareholders who will support him in a policy which the directors disapprove.

8.30   Transmission of shares by operation of law

Transmission of shares occurs by operation of law as a result of the death of a shareholder, his bankruptcy or that of a corporate which is a member. The procedure for transmission of shares is provided for under section 190.[225] In terms of section 190(1), '[d]espite the articles, shares in a company may pass by operation of law'. This provision overrides any provisions to the contrary in the articles. By section 190(2), '[i]n the case of the death of a shareholder of a company the—

(a)   survivor or survivors where the deceased was a joint holder; and

(b)   personal representative of the deceased where the deceased was a sole holder or last survivor of joint holders; shall be the only persons recognised by the company as having title to the deceased's interest in the shares'.

Be that as it may, by section 190(3), '[n]othing in this section shall release the estate of a deceased shareholder from liability in respect of a share with unpaid liability, whether the share was jointly held or not'. Further and by section 190(4) '[a] representative on whom the ownership of a share devolves, by reason of the person being the personal representative, receiver or assignee in bankruptcy of the holder or by operation of law may, on such evidence being produced as the board of directors may reasonably require—

(a)   be registered as the holder of the share; or

(b)   transfer the share to another person without first being registered as the holder of the share'.

Under the concept of transmission, '[t]he board of directors shall have the same right to decline or delay registration of a transfer by the representative as it would have had in the case of a transfer by the registered holder, but shall have no right to refuse registration of the representative'.[226] Additionally, in terms of section 190(6), '[a] representative or a transferee shall, prior to being registered as a member, be entitled to the same dividends, rights and remedies as if the representative were a member, except that the representative shall not, subject to an order by the Court made in accordance with this Act, be entitled to vote at a meeting of the company'. By section 190(7), '[t]he board of directors may

---

[225] Which replaces section 70 of CA 1994.

[226] Section 190(5).

give notice requiring the representative to elect to be registered as a member or to transfer the share, and if the notice is not complied with within ninety days, the company may suspend payment of all dividends or other moneys payable in respect of the share until the notice has been complied with'.

As evidence of transmission of shares by operation of law in terms of section 191(1), '[a] company shall accept the production of any document which is by law sufficient evidence that the ownership of a share has been transmitted by operation of law'. Additionally, '[a]person to whom ownership of a share is transmitted, in accordance with section 190, shall, within fourteen days of the transmission of the share, notify the Registrar of the transmission in the prescribed manner and form'.[227] A person who fails to comply with the foregoing is liable to what is termed an administrative penalty.[228]

8.31 Evidence of legal title to shares

The share certificate issued by a company to a person, in accordance with section 203, and entry of the name of the person in the company's share register shall be *prima facie* evidence that legal title to the shares vests in that person.[229] In terms of section197(2), '[a] registered holder of a share in a company shall be entitled to—

(a) exercise the right to vote and exercise other rights and powers attaching to the share; and

(b) receive notices and distributions in respect of the share'. As exemplified in *Woodhouse & Rawson Ltd v Hosack*[230] however, a share certificate cannot be equated to a register of members as it is not a document of title. 'The object of the certificate is to facilitate dealings with the shares, whether by way of sale or security, and so make them more valuable to their owner. On the other hand, a share certificate is not a negotiable instrument,...'.[231]

Be that as it may, the issuance of a share certificate being *prima facie* evidence of the title to the shares of the person named therein also raises the possibility of an estoppel against the company. In *Re Bahia and San Fransisco Railway Co*[232] the giving of a share certificate was held to amount to a statement by the company intended to be acted upon by purchasers of shares in the market which once acted upon, a company cannot deny. However, where the procuration of the share certificate is predicated on a falsified transfer or power of attorney as

---

[227] Section 191(2).
[228] Section 191(3).
[229] Section 197(1) which replaces section 68 and refines the language somewhat.
[230] [1894] 2 SLT (OH).
[231] Charlesworth on Company Law 279.
[232] [1868] LR 3 QB 584.

exemplified in the cases of *Sheffield Corporation v Barclays*[233] and *Starkey v Bank of England*[234] the rule in *Re Bahia* will not apply.[235] However, where, as in *Dixon v Kennaway & Co*[236] the company issues a share certificate and for some internal reason or because of an omission discovers that the same ought not to have been issued, it may be liable to pay damages to the transferee. Nor can the company deny the amount stated as being paid up with respect to the shares indicated in the share certificate.[237]

8.32   Procedure for Issuance of share certificate

In terms of section 203(1),[238] a company whose shares are not subject to a listing agreement with a securities exchange shall, within twenty-one days after the issue or registration of a transfer of shares in the company, as the case may be, send a share certificate to every holder of the shares stating the—

(a)   name of the company;

(b)   class of shares held by that person;

(c)   number of shares held by that person; and

(d)   amount paid on the shares and the amount, if any, remaining unpaid.[239]

After receiving an application for a share certificate, referred to in subsection (2), the company shall, in terms of section 203, within twenty-one days —

(a)   if the application relates to some of the shares, separate the shares shown in the register as owned by the applicant into separate parcels, one parcel being the shares to which the share certificate relates and the other parcel being any remaining shares; and

(b)   in all cases, send a certificate to the shareholder stating the—

     (i)   name of the company;

     (ii)   class of shares held by the shareholder; and

     (iii)   number of shares held by the shareholder to which the certificate relates.

Section 203(4) specifically provides that '[d]espite this Act, where a share certificate has been issued, a transfer of shares to which the share certificate issued relates shall not be registered by the company, unless a share transfer form as specified in this Act, is accompanied by—

---

[233] [1905] AC 392.

[234] [1903] AC 114.

[235] The principle applies with equal force to a counterfeit share certificate: *Ruben v Great Fingall Consolidated* [1906] AC 439.

[236] [1900] 1 Ch 833.

[237] *Bloomenthal v Ford* [1897] AC 156.

[238] In terms of section 203(6), '[i]f a company fails to comply with subsection (1) or subsection (3), every director of the company commits an offence.

[239] This must be read together with section 203(2), '[a] shareholder may apply to the company for a certificate relating to some or all of the shareholder's shares in the company'.

(a)   the share certificate relating to the share; or

(b)   evidence as to the loss or destruction of the share certificate; and if required, an indemnity in a form determined by the board of directors'.

'[W]here shares to which a share certificate relates are to be transferred, and the share certificate is sent to the company to enable the registration of the transfer, the share certificate shall be cancelled and no further share certificate shall be issued, except at the request of the transferee'.[240]

8.33   Perpetual debenture

According to section 204, '[a] term that is expressed in a debenture or in a deed securing a debenture, that is issued or executed by a company, shall not be valid by reason only that it provides that the debenture is—

(a)   irredeemable; or

(b)   redeemable only on the occurrence of a contingency, however remote, or on the expiration of a period, however long'.

In terms of section 205(1), '[a] company that has redeemed [a] debenture previously issued by it may—

(a)   re-issue the debentures; or

(b)   issue other debentures in their place'.

According to section 205(2), '[s]ubsection (1) shall apply, unless the company—

(a)   enters into a contract providing otherwise, or the articles contain a provision to the contrary; or

(b)   has, by passing a resolution or by some other act, indicated its intention that the debentures are cancelled'. Also, '[t]he debentures shall, on a re-issue of redeemed debentures or of other debentures in their place, be treated as having, and as always having had, the same priority as the redeemed debentures'.[241]

Further to the foregoing and in terms of section 203(4), '[t]he debentures of a company deposited to secure advances, whether on current account or otherwise, shall not be treated as redeemed by reason that the company's account is no longer in debit while the debentures are deposited'. Further, and according to section 203(5), '[t]he re-issue of a debenture or the issue of another debenture in its place in terms of this section, shall not be treated as the issue of a new debenture for the purposes of any provision limiting the amount or number of debentures to be issued'. Finally, according to section 206(1), '[t]he Court may order the specific performance of a contract with a company to take up and pay for any debenture of the company'. In fact, in terms of section 206(2), '[t]he Court shall not refuse to order the specific performance of a contract of that kind on the ground that the contract is one to lend money'.

---

[240] Section 203(5).
[241] Section 203(3).

8.34   Conclusion

In this chapter we have explored the matter of share capital noting as we have, that there are different types of share capital including nominal capital; Authorised Capital; Issued capital; Subscribed capital; Uncalled Capital; Called-up capital; Paid-up capital; Reserved capital; Premium capital. That share capital can be altered is statutory. There are mainly two different classes of shares namely preference shares and ordinary/equity shares. We noted that certain actions by the company may lead to variation of class rights. Chief among those is as a result of the alteration of capital. We have also discussed the significance of the concept of pre-emptive rights which entails that any sale of shares by either the company or a member of the company must first be offered to current and existing shareholders. Failure to observe this will invalidate any such sale. Shares can be forfeited. Quite apart from the foregoing, alteration of share capital may be in the form of reduction though this distinction is now patent in the Act. We have discussed reasons to why a company may reduce its share capital and the consequences of any such reduction to creditors. We have further noted that the Act now makes substantive provisions for dividends which is a break with the past where they were only provided for under model articles of association. We have also made the point that a company can acquire fully paid up shares and hold its own shares. We have discussed at length the matter of redeemable shares; holding companies and subsidiary companies; restrictions on transferability; transmission of shares by operation of law; evidence of legal title to shares; procedure for issuance of share certificate; and perpetual debenture.

FURTHER READING

Articles

Armour, J, 'Share Capital and Creditor Protection: Efficient Rules for a Modern Company Law' (2000) 63 MLR 355.

Steele, A, 'Rights issue reform' (2009) 32 CSR 158.

Worthington, S, 'Shares and shareholders: property, power and entitlement (Part 1)' (2001) 22 Comp Law 258.

Worthington, S, 'Shares and shareholders: property, power and entitlement (Part 2)' (2001) 22 Comp Law 307.

Simkovic M "The Effect of Enhanced Disclosure on Open Market Stock Repurchases", 6 Berkeley Bus. L.J. 96 (2006).

Books

Dine J and Koutsias M *Company Law* 6th edn (Palgrave Macmillan Hampshire 2007).

Farrah JH and Hannigan BM *Farrar's Company Law* 4th edn (Butterworths London 1998).

Gates RB *Gates Company Law and Practice in Zambia* (Reagan Blankfein Gates Lusaka 2017).

Sealy L and Worthington S *Sealy & Worthington's Cases and Materials in Company Law* 10th edn (Oxford University Press Oxford 2013).

Wild C and Weinstein S *Smith and Keenan's Company Law* 15th edn (Pearson Education London Ltd 2011).

9

PUBLIC ISSUE OF SHARES

AIMS AND OBJECTIVES

 After reading this chapter you should appreciate:
- ➢ The allotment of shares revisited
- ➢ The invitations to public to acquire shares and debentures
- ➢ The first publication of prospectus
- ➢ Contents of prospectus
- ➢ Expert's consent regarding the prospectus
- ➢ Registration of prospectus
- ➢ Over-subscription in debenture issue
- ➢ The reference to stock exchange listing in prospectus-allotment of shares
- ➢ Civil liability for misstatements or omissions in prospectus
- ➢ The offence of misstatement or omission in prospectus
- ➢ The liability for damages under the general law
- ➢ The Stop trading order
- ➢ A private placement

9.1 Introduction

Our discussion in this chapter relates purely to the issue of shares to the public by public companies or Plcs. It is worth remembering that though it is not always the case, most companies will be incorporated as private limited companies. They will usually be small and require very few resources to achieve the aims for which their promoters have them incorporated. However, if they survive the fate that most small companies face, namely failure, and then thrive, they will require more and more resources to finance their expansion by way of acquisitions or/and growth of market share. To do this, the company will ordinary invite members of the public to buy shares from it. However, because a private company limited by shares is precluded from making a public offer of shares,[1] it will have to convert to a public company to do so under the procedure provided for under section 53.

Responding to, and investing in the company by way of share purchase must, in the investor's mind, mean that he is expending resources for a stake in a company he is very likely to have very little control over. This downside is however tempered with the fact that in a liquid environment, the investor may still make a return on the investment irrespective of the influence he holds in the company in which he has shareholding. The obvious place for this liquidity is a stock or securities exchange. There are, for this reason, stringent requirements regulating the offer of shares to the public in the Act to protect the public from unscrupulous directors or companies. Invariably then, a public company will have to join a stock or securities exchange pursuant to the provisions of the Securities Act.[2] We must hasten to add that being a public company is not tantamount to being listed. For any public company that seeks to raise money from the public by way of offering shares, it must without fail, ensure that it meets the listing requirements of a securities exchange itself, licensed by the Securities and Exchange Commission.

The Securities Act,[3] we must note, goes further than providing for the manner of issuing shares by encompassing debt instruments such as bonds and other notes plus collective schemes.[4]In any case, as sections 4 and 5 of the Act make clear, where there are any inconsistencies between the Act and the Securities Act, the Securities Act will prevail. In view of the foregoing, and though incapable of being ignored, a highly structured and exhaustive discussion of securities law and regulation in Zambia is beyond the scope of this book and is better studied in a text whose focus is purely on securities law. Therefore, an attempt is made at giving a statutory delineation of the law in this area so far as the Act is concerned with only a few references where this is necessary, to the Securities Act.[5]

In summary then, the law governing the public issue of shares is to be found principally in the following:

(1)   The Companies Act No 9 of 2017;

(2)   The Securities Act No 41 of 2016; and

(3)   The Harmonised Listing Requirements of the Lusaka Stock Exchange "LUSE" also known as "Listing Rules."

---

[1]   See section 210 discussed below replaces section 122 of CA 1994.

[2]   No 41 of 2016.

[3]   No 41 of 2016.

[4]   See further, Mwenda, KK. Understanding Securities Law and Regulation in Zambia: Commentary & Legislation (Juta and Company Cape Town 2015) for a more focused but summarised discussion of securities law and regulation in Zambia.

[5]   No 41 of 2016.

9.2   Allotment of shares revisited

We have already made the point based on the holding in the case of *National Westminster Bank v IRC*[6] that 'shares are allotted when a person acquires the unconditional right to be included in the company's register of members in respect of those shares....' Thus, allotment of shares is the appropriation of a certain number of shares to a particular person. Unlike transmission, allotment is a direct divestiture from the company itself to a particular person.

Section 208[7] describes instances that amount to a public offer of shares. Section 208(1) makes the point that for purposes of the Act, where a company allots or agrees to allot any of its shares or debentures to the public by invitation' by any of the following that is to say—

(a)   to acquire any of its shares or debentures—

(i)   an invitation to the public so made shall be considered to be made by the company as well as by the person who in fact made it; and

(ii)   a person who acquires any of the shares or debentures in response to the invitation shall be considered to be an allottee from the company of those shares or debentures; and

(b)   in respect of any of the shares or debentures—

(i)   within six months after the allotment or agreement to allot; or

(ii)   before the company has received the whole of the consideration in respect of the shares or debentures; the allotment or agreement to allot is made by the company, with a view to an invitation to the public, in respect of those shares or debentures.

It follows that a public company's wish to raise money by the issue of shares or debentures to the public may be undertaken either by way of

(1)   a 'direct offer' to the public, or 'offer by prospectus'; or

(2)   private placement

We discuss these in turn and within the context of the Act.

9.3   Invitations to public to acquire shares and debentures

Section 210(1) makes clear that the matter of inviting the public companies relates only to public companies which includes a public company proposed to be formed. This particular provision shows that a public company need not always start its journey as a private company that later converts to a public company in terms of section 53. It is clear from section 6(a) that '[a] company incorporated under [the] Act shall', among others, 'be—a *public company*' meaning that a company can start its life as a public company which is why,

---

[6]   [1995] 1 AC 119; [1994] 3 All ER 1; [1994] 3 WLR 159.
[7]   Replacing section 119 of CA 1994.

it is submitted, there is provision for such a company, presumably including that which starts its life off as such, to convert, to a private company limited by shares.[8] In terms of section 210(2), '[a] person shall not make an invitation to the public to acquire shares in a company unless the company is a public company and the invitation complies with this Part'.

This same proscription extends to debentures as in terms of section 208(3), [a] person shall not make an invitation to the public to acquire debentures in a company, unless the—

(a) company is a public company;

(b) debentures are created by deed under the common seal of the company in favour of assignees for the debenture holders; and

(c) invitation complies with this Part or is supervised by the Court.

In *Nash v Lynde*[9], the managing director of a company prepared a document which was in the form of a prospectus. The document was marked as 'strictly private and confidential'. But the document did not disclose all material facts required to be disclosed by the Companies Act. It was circulated among directors and their friends. An outsider received this document through some friend of a director. On the basis of this document, the outsider applied for the shares of the company. It was held that the document received by the outsider was not a prospectus as it was merely a 'private communication' between the directors and their friends.

In *Re South of England Natural Gas Petroleum Co Ltd*[10] however, a company prepared some documents in the form of a prospectus. The copies of this document were sent and distributed only among the members of certain 'gas companies'. It was held to be an offer of 'shares to the public', although the offer was not to the public at large. It was therefore shown in *Government Stock & Others Securities Investment Co. Ltd v. Christopher,*[11] that the test is "not who receives the offer, but who can accept it". The number of persons who constitute members of the section to whom the offer is given, is not material. What is material is who is entitled to accept the offer or invitation; if anyone brings money and applies for the shares or debentures offered, regardless of whether the offer was made to him or not, the offer to which he responds will be taken to amount to a public offer.

Further to the foregoing and by section 210(4), '[a] person shall not make an invitation to the public to acquire equity shares in a company unless—

(a) all the equity shares in the company are already issued;

(b) the shares to which the invitation relates carry an unrestricted right to vote at a general meeting; and

---

[8] Section 52.
[9] [1929] AC 158.
[10] [1911] 1 Ch 573.
[11] [1956] 1 All ER 490.

(c)   on a poll, a constant number of votes which, in proportion to nominal value, is the same in the case of every share'.

However, section 210(5) provides that '[s]ubsection (4) shall not prohibit an invitation to acquire equity shares that do not comply with that subsection, if the—

(a)   rights making them equity shares are expressed by the terms of issue to be conditional on the exercise by the holder of an option;

(b)   shares will comply with that subsection if the option is exercised; and

(c)   shares are issued, and the invitation made, in fulfilment of an obligation entered into by the company before the commencement of this Act'.

The consequences of contravening the provisions are twofold: firstly and in terms of section 210(6), '[i]f a person acquires shares or debentures in a company as a result of an invitation to the public, in contravention of this section, that person shall be entitled to recover compensation for any loss sustained by that person from the person making the invitation, and where the person making the invitation is a body corporate, from an officer in default'. Secondly and according to section 210(7), '[i]f an invitation to the public is made, in contravention of [section 210], each person making the invitation and, where such a person is a body corporate, each officer in default commits an offence and is liable, on conviction, to a fine not exceeding two hundred thousand penalty units or to imprisonment for a period not exceeding two years, or to both'.

9.3.1   *First publication of prospectus*

Section 209 provides for the law relating to the first publication of a prospectus. According to section 209(1), '[t]he first publication of a prospectus shall be the date of registration of the prospectus'. Further, '[w]here shares or debentures, to which an invitation relates, are dealt in on a securities exchange or where a prospectus states that an application has been or will be made for permission to deal in the shares or debentures on the stock exchange, and the company is required to advertise the prospectus in a newspaper to comply with the requirements of that stock exchange, the first publication of the prospectus shall be when the prospectus is first so advertised'.[12]

However, the foregoing requirements relating to the publication of a prospectus as stipulated in section 209(2) shall, in terms of section 209(3), … not apply to offers to the public of the following types of securities:

(a)   shares issued in substitution for shares of the same class already issued, if the issuing of such new shares shall not involve an increase in the issued capital;

(b)   securities offered in connection with a takeover by means of an exchange offer, provided that a document is available containing information

---

[12] Section 209(2).

which is regarded by the competent authority as being equivalent to that of the prospectus;

(c) securities offered, allotted or to be allotted in connection with a merger or division, provided that a document is available containing information which is regarded by the competent authority as being equivalent to that of the prospectus;

(d) dividends paid out to existing shareholders in the form of shares of the same class as the shares in respect of which such dividends are paid, provided that a document is made available containing information on the number and nature of the shares and the reasons for, and details of, the offer; and

(e) shares offered, allotted or to be allotted to existing or former directors or employees by their employer or by an affiliated undertaking, except that—

(i) the company has its head office or registered office in Zambia; and

(ii) a document containing information on the number and nature of the transferable securities and the reasons for, and details of, the offer is made.

9.3.2 Prospectus required for invitation to public to purchase shares or debentures

The invitation to the public for purposes of acquiring shares or debentures of a public company is only permissible under the following circumstances:

(a) within six months prior to the making of the invitation a prospectus relating to the shares or debentures, that complies with this Part, is registered by the Registrar;

(b) every person to whom the invitation is made is given a true copy of the prospectus at the time when the invitation is first made to that person; and

(c) every copy of the prospectus states on its face—

(i) that it has been registered by the Registrar; and

(ii) the date of registration.[13]

In terms of section 211(2), [a]n invitation published in a newspaper or magazine advertisement that summarises the contents of a prospectus shall be considered as satisfying subsection (1) *(b)*, if the advertisement—

(a) omits, or is not accompanied by any kind of application form for, shares or debentures;

---

[13] Section 211(1).

(b)   states with reasonable prominence—
      (i)   where copies of the full prospectus may be obtained;
      (ii)   that the prospectus has been registered;
      (iii)   the date of registration; and
(c)   is in terms previously approved, in writing, by the Registrar.

9.3.3   *Contents of prospectus*

Section 212 stipulates the requirements for a prospectus lodged with the Registrar in mandatory terms, specifically that it will—
(a)   not contain any untrue or misleading statement;
(b)   contain all information that prospective purchasers of the shares or debentures and their advisors would reasonably expect to be provided in order to make a decision on the purchase; and
(c)   either—
      (i)   deal with matters and provide for reports specified in the Third Schedule; or
      (ii)   be made only to existing members or debenture holders of the company, whether or not an applicant for shares or debentures shall have the right to renounce in favour of other persons.

The Third Schedule plainly specifies what should be indicated in a prospectus including the true nature of the company's activities to enable the public to make an informed decision. It follows that all the material facts relating to the nature, complexion and status of the company must not only truly but scrupulously and precisely be disclosed to the public being invited to buy shares to which the prospectus relates. Nor should the prospectus contain in any way shape or form, any mis–statements (i.e. statements which are untrue or misleading). Omission of important facts or a deliberate effort to not disclose material facts however peripheral will incur negative consequences. Known as the golden rule of framing a prospectus, it was laid down by Kingdersely VC in *New Brunswick Co v. Muggeridge,*[14] as follows:

> Those who issue a prospectus hold out to the public great advantages which will accrue to the persons who will take shares in the proposed undertaking. The public is invited to take shares on the faith of the representations contained in the prospectus, and it is at the mercy of the company promoters. Therefore, everything must be stated with strict and scrupulous accuracy. Nothing should be stated as a fact which is not so, no fact should be omitted the existence of which might, in any degree, affect the nature of quality of the privileges and advantages which the prospectus holds out as inducement to take shares.

---

[14] [1860] 3 LT 651.

9.3.4   Expert's consent

The law relating to a prospectus containing a statement purporting to be made by an expert is contained in section 213.[15] Such a prospectus cannot be lodged with the Registrar 'unless it is accompanied by the written consent of an expert, that the expert has given consent to the inclusion of the statement'.[16] In the event that 'the expert withdraws consent to the inclusion of the statement, the expert shall without delay, in the prescribed manner and form, notify the Registrar and the person responsible for issuing the prospectus to that effect'.[17] It is a requirement under section 213(4) that '[a] person responsible for issuing a prospectus … cease from issuing the prospectus, after receiving a notice from an expert, made in accordance with subsection (3)'. Finally, and in terms of section 213(5), '[a] person who contravenes subsection (4), and if that person is a body corporate, each officer, in default, commits an offence and is liable, on conviction, to a fine not exceeding two hundred thousand penalty units or to imprisonment for a period not exceeding two years, or to both'.

It should be noted however, that if the statement is made by or on the authority of an expert, such as an accountant, valuer or engineer, and is included with his consent, other persons responsible for the document have only to prove that they reasonably believed that the expert was competent and had consented to provide the statement in question.[18] There is no need to show that there was reasonable belief in the truth and a correction need only be to the effect that the expert was not competent or had not consented to the issuance of the statement ascribed to him. There is correspondingly no liability for statements by public officials or in official documents, provided that they have been fairly and accurately reproduced.[19]

9.3.5   Registration of prospectus

There are, in terms of section 214, several requirements which must be met before the Registrar can register a prospectus.[20] Section 214(2) provides that the prospectus shall be 'signed by each—
  (a)   person named in the prospectus as a director or proposed director of the company or by that person's agent, authorised in writing; and
  (b)   other person making the invitation or that person's agent, authorised in writing'.

---

[15] Subsection 1; section 213 replaces section 125 of CA 1994.
[16] Section 213(2).
[17] Section 213(3).
[18] Keenan D *Smith and Keenan, 'Company Law'*….
[19] Keenan D *Smith and Keenan, 'Company Law'*….
[20] Section 214(1).

According to section 214(3), '[f]or the purpose of subsection (2)*(b)*, where the invitation is made by a body corporate or members of a firm, it shall be sufficient if the copy is signed on behalf of the body corporate by not fewer than two directors or, in the case of a firm, by not less than two of the partners, and each such director or partner may sign by an agent, authorised in writing'.

Additionally, and in terms of section 214(4), '[t]here shall be endorsed on or attached to a copy of the prospectus, referred to in subsection (1)—

(a)   the consent of an expert required by section 213; and

(b)   a certified copy or translation of each of the documents required to be available for inspection in accordance with paragraph 49 of the Third Schedule'.

According to section 214(5), '[t]he Registrar may, where a company has already lodged with the Registrar a certified copy or translation, referred to in subsection (4)*(b)*, waive the requirement that it be attached or endorsed, if the Registrar is satisfied that the copy initially delivered is readily identifiable and accessible'.

There are further requirements in terms of section 214(6)(7) and (8) which include the fact that '[a] prospectus shall state at its head that a copy of the prospectus has been registered by the Registrar and the Registrar assumes no responsibility as to its contents'; '[a] prospectus shall be accompanied by a statutory declaration by a director and the secretary of the company stating that the prospectus complies with the requirements of this Part'; and that the '[t]he Registrar shall, on registering a prospectus, issue a certificate stating that the prospectus has been registered'.

9.3.6   *Over-subscription in debenture issue*

No company is allowed to 'accept or retain subscriptions to an issue of debentures in excess of the amount of the issue disclosed in the prospectus, unless the prospectus specifies—

(a)   that the company expressly reserves the right to accept or retain over-subscriptions; and

(b)   a limit, expressed as a specific sum or money, on the amount of over-subscriptions that may be accepted or retained, being an amount not exceeding twenty-five per cent above the amount of the issue as disclosed in the prospectus'.[21]

Additionally, 'where a company specifies in a prospectus relating to a debenture issue that it reserves the right to accept or retain over-subscriptions, the prospectus shall—

(a)   not contain any statement of, or reference to, the asset backing for the issue, other than a statement or reference to the total assets and the total liabilities of the company and of its guarantor companies; and

---

[21] Section 215(1).

(b)   contain a statement or reference as to what the total assets and total liabilities of the company would be if oversubscriptions to the limit specified in the prospectus were accepted or retained'.[22]

9.3.7   *Reference to stock exchange listing in prospectus-allotment of shares*

The law relating to any reference to a stock exchange listing in prospectus-allotment of shares is to be found in section 216.[23] Section 216(1) provides that '[w]here a prospectus states or implies that application has been or may be made for permission for the shares or debentures offered in the prospectus to be listed for quotation on the official list of a securities exchange, then, subject to subsection (8)[24], allotment of shares or debentures shall not be made on an application made in terms of the prospectus, except in accordance with this section'. In terms of section 216(2), '[a]n allotment may be made if the permission, referred to in subsection (1), has been—

(a)   applied for, in the form prescribed by the stock exchange, before the third day on which the stock exchange is open, after the date of issue of the prospectus; or

(b)   granted before the determination day'.[25]

According to section 216(3), '[a] company shall, within fourteen days after the determination day, if the conditions of subsection (2) are not satisfied on the determination day, repay, without interest, any money received from an applicant in respect of the prospectus'. By section 216(4), '[t]he directors shall, if the company fails to repay money in accordance with subsection (3), in addition to the liability of the company but subject to subsection (5), be jointly and severally liable to repay that money, with interest at the ruling bank rate, from the end of that period of fourteen days'. In terms of section 216(5), '[a] director shall not be liable, in accordance with subsection (4), if the director proves that the default in the repayment of the money was not due to any misconduct or negligence on that director's part'.

In terms of section 216(9), '…a statement in a prospectus to the effect that the articles comply with, or have been drawn up so as to comply with a condition

---

[22]   Section 215(2).

[23]   It is important to note from the outset that in terms of section 216(7), '[a] condition that requires or binds an applicant for shares or debentures to waive compliance with any requirement of this section is void'.

[24]   Subsection (8) provides that '[t]he Registrar may, on the application of a company made before the determination day, by notice in the *Gazette* and in a daily newspaper of general circulation in Zambia or other media, except that this section shall not apply to the allotment of the shares or debentures'. In terms of section 216(11) '…"the determination day" is, subject to subsection (12), the day forty-two days after the issue of the prospectus. Subsection (12) provides that '[a] securities exchange may, before the determination day, notify the applicant referred to in subsection (9), that a later day, not more than ninety days after the issue of the prospectus, shall be the determination day'.

[25]   By Subsection (6), '[a] company shall, for so long as the conditions of subsection (2) are not satisfied, keep in a separate bank account all money received in respect of a prospectus'.

imposed by a securities exchange shall, unless the contrary intention appears, be taken to imply that an application has been, or may be, made for permission for the shares or debentures offered by the prospectus to be listed for quotation on the official list of the securities exchange'. According to section 216(10) '...where a stock exchange grants the permission referred to in subsection (9), subject to any condition that may be imposed, the permission shall be considered to be granted when the board of directors gives to the securities exchange a written undertaking to comply with the condition'.

9.3.8   *Civil liability for misstatements or omissions in prospectus*

The law regarding civil liability for misstatements or omissions in a prospectus is encased in section 217.[26] Section 217(1) provides that '...where a prospectus—
   (a)   contains a statement which is untrue or, in the context, misleading;
   (b)   omits any matter which is material or fails to set out any report required by [the] Act; the persons specified in subsection' (2), are liable to pay compensation to a person who acquires shares or debentures on the faith of the prospectus for any loss that person sustains by reason of the untrue statement or omission'.

By section 217(2), '[t]he following persons are liable to pay compensation in accordance with subsection (1):
   (a)   a person making the invitation to which the prospectus relates;
   (b)   a person who was a director of a body corporate making the invitation, at the time when the prospectus was published;[27]
   (c)   where the prospectus was made by a company to whose shares or debentures the invitation relates, a—
      (i)   person who has consented to being named in the prospectus as a director immediately or after an interval of time; and
      (ii)   promoter of a company who was a party to the preparation of the prospectus; or
   (d)   the expert, if the untrue statement or omission is in a statement by an expert, who consented to the publication of the prospectus'.

Section 217(2) must be read within the context of section 217(5) which provides that, [a] person is not liable, in accordance with this section and subsection (2) *(d)*, if that person proves that—
   (a)   the person was competent to make the statement and had reasonable grounds to believe, up to the date of publication of the prospectus or, where the waiting period applies, up to the expiry of the waiting period, that the statement was true; or

---

[26] It replaces section 129 of CA 1994.

[27] By section 217(4), '[a] person is not liable in accordance with this section and subsection (2)*(b)*, if that person proves that, having consented to being named as a director, the person withdrew consent before the registration of the prospectus and the prospectus was published without the person's consent'.

(b)   after lodgment of the prospectus with the Registrar, but before publication of the prospectus, or where the waiting period applies, before the expiry of the waiting period, on the person becoming aware of the untrue statement or omission, the person withdrew consent in writing and gave notice[28] of the withdrawal and the reason for it.

In *Greenwood v Leather Shod Wheel Co*[29], the company was formed to work a patent for the manufacture of wheels with leather tyres. The prospectus contained statements as to the 'orders' received, when in fact the company had only received orders for trial sets for approval. The plaintiff who has subscribed and paid for 1,000 £1 on the faith of the prospectus, claimed rescission against the company on the ground of misrepresentation, and compensation from the directors. The prospectus stated in the relevant part as follows: orders have already been received from Bank of England, House of Commons, Royal Mint, the Secretary of State for War, the leading railways, omnibus and cab proprietors etc… instructions have been received to prepare trial sets of wheels for a number of public bodies and influential firms mentioned….

The court granted the relief sought, and the decision was affirmed by the EWCA. The court state upon considering the prospectus that it was convinced that, though it was cunningly drawn, it is not, in relation to the persons to whom it was addressed, an honest document. It was cunningly framed so as avoid as far as possible telling in so many words absolute untruths; but it was so framed as to convey as a whole a perfectly untrue meaning. It was in the courts opinion, calculated to convey and did convey to the ordinary reader, as it did to the plaintiff, that the invention referred to in it had passed the experimental stage in England, and that numerous orders, besides trial orders, had already come into the company from the influential bodies, firms or persons, from which the value of the invention and the first prospects of the company would be naturally inferred.

At the date of the prospectus the company had not a single order. Save for several public bodies, firms, and person named in the prospectus had expressed their willingness to test the invention by having trial sets of wheels sent to them for the purpose of experimenting upon and testing the invention; and as to some of these, the cost of wheels was to be paid for by the experimenters and not by the company. That was the true position of the company with regard to these so called orders at the time the prospectus was issued. The company had in fact no single ordinary order in its possession at the time. In the courts opinion, the prospectus was, in these respects, not only calculated to mislead, nut contained

---

[28] In terms of Section 217(7), '[a] notice that is required to be given in accordance with…section [217] shall be in the prescribed form and shall be published in a daily newspaper of general circulation in Zambia'.

[29] [1900] 1 Ch 421 CA.

untrue statements within the meaning of section 3(1) of the Directors Liability Act 1890.

It would appear from the foregoing that a statement is untrue if by reason of what it omits it is misleading, even though the parts of it, taken separately, are literally true.[30]

However, in terms of section 217(3), A person is not liable, in accordance with this section, if the person proves that—

(a)   as regards any untrue statement that is not—

     (i)   a statement or report made by an expert, other than that person;

     (ii) a public official document or statement; or

     (iii) an extract from a document referred to in paragraph (i) or (ii); the person had reasonable ground to believe and did believe up to the time of the publication of the prospectus or, where the waiting period applies, up to the expiration of the waiting period, that the statement was true;

(b)   any untrue statement or public official document or report by an expert, other than that person or an extract there from—

     (i)   was a correct and fair copy of the statement, report or extract; and

     (ii) the person had reasonable ground to believe, at the time of the publication of the prospectus, that the person making the statement was competent to make it, had given consent and had not withdrawn the consent before the date of registration of the prospectus;

(c)   the person was not aware of the omission, or that the matter omitted was material, up to the time of the publication of the prospectus or, where the waiting period applies, when the waiting period expires;

(d)   after the publication of the prospectus, but before expiry of the waiting period, the person, on becoming aware of any untrue statement in the prospectus or omission, after the publication of the prospectus but before the expiry of the waiting period, withdrew consent to the prospectus and gave notice of the withdrawal and the reason for the withdrawal; or

(e)   the prospectus was published without the person's knowledge, and on becoming aware of the publication, gave notice that the prospectus was published without the person's knowledge.

Section 217(6) attaches liability for indemnification to '[a] person making an invitation to which a prospectus relates and a person who was a director making the invitation at the time when the prospectus was published, except a person

---

[30] Sealy L and Worthington S *Cases and Material in Company Law* 10th edn (Oxford University Press Oxford 2013) 453.

without whose knowledge or consent the prospectus was published'. Such a person, according to the section is liable to indemnify any person—

(a)   named in a prospectus as a director or, having agreed to become a director, does not consent to becoming a director or had withdrawn consent before the publication of the prospectus and did not authorise or consent to the publication of the prospectus; or

(b)   whose consent is required for the publication of a prospectus and the person has not given consent or has withdrawn it before the publication of the prospectus; against all damages, costs and expenses to which the person may be made liable by reason of the person's name being inserted in the prospectus or the inclusion in the prospectus of a statement purporting to be made by the person as an expert or in defending legal proceedings brought against the person in respect of the prospectus.

9.3.9   *Remedies for misstatement*

The foregoing discussion has clearly demonstrated legislative efforts at ensuring that as much information as is possible is made available to would-be investors to enable them make an informed decision. Be that as it may, it sometimes happens that the information that is made available in the prospectus is the kind 'that contains an untrue statement'[31] or statements 'or omits truthfully to state any of the matters which it is required by [the] Act to state' or put another way: 'wrong or misleading or…the rules governing issuance of prospectuses are not complied with'.[32] Both the Act and the common law have provided not just offences and sanctions but remedies. We begin with a discussion of the offences relating to misstatements or omissions in prospectuses under the Act and thereafter explore other remedies open to investors within the context of the Misrepresentation Act 1968[33] and the general law.

9.3.9.1   *Offence of misstatement or omission in prospectus under the Act*

Section 218[34] places criminal liability for misstatement or omission in a prospectus in the following terms:

> Any, person who authorises the publication of a prospectus, advertisement or circular in relation to an invitation to the public to acquire shares or debentures of a company, that contains an untrue statement or omits truthfully to state any of the matters which it is required by this Act to state, commits an offence

---

[31] Section 218(1) discussed below.

[32] Davies PL *Gower and Davies' Principles of Modern Company Law* 7th edn…. 670.

[33] Chapter 69 of the Laws of Zambia.

[34] Section 218 replaces section 130.

and shall be liable, on conviction, to a fine not exceeding two hundred thousand penalty units or to imprisonment for a period not exceeding two years, or to both'.[35]

Be that as it may, the following defences are available:
  (a)   that the untrue or omitted statement was immaterial; or
  (b)   that the person had reasonable grounds to believe, up to the time of publication of the prospectus, that the statement was true.[36]

Further, and in terms of section 218(3) '…a person shall not be regarded as having authorised the publication of a prospectus by reason only of the person having given the consent, required by section 213,[37] and the Registrar shall not be regarded as having authorised the publication of an advertisement or circular by reason of the Registrar having issued the certificate referred to in section 214(8)'.[38]

The following case exemplify the application of the foregoing statutory provisions.

In *Progressive Aluminium Ltd v Registrar of Companies,*[39] the prospectus of a company stated that the company had the experience of two and half decades in its line of business. In fact, the experience was not of the company itself but that of the partners of a firm which had been taken over by the company. In this case, the management was held not liable for the untrue statement. It was held that there was no *malafide* intention behind the statement. The statement was not so materially false as to make the directors criminally liable.

In *R v Kylsant,*[40] by the Larceny Act 1861, section 84 a director of a public company was guilty of a misdemeanour if he made, circulated or published any written statement or account which he knew to be false in any material particular with intent to induce any to entrust or advance property to the company. The Royal Mail Steam Packet Company, of which Lord Kylsant was chairman of directors, issued a prospectus for £2m. 5per cent preference stock, in which it was stated *inter alia* that '[t]he average annual balance available… after providing for depreciation [etc.] has been sufficient to pay the interest on the present issue more than five times over,…And which listed the dividends paid during the last seventeen years. These and all other statements in the prospectus were true, but the prospectus did not reveal that for the past seven years the company had made substantial loses, and had been able to pay the dividends specified and so produce the 'balance available' by bringing into account the various reserve funds and items of non – recurring nature such as tax refunds.

---

[35] Section 218(1).
[36] Section 218(2).
[37] Which provides for procedure relating to 'Expert's consent'.
[38] Which provides that '[t]he Registrar shall, on registering a prospectus, issue a certificate stating that the prospectus has been registered'.
[39] [1997] 89 Comp Cas 157 (AP).
[40] [1932] KB 442.

It was held that the prospectus was false and the accused was convicted and sentenced to twelve months imprisonment.

9.3.10   Other remedies available under the general law: The Misrepresentation Act 1968[41]

The effect of section 218 is to make misstatements or omissions in prospectuses criminal offences punishable by way of a fine (for a first offender)[42] in 'a case where there are no aggravating circumstances which would render a fine inappropriate' or a fine and imprisonment or simply imprisonment for a repeat offender, the repetition of the offence being an aggravating circumstance, among others, that would make a fine inappropriate. As a deterrence this is effective but only to an extent. It must be remembered that the foregoing is in accordance with the principles laid down by the Zambian Supreme Court in the case of *Longwe v The People*[43] which was repeated in *Musonda v The people*[44]: Where the legislature has seen it fit to prescribe a sentence of a fine or imprisonment or both, a first offender in a case where there are no aggravating circumstances which would render a fine inappropriate, should be sentenced to pay a fine with imprisonment only in default.

For investors who rely on the misleading or wrong statements, neither the fine a percentage of which will be payable to the State as determined by the Court and is not to exceed 'two hundred thousand penalty units' and/or imprisonment of the offender[45] will be little comfort to the huge losses they may have suffered for relying on the misleading or wrong statements. It may also be the case that the misstatement or wrongful statement is the kind that falls within the defences provided for under section 218. Additionally, the complainant/plaintiff may seek a remedy beyond imprisonment or fine (a domain of criminal law and procedure), such as rescission. There are civil remedies at common law available for misrepresentations which result into loss for plaintiffs who relied on them. A law of contract concept, a misrepresentation is defined as a misstatement of fact.[46] It is neither an expression of opinion nor a forecast or promise. It must be appreciated that for misrepresentation to be actionable, the following elements must be present:

---

[41] Chapter 69 of the Laws of Zambia.
[42] *Longwe v The People* SCZ No 130 of 1976 (unreported).
[43] SCZ No 130 of 1976 (unreported).
[44] [1976] ZR 215 at 217
[45] As of this writing only (ZMW200, 000 X 0.30) = ZMK 60, 000.00.
[46] For a detailed, historical and yet concise analysis, see Mckendrick E *Contract Law* 7th edn (Palgrave Macmillan New York 2007) Ch 13 272-294.

(1)   It must be a false statement of fact or law;[47]

(2)   It must be addressed to the plaintiff misled;[48]

(3)   It must induce the plaintiff into entering the contract.[49]

9.3.10.1   Fraud or deceit

The term fraud may be defined as a misstatement of facts made with an intention to deceive a person. If the statement is made without such an intention and the person making such a statement believes it to be true, then the person who made such statement will not be liable in damages for fraud. In *Derry v Peek*,[50] the Plymouth, Devonport, and District Tramways Co had power under a special Act of Parliament to run trams by animal power and, with the consent of the Board of Trade, by mechanical and steam power. Derry and the other directors of the company issued a prospectus inviting the public to apply for shares in the company and stating that the company had power to run trams by steam power and claiming that considerable economies would result. The directors assumed that the Board Trade would grant its consent as a matter of course, but in the event the Board refused permission for certain parts of the tramway, and the company went into liquidation. Peek, who had subscribed for shares under the prospectus, brought this action against the directors for fraud. It was held that before a statement can be regarded as fraudulent at common law, it must be shown that it was made knowing it to be untrue, or not believing it to be true, or recklessly, not caring whether it be true or false. On the facts of the case, it appeared that the directors honestly believed that permission to run the trams by steam power would be granted as a matter of course by the Board of Trade, and thus they were not liable for fraud.

In *Peck v Gurney*,[51] where the contents of a prospectus of a company formed to purchase the business of a firm were under discussion, the court stated that a person making a force statement is not guilty of fraud, if he honestly believes that the statement made by him is true. The damages for fraud can, therefore, be recovered from the company only if the following conditions are satisfied and proved by the investor: The misstatement in the prospectus must be fraudulent i.e. must be made knowingly and with the intention to deceive.

The alleged fraudulent misstatement ought to relate to some existing facts which can be deemed material to the contract relating to the purchase of shares

---

[47] This is not the same thing as omitting to state a material fact and if omission is the basis of the claim, the remedy must come under criminal proceedings in terms of section 218.

[48] While the prospectus is an invitation to the public, this cannot be used as a basis for the claim. To have standing, the plaintiff must show that he was not only a member of the public who purchased shares and to whom the remedy of damages and/or rescission is available were the court to decide in his favour.

[49] It must be proved by the plaintiff that had the misrepresentation not been made, he would not have not entered the contract, or more specifically, purchased shares on the basis of the prospectus in question.

[50] [1889] 14 AC 337.

[51] [1873] 43 LJ Ch 19.

or debentures. In addition and as a necessary predicate, the investor must, as a result of the fraudulent misstatement, be induced to purchase the shares or debentures in the company. But the foregoing in and of themselves are not enough; the investor must have taken the shares directly from the company and not through a third party or the securities exchange from another member. It follows that a person who or entity that purchases shares on the open market has no remedy against the company or directors the fact that he/it bought the shares on the faith of a representation (now impugned and held to be a misrepresentation) contained in the prospectus notwithstanding.

The case of *Edington v Fitzmaurice*[52] demonstrates the foregoing. Edington claimed for damages for deceit against the directors of a provision company to recoup his loss in investing in the company's 6 per cent debenture. It was stated in the prospectus relating to the debentures that the object of the issue was to finance the extension of the company's buildings and plant; but the company was in fact in difficulties, and only a fraction of the money raised was applied in this way, the bulk being used to pay off pressing liabilities. It was held that the directors were liable for fraud. The statement in this case was of existing facts as the directors had misrepresented their state of mind, and the statement made in the prospectus was material to the contract of purchasing debentures. The court observed further that, '[a]ll man [*sic*] who lends money reasonably wishes to know for what purpose it is borrowed, and he is more willing to advance if he knows that it is not wanted to pay off liabilities already incurred.'

9.3.10.2   Negligence

Following *Derry v Peek*[53] the Misrepresentation Act 1967 (which does not apply to Zambia)[54] on which the Misrepresentation Act 1968[55] is based (and with which we are concerned as it applies to this jurisdiction) was enacted. Section 3(1) of the Misrepresentation Act, 1968 provides a remedy for negligent misstatement in the following terms:

> Where a person has entered into a contract after a misrepresentation has been made to him by another party thereto, and as a result thereof he has suffered loss, then, if the person making the misrepresentation would be liable to damages in respect thereof had the misrepresentation been made fraudulently, that person shall be so liable notwithstanding that the misrepresentation was

---

[52] [1885] 29 Ch D 459.

[53] [1889] 14 App Cas 337.

[54] See legal principle in *Kabwe Transport Company Limited v Press Transport (1975) Limited* [1984] ZR 43 (SC).

[55] Chapter 69 of the Laws of Zambia.

not made fraudulently, unless he proves that he had reasonable grounds to believe and did believe up to the time the contract was made that the facts as represented were true.

As much as providing a remedy, section 3(1) also reverses the burden of proof from the plaintiff to the defendant. The defendant must prove that the statement now impugned was in fact not a misrepresentation. It is not for the plaintiff to prove that the statement was indeed a misrepresentation. The Misrepresentation Act, 1968 must be considered, as it rightly is, a generalisation of section 218 of the Act. While action for misrepresentation may be brought against the company under section 3(1) in, *inter alia*, an open share offer or pre-emptive rights issue as the foregoing will inexorably lead to a new contract being executed between the company and the purchaser upon the purchaser being entered on the company's members' register as the owner of the securities in question, it does not appear that section 3(1) can, despite its general *modus operandi,* be used to bring an action against directors, advisors, such as accountants or lawyers or indeed others such as banks and individuals who have offered their expertise and were an integral part of the public offer.[56] This is because section 3(1) only extends to misstatements made by a party to a subsequent contract[57] and by the same token, gives a basis for action to the other party also.

Section 3(1) makes the misrepresenter, where applicable, liable for damages as if he had been fraudulent.[58]

In *Al – Nakib Investment (Jersey) Ltd v Longcroft*[59], a case in which a restrictive approach to liability in negligence applied by the House of Lords in *Caparo Industries v Dickman*[60], was followed, the plaintiff company sued the directors of a company, claiming that it had bought shares in the company under an allegedly false prospectus. This, it was said, had induced the purchase of 400,000 shares in the newly floated company under the prospectus and directly from the company and had also induced the purchase of other shares in the company on the stock market. The judge held that since the purpose

---

[56] However see the decision in *Hedley Byrne & Co Ltd v Heller & Partners Ltd* [1964] AC 465 where there was, and since then has been an acceptance of liability arising out of negligent misstatements at common law. As the principle is unencumbered by the statutory wording found in section 3(1) of the Misrepresentation Act, 1968, it is capable of being used to bring a cause of action against those one would not ordinarily sue under section 3(1) such as directors and advisers quite apart from the company for any negligent misstatements not only in the prospectus in question but any related documents with respect to public offers.; See further, *Peek v Gurney* [1877] LR 6 HL 377 HL; *Andrews v Mockford* [1892] 2 QB 372

[57] Davies PL Gower and Davies' *Principles of Modern Company Law*....679; *The Skopas* [1983] 1 WLR 857.

[58] See *Royscot Trust v Rogerson* [1991] 2 QB 297 CA; *Smith New Court Securities Ltd v Scrimgeour Vickers (Asset Management) Ltd* [1996] 4 All ER 769.

[59] [1990] 3 All ER 321.

[60] [1990] 1 All ER 568.

of the prospectus was to invite subscriptions directly to the company and not purchases through the stock market there was no duty of care in negligence in regard to the market purchases, though there was a duty of care in regard to the shares purchased directly from the company.

We must add, at the risk of sounding repetitive that in view of the foregoing, it appears that as regards claims in negligence, investors who purchase shares or debentures on the stock market cannot claim to be owed any duty of care by persons or entities who or which make false statements in a prospectus. By the same token, those investors who purchase shares or debentures directly from the company are owed a duty of care by the company. However, in *Possfund Custodian Trustee Ltd v Derek Diamond*,[61] the plaintiff claimed that the court should now recognise that stock market practice has since changed and that prospectuses are now intended to encourage subsequent trading in shares so that those responsible should be liable at common law to subsequent purchasers for negligent or deceitful misrepresentations. In preliminary proceedings, Lightman J refused to strike out this claim. He stated that nowadays it is at least arguable that those who are responsible for issuing listing particulars and prospectuses owe a duty of care to subscribers and those who purchase in what may be described as the after – market in reliance on the prospectus. Any negligence would make the directors and their advisors liable.

9.3.10.3 Rescission

Rescission is a common law concept that allows an innocent party in the event of a misrepresentation to rescind the contract irrespective of the nature of the misrepresentation, that is to say, whether the misrepresentation was wholly innocent, negligent or fraudulent. Its stated goal is to, as far as is possible to, to put back the parties in the positions they were before the misrepresentation. For an investor who is a victim of a misrepresentation, this is an advantageous remedy as it widens the range of options open to him specifically that quite apart from damages he is entitled to he may also rescind the contract or simply rescind it without seeking damages and simply return the securities and at the same time recover his money.

9.3.10.3.1 Damages in lieu of rescission

Section 3(2) of the Misrepresentation Act, 1968 however provides that, [w] here a person has entered into a contract after a misrepresentation has been made to him otherwise than fraudulently, and he would be entitled by reason of the misrepresentation to rescind the contract, then, if it is claimed in any

---

[61] [1996] 2 All ER 774.

proceedings arising out of the contract that the contract ought to be or has been rescinded, the court or arbitrator may declare the contract subsisting and award damages in *lieu* of rescission, if of opinion that it would be equitable to do so, having regard to the nature of the misrepresentation and the loss that would be caused by it if the contract were upheld, as well as to the loss that rescission would cause to the other party.

The effect of the section is to give the Court or arbitrator as the case may be, discretion to substitute damages for the right to rescission. The decision to make this substitution should be based, it appears, on equitable reasons. In all cases however, this should be done 'having regard to the nature of the misrepresentation and the loss that would be caused by it if the contract were upheld, as well as to the loss that rescission would cause to the other party'. This provision, it may be contended, was to a great extent informed by the consequences that may be brought to bear if rescission was allowed in all instances of misrepresentation including opportunism, speculation in securities by investors who may hide behind the cloak of misrepresentation to achieve their inequitable goals to the detriment of the company. It is also useful to remember that misrepresentation does not render the contract void and as such should not be taken to give the innocent part an automatic right to rescission.

In all cases, the necessity to prove that a person who sold shares misrepresented facts or that the company, where the misstatements or untrue or wrong statements are in the prospectus, even when the same may have been included by experts or advisers without the company's concurrence, was, on the face of it, the source of the misrepresentation and as such liable for the misrepresentation. It would appear from the decisions in *Mair v Rio Grande Rubber Estates Ltd*[62] and *Re Pacaya Rubber Co*[63] that the burden carried by the company to distance itself from the misrepresentation with which it is inextricably linked and which it uses to offer securities to the public is a heavy one indeed.

9.3.10.3.1 Bars to rescission

There are quite a number of limitations that may come to bear upon an innocent party even in the face of actionable misrepresentation. We discuss some below:

(1) Affirmation

If with full knowledge of the representation, the innocent party makes it clear expressly, impliedly or by conduct that he intends to see the contract through as

---

[62] [1913] AC 853 HL.
[63] [1914] 1 Ch 542 CA.

in *Long v Lloyd*[64] he or she will be taken to have affirmed the contract. Therefore, actions such as attending and voting at meeting, accepting the payment of dividends or dealing in the securities on which the action for misrepresentation may be predicated in the face of facts relating to the misrepresentation being known will be a bar to rescission.[65]

(2)   Lapse of time

It has been shown in *Leaf v International Galleries*[66] that the innocent party (the investor) must act within a reasonable time, otherwise the right to rescind will be lost. Inordinate delay is just as bad as mere delay. 'The reason for this strictness', it has been observed, 'is that the company may well have raised credit from third parties who have acted on the basis of the capital apparently raised by the company, which appearance the basis of the capital apparently raised by the company, which appearance the rescission of the shareholder's contract would undermine'.

(3)   Restitution in *integrum* impossible

Where it is impossible to, as is the stated aim of rescission and exemplified in *Vigers v Pike,*[67] restore the parties to their original position, the right to rescind is lost.[68]

(4)   Third party acquires rights in good faith

Where a third party acquires shares or any security for that matter to which the misrepresentation relates in good faith, the original shareholder cannot rescind the contract after discovery of the misrepresentation in order to acquire the shares from the new owner.[69]

(5)   Use of discretion under section 3(2) of Misrepresentation Act, 1968

As we noted above, the right to rescission can be lost if the court exercises its discretion under section 3(2) of Misrepresentation Act, 1968.

---

[64] [1958] 1 WLR 753; see further, *Peyman v Lanjani* [1985] Ch 457 in which the EWCA held that the plaintiff had not lost his right to rescind even though he had proceeded with the contract to which he knew the facts of misrepresentation because he did not know that he had the right to rescind.

[65] *Sharpley v Louth and East Coast Railway Company* [1876] 2 Ch D 663; *Scholey v Central Railway of Venezuela* [1869] LR 9 Eq 226n; and *Crawley's case* [1869] LR 4 Ch App 322.

[66] [1950] 2 KB 86.

[67] [1842] 8 CI & F 562.

[68] See however Lord Brown-Wilkinson's dicta in Smith *New Court Securities Ltd Scrimgeour Vickers (Asset Management) Ltd* [1996] 4 All ER 769 at 774 regarding instances in which the misrepresentation is discovered after an investor has sold his holding.

[69] *Phillips v Brooks* [1919] 2 KB 243.

It should be noted that under section 2(a) of the Misrepresentation Act the innocent party can rescind the contract the fact that a misrepresentation has become part of the contract notwithstanding. Further and by section 2(b) the innocent party can still rescind the contract even if it has already been executed. It must be remembered though that this removal of bars to rescission relates only to innocent misrepresentation. Be that as it may, the need for the investor to act quickly can however not be over-emphasised.

(6)   Insolvency or/and liquidation of the company

At liquidation, the creditors' claims crystallise. For this reason a claim for rescission may not succeed nor can it, as shown in *Tennent v The City of Glasgow Bank*.[70] To succeed, he must, as was shown in *Oakes v Turquand*[71] and *Re Scottish Petroleum Company*.[72]

9.3.11   Stop trading order

Section 219(1) empowers the Registrar to 'apply to the Court for an order where it appears to the Registrar that a prospectus that has been registered—
- *(a)*   contains a statement, promise, estimate or forecast that is false or misleading, whether or not the statement or other specified particular was false or misleading at the time the prospectus was lodged;
- *(b)*   fails to comply in a material respect with this Part; or
- *(c)*   conceals or omits to state a material fact so that a statement in the prospectus is rendered misleading in the context in which it appears'.

Where an application is made by the Registrar pursuant to section 219(1), the Court may make any of the following orders:
- *(a)*   cancel the registration of the prospectus and direct the person or persons making the invitation to the public to which the prospectus relates to—
    - (i)   withdraw the prospectus;
    - (ii)   cease to accept further subscriptions or purchases of shares or debentures offered in the prospectus; and
    - (iii)   repay, with interest, any money received from applicants with respect to the prospectus;
- *(b)*   declare any contract for the subscription or purchase of shares or debentures offered in the prospectus to be voidable;
- *(c)*   direct the person or persons making the invitation to the public, to which the prospectus relates, to immediately re-issue the prospectus amended in such terms as the court directs; or
- *(d)*   protect the rights of persons injuriously affected by the issue of the prospectus, as the Court considers just in the circumstances.

---

[70] [1879] 4 App Cas 615.
[71] [1867] LR 2 HL325.
[72] [1882] 23 Ch D 413.

Further and by section 219(3), '[t]he Court may, in exercising its powers in terms of this section, on the application of the Registrar and on being satisfied of the existence of a *prima facie* case, make such interim orders, as it considers necessary, applying for a period of not more than fourteen days after the date of the order'.

9.3.12   *Enforceability of agreement before end and withdrawal after waiting period*

The Act stipulates that '[w]here an invitation is made to the public to acquire shares or debentures of a company, an agreement for the acquisition of the shares or debentures made before the end of the waiting period, other than a *bona fide* underwriting agreement, is not enforceable by the company or promoters'.[73] Additionally, '[w]here an invitation is made to the public in respect of shares or debentures of a company, an application for such shares or debentures shall not be revocable during a period of seven days commencing on the expiry of the waiting period, unless, before the expiry of that period of seven days, a person responsible for the prospectus has given notice to the public which has the effect of excluding or limiting the responsibility of the person giving it for any misstatement or omission in the prospectus'.[74]

9.3.13   *Allotment and minimum subscription*

Allotment and minimum subscription as a concept and essential part of public offers of shares are provided for under section 222.[75] To that end, section 222(1) explicitly requires that before an allotment of shares offered by a company to the public is made, firstly, the minimum subscription must be subscribed in terms of the Act; and secondly that the 'sum payable on application for the shares so subscribed be received by the company which seeks to allot any shares offered to the public.[76] Where in fulfilling the requirements of section 222(1) payment is made by bespeaking a cheque, 'the sum shall not be regarded as having been

---

[73] Section 220.

[74] Section 221.

[75] An important note so far as compliance with this section is concerned is to be found in subsection (11) which stipulates with clarity and brevity that '[a] condition that requires or binds an applicant for shares to waive compliance with a requirement of this section shall be void'.

[76] It must be noted that in terms of section 222(5), '[i]f subsection (1) has not been complied with, after the expiry of four months from the first issue of the prospectus, any money received from an applicant for the shares shall, without delay, be repaid, without interest, to the applicant'. By section 222(6), '[s]ubject to section 222 (7), if any money referred to in subsection (5) is not repaid within five months after the issue of the prospectus, the directors shall be jointly and severally liable to repay that money with interest at the ruling bank rate, from the expiry of the period specified in this subsection. Additionally, section 222(7) specifies that '[a] director is not liable, as provided in subsection (6), if that director proves that the default in the repayment of the money was not due to any misconduct or negligence on that director's part'.

received by the company until the cheque is paid by the bank on which it is drawn'.[77]

There are further requirements under section 222 which are deserving of attention:

For starters, '[t]he minimum subscription shall be calculated on the value of each share'.[78] More to the point, '[t]he amount payable, on application, on each share offered to the public shall not be less than five per cent of the nominal amount of the share'.[79] Any 'allotment made by a company to an applicant in contravention of section[222] shall, despite that the company is in the course of being wound-up, be voidable at the option of the applicant by written notice given to the company within thirty days after the date of the allotment'. Wilful contravention, or wilful authorisation or permission of the contravention of section 222 by any director shall make such a director 'liable to compensate the company and the allottee for any loss, damages or costs which the company or the allottee has sustained or incurred as a result of the contravention'.[80] There is a limitation period of two years after the date of allotment as regards actions for the 'recovery of any compensation in terms of subsection (9).[81]

We must also note the significant provision that '[a] company shall not allot, and an officer or promoter of a company shall not authorise or permit the allotment of, shares or debentures to the public, on the basis of a prospectus, more than six months after the publication of the prospectus'.[82] However, according to section 222(13), '[a]n allotment of shares or debentures shall not be void or voidable by reason only that it was made in contravention of subsection (12)'. This prevents a company from unjustly profiting from its own default and ensures that the allottee is not deprived from the rights and benefits accruing from the allotment of shares already offered to him by the company.

9.3.14   *Statement in lieu of prospectus*

The basis regarding the matter of statement in *lieu* (place) of prospectus is section 223.[83] In terms of section 223(1), '[a] company which fails to issue a prospectus on, or with reference to, its formation shall not allot any of its shares or debentures, unless it has, not less than three days before the first allotment of the shares or debentures, lodged with the Registrar a statement in lieu of a prospectus'. According to section 223(2), A statement in lieu of a prospectus shall be—

---

[77] Section 222(2).
[78] Section 222(3).
[79] Section 222(4).
[80] Section 222(9).
[81] Section 222(10).
[82] Section 222(12).
[83] Which replaces section 135 but more or less retains its contents.

(a)   signed by every person who is named in the statement as a director or a proposed director or by that person's agent authorised in writing; and

(b)   in the form of a prospectus and deal with such matters specified in the Third Schedule[84] as apply to the formation of a company'.

9.3.15   *Prohibition of waiver and notice clause*

It is worth mentioning that any condition that entails or binds any person or entity to abandon compliance with Part X of the Act or otherwise attributes to that person or entity, 'notice of a contract, document or other matter not' unequivocally[85] mentioned 'in a prospectus, advertisement or circular, is void'.[86] This matter is one well within matters envisaged under section 330[87] and for which any of the persons with standing thereunder can seek and be granted injunctive relief. Binding a person or entity to act in contravention of the Act is obviously illegal. In the case of *Bigos v Boustead*[88] the parties to a contract agreed to terms and conditions which were contrary to exchange regulations. The contract was held to be unenforceable. Similarly, a contract to defraud revenue author is illegal and unenforceable[89] Illegality is a vitiating factor and renders a contract *void ab initio*. Public policy demands that illegal contracts[90] should be unenforceable because justice would be tainted and the dignity of the court lost were a court of law enforce an illegal undertaking such as the one envisaged in section 224.

'[N]otice of a contract, document or other matter not' explicitly mentioned 'in a prospectus, advertisement or circular' can similarly not be enforced as the tenor of this part of the Act leaves no doubt as to its intent which is to protect investors by ensuring that all the information regarding the company is clearly and unambiguously stated to enable would be investors, that is, the public to make informed decisions. To that end, one cannot be bound by a contract or terms of which he is unaware as this is tantamount to fraud. Where the foregoing has under currents of subliminal threats devoid of overt threats to a would-be

---

[84] Previously specified in Part A of the Schedule Four under CA 1994.

[85] Or 'specifically'.

[86] Section 224.

[87] In terms of section 330(1), '[t]he Court may, on the application of a person referred to in subsection (2), make an order restraining a company or a director from engaging in conduct that contravenes or would contravene the articles or this Act. By section 330(2), '[f]or the purposes of subsection (1), an application may be made by—(a) the company; (b) a director or member; (c) an entitled person; or (d) the Registrar'.

[88] [1951] 1 All ER 92.

[89] *Miller v Kalinski* [1945] 62 TLR 85; See further, *Alexander v Rayson* [1936] 1 KB 169 where a contract to defraud the ratings authority by showing the value of the property to be less than it was, was held to be illegal and void.

[90] Which include contracts tending to corrupt public morals; those promoting sexual immorality; trading with an enemy in times of war; restraint of marriage; attempting to oust the jurisdiction of the Court.

investor, it will come under the purview of duress and if proved, the contract, section 224 notwithstanding, will be held to be void and unenforceable. As regards the term 'specifically' as used in section 224, we must remember that the *contra proferentem rule* of construction states that a clause will be interpreted strictly against a party at whose instance it was included in the contract and who now seeks to enforce it. Section 224 therefore requires not only transparency but clarity and the avoidance of vagueness at every turn or the parts of the prospectus which contravene section 224 will be void and of no effect.

9.4   Private placement

It is patent from the foregoing that the offering of shares to the public can be and by any measure, a lengthy demanding and expensive process. The costs may be in the form of printing copies of the prospectuses; advertising; underwriting; legal fees; accounting fees; and regulatory fees. Not wanting to go this route but still desirous of offering their shares, companies will choose the avenue of private placement/placing/selective marketing. This process which is less complex, less involving and less costly involves the company selling its entire issue of shares to what may be termed an 'issuing house' or more familiarly, a broker who/which then finds persons/entities 'interested in acquiring shares in the company and places the shares with them'.[91]

9.5   Conclusion

In this chapter we have discussed the allotment of shares; the invitations to public to acquire shares and debentures; first publication of prospectus; prospectus required for invitation to public to purchase shares or debentures; contents of prospectus; expert's consent; registration of prospectus; over-subscription in debenture issue; reference to stock exchange listing in prospectus-allotment of shares; civil liability for misstatements or omissions in prospectus; remedies for misstatement; offence of misstatement or omission in prospectus under the Act; other remedies available under the general law specifically the Misrepresentation Act 1968 as it relates to fraud or deceit; Negligence; Bars to rescission. We have examined the enforceability of agreement before end and withdrawal after waiting period; allotment and minimum subscription. We also noted that the Act provides for statement *in lieu* of prospectus; and prohibition of waiver and notice clause; and private placement.

---

[91] Farrah JH and Hannigan BM *Farrar's Company Law* 4th edn (Butterworths London 1998) 545.

FURTHER READING

Books

Davies PL *Gower and Davies' Principles of Modern Company Law* 7th edn. (Thomson Sweet & Maxwell London 2003).

Dine J and Koutsias M *Company Law* 6th edn (Palgrave Macmillan Hampshire 2007).

Farrah JH and Hannigan BM *Farrar's Company Law* 4th edn (Butterworths London 1998).

Gates RB *Gates Company Law and Practice in Zambia* (Reagan Blankfein Gates Lusaka 2017).

Keenan D *Smith and Keenan's Company Law* 13th edn (Pearson Longman Essex 2005).

Mckendrick E *Contract Law* 7th edn (Palgrave Macmillan New York 2007).

Mclaughlin S *Unlocking Company Law* 3rd edn (Routledge New York 2015).

Ridley A and Shepherd C *Company Law: Key Facts Key Cases* (Routledge New York 2015).

Sealy L and Worthington S *Sealy & Worthington's Cases and Materials in Company Law* 10th edn (Oxford University Press Oxford 2013).

Wild C and Weinstein S *Smith and Keenan's Company Law* 15th edn (Pearson Education Ltd London 2011).

IO

DEBENTURES AND CHARGES

AIMS AND OBJECTIVES

 After reading this chapter you should appreciate:
- ➢ The Power to borrow
- ➢ A Debenture and classes of debentures
- ➢ Debenture stock
- ➢ Redeemable debenture and the re-issue proscription
- ➢ What an irredeemable debenture is
- ➢ What an unsecured debentures is
- ➢ How debentures are acquired
- ➢ The Liability of assignee
- ➢ The appointment as assignee for debenture holders
- ➢ The significance of the Register of debenture holders
- ➢ Meetings relating to other debenture holders
- ➢ The concept of Charges
- ➢ The distinction between a floating and fixed charge
- ➢ Crystallisation of floating charge
- ➢ Automatic crystallisation
- ➢ Avoidance of floating charges
- ➢ Restrictions on a floating charge
- ➢ The registration of charges
- ➢ The registration of charges by companies
- ➢ Entries of satisfaction and release of property from charge
- ➢ Variation of registered charge
- ➢ The registration of enforcement of security by mortgagee
- ➢ The endorsement of registration on debentures
- ➢ Remedies open to secured debenture holders

10.1   Introduction

In this chapter we explore provisions in Part XI specifically sections 225 to 245 of
the Act which relate to debentures and charges. We saw in chapter 9 that in terms

of section 210, raising money by way of a public issue of shares is a feature only open to public companies. We must realise however, that corporate finance or the financing of corporate activities goes over and above sourcing needed funds through the device of shares. A more expansive definition of capital includes debt/loan capital which, within the context of our present discussion, includes debentures, debenture stock and charges. Our focus therefore relates to loan capital and the means deployed to secure it by the company. The distinctive nature of limited liability that most companies possess has meant that banks and other financial lending institutions or would-be creditors generally and without question, secure any money lent to a company with some sought of security in case of insolvency. Depending on the nature of the company and the attendant risk involved as determined by the lender, there may be a further requirement of personal guarantees from the directors on top of the security. As Nourse LJ has noted in *Re New Bullas Trading Ltd*,[1] 'he who lends money to a trading company neither wishes nor expects it to become insolvent.... But against an evil day he wants the best security the company can give him consistently with its ability to trade meanwhile'.

By security is meant that, 'in addition to the ability to sue the company for the discharge of the debt, the creditor is able to look to some property in which the company has interest in order to enforce the discharge of the company's obligation to the creditor.'[2] At the same time as the lender seeks security, the company wants to be able to borrow without having to give such security to the lender that its ability to trade is affected by the constraints imposed by the security.[3] The typical devices used by lenders to obtain security include the following:

(i)   Debentures;
(ii)   legal mortgages;
(iii)   equitable mortgage;
(iv)   fixed charge; and
(v)   floating charges.

10.2   The Power to borrow

It will be remembered that Section 86(2)[4] of the Act confers upon company directors express power to borrow money; to charge any property or business of

---

[1] [1994] 1 BCLC 485 at 487.
[2] Hannigan B *Company Law* 3rd edn (Oxford University Press Oxford 2012) 533.
[3] Hannigan B *Company Law*....
[4] Replaces section 215 (3) of CA 1994 and provides that '[w]ithout limiting the generality of subsection (1), and subject to the articles, the board of directors may exercise the powers of the company to— (a) borrow money; (b) charge any property or business of the company, including any of its uncalled capital; and (c) issue debentures or give any other security for a debt, liability or obligation of the company or of any other person'. There is a slight change from the former section in that the power to so do is subject to the articles.

the company or all or any of its uncalled capital; and to issue debentures or give any other security for a debt, liability or obligation of the company or any other person. The clarity of this provision as regards the fact that the power to borrow is reposed in the board of directors cannot be questioned. That notwithstanding, the members of a company may, through the articles, place such limitations (e.g. placing a fixed sum beyond which the company cannot borrow) as they see fit on the company's borrowing power.[5]

In *General Auction Estate and Monetary Co v. Smith*,[6] a company established under the UKCA 1862, for the purpose of the sale and purchase of estates and property, the granting of advances on property intended for sale, and loans on deposit of securities, and the discounting of approved commercial bills, had under its memorandum and articles of association no express power to borrow money. The company received deposits and discounted bills; and one of its directors, who was also a depositor, advanced money to the company upon the security of an equitable charge on realty belonging to the company, in order to enable it to repay money due to himself and another depositor. The company was afterwards ordered to be wound-up, and, in an action by the liquidator to set aside the security as *ultra vires* the company. It was held, (1) that the company was a trading company, and as such had an implied power to borrow money for the purpose of its business; and (2) that the borrowing which had taken place was one properly incident to the course and conduct of the business of the company for its proper purposes; and accordingly, that as the deposits were valid loans, it was competent for the company to borrow money for the purpose of repaying the depositors, and to give security to the person who made the advance, in the manner they had done.

10.3 Debenture[7]

The term 'debenture' has, compared to its previous definition under section 2 of CA 1994, a more expanded definition which now defines not only what a debenture is but also what it is not. Specifically, section 2 of the Act defines the term "debenture" to mean, a document issued by a corporate that evidences or acknowledges a debt of the corporate, whether or not it constitutes a charge on property of the corporate in respect of money that is or may be deposited with or lent to the corporate, and includes a unit of a debenture, debenture stock and bonds and any other security issued by the corporate, whether constituting a charge on the assets of the corporate or not,…

---

[5] Section 86(2).
[6] [1891] 3 Ch 432.
[7] Sections 225–245 replacing sections 86–95 of CA 1994.

However, the following do not, according to the Act,[8] come within the foregoing definition, that is to say:

   (a)   document acknowledging a debt incurred by the corporate in respect of money that is or may be deposited with or lent to the corporate by a person in the ordinary course of business—
         (i)   carried on by the person; and
         (ii)   of the corporate as is not part of a business of borrowing money and providing finance;
   (b)   document issued by a bank in the ordinary course of its banking business that evidences or acknowledges indebtedness of the bank;
   (c)   cheque, order for the payment of money or bill of exchange; or
   (d)   document of a kind and in the circumstances prescribed in regulations issued by the Minister.

Hence Chitty J has, in *Levy v Abercorris Slate & Slab Co,*[9] defined a debenture as '…a document acknowledging indebtedness which may be (and in this context is) secured by a charge or charges'. It follows then that any form of document, as long as it acknowledges indebtedness is a debenture. For instance, in *British India Steam Navigation Co v Inland Revenue Commissioners,*[10] Lindley J held that a simple "acknowledgement of indebtedness" was a debenture, which meant that a paper on which a director promised to pay the holder 100 pounds in 1882 and 5% interest each half year was enough. A debenture therefore, means a document which either creates a debt or acknowledges it, and any document given it fulfills either of these conditions is a debenture.[11] Thus, in *Stamp Duty Commissioners v African Farming Equipment Company Limited,*[12] the question in the matter was whether or not stamp duty was chargeable on an instrument drawn in the particular terms it was held that a debenture which is the only security for payment of money is, for stamp duty purposes, classed under Head 8(1)[13] of the first schedule to the Stamp Duty Ordinance.

However, one must be careful for though '[n]early every document evidencing indebtedness by a company is commercially called a debenture,..it would be a mistake to equate the two completely'.[14] There are good and compelling reasons for this caveat which include the fact that the raising of loan capital is not

---

[8]   Section 2.
[9]   [1887] 37 Ch 260 at 264; 'Debenture means a document which either creates a debt or acknowledges it, and any document which fulfills either of these conditions is a debentures.'
[10]   [1880-81] LR 7 QBD 165 QBD.
[11]   *Per* Chitty J in *Levy v Abercorris Slate and Slab Co* [1883] 37 Ch D 260.
[12]   [1969] ZR 32 (CAZ).
[13]   Head 8(1) provided: 'Mortgage, charge debenture or covenant being the only or principal mortgage) for the payment of money - for every ú100 or part of ú100 of the amount secured.' See also *Fleetwood and Hesketh v The Commissioners of Inland Revenue,* [1936] 1 KB 351, *per* Lord Hanworth, M.R at 358 and 359
[14]   Farrah JH and Hannigan BM *Farrar's Company* Law 4th ed….256.

restricted to the device of debentures. A company could raise capital through bills of exchange and related negotiable instruments[15] which like debentures evidence debt but are not ordinarily referred to as debentures.[16]

The person in whose favour the debenture is issued or created is referred to as a debenture holder. Section 2 states that, '*a debenture holder includes a debenture stockholder.*' Debenture holders are creditors and not members of the company, and are entitled to interest on their debentures whether the company earns profits or not.[17]

10.3.1   *Classes of debentures*

The foregoing finds statutory confirmation in section 225.[18] Specifically section 225(1) provides that a company may, if it so wishes, raise loans by the issue of a debenture or a series of debentures.   In terms of section 225(3), [d]ebentures which are declared to be of the same series by virtue of the terms—

(a)   that are stipulated in the debenture;

(b)   of a resolution authorising the issue of the debenture; or

(c)   of a trust deed relating to a debenture issued by a company; shall rank equally in all respects, despite the debentures having been issued on different dates.

It follows from the foregoing that, in an instance where debentures are issued in a series as envisaged in section 225(3), there will normally be a provision in the debentures in question explicitly providing expressly that the debentures are to rank *paripassu* otherwise priority will rank according to the time they are made and priority of payment and security according to the date of issue, and if all were issued on the same day, they would rank in numerical order.

Thus, in *Gartside v Silkstone and Dodworth Coal and Iron Co Ltd*[19] it was demonstrated that when two deeds relating to the same subject-matter are executed on the same day the court will inquire which of them was executed first. But if there is anything in the deeds themselves to show an intention either that they shall take effect *paripassu*, or that one should take effect in priority to the other, the court will presume that they were executed in such an order as to give effect to the manifest intention.

---

[15] Section 238(5) explicitly provides that '[w]here a negotiable instrument has been given to a company to secure the payment of any debts owed to the company, the deposit of the instrument for securing an advance to the company, shall not, for the purposes of this section, be considered to be a charge on the debts owed to the company'.

[16] Farrah JH and Hannigan BM *Farrar's Company* Law 4th ed. . . .

[17] Wild C and Weinstein S *Smith and Keenan's Company Law* 14th edn (Pearson Educated Ltd London 2005) 441.

[18] Formerly section 86 under CA 1994.

[19] [1882] 21 Ch D 762.

In *Gartside*, one hundred and fifty debentures of a company, each for £100, were all sealed with the company's seal on the same day. They bore the numbers 501 to 650. Each of the first hundreds (Nos. 501 to 600) contained a provision that it "and all other debentures of the company to the amount of £10,000 (the amount intended to be now borrowed by the company), or such of them as shall for the time being be due and unpaid, shall be all taken and considered, as between the company and the several holders thereof, as one debenture, and shall not be entitled to any preference or priority by reason of priority of date or otherwise, but shall be paid *paripassu* out of the funds of the company." Each of the other fifty debentures contained a similar provision, subsisting the sum of £5000 for £10,000. There was evidence that the company's seal was affixed to the debentures in the order of their numbers, beginning with the earliest. It was held that the company being in liquidation that the holders of the debentures for £10,000 were entitled to priority over the holders of the debentures for £5000.

10.3.2   Debenture stock

We have already made the point that a debenture is an instrument that evidences indebtedness with or without security with the company being the debtor on the one hand and the loan issuer or creditor on the other.

10.3.2.1   General

In terms of section 225(4), '[a] debenture stock shall be created—
- *(a)* by deed, under the common seal of the company and in favour of assignees for the debenture stockholders; and
- *(b)* as stock, of a specified total amount, parts of which, represented by debenture stock certificates, are issued to separate holders'. Whether it be by deed or as stock, the latter being a term in line with our discussion, debenture stock is 'borrowed capital consolidated into one mass for the sake of convenience'.[20] One advantage for holding debenture stock may well be that while a single debenture holder can only dispose of his debenture entitlement in whole, debenture stock may disposed of in whole or in part.

10.3.2.2   Debenture trust deed

'The early forms of debenture trust deed supplemented individual debentures but usually contained the security offered by the company'.[21] By comparison,

---

[20] *Palmer's Company Law* (24ᵗʰedn 1995) vol. 1 para 44-04 quoted in Farrar JH and Hannigan BM *Farrar's Company Law*...257.

[21] Farrar JH and Hannigan BM *Farrar's Company Law*...257.

'[t]he modern form replaces individual debentures and the holder of loan stock is now not usually a direct creditor of the company'[22] Put another way, debenture stock holders, unlike debenture holders, are not creditors of the company. In *Re Dunderland Iron Ore Co Ltd*,[23] a trust deed for securing debenture stock, made between the company and the trustees for the stockholders, provided that the company would pay the half-yearly interest direct to the stockholders, whose receipt should be a good discharge to the trustees and the company. The certificate delivered to each stockholder stated the rate of interest and the dates of payment, and certified that the stockholder was the registered holder of the stock which "is issued subject to the provisions contained" in the trust deed, but it did not contain any covenant with the stockholder to pay him the interest. It was held, that stockholders whose interest was in arrear were not entitled to present a winding-up petition as creditors under s. 82 of the UKCA, 1862.

It is further observed that the modern day debenture stock holder is merely a beneficiary, as implied above, 'under a trust by which the trustee holds the debt in question'.[24] Additionally, a good number if not the majority of trust deeds make provision for any matters needing action to be commenced by the trustee thereby pre-empting singular actions by debenture stockholders.[25] There remedy understandably lies against the trustee whom they may compel, should they be minded to, under the trust deed, to take action by exercising powers availed to him by the trust deed. That power may, *inter alia,* be predicated on section 225(5) which provides that '[a] contract with a company to take up and pay for any debenture of the company may be enforced by an order for specific performance'.

We must, in addition to the foregoing, discuss a few matters relating to a trust deed which may ground an action by the trustee. They include the following:[26]

(i)   The debenture trust deed may restrict transfers to specific multiples of stock in accordance with section 189;

(ii)   The trust deed may contain covenants by the company to repay capital sum and interest;

(iii) The trust deed may contain covenants by the company to observe and perform any and all matters relating to its business;

(iv)   The trust deed will contain provisions relating to a fixed or floating charge or both and the usual mortgage provision; and

(v)   It may contain, as it ordinarily should, relating to transfer and meetings of debenture stockholders.[27]

---

[22] Pennington RR *Company Law* (7th ed 1995) Ch 2 cited in Farrar JH and Hannigan BM *Farrar's Company Law*...257.

[23] [1909] 1 Ch 446.

[24] Farrar JH and Hannigan BM *Farrar's Company Law*...257.

[25] Farrar JH and Hannigan BM *Farrar's Company Law*....

[26] Taken from Farrar JH and Hannigan BM *Farrar's Company Law*...257.

[27] See section 233.

Finally, in terms of section 232(1) provides that '[a] registered debenture holder shall have votes in proportion to the value of the debentures held with respect to debentures of a company that are secured by a trust deed, unless the trust deed provides otherwise'.

10.3.2.3   Right to copies of trust deed

According to section 229(1), '[a] copy of a trust deed, securing an issue of debentures, shall be provided to a holder of the debentures, at the holder's request and on payment of the sum of one hundred fee units, or such lesser sum as may be required by the company, within seven days after receipt of the request'. Further, and in terms of section 229(2), '[s]ubject to the Credit Reporting Act, 2017 a company shall, within seven days of a request being made by an assignee in the prescribed form, furnish the assignee with the names, addresses and other registered particulars of the debenture holder for whom that person is an assignee. Finally and by section 229(3), '[i]f a company fails to comply with this section, the company and each officer in default commit an offence and are liable, on conviction, to a fine not exceeding one thousand penalty units for each day that the failure continues'.

10.4   Redeemable debenture and the re-issue proscription

These are debentures payable after effluxion[28] of a fixed period. The company therefore has the right to pay back the principal amount to the debenture holder after the effluxion of a fixed period and have its property released from the charge created in favour of the debenture holder. Section 234(1)(a)[29] which replaces section 95(1) under CA 1994 prohibits a company from re–issuing any debenture which has been redeemed. It is equally prohibited under section 234(1)(a) which replaces 95(2) under CA 1994 to issue a new debenture in place of a redeemed debenture on terms that the new debenture shall have the same priorities as the redeemed debenture. As such, in terms of section 234(3) which replaces section 95(3) under CA 1994 the issue of a new debenture in place of a redeemed debenture cannot be treated as the issue of a new debenture for purposes of any provision limiting the amount or number of debentures which may be issued. Therefore, any transaction which involves the re – issuing of a redeemed debenture is void *ab initio*.[30]

---

[28] 'When this phrase is used in leases, conveyances, and other like deeds, or in agreements expressed in simple writing, it indicates the conclusion or expiration of an agreed term of years specified in the deed or writing, such conclusion or expiration arising in the natural course of events, in contradistinction to the determination of the term by the acts of the parties or by some unexpected or unusual incident or other sudden event.'(www.thelawdictionary.org/effluxion-of-time. Retrieved on 18/08/2016)

[29] 'a company shall not re – issue any debenture which has been redeemed.'

[30] Section 234(4) replacing section 95(4) under CA 1994.

10.4　Irredeemable debenture

Section 225(6)[31] provides that '[a] condition, contained in a debenture or in a trust deed for securing a debenture, is not invalid by reason only that the debenture has been made irredeemable or redeemable, only on the occurrence of a contingency, however, remote or on the expiration of a period, however, long'. According to section 86(6), '[a] condition in a debenture or in a trust deed for securing s debenture shall not be invalid by reason only of the fact that the debenture is hereby made irredeemable or redeemable only on the happening of a contingency, however remote, or on the expiration of a period, however long.' An irredeemable debenture is a debenture which has no specific date of redemption. However, such a debenture becomes payable on winding up of a company or where the company persistently defaults in paying interest as and when it is due.[32] The fact that there is no set date for repayment does not mean that the company can never pay off the principal when it wishes to do so but that the debenture holder cannot compel the company to redeem them unless some event occurs.[33]

In the case of *Knightbridge Estates Trust Ltd v Byrne and Others,*[34] the appellants in 1931 mortgaged their freehold properties to the respondents to secure a loan of £310,000 By the deed the appellants covenanted to repay the money so borrowed with interest by eighty half-yearly installments. By clause 2 of the deed the appellants demised the mortgaged land to the respondents for a long term of years with the usual proviso for cesser. A few years later the appellants, being desirous of redeeming the mortgaged property by the repayment of the principal sum borrowed, notwithstanding the stipulation contained in the deed as to the repayment by eighty half-yearly installments, sought a declaration that they were so entitled to redeem at any time by giving the usual notice. It was held as follows:

(1)　That the mortgage was a "debenture" within section 74 of the UKCA 1929, having regard to the definition in s. 380, and therefore was not rendered invalid by reason of being redeemable only after forty years.

(2)　That the rule against perpetuities has no application to mortgages; and

(3)　That the appellants were not entitled to the declaration claimed.

Correspondingly, in *Kreglinger v New Patagonia Meat & Storage Co Ltd,*[35] the court recognised that requiring the borrower to sell sheepskin to the lender of finance for a period of time could constitute an unfair clog on the equity of redemption. In the event, on the facts of the particular case, it was held not to

---

[31] Which replaces section 86(6).
[32] Morse G *Charlesworth's Company Law* 13th edn (Stevens & Sons London).
[33] Morse G *Charlesworth's Company Law* 13th edn (Stevens & Sons London).
[34] [1940] AC 613.
[35] [1914] AC 25.

be unreasonable. The agreement provided that for 5 years the borrower must sell skin to the lender so long as the lender was willing to buy at the best price offered by any other person.

10.5   Unsecured debentures

The permissive tenor of section 225(2) entails that the Act, as with CA 1921 and CA 1994, permits the creation of unsecured debentures. Put another way, a debenture need not 'be secured by a charge over property of the company'. There is the option of creating an unsecured one should the parties so choose. The foregoing must be read with section 230. In terms of section 230(1), '[a] company shall not issue an unsecured debenture, debenture stock certificate or prospectus relating to unsecured debentures, unless the term " unsecured debenture " or such other term is stated on the document issued by the company. Further and by section 230(2), '[i]f a company fails to comply with this section, the company and each officer in default commit an offence and are liable, on conviction, to a fine not exceeding two hundred thousand penalty units for each day that the failure continues'.

10.6   How debentures are acquired

A debenture may be acquired from the company itself, by transfer[36] or transmission.[37]

10.6.1   Issue by the company (transfer)

Section 225(1)[38] provides that a company may raise loans by the issue of a debenture or a series of debentures. Unlike shares, debentures can be allotted at a discount unless the articles state otherwise. Issuance of debentures at a discount tied with a right to change into shares at par value, while not fatal to the debentures so issued is fatal to the right to exchange rendering it void as this '…would be an invitation to evade the rule that shares may not be issued at a discount'.[39] Thus in *Mosely v Koffyfontein Mines Ltd*[40], a company proposed to issue to its shareholders debentures at a discount of 20 per cent, repayable on November 1, 1909, upon the terms of a circular whereby the registered holder was to have the right at any time prior to May 1, 1909, to exchange

---

[36] Sections 188 and 189 read within the context of section 226(2).

[37] Section 190 read within the context of section 226(2).

[38] Section 86(1) under CA 1994.

[39] Dine J and Koutsias M *Company Law* 6th edn….289. However, in terms of section 238(9), '[t]he deposit of debentures as security for a debt of the company shall not for the purposes of [that] section be regarded as an issue of such debentures at a discount'.

[40] [1904] 2 Ch 108.

the debentures for fully paid shares in the company at the rate of one 1*l*.fully paid share for every £1.00 of the nominal amount of the debentures; and by the conditions of the debentures, in the event of the debenture-holder giving to the company a written demand for shares in exercise of this right, the principle moneys were to become immediately repayable. It was held that the proposed issue of debentures was void, in as much as it was capable of being used as a means of issuing shares at a discount.[41]

10.6.2   *Transmission*

In terms of section 190 as read together with section 226(2), debentures may pass by transmission. In terms of section 190(1) despite the articles, [debenture] in a company may pass by operation of law'. By subsection (2), '[i]n the case of the death of a shareholder of a company the—

(a)   survivor or survivors where the deceased was a joint holder; and
(b)   personal representative of the deceased where the deceased was a sole holder or last survivor of joint holders; shall be the only persons recognised by the company as having title to the deceased's interest in the [debentures]'.

However, because debenture holders hold rights against the company and because a debenture is evidence of indebtedness by the company section 226(3) which relates to the 'liability in respect of a share with unpaid liability, whether the share was jointly held or not' is inapplicable.

According to section 190(4), '[a] representative on whom the ownership of a share devolves, by reason of the person being the personal representative, receiver or assignee in bankruptcy of the holder or by operation of law may, on such evidence being produced as the board of directors may reasonably require—

(a)   be registered as the holder of the share; or
(b)   transfer the share to another person without first being registered as the holder of the share.

Further and as in the case of shares, in terms of 190(5), '[t]he board of directors shall have the same right to decline or delay registration of a transfer by the representative as it would have had in the case of a transfer by the registered holder, but shall have no right to refuse registration of the representative'.

10.7   Liability of assignee

In terms of section 227(1), '[a] company shall not, indemnify or compensate a person, who is an assignee for debenture holders of the company or a related

---

[41] Reversing the decision of Buckley J.

company for any liability which would attach to the assignee or for the cost of meeting any such liability, in respect of a breach of trust or failure to show due care and diligence, having regard to the powers, authorities or discretion conferred on the assignee by the trust deed'. By subsection (2), '[a] term in a contract between a company and an assignee that purports to indemnify or compensate the assignee in contravention of subsection (1), is void'. According to subsection (3), '[a] debenture holder may, by special resolution, release anything done or not done by an assignee'. Subsection (4) provides that '[t] he Court may, on the application of a debenture holder, remove an assignee of any debenture, and appoint another assignee, if satisfied that the assignee has interests which conflict or may conflict with those of the debenture holders or that, for any other reason, is undesirable that the assignee should continue to act'. Finally, by subsection (5) provides that '[t]he Court may, on an application being made in accordance with subsection (4), order the applicant to give security for the payment of the assignee's costs'.

10.8   Appointment as assignee for debenture holders

In terms of section 228(1), '[t]he following persons are not eligible for appointment or competent to act as assignee for a holder of a debenture issued by a company:

(a)   an individual under the age of eighteen years;

(b)   a person—

    (i)   under any legal disability;

    (ii)   prohibited or disqualified from so acting by order of a court of competent jurisdiction;

    (iii)   who is an officer or auditor of the company or a related company or who has been such an officer or auditor within the preceding two years, save with the leave of the court;

    (iv)   who has been convicted within the preceding five years of an offence involving fraud or dishonesty; or

    (v)   who has been removed, by order of Court, within the preceding five years from an office of trust;

(c)   an undischarged bankrupt as provided in any other written law or, subject to an order by the Court, under the written laws of another country.

According to section 228(2), '[a] person who, in contravention of section [228], acts or continues to act as an assignee for debenture holders commits an offence and is liable, on conviction, to a fine not exceeding one thousand penalty units for each day that the contravention continues or to imprisonment for a period not exceeding twelve months, or to both'.

10.9   Register of debenture holders

By section 231(1), '[a] company which issues or has issued debentures shall maintain a register of debenture holders'.[42] According to subsection(2), '[i]f a company fails to comply with this section, the company and each officer in default commit an offence and are liable, on conviction, to a fine not exceeding two hundred thousand penalty units for each day that the failure continues'. In terms of section 226(1), '[a] company shall, within sixty days after the allotment of any debenture or after the registration of the transfer of any debenture deliver, to the registered holder, the debentures or a certificate of the debenture stock, under the common seal of the company'. We must further note that section 188 which provides for transfer of shares; section 189 which provides for restrictions on transferability; section 190 which provides for transmission of shares by operation of law; and section 191 which provides for evidence of transmission of shares by operation of law 'apply, with the necessary modifications, in relation to debentures and debenture holders'.

As respects sections 188 and 189, section 231(3) adds that '[w]here a company imposes a restriction on the right to transfer debentures, notice of the restriction shall be endorsed on the face of the debenture or debenture stock certificate, issued in accordance with [section231](1), and in the absence of such endorsement, the restriction shall not be effective with regards to a transferee for value, whether or not the transferee has notice of the restriction'.

We must note though, that the transferee of a debenture under section 188 takes it subject to equities, which may include claims which the company has against the transferor. The terms of the company's claims are however, normally excluded by the terms of the debenture. For example, in *Re Goy & Co Ltd, Farmer v Goy & Co Ltd*,[43] after a resolutions for the voluntary winding-up of a company had been passed and a liquidator appointed, and judgment had been given in a debenture-holder's action against the company, R. became transferee by way of security of a loan, of certain debentures from C., who had been a director for the company. The conditions of the debenture provided that transfers must be delivered at the registered office with a fee, and such evidence of identity or title as the company might reasonably require, and thereupon the transfer would be registered; and that the principal and interest secured by the debentures would be paid without regard to any equities between the company and the original or any inter mediate holder. After R. had taken his transfer it was discovered that C. was guilty of misfeasance, and he was ordered to pay a sum of money to the liquidator in respect thereof. R. who had no notice of

---

[42] In terms of section 231(4), '[i]f a company fails to comply with subsection (1), the company and each officer in default commits an offence and is liable, on conviction, to a fine not exceeding one thousand penalty units for each day that the failure continues'.

[43] [1900] 2 Ch 149.

any cross-claim by the company, duly sent his transfer to the liquidator, who was also receiver in the action, for registration, but the liquidator declined to register it, and claimed to deduct C.s debt to the company from the amount due on his debentures. It was held that the right to transfer and to have the transfer registered was not affected either by the winding-up or by the judgment in the action, and that consequently, R. was entitled to receive without deduction any dividend payable in respect of C.'s debentures.

10.10 Meetings of other debenture holders

The Act allows for '[a] debenture not secured by a trust deed' to 'provide for the convening of a general meeting of the debenture holders or classes of debenture holders and for the passing of resolutions binding on all the debenture holders or on all classes of debenture holders'.[44] However, in terms of section 233(2) '[t]he Court may, despite any provision in a debenture regarding meetings, direct a meeting, of debenture holders of any class, to be held and conducted in a manner, and to consider such matters, as the Court considers appropriate and may give such ancillary or consequential directions as it considers necessary'. It must be remembered that by section 233(4), '[a] registered debenture holder shall have votes in proportion to the value of the debentures held, unless a debenture provides otherwise'.[45]

10.11 Charges[46]

The starting point to statutory recognition of charges is section 225(2) which unambiguously provides that 'a debenture may be secured by a *charge*[47] over property of the company or be unsecured'.

Unlike CA 1994 which did not define the term 'charge' leaving the same to common law definitions, section 2 defines 'charge' as used in section 225(5) and elsewhere in the Act as including the following:

  (a) a security interest or security agreement;
  (b) a mortgage or an agreement to give or execute the mortgage whether on demand or otherwise;
  (c) a debenture; or
  (d) an agreement for sale and purchase of land under which the seller remains in occupation, until such time as the whole of the purchase price is paid.

---

[44] Section 233(1).
[45] According to subsection (3), '…section [233] shall, subject to subsection (4) and unless the debentures provide otherwise, apply to a meeting held in accordance with this section, with the necessary modifications'.
[46] Sections 225 – 245 replacing sections 96–106 of CA 1994.
[47] Emphasis added.

Strictly speaking, the foregoing is not a definition but an inexhaustive list of what may or may not be deemed a 'charge' according to the Act. Nonetheless, the term 'charge' as may be apparent from the foregoing list, means an interest or right which the lender or creditor obtains in the property of the company by way of security that the company will pay back the debt.[48]

The tenor of section 2 in this instance means that the list is not exhaustive and any arrangements incidental to the foregoing may well be deemed to be charges. This is an instance in which the Act can be deemed a flexible code on the one hand, seemingly leaving no doubt as to which types of securities are black and white 'charges' and on the other, even in instances of explicit specifics, allowing for enough vagueness and ambiguity as to permit for judicial interpretation not only here but judicial construction relating to other securities not explicitly covered under section 2 and as envisaged in section 225(5). In this instance at least, the Act becomes a malleable document from which inspiration can be drawn, permits creativity and avoids being an obdurate code stifling commerce. This it does, as already intimated, by not attempting to be a clear explication of all manner of 'charges' that could be conceived by the mind of the draftsperson or contrived by his heart.

For purposes of determining priority it is important to classify or indeed resolve the issue of whether a charge is floating or fixed (specific). However, as we show later, this is not as straight forward as it may seem.

10.11.1   *Floating and fixed charge distinguished*

The distinction as to whether a charge is fixed or floating was given by Lord Macnaghten in *Illingworth v Houldsworth*[49] which case was discussed in *Amiran & Others v Agriflora (Z) Ltd (In receivership)*[50] as follows:

> A specific[51] charge… is one that without more fastens on ascertained and definite property or property capable of being ascertained or defined. A floating charge, on the other hand, is ambulatory and shifting in its nature, hovering over and so to speak floating with the property which it is intended to affect until some event occurs or some act is done which causes it to settle and fasten on the subject of the charge within its reach and grasp.

---

[48] In *Re Charge Card Services Ltd* [1987] BCLC 17 at 40, Millet J states that, '… without any conveyance or assignment to the charge, specific property of the charger is expressly or constructively appropriated to or make answerable for the payment of a debt, and the charge is given the right to resort to the property for the purpose of having it realized and applied in or towards payment of a debt.'

[49] [1878] BCLC 17 at 40.

[50] 2004/HPC/0268 (unreported); see also *The Attorney General v Zambia Sugar Co. & Nakambala Estates Ltd* [1977] ZR 273.

[51] Or fixed.

10.11.1.1   *Floating charge*

A floating charge was first recognised by the EWCA in *Re Panama, New Zealand & Australian Royal Mail Co*[52] and the characteristics of a floating charge where given by Romer LJ in *Re Yorkshire Woolcombers Association,*[53] in the following terms:

> I certainly do not intend to attempt to give an exact definition of the term "floating charge" nor am I prepared to say that there will not be a floating charge within the meaning of the Act, which does not contain all the three characteristics that I am about to mention, but I certainly think that if the charge has the three characteristics that I am about to mention it is a floating charge: (1) if it is a charge on a class of assets of a company present and future; (2) if that class is one which, in the ordinary course of the business of the company, would be changing from time to time; and (3) if you find that by the charge it is contemplated that, until some future step is taken by or on behalf of those interested in the charge, the company may carry on its business in the ordinary way as far as concerns the particular class of assets I am dealing with.

In *Agnew v IRC (Re Brumark)*[54] Lord Millet observed that, 'a charge on the 'undertaking' is taken to mean a charge on all the assets of the company, both present and future, including its circulating assets, i.e. assets that are regularly turned over in the course of trade.' In *The Government Stock and Other Securities Investment Co Ltd v The Manila Railway Co Ltd and Others,*[55] a company issued debentures by which it undertook to pay the principal at a distant day and interest on fixed days half-yearly and charged by way of floating security all its property present and future. A condition endorsed on the debentures provided that "notwithstanding the said charge" the company might in the course and for the purpose of its business sell or otherwise deal with its property until default should be made in payment of interest for three months after the same should have become due, or until an order or resolution for winding-up. After an installment of interest had been due more than three months but before the debenture-holders had taken any step to enforce their security the company by an issue of bonds mortgaged specific assets. It was held, that upon the construction of the condition, after the expiration of the

---

[52]   [1878] LR 5 Ch App 318.
[53]   [1903] 2 Ch 284 at 289.
[54]   *Agnew v IRC (Re Brumark)* [2001] 2 BCLC 188 at 191.
[55]   [1897] AC 81 HL.

three months the debentures remained a floating security till the holders took some step to enforce it and prevent the company from dealing with its property, and that the debenture-holders were not entitled to an injunction restraining the company from paying interest to the bond-holders.[56]

Fundamentally then, a floating charge is one which, in the ordinary course of the business of the company, would be changing from time to time;[57] and by the charge it is contemplated that, until some future step is taken by or on behalf of those interested in the charge, the company may carry on its business in the ordinary way without encumbrance in the usage of the assets over which the charge floats. By the same token, no matter how seriously the company breaches the conditions under which the floating charge has been agreed on and no matter how legitimate the claims of the debenture holder, if, as exemplified in *The Government Stock* case, no vigorous steps are taken to have the floating charge crystallise, that is, fixing it to the assets the company has at the material time, (in which case the floating charge becomes indistinguishable from a charge originally conceived and agreed as fixed) it will remain floating and the company will continue with business as usual.

In *Attorney-General v Zambia Sugar Company Limited and Nakambala Estate Ltd,*[58] the respondents applied to the High Court for a declaratory order that prior written consent of the President was not required for a debenture creating a floating charge over assets which included land. It was contended that a floating charge is not within section 13(1) of the Land (Conversion of Titles) Act, 1975, because it does not affect any particular piece of land at present, and there is only a possibility that it may affect land in future if anything occurs which causes the floating charge to crystallise. It was held, that a floating charge operates as an immediate and continuing charge on the property charged and has the effect of charging all the property in the hands of the borrower at the date of the charge. Hence, Presidential consent under section 13(1) is required.

10.11.1.1.1   Crystallisation of floating charge

A floating charge will crystallise under the following circumstances:

(1)   In the circumstances specified in the debenture

It is possible in theory for a company to dispose of all the assets to which a floating charge relates and for the debenture holder to lose out as a result. For this reason, a debenture will specify instances in which a floating charge

---

[56] The decision of the EWCA [1895] 2 Ch 551, affirmed.

[57] Lord Scott in *Re Spectrum Plus Ltd* [2005] 2 BCLC 269 at 304 observes that, 'these are circulating assets used in the normal course of business and they are constantly changing so they are not amenable to a fixed charge.

[58] [1977] ZR 273 (ZMSC).

will crystallise without more. To that end, the parties may expressly agree on a specific date on which the floating charge will crystallise. Otherwise as exemplified in the case *Sheppard and Cooper Ltd v TSB Bank Plc,*[59] the charge will crystallise when the call in the overdraft which the company cannot pay is made. Section 235 provides for a charge meant to secure a fluctuating amount as follows:

[w]here a charge is made to secure—

(a)   an indeterminate amount; or

(b)   a fluctuating amount advanced on a current account by, or due and owing to, the person entitled to the charge; the charge shall not be considered to be redeemed by reason only that the current account ceases to be in debit or by reason only that no amount is due or owing, as the case may be.[60]

It was held *Sheppard* that where a bank has lent a company money that is repayable on demand with a security over the company's assets, the timing of the banks appointment of an administrative receiver is governed, where the company has the means to repay by the time it needs to set the mechanics of repayment in motion. If the company has made it clear that it cannot pay, the bank may make the appointment straightaway as could any secured creditor.

(2)   **Other circumstance specified include:**

   (i)   failure of the company to pay interest;

   (ii)   failure to pay the principal sum when due as agreed;

   (iii) appointment of a business rescue administrator;[61]

   (iv)   appointment of a receiver;[62]

   (v)   commencement of winding-up;[63]

   (vi)   cessation of business.

10.11.1.1.2   Automatic crystallisation

In *National Westminster Bank Plc v Jones,*[64] affirming *Evans v Rival Granite Quarries Ltd,*[65] the court observed that as a matter of law, a floating charge crystallizes on the appointment of administrator, or when the company goes into

---

[59] [1996] 2 All ER 654.

[60] Similarly, section 242(4) relating to variation of a registered charge provides that '[w]here a registered charge by its terms, secures a fluctuating amount, or an initial sum together with the words "further advances", the making of a further advance to the company shall not, for the purposes of this section, constitute a variation in the terms of the charge.

[61] Section 21(3)*(b)* of the Corporate Insolvency Act No 9 of 2017.

[62] Section 4 of the Corporate Insolvency Act No 9 of 2017.

[63] Under Parts V, VI and VII of the Corporate Insolvency Act No 9 of 2017.

[64] [2002] 1 BCLC 55, CA.

[65] [1910] 2 KB 979; see further Gower *Gower's Principles of Modern* Company Law 6th edn 367.

liquidation (on a resolution being passed or a compulsory winding up ordered) or there is otherwise a cessation of business on the part of the company, for the effect of these circumstances is to bring to an end the company's freedom to carry on business in the ordinary way.

National Westminster Bank Plc is distinguishable from the case of *Re Woodroffes (Musical Instruments)*.[66] In 1980 a company created a debenture secured by a fixed and first floating charge on all its undertaking and assets in favour of a bank. The debenture provided that during its currency no further charge on the company's assets was to be created without the bank's consent. The debenture further provided that all moneys secured thereby where to become repayable on demand and that the bank might by notice to the company convert the floating charge into a specific charge as regards any assets specified in the notice. The debenture was duly registered under s. 95 of the Companies Act 1948. On 9 August 1982, without the bank's consent, the company created a second debenture secured by a second floating charge on all its undertaking and assets in favour of a Mrs. W. The 1982 debenture expressly provided that the charge was to be subject to and rank immediately after the charge created by the 1980 debenture. It further provided that Mrs. W might by notice to the company convert the floating charge into a specific charge as regards any assets specified in the notice. The 1982 debenture was also duly registered under s. 95 of the 1948 Act. On 27 August 1982 Mrs. W gave the company a notice to convert the floating charge forthwith into a specific charge as regards all the company's undertakings and assets. On 1 September the bank served on the company a formal demand for repayment of the principal and interest owing under the 1980 debenture and, at the company's request, it appointed joint receivers of all the premises charged by, comprised in or subject to the 1980 debenture. Having completed the realization of the company's assets and there being insufficient to pay all the company's creditors, the receivers applied to the court under s. 369(1) of the 1948 Act for directions as to the order of distribution of moneys in their possession as between Mrs. W, the bank and the company's preferential creditors. It being accepted that Mrs. W's floating charge crystallised on 27 August 1982, the question also arose whether the bank's floating charge crystallised on 27 August 1982 at the same time as Mrs. W's or on 1 September 1982 when it appointed receivers, the bank not having served notice on the company converting its floating charge into a fixed charge. The bank and Mrs. W contend that there was an automatic crystallisation of the bank's floating charge on 27 August 1982 either on the crystallisation of Mrs. W's floating charge or on the cessation of the company's business which was necessarily caused thereby.

It was held, that the bank's charge did not automatically crystallise on 27 August 1982 on the crystallisation of Mrs. W's charge because the relationship

---

[66] [1985] 2 All ER 908.

between the company and the bank was governed by the 1980 debenture, which, although it prohibited the creation without consent of subsequent charges, did not provide for the bank's floating charge to crystallise either on the creation or the crystallisation of a subsequent charge, and there were no grounds for implying in the 1980 debenture any term to that effect.

The cessation of a company's business (rather than if there was any distinction the company's ceasing to be a going concern) caused an automatic crystallisation of any floating charge created by the company. Likewise, it was in accordance with the essential nature of a floating charge on the whole of a company's undertaking and assets that on its becoming a fixed charge it would prevent the company from dealing with its assets and thus paralyze it and prevent it from carrying on its business. Accordingly, if the company in fact ceased business on 27 August 1982, or some other date before 1 September, 1982, the bank's charge crystallised on that date and not on 1 September 1982 when the receivers were appointed.

On the agreed facts there was not sufficient evidence on which the court could be satisfies on the balance of probabilities that the company ceased to carry on its business before 1 September 1982. It followed therefore that the bank's charge crystallised on 1 September 1982, with the result that, the bank's charge ranking in priority to Mrs. W's charge, the order of priority was (a) the bank to the extent of Mrs. W's charge, (b) the preferential creditors, (c) the bank as to the balance of its charge and (d) Mrs W.

10.11.1.1.3   *Postponement of floating charges*

Upon the crystallisation of the floating charge, the lender to whom the charge relates is entitled to repayment of the loan out of the assets to which the charge has attached before the company's unsecured creditors.[67] So far as postponement of the debenture debt goes, same may only go so far as preferential payments accrued at the date of the appointment of an administrator are concerned and not to those which accrue subsequently.[68] Thus, the main preferential debts are:[69]

(i)   Wages or salaries of employee

It was illustrated in *Buchan v Secretary of State for Employment*[70] that the fees of non-executive directors are not preferential, though executive directors will normally be regarded as employees to the extent of their remuneration paid to them in respect of their duties as executives, except where they are also

---

[67] Keenan D *Smith and Keenan's Company Law* 13th edn 450.
[68] Kennan D *Smith and Keenan's Company Law*...450.
[69] Keenan D *Smith and Keenan's Company Law*...450.
[70] [1997] 565 IRLB 2.

controlling shareholders. However, in *Re Portbase (Clothing) Ltd, Mond v Taylor,*[71] it was demonstrated that a fixed charge is not postponed to preferential creditors and other creditors as is a floating charge and the charge holder will get more form the security on realization. This will not apply however, if the fixed charge is by agreement between lenders, to rank behind a floating charge, in which the second ranking fixed charge is subject to the floating charge and ranks after it and claims of the preferential debts To be considered therefore are the following:

(i)   *All remuneration relating to employee holidays;*
(ii) *Unpaid retirement income contributions which it must be stressed fall out of statutory contributions which must be claimed from the relevant statutory pension scheme.*

10.11.1.1.4   Avoidance of floating charges

Under section 129 of the Corporate Insolvency Act[72] '[a] floating charge on property of a company, created within one year before the commencement of the winding-up, is void, unless it is proved that the company, immediately after the creation of the charge, was solvent'.[73] It was held in *Power v Sharp Investment Ltd*[74] that no money paid to the company before the execution of the debenture would qualify for the invalidity exemption in section 245 unless the interval between the payment and execution of the debenture was minimal and could be regarded as contemporaneous. However, it should be noted that a floating charge is valid as security for loans made after the date it was created if the lender promised to make such loans (covenanted loans), and even if the lender did not (un-covenanted loan).[75] Consequently, advances made to an insolvent company by its bank on an overdraft facility during the year before it is wound-up are validly secured in the winding-up by a floating charge given before the advances were made.[76]

The debenture creating the charge must expressly cover covenanted and un–covenanted loans.[77] In *Re Yeovil Glove Co Ltd,*[78] a company had since its incorporation in 1934 maintained two accounts with its bank. No. 1 account

---

[71] [1993] 3 All ER 829.

[72] No 9 of 2017.

[73] Similarly, under section 245 of the UK Insolvency Act 1986, 'a floating charge created by a company within one year before the commencement of its winding up or the making of an administration order is void as a security for any debt other than cash paid or goods supplied to the company in consideration of the charge at the time the charge was created, or subsequently with interest, if any, thereon agreed': Keenan D *Smith and Keenan's Company Law*…460

[74] [1993] BCC 609.

[75] [1993] BCC 609.

[76] [1993] BCC 609.

[77] See sections 235 and 242.

[78] [1965] Ch 148.

was the main current account, and No. 2 account, fed from it, was a directors' private ledger account. In 1957, the company was, by overdraft on its No. 1 account, indebted to the bank for nearly £65, 000.00, that indebtedness being guaranteed in part by the directors, but otherwise unsecured. In February and March, 1957, at the instance of the bank, the company, with a view to giving the bank by subrogation the statutory preference under section 319 (1) (b) and (4) of the Companies Act, 1948, opened two further accounts, No. 3 for wages and No. 4 for salaries, and authorized the bank to transfer week by week and month by month from No. 1 or 2 account to No. 3 or 4 account, as the case might be, the exact amount of the wages or salaries paid in the week or month 18 weeks or four months earlier. On June 19, 1957, the company executed a legal charge in favour of the bank whereby certain of its land and hereditaments, the fixed and movable plant and machinery and fixtures, implements and utensils were mortgaged.

At the end of 1957, the bank threatened to call in the overdraft, which was by then up to or beyond the limit prescribed by the bank, £67, 500.00, unless further security was provided. As a result, the company, on January 24, 1958, executed a mortgage and general charge, which was made supplemental to the legal charge, and by which the company, by way of further securing payment of the moneys already covenanted to be paid by the legal charge, and by which the company, by way of further securing payment of the moneys already covenanted to be paid by the legal charge, charged to the bank further properties, its uncalled capital, and "(c) by way of floating security all the undertaking and goodwill of the company and its property…assets and rights whatsoever and wheresoever both present and future." The charge imposed no obligation on the bank to make any further advances, and no cash was either paid or promised by the bank to the company upon the taking of that security. The accounts of the company continued thereafter to be operated in the same way as before, and the overdraft remained at about the same level, some £111, 000.00 being paid into the No. 1 account by the company between the date of the charge and August 20, 1958, and the bank paying out during the same period about £110,000. On August 20, 1958, the bank appointed a receiver under the charges. On January 12, 1959, five trade creditors petitioned for the winding up of the company, and an order was made on January 26, 1959.

On March 13, 1959, a liquidator was appointed. Not enough was realized to satisfy the secured creditors and the unsecured creditors, for over £94, 000, liquidator issued a summons asking inter alia, for a declaration that the charge of January 24, 1958, (a) was invalid against the liquidator pursuant to section 322 of the Companies Act, 1948, alternatively, (b) was invalid except to the amount of any cash paid by the bank subsequent to the creation of, and in consideration for, the charge. Plowman J. held that the charge was not invalid as against the liquidator. The liquidator appealed, contending (1) that as neither had cash been nor a covenant to pay cash been entered into by the bank at the time of the execution of the document by which the charge had been created there was no consideration for it in the legal sense of that term other than the bank's immediate forbearance to call in the overdraft; (2) that the rule in Clayton's Case did not apply, and the bank was bound to treat all payments in after the creation of the charge as devoted to post-charge indebtedness, so that, since the payments-in subsequent to the creation of the charge were more or less equal to the payments-out by the bank during the same period, no "new money" had been provided by the bank so as to be secured by the charge. It was held,

(1)   That the words "in consideration for" in section 322 of the Act of 1948 were not used in their technical sense, but meant by reason of' or "having regard to the existence of," the charge; and that, on the facts of the case, each payment by the bank subsequent to the charge had clearly been made in reliance on it in this sense.

(2)   That, albeit the result was startling and largely nullified the effect of section 322 in the case of a company having at the date of the charge a largely overdrawn account with its bank and which continued to trade, there was no ground for not applying the rule in Clayton's Case; that each payment which had been made subsequent to the date of the charge had therefore, having regard to the state of the company's accounts, been a provision of "new money"; and that, therefore, there was no reason to compel the bank to treat payments in after the date of the charge as devoted to post-charge indebtedness.

10.11.1.1.5   Restrictions on a floating charge

In *Wheatley v Silkstone Haigh Moor Coal Co*[79] it was observed that the freedom of the chargor to deal with the assets in the ordinary course of business includes a freedom to create further fixed charges ranking in priority to the floating charge. We must however note the courts' disinclination to permit an unrestricted ability by the chargor to create subsequent floating charges. The second floating charge over all of the property comprised in the first charge and ranking *paripassu* with or in priority to that charge is incompatible with the first charge and ranks subject to it.[80] In this respect, 240 which replaces and expands on the provisions of section 101 of CA 1994 provides in subsection (1) that[81] '*(a)* any consent, whether express or implied, given by a person who would otherwise be entitled

---

[79] [1885] 29 Ch D 715.
[80] *In Re Benjamin Cope & Sons Ltd* [1914] 1 Ch 800.
[81] Subject to section 240(2) which provides that '[s]ubsection (1) shall not affect the priorities between successive charges affecting the same property, where any other written law provides for priorities between those charges'.

to priority, charges required by this Part to be registered shall have priority in relation to one another in accordance with the times at which they were lodged as provided in the Movable Property (Security Interest) Act'.[82] What this provision means is that a subsequent charge can only rank *pari passu* with or in priority to the first floating charge where the first floating charge permits expressly or impliedly of such a charge.[83] Otherwise, charges according to this provision rank in priority according to the times they were lodged. However, in terms of section 240(1)*(b)* 'where a charge, other than a floating charge, gives security over property required to be registered with the Registrar in accordance with this Part, and over other property, subsection (1)*(a)* shall apply, in respect of the first mentioned property, but not in respect of the other property'.

10.11.1.2   Fixed charge

A fixed (or specific) charge is typically taken over identified assets not commonly used or dealt with in the day-to-day business of the company.[84] A fixed charge gives the holder of the charge an immediate proprietary interest in the assets subject to the charge. The consequence of a fixed charge is that the company is not, like under a floating charge, free to deal with the asset to which the fixed charge relates without the consent of the charge holder. It thus becomes apparent that a fixed charge is incongruous to and is not fit for a company that needs to deal with its assets in the ordinary course of business such as supermarket chains, wholesalers or motor vehicle dealership whose assets will essentially constitute their core means of business. We must re-emphasise the point that though the definitional differences between a fixed and floating charge are quite clear, once active steps are taken such as by appointing a receiver, or an event provided for in the debenture document occurs necessitating a crystallisation, the floating charge becomes a fixed charge and from that date onwards, the company will no longer be free to deal with the assets to which the crystallised charge would become affixed on the material day. We will explore this matter a little further below.

10.11.1.3   Determining whether a charge is a floating or fixed: case law

Determining whether a charge is fixed or floating is no straight forward matter. The label is not nearly as important as the degree of liberty to exploit and dispose of the assets to which a particular charge relates. It would seem that a higher degree of meddling in the usage, exploitation or disposal of the asset in question is more likely to persuade the court to conclude that the charge

---

[82] No 3 of 2016.

[83] *In Re Automatic Bottle Makers Ltd* [1926] Ch 412.

[84] *Per* Lord Millett in *Agnew v IRC (Re Brumark)* [2001] 2 BCLC 188 at 192.

in question is fixed rather than floating, the description by the parties in the document creating the charge notwithstanding. The colossal range 'of clauses to be found in documents creating charges' makes it nearly 'impossible to arrive at an exhaustive definition of the difference between'[85] fixed and floating charges. A holistic approach is more profitable in interpreting the nature, complexion, range and breadth of the restriction borne out of charge creation. As we indicated at the beginning of our discussion, the dissimilarity between a fixed and floating charge is significant when dealing with and determining the priority of various claims under the relevant parts of section 240 and the pecking order under section 127 of the Corporate Insolvency Act.[86] We now explore several decided cases complete with brief facts in places, holdings and important observations on this issue.

In *Re Armagh Shoes Ltd*[87], the charge under consideration by the court was labeled in the charge document as a 'fixed' but was held by the court to be a floating charge. The basis for the Court's decision was the following clause contained in the charge document: 'the mortgagor pursuant to every power and by force of every estate enabling it in this behalf and as beneficial owner hereby charges in the favour of the bank by way of fixed charge all receivables debtors plant machinery fixtures fittings and ancillary equipment now or *at any time hereafter belonging to the mortgagor.*'

Hutton J observed as follows:

> The authorities establish that the description of a charge as a fixed or specific charge does not, in itself, operate to prevent the charge from being a floating charge; and the deed in this case contains no express provision restricting the company from dealing with the assets charged. In my judgment in the present case it is a necessary implication from the deed that the company was to have the right or licence to deal with the assets, comprised within the ambit of the charge, in the ordinary course of its business until the bank decided to enforce the charge. I can see no basis for the implication that it was the intention of the company and the bank that the company would deal with the charged assets in breach of its contract with the bank, to which breaches the bank would turn a blind eye, and that if a third party asked the company if it was entitled to transfer some of the charged assets to him the company would have to tell him to obtain the bank's consent to the transfer.

---

[85] Dine J and Koutsias M *Company Law* 6th edn 293.
[86] No 9 of 2017.
[87] [1982] NI 59.

In *Re Keenan Brothers Ltd*[88] the parties tried to craft a fixed charge on future company 'book debts'. Two questions arose: (i) whether it was possible in law to create a fixed charge on future book debts – the court answered in the affirmative; and (ii) whether the charge that had in fact been created in this case was a fixed charge or a floating charge. On this point, McCarthy J after underscoring the term in the agreement that read as follows: '[t]he company shall pay into an account with the Bank designated for that purpose all moneys which it may receive in respect of the book Lending Money and Securing Loans 311 debts and other debts hereby charged and shall not without the prior consent of the Bank in writing make any withdrawals or direct any payment from the said account' proceeded to observe as follows:

In my view, it is because it was described as a specific or fixed charge and was intended to be, such that the requirement of a special bank account was necessary; if it were a floating charge payment into such an account would be entirely inappropriate and, indeed, would conflict with the ambulatory nature of the floating charge .... In *Yorkshire Woolcombers Association Ltd* (above), Romer LJ postulated three characteristics of a floating charge, the third being that, if you find that by the charge it is contemplated that, until some future step is taken by or on behalf of those interested in the charge, the company may carry on its business in the ordinary way as far as concerns the particular class of assets I am dealing with. Counsel for the banks has argued that this latter characteristic is essential to a floating charge and that the banking provision in the instruments here negatives such a characteristic; I would uphold this view.

However, in *Re Brightlife Ltd*,[89] Hoffman J came to a different conclusion on facts similar to those in *Re Keenan Brothers* holding that the charge in question was a floating charge. It was, as he saw it, a charge over (among other things) future book debts. He further held that the existence of a floating charge was not dependent on the company over whose property it floated having complete freedom of action. Specifically that:

It is true that clause 5(ii) does not allow Brightlife to sell, factor or discount debts without the written consent of Norandex [who had the benefit of the charge]. But a floating charge is consistent with some restriction on the company's freedom to deal with its assets. For example, floating charges commonly contain a prohibition on the creation of other charges ranking prior to or pari passu with the floating charge. Such dealings would otherwise be open to a company in the ordinary course of its business. In this debenture, the significant feature is that Brightlife was free to collect its debts and pay the proceeds into its bank account. Once in the account, they would be outside the

---

[88] [1986] BCLC 242.
[89] [1987] Ch 200.

charge over debts and at the free disposal of the company. In my judgment a right to deal in this way with the charged assets for its own account is a badge of a floating charge and is inconsistent with a fixed charge.[90]

Another interesting authority on this rather tricky issue is *William Gaskell Group v Highley.*[91] The question of whether the charge in question was fixed or floating turned on whether a clause which required payment of the proceeds of debts into an account which could not be drawn on without the consent of the Midland Bank remained valid after the Midland Bank assigned the debenture. It was held that it was still commercially viable to require the Midland Bank's consent, the clause remained valid meaning that the charge was fixed.

In *Re G. E. Tunbridge Ltd*[92] a charge described as fixed ostensibly said to be over all the assets of the company excluding those covered by a floating charge was held not to create a fixed charge over intangible assets such as book debts or tangible assets which were likely to be changed or sold over time in spite of the fact that the company was not allowed to dispose of the assets under a fixed charge without the consent of the chargee. A rather curious case that quite clearly was decided on an unusual splitting hairs interpretation of the charge document and is distinguishable from *Tunbridge* is *Re Climex Tissues.*[93] In that case, a charge was held to be properly described as a fixed charge despite the fact that the company was apparently permitted to deal with the property subject to the charge *'in the ordinary course of business'*. It was held that the wording (here emphasised) was to be taken to refer only to the stock (toilet rolls) and not the capital machinery. Additionally, that in the specific circumstances and on the facts of this case, the existence of a limited power to deal with property was not necessarily inconsistent with a fixed charge.[94]

10.11.1.4   Registration of charges

The registration of charges is an indispensable aspect of regulatory character of the Act and one which, as we show later can have devastating consequences if not followed to the letter. From a statutory point, the registration of charges can be discussed under the following four headings:

---

[90] In *New Bullas Trading Ltd,*in which the EWCA found that the debenture in question in that case had created a fixed charge over book debts which would become a floating charge over the proceeds once they had been collected and paid into a specified account.

[91] [1994] 1 BCLC 197.

[92] [1995] 1 BCLC 409.

[93] [1995] 1 BCLC 409.

[94] It would appear that no blanket approach or general rule applies as each case will be taken on turns on its precise facts and the degree of liberty with which the company is able to deal with the property which is subject to the charge. See further, the case of *Re Cosslett (Contractors) Ltd, Clark v Mid Glamorgan County Council* [1996] 1 BCLC 407 and that of *Royal Trust Bank v National Westminster Bank Plc and Anor* [1996] 2 BCLC 682.

(i) Company's register of charges
(ii) Registrar's register of charges
(iii) Registration of charges by companies
(iv) Certificate to be issued by Registrar

We discuss the foregoing in turn.

10.11.1.4.1   Company's register of charges[95]

In terms of section 236(2) a company which has any property that is subject to a charge is required and expected to 'open and maintain a register of charges in which the company shall, on the creation of a charge over property of the company, or on the acquisition of property subject to a charge, enter the following particulars:

(a) the date of creation of the charge or the date of acquisition of the property, as the case may be;

(b) a short description of the liability whether present or prospective that is secured by the charge;

(c) a short description of the property charged;

(d) the name of the assignee, if the charge secures debentures under a trust deed; and

(e) if the charge does not secure debentures under a trust deed the name of the—

    (i) chargee; and

    (ii) person whom the company believes to be the holder of the charge'.

In terms of section 236(3), '[a] register, opened and maintained in accordance with subsection (1), shall be open for inspection by any—

(a) member or creditor of the company or by Registrar or an agent of the Registrar, without charge; and

(b) other person on payment of an amount required by the company, not exceeding one hundred fee units or such higher amount as may be prescribed.

By section 236(4), '[i]f a company fails to comply with…section [236], the company and each officer in default commit an offence and are liable, on conviction, to a fine, not exceeding two hundred thousand penalty units'.

---

[95] This is falls within the purview of section 236. Under subsection (1), '…section [236] shall apply to any charge on property of the company, whether or not it is required to be registered in accordance with this Act'.

10.11.1.4.2   Registrar's register of charges[96]

The Registrar is obliged to 'maintain a register containing, with respect to each company, the particulars of the charges of the company that are lodged in accordance with this Part'.[97] Further, and in terms of section 237(2), '[t]he register, maintained in accordance with subsection (1), shall include, with respect to each company, a chronological index of the charges of the company'.

10.11.1.4.3   Registration of charges by companies

Section 238[98] which provides for the registration of charges by companies begins in subsection 1 by listing instances in which for its purposes 'a charge over the property or undertaking of a company does not apply', that is,

(a)   on a charge and to the extent to which the Trade Charges Act[99] and the Movable Property (Security Interest) Act[100] apply;

(b)   on a ship or aircraft or any share in a ship or aircraft; and

(c)   over shares in another body corporate, not being a charge—

   (i)   in favour of a broker who has paid for a share purchased or applied for on behalf of the company; or

   (ii)   created or accompanied by delivery of the certificates for the shares.

According to section 238(2), '...if a company, (a) creates a charge to which this section applies; or (b) acquires property that is subject to a charge to which this section applies; the company shall, within twenty-one days after the date of the creation of the charge, or after the acquisition of the property, as the case may be, lodge with the Registrar in the prescribed form the particulars referred to in subsection'. The foregoing must be accompanied by '(a) particulars of the instrument by which the charge is created or evidenced, sufficient to identify the instrument, if the charge is created or evidenced by an instrument registered in accordance with this or any other Act; or (b) a certified copy of the instrument, if any, by which the charge is created or evidenced, in any other case'.

Section 238(3) lists the particulars required under subsection (2) as follows:

(a)   date of creation of the charge;

(b)   date of acquisition of the property by the company, where the property was subject to the charge when acquired by the company;

(c)   amount secured by the charge;

---

[96] Previously provided for under section 98 of CA 1994.

[97] Section 237(1).

[98] Which replaces section 99 of CA 1994. According to subsection(4), '...section [238] shall apply in relation to any instrument creating or evidencing or purporting to create or evidence a charge over property located outside Zambia, notwithstanding that further proceedings may be necessary to make the charge valid or effectual according to the law of the country in which the property is situated'.

[99] Chapter 415 of the Laws of Zambia.

[100] No 3 of 2016.

(d)   short particulars of the property charged;

(e)   names of the charges; and

(f)   other particulars of the charge, as may be prescribed.

The foregoing must, where relevant, be read within the context of section 238(7) which provides as follows:

Where a series of debentures is created by a company and contains, or gives by reference to any other instrument, any charge to the benefit of which the debenture holders of that series are entitled in all respects equally, subsection (3) shall be satisfied by the lodgement of the following particulars:

(a)   the total amount secured by the whole series;

(b)   the date of the resolution authorising the issue of the series and the date of the document, if any, by which the security is created or defined;

(c)   a description of the property charged; and

(d)   the names of the assignees, if any, for the debenture holders, accompanied by a certified copy of the document containing the charge, or, if there is no such document, a certified copy of one of the debentures of the series; accompanied by particulars of the date and amount of issue, where more than one issue of debentures is made in a series, which shall be lodged within twenty-one days after any issue.

It is important to note for practical purposes that '[a] debenture that entitles a holder to a charge on land shall not, for the purposes of this section, be considered to be an interest in land'.[101] It is also vital to remember that there is a statutory requirement[102] for a company to, where it 'pays, whether absolutely or conditionally a commission or allowance or gives a discount, to a person in consideration of that person—

(a)   subscribing or agreeing to subscribe for debentures of the company; or

(b)   procuring or agreeing to procure subscriptions for such debentures; the particulars required to be lodged, in accordance with this section, shall include the amount or rate per centum of the commission, allowance or discount paid or made'.

Under CA 1994, the consequence of failing to comply with the requirements to registration were set out under section 99(11) as being (i) the charge shall be void against the liquidator and any creditor of the company, and (ii) the full debt secured by the charge shall become payable immediately by the company. There appears to be no equivalent provision under section 238 of the Act. However, section 4 of the Lands and Deeds Registry Act[103] lists documents creating charges as requiring registration. The *proviso* to section 4 not requiring the registration of a floating charge under the Lands and Deeds Registry Act will

---

[101] Section 238(6).

[102] Section 238(7).

[103] Chapter 185 of the Laws of Zambia.

need to be amended to refer to section 238 of the Act which replaces section 99 of CA 1994. Further, the consequences of non-registration can still be found under section 6 of the Lands and Deeds Registry Act[104] which specifically provides that, '[a]ny document required to be registered as aforesaid and not registered within the time specified in the last preceding section shall be null and void....'

It has been observed in *Re Welsh Irish Ferries Ltd*,[105] that the object of registration is not to provide a comprehensive account of all of a company's charges but to warn unsuspecting creditors that the debtor company has charged it assets.

10.12   Extension of time for lodgement

Extension of time for lodgment is provided for under section 245. In terms of section 245(1), it is provided that '[w]here under [the] Act a document is required to be lodged with the Registrar within a specified period, the period shall be extended by fourteen days in relation to a document executed or made in a place outside Zambia'. Additionally, under section 245(2) '[t]he Registrar may, before the end of any period fixed for the lodgement of a document or particulars, at the request of the person concerned, extend the period for lodgement by such a period, and on such terms, as the Registrar considers reasonable in the circumstances'.

Further, under section 245(3), '...where any document or particulars are lodged with the Registrar after the end of the period fixed for its lodgement, the Registrar shall accept the documents or particulars for registration'. Section 245(4) gives the Registrar discretion to '...reduce or waive any prescribed fee in relation to the extension of time in this section if the Registrar is satisfied that the failure to lodge the document or particulars was caused or continued solely through administrative oversight and that no person is likely to have suffered damage or to have been prejudiced as a result of the failure'.

Finally, where 'the particulars and documents relating to a charge, that are required by [section 238] to be lodged with the Registrar, are lodged within the time required', the Registrar is mandated to, 'issue a certificate of registration of the charge within fourteen days stating the date of lodgement and, if applicable, the amount secured, and the certificate shall be conclusive evidence that the requirements of this Part as to registration have been complied with'.[106]

---

[104] Chapter 185 of the Laws of Zambia.
[105] [1985] BCLC 327 at 332.
[106] Section 239.

10.13 Entries of satisfaction and release of property from charge

Where a debt for which a charge was made has been paid in full or in part, '[a] creditor shall lodge a discharge for the release of property accordingly'.[107] Ordinarily and in terms of section 241(2), [i]f there is lodged, with the Registrar, a statement in the prescribed manner and form, signed on behalf of a company and by the person entitled to a charge to the effect that—

(a) the debt for which the charge was given has been paid or satisfied in whole or in part; or

(b) part of the property or undertaking charged has been released from the charge or has ceased to form part of the company's property or undertaking; the Registrar shall enter the fact stated in the register of charges and the statement shall, in favour of the liquidator and any creditor of the company, be binding on the person entitled to the charge who signed the statement and on any other person claiming through that person.

10.14 Variation of registered charge

The provisions relating to variation of a registered charge are found in section 242. According to section 242(1), '[w]here a variation is made to the terms of a charge registered in accordance with this Part, other than a satisfaction or release to which section 241[108] applies, particulars of the variation shall be lodged with the Registrar in the prescribed form, within twenty-one days of the making of the variation.

According to section 242(2), '[t]he particulars, referred to in subsection (1), shall identify the terms of the original charge that have been varied and shall indicate the nature of the variation made in each such term'. Where, according to section 242(3), '…the effect of a variation, referred to in subsection (1), is to increase the extent of the security or the amount for which security is available, the increase shall, for the purposes of determining priorities in charges, be treated as if it were a charge for an amount of the increase and whose particulars were lodged at the time that the particulars of the variation were lodged'.

10.15 Registration of enforcement of security by mortgagee

In terms of section 243(1), '[i]f a person enters into possession of any of the property of a company as mortgagee under any powers contained in a charge, the person shall, within seven days after so doing, lodge a notice to that effect in the prescribed form with the Registrar'. Further, where, in terms of subsection

[107] Section 241(1).
[108] Which provides for '[e]ntries of satisfaction and release of property from charge'.

(2) '...a person who is in possession as mortgagee of property of a company goes out of possession, the mortgagee shall, within fourteen days thereafter, lodge a notice to that effect in the prescribed form with the Registrar'. Finally, a person '...who fails to comply with this section commits an offence, and is liable on conviction, to a fine not exceeding one thousand fee units for each day that the failure continues'.[109]

10.16 Endorsement of registration on debentures

In instances '[w]here a company issues a debenture forming one of a series of debentures, or a certificate of debenture stock, and the payment of the debenture is secured by a charge registered in accordance with this Part, the company shall endorse on the debenture or certificate of debenture stock, a statement that registration has been effected and specifying the date of registration'.[110] By subsection (2), '[i]f a company fails to comply with subsection (1), the company and each officer in default commit an offence and are liable, on conviction, to a fine not exceeding two hundred thousand penalty units'.

Further, in terms of section 244(3), '[a] person who—

(a) causes to be endorsed on a debenture or certificate of debenture stock a statement that registration has been effected, which that person knows to be false in any particular; or

(b) authorises or permits the delivery of a debenture or certificate of debenture stock bearing an endorsed statement that registration has been effected, which that person knows to be false in any particular; commits an offence and is liable, on conviction, to a fine not exceeding two hundred thousand penalty units or to imprisonment for a period not exceeding two years or to both'.

10.17 Remedies of secured debenture holders

Secured debenture holders have the following remedies available to them:[111]

(1) The property charged may be sold or leased;

(2) A receiver may be appointed to take possession of the property

In England and Wales, these remedies are available to debenture secured by a fixed charge under section 101 of the Law of Property Act 1925.[112] However, it is inconceivable that a Zambian court would be unpersuaded by the acceptance of the same in English case law and adopt them in a relevant case.

---

[109] Section 243(3).
[110] Section 244(1).
[111] Keenan D *Smith and Keenan's Company Law* 13th edn 462.
[112] Keenan D *Smith and Keenan's Company Law* 13th edn 462.

A floating charge is however not covered by this Act as shown in *Blaker v Herts & Essex Waterworks*[113] where it was stated that section 19 of the Conveyancing and Law of Property Act, 1881,[114] conferring on a mortgagee, where the mortgagee is by deed, power of sale, does not apply to the debentures of a joint stock company. By a Provisional Order under the Gas and Water Works Facilities Act, 1870, authorizing a waterworks undertaking, two individuals, "and the survivor of them and the executors or administrators of such survivor of them and the executors or administrators of such survivor, their or his assigns" were declared to be the "undertakers" for the purposes of the Order, and power was conferred on the undertakers to acquire lands by agreement (but not compulsorily), to construct water-works, and to supply water to the inhabitants of a district and charge rates for such supply, the amount of the capital of the undertaking was specified and the amount of all moneys borrowed by the undertakers and "secured by mortgage of the undertaking" was not at any time to exceed a specified sum. The undertaking was assigned to a limited company formed for that purpose, and the company issued debentures whereby they "charged" their undertaking, lands, works, property and effects (both present and future) with repayment of the money borrowed, the charge being expressed to be a floating security not hindering any sale, exchange, or lease of the lands, or the receipt or payment of any moneys, or any other dealings in the course of the business of the company, but attaching to all the property for the time being, whether real or personal, of the company. By a subsequent Provisional Order further powers were conferred on the company, and they only were recognised as undertakers for the purposes of that order. The company afterwards made default in payment of the principal moneys secured by the debentures on the day named therein for payment. In an action by the debenture-holders claiming (amongst other relief) a sale of the undertaking and property comprised in the debentures as a going concern, and the appointment of a manager until sale.

It was held, that the waterworks undertaking being for a public purpose and not mere private undertaking, the principle of the decision in *Gardner v London, Chatham, and Dover Railway Company*[115] was applicable; that the debentures did not confer upon the holders of them a power to sell the undertaking; and that the court ought not to direct a sale of the undertaking or the appointment of a manager.

---

[113] [1889] 41 Ch D 399.

[114] Which applies to Zambia by virtue of section 2 of The British Acts (Extension) Act and the relevant schedule made thereunder.

[115] [1867] LR 2 Ch App 201.

10.18   Conclusion

In this chapter we have, among other things, noted that a debenture is a document signifying indebtedness. We have also noted that one of the powers reserved to the board of directors is to borrow. A device usually exploited in this respect is the debenture. There, are, as we noted, several classes of debentures. We discussed the matter of debenture stock; debenture trust deed; right to copies of trust deed; redeemable debenture and the re-issue proscription; irredeemable debenture; unsecured debentures. Debentures may be issued by the company or be acquired by transmission. Allied to the matter of debentures is the concept of charges. Charges fall into fixed or floating charges. The former relates to fixed property while the latter relates movable property where the company is free to deal with the property unless and until the floating charges crystalises at which time it becomes affixed to the present assets. Both fixed and floating charges must be registered. It must also be remembered that the Act provides remedies for secured debenture holders.

FURTHER READING

Books

Dine J and Koutsias M *Company Law* 6th edn (Palgrave Macmillan Hampshire 2007).

Farrah JH and Hannigan BM *Farrar's Company Law* 4th edn (Butterworths London 1998).

Gates RB *Gates Company Law and Practice in Zambia* (Reagan Blankfein Gates Lusaka 2017).

Sealy L and Worthington S *Sealy & Worthington's Cases and Materials in Company Law* 10th edn (Oxford University Press Oxford 2013).

Wild C and Weinstein S *Smith and Keenan's Company Law* 15th edn (Pearson Education Ltd London 2011).

II

ACCOUNTING RECORDS, AUDIT AND ANNUAL RETURNS

AIMS AND OBJECTIVES

 After reading this chapter you should appreciate:
- ➢ Accounting records and the need for a company to keep accounting records
- ➢ Inspection of accounting records
- ➢ Why annual financial statements must include amounts paid to directors
- ➢ Why annual financial statements must include particulars of loans to officers
- ➢ Why director should make disclosure of loans and receipts
- ➢ Why the statement of financial position of the company should be signed by directors
- ➢ The provisions relating to the appointment of auditors
- ➢ The status of auditing firm
- ➢ Who must signing the auditor's report and why
- ➢ Qualifications of auditors
- ➢ The requirement for an auditor to avoid conflict of interest
- ➢ The contents of the auditor's report
- ➢ The need for an auditor to have access to information
- ➢ The mandatory requirement for an auditor's attendance at annual general meeting
- ➢ The obligation and manner of furnishing auditor's report
- ➢ Why small private company are not bound to appoint auditor
- ➢ The appointment of the auditor for small private company
- ➢ The preparation of audited financial statement
- ➢ The standards for financial statement preparation
- ➢ The obligation to provide consolidated financial statement
- ➢ The requirement for a comprehensive income statement when company becomes subsidiary
- ➢ The date for financial statement of subsidiary
- ➢ Annual return to Registrar

> ➤ Filing of annual returns in receivership or liquidation
> ➤ The "No change" return
> ➤ The documents to be lodged with annual return of public company
> ➤ Notice of adopted date given to Registrar
> ➤ Obligation to prepare annual report
> ➤ The requirement relating to the submission of annual report to shareholders
> ➤ The content of the annual report
> ➤ The provisions relating to the inspection of company's records
> ➤ The requirement for records to be made available for inspection by members
> ➤ The manner of inspection
> ➤ The commencement of inspection

11.1   Introduction

This chapter explores the provisions under Part XII specifically sections 264 to 281.[1] The rationale for including this aspect of company administration under the Act is predicated on the notion that a company registered under the Act in terms of sections 6 and 12 ought to be transparent about its financial matters because shareholders and third parties who have business dealings with the company have a right to know the viability of the company. The simple reason for this is that no other facet of a company is as accurate an indicator of a company's viability as its financial affairs. Shareholders get to know whether they are getting a return on their investments and to that end whether the board of directors should continue. The board will also decide whether their strategy is working and whether the management team should be sustained. Creditors will get an indication of whether their money is likely to be paid or not, and if not, whether they should take active steps to secure the money the company owes. Another part of our discussion relates to audits. The goal of an audit is to add trustworthiness to financial statements which form part of the annual accounts and 'to ensure that they comply with regulations and give a true and fair view though small companies may take exemption from audit'.[2] It is said, and must be deemed as a truism that, '[t]he keeping of accounts, the audit and filing with the Registrar are the price which the members and directors of a limited company must pay for limited liability'.[3]

---

[1] The focus is on aspects of company law as they relate to the topic of account records, audits and returns, it is not, and makes no attempt to explore and give a comprehensive take on the subject matter of accounting and auditing. Those who wish to explore these areas in greater technical depth are well advised to consult texts dedicated to accounting and auditing.

[2] Keenan D *Smith and Keenan's Company Law* 13th edn 467. Section 263, section 253 notwithstanding, places no obligation on a small private company irrespective, to appoint an auditor.

[3] Keenan D Smith and Keenan's Company Law 13th edn 467.

11.2   Accounting records

Accounting records and the requirement for the company to keep them are matters provided for under section 246.[4] This section is a vast improvement over the previous section 162 under CA 1994 which was more general and not as expansive by comparison. Under section 246(1) the board of directors is required to 'cause accounting records to be kept that—
- *(a)* correctly record and explain the transactions of the company; and
- *(b)* shall enable the financial—
  - (i)   position of the company to be determined with reasonable accuracy; and
  - (ii) statements of the company to be readily and properly audited'.

In terms of section 246(2) and without limiting the generality of subsection (1), 'the accounting records shall include—
- *(a)* entries of money received and spent each day and the matters to which it relates;
- *(b)* a record of the assets and liabilities of the company;
- *(c)* if the company's business involves dealing in goods, a record of goods bought and sold;
- *(d)* if the company's business involves providing services, a record of services provided and relevant invoices.

Retaining the contents of section 162(4) under CA 1994, section 246(3) maintains that '[t]he accounting records shall be kept in written form and in English'. Whether this is profitable given that there are many more languages in which the records could be kept is subject to anecdotal postulations. It appears though that since English is the language of commerce, this is a more cost effective and less confusing way of proceeding. 'If the board of directors fails to comply with the requirements of this section, every director of the company commits an offence and is liable, on conviction, to a fine not exceeding twenty thousand penalty units'.[5]

Under 247(1), '[a] company shall keep its accounting records at the company's registered office'. By section 247(2), '[i]f a company fails to comply with subsection (1), every director commits an offence and is liable, on conviction, to a fine not exceeding one hundred thousand penalty units'. Additionally, in terms of section 248, '[a] company shall, at its registered office, make its accounting records available for inspection to the directors, secretary and auditors of the company, at all reasonable times, without charge'.

---

[4] By way of comparison, see section 386 of the UK CA 2006.
[5] Section 246(4).

11.3   Annual accounts

'Annual accounts' or 'annual financial statements' per Act nomenclature, is a term with roots in commercial jargon but as a case of the law following commerce, it has now come to be a term used by the Act to describe what accountants normally think of as encompassing the balance sheet, and the profit and Loss statement.[6]

11.3.1 Annual financial statements to include amounts paid to directors

According to 249(1), '...the annual financial statements of a company shall, in respect of the financial year concerned, state the total amount of—

    (a)   emoluments paid to, or receivable by, the directors for their services; and

    (b)   any compensation paid to, or receivable by, the directors or past directors in respect of loss of office'.

The Act adds to the foregoing by providing that [t]he amount to be shown, in respect of—

    (a)   subsection (1) *(a)*, shall include emoluments paid to, or receivable by, a person in respect of that person's services—

        (i)   as director or director of its subsidiary; or

        (ii)   in connection with the management of the affairs of the company or a subsidiary;

    (b)   subsection (1) *(b)*, shall include sums paid to, or receivable by, a director or past director by way of compensation for loss of office[7]—

        (a)   as director; or

        (b)   in connection with the management of the affairs of the company or its subsidiary, where the loss arose from the loss of office as director.[8]

Further, '[w]here an amount to be stated in subsection (1) or (2), includes an amount to be paid by, or receivable from, a person other than the company, the accounts shall state the subtotals of the amounts receivable from, or paid by—

    (a)   the company;

    (b)   the company's subsidiaries; and

    (c)   any other person'.[9]

---

[6] Also referred to as income statement; earnings statement, revenue statement; statement of financial performance; and statement of operations.

[7] In terms of section 249(4), '"compensation for loss of office" includes sums paid as consideration for or in connection with a person's retirement from office; and "emoluments" includes fees and percentages paid to a director, any sums paid by way of expenses and allowances and the estimated money value of any other benefits received by the director, other than in cash'.

[8] Section 249(2).

[9] Section 249(3).

11.3.2 *Annual financial statements to include particulars of loans to officers*

The mandate for annual financial statements to include particulars of loans to officers is contained under section 250. Under section 250(1), [t]he annual financial statements of a company shall state the—

(a) particulars of any relevant loan[10] made during the financial year to which the accounts apply, including any loan which was repaid during that year; and

(b) amount of any relevant loan, whenever made, which remained outstanding at the end of the financial year'. According to section 250(2), '[i]f the company fails to comply with this section, the auditors shall include in the auditors' report on the statement of financial position of the company, so far as they are reasonably able to do so, a statement giving the particulars specified in subsection (1).

The foregoing notwithstanding, we must note from the outset that in terms of section 250(4), section 250 does not apply to a loan that was made by a company or a subsidiary of the company and was not made under a guarantee from, or on a security provided by, the company or subsidiary—

(a) in the ordinary course of its business, where the ordinary business of the company includes the lending of money; or

(b) to an employee of the company, or by an employee of the subsidiary, if the loan does not exceed fifty monetary units and is certified by the directors or subsidiary of the company[11], as the case may be, to have been made in accordance with any practice adopted or about to be adopted by the company or subsidiary with respect to loans to its employees.

According to section 251(1), '[a] person who is, or has, at any time within the previous five years, been a director or officer of a company shall, on the request of the company, provide the company with such information relating to the person as may be necessary for the purposes of sections 249[12] and 250[13]'. Failure to comply with section 251(1) is a serious matter as any person who fails to comply with that subsection 'commits an offence and is liable, on conviction, to a fine not exceeding ten thousand penalty units.'[14]

---

[10] According to section 250(3), 'a relevant loan is a loan, other than a loan referred to in subsection(4), made by the company, a subsidiary of the company or any other person under a guarantee from, or on a security provided by, the company or a subsidiary of the company to—*(a)* an officer of the company; or*(b)* any person who, after the making of the loan, during the financial year, became an officer of the company'.

[11] In terms of section 250(5), '...a subsidiary of a company is a body corporate which was a subsidiary of the company at the end of the financial year of the company during which the loan concerned was made'.

[12] Which provides for '[a]nnual financial statements to include amounts paid to directors'.

[13] Which provides for '[a]nnual financial statements to include particulars of loans to officers'.

[14] Section 251(2).

11.3.3   *Statement of financial position to be signed by directors*

The requirement for directors to append their signatures to the statement of financial position of the company is the province of section 252. In terms of section 252(1), '[t]he statement of financial position of a company's annual financial statements, to be laid before the company in a general meeting or delivered to the Registrar, shall be signed on behalf of the company by not less than two directors or, where the company has only one director, by that director'.

Further, '[i]f the statement of financial position is—

(a)   laid before the company in a general meeting or delivered to the Registrar without being signed as required by this section; or

(b)   not a copy laid or delivered, but is issued, circulated or published without—

    (i)   being signed as required by this section; or

    (ii)   a copy of the signature or signatures; the company and each officer in default commit an offence and are liable, on conviction, to a fine not exceeding one hundred thousand penalty units'.[15]

By section 252(3), '[i]f a copy of the statement of financial position is issued, circulated or published without having annexed to it copies of—

(a)   the statement of income;

(b)   any group accounts; and

(c)   the auditors' report; the company and each officer in default commit an offence and are liable, on conviction, to a fine not exceeding one hundred thousand penalty units'.

11.4   Auditors

Auditors as the term suggests are concerned with *auditing,* itself a continuous tense derived from the term *audit* which can be said to be 'a process which is concerned to establish and confirm confidence in the accounting information yielded by the company's records and systems so that an opinion may be given upon the accounts which have been prepared by the company from those records and systems'.[16] The purpose of an audit is to primarily inform shareholders of the performance of directors in their role as stewards appointed by shareholders in terms of section 85, to create shareholder value. A secondary purpose is by and large to detail a company's financial performance to enable creditors which

---

[15]   252(2).

[16]   Wild C and Weinstein S *Smith and Keenan's Company Law* 15th edn (Pearson Education Ltd 2011 Essex) 516.

may include debenture holders[17] and potential investors to make an informed decision.

In view of the foregoing, in this part of the text we explore provisions and the law relating to appointment of auditors; auditing firm; signing of auditor's report; qualifications of auditors; reappointment of auditor; auditor to avoid conflict of interest; auditor's report; access to information; auditor's attendance at annual general meeting; furnishing auditor's report; small private company need not appoint auditor; appointment of auditor for small private company; preparation of audited financial statement; standards for financial statement preparation; obligation to provide consolidated financial statement; comprehensive income statement when company becomes subsidiary; and date for financial statement of subsidiary. In the foregoing are contained rules and regulations important to this important aspect of corporate governance. 'All the rules and regulations associated with auditors and their conduct of the audit are designed to increase the value of the audit without imposing too high a cost on either the companies or their auditors'.[18]

11.4.1 Appointment of auditors[19]

11.4.1.1 General

Generally, a company is required to, at every general meeting,[20] appoint auditors who will serve until the next annual general meeting or until a need arises due to resignation or otherwise termination of their services irrespective.[21] The Act however considers the issue starting with recently incorporated companies. In terms of section 253(1) and only subject to section 263,[22] 'a company shall, within three months after its incorporation, appoint an auditor of the company, who shall hold office until the close of the company's first annual general meeting'. The threshold to be met is that of 'an ordinary resolution'.[23]

According to section 253(3), '[d]espite an agreement between a company and an auditor, the company may, by ordinary resolution, remove the auditor before the expiration of the auditor's term of office, except that the auditor shall be remunerated for the work done'. It is a requirement for a company to appoint an auditor within ninety days after the end of the financial year. Failure to so do

---

[17] See chapter 10 above which explores Part XI: sections 225–245 of the Act.

[18] Sealy L and Worthington S *Sealy & Worthington's Cases and Materials in Company Law* 10th edn (Oxford University Press Oxford 2013) 504.

[19] This is provided for under section 253. However, in terms of section 253(5), '[t]he provisions of … section [253] do not apply to small private companies.

[20] See specifically sections 57 and 58; see also chapter 5 above that explores Part VI: sections 56 – 81.

[21] See section 253(3) below.

[22] Which provides that '[s]mall private company need not appoint [an] auditor[s]'.

[23] Section 253(2).

has consequences: each director is, by such failure, deemed to have committed 'an offence and is liable, on conviction, to a fine not exceeding one hundred thousand penalty units'.[24]

11.4.1.2   *Small private company need not appoint auditor*

Quite apart from the exemption of application of section 253 to small companies highlighted in section 253(5) section 263(1) provides that 'a small private company need not appoint an auditor'.   However, where 'a small private company appoints an auditor, the provisions relating to appointment of auditors, as specified in [the] Act, shall apply'. According to section 264(1), '[d]espite [the] Act, where, at or before the time required for the holding of an annual meeting of a small private company, notice of intention to appoint an auditor is given to the board of directors, signed by shareholders who hold not less than fifty percent of the shares of the company, the company shall appoint an auditor'. It is important to note in this regard that in terms of section 263(2) '[a] resolution to appoint an auditor shall cease to have effect at the next annual general meeting'.

11.4.2   *Qualifications of and eligibility for appointment*

11.4.2.1   *General*

It has been observed[25] that, no matter how loyal the auditors are to the interests of the shareholders, the latter (and others) will not benefit, and are likely to suffer considerable harm, if the auditors fail to detect impropriety in relation to the financial affairs of the company, whether that impropriety exists at the top management level or lower down in the company. The law uses three main techniques to promote auditor competence: control over those who may become auditors and their education and professional conduct; securing to auditors the necessary legal powers to discharge their duties; and liability for negligently conducted audits.

11.4.2.2   *Qualification and eligibility*

The starting point is section 256 which provides that '[a] person shall not be appointed as auditor of a company unless that person is qualified and is registered to practice as an auditor by a body regulating the audit practice in Zambia'. The fact that the Act sees qualification as applying to natural persons is patent. This is evidenced by the fact that even though the Act[26] makes an

---

[24] Section 253(4).

[25] Davies PL Gower and Davies' *Principles of Modern Company Law*…576.

[26] Section 254 which replaces section 172 under CA 1994.

auditing firm[27] eligible for appointment as an auditor[28] only if such a firm satisfies the following conditions, that is to say if—

(a) at least one partner of the firm is ordinarily resident in Zambia;

(b) all or some of the partners, including the partner who is ordinarily resident in Zambia, are qualified for appointment as auditors;

(c) the firm is not indebted to the company; or

(d) a partner of the firm is not a member, director or employee of the company or a related company.

To the foregoing must be added the requirement under section 255 that '[a]n auditor's report shall be signed, on behalf of a firm appointed as the auditor of a company, by a partner of the firm who is a qualified auditor'.

The desire that those appointed to act as auditors are persons who are appropriately qualified and supervised is unmistakable from the tenor of sections 254, 255 and 256. It is important that audits, given their significance, are done correctly, with integrity and with an appropriate level of independence not only from the directors who may be adversely affected by the audit but the shareholders in whose interests the audits are primarily carried out. It therefore comes as no surprise that section 256 recognises the role of 'a body[29] regulating the audit practice'. It would appear from section 256 that it is not enough for one to have a qualification from a qualifying body offering a professional qualification in accountancy, he must, in addition, be a member of a supervisory body regulating auditors in Zambia[30] which preserves and enforces rules relating to the eligibility of persons or entities thereof to be appointed as auditors in terms of the Act and the nature of audit work according to the rules and regulations made pursuant to the Accountants Act.[31]

In terms of section 257(1), '[a]n auditor may be reappointed by an ordinary resolution by the company at the annual general meeting'. However this reappointment is limited to a period of not more than 6 years.[32] Additionally, '[a]n auditor of a company shall not be reappointed at an annual general meeting if the auditor has given notice to the company that the auditor does not wish to be reappointed'.

---

[27] This is a welcome change even though a matter of semantics as previously under section 172 of CA 1994, the Act allowed a company to appoint a private company as an auditor as long as it met the conditions under section 172(2)-(4) which conditions are retained under section 254. There are no explicit disqualifying factors that were previously provided for under section 172(5)-(7). The rationale for this may be that not meeting the qualifications set out in sections 254 and 256 should be enough notice.

[28] According to section 2 of the Accountants Act, 2008 "Auditor" means a person holding a practicing certificate or a firm registered under this Act and appointed to perform any auditing functions'.

[29] Zambia Institute of Chartered Accountants (ZICA). See further, the Accountants Act, Chapter 390 of the Laws of Zambia.

[30] ZICA.

[31] Chapter 390 of the laws of Zambia.

[32] Section 257(3).

11.4.3   *Duties and powers of auditors*

11.4.3.1   *General*

'The duties of auditors derive from contract and tort. Promoters, too, may owe duties in contract and tort, but their more significant duties are imposed in equity, and map very closely the duties owed by the company's directors'.[33] Though in general, an auditor's duties may mainly be said to encompass (i) carrying out an audit[34] which in the Accountants Act[35] 'means the independent examination of evidence from which the financial statements of an enterprise are derived in order to give the reader of the statements confidence as to the truth and fairness of the state of affairs which the financial statement disclose, but does not include boo-keeping, cost accounting and business or cost systems' and (ii) reporting to the shareholders regarding their findings as we discuss below,[36] there are other roles which auditors will ordinarily be expected to perform in the course of their duties or by statutory injunction. These may include but are not limited to avoiding conflicts of interest, reporting fraud and money laundering.

11.4.3.2   *The duty to avoid a conflict of interest*

An auditor must ensure that in performing his duties, he does so loyally and competently in line with the relevant rules impressed upon him by his qualification and the standards expected of him by the supervisory body. He must carry out the audit by the book, with veracity and an unimpeachable degree of independence from the company, directors, shareholders and/ or creditors. He is therefore statutorily required to, in terms of section 258, '… ensure, in carrying out the duties of an auditor.., that the auditor's judgment is not impaired by reason of any relationship with, or interest in, the company or a related company'. He has a fiduciary responsibility to the members but at the same time is not beholden to them nor should they, or any of the class of individuals mentioned hereinbefore, colour, corrupt, pervert or water down his work.

11.4.3.3   *The duty to prepare an auditor's report*

This duty is impressed upon the auditor by section 259. In terms of section 259(1), '[a]n auditor of a company shall prepare an audit report and present it

---

[33] Sealy L and Worthington S *Sealy & Worthington's Cases and Materials in Company Law* 10th edn (Oxford University Press Oxford 2013) 504.

[34] By which is meant in terms of the decision in *Leeds Estate, Building and Investment Co* v *Shepherd* [1887] 36 Ch D 787, he ought, as he should, check and verify the company's accounts.

[35] No 13 of 2008.

[36] See section 259(1).

at an annual general meeting'. It is required that an auditor's report contains information, as required by the IFRSs[37] which ZICA has adopted.[38] In terms of section 259(3), '[a]n auditor shall, in addition to the report referred to in subsection (1), report on whether there, *(a)* is a relationship, interest or debt which the auditor has in the company; and *(b)* are serious breaches of corporate governance principles or practices by the directors. By section 259(4), '[a]n auditor shall, within ninety days of signing an audit report, issue a management letter highlighting major weaknesses, breaches or other concerns noted during the audit. According to section 259(5), '[a]n auditor who contravenes this section shall be charged in accordance with the law regulating the practice of auditing in Zambia'.

11.4.3.4   The duty to report fraud

This is a rather problematic area. Though it may appear to the public and in the public's minds and the minds of the media that there is a legal obligation placed on auditors to report what is termed 'fraudulent activities' that the auditor may come across during his work , the reality is far removed from this perception. However, it has been observed that,[39] '[a]s regards the role of the auditor *in combating corporate fraud*, expectations which the public and some in business have of the auditor often go beyond their role as auditors. 'Although the term 'fraud' is often mentioned, there is in fact no crime of that name and if auditors are to be responsible for exposing it or reporting on it, then there must first be legislation to define what it is they are to report upon'. Be that as it may, auditing standards such as the IFRSs which ZICA has adopted, oblige auditors to consider whether the public interest will be better served with such information.[40]

In *Sasea Finance Ltd v KPMG (a firm)*[41] it was complained on appeal that the auditors had failed to timeously warn the company of fraud by a senior employee. The appeal concerned an application to strike out heads of claim in an action brought by the company against its auditors for negligence. It was

---

[37] International Financial Reporting Standards.

[38] Section 259(2).

[39] Wild C and Weinstein S *Smith and Keenan's Company Law* 15th edn ...519.

[40] Davies PL *Gower and Davies' Principles of Modern Company Law*....

[41] [2000] 1 All ER 676, CA; Coram: Kennedy LJ Aldous LJ and Mantell LJ; See further, *Sasea Finance Ltd (In Liquidation) v KPMG* Ch D (Times 25-Aug-98) where an auditor had negligently failed to identify the insolvency of a company and to warn against payment of dividends. It was held that the auditor was liable in damages for dividends wrongly paid; and *Equitable Fire Insurance Society v Ernst and Young* [2003] EWCA Civ 1114; [2003] 2 BCLC 603; [2007] Lloyds Rep PN 22, [2004] PNLR 16 where the plaintiffs sought damages from its accountants, saying that had they been advised of the difficulties in their financial situation, they would have been able to avoid the loss of some £2.5 Billion, or sell their assets at a time when their losses could be minimalized. Held on appeal from judgment limiting the claim to £500 million that the claim should not be limited to a claim of any certain size the issues being an area of developing jurisprudence and fact dependent.

held, allowing the appeal that the submission that the auditor's duty did not extend to the losses claimed because the transactions from which they flowed arose in the normal course of business and were part of the ordinary risks associated with the carrying on of that business must fail it was held further, that the auditor's duties to the company, could, as a last resort, embrace, 'a duty to inform relevant third parties of suspected wrongdoing'.[42] The challenge in this case had been that the discovery which concerned fraud by those in control meant that reporting to the company was unlikely to yield any positive results.

11.4.3.5   Duty to report money laundering and terrorism financing

11.4.3.5.1   General

There are specific reporting obligations for auditors under the Anti-money laundering and combating financing of terrorism (AML/CFT) framework discussed in detail below:

11.4.3.5.2   AML/CFT framework[43]

The fight against money laundering and terrorist financing in Zambia and around the world is important to protect [...] citizens and to ensure the integrity of financial institutions and national Security. Strong and effective Anti-Money Laundering and Financing of Terrorism (AML/CFT) framework promote financial integrity by making it difficult to conceal illegal activities. The [...] Government endeavors to develop and implement AML/CFT systems that comply with the required international standards. Below is the outline of the Zambian AML/CFT framework

11.4.3.5.3   AML/CFT institutional framework

(a)   Anti-Money Laundering Authority (AMLA)

This is the AML/CFT Policy making body established under Section 3 of the Prohibition and Prevention of Money Laundering Act, No 14 of 2001, as amended by Act, No 44 of 2010. The AMLA is chaired by the Attorney General, and other members include; the Governor-Bank of Zambia, the Commissioner General of the Zambia Revenue Authority (ZRA), the Inspector General of Police, the Commissioner-Drug Enforcement Commission (DEC), the Director General-Anti Corruption Commission (ACC). The mandate of AMLA is to

---

[42] Davies PL *Gower and Davies' Principles of Modern Company Law…*580.
[43] All the material discussed under AML/CFT is, except for minor changes in grammar and for typesetting purposes, taken from the Financial Intelligence Centre website: https://www.fic.gov.zm/aml-cft-framework and was retrieved on 7/02/2018.

provide general or specific policy directives and to advise Government on measures required to prevent and detect money laundering in the Republic of Zambia.

(b) Task Force of Senior Officials on AML/CFT matters

The Zambia Government is cognizant about the importance of coordination among key stakeholders for the effective functioning of the AML/CFT framework. For this reason, Cabinet Office set up the National Task Force of Senior Officials on AML/CFT. The overall mandate of the National Task Force of Senior Officials is to coordinate AML/CFT matters among key stakeholders with a view to improving the effectiveness of existing policies to combat money laundering, financing of terrorism and other serious offences.

(c) The Financial Intelligence Centre ('the Centre')

The Financial Intelligence Centre was established to be the sole designated agency responsible for the receipt, requesting, analysing and disseminating of the disclosure of suspicious transaction reports to Law Enforcement Agencies (LEAs) and other foreign designated authorities pursuant to the Financial Intelligence Centre Act No 46 of 2010 ("The FIC Act" or "the Act"). Further, it is the responsibility of the FIC to issue guidelines to reporting entities to ensure reporting entities comply accordingly with the provisions of the FIC Act. The Financial Intelligence Centre is governed by the Board of Directors appointed by the Zambian Republican President. The primary purpose of the Board is to guide and control the overall direction of the business of the FIC as provided for under section 8 of the Act, and provide policy oversight on AML/CFT matters

(d) Law Enforcement Agency (LEAs)

Section 2 of the FIC Act designates the following as Law enforcement Agencies (LEAs) in Zambia:
  i. The Zambia Police Force, established under the Constitution;
  ii. The Zambia Security Intelligence Service, established under the Zambia Security Intelligence Act;
  iii. The Immigration Department, established under the Immigration and Deportation Act, 2010;
  iv. The Drug Enforcement Commission, established under the Narcotic Drugs and Psychotropic Subsistence Act;
  v. The Anti-Money Laundering Investigations Unit, established under the Prohibition and Prevention of Money Laundering Act, 2001
  vi. The Anti-Corruption Commission, established under the Anti-Corruption Act, 2010;

vii. The Zambia Revenue Authority, established under the Zambia Revenue Authority Act; and

viii. Any other Investigative Institution that the Minister may, by statutory Instrument designate.

(e) Supervisory Authorities

The FIC Act defines the Supervisory Authorities as:

i.   The Governor of the Bank of Zambia, appointed under the Bank of Zambia Act;

ii.   The Registrar of Co-operatives, appointed under the Co-operatives Act, 1998;

iii. The Registrar of Pensions and Insurance, appointed under the Pension Scheme Regulation Act, 1996;

iv.   The Commissioner under the Securities Act;

v.   The Registrar appointed under the Patents and Companies Registration Agency Act, 2010;

vi.   The Commissioner of Lands;

vii. The Zambia Development Agency, established under the Zambia Development Agency Act, 2006;

viii. The Licencing Committee, established under the Tourism and Hospitality Act, 2007;

ix.   The Registrar of Estate Agents appointed under the Estate Agents Act, 2001;

x.   The Law Association of Zambia, established under the Law Association of Zambia Act;

xi.   The Zambia Institute of Chartered Accountants established under the Accountants Act, 2008; and

xii. Any other authority established under any written law as a supervisory or as the Minister may prescribe.

(f) Reporting Entities

[The term 'reporting entities' refers to] institutions regulated by Supervisory Authorities and are required to make a suspicious transaction reports concerning Money Laundering, Terrorist Financing and any other serious offences to the Financial Intelligence Centre. *Inter alia*, reporting entities include:

i.   Financial institutions e.g. Commercial Banks and Non-Bank Financial Institutions e.g. micro finance institutions

ii.   Designated non-financial businesses and professions (DNFBPs) e.g. Casinos, Real estate agents, Accountants; and Legal Practitioners.

(g)   National Prosecution Authority

The National Prosecution Authority (NPA) is one of the stakeholders in AML/ CFT regime. NPA is the principal authority for all prosecutions in the country as it houses the Office of the Director of Public Prosecutions (DPP). All prosecutors in Zambia derive their authority to prosecute from the DPP pursuant to section 82 of the Criminal Procedure Code, Chapter 88 of the Laws of Zambia.

(h)   Judiciary

The Judiciary is considered to be a relevant stakeholder on AML/CFT related issues as it provides efficacy to the process by being an impartial arbiter in proceedings. All prosecuted cases and claims for forfeiture must come before the courts of law.

(i)   Others Relevant Government Agencies

The Office of the Auditor General, Ministry of Home Affairs, Ministry of Mines, Ministry of Defence, Zambia Air Force, and Registrar of Societies among others are considered very critical for the provision of intelligence Information on Money Laundering, Terrorist Financing and other serious offences.

11.4.3.5.4   AML/CFT Legal Framework

[Parliament] has enacted AML/CFT legislation, to deal with money laundering, Financing of Terrorism, forfeiture and seizure of proceeds of crimes, prevention of corruption, fraud, and financial crime among others.   The AML/CFT legal framework covers *inter alia* the following Legislation: Prohibition and Prevention of Money Laundering Act No 14 of 2001, amended by Act No 44 of 2010 (Defines and criminalizes Money laundering); Anti-Terrorism Act No 21 of 2007 (Criminalizes financing of terrorism (section 20); Forfeiture of Proceeds of Crime Act No 19 of 2010 (Provides civil and criminal forfeiture and seizure of proceeds of crimes); Financial Intelligence Centre Act No 46 of 2010 (Establishes the Financial Intelligence Centre, provides for duties of supervisory authorities and reporting entities); The Public Interest Disclosure (Protection of Whistleblowers) Act No. 4 of 2010 (Provides for disclosure of conduct inimical to public interest); Mutual Legal Assistance in Criminal Matters Act (MLACMA), 1993; The Plea Negotiations and Agreements Act, No. 20 of 2010; The Anti-Corruption Act, No 3 of 2012 (replacing the Anti-Corruption Act, No 38 of 2010) (vested with powers to investigate corruption offences; The Non-Governmental Organisations Act, No. 16 of 2009; and The Penal Code Act, Cap. 87 of the Laws of Zambia.

11.4.3.5.5   Duty of care and skill

An Auditor will be expected to carry out his duty with care and skill expected of a person with his level of training and skill. This does not mean that he must perform beyond what is reasonably expected or required given his role and the information availed to him. The level of skill and care expected of an auditor has long been a subject of disputation and litigation from which a wealth of judicial decisions have emanated. Part of the disputation has to do with the fact that the standard of care principle which has long been settled in law but seems to have found no home in the commercial world is 'that the auditor is not a guarantor of the accuracy of the directors' accounts'.[44]

In *Re London and General Bank*[45] the greater part of the capital of the bank, which was being wound-up, had for some years been advanced to four of the 'Balfour' companies and a few special customers on securities which were insufficient and difficult of realisation. The auditors drew attention to the situation in a confidential report to the directors, stressing its gravity, and ending by saying – *'We cannot conclude without expressing our opinion unhesitatingly that no dividend should be paid this year'*. The chairman, Mr. Balfour, persuaded the auditors to strike this sentence out before the report was officially laid before the board of directors. The certificate signed by the auditors and laid before the shareholders at the annual general meeting stated that *'the value of the assets as shown on the balance sheet is dependent on realisation'*. As originally drawn, it also said – *'And on this point we have reported specifically to the board.'* But again Mr. Balfour persuaded them to withdraw this statement by promising to mention this in his speech to the shareholders which he did without drawing special attention to it. The directors declared a dividend of 7 per cent.

It was held by the EWCA, that the auditors had been guilty of misfeasance, and were liable to make good the amount of dividend paid. It is the duty of an auditor to consider and report to the shareholders, whether the balance sheet exhibits a correct view of the state of the company's affairs, and the true financial position at the time of the audit. He must take reasonable care to see that his certification is true, and must place the necessary information before the shareholders and not merely indicate the means of acquiring it. In the course of his judgment Lindley LJ said:

> An auditor [. . .] is not an insurer; he does not guarantee that the books correctly show the true position of the company's affairs; he does not even guarantee that his balance sheet is accurate according to the books of the company [. . .] but, he must be

---

[44] Davies PL *Gower and Davies' Principles of Modern Company Law*…586.
[45] [1895] 2 Ch 166. Summarised in *Smith and Keenan's Company Law* 15th edn…520.

honest, i.e. he must not certify what he does not believe to be true, and he must use reasonable care and skill before he believes that what he certifies is true. What is reasonable care in any particular case must depend upon the circumstances of the case. Theobald, the auditor, stated the true position to the directors, and if he had done the same to the shareholders, his duty would have been discharged.

In *Re Kingston Cotton Mill Co (No 2)*.[46] The directors of a company were enabled to pay dividends out of capital because the stock in trade of the company was overstated for several years. The auditors had not required the production of the stock records but had accepted the certificate of the company's manager regarding the value of the stock. It was held by the EWCA that the auditors were not liable. It was stated that an auditor is 'a watchdog not a bloodhound'. He can assume that the company's servants are honest and can rely upon statements they make unless there are suspicious circumstances which would give reason for distrust. *Per* Lopes LJ:

> It is the duty of an auditor to bring to bear on the work he has to perform that skill, care and caution which a reasonably competent, careful and cautious auditor would use. What is reasonable skill, care and caution must depend on the particular circumstances of each case. An auditor is not bound to be a detective, or, as was said, to approach his work with suspicion, or with a foregone conclusion that there is something wrong. He is a watchdog, but not a bloodhound. He is justified in believing tried servants of the company in whom confidence is placed by the company. He is entitled to assume that they are honest and to rely upon their representations, provided he uses reasonable care. If there is anything calculated to excite suspicion, he should probe it to the bottom; but in the absence of anything of that kind he is only bound to be reasonably cautious and careful [. . .] It is not the duty of an auditor to take stock; he is not a stock expert; there are many matters on which he must rely on the honesty and accuracy of others.

It has been observed[47] that the principle pronounced in *Re Kingston* (above) 'depends in considerable part on how willing the courts are to find that no circumstances had arisen which were suspicious'. In any case, the rule in

---

[46] [1896] 2 Ch 279 CA, summarised in *Smith and Keenan's Company Law* 15th edn 522.
[47] Davies PL *Gower and Davies' Principles of Modern Company Law*…586.

Re Kingston appears to have been modified somewhat in *Westminster Road Construction and Engineering Company Ltd.*[48] A company paid dividend out of profits which were overstated by reason of the overvaluation of work in progress. This figure was supplied by the manager and secretary and it was held that the auditor was liable to repay the money paid out as dividend because he had accepted the certificate given by them without making proper enquiries which would have revealed that the valuation was inflated. Similarly, it has been held in *Re Thomas Gerrard & Son Ltd*[49] (see facts below) in what has been termed as courts willing to take 'a more demanding line than their predecessors',[50] that the discovery of altered invoices should have caused the auditors to carry out their own check on the stock.

We must, in view of the foregoing, look at the standard of care expected of an auditor not with the lenses of the foregoing old authorities decided without the benefit of the recent developments in accounting standards but in light of the extensive nature of the rules and their influence. The inimitable Lord Denning once opined in *Formento (Sterling Area) Ltd v Selsdon Fountain Pen Co Ltd*[51] that an auditor, in order to perform his task as it should be, 'must come to it with an inquiring mind-not suspicious of dishonesty, I agree-but suspecting that someone may have made a mistake somewhere and that a check must be made to ensure that there has been none'.

In *Re Thomas Gerrard & Son Ltd*[52] the managing director of the company had falsified the accounts by three methods one of which involved including non-existent stock and altering invoices. The auditors who were put on inquiry by alterations of invoices negligently failed to investigate the matter and gave a falsely favourable picture of the profits of the company as a result of which it declared dividends it would not otherwise have declared which in turn resulted in extra tax being payable. The company was wound-up and in misfeasance proceedings under what is now [section 135 of the Insolvency Act, 2017] against the auditors they claimed that they had not been given enough time to do their work. It was held that this was no defence and the auditors must repay the dividends, the cost of recovering the extra tax and any of the extra tax not recoverable. In the course of his judgment Pennycuick J made the following points:

(i)　if directors do not allow the auditors adequate time to make proper investigations, they must either refuse to make a report at all or qualify it;

---

[48] [1932] unreported. Summarised in *Smith and Keenan's Company Law* 15th edn...522.
[49] [1967] 2 All ER 525.
[50] Davies PL *Gower and Davies' Principles of Modern Company Law*...586.
[51] [1958] 1 WLR 45 HL.
[52] [1968] Ch 455, summarised in *Smith and Keenan's Company Law* 15th edn...523.

(ii)   while leaving open the question whether the auditors would have been in breach of duty had the only fraud been falsification of stock, the judge held that once they were on notice of the altered invoices, they had a duty to make an exhaustive inquiry. Having failed to do so, they were liable to the company under what is now [section 135 of the Insolvency Act, 2017].

We must at this point raise the question of whether, in this jurisdiction, misfeasance proceedings could be commenced against an auditor as shown in *Re Thomas* (above). The reason the question is important has to do with the definition of officer in the Act. According to section 2, '"officer" includes: (a) a director, company secretary or executive officer of a company; or (b) a local director.' This definition is in no way exhaustive and must be taken to mean that any person whose role by implication may, under the right facts and circumstances be deemed to be an officer within the context of section 2, may be included in that definition aside from those explicitly mentioned.[53] However, it will be remembered that under the same section 2, "auditor" has the same meaning assigned to the word in the Accountants Act, 2008[54] and other written laws relating to the regulation of auditors and appointed to perform auditing functions for a company'. There is no explicit inclusion of an 'auditor'. In fact, by section 254(d), an auditing firm which has as one of its partners a person who is, 'a member, director or employee of the company or a related company' would not qualify for appointment as an auditor. The same principle, it is submitted, must apply to a private individual auditor.

Section 212 of the UK Corporate Insolvency Act, 1986 on which action against auditors for misfeasance in *Re Thomas* (above) was commenced, and in which they were held liable as 'officers' is similar to section 135 of the Corporate Insolvency Act, 2017 which provides as follows:

135(1) Where, in the course of a winding-up, it appears that a promoter, liquidator or officer of a company may have—

(a)   misapplied, retained, become liable or accountable for any money or property of the company; or

(b)   committed a misfeasance or breach of trust or duty in relation to the company; the Court may, on the application of a liquidator, creditor or member, inquire into the conduct of that liquidator, officer or promoter.

(2) The Court may order a person to repay or restore money or property or to compensate the company, to the extent that the person was unjustly enriched, where the Court is, after conducting an inquiry specified in subsection (1), satisfied that a liquidator or officer had—

(a)   misapplied, retained, become liable or accountable for any money or property of the company, or

---

[53] 'Officer' is similarly defined under section 2 of the Corporate Insolvency Act, 2017.
[54] No 13 of 2008.

    (b)   committed a misfeasance or breach of trust or duty in relation to the company.

(3) This section shall apply to matters specified in subsection (1) that occurred during the two years preceding the commencement of a winding-up.

What is patent from the foregoing is that the actions envisaged therein are against 'a promoter, liquidator or functions for a company'. To repeat, there is no explicit reference to or inclusion of 'auditors' in the definition of the term 'officer' under section 2 of the Act, 2017, it is instructive to note not only the non-exhaustive definition of 'officer' under the Act or the Corporate Insolvency Act, 2017 but also the fact that an auditor has been held to be an officer in a number of corporate contexts in, among others, the cases of *Mutual Reinsurance Co Ltd v Peat Marwick Mitchell & Co;*[55] *Re London & General Bank;*[56] *Re Thomas* (above) and *Re Kingston Cotton Mills (No 1).*[57]

A few other points are worth noting. For example, an auditor will be liable for negligence under the rule in *Hedley Byrne & Co v Heller & Partners*[58] if, without the exercising proper skill and care he reaches a valuation of shares. In addition, because the auditor's valuation of shares is in the main, obligatory on the parties concerned even when incorrect, and the general reluctance by the courts 'to set aside a professional valuation in the absence of fraud, or collusion…the remedy against the auditors [is] more attractive provided, of course, negligence can be established'.[59] Finally, as shown in *Re Republic of Bolivia Exploration Syndicate Ltd*[60] no auditor should accept appointment and less so the responsibility to audit without a working knowledge of the company's articles of association.

11.4.3.5.6   *Whether a duty of care is owed to third parties*

The question of whether an auditor owes a duty of care to a third party has exercised the minds of the courts since the issue became part and parcel of the duty of care edifice as it relates to auditors. The premise on which the courts have approached this issue appears to be general principles of common law as they relate to liability for economic loss brought about by negligent misstatement. The leading authority in this regard is the case of *Caparo Industries Plc v Dickman and others.*[61] The respondents owned shares in a public company, F Plc, whose accounts for the year ended 31 March 1984 showed

---

[55] [1997] 1 BCLC 1 CA.
[56] [1895] 2 Ch 166 CA.
[57] [1896] 1 Ch 6 CA.
[58] [1963] 2 All ER 575.
[59] *Smith and Keenan's Company Law* 15th edn….521; See *Baber v Kenwood Manufacturing Co* [1978] 1 Lloyd's Rep 175.
[60] [1914] 1 Ch 139.
[61] [1990] 2 AC 605 HL.

profits far short of the predicted figure which resulted in a dramatic drop in the quoted share price. After receipt of the audited accounts for the year ended 31 March 1984 the respondents purchased more shares in F Plc and later that year made a successful take-over bid for the company. Following the take-over, the respondents brought an action against the auditors of the company, alleging that the accounts of F Plc were inaccurate and misleading in that they showed a pre-tax profit of some £1·2m for the year ended 31 March 1984 when in fact there had been a loss of over £400,000, that the auditors had been negligent in auditing the accounts, that the respondents had purchased further shares and made their take-over bid in reliance on the audited accounts, and that the auditors owed them a duty of care either as potential bidders for F Plc because they ought to have foreseen that the 1984 results made F Plc vulnerable to a take-over bid or as an existing shareholder of F Plc interested in buying more shares. On the trial of a preliminary issue whether the auditors owed a duty of care to the respondents, the judge held that the auditors did not. The respondents appealed to the Court of Appeal, which allowed their appeal in part on the ground that the auditors owed the respondents a duty of care as shareholders but not as potential investors. The auditors appealed to the House of Lords and the respondents cross-appealed against the Court of Appeal's decision that they could not claim as potential investors. It was held as follows:

(1)   The three criteria for the imposition of a duty of care were foreseeability of damage, proximity of relationship and the reasonableness or otherwise of imposing a duty. In determining whether there was a relationship of proximity between the parties the court, guided by situations in which the existence, scope and limits of a duty of care had previously been held to exist rather than by a single general principle, would determine whether the particular damage suffered was the kind of damage which the defendant was under a duty to prevent and whether there were circumstances from which the court could pragmatically conclude that a duty of care existed.[62]

(2)   Where a statement put into more or less general circulation might foreseeably be relied on by strangers for any one of a variety of different purposes which the maker of the statement had no specific reason to anticipate there was no relationship of proximity between the maker of the statement and any person relying on it unless it was shown that the maker knew that his statement would be communicated to the person relying on it, either as an individual or as a member of an identifiable class, specifically in connection with a particular transaction or a transaction of a particular kind and that that person would be very

---

[62] Dictum of Brennan J in *Sutherland Shire Council v Heyman* [1985] 60 ALR 1 at 43–44 adopted.

likely to rely on it for the purpose of deciding whether to enter into that transaction[63]

(3)   The auditor of a public company's accounts owed no duty of care to a member of the public at large who relied on the accounts to buy shares in the company because the court would not deduce a relationship of proximity between the auditor and a member of the public when to do so would give rise to unlimited liability on the part of the auditor. Furthermore, an auditor owed no duty of care to an individual shareholder in the company who wished to buy more shares in the company, since an individual shareholder was in no better position than a member of the public at large and the auditor's statutory duty to prepare accounts was owed to the body of shareholders as a whole, the purpose for which accounts were prepared and audited being to enable the shareholders as a body to exercise informed control of the company and not to enable individual shareholders to buy shares with a view to profit. It followed that the auditors did not owe a duty of care to the respondents either as shareholders or as potential investors in the company. The appeal would therefore be allowed and the cross-appeal dismissed.[64]

What the decision in *Caparo* accomplished was a clarification of the realm of the duty of care that auditors owe. The conclusions drawn by the House of Lords can be summarised thus,

The statutory provisions establish a relationship between those responsible for the accounts (the directors) or for the report (the auditors) and some other class or classes of persons and this relationship imposes a duty of care owed to those persons. Among these "persons" is the company itself, to which, apart altogether from the statutory provisions, the directors are in a fiduciary relationship and the auditors in a contractual relationship by virtue of their employment by the company as its auditors.[65]

At the same time however, it could not be said that the relevant provisions in the Act establish the kind of relationship described above with any and all persons, that is 'members of the public who relied on the accounts to buy shares in the company' purely because the court would not be in a position to infer a relationship such as is envisaged in the Act as regards liability of auditors. The court refused to make a distinction between a third party already discussed here, and a shareholder who wished to buy additional shares in the company so far

---

[63] See *Cann v Willson* [1888] 39 Ch D 39; dictum of Denning LJ in *Candler v Crane Christmas & Co* [1951] 1 All ER 426 at 433–436; *Hedley Byrne & Co Ltd v Heller & Partners Ltd* [1963] 2 All ER 575; and *Smith v Eric S Bush (a firm), Harris v Wyre Forest DC* [1989] 2 All ER 514 which were considered.

[64] (Dictum of Richmond P in *Scott Group Ltd v McFarlane* [1978] 1 NZLR 553 at 566–567 adopted; *Al Saudi Banque v Clark Pixley (a firm)* [1989] 3 All ER 361 approved; dictum of Woolf J in *JEB Fasteners Ltd v Marks Bloom & Co (a firm)* [1981] 3 All ER 289 at 296–297 disapproved; Decision of the EWCA [1989] 1 All ER 798 reversed.

[65] Davies PL *Gower and Davies' Modern Principles of Company Law* 7th edn 582.

as the auditors owing a duty of care was concerned, because as the court saw it, such a shareholder was in no better position than a member of the public as 'the auditor's statutory duty to prepare accounts was owed to the body of shareholders as a whole,.. to enable the shareholders as a body to exercise informed control of the company and not to enable individual shareholders to buy shares with a view to profit'.

Thus Caparo rejected the prevailing notion in the commercial world and certain legal circles that negligent auditors were and could be held liable to any and all whom it could reasonably be foreseen would rely on the audited accounts and whom, as a result of such reliance would suffer loss. The consequence of this approach was to confine the common law duty of care within the realm of the Act's provisions relating to preparation of accounts and audits we have discussed elsewhere in this chapter.[66]

That said, *Caparo* is distinguishable from the decision in New Zealand in the case of *Scott Group Ltd v Mc Farlane*[67] where, the auditor's disclaimer did not exclude liability to the general public which opened them to unrestricted liability to third parties who relied on the audited accounts or 'liability in an indeterminate amount for an indeterminate time to an indeterminate class'.[68] The brief facts of the case were that G M McFarlane, a chartered accountant, audited the 1970 John Duthie Holdings Ltd financial statements, and through a simple mathematical error, resulted in John Duthie Holdings net worth being overstated by $38,000. At the same time, Scott Group Limited were considering making a takeover offer, and after reading the audited reports in question, valued the company at over $1 million, and offered to take over the company on the basis of two shares for every one share. However, just as the takeover was finalised, the mistake was discovered. As a result, Scott Group argued that it paid $38,000 too much for the shares, and sought compensation from the auditors for this amount. The auditors in response denied any liability for this mistake, on the basis there was no contractual relationship between the auditors and the takeover company, and neither did they owe Scott Group a duty of care for the mistake.

It was held by the NZCA[69] that as J D Holdings financial position was so poor, it made a takeover by another company a strong possibility, and that as a result, the auditors owed Scott Group a duty of care. However, despite succeeding on this important point, when it came to damages, as the court held that Scott Group had not suffered any financial loss and as, were not awarded any damages. Whilst the financial statements were overstated by $38,000, the

---

[66] See a similar rejection relating to the New Zealand Securities Act 1978 in *Deloitte Haskins & Sells v National Mutual Life Nominees* [1993] AC 774 PC.

[67] [1978] NZLR 553.

[68] *Ultramares Corp v Touche* [1931] 174 NE 441 at 441 *per* Cardozo CJ.

[69] New Zealand Court of Appeal.

evidence suggested that the shareholders of John Duthie Holdings were unlikely to have accepted any offer lower than the two for one share swap that was offered. Furthermore, the evidence on hand was that Scott Group paid $263,885 less than what the company was worth, making the purchase a good bargain irrespective of the $38,000 mistake.

We must end this part by submitting that given the extensive nature of auditing standards in recent years and specifically, in this jurisdiction's case, the adoption of IFRSs by ZICA, it would be a very brave thing indeed but one fraught with the grave danger of humiliation bringing the judiciary into disrepute and endangering the dignity of the court system from a a commercial stand point were a court to refuse to be guided to a substantial degree by the said standards as Woolf J was in *Lloyd Cheyham & Co Ltd v Littlejohn & Co*[70] in determining the common law standard of care as it relates to auditors.

11.4.4   Rights of auditors

11.4.4.1 General

There is no guarantee that because the statutory rules as provided in the Act and the Accountants Act result in law abiding and proficient auditors, they will under any and all circumstances (including inaccessibility to requisite information), as they are expected and required to, discover impropriety in the company. He cannot. It is therefore desirable and ultimately for the company's own good that the auditor is availed any and all the information needed in order for him to evaluate the company's accounts. To impede him becomes as most companies have ultimately found out to their humiliation, counter-productive. Section 262 mandates '[t]he auditor of a company' to, 'on completing an audit report, submit the report to the board of directors within an agreed time frame and reserve a copy of the report for the debenture holders or their assignees, except that where there is no agreed time frame, submit the report within ninety days after completion of the audit'. Where he has been impeded however, the auditor will 'qualify' the report to the shareholders reflecting that his audit was impeded and that the audit report is based only on the information he was allowed to gauge. To that end, section 260 codifies the auditor's right to access information.

11.4.4.2 Access to information

In terms of section 260(1), the board of directors or an officer of the company is mandated to guarantee that 'an auditor of the company has access to information,

---

[70] [1987] BCLC 303.

explanations, accounting records and other documents of the company'.[71] Under section 260(2), it is explicitly provided that '[w]here the board of directors or an officer of the company fails to comply with subsection (1), the board of directors or an officer of the company commits an offence and is liable, on conviction, to a fine not exceeding one hundred thousand penalty units'. However, in terms of section 260(3), [i]t shall be a defence to a member of the board or an officer of the company charged with an offence, in accordance with subsection (1) that the officer was—

(a)   not in possession or control of the information required; or
(b)   unable to give the explanations required, by reason of the duties assigned, or the position held by, the officer.

11.4.4.3   Auditor's attendance at annual general meeting

Auditors have a right of attendance at annual general meetings for obvious reasons. It will be remembered that the auditor is, under section 62(1)(d), entitled to receive notice of meetings and by section 66(e), not only to attend a general meeting of the company but speak. In terms of section 261,[72] [t]he board of directors shall ensure that an auditor of the company—

(a)   attends an annual general meeting and is heard on any part of the business of the meeting which concerns the auditor; and
(b)   receives the notices and communications that members are entitled to receive relating to an annual general meeting.

11.4.5   Liability for negligence

While we may have touched on this subject in the preceding sections of this chapter, it is worth emphasising that liability for negligence as it relates to auditors can be classified under statute, contract and tort. We briefly discuss these below. In addition, we look at the relevant issue of breach of duty, damages, and developments in exclusion of liability following from the New Zealand decision in *Scott Group* (above) and efforts in the recent past for capping auditors' liability given the danger expressed by Cardozo CJ in *Ultramares Corp* (above).

11.4.5.1   Statute

Section 135 of the Corporate Insolvency Act shows that an auditor may be liable '[w]here, in the course of a winding-up, it appears…' that he may have '… misapplied, retained, become liable or accountable for any money or property

---

[71] Replacing section 173(6) under CA 1994.
[72] Similar to section 173(10) under CA 1994.

of the company; or '…committed a misfeasance or breach of trust or duty in relation to the company…on the application of a liquidator, creditor or member', and upon the court inquiring into his conduct. The result may be, as shown in *Mutual Reinsurance Co Ltd v Peat Marwick Mitchell & Co;*[73] *Re London & General Bank* (above);[74] *Re Thomas* (above) and *Re Kingston Cotton Mills (No 1)*[75] the Court ordering the auditor '…to repay or restore money or property or to compensate the company, to the extent that the person was unjustly enriched, where the Court is, after conducting an inquiry specified in [section 135](1), satisfied that' an auditor 'had committed a misfeasance or breach of trust or duty in relation to the company'. It is also worth remembering that in terms of subsection (3), '…section [135] shall apply to matters specified in subsection (1) that occurred during the two years preceding the commencement of a winding-up'.

11.4.5.2 Contract

As held in *Caparo* (above), an auditor is under a contractual obligation to, in terms of section 2 of the Accountants Act, 2008, conduct an "audit" meaning 'the independent examination of evidence from which the financial statements of an enterprise are derived in order to give the reader of the statements confidence as to the truth and fairness of the state of affairs which the financial statement disclose, but does not include boo-keeping, cost accounting and business or cost systems'. The terms will obviously be explicitly spelt out in the engagement document but as we have also seen, he will be guided by provisions of the Act, ZICA adopted IFRSs and provisions of the Accountants Act, 2008. His failure to adhere to the terms and conditions of the contract gives the company the right to sue him for breach.

11.4.5.3 Tort

The claim here is in the tort of negligence. Where, an auditor knowingly makes a false statement or statements calculated to dishonestly deceive the company, the claim would fall under the tort of deceit. Making a claim is the easy part, proving it is a bit more difficult. In order to succeed the company must not only show that it was owed a duty but that the duty was breached causing the company loss and damage.

---

[73] [1997] 1 BCLC 1 CA.
[74] [1895] 2 Ch 166 CA.
[75] [1896] 1 Ch 6 CA.

11.4.5.3.1   Duty of care

As we have noted already the matter of duty of care as respects negligent misstatements by auditors has was ably considered by the House of Lords in *Caparo Industries Plc v Dickman*.[76] To recap:

- (a)   Auditors do not owe a duty of care to potential investors in the company;[77]
- (b)   Auditors do not owe a duty of care to potential investors even if they already hold shares in the company since as their duty is to the shareholders as a whole and not individual shareholders;
- (c)   Barring situation where they know that the audited accounts will be used for purposes of a takeover bid, auditors are not liable even in instances where they are aware of the person(s) who will rely upon the audited accounts;
- (d)   Where, as in *Morgan Crucible Co Plc v Hill Samuel Bank Ltd*[78] there is knowledge of user and use, a duty of care would exist in regard to the user.[79]

11.4.5.3.2   Breach of duty

We have already made the point, it will be remembered, that proving that an auditor owed a duty is only part of the challenge in an action for negligence against an auditor. To succeed in a case against a negligent auditor, the plaintiff, including the company, must prove that the auditor was in breach of his duty minus which he will not be held liable. 'An auditor is not likely to be in breach of duty if he follows Auditing Standards and Guidelines, Statements of Standard Accounting Practice and Financial Reporting Standards devised and issued by the profession'.[80] McNair J has held in *Bolam v Friern Hospital Management*

---

[76] [1990] 1 All ER 568; See further, *Al Saudi Banque v Clarke Pixley* [1989] 3 All ER 361; and *Abbott v Strong* (1998) *The Times*, 9 July; and *Yorkshire Enterprises Ltd v Robson Rhodes New Law Online* (1998) 17 June, Transcript Case No 2980610103 approved judgment.

[77] It has been held in *James McNaughton Paper Group v Hicks Anderson* [1991] 1 All ER 134 that even if an auditor knew that the audited accounts would be used by a bidder as the basis of a bid, he would not be liable if he reasonably believed and was entitled to assume that the bidder would also seek the advice of his own accountant (Summary taken from *Smith and Keenan's company law* 15th ed 524).

[78] [1991] 1 All ER 148.

[79] However, see the *James McNaughton Paper Group v Hicks Anderson* [1991] 1 All ER 134 where it was shown that, it may well be that the auditor will be deemed not be liable if, in the circumstances, he could reasonably assume that the user would seek a second opinion from his own accountant; See further, *Coulthard v Neville Russell* [1998] 1 BCLC 143, where the EWCA appeared to widen liability regarding misstatements by holding *inter alia* that auditors have, as a matter of principle, a duty of care to advise where there is a likelihood that a proposed transaction by the company and/or its directors may be in breach of the financial assistance provisions specifically, sections 183 – 186 of the Act.

[80] Wild C and Weinstein S *Smith and Keenan's Company Law* 15th edn 525.

Committee[81] that '[a] doctor is not guilty of negligence if he has acted in accordance with a practice accepted as proper by a responsible body of medical men skilled in that particular art . . . merely because there is a body of opinion who would take a contrary view.' While the statement related to the medical profession, the principle applies with equal force to others including auditors. As shown elsewhere in this chapter, courts are well advised to follow professional pronouncements as observed by Woolf J in *Lloyd Cheyham v Littlejohn*[82]:

[W]hile SSAPs[83] are not conclusive so that a departure from their terms necessarily involves a breach of duty of care and they are not rigid rules, they are very strong evidence as to what is the proper standard which should be adopted, and unless there is some justification, a departure will be regarded as constituting a breach of duty.

11.4.5.3.3 Damage

As a final point, it must be proved on a balance of probabilities that the breach in question caused the damage complained of. The case of *JEB Fasteners Ltd v Marks Bloom & Co*[84] demonstrates this. In 1975 the plaintiffs entered into negotiations to take over a manufacturing company which had recently started trading in the same products as the plaintiffs. During the negotiations the defendants, who were the company's accountants and who knew that the plaintiffs were negotiating to take over the company, produced audited accounts for the company's first trading year, being the year ended 31 October 1974, and having certified them as being accurate made the accounts available to the plaintiffs. The figures in the accounts were in certain respects substantially inaccurate. In particular, they showed that the company had done reasonably well in its first year and put an inflated value on its stock. The plaintiffs decided to take over the company, their primary motive for doing so being to acquire the services of the company's two directors, who had considerable experience in the trade. Accordingly, in June 1975 the plaintiffs completed the take-over of the company. At the time of the take-over the plaintiffs knew that the company had experienced financial difficulties in its first year and that its stock was worth less than the figure put on it in the accounts. The plaintiffs therefore

---

[81] [1957] 2 All ER 118.

[82] [1987] BCLC 303; as regards distributions *vis-à-vis* breach of duty by auditors, see *Bolitho v City and Hackney Health Trust* [1997] 4 All ER 771.

[83] Or 'Statements of Standard Accounting Practice'. Issued in 1990, 'they are edicts', now referred to as FRSses 'by which trading companies that are listed on the stock market must adhere to when constructing their financial reports. They form part of the Generally Accepted Accounting Practice, or GAAP, which is statutory in the United Kingdom through the Taxes Act'. The statement by Woolf J must be taken to be applicable to ZICA adopted IFRSs which guide accounting and auditing reporting procedures in Zambia.

[84] [1983] 1 All ER 583.

knew that the accounts were inaccurate but did not appreciate the full extent of the inaccuracy. The take-over was unsuccessful and the plaintiffs suffered considerable loss as a result. They brought an action against the defendants claiming damages for breach of the defendants' duty of care to the plaintiffs, as prospective buyers of the company, to take care in preparing the company's accounts, alleging that the defendants were negligent in the preparation of the accounts and that the plaintiffs had relied on the accuracy of the accounts in deciding to take over the company. The judge held that the defendants had been negligent in the preparation of the accounts and that the plaintiffs did 'rely on' the accounts in the sense that they had studied the accounts before the take-over and the picture of the company presented by the accounts had encouraged them to proceed with the take-over. However, the judge went on to hold that, because the plaintiffs' motive for the take-over was to obtain the services of the company's two directors and because the plaintiffs had formed their own view as to the value of the company's stock, the plaintiffs would have proceeded with the take-over in any event and therefore the defendants' negligence had not been a cause of the plaintiffs' loss. The judge accordingly dismissed the plaintiffs' action. The plaintiffs appealed, contending that as a matter of law and logic the judge could not on the one hand find that the plaintiffs had relied on the accounts and yet on the other hand dismiss their claim on the ground that the defendants' negligence was not a cause of their loss.

It was held that the terms 'reliance' and 'relied on' were capable of bearing either a narrow and precise meaning of 'induced' or 'wholly dependent on' or a wider meaning of 'being encouraged or supported in' taking a decision by subsidiary factors which if untrue would be a matter of disappointment but would not effect the taking of the decision. Furthermore (per Stephenson LJ), in the context of negligent misrepresentation the false misrepresentation had to play a real and substantial, although not necessarily decisive, part in inducing the plaintiff to act if it was to be a cause of the loss because the plaintiff 'relied on' it (in the narrow sense of that term). The judge had been ambiguous in using the term 'rely on' to mean 'encouraged' rather than 'induced' and he had been wrong to separate out as different issues the question whether the plaintiffs relied on the accounts and the question whether the plaintiffs had suffered loss by relying on the accounts: both were merely different ways of stating the issue of causation. Nevertheless, it was clear that the judge's underlying reasoning had been that although the plaintiffs had been aware of and had considered the accounts they had not to any material degree affected the plaintiffs' judgment in deciding to take over the company, and, on the facts, there was ample evidence to support that conclusion. The appeal would therefore be dismissed.[85]

---

[85] Decision of Woolf J [1981] 3 All ER 289 affirmed.

11.4.5.3.4   Developments in exclusion of liability[86]

The leading case with regard to auditors' liability and exclusion of liability is the New Zealand case of *Scott Group Ltd v McFarlane* (above). A recent Scottish case has recently followed its lead. In *Royal Bank of Scotland Plc v Bannerman Johnstone Maclay (a firm)*,[87] the bank lent money to a company APC Ltd on the strength of accounts audited by the defendants. It was alleged by the claimant that the audited accounts were less than adequately informative in terms, for example, of the going concern factor. The bank had later to appoint a receiver to the company which was insolvent. The auditors had notice that under overdraft facility letters the bank was entitled to see management accounts and annual audited accounts. However, they contended that the claimant had to prove that as auditors they *intended* the bank to rely on the accounts to make further loans or advances. The auditors said in effect 'when auditing the accounts our only intention was to carry out Companies Act duties to audit the accounts'.

The Scottish Court of Session (Outer House) in this case, equally applicable in England and Wales, ruled that the case law did not support a requirement of intention. The compelling effect of the authorities was that knowledge of user and use formed the basis of a duty of care for those making information or advice available. The auditors had the requisite knowledge and therefore owed a duty of care.

On appeal to the Inner House of the Court of Session in May 2005, it was held that the element of positive intention was not a *sine qua non* of the existence of a duty of care and the pursuers were entitled to inquiry on the averments made. The absence of a disclaimer might be a relevant circumstance pointing to an assumption of responsibility in respect of the information or advice tendered.

As was the case in *Scott Group Ltd v McFarlane* (above) the auditors in *Royal Bank of Scotland Plc* had not disclaimed liability to third parties such as the bank. The Institute of Chartered Accountants in England and Wales (ICAEW) (ZICA's rough equivalent) has specified that auditors must, in terms of section 495 of the UK CA 2006 [which is the rough equivalent of section 259 of the Act] be taken to assume responsibility for the contents of the audit report to shareholders as a body. Further, that the effect of the absence of a disclaimer may in certain instances lead the court, as it should, under the circumstances, to draw the conclusion such responsibility has indeed been assumed by the auditors as respects the audit report to a third party. To that end, ICAEW suggests that auditors include the following in audit reports in order to spell out their duty of care to third parties which is indicative of the non-existence of such a duty and that none is owed:

---

[86] See generally Davies LP *Gower and Davies' Principles of Modern Company Law* 7th edn Ch 22 581 -589; and Wild C and Weinstein S *Smith and Keenan's Company Law* 15th edn 526.

[87] 2003 SLT 181; summarised in *Smith and Keenan's Company Law* 15th edn 526.

This report is made solely to the company's members as a body, in accordance with [section 259 of the Companies Act 2017]. Our audit work has been undertaken so that we might state to the company's members those matters we are required to state to them in an auditor's report and for no other purpose. To the fullest extent permitted by law, we do not accept or assume responsibility to anyone other than the company and the company's members as a body, for our audit work, for this report, or for the opinions we have formed.

11.4.5   Preparation of audited financial statement

Under section 265(1), which must be read within the context of section 253, the board of directors must make certain that, 'within three months following the end of the financial year, an audit is conducted, in accordance with subsection (2), and the report of the financial affairs is signed by not less than two directors or, where the company has only one director, by the director'. This is because the company, if it is public, is required and expected to, under section 265(2) submit, 'to the Registrar, within thirty days of it being adopted by the shareholders' the audited financial statement of the company. This is a serious requirement because in terms of section 265(3), '[a] company which fails to submit audited financial statements, as required by subsection (2), commits an offence and is liable, on conviction, to a fine not exceeding one thousand penalty units for each day that the failure continues'. It is also a requirement under section 266 that '[t]he financial statements of a company'…'comply with standards prescribed by the body regulating the practice of accountancy in Zambia'. Since 1994, ZICA has adopted International Financial Reporting Standards (IFRSs) in full and without modification but these are not mandatory for small and medium companies.

11.4.6   Obligation to provide consolidated financial statement

Under section 267(1), '[a] company that has one or more subsidiaries shall prepare, within six months after the end of its financial year, consolidated financial statements'. According to section 267(2), [a] consolidated financial statement shall—

(a)   be signed by not less than two directors of the holding company or, where the holding company has only one director, by the director;

(b)   not be required in the case of a subsidiary of a company incorporated in Zambia; and

(c)   in the case of a company which is required to comply with International Accounting Standards, contain a consolidated—

(i)   financial statement for the group, as at the date of that financial statement; and

(ii) statement of comprehensive income.

11.4.7   *When company becomes subsidiary*

This is covered under section 268 which provides that '[w]here a company becomes a subsidiary of another company during the accounting period to which group financial statements relate, the consolidated profit and loss statement, or the consolidated income and expenditure statement for the group, shall relate to the profit or loss of the subsidiary for each part of that accounting period during which it was a subsidiary and not to any other part of that accounting period'.

Under section 269, [w]here the date of a financial statement of a subsidiary is not the same as that of the holding company, the group financial statements shall—

(a) where the date of the financial statement of the subsidiary does not precede that of the company by more than ninety days, incorporate the financial statements of the subsidiary for the accounting period ending on that date; or

(b) incorporate interim financial statements of the subsidiary completed for a period that is the same as the accounting period of the company.

11.5   Annual return to Registrar

Under section 270(1), '[a] company shall, within ninety days after the end of each financial year, lodge, with the Registrar, an annual return in the prescribed form'. However, section 272(1) provides that '[w]here the status of a company has not changed during the financial year, the company shall file a "no change" return, in the prescribed form, indicating the financial year in which the return is filed and containing a general statement that there has been no change in any given particulars in the return, since the filing of the previous return'.[88] Further to the foregoing, '[a]n annual return that is not filed, within the period specified in subsection (1), shall attract a penalty as prescribed'.[89] It is provided under section 270(3) that '[a]n annual return shall be signed by a director or the secretary and shall, in the case of a public limited company, include annual audited financial statements and updated beneficial ownership information'. By section 270(4), the Registrar is mandated to 'cause to be published in the *Gazette* or in a daily newspaper of general circulation in Zambia or on the website of the Agency or in any other media, a list of companies whose annual returns are

---

[88] That notwithstanding, in terms of section 272(2), provides that '[d]espite the filing by a company of a "no change" return, the Registrar may cause to be inspected any records of a company which the Registrar considers necessary for the better carrying out of this Act'.

[89] Section 270(2).

overdue'. Be that as it may, '[t]he Registrar is not liable for any publication made in good faith in terms of subsection (4)'.[90]

In terms of section 273, [a] public company shall lodge, with the Registrar, together with the annual return required under section 271 the following documents:

(a)   a certified copy of every financial statement;
(b)   statement of comprehensive income;
(c)   group accounts;
(d)   directors' report; and
(e)   auditors' report sent to members and debenture holders since the last annual return was made.

Finally, '[w]here a company adopts a date other than the one recognised for the financial year, it shall give notice of the adopted date to the Registrar, in the prescribed manner and form'.[91]

11.5.1   Filing of annual returns in receivership or liquidation

By section 271, the fact that a company has been placed under receivership or is in the process of being wound-up in accordance with the Corporate Insolvency Act, 2017 is not a bar to filing annual returns. '[T]he receiver or liquidator of the company shall cause an annual return to be filed until the completion of the receivership or winding up'. The rationale is that until the company is dissolved and its name removed from the register of companies, it is still a corporate body subject to the regulatory edifice under the companies Act and related laws.

11.6   Annual reports

11.6.1   Obligation to file and submission to shareholders

The two matters namely the obligation to file returns and the submission of such returns to shareholders are covered under sections 275 and 276. Under section 275 which is subject to section 277, 'the board of directors shall prepare an annual report on the affairs of the company during the accounting period ending on that date'. In terms of section 276, '[t]he board of directors shall cause a copy of the annual report to be sent to every shareholder not less than twenty-one days before the date fixed for the annual general meeting'.

Section 277(1)[92] stipulates that, [a]n annual report will, for obvious reasons of record keeping and solemnity not be orally made or by video or audial recording but be (1) in writing, (2) dated and (3) shall—

---

[90] Section 270(5).
[91] Section 274.
[92] By section 277(2), '[a] company whose subsidiary company is located outside Zambia shall comply with this section within sixty days after the dates specified in this section'.

(a)   contain information describing—

    (i)   the company's affairs, so far as is reasonable for the members to have an appreciation of such affairs, being information which is not harmful to the business of the company or a subsidiary; and

    (ii)   any change in the nature of the business of the company or its subsidiary and the classes of business in which the company has an interest, whether as a member of another company or otherwise, during the accounting period; and

(b)   include the financial statements and any group financial statements for the accounting period completed and signed in accordance with this Act;

(c)   include an auditor's report, where an auditor's report is required to be included in relation to the financial statements or group financial statements;

(d)   include updated beneficial ownership information in respect of shares;

(e)   state particulars of entries in the interests register made during the accounting period;

(f)   state the amount which represents the total of the remuneration and benefits due or received by the company and any related company, corporation or institution by—

    (i)   executive directors engaged full-time by the company and related companies, corporations, or institutions, including all bonuses and commissions received by the executive directors; and

    (ii)   non-executive directors;

(g)   state the total amount of donations made by the company and any subsidiary during the accounting period;

(h)   state the names of the persons—

    (i)   holding office as directors at the end of the accounting period; and

    (ii)   who ceased to hold office as directors during the accounting period;

(i)   state the amounts payable as audit fees by the company to an auditor of the company and, as a separate item, fees payable by the company for other services provided by the auditor; and

(j)   be signed on behalf of the company by not less than two directors or, where the company has only one director at the completion of the annual financial statements, by the director.

11.7   Inspection of company's records

11.7.1   General

Under section 278(1), '[a] company shall make available for inspection, by the Registrar, a delegate of the Registrar or a member or a person authorised in writing by the member, the records specified in section 279, if the Registrar or the member suspects any non- compliance by directors or executive officers'. Subsection (2) mandates that '[a] written notice of intention to inspect records of a company'[…] 'be served on the company not less than three days in advance of the inspection'.

11.7.2   Records to be made available for inspection by members

The records to be made available for inspection, according to section 279 for the purposes of section 278 include but may not be limited to the following—
- *(a)*   minutes of meetings and resolutions of members;
- *(b)*   copies of written communications to shareholders or to holders of a class of shares during the preceding five years, including annual reports, financial statements and group financial statements;
- *(c)*   beneficial ownership records;
- *(d)*   certificates given by directors;
- *(e)*   records relating to directors; and
- *(f)*   the interests register, where applicable.

11.7.3   Manner of inspection and commencement

According to section 280, '[d]ocuments that are to be inspected shall be available for inspection during business hours at the place where the company's records are kept for the inspection period specified in section 281'. To that end, section 281(1) provides that '[a]n inspection period is the period commencing on the third weekday after the day on which notice of intention to inspect is served on a company by a person referred to in section 278, and ending on the eighth weekday after the notice is received'. Finally, in terms of section 281(2), '[a]' member or a person authorised in writing by the member may, on a written request and after payment of a fee, request for a copy of, or extract from, a document which is available for inspection.

11.8   Conclusion

This chapter has explored the provisions under sections 264 to 281. We have noted that the basis for including this aspect of company administration under the Act is founded on the view that the company ought to be transparent about its financial matters because shareholders and third parties who have business dealings with the company have a right to know the viability of the company. We have noted that this is for good reason as the viability of a company is more often than not determined by the health of its finances. By these, shareholders can determine whether the board of directors are adding to shareholder value. The finances are also a useful guide to the board of directors as to whether they should maintain or change course. For creditors the financial indicators help them determine whether they should take active steps to secure the money the company owes. Another part of our discussion has related to audits. We have noted that the goal of an audit, among other things, is to add trustworthiness to financial statements which form part of the annual accounts.

FURTHER READING

Books

Davies PL *Gower and Davies' Principles of Modern Company Law* 7th edn (Thomson Sweet & Maxwell London 2003).

Farrah JH and Hannigan BM *Farrar's Company Law* 4th edn (Butterworths London 1998).

Gates RB *Gates Company Law and Practice in Zambia* (Reagan Blankfein Gates Lusaka 2017).

Sealy L and Worthington S *Sealy & Worthington's Cases and Materials in Company Law* 10th edn (Oxford University Press Oxford 2013).

Wild C and Weinstein S *Smith and Keenan's Company Law* 15th edn (Pearson Education Ltd Essex 2011).

12

SCHEMES OF ARRANGEMENT, RECONSTRUCTION AND AMALGAMATION

AIMS AND OBJECTIVES

 After reading this chapter you should appreciate the following:

- ➢ Compromise between company, creditors and members
- ➢ Effect of compromise or arrangement with creditors and members
- ➢ Reconstruction and amalgamation of companies
- ➢ Amalgamation
- ➢ Amalgamation proposal
- ➢ Amalgamation resolution
- ➢ Documents for submission to shareholders
- ➢ Procedures before amalgamation
- ➢ Approving amalgamation proposal
- ➢ Notice of amalgamation to creditors
- ➢ Lodgement of documents for amalgamation
- ➢ Certificate of amalgamation or of incorporation
- ➢ Removing amalgamating companies from register
- ➢ Property, rights, powers and privileges of amalgamated company
- ➢ Liabilities and obligations of amalgamated company
- ➢ Enforcement of Court ruling by or against amalgamated company
- ➢ Objection to amalgamation
- ➢ Conversion of shares and rights in amalgamation proposal

12.1   Introduction

We have already considered in the chapters preceding our current discussion, methods in and by which a company can alter its structure including the fact that in terms of section 25(2), '[t]he articles *may* contain restrictions on the type of business that a company may carry on or the powers exercisable by the company'. Further, in terms of section 25(3), the company is, unless its articles, restrict it from doing so in terms of section 25(1), at liberty to '…carry on any business or exercise…. any powers'. Put another way, a company's power to change its objects over the course of its life is virtually unlimited unless its articles provide otherwise. Other methods we considered through which structural change may come about include conversion from one form to another under sections 48 to 55; alteration of shareholder rights under section 136; variation of class rights under section 143; reduction of share capital under sections 150 and 151;[1] and acquisition by a company of its own shares in terms of sections 163 to 166.

Given the foregoing, it begs the question why we have to specifically deal with the topic of schemes of arrangement, compromise and reconstruction now provided for under sections 46, 47 and 48[2] of the Corporate Insolvency Act, 2017[3] and amalgamation under sections 282 to 296 of Part XIII of the Act.[4] It has been contended by two jurists[5] that,

> [t]he reason is that the provisions referred to above do not permit a company to *compel* a shareholder to sell or otherwise dispose of his shares, except as part of a reduction when he is, for example, paid off,… Nor do they allow the rights of creditors to be affected or enable the liability of members to be increased without their individual consent. Nor, again, do they provide a means of amalgamating two or more companies or the transfer of the undertaking of one company to another, or the demerger or partition of a company into separate management in another company or companies.

It ought to be remembered also that certain company species such as those limited by guarantee may not have the procedures we have considered so far in this text open to them due to want of share capital. Under such circumstances, recourse can only be had by invoking sections 46, 47 and 48 of the Corporate Insolvency Act, 2017.

This chapter therefore explores other methods exploited by companies to alter their structures due to problems brought about by and arising from the company's relationship with its creditors. The problems have the potential to have the company wound-up. As may be discernible however,[6] the winding-up route is an extreme step with far reaching consequences. It follows therefore that continuing to run the company under the devices of a scheme of arrangement,

---

[1] But according to 46(1),… "arrangement" includes a reorganisation of the share capital of the company by the consolidation of shares of different classes, or by the division of shares in shares of different classes or by both methods'.

[2] By way of comparison see sections 895, 896 and 897 of the UK CA 2006.

[3] Replacing sections 234 and 235 under Part XI of CA 1994.

[4] Which are expanded provisions replacing section 236 under Part XI of CA 1994.

[5] Wild C and Weinstein S *Smith and Keenan's Company Law* 15th edn 532.

[6] See Part V-VII of the Corporate Insolvency Act No 9 of 2017.

reconstruction and/or amalgamation may be more appropriate. The chapter is arranged in two major parts with the first dealing with schemes of arrangements and compromise and the second with reconstruction amalgamation of companies. We discuss these in turn.

12.2   Schemes of arrangement and compromise

12.2.1   General

The Corporate Insolvency Act, 2017 seems to make no distinction in dealing with the issue of arrangement and compromise. As such, sections 46 and 47 of that Act provide for these processes together and make no separation. Section 48 also under the Corporate Insolvency Act, 2017 while dealing with reconstruction, also makes provision for amalgamation.[7] While this drafting style seems to have been preferred and may have a theoretical justification, the practical realities are far removed from the picture it seems to create and can be a source of confusion for some. We have therefore attempted to discuss these matters separately, while at the same time acknowledging the statutory provisions relating to arrangement, compromise, reconstruction and amalgamation both in the Corporate Insolvency Act, 2017 and the Companies Act, 2017.[8]

12.2.2   Compromise

The expression compromise has been defined as follows: A settlement or adjustment of dispute or controversy by mutual concessions. In case of compromise, the parties agree to settle their controversy by mutual concessions. In case of compromise, the parties agree to settle their dispute by some [give and take] arrangement. It may be noted that the compromise presupposes the existence of some dispute, because there can be no compromise unless there is some dispute. The need for compromise may arise for the settlement of some dispute between the company and its creditors or members.[9]

12.2.3 Compromise between company, creditors and members

The starting point in this discussion is section 46. In terms of subsection (2), section 46, 'applies to a company, irrespective of whether or not it is financially distressed'.

According to section 46(3), '[a] company, creditor or member of a company may apply to the Court for an order that a meeting of the creditors or members

---

[7] Also provided for as shown below under Part XIII: sections 282-296 of CA 2017.

[8] By way of comparison provisions relating to arrangements and reconstruction are provided for under CA 2006, sections 895, 896 and 899 of the UK CA 2006 sections 110 *et seqs* of the UK Insolvency Act 1986.

[9] Gogna PPS *A Textbook of Company Law* (S. Chand & Company Ltd New Delhi 2004) 374.

or class of members, as the case may be, be convened and conducted to consider the compromise or arrangement'. Further and according to section 46(4), '[w]here a compromise or arrangement is proposed between—

    (a)   a company and its creditors or any class of its creditors; or

    (b)   a company and its members or any class of its members; the Court may, on the application referred to in subsection (3), or, in the case of a company being wound-up, of the liquidator, order a meeting of the creditors, class of creditors, members or class of members, as the case may be, to be convened and conducted to consider the compromise or arrangement'.[10]

By subsection (7), '[u]nless the Court orders otherwise, the voting power at a meeting of creditors ordered to be convened as specified in this section shall be assigned to the creditors in proportion to the amount of the debt outstanding from the company to each creditor'. Additionally, subsection (8) provides that '[w]here a meeting, by extraordinary resolution, agrees to a compromise or arrangement, the compromise or arrangement—

    (a)   shall be binding on all the creditors or class of creditors or on the members or class of members, as the case may be; and

    (b)   shall be binding on the company if and when—

        (i)   it has been approved by order of the Court; and

        (ii)   a copy of the order of the Court has been lodged with the Registrar'.

'Where an extraordinary resolution agreeing to a compromise or arrangement has been passed at a meeting convened as specified in this section, the company or any person who was entitled to vote at the meeting may apply to the Court for approval of the compromise or arrangement'.[11] By subsection (10), '[a]t a hearing by the Court of the application for approval of the compromise or arrangement, a member or creditor of the company claiming to be affected thereby is entitled to be represented and to object'. It has to be noted that '[t]he Court may prescribe such terms, as it considers appropriate, as a condition of its approval, including a condition that a member shall have the right to require the company to purchase shares at a price fixed by the Court or to be determined in a manner provided in the order, and, in that case, for the reduction of the company's capital accordingly'.[12]

---

[10] In terms of subsection (5), '[s]ubject to an order of the Court, the Companies Act, 2017 shall apply to a meeting of members or a class of members ordered to be convened as specified in this section'. By subsection(6), '[s]ubject to an order of the Court, the Companies Act, 2017 shall apply, with the necessary modifications, to a meeting of creditors or class of creditors ordered to be convened as specified in this section'.

[11] Section 46(9).

[12] Section 46(11).

In the event that '…an order is made approving the compromise or arrangement: *(a)* the company shall lodge a copy of the order with the Registrar within twenty-one days after the making of the order;[13] and *(b)[14]* a copy of the order shall be annexed to or incorporated in every copy of the articles issued after the order was made'.[15] We must also be alive to the fact that '[w]here an order, made under this section, has the effect of altering the share capital of the company, the Registrar, on lodgment of the copy of the order, shall issue a replacement certificate of the share capital of the company, worded to meet the circumstances of the case'.[16]

12.2.4 *Effect of compromise or arrangement with creditors and members*

The 'effect of compromise or arrangement with creditors and members is covered under section 47. In terms of section 47(1), [w]here a meeting of creditors or any class of creditors or of members or any class of members is convened in accordance with this Part, the company shall prepare a statement explaining the effect of the compromise or arrangement and in particular stating any material interests of the directors in the company or a related body corporate, whether as directors or as members or as creditors of the company or otherwise, and the effect of the compromise or arrangement, in so far as it is different from the effect on the like interests of other persons.

In terms of section 47(2), '[w]here a compromise or arrangement affects the rights of debenture holders of the company, the statement, prepared in accordance with subsection (1), shall apply to debenture holders of a company or trustee related thereto'. It is a requirement that '[a] copy of the statement of the kind specified in subsection (1) '…be sent to every creditor or member with the notice of the meeting to be convened….'[17]

There is a further requirement in terms of section 47(4) that '[a] notice of a meeting', to be convened mentioned above, '…be issued by advertisement in a newspaper of general circulation in Zambia and in any other media and shall include a copy of the statement or specify where the members or creditors entitled to attend the meeting may obtain copies of the statement, which statement shall be given free of charge to any creditor or member'. By section 47(5), '[i]f a company fails to comply with this section, the company, and each officer in

---

[13] By subsection (14), '[i]f a company fails to comply with subsection (12) *(a)*, the company, and each officer in default, commits an offence and is liable, on conviction, to a fine not exceeding three thousand penalty units for each day that the failure continues'.

[14] By subsection (15), '[i]f a company issues a copy of its articles that does not comply with subsection (12) *(b)*, the company and each officer in default commits an offence and is liable, on conviction, to a fine not exceeding three thousand penalty units in respect of each copy issued'.

[15] Section 46(12).

[16] Section 46(13).

[17] Section 47(3).

default, commits an offence and shall be liable, on conviction, to a fine not exceeding fifteen thousand penalty units'. In terms of section 47(6) however, '[i]t is a defence to a prosecution under subsection (5) to show that failure was due to the refusal of another person to supply the necessary particulars relating to an interest in the company or related body corporate'.

12.2.5 Arrangement

The term 'arrangement' has, by comparison to the term 'compromise' a wider meaning. In terms of 46(1), '…"arrangement" includes a reorganisation of the share capital of the company by the consolidation of shares of different classes, or by the division of shares in shares of different classes or by both methods. This is exemplified in the case of *In Re Guardian Assurance Co*[18] where an assurance company presented a petition under s.120 of the UK (Consolidated) Act, 1980, for the sanction of the Court to a proposed arrangement for the fusion of the company's interests with those of a marine insurance company, and for the subdivision of its shares in order to carry out the arrangement. The scheme involved that each of the petitioning company's shareholders should contribute a portion of his holding in the company to be transferred to the marine insurance company and its shareholders, and it had been approved by the requisite majority of the shareholders n general meeting. Younger J., while approving the scheme as being advantageous to the interests of the company, refused to sanction it on the ground that s.120 necessarily involved some kind of dispute or difficulty to be resolved by a compromise or arrangement, and that there was none shown to him in the present case. It was held on appeal, that the scheme, though not a 'compromise', was an 'arrangement' within the section, and that there was no ground for limiting the meaning of the word 'arrangement' to something analogous to a compromise.[19]

In addition, it has been shown that an arrangement may also include on the one hand, a procedure of debenture holders who are agreeable to an extension where the company may pay back the debt owed and on the other, one where the debtors agree to taking a 'hair cut' or are compelled to lose the entire value of the debentures[20] as exemplified in the case of *The Philadelphia Securities Co v The Realisation Corp of Scotland Ltd.*[21] To be included in the term 'arrangement', as exemplified in the case of *Re Empire Mining Co*[22] is an agreement where there is an exchange of debentures for shares in the company in question or in another company. In that case, it was shown that the power given to the Court by

---

[18] [1917] 1 Ch 431 (CA).
[19] Decision of Younger J. reversed.
[20] Or less than the face value of the debentures in question.
[21] [1903] 11 SLT 217 (OH).
[22] [1890] 44 Ch D 402.

joint Stock Companies[23]Arrangement Act, 1870, to sanction a scheme between a company and its creditors, extends to debenture-holders, and the Court has jurisdiction to deprive dissentient debenture-holders, of their security, and to sanction a scheme which provides that they shall accept fully paid shares in satisfaction of their claims. But the Court will not sanction a scheme merely because it has been approved by a large majority of creditors; it will require to be satisfied that the proposed arrangement is fair and equitable.

As illustrated in *Wright & Greig Ltd., Petitioners,*[24] an arrangement may entail the variation of creditor or debenture holder rights only in some respects. Additionally, debenture holders or creditors may choose to be paid partly in cash and partly in shares or debentures as the case may be in the new company. By the same token, preference shareholders may be compelled to drop their claim to arrears owed to them by the company involved in the arrangement and instead, agree to a reduced dividend or a variation of their class rights.

In *In Re Calgary and Edmonton Land Co Ltd*[25] a company had been in a creditors' winding up since May 21, 1970. The applicant, as a shareholder and director of the company, took out a summons for a stay of the winding up and other relief. He presented no proposals for discharging the claims of the remaining creditors or the liquidator's expenses, nor did he present any scheme to give effect to the rights of shareholders who might oppose the stay. The registrar dismissed the summons on the ground that it ought to have been preceded by a scheme under section 206 of the UK CA., 1948 giving members an opportunity of putting forward their views. It was held on the applicant's motion that the registrar's order be discharged:

(1)   That section 307(1) and (2) of the UK CA of 1948 extended section 256(1) to a voluntary winding up, that the jurisdiction of the court under section 256 was discretionary, and that it was for those who sought a stay to make out a sufficient case.

(2)   That although, on a winding up, section 302 of the UK CA 1948 entitled each member to an aliquot share of the company's surplus assets, the member's rights could not be quantified until the liquidation was complete; and that, normally, no stay should be granted unless each member either consented to it, or was bound not to object to it (whether by a scheme under section 206 of the UK CA, 1948 or otherwise), or there was secured to him the right to receive all that he would have received had the winding up proceeded to its conclusion; and that as this was not the case, the motion ought to be dismissed.[26]

---

[23] Or simply companies.

[24] 1911 1 SLT 353

[25] [1975] 1 WLR 355; [1975] 1 All ER 1046.

[26] *In re Trix Ltd* [1970] 1 WLR 1421 applied.

As the term pertains to members, Megarry J. has opined that, The word arrangement [...] is very wide in its meaning, and if the members of a company in liquidation agree with the company to seek or not to oppose a stay of the winding up, where under the members will give up their existing right to have all the proceeds of the company's assets distributed among them and instead be remitted to their contractual rights under the articles of the company, I do not see why that cannot be described as an "arrangement" between "the company and its members"[....][27]

Two further authorities merit our consideration: The first is *Re NFU Development Trust Ltd.*[28] The NFU Development Trust Ltd was a company limited by guarantee without a share capital, its objects being generally to further, encourage and assist the farming community and in particular farmers engaged in the production of fat stock. The NFU Development Co Ltd was a member of the company. In addition there were about 94,000 other members all of whom were farmers, farming companies or retired farmers. The company's assets exceeded £3,000,000.00 and its liabilities were less than £25,000.00. Members were elected by the board. Their only obligation was to pay an entrance fee of 25p and to contribute 5p should the company's assets be deficient. The articles provided that no dividends should be paid to members but that , on winding-up, surplus assets would be divided among members in such proportion as the board might determine and in default of such determination equally between the members. Members had the right to elect members of nine area 'electoral colleges' each of which appointed a member of the board, other members of the board being appointed by the NFU Development Co Ltd and the farmers' unions. Every member had a right to vote at a general of the company save that on a resolution to alter the memorandum or articles, to wind up the company or to remove or appoint a director, the NFU Development Co Ltd had three times the number of votes cast by all other members who voted. In order to reduce the expenses of administration the board proposed a scheme reducing the membership of the company to seven, one of the seven being the NFU Development Co Ltd, and depriving all other members of their membership. At the meeting directed by the court 1,439 votes were cast, seven in person and the remainder by proxy. 1,211 votes were cast in favour of the scheme and 228 against, a majority of almost 85 per cent. On a petition to sanction the scheme under s 206 of the UK CA 1948 the objectors contended, inter alia, that, as the company had no share capital and the right of membership was non-transferable and ceased on death, it was impossible to ascertain whether a particular majority represented three-fourths in value of those present and voting as required by s 206(2) of the 1948 Act. It was held as follows:-

---

[27] [1975] 1 WLR 355 at page 363.
[28] [1973] 1 All ER 135.

(1)   In a case such as the present where each member had precisely the same financial stake in the company, every member had in law an identical stake. The position was therefore the same as if each member owned a single share in the company, with the result that a three-fourths majority of members present and voting satisfied the requirements of s 206(2)[29]

(2)   However the scheme would not be sanctioned because the terms of the scheme were such that it did not qualify as a 'compromise or arrangement' between the company and its members within s 206 of the 1948 UK CA. The words 'compromise' and 'arrangements' implied some element of accommodation on each side and were not apt to describe a total surrender of the rights of one side. Since the rights of members were being expropriated without any compensation advantage, it could not be said that they were entering into a compromise or arrangement with the company.[30]

The second is *Re Savoy Hotel Ltd.*[31] In that case, the issued ordinary share capital of a company was divided into A and B shares. The A and B shares carried 40 times as many votes as A shares of an equivalent nominal value. Accordingly, the holders of the A shares, who together owned 97.7 percent of the equity, were entitled to only 51.45 percent of the votes whilst the holders of the B shares, who together owned only 2.3 percent of the equity, were entitled to 48.55 percent of the votes. Moreover, some 65 percent of the B shares (carrying about 31.68 percent of the votes) were held by members of the company's board either beneficially or as trustees. In practice, therefore, the B shareholders controlled the company in general meetings and could block an outside offer to acquire the company's share capital. The applicant, another company, was the beneficial owner of 88,000 A shares, of which 44,000 were registered in its name. The applicant did not own or hold any B shares. The applicant wished to acquire control of the company and proposed to the company a transfer scheme of arrangements to be sanctioned by the Court under section 206 of the UK CA 1948, whereby the applicant was to acquire all the company's A and B shares (other than those it already held) in exchange for shares in the applicant or cash sums. The applicant applied to the court under section 206(1) for an order giving it liberty to convene separate meetings of the A and B shareholders to implement the scheme. The applicant's purpose in convening separate meetings was to obtain at the meeting of the A shareholders at 75 percent majority in favour of the scheme and thereby to make the scheme binding on the company, under section 206(2). The scheme did not provide for the company's approval to be obtained in general meetings

---

[29] *Re Albert Life Assurance Co* [1871] 6 Ch App 381 distinguished.
[30] Dictum of Bowen LJ in *Re Alabama, New Orleans, Texas and Pacific Junction Railway Co* [1891] 1 Ch at 243 applied.
[31] [1981] 3 All ER 646.

and was disapproved of by the board of the company. The only provision in the scheme which in terms involved the company's participation was a clause conferring power on the applicant, in order to give effect to the transfer of the shares, to appoint a third party to execute a transfer of the shares in its favour in place of the existing shareholder and requiring the company to register a transfer of shares in favour of the applicant provided certain conditions were satisfied. The company opposed the application to convene separate meetings of the A and B shareholders on the ground that the court had no jurisdiction to sanction the proposed scheme, and submitted (i) that the scheme was not one "between" the company and its members or any class of them, within section 206(1), since it did not sufficiently materially affect the rights and obligations between it in the absence of the company's approval, and (iii) that therefore the court either had no power to convene the meetings or, in the exercise of its discretion, ought not to convene them in all the circumstance. It was held as follows:-

(1)   The word 'arrangement' in s 206 of the 1948 UK CA was to be interpreted widely, and, since the scheme would affect the contractual relationship subsisting between the company and its members by requiring the company to register the applicant in place of existing members as the holders of the company's shares, the rights and obligations between the company and its members were sufficiently affected for the proposed scheme to be an 'arrangement...between' them within section 206(1)[32]

(2)   However, since section 206(1) of the UK CA 1948 referred to an arrangement 'proposed between' a company and, *inter alios*, its members, that assumed consent by the company, as a legal personality separate from its members, to the arrangement. Accordingly, the court had no jurisdiction under section 206 to sanction an arrangement regarding the members of a company which did not have the company's approval, either through its board or by the majority of the members in a general meeting. It followed that the court had no jurisdiction to sanction the applicant's scheme.[33]

(3)   Furthermore, although the court had power under section 206(1) of the 1948 Act to order that separate meetings of the A and B shareholders be convened, in all the circumstances the court would exercise its discretion to refuse to exercise that power because the company's board had withheld approval of the scheme, the scheme did not provide for approval to be obtained in general meeting, the board was unlikely to reconsider its attitude or to approve the scheme and accordingly the

---

[32] *Re Guardian Assurance Co* [1917] 1 Ch 431, dictum of Plowman J in *Re National Bank Ltd* [1966] 1 All ER at 1012 and dictum of Megarry J in *Re Calgary and Edmonton Land Co Ltd* [1975] 1 All ER at 1054 applied.

[33] *Re International Contract Co, Hankey's Case* [1872] 26 LT 358 and *Re Oceanic Steam Navigation Co Ltd* [1938] 3 All ER 740 applied.

meetings would not serve any useful purpose. The application would therefore be dismissed.

It will be noted immediately that section 206(1) and (2) of the UK CA, 1948 on which the actions in *In Re Calgary and Edmonton Land Co Ltd*, *Re NFU Development Trust Ltd* and *Re Savoy Hotel Ltd* discussed above, among others, were premised and largely decided is similar to section 46(2)(6) and to some extent section 46(7) of the Corporate Insolvency Act, 2017. The foregoing authorities would therefore be of considerable persuasive value should a similar action be brought before the Zambian High Court under section 46 of the Corporate Insolvency Act. It is to the statutory provisions regarding schemes of arrangements and compromises that we now turn.

12.3   *Reconstruction and amalgamation*

While neither the Act nor the Corporate Insolvency Act, 2017 define the term 'reconstruction', the Act does define the term 'amalgamation'. It has been suggested that 'a reconstruction is said to occur 'where a company transfers its assets to a new company with substantially the same shareholders'.[34] In terms of section 2 of the Act, "amalgamation" means the combination of two or more companies to form a new body corporate as provided for in section 282 (discussed below) and the word amalgamating shall be construed accordingly'. Further, an "amalgamated company" means a company that comes into existence as a result of an amalgamation as specified in section 282. Put another way, an amalgamation means nothing more and nothing less than the merger of two or more companies to form one entity. In this portion of the chapter, we consider statutory procedures relating to reconstructions and agreed amalgamations[35]

12.3.1   *Reconstruction and amalgamation of companies: Corporate Insolvency Act, 2017*

This part of our discussion is based on section 48 of the Corporate Insolvency Act, 2017. According to section 48(1), [w]here an application is made to the Court, as specified in this Part, to approve a compromise or arrangement and it is shown to the Court that—

(a)   the compromise or arrangement has been proposed for the purposes of, or in connection with, a scheme for-

    (i)   the reconstruction of any company or group of companies; or

    (ii)   the amalgamation of any two or more companies; and

---

[34] Charlesworth's Company Law…94.

[35] Agreed amalgamations should be distinguished from "Take-overs" which are a contested species of amalgamations with which we are not concerned here and must be considered under the Competition and Consumer Protection Act, 2010 and the Securities Act, 2016.

(b)   under the scheme, the whole or any part of the undertaking or property of a company, in this section referred to as "the transferor company", is to be transferred to another company, in this section referred to as "the transferee company"; the Court may, by order approving the compromise or arrangement or by a subsequent order, provide for any of the following:

    (i)   the transfer to the transferee company of the whole or any part of the undertaking and property or liabilities of the transferor company;

    (ii)   the allotment or appropriation by the transferee company of any shares, debentures, policies or other like interests in the transferor company which under the compromise or arrangement are to be allotted or appropriated by the transferor company to or for any person;

    (iii) the continuation by or against the transferee company of any legal proceedings pending by or against the transferor company; (iv) the dissolution, without winding-up, of the transferor company; (v) the provision to be made for any persons who, within such time and in such manner as the Court directs, dissent to the compromise or arrangement; or (vi) such incidental, consequential and supplementary matters as are necessary to secure that the reconstruction or amalgamation is fully and effectively carried out.

In terms of section 48(2), [w]here an order, made in accordance with this section, provides for the transfer of property or liabilities—

(a)   the property shall, by virtue of the order, be transferred to, and vest in, the transferee company and shall, if the order so directs, be freed from any charge which is under compromise or arrangement to cease to have effect; and

(b)   the liabilities shall, by virtue of the order, be transferred to, and become the liabilities of, the transferee company'.

According to section 48(3), '[w]here an order is made, in accordance with this section, every company in relation to which the order is made shall cause a copy of the order to be lodged with the Registrar within fifteen days after the making of the order'. By subsection (4), '[i]f a company fails to comply with subsection (3), the company, and each officer in default, commit an offence and are liable, on conviction, to a fine not exceeding ten thousand penalty units for each day that the failure continues'.

12.3.2　Amalgamation under the Companies Act, 2017

The Act permits for a scenario where two or more companies can 'amalgamate and continue as one of the companies in the amalgamation or as an entity incorporated in accordance with this Act'. Such amalgamation will come under the purview of the Competition and Consumer Protection Act, 2010 in addition to the requirements under part XIII of the Act.

12.3.3　Amalgamation proposal

Section 283 stipulates that, …person undertaking an amalgamation shall, in a proposal to amalgamate, set out the terms of the amalgamation, in particular the—

- *(a)*　name of the amalgamated company;
- *(b)*　registered office of the amalgamated company;
- *(c)*　full names and residential addresses of directors of the amalgamated company;
- *(d)*　address for the registered office of the amalgamated company;
- *(e)*　share structure of the amalgamated company, specifying the
- (i)　number of shares of the company; and (ii) rights, privileges, limitations and conditions attached to each share of the company;
- *(f)*　manner in which the shares of each company that is proposed to be amalgamated are to be converted into shares of the amalgamated company;
- *(g)*　consideration that the holders of those shares are to receive;
- *(h)*　payment to be made, if any, to a shareholder or a director of the amalgamated company;
- *(i)*　details of any arrangement necessary to complete the amalgamation and the subsequent management and operation of the amalgamated company;
- *(j)*　copy of the articles of the amalgamated company; and
- *(k)*　date on which the amalgamation shall become effective.

12.3.4　Amalgamation resolution

In terms of section 284(1), '[t]he board of each company which is proposed to be amalgamated shall resolve that the—

- *(a)*　amalgamation is in the best interest of the company; and
- *(b)*　board of directors is satisfied, on reasonable grounds specified, that the amalgamated company shall, immediately after the amalgamation, satisfy the solvency test'. There is an additional stipulation under

subsection (2) for '[t]he directors who vote in favour of a resolution to amalgamate as specified in' subsection 1', to 'make a declaration as to the matters resolved' in the said resolution.

12.3.5   Documents for submission to shareholders

Under section 285, [t]he board of directors of each company which is to be amalgamated shall, not less than thirty days before the amalgamation is proposed to take effect, send to each shareholder—

(a)   a copy of the proposal for amalgamation;

(b)   copies of the declarations made by the directors in compliance with section 284;

(c)   a summary of the principal provisions of the articles of the company;

(d)   a statement—
  (i)   that a copy of the articles of the proposed amalgamated company shall be supplied to a shareholder who requests it;
  (ii)   setting out the rights of shareholders; and
  (iii)   of any material interests of the directors, whether in that capacity or otherwise; and

(e)   such other information and explanation as may be necessary to enable a shareholder to understand the nature and implications for the company and its shareholders of the proposed amalgamation.

12.3.6   Procedures before amalgamation

According to section 286, [t]he board of directors of each amalgamating company shall, not less than thirty days before the amalgamation is proposed to take effect—

(a)   send a copy of the proposal to amalgamate to every secured creditor;

(b)   give public notice of the proposed amalgamation, in the prescribed form, including a statement that—
  (i)   copies of the proposal to amalgamate are available at the registered offices of the companies to be amalgamated and at such other places, as may be specified for inspection, during normal business hours; and
  (ii)   a shareholder or creditor of the amalgamating company, or any person to whom the company is under an obligation, is entitled to be supplied at no cost, with a copy of the proposal to amalgamate on request.

It ought to be remembered that in terms of section 287, '[a] proposal to amalgamate be approved by special resolution of the shareholders of each amalgamating company to be amalgamated'. Additionally, in terms of section 288, '[t]he board of directors of each company to be amalgamated shall, not less than thirty days before the amalgamation is proposed to take effect, give written notice of the proposed amalgamation to every creditor of the company'.

12.3.7 Lodgement of documents for amalgamation

Section 289 provides that, for the purpose of effecting an amalgamation, the following documents shall be lodged with the Registrar:

(a) an application for registration of the amalgamated company in the prescribed form signed by each of the persons named in the proposal to amalgamate as a director or secretary of the amalgamated company consenting to act as a director or secretary of the amalgamated company;

(b) the special resolution required by section 287, together with the approved proposal to amalgamate;

(c) a declaration—

    (i) stating that the amalgamation has been approved in accordance with this Act which shall be signed by not less than two directors of each company to be amalgamated or, where a company has only one director, by the director; and

    (ii) signed by the board of directors of the amalgamated company stating that, where the proportion of the claims of creditors of the amalgamated company in relation to the value or the assets of the company is greater than theproportion of the claims of creditors of the amalgamated company in relation to the value of the assets of the amalgamated company, no creditor shall be prejudiced by that fact.

12.3.8 Certificate of amalgamation or/and incorporation et seq

According to section 290, [t]he Registrar shall, on receiving the documents specified in section 289—

(a) where the amalgamated company is the same as one of the companies being amalgamated, issue a certificate of amalgamation; or

(b) where the amalgamated company is a new company—

    (i) enter the particulars of the company on the Register; and

    (ii) issue a certificate of incorporation in the prescribed form and manner, to the company.

The foregoing must be followed by the removal of amalgamating companies from register in terms of section 291. The Registrar shall only retain the name of the amalgamated company. Related to the foregoing is the issue of how to deal with the property, rights, powers and privileges of amalgamated company.

In terms of section 292, the '[t]he property, rights, powers and privileges of each company which has been amalgamated, which has been removed from the Register, shall be the property, rights, powers and privileges of the amalgamated company'.

In terms of section 293, '[a]n amalgamated company shall continue to be liable for all the liabilities and obligations of each of the companies which have been amalgamated and all pending proceedings by or against such companies shall be continued by or against the amalgamated company'. Related to the foregoing is section 294 which provides that as regards any judicial proceedings, '[t]he decision of the Court in favour of, or against, a company which has been amalgamated may be enforced by, or against, the amalgamated company'. At the same time, '[a] shareholder, debenture holder, creditor or other interested person may make an objection to an amalgamation before the Court'.[36]

Finally, in terms of section 296, '[a] provision in a proposal to amalgamate relating to the conversion of shares and rights of shareholders in the companies to be amalgamated shall have effect according to the terms of the amalgamation'.

12.4   Conclusion

This chapter has explored methods other than conversion and alteration of capital that companies exploit to change their structures due to in part, to challenges brought about by and arising from the company's relationship with its creditors. These challenges have the potential to have the company wound-up, an extreme step with far reaching consequences. We have noted that it is far more profitable to run the company under the devices of a scheme of arrangement, reconstruction and/or amalgamation.

FURTHER READING

Articles

Hunter, M, 'The Nature and Functions of a Rescue Culture' [1999] JBL 491.

Xie, B, 'Regulating pre-packaged administration – a complete agenda' [2011] JBL 513.

Books

Davies PL *Gower and Davies' Principles of Modern Company Law* 7th edn. (Thomson Sweet & Maxwell London 2003).

Farrah JH and Hannigan BM *Farrar's Company Law* 4th edn (Butterworths London 1998).

---

[36] Section 295.

Gates RB *Gates Company Law and Practice in Zambia* (Reagan Blankfein Gates Lusaka 2017).

Goode R *Principles of Corporate Insolvency Law, Student* 4th edn (R) (Sweet & Maxwell London 2011).

Sealy L and Worthington S *Sealy & Worthington's Cases and Materials in Company Law* 10th edn (Oxford University Press Oxford 2013).

Wild C and Weinstein S *Smith and Keenan's Company Law* 15th edn (Pearson Education Ltd Essex 2011).

Reports

Insolvency Law and Practice, 'Report of the Insolvency Law Review Committee' (Cmnd. 8558, 1982) (The 'Cork Report').

DTI, 'Productivity and Enterprise – Insolvency: A second Chance' (Cm. 5234, 2001).

DTI/Treasury, 'Report by the Review Group on the Review of Company Rescue and Business Reconstruction Mechanisms' (2000).

13

FOREIGN COMPANIES[1]

13.1   Introduction

The dual role of the Act namely to enable the incorporation of the company and regulate its operations extends to companies that are incorporated outside this jurisdiction but which under the Act still need to be registered as foreign (registered) companies. In terms of section 2, '[a] "foreign company" means—

---

[1]   Formerly covered under Part XII: Sections 240 – 261 of CA 1994.

(a) a body corporate formed outside Zambia that has been registered under this Act;[2] or *(b)* an existing foreign company, subject to section 297'. Our goal in this chapter is to explore statutory provisions relating to foreign companies as regards the following: Application of Act to existing foreign company; Register of foreign Companies; Registration of foreign company; Established place of business; Financial year of foreign company; Returns required on alteration of registered particulars; Foreign company to appoint local director; Responsibilities of local directors; Service on foreign company; Annual accounts of foreign company; Maintenance of accounting records; Name of foreign company; Publication of name of foreign company; Registration of charges by foreign company; Notification of winding up of foreign company; Winding up of foreign company in Zambia; Cessation of business of foreign company; Invitation to the public relating to foreign companies; Invitation to public relating to other foreign corporates; and Penalties and disabilities. We discuss each in turn.

13.2   Application of Act to existing foreign company

Part XIV of the Act applies to any existing company deemed as such in any of the following situations, that is to say, if—

(a)   it had been duly registered in accordance with this Act as a foreign company; and

(b)   any document that, in accordance with the repealed Act, was duly lodged by it with the Registrar, or duly registered by the Registrar, had been duly lodged or registered in accordance with this Act.

13.3   Register and registration of foreign Companies

The Registrar is mandated under section 298 to 'maintain a Register of Foreign Companies for the purposes of Part XIV.

In terms of section 299(1),[3] a corporate formed outside Zambia may register as a foreign company by lodging with the Registrar an application for registration accompanied with the following documents and/or particulars:

(a)   the name of the company;

(b)   the nature of the company's business or main objects;

---

[2] In terms of section 364(2)(b), [a] person who, not being a body corporate— whose members have limited liability under the laws of the country of its incorporation, trades or carries on business in Zambia under a name or title the last word of which is "Limited" or any contraction or imitation thereof, or any equivalent in a language other than English; commits an offence and is liable, on conviction, to a fine not exceeding one thousand penalty units for each day that the person trades or carries on business under that name or title.

[3] By subsection(3) '[t]he application, referred to in subsection (1), may specify a date, not less than twelve months and not more than fifteen months after the date of lodgement of the application, on which the second financial year of the company shall begin'.

(c)   the beneficial ownership of the shareholding in the country of incorporation;

(d)   the relevant particulars of the persons who are to be the local directors specifying which person is to be the local chairperson;[4]

(e)   the number and par value, if any, of the company's authorised and issued shares, and the amount paid thereon, distinguishing between the amounts paid and payable in cash and the amounts paid and payable other than in cash, if the company has shares;

(f)   the address of the company's registered or principal office in the country of its incorporation;

(g)   subject to subsection (5), the physical address of an office in Zambia to be the company's registered office; and

(h)   a postal address of the company in Zambia.[5]

According to section 299(4), [t]he application, referred to in subsection (1), shall be accompanied by the following:

(a)   a certified copy of the charter, statutes, regulations, memorandum and articles, or other instrument constituting or defining the constitution of the company and, if the instrument is not written in English, a certified translation of the instrument;

(b)   in relation to each documentary agent and local director, a statement signed by the documentary agent or local director accepting appointment as such; and

(c)   the particulars and documents referred to in section 238(2) relating to a charge on any property in Zambia acquired by the company, not less than fourteen days before the lodgement of the application or, if there are no such charges, a statement in the prescribed form to that effect.

If at the time of lodging the application for registration aforementioned, the foreign company has not set up or acquired an established place of business[6] for registration as a foreign company, it is obliged to rectify this anomaly within twenty-eight days after the lodgement.[7]

13.4   Established place of business

What amounts to an established place of business for a foreign company is provided for under section 300. In terms of section 300(1), a foreign company has an " established place of business " if it has any of the following in Zambia—

---

[4] In terms of section 299(6) '…the relevant particulars of a person in the case of—*(a)* an individual are: (i) present, and if any, former forenames and surname; (ii) residential and postal address; and (iii) business occupation, if any; and *(b)* a body corporate, are its: (i) name and, if a company, its designating number; (ii) registered office; and (iii) registered postal address'.

[5] Section 299(2).

[6] As defined under section 300 discussed below.

[7] Section 299(5).

(a)   a branch or management office;

(b)   an office for the registration of transfer of shares;

(c)   a factory or mine; or

(d)   any other fixed place of business.

However, the following are not established places of business in terms of section 300:

(1)   [a]n agent, in Zambia, of a foreign company in which the agent does not—

    (a)   have, or habitually exercise, a general authority to negotiate and conclude contracts on behalf of the body corporate; or

    (b)   maintain a stock of merchandise belonging to that body corporate from which the agent regularly fills orders on behalf of the foreign company; is not an established place of business of the foreign company for the purpose of this Part.[8]

(2)   …[w]here a foreign company carries on business dealings in Zambia, through a broker or general commission agent acting in the ordinary course of business, the office of the broker or agent….[9]

(3)   Where a foreign company has a subsidiary which is incorporated in Zambia or has an established place of business in Zambia, the—

    (a)   office of the subsidiary; or

    (b)   established place of business of the subsidiary[10]

13.5   Financial year of foreign company

The "financial year" of a foreign company is, in terms of section 301(1), 'the period of twelve months that begins on one accounting date of the company and ends on the day before thenext'. By subsection (2), '[t]he first "accounting date" of a foreign company is the date—

(a)   of its registration as a foreign company; or (

b)   on which it first had an established place of business'. According to subsection (3), '…the subsequent accounting dates of a foreign company are the—

    (a)   date specified in the application for its registration as the date on which the second financial year of the company will begin, and anniversaries of that date, if the application for registration specified such a date; or

    (b)   anniversaries of the date of its incorporation, if the application for registration did not specify such a date.

---

[8]   Section 300(2).

[9]   Section 300(3).

[10]   Section 300(4).

Be that as it may, in terms of section 301(4), '[a] foreign company may change an accounting date, by lodging a notice of the change in the prescribed form with the Registrar, except that the change does not result in a financial year being longer than fifteen months'. By section 301(5) '[w]here a foreign company changes an accounting date pursuant to this section, the subsequent accounting dates of the company are unless changed in accordance with this section, the anniversaries of that date'.

13.6   Returns required on alteration of registered particulars

According to section 302(1), a foreign company shall lodge a notice with the Registrar, Within sixty days following the effective date of an alteration, a foreign company is obliged to lodge a notice with the Registrar thereof—

- *(a)* in the charter, statutes, regulations, memorandum and articles, or other instrument relating to the foreign company within sixty days of the alteration being made;
- *(b)* of the particulars contained in the application, referred to in section 299(2); or
- *(c)* to the particulars in section 299 (2) *(a)*, *(b)*, *(e)* or *(f)*.

It is mandatory for the foreign company to, in terms of subsection (2), 'in the case of an alteration to any of the particulars, referred to in section 299 (2) *(c)*, *(d)*, *(g)* or *(h)*, lodge a notice of the alterations with the Registrar, within twenty-eight days after the date on which the alteration takes effect'. Finally, in terms of subsection (3), '[w]here the particulars lodged in terms of this section include the name of a person appointed as a documentary agent or local director or manager, the notice shall be accompanied by a consent signed by the person to act in that capacity'.

13.7   Appointment of local director

The requirement under section 303(1) to appoint at least one local director is mandatory with no derogations. In terms of section 301(2), '[a] contravention by a foreign company of subsection (1) which continues for more than sixty days shall constitute a ground for winding up the company by the Court on the application of the Registrar'. Under subsection (3), '[a] company which intends to decrease the number of its local directors, where the company has more than one local director, shall notify the Registrar in the prescribed form and manner'. Finally, under subsection (4), '[a] company shall not appoint, as a local director, an individual who is not qualified to be a director as specified in this Act'.

13.8   Responsibilities of local directors

Acts[11] by a local director under the guise of his ostensibly on behalf of the foreign company, in the course of carrying on the business of the company shall bind the company except in the following situations:

    (a)   local director lacked the authority so to act; and

    (b)   person with whom the local director dealt with had actual knowledge of the lack of authority or, having regard to the person's position with, or relationship to, the foreign company the person ought to have known of the lack of authority.

In terms of section 304(2), A foreign company shall, in legible Roman characters, state the forenames or the initials and surname of the local director and any former forename or surname of the local director in all trade circulars and business correspondence on or in which the company's name appears and which are despatched by or on behalf of the foreign company—

    (a)   in Zambia, whether to persons in Zambia or not;

    (b)   outside Zambia, exclusively to persons in Zambia; or

    (c)   exclusively for the purposes of the company's operations in Zambia.

According to section 304(3), [t]he Registrar may, if special circumstances exist which justify an exemption from the requirements of subsection (2), by notice published in the *Gazette* and in a daily newspaper of general circulation in Zambia and subject to any conditions specified in the notice, exempt a foreign company from the requirements or this sub-section.

Finally, in terms of section 304(4), '[a] foreign company shall maintain a register of its local directors, at its registered office or the office notified to the Registrar for the purposes of section 307, and section 31 shall apply to the register, with the necessary modifications'.

13.9   Service on foreign company

According to section 305(1),[12] [a] document may be served on a foreign company by—

    (a)   leaving it at an address registered as the address of a documentary agent of the foreign company;

    (b)   personal service on a documentary agent of the company, if the agent is an individual;

    (c)   leaving it at the registered office of the foreign company, if the company has no registered documentary agent, or at the registered address of such an agent;

---

[11] Sections 304(1).

[12] By subsection (3), '[s]ervice, in accordance with subsection (1), other than paragraph 1(c), shall continue to be effective in relation to the foreign company for a period of two years after the company ceases to be registered as a foreign company'.

(d)   personal service on a local director;

(e)   leaving it at the registered office or principal place of business of the foreign company in the country of its incorporation; or

(f)   by personal service on a director or secretary of the foreign company in the country of its incorporation

Further, and in terms of section 305(2), [a] document sent by registered or other receipted post to the address registered as the postal address of a documentary agent shall be taken to have been served on the foreign company if it is proved, by a receipt issued or otherwise, that the document, or a post office notification of the document, was delivered to the registered postal address.

The foregoing notwithstanding, section 305(4) provides that '[n]othing in [section 305 as a whole] shall derogate from the power of the Court to direct how service of a document relating to legal proceedings before the Court shall be effected'.

13.10 Annual accounts of foreign company

It is a requirement under section 306(1) that '…within nine months after the end of each financial year of the foreign company', a foreign company 'lodge with the Registrar in the prescribed form, annual accounts and an auditors' report corresponding as nearly as practicable with the annual accounts and auditors' report in relation to the operations and assets of the company in Zambia as specified in Part XII, if the operations and assets were the whole operations and assets of a public company incorporated in accordance with this Act'.[13]

In terms of section 306(4), [i]f a foreign company is required by its articles or provisions of a constitutive document regulating its conduct, by whatever name called, or by the laws of the country in which it is incorporated, to circulate annual accounts to its members or lay them before its members at an annual general meeting, the company shall, within twenty-eight days after complying with the requirements, lodge with the Registrar a certified copy of the accounts, together with, if the accounts are in a language other than English, a certified translation of the accounts in English.

By section 306(5), A foreign company may, in its statement of comprehensive income, referred to in subsection (1), make such apportionments and add such notes and explanations as are, in the foreign company's opinion, necessary or desirable to give a true and fair view of the profit or loss on its operations in Zambia, and for this purpose may debit a reasonable rate of interest on capital employed in Zambia.

According to section 306(6), the Registrar may, in relation to the accounts and reports referred to in subsection (1), on the application or with the consent

---

[13] By subsection (2), '[f]or the purposes of subsection (1), a foreign company shall appoint an auditor or auditors' who according to subsection (3) '…shall be a—*(a)* qualified and registered to practice in Zambia by a body regulating the audit practice in Zambia; or *(b)* firm of registered accountants'.

of the local directors modify any of the requirements of this section or Part XII to suit the circumstances of the foreign company, except that the accounts and reports give a true and fair view of the profit or loss of the operations of the foreign company and the state of affairs of the company in Zambia.

13.11   Maintenance of accounting records

As is the case with 'local' companies, section 307(1) requires that, '[a] foreign company…keep the following:

(a)   such accounting records that correctly record and explain the transactions of the foreign company relating to its operations and assets in Zambia, including any transactions as trustee, and the financial position of the company in relation to the operations and assets'.

(b)   its accounting records in such a manner as will enable the—
  (i)   preparation of true and fair accounts of the operations and assets of the foreign company; and
  (ii)   accounts of the foreign company to be conveniently and properly audited in accordance with this Part;

(c)   its accounting records for a period of ten years after the completion of the transactions to which they relate; and

(d)   at its registered office, or at another office notified to the Registrar in writing, such statements and records, with respect to the matters dealt with in its accounting records, that would enable the foreign company to prepare true and fair accounts, together with any documents required by this Part to be attached to the accounts.

By subsection(3), '[a] company shall keep its accounting records in—

(a)   writing or any form that enables the accounting records to be readily accessible and readily convertible into writing; and

(b)   English, unless the use of another language is approved, in writing, by the Registrar'.

Further to the foregoing and in terms of subsection (4), '[a] foreign company shall make its accounting records available, in writing, at all reasonable times for inspection, without charge, by its auditors and local directors and the Registrar or a delegate of the Registrar'.

According to section 307(5), [i]f a foreign company fails to comply with this section the—

(a)   Registrar may apply for an order that the foreign company be wound-up in accordance with section 312; and

(b)   foreign company and each officer in default commit an offence and shall be liable on conviction to the general penalty specified in this Act.

Be that as it may, in terms of section 307(6), '[t]he Registrar may, if special circumstances of a company justify, exempt the foreign company generally or in respect of any particular financial year from any provision of this section'.

13.12   Name of foreign company

Section 308(1) provides the following requirements relating to the name of a foreign company under the Act, specifically, that it shall be—

(a)   the name of the foreign company as incorporated in the country of its incorporation, if that name is in English; and

(b)   a translation or transliteration in English of the name of the company as incorporated in the country of its incorporation, as the company chooses, if that name is not in English.

However, by section 308(2), '[t]he Registrar may, on the application of a foreign company, whether before or after registration of the company, permit the company to have a different name in Zambia'. Further and according to subsection (3), '[t]he Registrar may, where the name of the foreign company is likely to cause confusion with the name of another body corporate or is otherwise undesirable, direct the foreign company to change its name to another name, approved by the Registrar, for use in Zambia'. The foregoing is important as the Act in subsection (4) proscribes any registration by the Registrar of a body corporate as a foreign company '…unless it' 'complies with the direction made by the Registrar in subsection (3)'. In fact, by subsection (5), '[t]he Registrar shall, where the foreign company fails to comply with the direction made in accordance with subsection (3), within forty-two days after the issue of the direction, register the designating number of the company, together with the words "Foreign Company", as the name of the company'.

According to section 308(6), [a] change of name, in accordance with this section, or the use of a name different from the name used by the foreign company in the country of its incorporation, shall not affect any rights or obligations of the company, or render defective any legal proceedings instituted or to be instituted by or against the foreign company, and any legal proceedings that might have been continued or commenced by or against the foreign company by its former name may be continued or commenced by or against the company under its new name.

13.13   Publication of name of foreign company

In terms of section 309, '[s]ection 43[14] shall apply to a foreign company, as if its name included, at the end of it, the words—

(a)   "incorporated in" followed by the name of the country of its incorporation; and

(b)   "with limited liability"; if the liability of the members is limited; but shall not apply in relation to business correspondence of the foreign company despatched outside Zambia'.

---

[14] Which empowers the Registrar to, under certain circumstances, direct change of name.

13.14   Registration of charges by foreign company

As regards registration of charges by foreign companies, section 310 stipulates as follows:

[s]ection 238[15] shall apply in relation to a foreign company as if a reference to—

(a)   a company were a reference to the foreign company;

(b)   a charge were a reference to a charge over property of the foreign company situated in Zambia; and

(c)   the acquisition of property by the foreign company included a reference to the acquisition of property before its registration as a foreign company.

13.15   Notification of winding up of foreign company

The procedure for notification of winding up of a foreign company is to be found in section 311 which provides as follows:

(1)   Where—

     (a)   a winding-up order is made by a court of the country of incorporation of a foreign company;

     (b)   a resolution is passed or other appropriate proceedings are taken in the country of incorporation of a foreign company leading to the voluntary winding up of the company; or

     (c)   the company is dissolved or otherwise ceases to exist, according to the law of the country of incorporation of the foreign company; the foreign company or if the company is dissolved, the documentary agents and local directors of the company shall lodge a notice with the Registrar within twenty-eight days after the event occurs.

(2)   A foreign company shall, where an event referred to in subsection (1)(a) or (b) occurs, cause a statement to appear, in legible Roman characters, on every invoice, order or business letter thereafter issued in Zambia by or on behalf of the foreign company, to the effect that the company is being wound-up in the country of its incorporation.

(3)   A person who carries on, or purports to carry on, business in Zambia on behalf of a foreign company after the date on which it was dissolved or otherwise ceased to exist in the country of its incorporation commits an offence and is liable, on conviction, to a fine not exceeding thirty thousand penalty units for each day that the person carries on business.

(4)   Nothing in this section shall derogate from the provisions of section 312.[16]

---

[15] Which provides for Registration of charges by companies.
[16] Which provides for 'winding up of foreign companies in Zambia.

13.16 Winding up of foreign company in Zambia

The procedure as it is provided for under section 312 is as follows:
(1) A foreign company may be wound-up in accordance with this section whether or not the foreign company has been dissolved or has otherwise ceased to exist according to the law of the country of its incorporation.
(2) For the purposes of a winding-up, in accordance with this section, the foreign company shall be treated as if it were a company incorporated in Zambia whose whole operations and assets were the operations and assets in Zambia of the foreign company.
(3) Subject to this section, the Corporate Insolvency Act, 2017, shall apply, with necessary modifications, to the winding up of a foreign company.
(4) A foreign company may be wound-up by the Court on the following grounds, in addition to the grounds referred to in the Corporate Insolvency Act, 2017, if the—
   (a) foreign company is in the course of being wound-up, voluntarily or otherwise, in the country of its incorporation;
   (b) company is dissolved in the country of its incorporation or has ceased to carry on business in Zambia, or is carrying on business for the purposes only of winding up its affairs; or
   (c) Court considers that the foreign company is being operated in Zambia for an unlawful purpose.
(5) The Court may, in the winding-up order, made in accordance with this section or on subsequent application by the liquidator, direct that all transactions in Zambia by or with the foreign company shall be considered to be, or have been, validly done despite the transactions occurring after the date when the company was dissolved or otherwise ceased to exist according to the law of the country of its incorporation, and may make the order on such terms and conditions as the Court considers appropriate.

13.17 Cessation of business of foreign company

As it relates to foreign companies, cessation of business the law and procedure is to be found in section 313 which provides as follows:
(1) If a foreign company ceases to have an established place of business in Zambia, it shall, within twenty-eight days thereafter, lodge with the Registrar a notice of that fact, in the prescribed form.
(2) The Registrar shall register the notice, referred to in subsection (1), and the company shall, subject to this section, cease to be a foreign company registered in Zambia.
(3) A foreign company shall maintain a documentary agent and continue to notify the Registrar of the particulars of its documentary agents, for

a period of two years after lodging the notice of its ceasing to have an established place of business in Zambia.

(4)   Where the Registrar has reason to believe that a foreign company has ceased to have an established place of business in Zambia, the Registrar shall serve a notice on the foreign company of the fact and stating the effect of subsection (5).

(5)   If, at the end of ninety days after the giving of a notice as specified in subsection (4), the Registrar is not satisfied that the foreign company is maintaining an established place of business in Zambia, the foreign company shall be considered as having lodged a notice in accordance with subsection (1) on that day.

(6)   A person who, while a body corporate was registered as a foreign company, would have had the right to inspect a document or register held by the Registrar in relation to the foreign company shall have the right to do so during a period of two years following the lodging by the company of the notice specified in subsection (1).

13.18   Invitation to public relating to other foreign corporates

The provisions here are not any different from those under sections 208 - 224 under Part X of the Act as discussed in chapter 9 of this text. *A fortiori,* section 315 which relates to the 'invitation to the public relating to other foreign corporates' provides as follows:

(1)   In this section, "non-Zambian company" means a body corporate formed or proposed to be formed outside Zambia, other than a foreign company.

(2)   Part X shall apply, with the necessary modifications, to a non-Zambian company as if it were a public company.

(3)   The Registrar may, at the request of a non-Zambian company, waive or modify the provisions of Part X in relation to a non-Zambian company.

(4)   A prospectus registered by a non-Zambian company for the purposes of an invitation to the public to acquire shares or debentures shall, in addition to complying with Part X and subject to any modifications made in terms of subsection (2), also contain particulars of the—

 (a)   instrument constituting or defining the constitution of the company;

 (b)   law, or provisions having the force of law, by or under which the incorporation of the foreign company was effected;

 (c)   address in Zambia where copies of the foregoing, or, if the same are in a language other than English, certified translations thereof, may be inspected;

    (d) date on which and the country in which the company was incorporated; and

    (e) nature of the liability of the member.

(5) A breach of subsection (3) shall be deemed to be a breach of section 218.[17]

13.20 Penalties and disabilities

Section 316 which provides for penalties and disabilities as they relate to foreign companies stipulates the following consequences for any default or contravention of any, part, most or all of the provisions of Part XIV: sections 297 - 316:

(1) If a foreign company fails to comply with any obligation imposed on it by this Part, the foreign company and any officer or documentary agent in default commit an offence and is liable, on conviction, to the general penalty specified in this Act.

(2) If a local director or a documentary agent of a foreign company wilfully fails to comply with any of the obligations imposed by this Part, the local director or documentary agent commits an offence.

(3) Subsections (1) and (2) shall not apply to an act or omission which constitutes an offence under another provision of this Part or Act.

(4) Subject to this section, if a foreign company fails to lodge with the Registrar a document required by this Part to be lodged, the rights of the foreign company under or arising out of, or incidental to, a contract made in Zambia while the failure continues shall not be enforceable by action or other legal proceedings.

(5) The Court may, on the application of a foreign company to which subsection (4) applies and if it is satisfied that it is just and equitable to do so, grant relief, either generally or on conditions, from any disability imposed by subsection (4).

(6) Nothing in this section shall prejudice the rights of any other party against the foreign company in respect of a contract referred to in subsection (4).

(7) If another party commences an action or proceedings against a foreign company to which subsection (4) applies, this section shall not preclude the foreign company from enforcing in the action or proceedings by way of counter-claim, set-off or otherwise, such rights as it may have against the party in respect of that contract.

---

[17] Which provides for offence of misstatement or omission in prospectus.

13.21 Conclusion

In this chapter we have discussed the dual role of the Act to enable the incorporation of the company and regulate its operations extends to companies that are incorporated outside this jurisdiction but which under the Act still need to be registered as foreign (registered) companies. We have explored statutory provisions relating to foreign companies as regards the following: Application of Act to existing foreign company; Register of foreign Companies; Registration of foreign company; Established place of business; Financial year of foreign company; Returns required on alteration of registered particulars; Foreign company to appoint local director; Responsibilities of local directors; Service on foreign company; Annual accounts of foreign company; Maintenance of accounting records; Name of foreign company; Publication of name of foreign company; Registration of charges by foreign company; Notification of winding up of foreign company; Winding up of foreign company in Zambia; Cessation of business of foreign company; Invitation to the public relating to foreign companies; Invitation to public relating to other foreign corporates; and Penalties and disabilities.

FURTHER READING

Books

Davies PL *Gower and Davies' Principles of Modern Company Law* 7th edn. (Thomson Sweet & Maxwell London 2003).

Farrah JH and Hannigan BM *Farrar's Company Law* 4th edn (Butterworths London 1998).

Gates RB *Gates Company Law and Practice in Zambia* (Reagan Blankfein Gates Lusaka 2017).

Goode R *Principles of Corporate Insolvency Law, Student* (ed) 4th edn (Revised). (London Sweet & Maxwell 2011)

Sealy L and Worthington S *Sealy & Worthington's Cases and Materials in Company Law* 10th edn (Oxford University Press London 2013).

Wild C and Weinstein S *Smith and Keenan's Company Law* 15th edn (Pearson Education Ltd London 2011).

Reports

European Commission Communication, Modernising Company Law and Enhancing Corporate Governance in the EU – A Plan to Move Forward (COM (2003) 284).

European Commission Green Paper, The EU corporate governance framework (COM (2011) 164).

European Commission Internal Market and Services, Report of the Reflection Group on the Future of EU Company Law, Brussels 5 April 2011.

14

ADMINISTRATION OF ACT, ENFORCEMENT AND GENERAL PROVISIONS

AIMS AND OBJECTIVES

 After reading this chapter you should appreciate the following:

- ❖ *As respects the administration of the Act:*
  - ➤ Establishment of Companies Office Companies
  - ➤ Powers of Registrar
  - ➤ Appointment of officers
  - ➤ Seal of Agency
  - ➤ Keeping of registers and lodged documents
  - ➤ Inspection of registers
  - ➤ Inspection of records
  - ➤ Waiver of fees
  - ➤ Collection of information
- ❖ *As respects enforcement and general provisions under the Act:*
  - ➤ Injunction
  - ➤ Derivative actions
  - ➤ Costs of derivative action to be met by company
  - ➤ Powers of Court where leave is granted
  - ➤ Compromise, settlement, or withdrawal of derivative action
  - ➤ Actions by member against director/company/company to act
  - ➤ Representative actions
  - ➤ Ratification of certain actions of directors
  - ➤ Exercise of discretionary power
  - ➤ Appeal against a decision of Registrar
  - ➤ Registrar to sit with assessors in determining matter
  - ➤ Registrar to act as soon as practicable
  - ➤ Registrar to act in accordance with decision of Court
  - ➤ Reference to Court by Registrar
  - ➤ Registrar to appear in legal proceedings
  - ➤ Immunity of officers as regards official acts

- Requests for information
- Registration of documents
- Extension of time
- Documents to be in official language
- Oaths and affirmations
- Evidence of entries and documents
- Loss or destruction of certificate
- Electronic Transactions
- Retention of records
- Failure to keep books
- Failure to provide documents 404 No. 10 of 2017 Companies
- Furnishing false document
- Fraudulent use or destruction of property
- Falsification of records
- Penalties for carrying on business fraudulently
- Persons prohibited from managing companies
- Failure to comply with registration requirements and
- The consequences for improper use of " Plc " or "Limited"
- Imprisonment for failure to pay fine
- Exemption from liability for actions or omissions
- The consequences for deceiving or influencing Registrar or officer
- The consequences for aiding and abetting offences
- The consequences for false representation about Companies Office
- Administrative penalties
- Offences by body corporate or unincorporated body
- General offences
- General penalty for offences without specific penalty
- Prescribed fee
- Regulations
- Repeal of CA1994
- Transitional provisions

14.1   Introduction

This chapter focuses on the last two parts of the Act namely Part XVI: sections 320 - 329 and Part XVII: sections 330 – 377. We are therefore concerned with exploring firstly, provisions relating to the administration of the Act and secondly, enforcement and general provisions that affect how all the other parts of the Act we have discussed so far are effected in practice. The foregoing may be clear from our approach so far in that in the preceding chapters we have, where necessity has demanded it, alluded to several provisions contained in the two parts we will now explore a little further.

14.2 Administration of Act[1] appointment of officers and seal of PACRA

The power to administer the Act is reposed in the Patents and Companies Registration Agency (PACRA).[2] To help with all matters relating to companies, the Act provides for the establishment of a 'Companies Office'[3] under PACRA.[4] There is provision for the appointment of PACRA officers under section 323 in the following terms: '[t]he Agency may, on such terms and conditions as it may determine, appoint such officers as it considers necessary for the carrying out of its functions in accordance with this Act'.

There are further provisions for the seal of PACRA under section 324 in the following terms:

(1) The seal of the Agency, kept in terms of the Patents and Companies Registration Act, 2010, shall be used for the purposes of this Act and the impression thereof made for such purposes, shall be judicially noticed.

(2) On the commencement of this Act, any impression of a seal made for purposes of this Act before the commencement of this Act, shall be considered to be an impression of the seal of the Agency.

14.2.1 *Role and power of the Registrar*

The starting point as regards the role and power of the Registrar is to be found in section 322. It stipulates as follows: [t]he Registrar shall exercise the powers and perform the functions assigned to the Registrar by this Act and the Patents and Companies Registration Agency Act,[5] except that any power conferred or duly imposed on the Registrar by this Act may be exercised or performed by the Registrar personally or by an officer acting under the delegation or control or direction of the Registrar.

The foregoing shows that the Registrar is empowered to exercise the powers and perform the duties assigned to the Registrar by the Act and the Patents and Companies Registration Agency Act.[6] In relation to incorporation, his role is purely administrative. He has to satisfy himself that the incorporation

---

[1] Previously under Division 14.1: sections 366-380 of CA 1994.
[2] Section 320.
[3] This section must be read together with section 369 which provides for matters regarding '[f]alse representation about Companies Office'.
[4] Section 321.
[5] No 15 of 2010.
[6] No 15 of 2010.

documents are in order and that all the formalities prescribed by the Act have been complied with. The following are further roles of the Registrar:

14.2.1.1   Keeping of registers and lodged documents

Section 325 provides for the Registrar's role in keeping registers and lodged documents in the following terms:

(1)   The Registrar shall maintain the registers required by this Act, together with any other registers that the Registrar considers necessary or convenient for the purposes of this Act.

(2)   The Registrar shall, where a document is lodged in accordance with this Act, register the document, or a copy thereof, and keep it.

(3)   The registers and other documents kept by the Registrar, for purposes of this Act, may be recorded or stored in handwritten, typed form or by electronic or photographic process.

(4)   For the purposes of this section—

　　　(a)   the information in a register, kept in accordance with the repealed Act, shall, if it is information that would have been required to be kept on a register had this Act been in force, be deemed to be information required to be kept on a register in compliance with this Act; and

　　　(b)   a document lodged for the purposes of the repealed Act shall be deemed to be a document lodged in accordance with this Act.

14.2.1.2   Inspection of registers

The power of the Registrar to inspect registers is provided for under section 326 and is stated as follows:

(1)   Subject to this Act, the registers, or any document lodged at the Companies Office shall, on payment of the prescribed fees, be open to inspection by the public during prescribed hours.

(2)   The Register of Companies shall be *prima facie* evidence of any matters required or authorised in accordance with this Act to be entered therein.

14.2.1.3   Inspection of records

Records inspection is another power reposed in the Registrar under section 327 which provides as follows:

(1)   The Registrar may, for the purpose of ascertaining whether a company or an officer of the company is complying with this Act or regulations made in accordance with this Act, on giving fourteen days' written notice to the company, call for the production of, or inspect, any book required to be kept by the company.

(2)   The Court may, on application by the Registrar or by a member or creditor of the company, or a person claiming an interest which the Court considers sufficient, where a company or an officer, receiver or liquidator of the company—

    (a)   fails to comply with a provision of this Act which requires the company, or the officer, receiver or liquidator of the company to lodge or deliver a return, account, or other document, or to give notice of any matter; and

    (b)   continues to fail to comply with the provision for the period of fourteen days after receiving the notice requiring compliance with that provision; make an order directing the company and any officer thereof, or the receiver or liquidator, to comply with the provision within such time as may be specified in the order, and may provide that all costs of and incidental to the application shall be borne by the company or by the officer, receiver or liquidator of the company responsible for the failure.

14.2.1.4   Waiver of fees

The power to waive fees and the circumstances thereof by the Registrar is stipulated under section 328 in the following terms:

(1)   The Registrar may waive the whole or any part of a fee payable in accordance with this Act, subject to rules issued by the Board of the Agency.

(2)   Where a provision in this Act refers to a prescribed fee and no fee has been prescribed for the purposes of the provision, the fee applicable to lodgements in general shall apply.

14.2.1.5   Collection of information

The power of the Registrar to collect information and its limits are provided for under section 329 as follows:

(1)   The Registrar may, by notice in writing, direct a—

    (a)   company; or

    (b)   person who is, or has been an officer or director of a company; to submit to the Registrar, within the period stated in the notice, specified information with regard to the operations of the company.

(2)   The notice, referred to in subsection (1), shall—

    (a)   not require a company or person to submit information, less than fourteen days after the date on which the notice is served;

(b) be published in the *Gazette* and may be published in a daily newspaper of general circulation in Zambia; and

(c) be served on the company or person named in the order.

(3) A company or person shall be considered to have received the notice, served in accordance with subsection (1), on the earliest of the dates on which the notice was served.

(4) The Registrar may, for the purpose of ensuring that the information, submitted following a notice served, in accordance with this section, is correct and complete, require a company or person to whom the notice applies to—

(a) produce specified records or documents for inspection, before a specified officer and at a specified time; or

(b) submit other information, within a specified period.

(5) The Registrar may, in writing, authorise a person to make an enquiry for the purpose of—

(a) obtaining information which a company has failed to furnish, as required of it in accordance with subsection (1);

(b) satisfying the Registrar that the information furnished by a company, following a notice served in accordance with subsection (1), is correct and complete;

(c) obtaining such information as may be necessary to make the information or statistics furnished correct and complete; and the powers of the person authorised shall extend to the investigation of any matter relevant for the purposes of the enquiry.

(6) If a company, served with a notice in accordance with this section, fails to provide the information or furnishes information which is incorrect or incomplete in a material respect, the company and each officer in default commit an offence, and are liable on conviction to a fine not exceeding one hundred thousand penalty units.

(7) A person who fails to comply with a notice served in accordance with this section commits an offence.

14.3   Enforcement and general provisions

In this part of our discussion we make no attempt to add, amplify or subtract from the provisions of the Act.

14.3.1 *Injunction*

Injunctions or the right to seek injunctive relief are/is provided for under section 330 as follows:

(1)   The Court may, on the application of a person referred to in subsection (2), make an order restraining a company or a director from engaging in conduct that contravenes or would contravene the articles or this Act.

(2)   For the purposes of subsection (1), an application may be made by—

    (a)   the company;

    (b)   a director or member;

    (c)   an entitled person; or

    (d)   the Registrar.

(3)   The Court may not make an order in terms of this section, in relation to conduct or a course of conduct that has been completed.

14.3.1 *Derivative action and minority protection*[7]

14.3.1.1   *General*

A derivative claim is one for which, as the name suggests, the right of action is derived from and exercised on behalf of the company. That said, the principle of majority rule within the company's juristic edifice is well established. To the majority is reserved the power to determine the direction of the company. Be that as it may, the emphasis on majoritarian rule in company decision made through simple, special or/ and extraordinary resolutions is liable to abuse to the detriment of minority shareholders. This can be source of injustice to shareholders in the minority. For this reason and as we show below, both the common law and statute have drawn rules which attempt to strike a balance between the hegemony of shareholders in with majority power and the protection of those in the minority.

   We must note from the outset that the issue of minority rights within the context of company law administration and legal interpretation is more a matter of procedure. It has been observed in *Nurcombe v Nurcombe*[8] that the nature of a derivative action is that it is 'a procedural device for enabling the court to do justice to a company controlled by miscreant directors or shareholders. Lord Denning has also observed in *Wallersteiner v Moir (No 2)*[9] that 'the form of the action is always "A.B. (a minority shareholder) on behalf of himself and all other shareholders of the company "against the wrongdoing directors and the

---

[7]   This is portion of the discussion is a revised and updated excerpt from Gates RB *Gates Company Law and Practice*....

[8]   [1985] 1 WLR 370 per Lawton LJ at 376

[9]   [1975] QB 373 at 390.

company. In *Burland v Earle*[10] Lord Davey held that the foregoing was a "mere matter of procedure in order to give a remedy for a wrong which otherwise would escape redress." than company law. Derivative claims, as they are called, are covered by rules of court procedure. A derivative claim is an action by a minority shareholder on behalf of the company where there is an abuse of power by the majority in the company, whether acting as directors/shareholders.[11] The right to sue in essence is derived from the company.

14.3.1.2   The Rule in Foss v Harbottle[12]

The supremacy of the majority as a concept in company law jurisprudence has as its genesis the case of *Foss v Harbottle*.[13] Two shareholders in a company incorporated by parliament, on behalf of themselves and all other shareholders except the defendants brought an action against the five directors (three of whom had become bankrupt), and against a shareholder who was not a director, and the solicitor and architect of the company, charging the defendants with concerting and effecting various fraudulent and illegal transactions, whereby the property of the company was misapplied, alienated and wasted; that there had ceased to be a sufficient number of qualified directors to constitute a board; that the company had no clerk or office; that in such circumstances the shareholders had no power to take the property out of the hands of the defendants, or satisfy the liabilities or wind up the affairs of the company; praying that the defendants might be decreed to make good to the company the losses and expenses occasioned by the acts complained of; and praying the appointment of a receiver to take and apply the property of the company in discharge of its liabilities, and secure the surplus: the defendants objected.

The Court held that the continued existence of a board of directors *de facto* must be intended; that the possibility of convening a general meeting of proprietors capable of controlling the acts of the existing board was not excluded by the allegations of the action; that in such circumstances there was nothing to prevent the company from obtaining redress in its corporate character in respect of the matters complained of; that therefore the plaintiffs could not sue in a form of pleading which assumed the practical dissolution of the corporation; and that the objectors must be allowed.

The fundamental point to remember from this seminal decision is that the proper plaintiff, in order to redress an incorrect action done to a company or to the property of the company, or to make obligatory, rights of the company, is the

---

[10] [1902] AC 83 at 93.
[11] Keenan D *Smith and Keenan's Company Law*.
[12] [1843] 2 Hare 461; 67 ER 189.
[13] [1843] 2 Hare 461; 67 ER 189.

company itself.[14] It follows that the court will, as a general rule, be disinclined to consider an action brought on behalf of the company by a shareholder if only to thwart or interfere with will of the majority. Further, that the court will be disinclined to get in the way of a company's internal management if the same is within the articles of the company.[15] Further, in *Burland v Earle*[16] it was held *inter alia* that, it is an elementary principle of the law relating to joint stock companies that the court will not interfere with the internal management of companies acting within their powers, and in fact has no jurisdiction to do so. Again, it is clear law that in order to redress a wrong done to the company or to recover moneys or damages alleged to be due to the company, the action should prima facie be brought by the company itself.

14.3.1.2   Foundation of the rule in Foss v Harbottle

The rule in *Foss v Harbottle* is predicated on at least four principles derived from decisions made following the establishment of the rule which we discuss below:

(1)   The company is a legal person

The cases of *Associated Chemicals Limited v Hill and Delamain Zambia Limited and another* and *BP Zambia v Interland Motors* (above) demonstrate this point.

(2)   Prevention of a multiplicity of actions

Again, the futility of an action by the minority if against the will of the majority cannot be overemphasised. It has been noted by Mellish LJ in *MacDougall v Gardiner*[17] that, if the thing complained is a thing which, in substance, the majority of the company are entitled to do, or if something has been done irregularly which the majority of the company are entitled to do, or if something has been done irregularly which the majority of the company are entitled to regularise, or if something has been done illegally which the majority of the company are entitled to legalise, there can be no use of having litigation about it, the ultimate end of which is only that a meeting has to be called, and then ultimately the majority gets its wishes.[18]

---

[14] This is predicated on the separate legal personality principle in the *Salomon case* as approved in *Associated Chemicals Limited v Hill and Delamain Zambia Limited and another* and *BP Zambia v Interland Motors* discussed in chapter 1 above.

[15] See further, the case of *Pavlides v Jensen* [1956] Ch 565.

[16] [1902] AC 83.

[17] [1875] 1 Ch D 13.

[18] See also *Gray v Lewis* [1873] 8 Ch App 1035 at page 1051.

It is not inconceivable that if allowed, or so the reasoning goes, such an action would risk bringing about the sort of multiplicity which the Zambian Supreme Court disapproved of in the case of *Development Bank of Zambia and KPMG Peat Marwick v Sunvest Limited and Sun Pharmaceuticals Limited*[19] specifically stating: 'We...disapprove of parties commencing a multiplicity of procedures and proceedings and indeed a multiplicity of actions over the same subject matter.' This received approval in the case of *BP Zambia v Interland Motors Ltd*[20]

(3)   The right of the majority to rule

It is said that an action by a single shareholder cannot be entertained because the views of the majority have not been tested. As shown in *Associated Chemicals Limited v Hill and Delamain Zambia Limited and another* and *BP Zambia v Interland Motors,* a company is a metaphysical entity, a fiction of law, which only has legal but no physical existence, and although it is a separate legal and distinct person from its members, it can only act through humans charged with its management and control of its affairs. It follows that an action can only be brought by a company's agents namely directors if such power has been delegated to them in the articles or through a company resolution.

(4)   The court's order may be made ineffective

This may be accomplished by the company passing an ordinary resolution of members in a subsequent general meeting. In *MacDougall v Gardiner*[21] the articles of the company empowered the chairman, with the consent of the meeting, to adjourn a meeting, and also provided for taking a poll if demanded by five shareholders. The adjournment was moved, and declared by the chairman. A shareholder suing on behalf of himself and all other shareholders except those who were directors brought an action against the directors and the company for a declaration that the chairman's conduct was illegal and an injunction to restrain the directors from carrying out certain arrangements without the shareholders' approval. It was held that the action could not be brought by a shareholder; if the chairman was wrong, the company alone could sue.

It is patent from the foregoing that the rule in *Foss v Harbottle* is, as far as minority actions are concerned, most unhelpful. The framing of the rule has been a source of considerable difficulties instances where the wrong doers are directors to whom, going by the rule, the right to sue is reserved.[22]

---

[19] [1997] SCZ Judgment No 10.

[20] [2001] ZR 37.

[21] [1875] 1 Ch D 13.

[22] *Breckland Group Holdings Ltd v London & Suffolk Property Holdings Ltd* [1989] BCLC 100.

14.3.1.3　Derivative action at common law: exceptions to the general rule

(1)　Acts which are ultra vires or illegal

No majority of members can authenticate or sanction an illegal act. So far as illegality is goes, the minority is not prevented from bring an action to stop the illegality and to compel the company or more specifically the directors to comply with the law. This may relate to e.g. loans, quasi-loans, and credits granted by the company to its directors.

(2)　Acts requiring a special resolution

Where the act disputed by the minority and which forms the necessary predicate for the action before court is one where only a special resolution is required such as the alteration of articles or capital, a simple majority of the members cannot be allowed to confirm the same. In *Ballie v Oriental Telephone Co Ltd*[23] a shareholder was able to bring a minority shareholders' action to restrain the company from acting on a special resolution of which insufficient notice had been given.

In *Edwards v Halliwell*[24] rule 19 of the rules of the defendant trade union provided: "The regular contributions of employed members shall be as per tables … and no alteration to same shall be made until a ballot vote of the members has been taken and a two-thirds majority obtained." In December, 1943, a delegate meeting of the union, without taking any ballot, passed a resolution increasing the amount of the contributions of employed members. The plaintiffs, two members of the union, claimed against two members of the executive committee of the union and the union itself a declaration that the alteration adopted at the delegate meeting was invalid. It was *held,* (i) that as the matter in question was not a mere irregularity in the internal management of the union, but was a matter of substance and tinctured with oppression, the court would grant the plaintiffs relief if it was proper to do so.[25] (ii) that, it was implicit in the rule in *Foss v Harbottle* that the matter relied on as constituting the cause of action should be a cause of action properly belonging to the general body of members of the association in question as opposed to a cause of action which some individual member could assert in his own right. In the present case, the personal and individual rights of membership of the plaintiffs had been invaded and particular damage inflicted by the invalid alteration of the tables of contributions, and in such circumstances the rule in *Foss v Harbottle* had

---

[23] [1915] 1 Ch 503 (CA).
[24] [1950] 2All ER 1064.
[25] *Amalgamated Society of Engineers v Jones* (1913) (29 TLR 484), distinguished.

no application to individual members who were suing, not in the right of the union, but in their own right to protect from invasion their individual rights as members, and, therefore, the plaintiffs were entitled to their declaration.[26]

(3)   Where there is a fraud on the minority

As we have noted already, taken to the hilt the rule in *Foss v Harbottle* is capable of doing grave injustice in that it would grant the majority carte blanche to do as they please because no action could be brought against them in respect of the wrong complained of. A line of authorities seem to have accepted the need for the somewhat amorphous exception termed "Fraud on the Minority". They also show the development trajectory of the exception from the days of *Burland v Earle*[27]where Lord Davey noted as follows concerning a derivative action and fraud: 'The cases in which the minority can maintain such an action are, therefore, confined to those in which the acts complained of are of a fraudulent character or beyond the powers of the company. A 'familiar example' he said, 'is where the majority are endeavouring directly or indirectly to appropriate to themselves money, property, or advantages which belong to the company, or in which the other shareholders are entitled to participate,...'[28] to *Estmanco (Kilner House) Ltd v Greater London Council*[29] wherein Sir Robert Megarry V-C noting at page 445 that '[fraud on the minority] does not seem to have yet become very clear exactly what the word 'fraud' means in this context; but I think it is plainly wider than fraud at common law....'[30] and went on to indicate his desire for the term 'fraud' to extricate itself from its fetters.[31] It has been noted that '...that fraud in this context is not confined to literal or common law fraud and may include the misappropriation of corporate property; mala fide abuse of power[...]; discrimination against a section of the membership; as well as errors of judgment from which the directors have benefited.'[32]

---

[26] *Pender v Lushington* [1877] (6 Ch.D. 70), applied.

[27] [1902] AC 83.

[28] [1902] AC 83 at 93; *see Prudential Assurance Co Ltd v Newman Industries Ltd (No. 2)*[1982]1 All ER 354 (CA);[1980] All ER 841wherein Templeman J expressed the view that the term 'fraud in this case should be extended to directors who may not have majority voting power but exercise actual or practical control of the company.

[29] [1982] 1 All ER 437.

[30] In the sense of *Derry v Peek* [1889] 14 App Cas 337; [1886-90] All ER Rep 1.

[31] Additional circumstances such as a substantial profit made on property sold to a director as exemplified in *Daniels v Daniels* [1978] Ch 406 and a loss caused to a company through the negligence of its directors who derived no personal gain as in *Pavlides v Jensen* [1956] 2 All ER 518 have successfully and unsuccessfully been held to constitute a fraud on the minority in the former and latter case respectively.

[32] Keenan D *Smith and Keenan's Company Law* 305.

There are two heads under which the fraud of the minority may be considered. They are as follows:

(i) Where the company is defrauded

Two cases illustrate this scenario. The first is *Menier v Hooper's Telegraph Works Ltd.*[33] Company A (European and South American Telegraph Co) was formed to lay a transatlantic cable to be made by Hooper's, the majority shareholder in company A, from Portugal to Brazil. Hooper's found that they could make a greater profit by selling the cable to another company B, but B did not have the government concession to lay the cable which company A had. After much intrigue with the Portuguese government trustee to the concession, he agreed to transfer the concession to company B, and company B then bought the cable from Hooper's. To prevent company A from suing for loss of the concession Hooper obtained the passing of a resolution to wind up company A voluntarily and arranged that a liquidator should be appointed whom Hooper could trust not to pursue the claim of company A in respect of the loss of its contract. Menier, a minority shareholder of company A, asked the court to compel Hooper to account to company A for the profits made on the sale of the cable to B.

It was held by the EWCA in Chancery, that where the majority shareholders of a company propose to gain a benefit for themselves at the expense of the minority, the court may interfere to protect the minority. In such a case one shareholder has a right to bring a derivative claim to seek relief and the claim is not barred by the rule in *Foss v Harbottle*. This was a blatant case of fraud and oppression and Hooper's were trustees of the profit and had to account to company A for it.

The second is Cook v Deeks.[34] *In that case,* three directors of a company carrying on the business of railway construction contractors obtained a contract in their own names to the exclusion of the company. The contract was obtained under circumstances which amounted to a breach of trust by the directors and constituted them trustees of its benefits on behalf of the company. By their votes as holders of three-quarters of the issued shares they subsequently passed a resolution as a general meeting of the shareholders declaring that the company had no interest in the contract.

It was held, that the benefit of the contract belonged in equity to the company, and the directors could not validly use their voting power to vest it in themselves.[35]

---

[33] [1874] 9 Ch App 350.
[34] [1916] 1 AC 554.
[35] *North-West Transportation Co v Beatty* [1887] 12 App Cas 589 and *Burland v Earle* [1902] AC 83 distinguished.

(ii)   Where the minority as individuals are defrauded

(a)   Expulsion of the minority from the company

In *Brown v British Abrasive Wheel Company,*[36] a company was in great need of further capital. The majority, representing 98 per cent of the shares, were willing to provide this capital if they could buy up the 2 per cent minority. Having failed to effect this by agreement, they proposed to pass an article enabling them to purchase the minority shares compulsorily on certain terms therein mentioned, but were willing to adopt any other mode of ascertaining the value that the Court thought fit.

It was held that in the circumstances, the proposed article was not just or equitable or for the benefit of the company as a whole, but was simply for the benefit of the majority. It was not therefore an article that the majority could force on the minority under section 13 of the Companies (Consolidation) Act, 1908.

The foregoing position can be contrasted with the decision in *Dafen Triplate Company Ltd v L'anelli Steel Company* (1907) *Ltd*[37] The defendant company, not having power under its original articles of association to acquire compulsorily the shares of members, passed special resolutions altering its articles and introducing a power enabling the majority of the shareholders to determine that the shares of any member (other than a certain named company) should be offered for sale by the directors to such person or persons (whether a member or members or not) as they should think fit at the fair value to be fixed from time to time at stated intervals by the directors.

The shareholders in the defendant company were principally companies and persons manufacturing tin plates who were originally invited to become shareholders on the understanding that, although under no legal obligation to do so, they were to take the steel bars required for their tin plates from the defendant company which was formed as a private company, with the object of providing such supply. The plaintiff company, which was an original shareholder of the defendant company, subsequently withdrew its custom and transferred it to a new rival steel company which the plaintiff company had been instrumental in forming. Being unable to acquire the plaintiff company's shares by agreement, the defendant company passed the resolutions in question with the object of acquiring the plaintiff company's shares and of protecting the defendant company against conduct on the part of its shareholders detrimental to the interests of the company.

It was held, that the resolutions in conferring an unrestricted and unlimited power on the majority of the shareholders to expropriate any shareholder they

---

[36] [1919] 1 Ch 290.
[37] [1920] 2 Ch. 124.

might think proper at their will and pleasure, went much further than was necessary for the protection of the company from the conduct of the shareholders detrimental to the company's interests, and that the power thereby conferred could not be bona fide or genuinely for the benefit of the company as a whole and was not such a power as could be assumed by the majority.

It was held also, that in the alteration of the original articles by the introduction of a power of expropriation the exception of one particular member from the operation of the power, whereby a privilege was conferred upon the excepted member over other members of his class, was invalid.[38]

(b)   Inequitable case of majority power

In *Clemens v Clemens Brothers*[39] the plaintiff held 45 per cent, and her aunt 55 per cent, of the issued share capital of a family company. The company had been incorporated in 1913 and carried on a highly successful business in the building trade. The capital of the company consisted of 200 preference shares, of which the plaintiff and the aunt each held 100, and 1,800 ordinary shares of £1 each fully paid, of which the plaintiff held 800 and the aunt 1,000. Under the articles of association members of the company had a right of pre-emption if another member wished to transfer his shares. The aunt was a director of the company but the plaintiff was not. There were four other directors. The total directors' emoluments exceeded the company's net profits before taxation in each of the years 1971 to 1974. The directors proposed to increase the company's share capital from £2,000 to £3,650 by the creation of a further 1650 ordinary shares all of which were to carry voting rights. The directors other than the aunt would receive 200 shares each, and the balance of 850 shares would be placed in trust for long service employees of the company. The secretary wrote to the plaintiff on 1 November 1974 setting out the proposals and enclosing notice of an extraordinary general meeting to be held on 27 November to approve the setting up of a trust for the company's employees, to increase the company's capital and to provide for the proposed allotments. Resolutions to that effect were set out in the notice and a draft of the proposed trust deed was enclosed.

On 22 November the plaintiff's solicitor wrote a letter to the aunt pointing out the scheme would reduce the plaintiff's shareholding to under 25 per cent and stating that the plaintiff was opposed to it. The aunt replied that she was fully aware of the implications of the changes in the company's structure but intended to support the scheme. The plaintiff's solicitor attended the meeting on 27 November as her proxy and proposed an adjournment. The aunt voted against the adjournment, and the three resolutions were then passed. The plaintiff

---

[38] See also *Sidebottom v Kenshaw Leese and Company* [1920] 1 Ch 154.
[39] [1976] 2 All ER 268.

brought an action against the company and the aunt, seeking a declaration that the resolutions were oppressive of the plaintiff and an order setting them aside. The defendant contended that, if two shareholders both honestly held differing opinions, the view of the majority should prevail, and that shareholders in general meeting were entitled to consider their own interests and to vote in any way they honestly believed proper in the interests of the company.

It was held, that the aunt was not entitled as of right to exercise her majority votes as an ordinary shareholder in any way she pleased; her right was subject to equitable considerations which might make it unjust to exercise it in a particular way. Although it could not be disputed that she would like to see the other directors have shares in the company and a trust set up for long service employees, the inference was irresistible that the resolutions had been framed in order to put complete control of the company into the hands of the aunt and her fellow directors, to deprive the 268 plaintiff of her existing rights as a shareholder with more than 25 per cent of the votes and to ensure that she would never get control of the company. Those considerations were sufficient in equity to prevent the aunt using her votes as she had, and the resolutions would accordingly be set aside.[40]

(4)   Fraud and Negligence

There are two authorities in which two different decisions were reached regarding the question of whether damage resulting from negligence by a company's directors can be brought under 'fraud'. The brief facts and holdings are set out below:

In *Pavlides v Jensen*[41] TAC Ltd had a capital divided into six hundred thousand ordinary shares of 10s each and six hundred thousand deferred shares of 1s each. Five hundred and seventy-eight thousand of the ordinary shares of TAC Ltd and the greater part of the deferred shares were held by another company. The individual defendants were directors of T AC Ltd and had been at the material times and were directors of, and a majority of the board of, the holding company. Holders of deferred shares of TAC Ltd were not entitled to receive notice of or to attend or vote at general meetings. In 1947 TAC Ltd sold an asbestos mine for £182,000 to another (i.e, a third) company in which TAC Ltd held twenty-five per cent of the issued capital. The sale was not submitted to the approval of T AC Ltd in general meeting. The plaintiff, who was the holder of 1,980 deferred shares in TAC Ltd alleged that the sale was grossly negligent because it was at an undervalue, the true value being about £1,000,000. The

---

[40] See also *Smith v Croft (No 2)* [1988] Ch 114 where the procedure under RSC, Ord 18 r 9 and Ord 33 r 3 were discussed.

[41] [1956] 2 All ER 518.

plaintiff claimed on behalf of himself and all other shareholders of TAC Ltd except the defendant directors against the defendant directors and TAC Ltd a declaration that the directors were guilty of a breach of duty, and inquiry as to the damages caused to TAC Ltd by such breach of duty, and payment by the directors to TAC Ltd of the amount of such damages. The plaintiff did not allege that the sale was ultra vires, or that the directors had acted fraudulently. On a preliminary point as to the competence of the plaintiff, as a minority shareholder, to bring the action, it was held, that the action was not maintainable by the plaintiff because, the sale of the mine being within the powers of TAC Ltd and no acts of a fraudulent character being alleged by the plaintiff, the sale could be approved or confirmed by the majority of shareholders.[42]

In *Daniels v Daniels*[43] the plaintiffs were minority shareholders in the third defendant ('the company'). The first and second defendants were majority shareholders and directors of the company. In October 1970 the company sold certain land to the second defendant for £4,250 on the instructions of the first and second defendants as directors. In 1974 the land was sold by the second defendant for £120,000. The plaintiffs brought an action against the defendants alleging that the price at which the land had been sold to the second defendant was well below its market value and that the first and second defendants knew that that was so, but had purported to adopt the probate value of the land although a probate value was usually much less than the open market value. The defendants applied to strike out the statement of claim as disclosing no reasonable cause of action since it did not allege fraud or any other ground that would justify an action by minority shareholders against the majority for damage caused to the company.

It was held, that the application would be dismissed. The confines of the rule that minority shareholders could not maintain an action on behalf of the company should not be drawn so narrowly that directors were able to make a profit out of their own negligence. Accordingly, minority shareholders were entitled to bring an action where the majority of the directors negligently, though without fraud, had benefited themselves at the expense of the company.[44]

(5) Where a member's personal rights are infringed

The majority cannot use the rule in *Foss v Harbottle* (above) to infringe the rights of a member who by virtue of owning shares will enjoy a bundle of

---

[42] Dictum of Lord Davey in *Burland v Earle* [1902] AC at 93 applied. Dicta of Sir George Jessel MR, in *Russell v Wakefield Waterworks Co* (1875) LR 20 Eq 480, 482), considered.

[43] [1978] 2All ER 89.

[44] *Alexander v Automatic Telephone Co* [1900] 2 Ch 56 *and Cook v Deeks* [1916–17] All ER Rep 285 applied; *Foss v Harbottle* [1843] 2 Hare 461 explained; *Atwool v Merryweather* [1867] LR 5 Eq 464, *Turquand v Marshall* [1869]LR 4 Ch App 376 and *Pavlides v Jensen* [1956] 2 All ER 518 distinguished.

rights including the right to vote, to dividends, to attend meetings among others. Therefore any act by the majority is liable to a challenge. This is exemplified in the case of *Pender v Lushington*[45] wherein A was a shareholder of a company and had a right to vote. At company's meeting, he cast his vote, but his vote was rejected. He brought an action to compel the directors to record his vote. It was held that he had a right to cast his vote and to have it recorded. The court observed that a member has a right to vote as he likes. It is no ground for rejecting a member's vote that he has voted against the interest of the company.

(6)   Where the wrongdoers are in control of the company

Where a wrong against the company has been committed and the wrongdoers remain in the control of the company using their control to prevent an action being brought against them by the company for the wrong, it is permissible by way of exception to the *Foss v Harbottle* rule for any member to commence an action in the name of the company against the wrong doers. In *Glass v Atkin*[46] A company was under the control of four members namely B,C,D and E, each of whom had equal shares. B and C brought an action against D and E on the ground that D and E had fraudulently converted the company's property to their own use. Allowing the action by B and C, and at the same time noting that it was for the company itself to bring such an action, the court was of the view that there was nothing inappropriate about this particular action for the simple reason that D and E who were the wrongdoers would have prevented the action from being commenced by the company as they had control of the company.

14.3.1.4   Derivative actions under the Act[47]

Section 331 provides for the manner of and circumstances under which a derivative action in the following terms:

(1)   Except as provided in this section, a director or an entitled person shall not bring or intervene in any proceedings in the name of, or on behalf of, a company or its subsidiary.

(2)   Subject to subsection (4), the Court may, on the application of a director or an entitled person, grant leave to—

    (a)   bring proceedings in the name and on behalf of the company or any subsidiary; or

    (b)   intervene in proceedings to which the company or any related company is a party for the purpose of continuing, defending, or discontinuing the proceedings on behalf of the company or subsidiary, as the case may be.

---

[45] [1877] 6 Ch.D. 70.

[46] [1967] 65 DLR (20) 501.

[47] For a detailed common law perspective, see generally Gates RB *Gates Company Law and Practice in Zambia* Ch.

(3)   Despite the generality of subsection (2), the Court shall, in determining whether to grant leave in accordance with that subsection, have regard to the—

    (a)   likelihood of the proceedings succeeding;

    (b)   costs of the proceedings in relation to the relief likely to be obtained;

    (c)   action already taken, if any, by the company or its subsidiary to obtain relief; or

    (d)   interests of the company or its subsidiary in the proceedings being commenced, continued, defended, or discontinued, as the case may be.

(4)   The Court may grant leave, in accordance with subsection (2), if satisfied that—

    (a)   the company or its subsidiary does not intend to bring, diligently continue or defend, or discontinue the proceedings, as the case may be; or

    (b)   it is in the interests of the company or subsidiary that the conduct of the proceedings should not be left to the directors or to the determination of the members as a whole.

(5)   A notice of the application, made in accordance with subsection (2), shall be served on the company or subsidiary.

(6)   A company or its subsidiary—

    (a)   may appear and be heard; and

    (b)   shall inform the Court, whether or not it intends to bring, continue, defend, or discontinue the proceedings, as the case may be.

14.3.1.4.1   *Unfair Prejudice*

The starting point in this discussion is sections 56 and 57 of the Corporate Insolvency Act, 2017. Any member of the company or a personal representative of a deceased member may petition the court on the grounds that the affairs of the company are being, or have been, or will be conducted in a manner unfairly prejudicial to the interests of the members generally or some part thereof including the petitioner himself.[48] Where this is the case, the court ought to satisfy itself that the petition is well founded. In *re Belladot Silk Ltd*[49] a member of the company presented a petition to the court for relief, but mainly as a form of harassment of the board in order to make them pay an alleged debt to one of his companies. The court held that there being a collateral purpose to the

---

[48] Wild C and Weinstein S *Smith and Keenan's Company Law* 13th edn.

[49] [1965] 1 All ER 667.

petition it could not, as it lacked the necessary proof of being a genuine attempt to get a relief be upheld. It has been held in *Re Kenyon Swansea Ltd*[50] that it is sufficient as a basis for a petition that there is a proposal which if effectuated would be prejudicial to the petitioner.

14.3.1.4.1.1   Relief Available

(1)   Specific relief

The court may make an order regulating the company's affairs for the future. The court may also restrain the doing of or the continuing of prejudicial acts as in *Re H R Harmer Ltd.*[51] On 1 July 1947, a company was formed to acquire a business which had been founded many years earlier by H (referred to hereinafter as "the father"), who was born in 1869. Two of his sons, C and B, went into the business on leaving school (C in 1921 and B in 1931). The nominal capital of the company was £50,000 divided into thirty-nine thousand preference shares of £1 each (which for present purposes could be disregarded), ten thousand "A" ordinary shares of £1 each, and one thousand "B" ordinary shares of £1 each. All the ordinary shares had been issued. The residue of profits in each year available for dividend was divisible among the holders of the "A" ordinary shares. The "B" ordinary shares conferred no right to participate in the profits but carried the whole of the voting power. In a winding-up the "A" and "B" shares were to rank equally as regards return of capital and participation in surplus assets. In July, 1947, the father sold all the assets of his business to the company for 33,325 the consideration being satisfied by the issue of shares. He nominated his sons as allottees equally of (apart from preference shares) 6,750 "A" ordinary shares and 240 "B" shares. The holdings of "A" and "B" shares at the date of the petition subsequently mentioned were that the father held 1,028 "A" shares and he and his wife (who voted as he wished) held 786 "B" shares; C held 4,611 "A" shares and C and his wife held 107 "B" shares, and B held 4,361 "A" shares and B and his wife held 107 "B" shares. By the company's articles, the father was appointed governing director for life, but no special rights were attached to that office; C and B each became a life director; and the father was appointed chairman of the board of directors with a casting vote. The father considered that he was entitled to disregard resolutions of the board as long as he held the voting control. He assumed powers which he did not possess and exercised them against the wishes of shareholders (namely C and B) who had major beneficial interests but a minority of votes. It was conceded that at the time of the presentation of the petition next mentioned the facts would justify the making of a winding-up order on the ground that it was just and equitable

---

[50] [1987] The Times 29 April.
[51] [1958] 3 All ER 689.

that the company should be wound-up. By a petition presented on 1 October 1957, C and B applied to the court for an order under s 210a of the Companies Act, 1948, complaining that, owing to the actions of the father, the affairs of the company were being conducted in a manner oppressive to some part of the members, including themselves. On appeal from an order granting relief under s 210, it was contended on behalf of the father that the sons were not entitled to the order for the following reasons, among others, viz, (a) it was not shown that the affairs of the company were "being conducted in a manner oppressive to" the sons as members, but only as directors; (b) the sons were not entitled to complain of the father's conduct, because they had acquired their ordinary shares as a gift from him, and because it had been recognised from the time when the company was formed that the father intended to retain control of it; (c) the acts complained of might have been lawfully done by calling a general meeting 689 and passing the requisite resolutions; and (d) this was not a case of discrimination between different shareholders or classes of shareholders.

It was held that in s 210 of the Companies Act, 1948, the word "oppressive" meant "burdensome, harsh and wrongful".

The definition given by Viscount Simonds in *Scottish Co-operative Wholesale Society v Meyer*[52] relief under s 210 had been rightly granted because, viewing the events proved as a consecutive whole, the affairs of the company had been conducted in a manner oppressive to the sons as members, not merely as directors, and, even if the father's acts might lawfully have been done with the authority of a general meeting, the sons were entitled to require that the proper procedure should be followed, it being irrelevant, if it were indeed the fact, that the original acquisition of shares by the sons was a gift from the father; moreover, s 210 was not confined to discrimination between classes of shareholders, nor was oppression limited to such as was designed to obtain pecuniary advantage, as distinct from such as expressed an overweening desire for power.

Per Romer LJ (adopting a passage from the judgment of Roxburgh J): 'to assume power that one does not possess and to exercise that against the wishes of shareholders who have major beneficial interests but a minority of votes is *prima facie* oppression, and shifts the burden of proof'.

(2)   General

Here under, the court may make any order as it thinks fit for giving relief in respect of matters complained of. The case of *Re a company*[53] illustrates this. In that case, the shares of a private family company were held by F., his wife

---

[52] [1959] AC 324; [1958] 3 WLR 404 HL.
[53] (No 005287 of 1985) [1986] 1 WLR 281.

and their four daughters. 1982 it was agreed that H., the husband of one of the daughters, should acquire a controlling interest in the company. The agreement was implemented by transfers of shares by F., his wife and the four daughters, but the daughters each retained a substantial minority interest. Between 1982 and 1984 the petitioners, three of F.'s daughters, complained that H. had conducted the company's affairs in a way contrary to the agreement and unfairly prejudicial to their interests, inter alia, by paying to himself and to a company which he controlled management fees which he ought not to have paid, and that he had acted in other ways without authority, and in breach of his fiduciary duties to the company. In May and June 1985 negotiations were commenced for the purchase by H. of the petitioners' shares but on 25 July their solicitors received a letter informing them that H.'s shares had been acquired by a Gibraltarian Company. The petitioners presented a petition seeking relief under section 461 of the Companies Act 1985, requiring H. to account for payments made without authority. The petitioners were unable to discover what had happened to the company's assets, the company's business having been sold in February 1985 for £520,800.

On H.'s application to be struck out as a respondent to the petition on the ground that he was no longer a member, it was held, is missing the application, that the wording of section 461(1) of the Companies Act 1985 was wide enough to allow the court to grant relief in respect of a complaint that the company's affairs had been conducted by a respondent, who was no longer a member of the company in a manner unfairly prejudicial to the interests of the members; that, accordingly, the matter should proceed without requiring the petitioners to bring a separate derivative shareholders' action against H. and the issue whether the petitioners in section 461 proceedings could obtain an order that H. personally purchase their shares should be deferred to the hearing of the petition.

Further to the foregoing, it is also open to the court to, in its discretion, authorise a claim to be brought by the company wronged by majority itself in keeping with the rule in *Foss v Harbottle*. Finally, the court may order the purchase of the minority shares at a fair price either by other members or the company itself in which case the court will order a reduction of capital.

14.3.1.4.2 *Where the shareholding is equal*

Equal shareholding is, where the personal relationship of shareholders deteriorates, a situation that may lead to deadlock. This is well illustrated in the case of *West v Blanchet and Anor.*[54] The company's business was teaching English under the name of Leicester Square School of English Ltd. It was a joint venture between Jason West, the petitioner, and Stephen Blanchet. The

---

[54] [2000] 1 BCLC 795.

nominal capital was £100 divided into 100 £1 shares. The paid-up capital was £2, of which West and Blanchet held one share each. West was responsible for marketing and Blanchet for management. The second respondent, who was a director with no shares, was responsible for teaching. The parties' relationship broke down and the respondents terminated West's employment. He played no part in management after this but continued as a director/shareholder. West later offered to buy Blanchet's shares and Blanchet made an offer for West's. However, they could not agree on who should leave the company. West applied to the court for an order under [the equivalent of s 996 of the UKCA 2006] that Blanchet be required to sell him the shares, alleging that the two respondents had conducted the company's affairs in a manner prejudicial to him in that they had excluded him from the company's affairs and management decisions. The respondents asked the court to strike out the claim as an abuse of court process.

It was held, that in a case such as this the issue was which offer was the more reasonable and realistic. Blanchet had funds readily available to buy West's shares, but West had no available personal funds and his offer was short on details. Blanchet's offer was therefore the more reasonable and realistic, so the court should strike out West's claim.[55]

14.3.1.4.3   The motives of the minority: when there is abuse of procedure

The unfair prejudice procedures cannot be used where they would achieve a collateral purpose, as where the board of a company would be requested to make a takeover bid at a higher price than that intended. The case of *Re Astec (BSR) Plc*[56] demonstrates this scenario. In 1989, Emerson Electric, US company, acquired 45 per cent of the Astec shares. It made further acquisitions over the subsequent period so that in March 1997 it held 51 per cent of Astec. In January 1998, Emerson issued a press release stating that it would buy the remainder of the shares in Astec at no premium to market value, and would stop making dividend payments.

The minority shareholders petitioned the court under [the equivalent of s 459 of the UKCA 2006], accusing Emerson of bullying tactics and asking the court to order it to purchase the remaining shares in Astec at a fair value-in effect to undertake a takeover of Astec at an increased price.

Held, inter alia, that the petition was an abuse of process and should be struck out.[57]

---

[55] *Townap Textiles Zambia Ltd and Chhaganlal Distributors Ltd v Tata Zambia Ltd* [1988 - 1989] Z.R. 93 (SC) discussed below under "minority petition for a just and equitable winding-up."

[56] [1999] 2 BCLC 536.

[57] *Per* Parker j: '...the petition is, in my judgment, being used for the purpose of exerting pressure in order to achieve a collateral purpose....'

Nor will it be appropriate to use the unfair prejudice procedures to foist onto the company an order for purchase of shares for the sheer reason that the plaintiff has lost faith and assurance in the way in which the company is being run by the other members without more. To form a basis for such an action there must be some breach of the terms on which there has been concurrence as regards the way the company should be run. In the case of *O'neill and Anor v Phillips and Others*[58] the company, which provided specialist service for stripping asbestos from buildings, employed Mr O'Neill as a manual worker in 1983. Mr Phillips, who held the entire issued share capital of 100 £1 shares, was so impressed by Mr O'Neill that in 1985 he gave him 25 shares and appointed him a director. Shortly afterwards, Mr Phillips had informally expressed the hope that Mr O'Neill would be able to take over the day-to-day running of the company and would allow him to draw 50 per cent of the profits. Mr O'Neill took over on Mr Phillips' retirement from the board, and was duly credited with half the profits. In 1991, the industry went into recession, the company struggled and Mr. Phillips, who had become concerned by Mr O'Neill's management, resumed personal command. He told Mr. O'Neill that he would only be receiving his salary and any dividends on his 25 shares, but would no longer receive 50 per cent of the profits. In January 1992, Mr O'Neill petitioned the court for relief against unfair prejudice in respect both of his termination of equal profit-sharing and the repudiation of an alleged agreement for the allotment of more shares.

The House of Lords Unanimously allowed an appeal by Mr. Phillips and others from the Court of Appeal. Lord Hoffmann said that, as to whether Mr. Phillips had acted unfairly in respect of equality of shareholding, the real question was whether in fairness or equity Mr. O'Neill had had a right to the shares. On that point, one ran up against the insuperable obstacle of the judge's finding that Mr. Phillips had never promised to give them. There was no basis consistent with established principles of equity for a court to hold that he had behaved unfairly in withdrawing from the negotiations. The same applied to the sharing of profits. A member who had not been dismissed or excluded from management could not demand that his shares be purchased simply because he felt that he had lost trust and confidence in the others and in the way the company was run.[59]

---

[58] [1999] I WLR 1092.

[59] See the case of *Harbourne Road Nominees Ltd v Karvaski* [2011] EWHC 2214 (Ch) which explored the principle established in *O'Neill v Phillips* [1999] I WLR 1092; *Re Bird Precision Bellows* [1984] 2 WLR 869; *Re London School of Economics* [1985] 3 WLR 474; *Re a Company (No 007623 of 1984)* [1986] BCLC 362; *Re Macro (Ipswich)Ltd* [1994]2 BCLC 354; *Fulham Football Club (1987) Ltd v Richards &Anor* [2011]EWCA Civ 855 and *Glamlestaden Fastigheter AB v Baltic Partners Ltd* [2007] UKPC 26 (Privy Council). It was shown in the last case that creditor interest may be protected by way of unfair prejudice actions.

14.3.1.4.4   Minority protection and the shareholders' agreement

We visited this issue earlier in the text. It is worth re-emphasing the point from the perspective of the interplay between minority protection and shareholder agreements. Minority shareholders can expect to be protected from what may be called the inherent oppression of the minority by the majority through the existence of shareholders' agreements. It means that majority shareholders cannot in all cases impose their will on the minority.

14.3.1.4.5   Minority petition for just and equitable winding-up

The High Court has jurisdiction under section 57(1)(g)[60] 275 of the Corporate Insolvency Act to wind up a company on the petition of minority shareholders on the ground that it is just and equitable to do so. Specifically, section 57(1)(g) provides that '[t]he Court may order the winding-up of a company on the petition of a person other than the Official Receiver if—in the opinion of the Court, it is just and equitable that the company should be wound-up'[61]

The issue was considered in *Townap Textiles Zambia Ltd and Chhaganlal Distributors Ltd v Tata Zambia Ltd.*[62] To allow the respondent to take part in industrial activities in Zambia the second appellant and the respondent acquired the shares in the first appellant company. Four directors were appointed, two directors from each of the second appellant and respondent. Subsequently, a director representing the respondent company resigned and thereafter the respondent's representation in the company was reduced to one director. From then on the relationship between the directors representing their respective companies deteriorated. The respondent's director wanted parity of directors, the second appellant's director wanted a majority in their favour. A petition was then presented to a Court for a winding up order. At the hearing the original director of the respondent who had resigned gave evidence that parity of directors between the parties was never intended. At one stage he was invited by a director of the second appellant company to rejoin the Board of Directors but this was objected to by a director of the respondent company. Three directors were then proposed by the director of the respondent company but these were rejected by a director of the second appellant. Therefore, no director of the respondent

---

[60] Which replaces what used to be section 275 under CA 1994. Section 57(1)(g) of the Corporate Insolvency Act, 2017 must however be read together with section 56 in that same Act which though allowing a member of a company to commence winding-up proceedings places restrictions under section 57(2) when such a petition relates to public or private company limited by shares.

[61] *Loch v John Blackwood Ltd* [1924] AC 783 shows the flexibility with which section 122(1)(g) of the UK Insolvency Act 1986 a similar provision to section 57(1)(g) of the Corporate Insolvency Act, 2017 where an order for winding up was made in the face of a refusal by the managing director who represented the majority.

[62] [1988 - 1989] ZR 93 (SC); See also *Pan Electronics Limited and Savvas Panayiotides and Others v Andereas Miltiadous and Others* [1988] SCZ Judgment No 1 (ZMSC).

attended further directors' meetings. The respondent presented a petition to wind up. The petition, inter alia, alleged that the respondent's sole director was wrongly removed, that the first appellant company failed to maintain proper accounts and records, that the first appellant company had not obtained title to the land on which its factory stands and that the company had sold goods at discount prices to a company in which the directors of the first appellant company had interests. It was also alleged that the petitioner was prevented from taking part in the management of the first appellant company. In reply the first appellant company averred that the respondent made no contribution under a management agreement and gave no financial and management support so that the first appellant company was in a financial crisis. The Court was urged, under a clause in the articles to make an order to allow arbitration. The trial Judge found that the respondent had been completely removed from management, there was a complete breakdown of trust and confidence and total deadlock between the parties. He ordered the company be wound-up. The appellant appealed. It was held as follows:

(i)   Where a petitioner is effectively prevented from taking part in the management of the affairs of a company through representation on the board of directors and this was contrary to the spirit of the joint ventures between the parties which had been completely destroyed, arbitration proceedings can serve no useful purpose.

(ii)   Where the circumstances exist in (i), and there is no other order which it is desirable or competent for the Court to make, a winding-up order is appropriate.[63]

That said, in general an order for winding up will be made under the following circumstances:

(1)   Where as in *Re Thomas Edward Brinsmead & Sons*[64] the company in question is incorporated for fraudulent or illegal reasons. It was held in that case that on the petition of a shareholder, that-notwithstanding only a part of the substratum had gone, inasmuch as the company still had a valuable business which could be carried on consistently with obedience to the injunction, and that the majority of the shareholders in general meeting had voted against winding-up it was "just and equitable" that the company should be wound-up.[65]

---

[63] See *Jesner v Jarred* [1992] The Times, 26 October.

[64] [1897] 1 Ch.45.

[65] In *Re Haven Gold Mining Co* [1882] 20 Ch D 151 CA and *Re Medical Battery Co* [1894] 1 Ch.444, fraudulent misrepresentation in the particulars relating to listing and fraud in the course of the business with third parties without more were held not to constitute a ground on which a petition could be brought to wind up the company by the minority; *Re London and County Coal Co* [1866] LR 3 Eq355.

(2)   Where there is no genuine intent on the part of the directors to run a legitimate business. The case of *Re London and County Coal Co*[66] demonstrates this.[67]

(3)   Where as illustrated in the case of *Ebrahimi v Westbourne Galleries*[68] there is a breakdown in the administration of the company or deliberate if not unfair exclusion of a member who is also a director from the management of the company.

(4)   Where the articles of the company restrict the business of the company to specific objects but the same have failed e.g. mining or banking. The case of *Re Bleriot Aircraft Co*[69] exemplifies this point. In it, a company was wound-up because its substratum namely the acquisition of the English portion of the aircraft business from M who refused to carry out the contract could not be carried out.

'Whether it is just and equitable to wind up a company depends on the facts which exist at the time of the hearing and a petitioner is confined to heads of complaint set out in his petition.[70] A shareholder is not entitled to a winding-up order on the "just and equitable" ground if his object is not a company purpose but the securing for himself of an advantage in a question between himself and other shareholders.'[71] A point must be made at this juncture that 'as soon as a prayer for winding-up has been made, the company becomes paralysed, resulting in the fact that no transactions relating to the company's property can be entered into after this point. Consequently, this is a drastic course of action and as such should be viewed as one of last resort for any minority shareholder'[72] It will be remembered that in terms of section 57(1)(g) of the Corporate Insolvency Act, winding-up the company will only be made where no other alternative exists and only when 'it would be just and equitable that the company should be wound-up.' Should the court be of the opinion both that some other remedy is available to the petitioners and that they are acting unreasonably in seeking to have the company wound-up instead of pursuing that other remedy, it will not make the winding-up order.[73]

---

[66] [1866] L.R.3 Eq.355.

[67] However as has been shown in *Re Suburban Hotel Co* [1867] L.R. 2 Ch.App.737 and *Cox v "Gosford" Ship Co Ltd* [1894] 21 R. 334 neither loss making nor high indebtedness can, without more, form a basis for a successful winding up petition.

[68] [1972] 2 All ER 492. See facts and discussion in chapter 2 above under the subheading "the personal relationship company"; See also *Re Five Minute Car Wash Service Ltd* [1966] 1 All ER 242; *Virdi v Abbey Leisure Ltd* [1990] BCLC 342 and *Re a company (No 002567 of 1982)* [1983] 2 All ER 854 where the point was made that in circumstances where there is a fair offer for shares the court will be disinclined to wind up the company upon a petition.

[69] [1916] 32 T.L.R.253; *Pirie v Stewart* [1904] 6 F 847.

[70] *Re Fildes Bros. Ltd* [1970] 1 All ER 923.

[71] *Charlesworth's Company Law* 445.

[72] *Smith and Keenan's Company Law* 15th edn 348.

[73] It cannot be emphasised enough that this is a remedy grounded in equity and in terms of *Ebrahimi v Westbourne Galleries* [1972]2 All ER 492 those that seek to use it must come to equity with clean hands. We cannot say the same for section 57 of the Act.

14.3.1.4.6   Costs of derivative action to be met by company

The costs of derivative action and how they are to be met is provided for under section 332 which stipulates as follows:

(1)   The Court may, on the application of a director, or an entitled person to whom leave was granted, in terms of section 331,[74] order that the whole or part of the costs of bringing or intervening in proceedings be met by the company, including any costs relating to any settlement, compromise or discontinuance approved in accordance with section 334.[75]

(2)   A director or an entitled person may bring an application for costs as specified in this section at the same time an application is brought in terms of section 331 to bring or intervene in the proceedings, and the Court may make an order on that application at the same time that the Court grants leave in accordance with section 331.

14.3.1.4.7   Powers of Court where leave is granted

According to section 333, (1) The Court may make any order as it may consider appropriate in relation to proceedings commenced with leave of the Court in accordance with section 331. (2) Without limiting the generality of subsection (1), the Court may—

(a)   make an order—

(i)   authorising a member or any other person to control the conduct of the proceedings;

(ii)   requiring the company or the board of directors to provide information or assistance in relation to the proceedings; or

(iii)   directing that any amount ordered to be paid by a defendant in the proceedings shall be paid, in whole or in part, to its subsidiary or an entitled person rather than to the company; or

(b)   give directions for the conduct of the proceedings.

It must be added that by section 334, '[p]roceedings commenced with leave of the court in accordance with section 331, may not be settled, compromised or discontinued, without leave of the Court'.

14.3.1.4.8   Actions by members

14.3.1.4.8.1   Actions by member against director/company

Under section 335(1), '[a] member or former member of a company may bring an action against a director for breach of a duty owed to the member or former

---

[74] Which provides for derivative action.

[75] Which provides for Compromise, settlement, or withdrawal of derivative action.

member'. Additionally, and in terms of section 335(2) '[a]n action may not be brought as specified in subsection (1), to recover any loss in the form of a reduction in the value of shares in a company or a failure of the shares to increase in value by reason only of a loss suffered, or a gain forgone, by the company'. The foregoing power is extended to a member under section 336 which permits '[a] member'…to 'bring an action against the company for breach of a duty owed by the company to the member'.

Section 336 must be read within the context of section 337 which provides that, '[d]espite section 336, the Court may, on the application of a member, make an order requiring the board of directors to take any action that is required by the articles or this Act to be taken and, on making the order, the Court may grant such other consequential relief as it considers appropriate'.

14.3.1.4.8.2   *Representative actions*

Representative actions are permitted under section 338 which provides as follows:

> The Court may, where a member brings proceedings against the company or a director and other members have the same or substantially the same interest in relation to the subject matter of the proceedings, appoint that member to represent all or some of the members having the same or substantially the same interest and may, for that purpose, make such order as it considers appropriate including an order—
>
> (a)   as to the control, conduct and costs of the proceedings; or
>
> (b)   directing the distribution of any amount ordered to be paid by a defendant in the proceedings among the members represented.

We have noted that as was shown in *Pender v Lushington*[76] the rule in *Foss v Harbottle* (above) will not apply to instances where a member sues not in the name of the company but in their own name in order to protect their bundle of rights. Such a member may in addition to himself, sue on behalf of others in what is referred to as a representative action. Such representative actions may include enforcing articles given rights such as voting receipt of dividends when they are due or a claim for damages. Therefore, where, as in *Brown v British Abrasive Wheel Co*[77] the majority attempt to carry out an act which is contrary

---

[76] See note 416 above.

[77] [1919] 1 Ch 290.

to its articles or as in *Lowe v Fahey*[78] the company acts *utra vires* its articles where for example the articles restrict its business or as in *Edwards v Halliwell*[79] where a special majority is required to make a resolution on a particular issue for example alteration of capital or the articles themselves, and it has not been obtained, an individual will not be precluded from suing in a representative action using the *Foss v Harbottle* rule.

14.3.1.4.9   Ratification of certain actions of directors and exercise of discretionary power

As regards the ratification of certain actions of directors, section 339 provides as follows:

(1)   The exercise by the board of directors of a power vested in the members, or any other person, may be ratified or approved by those members or that person, in the same manner in which the power may be exercised.

(2)   The exercise of a power that is ratified, as specified in subsection (1), shall be considered to be a proper and valid exercise of that power.

(3)   The ratification or approval specified in this section of the exercise of a power by the board of directors shall not prevent the Court from exercising a power which might, if it were not for the ratification or approval, be exercised in relation to the action of the board of directors.

In terms of section 340, '...[w]here any discretionary or other power is given to the Registrar, the Registrar shall not exercise that power adversely or arbitrarily and a person challenging a decision of the Registrar shall have the right to apply to the Court'.

It must be remembered that under section 341, '...a person aggrieved by a decision of the Registrar may within thirty days after the date on which the person is notified of the decision, appeal to the Court against the decision, and the Court may confirm, reverse or vary the decision or make such order or give such directions in the matter as it considers just and equitable.

The decisions which are appealable include all decisions we have discussed above which the Registrar makes in his administrative role including those under Part II: sections 6 – 21 relating to the registration and incorporation of companies; Part IV: sections 36 – 47 relating to company name and change of name; Part V: sections 48 – 55 relating to conversion of companies; and those under Part XVI: sections 320 – 329 relating to the administration of the Act. Section 320 thereunder gives PACRA general power to administer the entire Act and stipulates the general powers of the Registrar under section 322 which have already considered.

---

[78] [1996] 1 BCLC 262 Ch.D.

[79] [1950] 2 All ER 1064.

Other powers are stipulated under the following sections already considered:

(1) Section 325 on his role in keeping of registers and lodged documents
(2) Section 326 on his role and power in the inspection of registers
(3) Section 327 on his role in, and power to inspect company records
(4) Section 328 which gives the Registrar power to waive fees; and
(5) Section 329 which gives him power to collect desired information on companies.

However, the decisions envisaged under section 341 include those decisions made by the Registrar when performing *quasi*-judicial functions under section 342 *et seqs* discussed below. It will be good to note that generally speaking, in terms of section 343, '[w]here the Registrar is required…to do any act or thing and no time or period is provided within which the act or thing is to be done, the Registrar shall do the act or thing as soon as practicable'.

14.3.2   *Quasi-judicial functions of the Registrar*

14.3.2.1 *Registrar to sit with assessors in determining matter*

In terms of section 342(1), '[t]he Registrar may sit with such number of assessors, in all proceedings brought before the Registrar, as the Board of the Agency may determine'. Subsection (2) appears to suggest that the Assessors will be appointed on an ad hoc basis. Even so, they '…shall be remunerated by the Agency as may be prescribed'. However, in terms of section 345,

[w]hen a matter to be decided by the Registrar, in accordance with this Act, appears to the Registrar to involve a complex point of law or is of unusual importance, the Registrar may, after giving notice to the parties, refer such a matter to the Attorney-General for advice or to the Court for determination, and shall thereafter act in accordance with the advice of the Attorney-General or decision of the Court or a decision substituted therefor on appeal to the EWCA or Supreme Court, as the case may be.

14.3.2.2 *Registrar to act in accordance with decision of Court*

According to 344(1), '[w]here an aggrieved person appeals to the Court', [in terms of section 341 or from a specific decision made in terms of proceedings under section 342], 'the Registrar shall act in accordance with the decision of the [High Court], subject to any further appeal', and only if there is an application for stay of execution of judgment.[80] In terms of subsection (2), [u]nless otherwise directed by the Court, the Registrar may submit to the Court a statement, in writing, signed by the Registrar, giving particulars of the proceedings that were before the Registrar in relation to the matter in issue, the practice of the Companies Office in similar cases and such other matters within the particular knowledge of the Registrar and the statement shall form part of the evidence in the proceedings before the Court.

14.3.2.3   *Registrar to appear in legal proceedings*

According to section 346(1), and as regards legal proceedings in '…which the relief sought includes alteration, revocation or rectification of the register, the Registrar shall have the right to appear and be heard and shall appear if so directed by the Court'.

In terms of section 346(2), [t]he Registrar may, unless otherwise directed by the Court, in lieu of appearing and being heard, submit to the Court a statement in writing, signed by the Registrar, giving particulars of the

   (a)   proceedings before the Registrar in relation to the matter in issue;
   (b)   grounds of any decision given by the Registrar affecting the matter in issue;
   (c)   practice of the Companies Office in like cases; or
   (d)   matters relevant to the issue as the Registrar considers necessary; and the statement shall be considered to form part of the evidence in the proceedings.

14.3.2.3   *Immunity of officers as regards official acts*

It ought to be noted that in terms of section 347,

   (1)   The Registrar and any officer of the Agency shall not be liable for any act or omission by reason of, or in connection with, any action or investigation required or authorised by this Act, any treaty or convention or any report or other proceedings consequent on any such action or investigation.
   (2)   The Registrar shall not be liable for any damage that may be caused by the publication, in good faith, of a matter relating to the affairs of a company in the *Gazette*, in a daily newspaper of general circulation in

---

[80] See, *Ndola City Council v Charles Mwansa* [1994] ZMSC Judgment No 78 (SC) where it was reiterated that [i]t is trite law that an appeal *per se* from the Subordinate Court's decisions to the High Court do not operate as stay of execution. This is specifically provided for in the High Court Act. The appellant must apply for stay to the High Court and the matter becomes discretionary. The same situation applies to the appeals to the Supreme Court. There is a specific provision to the effect that the appeal does not operate as stay of execution, it must be applied for and the decision is discretionary.

Zambia, other media or displaying such matter in a prominent public place or on the website of the Agency or in any other media.

Be that as it may, section 348 mandates the Registrar to, 'on the request of any person and on payment of the prescribed fee, or furnish a certificate in respect of the document or copies of any document, which is open to public inspection and which is lodged in the Register or any other register, maintained in accordance with this Act'. Any refusal for whatever reason would make the Registrar liable to a suit under section 341. Barring an appeal, he would also be bound to follow the decision of the High Court in terms of section 344(1).

14.3.2.4 *Registration of documents*

The registration of documents is provided for under section 349[81] which stipulates as follows:

(1)　Where this Act requires a document or particulars to be lodged with the Registrar, the Registrar shall register them in the form and manner prescribed or, if no manner is prescribed for the document or particulars, the Registrar shall determine them manner and form of lodgement.

(2)　For purposes of this Act, a document or particulars shall be taken not to have been lodged with the Registrar until a fee, prescribed in accordance with this Act, has been paid to the Registrar.

(3)　Subject to this Act, where this Act requires a document or particulars to be lodged, a company shall lodge a separate document or set of particulars.

(4)　[82]Where the Registrar considers that a document or particulars lodged with the Registrar—

　　(a)　contain matter which is contrary to any written law;

　　(b)　by reason of an error, omission or misdescription, have not been duly completed;

　　(c)　are insufficiently legible;

　　(d)　are written on material insufficiently durable; or

　　(e)　otherwise do not comply with the requirements of this Act; the Registrar may refuse to register the document or particulars in that state and direct that they be amended or completed in a specified manner and re-submitted.

---

[81] Section 349 must be read together with section 351 which provides as follow, (1) Subject to this Act, where this Act requires a document or register to be prepared, kept, maintained or lodged, the document shall be in English. (2) Where the Registrar approves the lodgement of a document which, or part of which, is in a language other than English, the Registrar may require a certified translation into English to be annexed to it.

[82] In terms of subsection (5), '[w]here the Registrar gives a direction, as specified in subsection (4), the document or particulars shall be considered not to have been lodged'.

(6)   The Registrar may require a document or a fact stated in a document, lodged with the Registrar, to be verified by statutory declaration.

(7)   Where the Registrar is required or permitted by this Act to cause a copy or particulars of a document lodged, with the Registrar, to be published in the *Gazette* or in a daily newspaper of general circulation in Zambia or other media, the Registrar may require the lodgement, with the Registrar, of any such document in duplicate or the provision of any such particulars, and may withhold registration of the document until the requirement has been complied with.

(8)   Where this Act provides that a document to be lodged shall be "in the prescribed form", the Registrar shall accept for lodgement and registration a document that contains all the information required and varies from the prescribed form in essential respects only.

14.3.2.5   Extension of time

According to section 350,

(1)   [t]he Registrar may, before the end of the period fixed for lodgement of a document or particulars, at the request of the person concerned, extend the period for lodgement by such period, and on such terms as the Registrar considers reasonable in the circumstances.

(2)   Subject to this section, where a document or particulars are lodged with the Registrar, after the end of the period fixed for their lodgement, the Registrar shall accept the document or particulars for registration on payment of such additional fee as may be prescribed.

(3)   The Registrar may reduce or waive an additional fee imposed, in terms of subsection (2), if the Registrar is satisfied that the failure to lodge the document or particulars was caused or continued solely through administrative oversight and that no person is likely to have suffered damage or to have been prejudiced as a result of the failure.

14.3.2.6   Oaths and affirmations, evidence of entries and loss or destruction of certificate

Matters to do with oaths and affirmations, evidence of entries and loss or destruction of certificate are provided for under sections 352, 353 and 354.

Section 352 provides as follows:

> A person who is required by this Act to take an oath or swear to the truth of an affidavit may, in lieu thereof, make an affirmation or declaration in accordance with the law relating to affirmations or declarations in Zambia.

Section 353 provides as follows:

(1)   A certificate signed by the Registrar and certifying that an entry which the Registrar is authorised by this Act to make, has or has not been made, or that any other thing which the Registrar is so authorised to do has or has not been done, shall be *prima facie* evidence of the matter so certified.

(2)   A copy of any entry in any register or of any document kept in the Companies Office or an extract from any such register or document, certified by the Registrar, may be admitted in evidence without further proof and without production of the original.

Finally, section 354 provides as follows: Where the Registrar is satisfied that a certificate of incorporation has been lost or destroyed or cannot be produced, the Registrar may cause a duplicate of it to be sealed, on payment of such fees as may be prescribed.

14.3.2.7   *Electronic Transactions*

Section 355 provides for electronic transactions in the following terms:

(1)   A document authorised or required to be filed with, or delivered to the Registrar in accordance this Act, may be filed or delivered by means of a device or facility that records or stores information electronically or by other means and permits the information so recorded or stored to be readily inspected or reproduced in usable form.

(2)   A document or certificate required to be signed, issued or kept by the Registrar may be signed, issued or kept in electronic form.

(3)   Meetings or resolutions, required by this Act, may be held or passed by electronic means.

(4)   A document delivered to the Registrar, which appears to the Registrar to be incomplete or internally inconsistent, may be corrected by the Registrar, but only—

    (a)   on instructions given by the company or as required by any other written law; and

    (b)   if the company has not withdrawn its consent to instructions given in accordance with this section.

(5)   For purposes of subsection (4), the following requirements shall be met as regards instructions:

    (a)   instructions must be given in response to an enquiry by the Registrar;

    (b)   the Registrar shall be satisfied that the person giving the instructions is authorised to do so by the—

        (i)   person by whom the document was delivered; or

        (ii)   company to which the document relates; and

(c) the instructions shall meet requirements by the Registrar as to—

    (i)   the form and manner in which they are given; and

    (ii) authentication.

(6)   The company's consent to instructions, given in accordance with this section, and any withdrawal of such consent, shall be notified to the Registrar in hard copy or electronic form

(7)   A document that is corrected in accordance with this section shall be treated as having been delivered when the correction is made.

(8)   The Registrar may accept a replacement for a document previously delivered that did not comply with the requirements for proper delivery or contained unnecessary or erroneous material.

(9)   A replacement document shall not be accepted, unless the Registrar is satisfied that it has been delivered by the—

    (a) person by whom the original document was delivered; or

    (b) company to which the original document relates; and that it complies with the requirements for proper delivery.

(10) The power of the Registrar to impose requirements as to the form and manner of delivery includes power to impose requirements as to the identification of the original document and the delivery of the replacement in a form and manner enabling it to be associated with the original.

14.3.2.8   *Retention of records, failure to keep records and failure to provide documents*

According to section 356, '[a] company shall retain records or books required to be kept in accordance with this Act for a minimum period of ten years and in accordance with the Financial Intelligence Centre Act'.[83] In terms of section 357, '[a] company that fails to keep records or books, as required to be kept in accordance with this Act, commits an offence and is liable, on conviction, to a fine not exceeding one hundred thousand penalty units'.

Section 358 relates to failure to provide documents and specifically provides as follows:

(1)   A company that fails or delays to provide the Registrar with documents, as required by this Act, commits an offence and is liable, on conviction, to a fine not exceeding one hundred thousand penalty units.

(2)   Where the documents, referred to in subsection (1), are fraudulent, a company that wilfully provides them commits an offence and is liable, on conviction, to a fine not exceeding one hundred and fifty thousand penalty units.

---

[83] Act No 46 of 2010.

14.3.2.9   Furnishing false document, fraudulent use or destruction of property and falsification of records

Section 359 provides for matters relating to furnishing false documents in the following terms: Without prejudice to the Penal Code, a director or employee of a company who knowingly makes, submits or authorises the making or submission of a false or misleading statement or report with regard to—

(a) a director, officer, employee, inspector, shareholder, debenture holder or assignee for debenture holders of the company;

(b) where the company is a subsidiary, a director, officer, employee or inspector of its holding company;

(c) a stock exchange or an officer of a securities exchange; or

(d) the property of the company; commits an offence and is liable, on conviction, to a fine not exceeding two hundred thousand penalty units or to imprisonment for a period not exceeding two years, or to both.

Section 360 provides for matters relating top fraudulent use or destruction of property in the following terms: Without prejudice to the Penal Code, a director, officer, employee or shareholder of a company who fraudulently—

(a) takes or applies property of the company for that director's, officer's or employee's or shareholder's own use or benefit or for a use or purpose other than the use or purpose of the company; or

(b) conceals or destroys property of the company; commits an offence and is liable on conviction, to a fine not exceeding two hundred thousand penalty units or to imprisonment for a period not exceeding two years, or to both.

Section 361 provides for the falsification of records in the following terms: Without prejudice to the Penal Code, a director, officer, employee, or shareholder of a company who, with intent to defraud or deceive a person

(a) destroys, displaces, mutilates, alters, falsifies or is a party to the destruction, mutilation, alteration or falsification of any register, accounting records, book, paper or other document belonging or relating to the company; or

(b) makes, or is a party to the making of a false entry in a register, accounting record, book, paper, or other document belonging or relating to the company; commits an offence and is liable, on conviction, to a fine not exceeding five hundred thousand penalty units or to imprisonment not exceeding five years or to both.

14.3.2.10   Penalties for carrying on business fraudulently

The Act provides for penalties for carrying on business fraudulently under section 362 in the following terms: Without prejudice to the Penal Code, a director of a company who—

(a) by false pretences or other fraud, induces a person to give credit to the company; or

(b) with intent to defraud a creditor of the company—

  (i) gives, transfers or causes a charge to be given on property of the company to another person;

  (ii) causes property of the company to be given or transferred to a person; or

  (iii) causes or is a party to an execution being levied against property of the company; commits an offence and is liable, on conviction, to a fine not exceeding two hundred thousand penalty units or to imprisonment for a period not exceeding two years, or to both.

14.3.2.11   *Persons prohibited from managing companies*

Section 363 provides for matters relating to persons prohibited from managing companies in the following terms: Without prejudice to the Penal Code, where a person has been convicted of—

(a) an offence in connection with the promotion, formation or management of a company;

(b) an offence involving fraud; or

(c) a breach of professional confidentiality; that person shall not, during the period of three years following the conviction or the judgment, be a director or promoter of, or in any way, whether directly or indirectly, be concerned with, or take part in, the management of a company, unless that person first obtains leave of the Court, which may be given on such terms and conditions as the Court considers appropriate.

14.3.2.12   *Failure to comply with registration requirements and improper use of "Plc" or "Ltd"*

We discussed the requirements pertaining to registration of companies under chapter 1 in which we explored sections 6–21. We also discussed the requirement for a registered company names to end with "Plc" and "Ltd", under section 36. Additionally, we discussed provisions relating to foreign companies and in particular, section 297(a) which references the need to meet the requirements under sections 6 – 21 for a company to be called a foreign registered company under the Act in chapter 13. The foregoing must all be considered within the context of section 364 which stipulates as follows:

(1) A person who fails to comply with this Act regarding the requirement to be registered, commits an offence, and is liable, on conviction, to a fine not exceeding one hundred thousand penalty units.

(2)   A person who, not being a body corporate—

    (a)   trades or carries on business in Zambia under a name or title which includes the word "Limited", "Plc", "Corporation" or any contraction or imitation thereof, or any equivalent in a language other than English; or

    (b)   whose members have limited liability under the laws of the country of its incorporation, trades or carries on business in Zambia under a name or title the last word of which is "Limited" or any contraction or imitation thereof, or any equivalent in a language other than English; commits an offence and is liable, on conviction, to a fine not exceeding one thousand penalty units for each day that the person trades or carries on business under that name or title.

14.3.2.13   *Imprisonment for failure to pay fine*

To the preceding discussion relating to certain offences and their consequences under the Act must be added the stipulation under section 365 that, [w]here a court issues a warrant in accordance with section 312 of the Criminal Procedure Code for the commitment of a person to prison for a failure by the person to pay a fine imposed on the person for an offence provided for in this Act, the period of imprisonment specified in the warrant shall not exceed one day for every three penalty units of the fine that remain unpaid.

It must, in addition, be read within section 366 which provides as follows:

> a person shall not be liable to an action in damages for anything done or omitted to be done by that person in the exercise or performance of a power or function conferred or imposed on that person by or in accordance with this Act, unless the act or omission was in bad faith or was due to want of reasonable care or diligence.

14.3.2.14   *Deceiving or influencing Registrar or officer*

According to section 367 which provides for matters relating to deceiving or influencing the Registrar or any officer of PACRA,

    (1)   A person who, for the purpose of—

        (a)   deceiving the Registrar or an officer in the administration of this Act; or

        (b)   procuring or influencing the doing or omission of anything or matter as specified in this Act; or makes or submits a false statement or representation, whether orally or in writing,

knowing the same to be false, commits an offence and is liable, on conviction, to a fine not exceeding two hundred thousand penalty units or to imprisonment for a period not exceeding two years, or to both.

(2)   A person who, having innocently made a false statement or representation, whether orally or in writing, for the purpose of procuring or influencing the doing or omission of anything in relation to any matter in this Act and who on becoming aware that such statement or representation was false, fails to advise the Registrar of such falsity within a reasonable time, commits an offence and is liable, on conviction, to a fine not exceeding two hundred thousand penalty units or to imprisonment for a period not exceeding two years, or to both.

14.3.2.15   *Aiding and abetting offences*

According to section 368, (1) A person commits an offence if the person—
(a)   aids, abets, counsels or procures; or
(b)   is in any way, directly or indirectly, knowingly a party to; the doing of an act outside Zambia which, if it were done in Zambia, would be an offence against this Act, commits an offence and is liable, on conviction, to a fine not exceeding two hundred thousand penalty units or to imprisonment for a period not exceeding two years, or to both.[84]

14.3.2.16   *False representation about Companies Office*

Provisions relating to false representation about the Companies office whose establishment is provided for under 321 are to be found under section 369[85] which provides as follows:
(1)   A person who in connection with the person's business, uses any means that would reasonably lead other persons to believe that the person's office is, or is officially connected with, the Companies Office, by
(a)   placing, or allowing to be placed, the name of the company, on a building in which the person's office is situated;
(b)   placing on a document, as a description of the person's office or business the words "Companies Office" or "office for registration or incorporation of companies", or words of similar import, whether alone or together with other words;
(c)   impersonating or falsely purporting to be an employee or agent of the Agency; or

---

[84] Subsection (2) however provides that '[s]ubsection (1) shall not affect the provisions of the Penal Code'.
[85] Subsection (2) provides that '[a]n offence specified in this section is an offence of [the tortious] strict liability'. For a detailed discussion of the concept of strict liability, see Rogers WVH *Winfield & Jolowicz Tort* 18th edn. Ch 15: 'Strict Liability: The Rule in *Rylands v Fletcher* [[1868] LR 3 HL 330]]' 763 – 797.

(d)   using when advertising the person's office or business; commits an offence and is liable, on conviction, to a fine not exceeding two hundred thousand penalty units or imprisonment for a period not exceeding two years, or to both.

14.3.2.17   Administrative penalties

According to section 370,

(1)   The Registrar may impose an administrative penalty on a person for any failure to comply with this Act.
(2)   An administrative penalty, referred to in subsection (1), shall not exceed the amount prescribed by the Minister for each day during which such failure continues.
(3)   An administrative penalty, imposed in accordance with subsection (1), shall be paid to the Agency within the period specified by the Registrar.
(4)   If any person fails to pay an administrative penalty, within the period specified in subsection (2), the Registrar may, by way of civil action in a competent court, recover the amount of the administrative penalty from such person as an amount due and owing to the Agency.

14.3.2.18   Offences by body corporate or unincorporated body

Matters relating to offences by a body corporate or an unincorporated body is provided for under section 371 as follows:

Where an offence under this Act is committed by a body corporate or unincorporated body, and the director, manager or shareholder of that body is suspected to have committed the offence and is charged of that offence, that director, manager or shareholder of the body corporate or unincorporated body is liable, upon conviction, to the penalty specified for the offence, unless the director, manager or shareholder proves to the satisfaction of the court that the act constituting the offence was done without the knowledge, consent or connivance of the director, manager or shareholder or that the director, manager or shareholder took reasonable steps to prevent the commission of the offence.

14.3.2.19   General offences and general penalty

Section 372 provides for general offences, specifically that '[w]ithout prejudice to the Penal Code', a person who—

(a)   fails to comply with a request, direction or order issued in accordance with this Act, by the Court, the Registrar or any other authorised person;

(b)   is knowingly a party to the carrying on of any business of a company for a fraudulent purpose;

(c)   makes use of a name or title which the person is not, in accordance with this Act, authorised to use;

(d)   knowingly is a party to a company carrying on business with intent to defraud a creditor of the company or any other person;

(e)   divulges or makes use of information obtained in accordance with this Act which the person is not otherwise authorised to disclose;

(f)   wilfully falsifies any information required in accordance with this Act;

(g)   is required to provide a document and wilfully

    (i)   makes, or authorises the making of, a statement that is false or misleading; or

    (ii)   omits or authorises the omission of, anything, the omission of which makes the document false or misleading in a material respect;

(h)   in relation to a mechanical, electronic, or other device used in connection with the keeping or preparation of a register, accounting book, paper, or other document belonging to a company in accordance with this Act, knowingly—

    (i)   records or makes available to a person false information on a matter; or

    (ii)   omits or authorises the omission of, anything, the omission of which makes the document false or misleading in a material respect;

(i)   impersonates a shareholder or debenture holder for the purpose of obtaining an advantage;

(j)   makes or causes to be made—

    (i)   a false entry in a register established in accordance with this Act; or

    (ii)   writing falsely purporting to be a copy of an entry in the register; or

    (iii)   produces or tenders or causes to be produced or tendered in evidence any such writing;

(k)   uses the name or unique registration number or seal of a company, or issues a letter, bill or document relating to the company otherwise than in accordance with this Act or any other law;

(l)   alters, defaces, makes additions to, or partly removes, erases or obliterates a document issued by the Registrar;

(m)   in the exercise of any powers or functions conferred upon that person by this Act or by regulations made in accordance with this Act, fails

to act in accordance with the instrument which confers the function or power; or

(n) otherwise contravenes this Act or regulations made under it; commits an offence and is liable, on conviction, to a fine not exceeding two hundred thousand penalty units or to imprisonment for a period not exceeding two years, or to both.

Section 373 provides for a general penalty in the following terms,

> A person who contravenes any provision of this Act, where no specific penalty has been provided is liable, on conviction, to a fine not exceeding four hundred thousand penalty units or to imprisonment for a term not exceeding four years, or to both, and, if the person is a foreigner, to the variation or revocation of that person's immigration permit.

14.3.2.20   *Prescribed fee and regulations*

Section 374 provides that '[t]he Minister may, prescribe a payable fee for any act to be performed by the Registrar or any document to be lodged with the Agency'.

Section 375 provides for regulations in the following terms:

(1) The Minister may, by statutory instrument, make regulations for or with respect to any matter that by this Act is required or permitted to be prescribed, or that is necessary or convenient to be prescribed for carrying out or giving effect to this Act, other than a matter required or permitted to be prescribed by any other person or body.

(2) Without limiting the generality of subsection (1), such regulations may be made on the—

   (a) conduct of the business of the Companies Office;

   (b) form and content of any application, notice, return, account, book, record, certificate, licence or other document required for the purposes of this Act;

   (c) payment of fees and charges in respect of any matter or anything done or provided for by this Act;

   (d) procedure to be followed in connection with any application or request to the Registrar or any proceeding before the Registrar;

   (e) additional obligations and procedures for the determination of beneficial ownership and timely access to beneficial ownership information by the public;

   (f) the provision of copies of any documents required in accordance with this Act, and the certification of such copies;

(g)   the making of inspections and searches in accordance with this Act, including the times when they may be made;

(h)   the conduct of any proceeding or transaction in accordance with this Act;

(i)   the service of notices and other documents in accordance with this Act; and

(j)   any matter necessary or convenient to be provided for in relation to the transition between the repealed Act and this Act.

14.3   Conclusion

In this chapter we have explored on the last two parts of the Act namely Part XVI: sections 320 - 329 and Part XVII: sections 330 – 377. We have examined firstly, provisions relating to the administration of the Act and secondly, enforcement and general provisions that affect how all the other parts of the Act we have discussed so far are enforced in practice. This has been clearly detailed in the preceding chapters where we have alluded to several provisions contained in the two parts relating to the administration of Act and the enforcement and general provisions contained in the Act.

FURTHER READING

Articles

Cain, B, 'Company Names Adjudicator Rules' (2008) 32 CSR 25.

Ireland, P, 'Capitalism Without the Capitalist: the Joint Stock Company Share and the Emergence of the Modern Doctrine of Separate Corporate Personality' (1996) 17 *Journal of Legal History* 63.

Mayer, T, 'Personal liability for trading in a prohibited name: sections 216–217 Insolvency Act 1986' (2006) 27 Comp Law 14.

Pekmezovic, A, 'Determinants of corporate ownership: the question of legal origin: Part 1' (2007) 18 ICCLR 97.

Pekmezovic, A, 'Determinants of corporate ownership: the question of legal origin: Part 2' (2007) 18 ICCLR 147.

Pennington, R, 'The Validation of Pre-Incorporation Contracts' (2002) 23(9) Comp Law 284.

Books

Davies PL *Gower and Davies' Principles of Modern Company Law* 7th edn (Thomson Sweet & Maxwell London 2003).

Dine J and Koutsias M *Company Law* 6th edn (Palgrave Macmillan Hampshire 2007).

Farrah JH and Hannigan BM *Farrar's Company Law* 4th edn (Butterworths London 1998).

Gates RB *Gates Company Law and Practice in Zambia* (Reagan Blankfein Gates Lusaka 2017).

Keenan D *Smith and Keenan's Company Law* 13th edn (Pearson Longman Essex 2005).

McCahery J and Vermeulen E *Corporate Governance of Non-listed Companies* (Oxford University Press Oxford 2008).

Sealy L and Worthington S *Sealy & Worthington's Cases and Materials in Company Law* 10th edn (Oxford University Press Oxford 2013).

Wild C and Weinstein S *Smith and Keenan's Company Law* 15th edn (Pearson Education Ltd London 2011).

APPENDICES

Appendix 1

FIRST SCHEDULE
(Section 12(3))

STANDARD ARTICLES REGULATIONS FOR MANAGEMENT OF A COMPANY LIMITED BY SHARES, UNLIMITED AND PUBLIC LIMITED COMPANIES

Table of Divisions

1. Interpretation

1. (1) In these regulations, unless the context otherwise requires:

   "Act" means the Companies Act;

   "prescribed rate of interest" means the rate of interest prescribed in regulations made in accordance with the Act for the purposes of the Standard Articles;

   "seal" means the common seal of the company and includes any official seal of the company;

   "resolution" means an ordinary resolution of the company;

   "secretary" means any person appointed to perform the duties of a secretary of the company.

   (2) Unless the context otherwise requires, an expression if used in a provision of these regulations that deals with a matter dealt with by a particular provision of the Act, has the same meaning as in that provision of the Act.

2. Share Capital and Variation of Rights

2. Without prejudice to any special rights previously conferred on the holders of any existing shares or class of shares, but subject to the Act, shares in the company may be issued by the directors and any such share may be issued with such preferred, deferred or other special rights or such restrictions, whether with regard to dividend, voting, return of capital or otherwise, as the director may determine.

3. The directors shall not issue any rights or options to shares in favour of any persons unless the issue has been authorised at a general meeting by a special resolution.

4. Subject to the Act, any preference shares may, with the sanction of a resolution, be issued on the terms that they are, or at the option of the company are liable to be redeemed.

5. (1) If at any time the share capital is divided into different classes of shares, the rights attached to any class (unless otherwise provided by the terms of issue of the shares of that class) may, whether or not the company is being wound-up, be varied with the consent in writing of the holders of three-quarters of the issued shares of that class, or with the sanction of a special resolution passed at a separate meeting of the holders of the shares of the class.

   (2) The provisions of the Act and these regulations relating to general meetings apply so far as they are capable of application and with the necessary modifications to every such class meeting except that—

(a) where a class has only one member-that member shall constitute a meeting;

(b) in any other case- a quorum shall be constituted by two persons who, between them, hold or represent by proxy one third of the issued shares of the class; and

(c) any holder of shares of the class, present in person or by proxy, may demand a poll.

(3) The rights conferred upon the holders of the shares of any class issued with preferred or other rights shall, unless otherwise expressly provided by the terms of issue of the shares of that class, be varied by the creation or issue of further shares ranking equally with the first-mentioned shares.

6. (1) The Company may make payments by way of brokerage or commission on the issue of shares.

(2) Such payments shall not exceed the rate of 10 per cent of the price at which the shares are issued or an amount equal to 10 per cent of that price, as the case may be.

(3) Such payments may be made in cash, by the allotment of fully or partly paid shares or partly by the payment of cash and partly by the allotment of fully or partly paid shares.

7. (1) Except as required by law, the company shall not recognise a person as holding a share upon any trust.

(2) The company shall not be bound by or compelled in any way to recognise (whether or not it has notice of the interest or rights concerned) any equitable, contingent, future or partial interest in any share or unit of a share or (except as otherwise provided by these regulations or by law) any other right in respect of a share except an absolute right of ownership in the registered holder.

8. (1) A person whose name is entered as a member in the register of members shall be entitled without payment to receive a certificate in respect of the share under the seal of the company in accordance with the Act but, in respect of a share or shares held jointly by several persons, the company shall not be bound to issue more than one certificate.

(2) Delivery of a certificate for a share to one of several joint holders shall be sufficient delivery to all such holders.

(3) If a share certificate is defaced, lost or destroyed, it may be renewed on payment of the fee allowed by the Act, or such lesser sum, and on such terms (if any) as to evidence and the payment of costs to the company of investigating evidence, as the directors decide.

3.   Calls on Shares

9.   (1)   The directors may make calls upon the members in respect of any money unpaid on the shares of the members (whether on account of the nominal value of the shares or by way of premium) and not by the terms of issue of those shares payable at fixed times, except that no call shall exceed one-quarter of the sum of nominal values of the shares or be payable earlier than thirty days from the date fixed for the payment of the last preceding call.

(2)   Each member shall, upon receiving at least fourteen days' notice specifying the time or times and place of payment, pay to the company, at the time or times and place so specified the amount called on his shares.

(3)   The directors may revoke or postpone a call.

10.   A call shall be considered to have been made at the time when the resolution of the directors authorising the call was passed and may be required to be paid in instalments.

11.   The joint holders of a share are jointly and severally liable to pay all calls in respect of the share.

12.   If a sum called in respect of a share is not paid before or on the day appointed for payment of the sum, the person from whom the sum is due shall pay interest on the sum from the day appointed for payment of the sum to the time of actual payment at such rate not exceeding the prescribed rate of interest as the Directors determine, but the directors may waive payment of that interest wholly or in part.

13.   Any sum that, by the terms of issue of a share, becomes payable on allotment or at a fixed date, whether on account of the nominal value of the share or by way of premium, shall for the purposes of these regulations be deemed to be a call duly made and payable on the date on which by the terms of issue the sum becomes payable, and, in case of non-payment, all the relevant provisions of these regulations as to payment of interest and expenses, forfeiture or otherwise apply as if the sum had become payable by virtue of a call duly made and notified.

14.   The directors may, on the issue of shares, differentiate between the holders as to the amount of calls to be paid and the times of payment.

15.   (1)   The directors may accept from a member the whole or a part of the amount unpaid on a share although no part of that amount has been called up.

(2)   The directors may authorise payment by the company of interest upon the whole or any part of an amount so accepted, until the

amount becomes payable, at a rate agreed upon between the directors and the member paying the sum subject to sub-regulation (3).

(3)   For the purposes of sub-regulation (2), the rate of interest shall not be greater than—

       (a)   if the company has, by resolution, fixed a rate, the rate so fixed; and

       (b)   in any other case, the prescribed rate of interest.

4.   Lien

16. (1)   The company has a first and paramount lien on every share (not being a fully paid share) for all money (whether presently payable or not) called or payable at a fixed time in respect of that share.

     (2)   The company also has a first and paramount lien on all shares (other than fully paid shares) registered in the name of a sole holder for all money presently payable by him or his estate to the company.

     (3)   The directors may at any time exempt a share wholly or in part from the provisions of this regulation.

     (4)   The company's lien (if any) on a share extends to all dividends payable in respect of the share.

5. Forfeiture of Shares

17. (1)   If a member fails to pay a call or instalment of a call on the day appointed for payment of the call or instalment, the directors may, at any time thereafter during such time as any part of the call or instalment remains unpaid, serve a notice on him requiring payment of so much of the call or instalment as is unpaid, together with any interest that has accrued.

     (2)   The notice shall name a further day (not earlier than the expiration of fourteen days from the date of service of the notice) on or before which the payment required by the notice is to be made and shall state that, in the event of non-payment at or before the time appointed, the shares in respect of which the call was made will be liable to be forfeited.

18. (1)   If the requirements of a notice served under regulation 17 are not complied with, any share in respect of which the notice has been given may at any time thereafter, before the payment required by the notice has been made, be forfeited by a resolution of the directors to that effect.

(2) Such a forfeiture shall include all dividends declared in respect of the forfeited shares and not actually paid before the forfeiture.

19. A forfeited share may be sold or otherwise disposed of on such terms and in such manner as the directors think fit, and, at any time before a sale or disposition, the forfeiture may be cancelled on such terms as the directors think fit.

20. A person whose shares have been forfeited shall cease to be a member in respect of the forfeited shares, but shall remain liable to pay to the company all money that, at the date of forfeiture, was payable by him to the company in respect of the shares (including interest at the prescribed rate of interest from the date of forfeiture on the money for the time being unpaid if the directors think fit to enforce payment of the interest), but his liability shall cease if and when the company receives payment in full of all the money (including interest) so payable in respect of the shares.

21. A statement in writing declaring that the person making the statement is a director or a secretary of the company, and that a share in the company has been duly forfeited on a date stated in the statement, shall be prima facie evidence of the facts stated in the statement as against all persons claiming to be entitled to the share.

22. (1) The company may receive the consideration (if any) given for a forfeited share on any sale or disposition of the share and may execute a transfer of the share in favour of the person to whom the share is sold or disposed of.

(2) On the execution of the transfer, the company shall register the transferee as the holder of the share.

(3) The transferee shall not be bound to see to the application of any money paid as consideration.

(4) The title of the transferee to the share shall not be affected by any irregularity or invalidity in connection with the forfeiture, sale or disposal of the share.

23. The consideration referred to in regulation 22 shall be applied by the company in payment of such part of the amount in respect of which the lien exists as is presently payable, and the residue (if any) shall (subject to any like lien for sums not presently payable that existed upon the shares before the sale) be paid to the person entitled to the shares immediately before the transfer.

24. The provisions of these regulations as to forfeiture shall apply in the case of non-payment of any sum that, by the terms of issue of a share, becomes payable at a fixed time, whether on account of

the nominal value of the shares or by way of premium, as if that sum had been payable by virtue of a call duly made and notified.

6. Transfer of Shares

25. (1) Subject to these regulations, a member may transfer all or any of his shares by instrument in writing in a form prescribed for the purposes of section 188 of the Act or in any other form that the directors approve.

(2) An instrument of transfer referred to in sub-regulation (1) shall be executed by or on behalf of both the transferor and the transferee.

26. The instrument of transfer shall be left for registration at the registered office of the company, together with such fee (if any) not exceeding two penalty units as the directors require, accompanied by the certificate of the shares to which it relates and such other information as the directors properly require to show the right of the transferor to make the transfer, and thereupon the company shall subject to the powers vested in the directors by these regulations, register the transferee as a shareholder.

27. The directors may decline to register a transfer of shares, not being fully paid shares, to a person of whom they do not approve and may also decline to register any transfer of shares on which the company has a lien.

28. The directors may refuse to register any transfer that is not accompanied by the appropriate share certificate, unless the company has not yet issued the share certificate or is bound to issue a renewal or copy of the share certificate.

29. The registration of transfers may be suspended at such times and for such periods as the directors from time to time determine, provided that the periods do not exceed in the aggregate thirty days in any year.

7. Transmission of Shares

30. In the case of the death of a member, the survivor where the deceased was a joint holder, and the legal personal representatives of the deceased where that person was a sole holder, shall be the only persons recognised by the company as having any title to his interest in the shares, but this regulation does not release the estate of a deceased joint holder from any liability in respect of a share that had been jointly held by him with other persons.

31. (1) Subject to any written law relating to bankruptcy, a person becoming entitled to a share in consequence of the death or

bankruptcy of a member may, upon such information being produced as is properly required by the directors, elect either to be registered as a holder of the share or to have some other person nominated by that person registered as the transferee of the share.

(2) If the person becoming entitled elects to be registered, that person shall deliver or send to the company a notice in writing signed by that person stating that that person so elects.

(3) If he elects to have another person registered, he shall execute a transfer of the share to that other person.

(4) All the limitations, restrictions and provisions of these regulations relating to the right to transfer, and the registration of the transfer of share are applicable to any such notice or transfer as if the death or bankruptcy of the member had not occurred and the notice or transfer were a transfer signed by that member.

32. (1) Where the registered holder of a share dies or becomes bankrupt, his personal representatives or the assignee of his estate, as the case may be, shall be upon the production of such information as is properly required by the directors, entitled to the same dividends and other advantages, and to the same rights (whether in relation to meetings of the company, or to voting or otherwise), as the registered holder would have been entitled to if he had not died or become bankrupt.

(2) Where two or more persons are jointly entitled to any share in consequence of the death of the registered holder, they shall, for the purposes of these regulations, be deemed to be joint holders of the shares.

8. Conversion of shares into stock

33. The company may, by resolution, convert all or any of its paid up shares into stock and reconvert any stock into paid up shares of any nominal value.

34. (1) Subject to sub-regulation (2), where shares have been converted into stock, the provisions of these rules relating to the transfer of shares apply, so far as they are capable of application, to the transfer of the stock or of any part of the stock.

(2) The directors may fix the minimum amount of stock transferable and restrict or forbid the transfer of fractions of that minimum, but the minimum shall not exceed the aggregate of the nominal values of the shares from which the stock arose.

35. (1) The holders of stock shall have, according to the amount of the stock held by them, the same rights, privileges and advantages as

regards dividends, voting at meetings of the company and other matters as they would have if they held the shares from which the stock arose.

(2) No privilege or advantage shall be conferred by any amount of stock that would not, if existing in shares, have conferred that privilege or advantage.

9. Alteration of Capital

36. The provisions of these regulations that are applicable to paid up shares shall apply to stock, and references in those provisions to share and shareholder shall be read as including references to stock and stockholder, respectively.

37. The company may by resolution increase its authorised share capital by the creation of new shares of—

   (a) such amount as is specified in the resolution;

   (b) consolidating and dividing all or any of its authorised share capital into shares of larger amount than its existing shares;

   (c) by subdividing all or any of its shares into shares of smaller amount than is fixed by the certificate of share capital, so that in the subdivision the proportion between the amount paid and the amount (if any) unpaid on each such share of a smaller amount is the same as it was in the case of the share from which the share of a smaller amount is derived; and

   (d) by cancelling shares that, at the date of passing of the resolution, have not been taken or agreed to be taken by any person or have been forfeited, and reduce its authorised share capital by the amount of the shares so cancelled.

38. (1) Subject to any resolution to the contrary, all unissued shares shall, before issue, be offered to such persons as at the date of the offer are entitled to receive notices from the company of general meetings in proportion, as nearly as the circumstances allow, to the sum of the nominal values of the shares already held by them.

   (2) The offer shall be made by notice specifying the number of shares offered and delimiting a period within which the offer, if not accepted, will be deemed to be declined.

   (3) After the expiration of that period or on being notified by the person to whom the offer is made that he declines to accept

the shares offered, the directors may issue those shares in such manner as they think most beneficial to the company.

(4) Where, by reason of the proportion that shares proposed to be issued bear to shares already held, some of the first-mentioned shares cannot be offered in accordance with sub-regulation (1), the directors may issue the shares that cannot be so offered in such manner as they think most beneficial to the company.

39. Subject to the Act, the company may, by special resolution, reduce its share capital, any capital redemption reserve fund or any share premium account.

10. General Meetings

40. (1) A director may, whenever he thinks fit, convene a general meeting.

(2) If no director is present within Zambia, any two members may convene a general meeting in the same manner, or as nearly as possible, as that in which such meetings may be convened by a director.

(3) A general meeting shall be held in Zambia unless all the members entitled to vote at that meeting agree in writing to a meeting at a place outside Zambia.

41. (1) A notice of a general meeting shall specify the place, the day and the hour of meeting and, except as provided by sub-regulation (2), shall state the general nature of the business to be transacted at the meeting.

(2) It shall not be necessary for a notice of an annual general meeting to state that the business to be transacted at the meeting includes the declaring of a dividend, the consideration of annual accounts and the reports of the directors and auditors, the election of directors in the place of those retiring or the appointment and fixing of the remuneration of the auditors.

11. Proceedings at General Meetings

42. (1) No business shall be transacted at any general meeting unless a quorum of members is present at the time when the meeting proceeds to business.

(2) For the purpose of determining whether a quorum is present, a person attending as a proxy, or as representing a body body corporate or association that is a member, shall be deemed to be a member.

43.   If a quorum is not present within half an hour after the time appointed for the meeting—

    (a)   where the meeting was convened upon the requisition of members, the meeting shall be dissolved; or

    (b)   in any other case—

        (i)   the meeting shall stand adjourned to such day, and at such time;

        (ii)   place, as the directors determine or, if no determination is made by the directors, to the same day in the next week at the same time and place; and

        (iii)   if a quorum is not present at the adjourned meeting within half an hour after the time appointed for the meeting—

            A.   two members shall constitute a quorum; or

            B.   the meeting shall be dissolved, if two members are not present.

44. (1) If the directors have elected one of their number as chairman of their meetings, he shall preside as chairman at every general meeting.

    (2) Where a general meeting is held and—

    (a)   a chairman has not been elected as provided by sub-regulation (1); or

    (b)   the chairman is not present within fifteen minutes after the time appointed for the holding of the meeting or is unwilling to act;

    (c)   the member present shall elect one of their number to be chairman of the meeting.

45. (1) The chairman may with the consent of any meeting at which a quorum is present, and shall if so directed by the meeting, adjourn the meeting from time to time and from place to place, but no business shall be transacted at any adjourned meeting other than the business left unfinished at the meeting from which the adjournment took place.

    (2) When a meeting is adjourned for thirty days or more, notice of the adjourned meeting shall be given as in the case of an original meeting.

  (3) Except as provided by sub-regulation (2), it shall not be necessary to give any notice of an adjournment or of the business to be transacted at an adjourned meeting.

46. (1) At any general meeting a resolution put to the vote of the meeting shall be decided on a show of hands unless a poll is (before or on the declaration of the result of the show of hands) demanded—

   (a) by the chairman;

   (b) by at least three members present in person or by proxy;

   (c) by a member or members present in person or by proxy and representing not less than one tenth of the total voting rights of all the members having the right to vote at the meeting; or

   (d) by a member or members holding shares in the company conferring a right to vote at the meeting being shares on which an aggregate sum has been paid up equal to not less than one-tenth of the total sum paid up on all the shares conferring that right.

   (2) The demand for a poll may be withdrawn.

47. (1) If a poll is duly demanded, it shall be taken in such manner and (subject to sub-regulation (2)) either at once or after an interval or adjournment or otherwise as the chairman directs, and the result of the poll shall be the resolution of the meeting at which the poll was demanded.

   (2) A poll demanded on the election of a chairman or on a question of adjournment shall be taken forthwith.

48. In the case of an equality of votes, whether on a show of hands or on a poll, the chairman of the meeting at which the show of hands takes place or at which the poll is demanded, in addition to his deliberative vote (if any), shall have a casting vote.

49. Subject to any rights or restrictions for the time being attached to any class or classes of shares at meetings of members or classes of members—

   (a) each—

   (i) registered member, or registered member of that class;

   (ii) person on whom the ownership of a share of such a registered member has evolved by operation of law;

   (iii) proxy or attorney of a person referred to in paragraph (i) or (ii); if the person is not present at the meeting; shall be entitled to vote;

   (b) on a show of hands, each person present who is entitled to vote shall have one vote; and

   (c) on a poll, every person present who is entitled to vote shall have votes.

50. In the case of joint holders, the vote of the senior who tenders a vote whether in person or by proxy or by attorney, shall be accepted to the exclusion of the votes of the other joint holders and, for this purpose, seniority shall be determined by the order in which the names stand in the register of members.

51. If a member is of unsound mind or is a person whose person or estate is liable to be dealt with in any way under the law relating to mental health, his committee or assignee or such other person as properly has the management of that persons estate may exercise any rights of the member in relation to a general meeting as if the committee, assignee or other person were the member.

52. A member shall not be entitled to vote at a general meeting unless all polls and other sums presently payable by him in respect of shares in the company have been paid.

53. (1) An objection may be raised to the qualification of a voter only at the meeting or adjourned meeting at which the vote objected to is given or tendered.

   (2) Any such objection shall be referred to the chairman of the meeting, whose decision shall be final.

   (3) A vote not disallowed pursuant to such an objection shall be valid for all purposes.

54. (1) An instrument appointing a proxy shall be in writing under the hand of the appointer or of his attorney duly authorised in writing or, if the appointer is a body corporate, either under seal or under the hand of an officer or attorney duly authorised.

   (2) An instrument appointing a proxy may specify the manner in which the proxy is to vote in respect of a particular resolution and, where an instrument of proxy so provides the proxy shall not be entitled to vote in the resolution except as specified in the instrument.

   (3) An instrument appointing a proxy shall be deemed to confer authority to demand or join in demanding a poll

   (4) A proxy need not be a member of the company.

   (5) An instrument appointing a proxy shall be in the following form or in as similar a form as the circumstances allow.
   Name of Company: ....
   I/we .... , of being a member/members of the above named company, hereby of or, in his absence of as my/our proxy to vote for me/us on my/our behalf at the annual/extraordinary general meeting of the company to be held on the...........day of..........20......and at

any adjournment of that meeting:

*in favour of/against resolution No.: ....

*in favour of/against resolution No.: ....

*in favour of/against resolution No.: ....

Unless otherwise instructed, the proxy will vote as that person thinks fit.

Signed:...

Date:...

*Strike out whichever is not desired.

55.   An instrument appointing a proxy shall not be treated as valid unless the instrument, and the power of attorney or other authority (if any) under which the instrument is signed or a notarially certified copy of that power or authority, is or are deposited, not less than forty-eight hours before the time for holding the meeting or adjourned meeting at which the person named in the instrument proposes to vote, or, in the case of a poll, not less than twenty-four hours before the time appointed for the taking of the poll, at the registered office of the company or at such other place in Zambia as is specified for that purpose in the notice convening the meeting.

56.   A vote given in accordance with the terms of an instrument of proxy or of a power of attorney shall be valid notwithstanding the previous death or unsoundness of mind of the principal, the revocation of the instrument (or of the authority under which the instrument was executed) or of the power, or the transfer of the share in respect of which the instrument or power is given, unless notice in writing of the death, unsoundness of mind, revocation or transfer has been received by the company at the registered office before the commencement of the meeting or adjourned meeting at which the instrument is used or the power is exercised.

12. Directors

57.   The company may by ordinary resolution fix a share qualification for directors, but unless and until a qualification is so fixed, there shall be no share qualification.

58.   In addition to the circumstances in which the office of a director becomes vacant by virtue of the Act, the office of a director shall become vacant if the director makes any arrangement or composition with his creditors generally.

13. Borrowing powers

59. (1) Subject to sub-regulation (2), the directors may exercise the powers of the company to borrow money, to charge any property or business of the company or all, or any of its uncalled capital and to issue debentures or give any other security for a debt, liability or obligation of the company or of any other person.

    (2) The amount of any borrowings outstanding at any time shall not exceed the amount of issued share capital of the company at the time.

14. Proceedings of Directors

60. The provisions of section 107 of the Act (providing that a director who is materially interested in a contract or arrangement to be considered at a meeting of the company or of the directors should not be counted in the quorum or vote on the matter) may be suspended or relaxed, whether generally or in respect of a particular transaction, by a resolution of the company.

61. (1) A director may, if the other directors approve, appoint a person as an alternate director in accordance with the Act.

    (2) An alternate director shall be entitled to notice of meetings of the directors.

    (3) An alternate director may, subject to the instrument of appointment, exercise any powers that the appointer may exercise.

62. At a meeting of directors, the quorum shall be two, or such larger number as is determined by resolution of the company.

63. In the event of a vacancy or vacancies in the office of a director or offices of directors, the remaining directors may act but, if the number of remaining directors is not sufficient to constitute a quorum at a meeting of directors, they may act only for the purpose of increasing the number of directors to a number sufficient to constitute such a quorum or of convening a general meeting of the company.

64. (1) The directors shall elect one of their number as chairman of their meetings and may determine the period for which he shall hold office.

    (2) Where meeting of directors is held and—

    (a) a chairman has not been elected as provided by sub-regulation (1); or

    (b) the chairman is not present within ten minutes after the time appointed for the holding of the meeting or is unwilling to act; the directors present shall elect one of their number to be a chairman of the meeting.

65. (1) The directors may delegate any of their powers to a committee or committees consisting of such of their number as they think fit.

(2) A committee to which any powers have been so delegated shall exercise the powers delegated in accordance with any directions of the directors and a power so exercised shall be deemed to have been exercised by the directors.

(3) The members of such a committee may elect one of their number as chairman of their meetings.

(4) Where such a meeting is held and—

    (a) a chairman has not been elected as provided by sub-regulation (3); or

    (b) the chairman is not present within ten minutes after the time appointed for the holding of the meeting or is unwilling to act; the members present may elect one of their number to be chairman of the meeting

(5) A committee may meet and adjourn as it thinks proper.

(6) Questions arising at a meeting of a committee shall be determined by a majority of votes of the members present and voting.

(7) In the case of an equality of votes, the chairman, in addition to his deliberative vote (if any), has a casting vote.

15. Managing Director

66. (1) The directors may, upon such terms and conditions and with such restrictions as they think fit, appoint a executive director in accordance with the Act and confer upon the executive director any of the powers exercisable by them.

(2) Any powers so conferred may be concurrent with, or be to the exclusion of the powers of the directors.

(3) The directors may at any time withdraw or vary any of the powers so conferred on a managing director.

16. Associate Directors

67. (1) The directors may from time to time appoint any person to be an associate director and may from time to time terminate any such appointment.

(2) The directors may from time to time determine the powers, duties and remuneration of any person so appointed.

(3) A person so appointed shall not be required to hold any shares to qualify him for appointment but, except by the invitation and with the consent of the directors, shall not have any right to attend or vote at any meeting of directors.

17. Secretary

68. A secretary of the company shall hold office on such terms and conditions, as to remuneration and otherwise, as the directors determine.

18. Seal

69. (1) The directors shall provide for the safe custody of the seal.

(2) The seal shall be used only by the authority of the directors, or of a committee of the directors authorised by the directors to authorise the use of the seal, and every document to which the seal is affixed shall be signed by a director and be countersigned by another director, a secretary or another person appointed by the directors to countersign that document or a class of documents in which that document is included.

19. Inspection of Records

70. Subject to the Act, the directors shall determine whether and to what extent, and at what time and places and under what conditions, the accounting records and other documents of the company or any of them will be open to the inspection of members other than directors, and a member other than a director shall not have the right to inspect any document of the company except as provided by law or authorised by the directors or by a resolution of the company.

20. Dividends and Reserves

71. (1) The company by resolution may declare a dividend if, and only if, the directors have recommended a dividend.

(2) A dividend shall not exceed the amount recommended by the directors.

72. The directors may authorise the payment by the company to the members of such interim dividends as appear to the directors to be justified by the profits of the company.

73. Interest shall not be payable by the company in respect of any dividend.

74. A dividend shall not be paid except out of profits of the company.

75. (1) The directors may, before recommending any dividend, set aside out of the profits of the company such sums as they think proper as reserves, to be applied, at the discretion of the directors, for any purpose for which the profits of the company may be properly applied.

(2) Pending any such application, the reserves may, at the discretion of the directors, be used in the business of the company or be invested in such investments as the directors think fit.

(3) The directors may carry forward so much of the profits remaining as they consider ought not to be distributed as dividends without transferring those profits to a reserve.

76. (1) Subject to the rights of persons (if any) entitled to shares with special rights as to dividend, all dividends shall be declared and paid according to the amounts paid or credited as paid on the shares in respect of which the dividend is paid.

(2) All dividends shall be apportioned and paid proportionately to the amounts paid or credited as paid on the shares during any portion or portions of the period in respect of which the dividend is paid, but, if any share is issued on terms providing that it will rank for dividend as from a particular date, that share shall rank for dividend accordingly.

(3) An amount paid or credited as paid on a share in advance of a call shall not be taken for the purposes of this regulation to be paid or credited as paid on the share.

77. The directors may deduct from any dividend payable to a member all sums of money (if any) presently payable by him to the company on account of calls or otherwise in relation to shares in the company.

78. (1) If the company declares a dividend it may by resolution direct the directors to pay the dividend wholly or partly by the distribution of specific assets, including paid up shares in, or debentures of, any other corporation.

(2) Where a difficulty arises in regard to such a distribution, the directors may settle the matter as they consider expedient and in particular may issue fractional certificates and fix the value for distribution of the specific assets or any part of those assets, and may determine that cash payments will be made to any members on the basis of the value so fixed in order to adjust the rights of all parties, and may vest any such specific assets in assignees as the directors consider expedient.

79. (1) Any dividend, interest or other money payable in cash in respect of shares may be paid by cheque sent through the post directed to—

(a) the registered address of the holder or, in the case of joint holders, to the registered address of the joint holder named first in the register of members; or

(b) to such other address as the holder or joint holders in writing directs or direct.

(2) Any one of two or more joint holders may give effectual receipts for any dividends, interests or other money payable in respect of the shares held by them as joint holders.

21. Capitalisation of Profits

80. (1) Subject to sub-regulation (2), the company may resolve—*(a)* to capitalise any sum, being the whole or a part of the amount for the time being standing to the credit of any reserve account or the statement of comprehensive income or otherwise available for distribution to members; and *(b)* to apply the sum, in any of the ways mentioned in sub-regulation (3), for the benefit of members in the proportions to which those members would have been entitled in a distribution of that sum by way of dividend.

(2) The company shall not pass a resolution under sub-regulation (1) unless it has been recommended by the directors. (3) The ways in which a sum may be applied for the benefit of members under sub-regulation (1) shall be—

(a) in paying up any amounts unpaid on shares held by members;

(b) in paying up in full unissued shares or debentures to be issued to members as fully paid; or

(c) partly under paragraph *(a)* and partly under paragraph *(b)*.

(4) The directors shall do all things necessary to give effect to the resolution and, in particular, to the extent necessary to adjust the rights of the members among themselves and may—

(a) issue fractional certificates or make cash payments in cases where shares or debentures become issuable infractions; and

(b) authorise any person to make, on behalf of all the members entitled to any further shares or debentures upon the capitalisation, an agreement with the company providing for the issue to them, credited as fully paid up, of any such further shares or debentures or for the paying up by the company on their behalf of the amounts or any part of the amounts remaining unpaid on their existing shares by the application of their respective proportions of the sum resolved to be capitalised; and any agreement made under an authority referred to in paragraph *(b)* shall be effective and binding on all the members concerned.

22. Winding-up

81. (1) If the company is wound-up, the liquidator may, with the sanction of a special resolution, divide among the members in kind the whole or any part of the property of the company and may for that purpose set such value as the liquidator considers fair upon any property to be so divided and may determine how the division is to be carried out as between the members or different classes of members.

(2) The liquidator may, with the sanction of a special resolution, vest the whole or any part of any such properly in assignees upon such trusts for the benefit of the contributories as the liquidator thinks fit, but so that no member is compelled to accept any shares or other securities in respect of which there is any liability.

23. Indemnity

82. Every officer, auditor or agent of the company shall be indemnified out of the property of the company against any liability incurred by him in his capacity as officer, auditor or agent in defending any proceedings, whether civil or criminal, in which judgment is given in that favour or in which that person is acquitted or in connection with any application in relation to any such proceedings in which relief is under the Act granted to him by the court.

APPENDIX 2

SECOND SCHEDULE
(Section 12(3))

ARTICLES OF ASSOCIATION OF
REGULATIONS FOR MANAGEMENT OF A COMPANY
LIMITED BY GUARANTEE

Table of Divisions

1. Name and Location
2. Purpose and Mission
3. General Policies
4. Membership
5. Government and Representation
6. Means
7. Prohibitions
8. Statement of Faith
9. Amendments
10. Dissolution
11. Board of Directors
12. Executive Committee
13. National Workers
14. National Coordinator/Director
15. Sub-Committees
16. Branches
17. Inspection of Accounts and List of members
18. Body Corporate
19. Winding-up
20. Indemnity

1. (1) In these regulations, unless the context otherwise requires
"Articles" means the articles of the Company;
"The Office" means the registered office of the company; and
"The Seal" means the common seal of the Company.

  (2) Unless the context otherwise requires, words or expressions contained in these regulations bear the same meaning as in the Act.

Members

2.   Each subscriber to an application for incorporation of the company and such other persons as are admitted to membership in accordance with the articles shall be the members of the company. No person shall be admitted as a member of the company unless by a resolution of the company, and by signing a declaration of guarantee and delivering it to the company.

3.   A member may at any time withdraw from the company by giving at least seven days' written notice to that effect.

General Meetings

4.   All general meetings other than annual general meetings shall be called extraordinary general meetings.

5.   The Directors may call a general meeting whenever they consider necessary and, on the requisition of members pursuant to the provisions of the Act, shall forthwith proceed to convene an extraordinary general meeting on a date not later than six weeks after receipt of the requisition. If there are no sufficient directors present within Zambia to call a general meeting, any one Director, or any two members may convene a general meeting in the same manner, or in a manner as similar as possible to that in which such a meeting may be convened by a Director.

6.   A general meeting shall be held in Zambia unless all the members entitled to vote at the meeting agree in writing to hold the meeting at a place outside Zambia.

Notice of General Meeting

7.   An annual general meeting and a general meeting called for the passing of a special resolution or resolution appointing a person as a Director shall be called by at least twenty-one days' notice. All other general meetings shall be called by at least fourteen days' notice, but a general meeting may be called by shorter notice if it is so agreed by all the members entitled to attend and vote at the meeting.

8.   A notice of a general meeting shall specify the date, place, and hour of the meeting and the general nature of the business to be transacted and, in the case of an annual general meeting, shall specify the meeting as such.

9.   The accidental omission to give notice of a meeting to, or the non-receipt of notice of a meeting by, any person entitled to receive notice shall not invalidate the proceedings at the meeting.

Proceedings at General Meetings

10.   A business shall not be transacted at any general meeting unless a quorum of members is present at the time when the meeting proceeds to business. For the purpose of determining whether a quorum is present, a person attending as a proxy, or as a representative of a body corporate or association that is a member shall be deemed to be a member.

11.   If a quorum is not present within half an hour after the time appointed for the meeting—

    (a)   where the meeting was convened upon the requisition of members, the meeting shall be dissolved; or

    (b)   in any other case—

        (i)   the meeting shall stand adjourned to such day, and at such time and place, as the directors determine or, if no determination is made by the directors, to the same day in the next week at the same time and place; and

        (ii)   if a quorum not present at the adjourned meeting within half an hour after the time appointed for the meeting—A. two members shall constitute a quorum; or B. the meeting shall be dissolved, if two member are not present.

12. (1)   If the directors have selected one of their number as chairman of their meetings, that person shall preside as a chairman at every general meeting of the company.

    (2)   Where a general meeting is held and—

    (a)   a chairman has not been elected as provided above; or

    (b)   the chairman is not present within fifteen minutes after the time appointed for the holding of the meeting or is unwilling act; the members present shall elect one of their number to be chairman of the meeting.

13. (1)   The chairman may, with the consent of a meeting at which a quorum is present (and shall if so directed by the meeting), adjourn the meeting from time to time and from place to place, but no business shall be transacted at an adjourned meeting other than the business left unfinished at the meeting from which the adjournment took place.

    (2)   When a meeting is adjourned for thirty days or more, notice of the adjourned meeting shall be given as in the case of an original meeting. Except as provided in the preceding paragraph, it shall not be necessary to give notice of an adjournment or of the business to be transacted at an adjourned meeting.

14. (1) At a general meeting, a resolution put to the vote of the meeting shall be decided on a show of hands unless a poll is demanded (before or on the declaration of the result of the show of hands)—

    (a) by the chairman;

    (b) by at least three members present in person or by proxy; or

    (c) by a member or members present in person or by proxy and representing not less than one tenth of the total rights of all the members having the right to vote at the meeting.

  (2) The demand for a poll may be withdrawn.

15. (1) If a poll is duly demanded, it shall be taken in such manner, either at once or after an initial meeting, adjournment or otherwise, as the chairman directs and the result of the poll shall be the resolution of the meeting at which the poll was demanded.

  (2) A poll demanded on the election of the chairman or on a question of adjournment shall be taken forthwith.

16. In the case of an equality of votes, whether on a show of hands or on a poll, the chairman of the meeting at which the show of hands takes place or at which the poll is demanded, in addition to the chairman's deliberate vote (if any), shall have a casting vote.

17. Subject to any rights or restrictions for the time being, at a meeting of members, each registered member, proxy or attorney of a member who is not present at the meeting shall be entitled to vote.

18. On a show of hands, each person present who is entitled to vote shall have one vote, and on a poll, every person present who is entitled to vote shall have a vote in accordance with section 67 of the Act.

19. (1) An objection may be raised to the qualification of a voter only at the meeting or adjourned meeting at which the vote objected to is given or tendered. Any such objection shall be referred to the chairman of the meeting, whose decision shall be final. A vote not disallowed pursuant to such objection shall be valid for all purposes.

  (2) An instrument appointing a proxy shall be in writing under the hand of the appointed or his attorney duly authorized in writing or, if the appointer is a body corporate, either under seal or under the hand of an officer or attorney duly authorized.

  (3) An instrument appointing a proxy may specify the manner in which the proxy is to vote in respect of a particular resolution

and, where an instrument of proxy so provides, the proxy shall not be entitled to vote in the resolution except as specified in the instrument.

(4)   An instrument appointing a proxy shall be deemed to confer authority to demand or join in demanding a poll.

(5)   A proxy need not be a member of the company.

(6)   An instrument appointing a proxy shall be in the following form or in similar form as the circumstances require.

Name of Company:..

I/ We...

.............of...

Being a member/members of the above named accompany.

Companies [**No. 10 of 2017 615**

Hereby appoint..

of...

....

....

Or in his absence..

of...

....

As my/our proxy to vote for me/us on my/our behalf at the annual/extraordinary general meeting of the company to be held on the ....day of...................................20.......................................

* in favour of/against resolution No.:..............................

* in favour of /resolution No.:....................................

* in favour resolution No.:...

Unless otherwise instructed, the proxy will vote as he thinks fit.

Signed:..

Date:..

*Strike out whichever is not desirable.

20.   An instrument appointing a proxy shall not be treated as valid unless the instrument and the power of attorney or other authority (if any) under which the instrument is signed or a notarially certified copy of that power or authority are deposited, not less than forty-eight hours before the time for holding the meeting or adjourned meeting at which the person named in the instrument proposes to vote, or in the case of a poll, not less that twenty-four hours before the time appointed for the taking of the poll, at the registered office of the company or at such other place in Zambia as shall be specified for that purpose in the notice convening the meeting.

21.   A vote given in accordance with the terms of an instrument of proxy or of a power of attorney shall be valid notwithstanding that the principal has since died, become of unsound mind or revoked the instrument (or the authority under which the instrument was executed) or the power, unless notice in writing of the death, unsoundness of mind or revocation has been received by the company at the company's registered office before the commencement of the meeting or adjourned meeting at which the instrument is to be used or the power exercised.

Directors

22.   In addition to the circumstances in which the office of director becomes vacant by virtue of the Act, the office of director makes any arrangement or composition with his creditors generally

Borrowing Powers

23.   The board of directors may exercise the powers of the company to borrow money, to charge any property or business of the company and to issue debentures or give any other security for a debt, liability or obligation of the company or of any person.

Powers and Duties of Directors

24.   The affairs of the company shall be managed by the directors, who may pay all expenses incurred in registering the company and may exercise all such powers of the company as are not, by the Act or these articles, required to be excised by the company in a general meeting, subject nevertheless to the provisions of the Act and these articles.

25.   The board may from time to time and at any time by power of attorney appoint a body corporate, firm or person or body of persons, whether nominated directly or indirectly by the directors to be the attorney or attorneys of the company for such purposes and with such powers, authorities and discretion (not exceeding those vested in or exercisable by the directors under these articles) and for such period and subject to such conditions as they consider necessary.

Proceedings of Directors

26.   The provisions of section 107 of the Act providing that a director who is materially interested in a contract or arrangement to be considered at a meeting of the company should not be counted in quorum or vote on the matter may be suspended or relaxed,

whether generally or in respect of a particular transaction, by a resolution of the company.

Alternate Directors

27. (1) A director may, if the others approve, appoint a person as an alternate director in accordance with the Act.

    (2) An alternate director may, subject to the instrument of appointment, exercise any powers that the appointer may exercise.

28. (1) At a meeting of directors, the quorum shall be two, or such larger number as shall be determined by resolution of the company.

    (2) In the event of a vacancy or vacancies in the office of director, the remaining directors or director may act but if the number of remaining directors is not sufficient to constitute a quorum at a meeting of directors, the remaining directors or director may act only for purposes of increasing the number of director to a number sufficient to constitute such quorum or of convening a general meeting of the company.

29. (1) The directors may delegate any of their powers to committees consisting of such of their number as they consider appropriate. Powers so delegated and exercised shall be deemed to have been exercised by the directors.

    (2) The members of such a committee may elect one of their number as chairman of their meetings. Where such a meeting is held, and a chairman has not been elected as provided above, or the chairman is not present within ten minutes after the appointed time for the holding of the meeting or is unwilling to act, the members present may choose one of their number to be chairman of the meeting.

    (3) Questions arising at a meeting of a committee shall be determined by a majority of votes of the members present and voting. In the event of an equality of votes, the chairman, in addition to his deliberate vote (if any) shall have a casting vote.

Executive Director

30. The board of directors may, upon such terms and conditions and with such restrictions as it considers necessary, appoint an executive director in accordance with the Act and confer upon the executive director any of the powers exercisable by the board. Any powers so conferred may be concurrent with, or to the exclusion of the powers of the board. The board may at any time withdraw or vary any of the power so conferred on the executive director.

Remuneration of Directors

31.   The directors shall be entitled to such remuneration as the company may, by ordinary resolution, determine and, unless the resolution provides otherwise, the remuneration shall be deemed to accumulate from day to day.

Directors' Expenses

32.   The directors may be paid all travelling, hotel, and other expenses properly incurred by them in connection with their attendance at meetings of directors or committees of directors or general meetings of the company or otherwise in connection with the discharge of their duties as directors.

Secretary

33.   A secretary of the company shall hold office on such terms and conditions as to remuneration and otherwise, as the board may determine.

Minutes

34.   The board shall cause minutes to be recorded in books kept for that purpose—

(a)   of all appointments of officers made by the directors; and

(b)   of all proceedings at meetings of the company, of the directors and of committees of directors, including the names of the directors present at such meetings.

The Seal

35.   The board shall provide for the safe custody of the seal. The seal shall be used only with the authority of the board, or of a committee of directors authorized by the board and every document to which the seal is affixed shall be signed by a director and countersigned by the directors to counter-sign that document or a class of documents in which that document is included.

Inspection of Records

36.   Subject to the Act, the board shall determine whether and to what extent, at what time, places and under what conditions, the accounting records and other documents of the company or any of them will be open to the inspection of members other than directors, and a member other than a director shall not have the right to inspect any document of the company except as provided by law or authorized by the board or by a resolution of the company.

Indemnity

37.   An officer, auditor or agent of the company shall be indemnified out of the property of the company against any liability incurred by the officer, auditor or agent in that capacity in defending any proceedings, whether civil or criminal, in which relief is granted to the officer, auditor or agent by the court under the Act.

38. (1) We the several persons whose names and addresses are subscribed, wish to be formed into a COMPANY LIMITED BY GUARANTEE in pursuance of this application, and—

(2) We agree that if, upon the winding up of the company, there remains after the discharge of all its debts and liabilities any property of the company, that property will not be distributed among the members, but will be transferred to some other company having similar objects, or applied to some other charitable object, such other company or charity to be determined by ordinary resolution of the members in a general meeting prior to the dissolution of the company.

(3) We respectively declare that if, upon the winding up of the company, the assets of the company prove insufficient to discharge all the debts and liabilities of the company, we guarantee to contribute to the discharge of those debts and liabilities an amount set against our respective names.

SUBSCRIBERS' NAMES, ADDRESSES AND
GUARANTEED AMOUNT **WITNESS:**

Full Name: ....

Occupation: ....

Address: ....

Signature: ....

APPENDIX 3

THIRD SCHEDULE
(Section 212)
CONTENTS OF PROSPECTUS

1.   In this Schedule, unless the context otherwise requires—
"company" includes a company proposed to be formed; "proposed subsidiary" in relation to a company, means a body corporate in which the company proposes to acquire securities and which, by reason of the acquisition or anything to be done in consequence thereof or in connection therewith, will become a subsidiary of the company.

2.   The prospectus shall state at its head -"A copy of this prospectus has been delivered to the Registrar of Companies for registration. The Registrar has not checked and will not check the accuracy of the statements made and accepts no responsibility therefor or for the financial soundness of the company or the value of the securities concerned."

3.   The reports set out in a prospectus for purposes of this Schedule shall be made by a person or persons duly qualified under Part XII of this Act to be appointed as auditors of the company.

4.   Where reports prepared for the purposes of this Schedule would not otherwise give a true and fair view of the matters required to be covered by the reports, the persons charged with the preparation of the reports shall add such information and explanations as well to give a true and fair view of those matters.

5.   If any of the information required for the purposes of reports for this Schedule is for reasons beyond the power of the company not available, that fact and the reasons therefor shall be stated.

Matters to be specified in Prospectus
6.   The full name of the company.
7. (1) A full description of the securities which the public are being invited to acquire, and of the terms on which they are being invited to acquire them, including—

        (a) the date prior to the expiration of which applications will not be accepted or treated as binding;

(b) the total amount payable for each share or debenture and the amount thereof payable on application and allotment, if securities are being offered for subscription or purchase; and *(c)* the policy which will be adopted if applications exceed the shares or debentures on offer. (2) Where the securities are unsecured debentures they shall be described as "unsecured".

8. Whether or not an application has been or is being made to a stock exchange for permission to deal in the securities concerned and—

    (a) if so, the name of the stock exchange; or

    (b) if not, a statement that there will not be a market for the securities and that any holder wishing to dispose of his securities may be unable to do so.

9. The full name (including any former or other names), residential and postal addresses and business occupation of each person making the invitation, other than the company.

10. The situation of the company's registered office, and its postal address.

11. The full name (including any former or other names), residential and postal addresses and business occupation of every director or proposed director and of the secretary or proposed secretary of the company, and particulars of all other directorships held by each director or proposed director.

12. Other than for a proposed company, the names, addresses and professional qualifications of the company's auditors.

13. The name and address of any underwriter of the invitation.

14. The names and addresses of the company's bankers, stockbrokers and legal practitioners.

15. If the invitation relates to debentures, the names and addresses of any trustees for debenture holders, the date of the resolutions creating the debentures, and short particulars of the security therefor or, if the debentures are unsecured, a statement to that effect.

16. The nature of the business or businesses of the company or, if the company has no business, its principal objects.

17. The restrictions, if any, upon the business of the company contained in the articles.

18. A brief summary of the history of the company.

19. The names, countries of incorporation, and nature of the businesses of all subsidiaries of the company and of all bodies

body corporate in which the company is beneficially entitled to equity shares conferring the right to exercise more than twenty-five per cent of the votes exercisable at a general meeting of the body corporate.

20.   If the company is a subsidiary, the name, country of incorporation and nature of the business of each holding company and, in the case of a holding company that is a member of the company, the number of shares in each class of the company held by the holding company.

21.   The name, country of incorporation, and nature of the business of any proposed subsidiary of the company.

22.   Where the company is proposing to acquire a business, a full description, of the nature of that business.

23.   The situation, area and tenure (including, where appropriate, the rent and unexpired term of any lease or concession) of the main places of business of the company and its subsidiaries and proposed subsidiaries.

24.   A statement as to—

    (a)   the financial and trading prospects of the company together with any material information which may be relevant thereto; and

    (b)   any material changes in the financial or trading position of the company which may have occurred since the end of the last completed financial year of the company.

25.   A statement by the directors of the company that in their opinion the company's working capital is sufficient or, if not, how it is proposed to provide the additional working capital thought by the directors to be necessary.

26.   The amount or estimated amount of the expenses incidental and preliminary to the invitation (including the expenses of any application to a stock exchange for permission to deal in the securities concerned in the invitation) and by whom such expenses are payable.

27.   Particulars of any commissions payable, or paid within the two preceding years, as commission for acquiring any shares or debentures of the company or of any of its subsidiaries and proposed subsidiaries.

28.   Where the company is inviting the public to subscribe for any of its shares or debentures—

    (a)   a statement or an estimate of the net proceeds of the issue and a statement as to how such proceeds were or are to be applied;

(b) the minimum amount which in the opinion of the company's directors must be raised by the issue in order to provide the sums, or, if part thereof is to be defrayed in any other manner, the balance of the sums, required to be provided in respect of each of the following matters:

    (i) the purchase price of any property purchased or to be purchased which is to be defrayed in whole or in part out of the proceeds of the issue;

    (ii) any expenses incidental and preliminary to the invitation and issue (including the expenses of any application to a stock exchange for permission to deal in the shares or debentures) payable by the company, and any commission be payable to any person in consideration of his agreeing to subscribe for, or of his procuring or agreeing to procure subscriptions for any share or debentures of the company;

    (iii) the repayment of any moneys borrowed by the company in respect of any of the foregoing matters; (iv) working capital; and

(c) the amounts to be provided in respect of the matters stated in paragraph (b) otherwise than out of the proceeds of the issue, and the sources out of which these amounts are to be provided.

29. Where a person other than the company is inviting the public to purchase any shares or debentures of the company (whether or not the invitation is also made by the company)—

(a) if the shares or debentures were issued by the company for cash-a statement of the price per share or debenture at which those shares or debentures were issued, and of the total net proceeds of the issue;

(b) if the shares or debentures were issued by the company for a consideration other than cash-a statement of the nature of the consideration and an estimate by the directors of its fair value and of the price per share or debenture which it represents;

(c) if the person making the invitation did not acquire the shares or debentures directly from the company on their issue—

    (i) if he purchased them for cash-a statement of the price per share or debenture at which he purchased them (or, if purchased over a period of time at different prices, the lowest and highest prices) and the total purchase price paid by him; or

      (ii)   if he acquired them for a consideration other than cash-a statement of the nature of the consideration and an estimate by him of its fair value and of the price per share or debenture which it represents.

30.   The authorised capital of the company and the number and description of the company's authorised shares of each class and issued shares of each class.

31.   The amount paid on the issued shares of each class—

      (a)   in cash; and

      (b)   otherwise than in cash.

32.   The amount, if any, remaining payable on the shares of each class previously issued, distinguishing between the amount presently due for payment and the amount not yet due for payment.

33.   The number of unissued shares of each class agreed to be issued and the amounts payable therefor, distinguishing between amounts payable in cash and amounts payable otherwise than in cash.

34.   If the company's shares are divided into different classes, the rights in respect of voting, repayment, and dividends and other special rights attached to the several classes and a statement as to the consents necessary for the variation of such rights.

35.   The amounts of the dividends (if any) per share paid by the company in respect of each class of shares in each of the ten completed financial years of the company immediately preceding the date of publication of the prospectus, or in respect of each of the financial years since the incorporation of the company if this occurred less than ten years before the publication, and particulars of any cases in which no dividends have been paid in respect of any class of shares in any of those years.

36.   If any of the company's shares are redeemable preference shares, the earliest date on which the company has power to redeem them.

37.   The name of each person who holds more than 25 per cent of the company's shares or any class of shares and the number and description of the shares held or owned.

38.   The name of each person who is the beneficial owner of the company's shares or any class of shares and the number and description of the shares held or owned.

39.   The amount of the outstanding debentures issued or agreed to be issued by the company and any of its subsidiaries and proposed subsidiaries or, if none, a statement to that effect.

40.   Particulars of any bank overdrafts of the company and any of its subsidiaries and proposed subsidiaries as at the latest practical date (which shall be stated) or, if there are no bank overdrafts, a statement to that effect.

41.   The nature of the consideration for the issue of any of the company's shares or debentures issued or proposed to be issued otherwise than for cash.

42.   Particulars of any share or debentures of any of the company's subsidiaries and proposed subsidiaries which have, within two years immediately preceding the publication of the prospectus, been issued, or which are proposed to be issued otherwise than for cash and the nature of the consideration.

43.   Particulars of any shares or debentures of the company or any of its subsidiaries and proposed subsidiaries which have, within two years immediately preceding the publication of the prospectus, been issued, or which are proposed to be issued, for cash, the price and terms upon which the same have been or are to be issued and (if not already fully paid) the dates when any instalments are payable.

44.   Particulars of any shares or debentures of the company or any of its subsidiaries and proposed subsidiaries which are under option, or agreed conditionally or unconditionally to be put option, with the price to be paid for the securities option, the duration of the option, the consideration for which the option was granted and—*(a)* where the option is to all the shareholders or debenture holders or any class thereof or to employees generally a statement of that fact; or *(b)* in any other case-the name and address of each grantee.

45. (1) Subject to sub-clause (2), where any property has been acquired or is proposed to be acquired by the company or any of its subsidiaries and proposed subsidiaries—

      (a)   the names and addresses of the vendors;

      (b)   the amount paid or to be paid in cash, shares, debentures or otherwise to the vendor, and, where there is more than one separate vendor or the company or subsidiary or proposed subsidiary is a sub-purchaser, the amount so paid or to be paid to cash vendor, distinguishing between the amounts paid or to be paid—

(i)　in cash;

(ii)　in shares;

(iii)　in debentures; *(c)* the nature of, and value attributed to, any other consideration; *(d)* the amount (if any) paid or payable for goodwill; *(e)* full particulars of the nature and extent of the interest, direct or indirect, of every director or proposed director of the company or any of its subsidiaries and proposed subsidiaries in the property; and *(f)* short particulars of the property.

(2)　Sub-clause (1) shall not apply where the contract for the acquisition of the property was—

　　(a)　completed, and any purchase money fully paid, more than two years before the date of publication of the prospectus; or

　　(b)　entered into in the ordinary course of business and there is no connection between the contract and the invitation.

46.　Unless more than two years have elapsed since the registration of the company—

　　(a)　the amount or estimated amount of the expenses incidental or preliminary to the promotion and registration of the company and by whom those expenses have been paid or are payable;

　　(b)　the names of the promoters of the company;

　　(c)　the amount of any cash or securities paid, or benefit given or proposed to be given, to any promoter and the consideration for such payment or benefit; and

　　(d)　full particulars of the nature and extent of the interest of every director and proposed director in the promotion of the company.

47.　Where the prospectus includes a statement purporting to be made by an expert, a statement that the expert has given and has not withdrawn his written consent to the publication of the prospectus with the statement included in the form and in the context in which it is included.

48.　The dates of, parties to, and general nature of, every material contract (other than contracts entered into in the ordinary course of business or completed more than two years before the date of publication of the prospectus).

49. (1) A reasonable time (not being less than twenty-eight days) during which, and place at which, subject to this clause, the following documents (or certified copies thereof), may be inspected—

    (a) the company's certificate of incorporation, certificate of share capital and articles;

    (b) where the invitation relates to debentures-the debenture trust deed;

    (c) each contract disclosed pursuant to clause 48 of this Schedule or, in the case of a contract not reduced to writing, a memorandum giving full particulars thereof;

    (d) the annual accounts (including any group accounts), auditor's report and directors' report for each of the last five financial years, or, where part of that period fell before the commencement of this Act, all similar accounts and reports produced by the company in respect of that part of the period;

    (e) the annual accounts (including any group accounts), auditors' report and directors' report in respect of each subsidiary and proposed subsidiary, for each of the last five financial years, or where—

        (i) part of that period fell before the commencement of this Act; or

        (ii) the subsidiary or proposed subsidiary is not a company to which this Act applies; all similar accounts and reports produced by the subsidiary or proposed subsidiary in respect of that period or part of the period;

    (f) all other reports, letters, statement of financial positions, valuations and statements by an expert any part of which is extracted or referred to in the prospectus; and

    (g) a written statement, signed by the accountants making the report required under this schedule, setting out the adjustments made by them in arriving at the figures shown in their report and giving the reasons therefor.

(2) If any part of any of the above-mentioned documents is in a language other than English, a certified translation into English of that part of the document shall be made available for inspection instead of the original or a certified copy.

(3) Paragraph (1) *(e)* shall not require to be made available for inspection the profit and loss accounts and statement of financial position s of a subsidiary or business in respect of any financial

years in which the profits or losses and assets and liabilities of the subsidiary or business are dealt with in the accounts or group accounts of the company.

50.   The names and addresses of the persons making the reports required under this Schedule.

Reports to be set out in Prospectus

51.   A report with respect to—

    (a) the profits or losses of the company in respect of—

        (i) each of the ten completed financial years immediately preceding the publication of the prospectus, (or since the incorporation of the company if less than ten years); and

        (ii) the period from the end of the last financial year to the latest practicable date being a date less than ninety days before the date of the publication of the prospectus, if the last financial year of the company ended ninety days or more before the date of the publication of the prospectus; or

    (b) if the company has subsidiaries-a report as required by paragraph *(a)* with respect to the profits or losses of the company and of its subsidiaries, so far as such profits or losses can properly be regarded as attributable to the interests of the company.

52.   A report with respect to—

    (a) the assets and liabilities of the company as at the end of its last financial year or, if the financial year ended ninety days or more before the date of publication of the prospectus, as at the latest practicable date, being a date less than ninety days before the date of publication of the prospectus; or

    (b) if the company has subsidiaries-a report of the kind required by paragraph *(a)* with respect to the assets and liabilities of the company, and of its subsidiaries so far as such assets can properly be regarded as attributable to the interests of the company.

53.   A report with respect to the aggregate emoluments paid by the company to the directors of the company or any related body corporate during the last period for which the accounts have been made up and the amount, if any, by which such emoluments would differ from the amounts payable under any arrangement in force at the date of publication of the prospectus.

54. (1) A report with respect to profits or losses of—

    (a) each proposed subsidiary of the company;

    (b) each business acquired by the company within ten years before the date of publication of the prospectus; and

    (c) each body corporate that became a subsidiary of the company within ten years before the date of publication of the prospectus; in respect of—

        (i) each of the ten financial years immediately preceding the publication of the prospectus, (or each financial year since the commencement of that business or the incorporation of that subsidiary or proposed subsidiary, if less than ten years); and

        (ii) if the last financial year of that business, subsidiary or proposed subsidiary ended ninety days or more before the date of the publication of the prospectus-the period from the end of the last financial year to the latest practicable date, being a date less than ninety days before the date of the publication of the prospectus.

(2) The report shall deal with such of the profits or losses of a subsidiary or proposed subsidiary as can properly be regarded as attributable to the interests of the company.

(3) Where the report relates to any financial year before the subsidiary became a subsidiary of the company or relates to a proposed subsidiary, only such of its profits or losses shall be regarded as attributable to the interests of the company as would have been properly so attributable if the company had held the securities in the subsidiary or proposed subsidiary which it holds at the date of publication of the prospectus or proposes to acquire.

(4) Where any such subsidiary or proposed subsidiary itself has subsidiaries, the report shall extend to the profits or losses of its subsidiaries so far as the same can properly be regarded as attributable to the interests of the company.

(5) The report need not extend to any period in respect of which the profits or losses of that business or the appropriate part of the profits or losses of that subsidiary are dealt with in the report required under clause 51.

55. (1) A report with respect to the assets and liabilities of each proposed subsidiary of the company and each business or subsidiary acquired since the latest date up to which the accounts of the

company have been made, as at the end of the last financial year of the business, subsidiary or proposed subsidiary, or, if the financial year ended ninety days or more before the date of publication of the prospectus, as at the latest practicable date not being more than ninety days before the date of publication of the prospectus.

(2) The report shall deal with the assets and liabilities of the business, subsidiary or proposed subsidiary so far as such assets and liabilities can properly be regarded as attributable to the interests of the company.

(3) In relation to a proposed subsidiary, only such assets and liabilities shall be regarded as attributable to the interests of the company as would have been properly so attributable if the company had held the securities in the proposed subsidiary which it proposes to acquire.

(4) Where any such subsidiary or proposed subsidiary itself has subsidiaries, the report shall extend to the assets and liabilities of its subsidiaries so far as the same can properly be attributable to the interest of the company.

56. A report with respect to any other matters which appear to the persons charged with making the reports to be relevant having regard to the purposes of the reports.

APPENDIX 4

FOURTH SCHEDULE
(Section 376(2))
TRANSITIONAL PROVISIONS

1.   A person holding office at the commencement of this Act shall remain in office as if that person had been appointed in accordance with this Act but shall comply with the requirements of this Act within two years of the commencement of this Act.

2.   Any act done or executed in accordance with the repealed Act and in force and operative at the commencement of this Act shall have effect as if done or executed in accordance with this Act.

3.   (1)   Existing companies' articles of association in force and operative at the commencement of this Act shall have effect as if made in accordance with this Act.

    (2)   Where a company formed prior to the commencement of this Act has, pursuant to its articles of association, or a resolution of the meeting of shareholders, authorised the board of the company to issue shares and some part of the authorised capital remains unissued, the board shall have authority to issue shares under this Act on the terms and conditions, and up to the limit expressed, in the articles of association, or the resolution, without requiring the authority of a further resolution of the shareholders.

    (3)   Where an existing company incorporated in accordance with the repealed Companies Act, adopts articles of association in accordance with this Act the Registrar shall issue to the company a replacement certificate of incorporation worded to meet the circumstances of the case upon payment of the prescribed fee.

    (4)   An existing company shall not amend its articles unless, after the amendment, the articles are expressed in terms of and consistent with this Act.

    (5)   If an existing company fails to comply with subsection (4), the company and every officer of the company commit an offence, and is liable on conviction to a fine not exceeding one hundred thousand penalty units or, in the case of the officer, to imprisonment for a period not exceeding two years, or to both.

4.   All proceedings, judicial or otherwise, commenced and pending before the commencement of this Act shall be continued as if commenced in accordance with this Act.

5.   A register, fund or account kept in accordance with the repealed Act, relating to organisation of companies shall be considered to be part of the register, fund or account kept in accordance with this Act.

6.   (1)   A company registered in accordance with the repealed Act, shall be considered to be registered under this Act, and this Act shall extend and apply to the company accordingly.

     (2)   A reference in this Act, express or implied, to the date of registration of a company referred to in subsection (1) shall be construed as a reference to the date on which the company was registered in accordance with the repealed Act.

7.   A fee, charge or sum paid or unpaid before the coming into force of this Act shall be considered to be paid or unpaid, as the case may be, in accordance with this Act.

8.   An approval given, or authorisation granted, and in force before the coming into force of this Act or any act or thing done in accordance with the repealed Act, shall be considered to have been given, granted or done in accordance with the relevant provisions of this Act and any such approval or authorisation shall remain valid for the period specified under the repealed Act.

APPENDIX 5

SUGGESTED STEPS FOR TACKLING ESSAY QUESTIONS[1]

SAMPLE QUESTION 1[2]

Critically analyse the concepts of limited liability and separate corporate personality explaining how they complement one another.

(1) *Unpack the question*

This is the first essential step which you must take time to do properly. You should separate out:

The concept of limited liability

- The concept of separate corporate personality
- The need to consider how these two concepts relate to/complement one another
- The need for analysis
- The need for evaluation, i.e., critique of the concepts/relationship.

(2) *Explain the meaning of limited liability*

- Show that you understand the concept
- Explain that it is the liability of the shareholders/ members to contribute to the assets of the company to enable it to pay its debts that is limited
- The starting point is that on a winding up the members of a company are liable to contribute to the company to any amount sufficient for payment of its debts and liabilities, i.e., liability is not limited: section 51(2) subject to section 40 Insolvency Act, 2017.
- For shareholders of a limited company, this liability is restricted to the amount, if any, unpaid on his shares: section 52 of the Insolvency Act, 2017.

[1] Excerpted and adapted from McLaughlin S *Unlocking Company Law* 2nd edn (Routledge Oxon 2013) 85-86; 135-136; and 264 – 266.
[2] McLaughlin S *Unlocking Company Law....* 85-86.

(3) *Explain the meaning and consequences of separate corporate personality*

- Show that you understand the concept
- The debts of the company are not the debts of one or more of the owners of the company, therefore the owner is not liable to pay any sum owed by the company to the lender/creditor
- Illustrate with cases any/all of the following consequences: a company can own property, can be a party to a contract, can act tortiously, can be a victim of tortious behaviour, has human rights, can commit a crime, can be the victim of a crime, can sue and be sued, has perpetual existence until dissolved
- Emphasize that a company's liability is unlimited, as in the case of individuals, unless limited under a contract/by effective notice, but its ability to meet its liabilities when it is trading is limited to the value of its own assets/resources.

(4) *Explore the relationship between the two concepts*

- Note that it is possible to establish a separate corporate personality able to incur debts and liabilities, without limiting the liability of its members (an unlimited company)
- Consider whether the reverse is true. It would be extremely diffcult to implement limited liability without a separate corporate personality, and legal regulation of exclusion and limitation of liability (clauses/notices etc) would almost certainly preclude an effective outcome.

Reflect on the concepts

- Move beyond a technical explanation of the concepts to consider the implications and attractiveness of the concepts
- You should refer to the basic debate between those who see limited liability as encouraging under-capitalised and irresponsible business initiatives and those who so it as essential to facilitate investment in business
- You could also discuss the plight of the tort victim who did not choose to do business with the company.

CONCLUDE

QUESTION 2[3]

Critically analyse case law on the rights of shareholders to enforce the articles of association to demonstrate why you agree or disagree with the proposition that the contractual effect of the articles is limited to provisions of the articles concerned with the membership and constitution of the company.

Unpack the question

This is the first essential step which you must take time to do properly. You should separate out:

- Explaining what the articles of association are
- Identifcation of the articles as a contract
- Identifying the types of rights protected under section 17 and the case law
- The concept of a membership right/outsider right and the case law
- Provisions concerned with the constitution of the company and the internal management and majority rule principle and the case law
- Your reasoned views on the accuracy of the proposition.

The articles: what they are and contractual character

- The internal rules of the company registered on incorporation or appropriate Model Articles under section 12(3) and schedule 1 apply: sections 25(7)(8) and 26.
- A contract between the company and members and between the members *inter se*: sections 26
- Explain ways in which the articles are a unique type of contract. *The types of rights protected under s 17 and the cases, discuss the cases on membership rights and outsider rights:*
- *Eley v Positive Govenment Security Life Assurance Co* [1876] 1 Ex D 88 CA
- *Browne v La Trinidad* [1887] Ch D 1
- *Beattie v Beattie* [1938] Ch 708
- *Hickman v Kent or Romney Sheep Breeders Association* [1915] 1 Ch 881 Ch: Note classic words of Astbury J).

Discuss constitutional rights and the internal management and majority rule principle
- Discuss *Salmon v Quinn & Axtens* [1909] AC 442
- Discuss the internal management and majority rule cases: *Grant v UK Switchback Railways Company; MacDougall v Gardiner* [1888] 40 Ch D 135 CA

CONCLUDE

Express your reasoned opinion as to the accuracy or otherwise of the statement.

SAMPLE QUESTION 3[4]

Critically analyse the proposition that objects clauses are now legally unimportant because the ultra vires doctrine no longer applies to registered companies.

(1)   ***Unpack the question: This is the first essential step which you must take time to do properly. You should separate out:***
- Explanation of the meaning of *"the ultra vires doctrine"*
- Explanation of what an objects clauses is
- Explanation of the incremental reform of the doctrine *vis-a-vis* companies
- The remaining issue of the effect of an objects clause on the authority of the board to exercise the powers of the company
- Explanation of the operation of the constructive notice doctrine and *Royal British Bank v Turquand* [1856] 6 E & B 327; [1843-60] All ER Rep 435; 119 ER 886.
- Explanation of the effect of section 86
- Assessment of whether or not it is correct to say that objects clauses are unimportant.

(2)   ***Explain the incremental reform of the doctrine vis-a-vis companies***

In particular:
- Explain the effect of sections 23 and 24
- Explain the effect of the…Act on existing companies with objects clauses: s 28
- Note that there is no requirement for objects clauses for companies registered pursuant to the Companies Act 2017 section 12

---

[4] McLaughlin S *Unlocking Company Law*.... 264-266.

(3)   *Discuss the effect of an objects clause*

- Note the right to seek winding-up by the court because just and equitable to do so if object no longer possible: *Re Baku Consolidated Oil Fields Ltd* Times 7 July 1993

- Note the right of an individual shareholder to seek an injunction: *Stevens v Mysore Reefs* [1902] 1 Ch 745

- Identify a failure to respect an objects clause as resulting in a breach of directors' duty to act otherwise than in accordance with the constitution: section 12(4)(viii); 25(1)(2)(3); and 330

- Explain that the clause operates as a limit on the powers of the directors which, without more, stops a contract inconsistent with it from being binding on the company.

The doctrine of ultra vires and objects clauses explained

- Explain what an objects clause is and its common law effect: *Ashbury Carriage and Iron Company Ltd v Riche* [1875] LR HL 653

- Explain what an objects clauses is, the evolution to extensive objects clauses encompassing comprehensive purposes and powers and endorsement of this trend in section

- Explain that ultra vires is about acts beyond the legal capacity of a company, which is now only going to arise in relation to charitable companies and note that it is important to distinguish discussion of acts outside the authority of the directors, which remains an important issue.

Made in the USA
Monee, IL
21 April 2022

95103795R10295